The
Unapologetic Hippie

— a trilogy —

Leaving the Earth's Atmosphere

Orbiting the Planet

Down to Earth

Phil Polizatto

The Unapologetic Hippie
All Rights Reserved.
Copyright © 2023 Philip Polizatto
v4.0

This is a work of pure fiction. Pure fiction and nothing else. Characters, even those based on real people, are entirely fictional. All names are fabricated. Dialogue is grossly exaggerated. Incidents are wildly embellished for dramatic or comedic effect. Time is collapsed for cohesiveness. Resemblance to any person, place, mineral, or vegetable, living or dead, is entirely coincidental. If the reader infers a resemblance, it is in no way intended, and is only a figment of the reader's vivid imagination. To those who participated in this era, you are not supposed to be able to remember anything anyway or may still be hallucinating. Nevertheless, no matter how unbelievable, implausible, or outrageous something may sound, it is not even close to the truth.

The opinions expressed in this manuscript are solely the opinions of the author and do not represent the opinions or thoughts of the publisher. The author has represented and warranted full ownership and/or legal right to publish all the materials in this book.

This book may not be reproduced, transmitted, or stored in whole or in part by any means, including graphic, electronic, or mechanical without the express written consent of the publisher except in the case of brief quotations embodied in critical articles and reviews.

Hunga Dunga Press
ISBN: 978-0-578-27743-1
Registration Number: TXu 2-346-236

Cover Photo © 2023 www.gettyimages.com. All rights reserved - used with permission.
PRINTED IN THE UNITED STATES OF AMERICA

To Tim, without whom this book would not exist. He kept me healthy, happy and never allowed mundane chores to distract me from my work.

To my Mom and Dad, who were wise not to read this book.

To Giacco Giordano, for letting me tell his amazing story.

Phil Polizatto

To those whom I never heard from nor ever saw again, I love you all.

Giacco Giordano

BOOK ONE

Leaving the Earth's Atmosphere

ARCTIC CIRCLE
October 1976

As we touched down in a spray of fine snow, I saw no one on my left or right. The plane came to a jerky halt. I collected what was left of my brain and nerves and fiddled anxiously with the door handle. I swung my left foot onto the tiny step beneath the door and immediately lost my footing on its ice and tumbled to the ground.

The pilot laughed as he threw down my gear and laughed again when he saw the deformed ice angel I'd made in the snow. He waited impatiently as I snailed my body and belongings out of the way and I caught a blast full of icy crystals that hurt my face as he pushed the throttle forward and took off.

The runway next to the river was as slick as snot, but the single engine Cessna took off with far fewer problems than I had, just trying to walk to the edge of the landing strip. Pushing some gear in front of me and dragging a duffel bag behind me, I spent more time sliding in place than I did actually covering any ground. The Cessna circled me once and as it dipped a wing, I could see the pilot crack a smile.

So here I was. Alone. Twenty below, not counting the wind chill. Alone never quite had so much meaning. There was that kind of sweet alone I used to feel as a kid back in New Jersey, when I'd move the little lever on the thermostat to the right and hide next to the living room heating vent that was between the curved back of the sofa and the wall. A little skinny cave that only I could fit into. The whoosh of the heat going on would immediately make me feel good all over. The forced air blowing out of the vent would muffle even the sound of my father's voice, most always loud and angry, usually at himself, but always with a threat for me in it.

Everything would be just fine until Dad started screaming in Italian about how damned hot it was and start throwing open all the doors and windows. Mom's shoes would appear at the opening of my cave, so I knew she was lowering the heat. She'd bend down, stick her face in, and give me one of those *why-are-you-always-instigating-trouble* looks? Maybe even mouth the word *scutch,* which in our house, was Sicilian slang for *troublemaker.* I'd belly-shuffle backwards deeper into the recesses of the cave where I could be even more alone.

Then there would be Hunga Dunga, and alone at Hunga Dunga meant sitting in a circle of anywhere between eight and twenty people around a table of straw mats rolled out on the floor, holding hands, emulating Quaker quiet time before the evening meal. Who knows what each of us was thinking to ourselves? *Everything was needless to say.* And to say anything was only an admission of not being in the here and now.

With our eyes closed, and everyone agreeing to be quiet for at least 30 seconds before diving into the food, this was as *alone* as you could get. Some of us took advantage of it, while others may have been worrying someone knew something *they* didn't about the meaning of life.

Alone in Twisp meant Cascade-country post card views and the assurance your double-barrel wood stove would put out all the heat you'd need to keep you toasty warm forever.

Nevertheless, here I was now, wondering why no one had come to greet me. I did a slow 360-degree turn. The moon was rising even before the sun had set. And when it did, the blackness arrived quickly. A more brilliant star-filled sky I had never seen. I could just make out the cabins of Alatna across the river. The light coming through their windows looked warm and soothing and the bonfire on the bank of the river so aboriginal.

Allakaket was hidden from view by a bend in the river and a rise in its bank. From behind the rise about a quarter mile away appeared a sight, small as it was, that brought more romance to the already spectacular picture. Crossing the frozen Koyukuk was a sled pulled by a team of dogs. I could make out the silhouette of the driver, his body rocking forwards and backwards, urging them on toward the light of the bonfire on the other side. It was an inviting scene. An understatement considering it was the only picture playing in town.

I left my gear on the bank. I was wearing new grey itchy wool one-piece long-johns, brown wool ski pants, a forest green flannel shirt, a turtleneck sweater, felt lined boots, and white wool gloves inside oversized black leather mittens. Joel's old air force flight suit was my outermost defense against the cold, along with a scarf to wrap around my face.

I guess you could say it was foolish of me to try to cross the river. Say stupid, perhaps, but don't be completely unsympathetic. It's just that, well, this was Alaska! I was standing on the Arctic Circle! Everyone knows the rivers freeze two stories thick! Besides that, a sled with dogs and a man just did it. I'm sure everyone did it.

Suddenly it became exquisitely beautiful, standing there halfway to the other side. So quiet and still. So white and black with accents of blue. Glistening. Every crystal of snow is distinct from another. They fall from the pile I pick up in one hand and pour into the other like sand. It's so very dry, so very cold, the individual flakes remain unique, and the warmth of my hand inside its two gloves can't begin to reach the flakes to make them want to melt together. So they remain apart, and I feel like I've never really seen a snowflake before, the details of one so clear and different from the one next to it. I'm seeing them with the microscopic clarity you get sometimes with mescaline, and I am amazed.

I look up and the full moon is halfway to the enormous stars above me. The moment she catches my eye, I feel the whole earth move toward her with such a force, I hear a huge creaking sound. Like some old, big, rusty, many-bearinged motor suddenly set into gear.

I'm looking up, but I'm falling through. Faster and faster. The speed is dizzying, and I feel the water rushing past my body. My elbows catch on the edge of the ice. Water is up to my armpits. The rest of me is sucked at an angle not too far from parallel to the ice itself. The current is strong and enraged. For a long time it seems inevitable that I'll surrender. Much to my surprise, I'm not panicking. I do know I should be very concerned. However, my concern seems to be preempted by an overpowering sense of timelessness. Like the extreme slow motion of a car accident.

I look up and see myself looking down at me. *There's no hurry*, I am saying. *Make no appointments and there'll be no disappointments.* That's what Swami Satchitananda always used to say. *No mind, never matter. No matter, never mind.* That's what Swami

Guaribala always used to say.

So I take the time to notice me noticing how the water is starting to fill up my flight suit. How I am getting heavier. I wonder how much a gallon of water weighs. I am impressed by the power of the current. It reminds me of a Chinese finger puzzle, the kind where the more you try to pull your finger out, the tighter the hold it gets on you.

The current is the puzzle. My body is one of the fingers. The other finger must belong to the Goddess. I figure it must be her middle finger because she's really trying to screw me over. She's pulling just as hard, twisting, turning, and flinging me from one side of the hole to the other.

The puzzle is the current. I know the secret is to relax. *To struggle is hell. To relax is divine.* So I relax under the most dazzling sky I've ever seen. I am flying toward the moon. I am spinning into the current. I am alone in a sofa cave with no one to hear me or see me.

Suddenly I hear Richie Havens singing "Freedom" wafting over thousands of stoned, semi-naked, long-haired people. I see through my eyelids a glowing light. I see that it is Psylvia's, and she is gazing at me with smiling eyes that are outlined with black kohl. She winks a wink that is forever. On her eyelid is the most beautiful tropical setting I've ever seen. Pillow clouds. A wide, sandy beach. Coconut palms heavy with fruit. A seagull flies by. The surf is warm and gentle.

"It just doesn't get any better than this!" That's what I heard Swami JonPon saying as I prepared to go for the long swim.

CHAPTER 1
June 1969

Suzanne made love to me a day before I knew about it. The last thing I remember was snorting some PCP. Angel dust. Elephant tranques. Gary was about to cut it with baking powder and cap it, but insisted I try some of the raw stuff first. It must've been too much. He should've known. Maybe he did. I walked into the living room. Dean, who owned the house, and Lisa, his lover (who was supposed to be *our* lover) were watching TV. Hilton was in a corner of the room thumbing through a stack of albums leaning against the wall.

Suddenly I was scared. Everything became two and a half dimensional. Somewhere between a cartoon and a Dali. My frames of reference dissolved, and my ego fought to keep them intact. I knew from LSD, the worst thing was to fight it. There was a certain plausibility to the "hallucinations" of psychedelics. A feeling that but for our limited consciousnesses, they could be recreated naturally. Why else would Richard Alpert go to India and become Baba Ram Dass? To fight them was to deny how expansive reality could be. The secret of a good acid trip was to destroy all frames of reference. The secret of a good acid trip was not to fight it. PCP was different. I *wanted* to fight it. Its hallucinations were distortions bordering on the preposterous and it was inconceivable anyone would ever want to recreate them on the natch.

I called out for help to those people who were in the living room. I called out loudly, or so I thought. There was no response. The guy on the couch turned once when I walked into the room and smiled at me, then went back to watching TV.

I saw what the problem was. The words coming out of my mouth were hanging in mid-air spelled out like Superman letters. They hung there halfway to the people on the other side of the room and then crumbled like crushed cornflakes to the floor before they could reach their ears. The carpet was thick with letters. No wonder they couldn't hear me!

I started sweating. It was so hot I couldn't bear it. I took off my shirt. I fought my way through the heavy air to the screen door and barely had the strength to open it. The cool night air helped a little. The moon was full for all practical purposes. For other purposes it was a traveling spotlight. It followed me to the sidewalk. It followed me following the sidewalk. It followed me walking but not getting anywhere. Of course I couldn't remember that Dean's house sat in the middle of a traffic circle!

Eventually I stopped walking. I looked up at the moon and rocking forth and back like a Sephardic Jew saying prayers, closed my eyes and fell into it.

The moon turned into Suzanne's face looking into mine. Long brown hair bothered and confused my eyelids. I was dreaming I was caught in cobwebs when I opened them. On either side of her were Jimi Hendrix posters. The posters were on the ceiling and Suzanne was straddling me, her hips grinding rhythmically in a figure-eight motion. Her breasts bungeed up and down and once in a while dipped into my skin. I came right after an orgasm shuddered through her and she collapsed on top of me.

She raised herself up and said, "Well, I see you're doing better today."

"Better than what?" I asked.

"Better than when Sandy and I picked you up two days ago walking stark naked around Anthony Circle in the middle of the night!"

She got off me and stepped into a puddle of clothing which shimmied up her body and became a thrift shop 1940s pale yellow-flowered dress. It hung on her softly and sexily as she walked into the kitchen just a few steps away.

Everything in the house was just a few steps away. In fact, I guess it was more of a hobbit's dwelling than a house. I rolled my head away from the yellow flowers stirring something on the stove. My eyes were still having problems focusing. Jimi Hendrix was much too close. I was ordering my eyes to adjust when I realized the ceiling was probably only six and a half feet high. I rolled my head to the right. I could see a tiny bedroom, a bathroom, and a little porch. I lifted myself up to my elbows. I was lying on a foam pad in the middle of a small living room, surrounded by overstuffed pillows and a beanbag chair. I looked back to the kitchen and sat up when Suzanne brought in some miso soup in a fine china bowl. Mint tea steeped in a stoneware pot. Two small cups painted with birds balanced precariously upside down on the lid. A freshly rolled joint stuck out from between Suzanne's lips. She set everything down on the floor next to the bed, poured the tea, lit the joint and after a deep drag, passed it to me.

"Me and Sandy almost didn't pick you up, you know," she said through a smoky exhale and stifled cough. "But then she thought maybe you were a rock star or something because she's seen you going into Eric Burdon's house up the street and we didn't want the cops to get you or anything."

I opened my mouth to say something, but Suzanne kept right on going. "And Sandy's been dying to have an excuse to knock on Eric's door. So we brought you here and you've been a complete zombie bore. Except for those enormous hard-ons you kept getting, and I thought maybe what you needed was me. And I guess I was right! So eat your miso soup and tell me are we good detectives or not?"

I told her.

"Well, first of all, I'm not a rock star, although I do get to hang out with some of the bands."

"Like the Animals?" Suzanne asked hopefully.

"Well, with some of them," I answered. "Actually, two of them are my roommates."

Suzanne's eyes widened with expectations.

"You know where you picked me up?"

Suzanne nodded vigorously.

"Well, that's where I'm living. Or crashing at least. For the time being. With my friends Dean, John, and Hilton."

Suzanne looked stumped.

"You know. From the Animals? John on drums, Hilton on guitar?"

"Oh! And Eric?" Suzanne asked. "You know him pretty good then?"

"Naw! Not really. He likes my acid. I like his swimming pool. That's the extent of our relationship."

"So you're a dealer, is that it?"

"Well, if you say so," not really wanting to discuss it. "I'm just helping out friends."

I stared out the window, finding it difficult to meet Suzanne's eyes. I could feel hers looking directly into my brain, trying to find the crosshairs to what might be most vulnerable. Feeling a need to further qualify my entire life as she knew it, I added, "But I only deal in natural stuff like good herb and hash. Mushrooms and peyote buttons. Pure LSD. You know. Your everyday stuff."

Suzanne rolled her eyes. They said, *Oh please, give me a break!* "LSD isn't natural. It's a chemical!" she said, trying to bust me. "I love acid! So don't get paranoid or anything. I'm not a cop!"

I chuckled. "Well, I didn't think so from the bong on the windowsill over there and the joint that you're bogarting. As far as I'm concerned," I insisted, "if the acid's really pure, it *is* natural."

"So you're just the high priest around here? Is that it?" Suzanne summed me up with a little smile. "Dispensing sacraments to the canyons' multitudes, so fervent to receive them?"

The way she said it revealed a quickness of wit and an intelligence that made her more beautiful. And I liked her public relations.

"Well, you certainly put it nicely. But I'm no high priest. I just like getting high!" We both laughed.

"I don't even know your name." She cocked her head to look at me and waited for the answer.

"Giacco. Giacco Giordano," I said, sticking out my hand.

"Suzanne. Suzanne Friendly," she took mine and shook it once.

I couldn't tell whether that was her real name or a handle she gave herself to reflect her personality. I decided not to ask.

Suzanne poured another cup of tea and took four or five small tokes in a row off the joint while she continued talking. "But… *suck*… in Laurel Canyon… *suck*… most of the prayers are… *suck*… musical. So I imagine you have a… *suck*… pretty interesting clientele, eh?" … *suck*.

Clientele? I didn't like that word. Suzanne wasn't getting it. It wasn't a business. It just was. On the other hand, she was right. I did hang out with some pretty interesting characters. It was no big deal. You couldn't help it. The canyon was riddled with celebrities. With their groupies. With the groupies of the groupies.

Frank Zappa lived down the hill toward Laurel Canyon Boulevard. You could see Joni Mitchell's house from the roof of Dean's garage. Ray Manzarek, drummer with the Doors used to give me rides down the canyon on the back of his Harley. Papa John Phillips' house on the ridge above the canyon had an awesome view. Dean's house looked like a bull's eye from up there. Lee Michael's wasn't far, and he and I had dropped acid a couple of times together.

Dropping acid and dropping names. In Laurel Canyon, it was impossible not to. I was a drug dealer when the *Names* bought the acid. I was a drug dealer when the *Names* dropped the acid. I was a *high priest* when the *Names* were peaking on the acid. I was a drug dealer when the *Names* wanted some more.

"So your friend's house… Dean? Is that his name? I guess that's a pretty happenin' place, huh?"

"Yeah! I'll say! Too happenin' for me! And if it's too happenin' for me, you know it's gotta be too happenin' for Dean! That's one of the reasons I'm getting out!"

Suzanne tilted her head and wrinkled her nose. "So where are you going?"

"A friend of mine thinks he can score me a studio in one of those old storefronts down at Pacific Ocean Park."

"You mean that old, dilapidated amusement park down in Santa Monica?"

"Yeah, that's the one," I said.

"What kind of studio?"

"Oh, just a place where I can move around," I answered vaguely.

Suzanne didn't want vague. She wanted specifics. "What do you mean move around?"

"Well, it's sort of like dance, but it's not. It's something else." I tried to end it with that.

"More. Keep going!"

"Well, it's hard to explain," I began to explain, "But it's like getting out of your body and *becoming* the music."

"You know, Giacco," Suzanne said excitedly, "I know exactly what you mean! I have a friend, Frank. He's a great guitarist. I mean brilliant! And sometimes we get so high… him jammin' on the guitar… me jammin' with my body… that we get to the point where I can play his guitar through my body, and he can play my body through his guitar."

I looked at Suzanne curiously. "You have achieved synesthesia! The senses trade places. You hear colors. You touch music. You move the notes through the air."

"That's it, Giacco! That's it! It's like having superpowers or something! It's not like we can't remember later on what happened. When it's happening we both know it. I mean just with the tiniest look or gesture or sound we can trade places. It's simply amazing and a total mind-fuck! It's like being a god!"

"It's like being a Sufi!" I explained. "It's like a meditation!"

Suzanne stared at me with an affection that I hadn't noticed before but could now definitely feel. I didn't know it yet, but I was striking all the right chords in her. And I guess, she in me.

CHAPTER 2
June 1969

From the very first time I took acid, I knew music was my element. It filled the room like a sea. I swam in it like a fish. When a record stopped, I felt like a trout who'd been hooked and brought to the surface, struggling for air. But when another record was put on, I came alive like the fish being thrown back into the water.

When I wasn't tripping, I talked incessantly. But when I was high, I talked almost not at all. My body did all the talking. And I saw everyone's movements as a dance. Opening a refrigerator door. Getting a glass of water. Sweeping the floor. Making love.

"Just move around," I told Suzanne as I got up off the foam pad, walked to the window and pushed aside the curtain. "Use the props. Watch what you're doing," I said as I let the curtain fall back into place and retraced my steps. "Pay attention. When you find a movement you like, repeat it."

I sat back down on the pad, got up again and walked to the window and pushed back the curtain. "Repeat it over and over exactly the same way each time." Which I did, making my movements more deliberate and ever slower.

"Pick out one instrument from the music that's playing and use it to create your own unique rhythm and mood. Become aware of the locus of points in the movements you choose."

"Meditate on those points. Become the music. Be a *witness* to what you're doing. Don't go into a trance but stay in control." I kept retracing my steps until they were in slow motion. I was the equivalent of a 45 RPM record played at 33. Suzanne just stared at me.

"Then witness the whole process until you slowly return to your original starting point." I lay back down on the bed in exactly the same position I began with.

"That is very cool!" Suzanne said, "*very* cool!"

"Now imagine seven, eight, nine people all doing this. All picking out their own instrument, their own movement. Can you see how it becomes a dance?"

"Of course!" Suzanne said. "It's beautiful!"

"Well, I'm glad someone gets it!"

"What do you mean?" Suzanne asked.

"Most people don't get it, Suzanne. I don't understand why they don't get it, but they don't. Therefore most people don't want to pay money to see it." I lifted my head off the pillow. My neck was taut from the effort and rigid with frustration.

"And the ones who do get it are as stoned as the dancers. They're not such a great source of funding for the arts now, are they? They're too high to hold a fuckin' steady job!"

As soon as I said it, I was sorry. How ironic I, of all people, should get on anyone's case for not having a steady job. Too absurd! I knew my problems were caused by the United States Government and its inability to lead the nation in the huge societal change that was coming, and that would allow all artists to thrive. What the fuck was the country waiting for? A written invitation?

I felt Suzanne's eyes on me. I turned and found her looking at me like I had been berating her! I had been getting all worked up and she felt the brunt of it though she was the last person who deserved it. She deserved mellow. So I relaxed the muscles in my neck and let my head fall back on the pillow. I mellowed out as best I could and tried to change my attitude.

"I need to do something to help the slow learners." I laughed, but with a hint of aggravation.

"I was thinking maybe invisible day-glow paint and black lights might help. The dancers could paint themselves with it. They'd have to be nude of course. Broad strokes along their arms and legs. Maybe a dab on their forehead and buttocks and anywhere else they were brave enough to smudge it on.

"Then when they're in the groove, I'd bring the house lights down and the black lights up. The audience would see only the designs made by their movements! The designs would repeat themselves over and over.

When the dancers started to return to their original positions, I'd gradually dim the black lights and bring the house lights back up. If they started sitting at a kitchen table or whatever, they'd end up in the exact same spots. And maybe *then* the audience would get it! They'd realize that what'd happened in between *was* the dance!"

Suzanne stared at me wide-eyed. I thought maybe she thought I was a wacko or loony tune. But instead she said, "Giacco, you are beautiful, and you get me high! How many dancers do you have? Do you need more?"

"Well, so far, I've got five girls who I think are runaways and probably jailbait. That bothers me some. Then there's maybe three young hot studs who love to exhibit themselves. We call ourselves The Movement. If we take just the right amount of acid, it seems to work. But there's really only one guy and one girl who seem to really know what's going on, who've had that 'aha' experience and don't even need to get high. The others always drift off into some kind of Isadora Duncan free form or whatever and screw it all up."

"Do you make any money at it?"

"The only time we make any money is when we do rock concerts," I answered. "And we owe that to Saul."

"Who's he?" Suzanne wanted to know.

"Saul! About the only person who appreciates what I'm trying to do. He caught me dancing at a party one night and told me to do something with it. To get some true freaks together and turn it into something very far out. Something he could market."

Saul was an establishment impresario by day, undercover hippie by night. Like Dean, he was what I called a "straddler," still reconciling truths he experienced on psychedelics with the piece of the American pie he wanted. He was unable to wean himself of the green-milked teat. He wasn't ready yet to give up the material world completely. And for those of us who said we were… well thank god for the "straddlers." It was because of people like Saul that we made any money at all. He hired us to work rock concerts. For two reasons.

At night, when the strobe lights were most effective, we'd dance on tall scaffolds next to the stage that topped the speakers. Acrophobia was not a good trait to have. As a safety precaution, we were harnessed to a three-foot tether. That encumbrance, added to the one square yard of the platform, wasn't exactly conducive to interpretive dance.

During the day, our mission was to keep the vibes positive. Stroll through the crowds, entertain them, keep them mellow. Mobs can be strange things. The light and dark forces were always at work. Keep the crowds choosing the light. The vibes made all the difference. That's what it had come to. Either go-go dancing on tall, swaying, vibrating platforms, or sweeping through the crowds as jesters. It was demeaning. Saul said I was just paying my dues.

He had confidence in me. It was Saul who was looking for a studio for me. It was Saul who was going to pay the bills. It was Saul who introduced me to a lot of well-connected, if not *yet* well-known people. Some of these minor Hollywood luminaries would hire me to dance for them at their parties, a la 17th century command performances at a royal court.

Though these rising stars were always very tuned in to my "performance art," it was probably because they were so high on the psychedelics I had previously sold them. The same ones *I* would be dancing on. So whether they were paying me to dance or paying for the drugs, it was all the same. They went hand in hand.

Dropping names. Dropping acid. It was all part of the Big Joke. Life was a *lila*, a cosmic dance, and it didn't matter what steps you were doing. You were just doing them. All you could really do was watch yourself tango.

"Saul's big problem with me is that he thinks I might up and disappear at any moment," I told Suzanne. "He's right."

"He says, 'Well all your cosmic jabber is just *reeeaaally* groovy! Too far fucking out! But the fact is that *I* think you're really on to something, Giacco! I think you could really make it if you just showed a little… *just a little*… perseverance! You're onto something very edgy, but you just don't want it bad enough! If you would just say to yourself, *this is what I really want!* and work for it, I know you would make it!'"

"Maybe he's right," I admitted. "I don't know if I just don't care… or if I don't know what IT is! And until I do, what's to care about?"

Suzanne just stared. I wondered how long I had been talking. Once again, I was probably running at the mouth.

I made a vow to become the deep, silent type.

Suzanne set down her cup and brushed her long hair off her neck. She looked up at the sun coming through the window and then back at me. A contemplative expression passed across her face.

"It's the old dilemma," she said with grandmotherly wisdom.

"What old dilemma?" I asked, trying to keep my vow.

She offered her answer tentatively, looking into my eyes for some kind of affirmation. "Whether to have a goal and make reaching it the *art* of your life, or to have *no* goals and let your *life* be your art."

"Maybe having no goals and letting your life be your art is a goal in itself," I said, "and when I get to that point, I get so confused, I feel like it's time to pack up and hit the road!"

So much for the deep silent type!

The words "hit the road" jarred her. Just slightly, but enough to make me notice. The tone in her voice got deliberately lighter. She leaned forward onto her knees and began gathering up the teacups and stuff. Before she rose, she gave me a small kiss on the lips.

"You know for someone who was practically comatose for the past two days, you sure make up for it when you're awake!"

"Yeah. I know. I'm just a motormouth."

"You're just a motor mind!" Suzanne corrected.

As it turned out, the reason for her interest in all my ramblings was that she was a dancer as well. A topless dancer. In a club at the east end of the strip. The Razz and Jazz Club. To anyone who knew her it was a total disconnect. It didn't fit. Her middle-class domesticity at home. Her erotic gyrations at work.

Suzanne was a very good dancer. She dazzled the crowd down at the club. And she flattered me one night when she went off on a little trip. She started off serving drinks as usual, but slowly and sensually, exaggerated the locus of points of her movements into an extremely erotic dance. She was turned totally inward, oblivious to the crowd. Whichever way she found herself moving, she simply watched herself from someplace above. She *became* the music in the middle of a small, raised, oval stage, circled by completely entranced and lusting men. I thought maybe, just maybe, she was resolving the "old dilemma" right there and then. She was making her life an art, and her art, her life.

Her job raised the eyebrows of some of her friends and definitely her Mom and Dad who hated me. She regarded what she did as no more eyebrow raising than being a receptionist, except that it paid a whole lot more. I regarded it the same way. And it was ironic, that her profession made *me* look like a stud.

Sometimes, I'd go down to the club to watch her dance. Her customers would shoot the bull with me. They were such aroused and horny men, they often seemed willing, if not eager, to try new things. If only they could find someone to take them on a tour of the sexual possibilities. A regular guy. Trustworthy. Like the boyfriend of a hot topless dancer. Someone like me!

But in the meantime, it was primarily Suzanne. We wound up living together for a couple of months, though I kept a United Airlines "Ocupado" sign on a mattress in Dean's finished basement just in case. I divided my time almost equally between the two places, but Suzanne invariably found me in her bed when she got home from work. Suzanne and I got to know each other very well. She worked hard at pleasing me. Sexually and in other ways. Maybe the qualities she had that made me stick around gave her confidence in her feminine charms. I should have warned her that gender had nothing to do with it. All my romantic involvements ended up cerebral ones.

Suzanne was beautiful. Tender. Caring and nurturing. Just short of mothering, which she knew would drive me crazy. I thought it was surprising that she would so readily take on the role of a middle-class wife. I wasn't used to it. But I liked to be indulged, and, in the daily business of life… cooking, eating, washing dishes, straightening up… I was lazy. She liked doing it. So it was easy. I settled into a relationship with Suzanne because it was easy. And lazy.

I was lazy in making love to her. But she enjoyed taking the initiative and never complained. I relished our lovemaking. But I felt I had to tell her that even *I* wasn't sure in which direction I was bent. Not that I even *wanted* a direction!

If someone inquired, I'd say, "I'm Giacco. And Giacco sleeps with whomever turns him on." If they insisted I was bisexual, I'd insist more. "I'm Giacco, and Giacco sleeps with whomever turns him on… *and if you're not careful, it might even be you!*" And sometimes it was. Especially if the someone were attractive, and I were particularly glib that evening.

Suzanne said she was cool with it. That's the way it should be. But Suzanne was full of contradictions like everyone else. Just when I thought she was a really *here-and-now* kind of gal, she started setting goals for us. Scary goals. She started talking about kids. About settling down.

Our relationship was meaning too much too fast. In her eyes, we were lovers with a future she was imagining, or maybe devising, waiting just around the corner. I didn't know what was waiting for me just around the corner and I liked it that way.

I found myself reminding Suzanne that if the space at the beach came through, I'd probably move down there. She knew what that meant. The grieving process we went through over our impending separation lasted about thirty minutes. It may have been accelerated by this new drug making the rounds called The Peace Pill. Half heroin. Half mescaline. Very useful for conflict resolution.

Within a month after I left, she was hot and heavy with her guitarist friend Frank. He was an old high school chum who was always hanging around anyway. And he loved her. I knew they'd be good for each other. As for me, I was up to my old tricks looking for "adventures" on the Strip. Hanging out at the Whiskey with Miss Lucy, Miss Mercy, Obie, and cutie pie Carlos. Slummin' the canyons. Dropping acid. Dropping names. Dancing at the drop of either.

Suzanne and I became good friends. Up until I borrowed her VW bug and rear-ended some Orange County matron, who, for a measly three-hundred-dollar dent in the back of her BMW, caused both Suzanne and I to lose our licenses. Except for Suzanne, all my lovers ended up my best friends. And she promised she would too, upon payment of three hundred dollars and court costs. I guess it could have been worse.

I never saw nor heard from her ever again.

CHAPTER 3
August 1969

I set out from Laurel Canyon with hopes of making it to Reno by nightfall. Fat chance. I thought Peter would make hitching easier. I was scruffy with long wild hair, wilder clothes, and a poor excuse for a beard. Peter was so clean-cut looking he stuck out like an orderly in a loony bin. At least in my crowd.

He was clean-shaven and had a buzz-cut, something we always razzed him about. He had on new jeans and a white T-shirt one size too small so it really showed off his muscular chest. He had the ideal body as far as I was concerned. The kind I thought I might have if I worked at it a lot, but didn't. He was short, but with a compact gymnast's physique, every muscle group well-honed and defined. His family had recently moved to LA from New York, but, unlike most refugees from the Big Apple, he was already homesick for the dirt and noise of the Lower East Side.

Miss Mercy and Miss Lucy discovered him in a juice bar on the strip and brought him back to my house, or rather Dean's house. From then on, he was a regular. It was really all the teenage girls hanging around that intrigued him. Especially Mimi. But he soon figured out that he had to be intrigued by everyone if he were going to fit in at all. That included guys whose sexual proclivities, like mine, were moving targets or works in progress. Besides, Mimi had the hots for Rod Stewart and was "saving" herself for backstage antics.

So like most reasonable boys, primarily straight but predominantly horny, he convinced himself that skin was skin, lips were lips, and a blow job was a blow job, and rose to the occasion. On many more occasions than one.

I liked Peter a lot. He was different from most of my friends. He was more judicious in his use of drugs. He was quiet and introspective. But when he did get high he displayed a keen wit and wild streak. It was Peter who turned me on to Woodstock. His friends back east told him it was going to be an all-out explosion of music and a libertarian free-for-all. It was going to be so high the place would probably levitate.

To us, though we weren't cynics, it was hype we could live with. Peter was more interested in an excuse to head back east for a while. I was more interested in getting him alone on a backcountry road. Besides, I was planning to move to the beach in a few weeks and was sort of in a transitional stage. For me, the timing was perfect.

The weather was great. Hitchhiking was in. It was the hippies' rapid transit system… most of the time. Anyone who was the least bit hip would pick you up. We were traveling light. Each of us had a small backpack stuffed loosely with a few changes of clothing. Peter, surprisingly, didn't own a sleeping bag and brought just a bedroll. I think he thought it made him look macho and cowboy-like. It did look good. The blanket you could see on the outside of the roll was earth-colored with some wide faded teal blue stripes down it. Very masculine. It was strapped to the bottom of his pack and rested comfortably on his nice rump.

It took a number of rides to get across the San Fernando Valley, but they came one right after the other. In the little town of Mohave, we had to wait a bit, but we were never bored from lack of conversation. The next ride let us off just north of Fresno. It had turned into a scorcher of a day and we raced for the stream at the bottom of the embankment off the road. We both got naked and splashed each other like six-year-olds in a backyard wading pool. I admired his body all tanned and sparkling with droplets dripping from his nose, chest, ass and cock. I couldn't wait until it was time to crash for the night.

That would happen at a cloverleaf interchange somewhere around Sacramento at around two in the morning. It wasn't exactly what I had in mind, but all the rides seemed to be gone for the night. And those that were on the road would likely be cops. No sense in inviting trouble. So we picked one of the four grassy leaves of the clover, the one that was most in the shadows, and made a beeline for the penumbra.

The grass was still a little damp from the sprinklers that must've been going that afternoon. Relative to the heat of the day, the night seemed unusually cool. Peter rolled out his blankets, but I warned him they were going to sop up the moisture and he'd be cold, wet and miserable by dawn. So we laid out our light, but waterproof, jackets as a ground cloth, put the blankets on top of them for padding, and tried to squirm into my sleeping bag with our clothes on.

We were halfway in the bag, but it was obvious clothes were going to be a major obstacle. So we wrestled our way back out and quickly took them off and stuffed them in our packs. When we tried to get back in the second time, it was as if the bag had been coated with oil. We slid in effortlessly and by the time our feet touched the bottom of the bag, our bodies had done some major exploring.

We were both hard. We really wanted to get our rocks off. But despite the desire, despite the arousal, we were so tired, we just fell asleep, spooning. My front to his back. My hand across his chest, slipping lazily from his nipple to his stomach. Had I known then that there would never be another opportunity to get it on with Peter, and that once we got to Woodstock I would never see him again, I would have been more demanding of myself.

We woke up early to the sounds of trucks loudly down shifting as they exited off ramps or up shifting as they merged with the traffic. Bleary-eyed and in need of showers, we dressed, pulled on our packs and stuck out our thumbs. Peter wasn't looking quite as clean-cut as the day before, but after half an hour we got a ride in the back of a pickup all the way to Donner Pass where we were let out in the middle of nowhere.

We waited and waited. For some reason all the traffic had dried up and the people in the few cars that whizzed by either gave us the finger or just snarled. We waited for hours. In desperation, I scavenged a piece of cardboard and penciled the message, "Put A Little Love In Your Heart!" I admit it was a little schmaltzy, but since the song was on all the mainstream charts, I figured that maybe it would strike a sympathetic chord in somebody.

A car with an elderly couple slowed as they passed to read the sign. They pulled over to the side of the road. Peter and I grabbed our gear and ran as fast as we could. When we got to the car window, the woman rolled it down. Her husband leaned over and in a loud bark yelled, "No"! Then he put the car in drive and they sped away. Peter and I looked at each other flabbergasted and dispirited. A rude awakening that rural Amerika was not LA or New York or any of the islands of civilization we were accustomed to.

Finally, two teenagers in a Chevy convertible picked us up. Buddy, driving. Hank, shotgun. They were shorthaired country boys living on the outskirts of Truckee. The area was so thoroughly redneck, the consummate teenage rebellion was to be nice to hippies. They said they'd give us a ride as far as Truckee but if we got them stoned and gave them some bucks for gas, they'd take us all the way to Reno. "Friday night, looking for somethin' to do anyway."

Fortunately, I had some stash that Saul gave me as a *bon voyage* present. It was one-toke stuff. Two would get you psychedelic. I hadn't told Peter about it yet because he told me not to bring anything. He didn't want to have to worry about being caught "holding." He was a bit chagrined, but given the circumstances, glad I had brought it along and also glad I hadn't told him about it.

We got through Truckee with no problems. Then, as we came down a hill into the tiny town of Boca, the kids recognized some trucks parked in front of the local beer joint. Suddenly Buddy and Hank got totally paranoid. They pulled over to the side of the road and asked us to get in the trunk of the car. Peter was completely against that idea. So was I. But Hank begged us to trust them and Buddy begged harder when one of the trucks pulled out and headed up the road in our direction.

Peter and I got in the trunk and the kids hurriedly threw our gear on top of us. When we heard the trunk latch, we were immediately angry with ourselves for being so gullible. Something in the kids' faces had made me trust them, but now that I was in a confined, dark hole, I felt like an idiot allowing myself, ourselves, to be completely at the mercy of these two teenagers.

The Chevy shook as Buddy turned the ignition just as the truck came over the crest of the hill. It pulled into the wrong lane of traffic and slowed to a stop next to the car. We could hear them talking outside.

"Whatchoo boys up to?" a raspy, deep voice bellowed.

I could imagine Buddy shading his bloodshot eyes, trying not to look up. "Aw, we're just comin' back from the lake. Tried to get some guy to buy us some beer in Truckee. No luck though. How about you, Jake?"

Jake studied Buddy, then Hank. "Then why's your eyes so red? Been smokin' some maryjane? You been hangin' with some o' those fuckin' queero hippies moved in up the middle fork?"

Buddy started stuttering, but Hank kept it together. "We just been swimmin' too much, Jake. That's all."

"You know your Poppa hates those pinko faggots!" Jake reminded Hank. "He's got good reason to bust 'em as often as he does! They ain't nothin' but fuck-ups living off the rest of us. Every time I see 'em pull out some o' those stamps in the store to pay for food, makes me want to spit on 'em!"

"Yea, Jake. If we see any of them, we'll let them know how you feel," Buddy regrouped nicely, regaining his composure and lassoing in his drug induced paranoia.

"Naw. You don't tell them how I *feel*! You steer 'em to me so I can let my fists tell 'em themselves! Better yet, you send 'em down to Elma's. Tell 'em there's beers on the house waitin' for 'em. And a whole bunch of hard-workin' real men wanna shove some beer bottles up their faggot asses! That's whatcha do!"

Hank said, "Hey Jake… a pair o' headlights aimin' for ya! Better flash em' 'fore ya get into a head-on!" I could almost feel Jake giving Buddy and Hank a dirty look. He put the truck in low, and lurched away down the right side of the road.

Buddy put the Chevy in gear and pulled onto the pavement. As we passed Elma's Tavern at a crawl, I could hear Hank and Buddy exchanging friendly expletives and put-downs with guys hanging out in front. Then the Chevy picked up speed and everything was quiet for a long time. Buddy yelled toward the back seat. "You guys OK back there?"

"Claustrophobic!" I yelled back, and then wondered if they knew what that meant.

"How about letting us out, now?" Peter asked, trying to sound firm.

"Few more miles," Hank yelled. "As soon as we're out of my Dad's jurisdiction."

Peter and I looked at each other in the dark. I could hear him swallowing hard.

When the car stopped, and the trunk opened, we were at the far end of a rest stop. Hank and Buddy smiled at us, proud of themselves. Peter crawled out first.

"I think you guys've been sneakin' into too many drive-in movies," he said wiping sweat off his face.

"Told ya we'd get ya through," Buddy laughed confidently. "But ya gotta remember, beatin' up and bustin' the likes of you two, especially *you*," he said pointing at me, "is the local sport around here. So be cool!"

As we drove through Reno, happy to be in the fresh air, mocking all the glitter and lights but relieved to be in the middle of some semblance of civilization, Peter and I knew these guys had really done us a big favor. Their tactics were a bit dramatic, but their hearts were in the right place. We could tell they felt good about themselves. As if they had done what one "brother" would have expected of another. We gave them hearty hippie handshakes and left them a little weed and a couple of bucks for gas. When they dropped us off at an on-ramp, we were just shy of Sparks, Nevada.

Peter and I were exhausted and stressed out. It was already past midnight. The chances of getting any worthwhile rides were slimmer than a speed freak. We knew from here on we'd have to make sure we only got dropped off in decent areas, not the middle of nowhere. Worse yet, in the middle of somewhere where the locals would love to pummel us to death and with the sheriff's blessing.

We found some shelter behind a highway department shed, but Peter was too nervous about sharing my bag. It was too easy for the wrong people to discover us. I agreed. I took out my stash and hid it under a rock a few yards from the shed. Just in case some cops came along I didn't want to be caught holding, although I had heard stories many times about The Man slipping something into your back pocket as he frisked you. We didn't sleep well. The cement floor was cold and hard and every car that drove by sounded like it belonged to Jake.

In the morning, not too long after the sun rose, we washed up with cold water from the outdoor spigot, brushed our teeth and combed our hair. I tried to comb it. It needed a wash badly. It was getting all matted and tangled. I looked like shit. Peter looked like a hobo. After packing up our stuff and retrieving my pot, we walked to the on-ramp.

There stood an assortment of at least twelve hippies. Men. Women. Some outlandish looking, others more tame. They all stood there, traffic vrooming by, strung out along the ramp far enough apart to tell who went with whom and who went alone. None of them had their thumbs out. Our hearts sank when we saw the state trooper parked at the bottom of the ramp. He just sat there smugly waiting for the first car to stop so he could bust both the hiker and the driver.

Peter and I took our place at the end of the line and waited. No one had the nerve to stick out his or her thumb. Most cars whizzed by. A few slowed down. They were people you knew would stop and pick you up under other circumstances. But then they'd see the trooper and speed up again. Sometimes they'd shrug their shoulders and smile guiltily, sympathetically.

We waited and waited. Noon passed. Someone made a run to a store a few blocks away to pick up food for everyone. Except for a couple on their way to Denver, all were on their way to Woodstock. It was in Sparks, waiting for a ride, talking to the other hitchhikers, that I realized Woodstock *did* have the makings of a very special event. I really had no expectations about this Woodstock thing. It could be a total flop for all I cared. Taking a trip with Peter was what I cared about. Woodstock was secondary, almost inconsequential. But now, I began to feel a little psyched up about it.

Around two in the afternoon, one of the hitchhikers, hair tied neatly behind him in a long ponytail, approached the trooper and asked him to consider disappearing for a while. After all, what were we to do? Give us a break. Go away and let us get rides and we'll never come back here again! The trooper laughed. Said something about how he had all day. This was his assignment. Too cushy to pass up!

I noticed a car pull over about a block and a half down the street before the on-ramp. It had a flat tire. By the time I decided what to do and started walking toward him, the driver had the rear of the car jacked up and most of the lugs on the wheel removed. As he raised his head, I guessed he was a salesman, about forty-five, and not a likely person to solicit. I tried anyway.

"Need any help?" I asked.

"No, thanks. Just about got this done. Glad it happened now though before I get on the freeway."

"Where you heading?" I hoped he noticed the hint in my voice.

"Goin' up to Lovelock. Route 40. Sorry, I don't give rides to strangers."

He *had* noticed the hint in my voice. There was nothing to do but lay it on the line. I told him what was happening and that all we needed was a ride away from here. Once we got out of town a few miles, we'd have a better chance of getting a ride. We were going to take Route 50, dead east, but going north a little bit and then east would do. East was east. We were flexible.

"What's it worth to you?" he asked like maybe he *was* a used car salesman, ready to deal.

Peter and I had some money with us, but not a lot. I mean what's the point of hitchhiking if you had to pay for your rides? That was the whole point. To get somewhere on almost nothing and meet groovy people along the way. To me, hitchhiking was better than taking the bus any day, even when I could afford it. Usually. Not today. Not now. Now I was desperate and wished I were on a fleet-footed Greyhound.

"How many of us are you willing to take?"

"I'll take no more than five. And I'll let you out one at a time along the way. Ya know, spread you out so you can get rides easier."

"I'll be back before you can get your tire on." I promised as I ran back to Peter and the others to talk it over. Surprisingly, only one other person wanted to do it, the only woman in the group traveling solo. Jamie was her name. The others were set on Route 50 and didn't want to take the chance on fucking up their itinerary. They felt the trooper just couldn't stay there forever.

Jamie, Peter and I ran back to the salesman. The tire was on, the jack back in the trunk, and as he slammed it shut, I saw his eyes light up at the sight of Jamie. She *was* a bit of a fox with her long straight brown hair and light brown eyes. She was wearing a longish summer skirt made of some sort of flimsy, sheer material. Not sheer enough to be revealing, but enough to spark the imagination. On top, she wore a sleeveless, tie-dyed, silk undershirt. She wore no bra and the sweat of her breasts soaked through the silk and darkened the colorful mandalas that cupped them as we stood there out of breath.

"So how much did you come up with?" the salesman asked me though his eyes were targeted on Jamie's breasts.

"Fifteen dollars for the three of us. As far as Lovelock."

"Please! Please, please, please, please!" Jamie besccched so seductively, it seemed more like cooing than begging. That's all it took to make the deal.

"I'll sit up front with you," she smiled at the salesman. "If that's OK with you guys." She looked back at us and winked as she opened the back door for us, slammed it, and slid into the front seat.

As we approached the on-ramp, we scrunched down so the trooper wouldn't see us go by. In another 15 minutes, Jamie had the salesman completely in her spell. In another 20, she had persuaded him to take her all the way to Salt Lake City. The salesman would exact an added fee. The price would be Peter and me. We'd have to get out as planned in Lovelock. She went for it and we couldn't blame her.

When they sped away, Peter and I dropped our packs to the ground and surveyed the area. We were just on the far side of Lovelock. Nothing to the west but empty road. Same to the east. But directly across the road was a dilapidated cafe. The setting sun brought out the red of the earth and swirls of dust on the fallow fields and the dripping rust of nails that stained the pillars on the porch of the cafe.

Peter stuck his thumb out into the dry, warm air. For which invisible car I don't know. I bent over my pack looking for the dried fruit we'd been rationed in Sparks, spied the weed instead, and hid it behind a fence post while we waited for a ride.

When I stood up and turned around, I saw an old man step out of the cafe. He creakily stretched up to grab a pillar with each hand and leaned over the porch to spit. His enormous stomach sagged forward with the gravity and spilled over the top button of his pants. Each time he spit his distended belly shook. He stared at us intently with disgust. Then he sat back in an old rocker, his eyes never leaving us.

We saw an old jalopy of a pickup coming up the road from the west. A likely vehicle, I forced myself to think positively. As it got closer, I guessed it was a '49 Ford. My hopes picked up. Yes, yes, yes! You are ours! But when it passed it was filled with young, scruffy cowboys who hooted and jeered at us. Three in the cab. Two in the bed. As it got smaller I could make out one of the guys in the back giving us the finger. Oh well.

The old man chuckled as he rocked.

A blotch of a vehicle in the distance coming from the other direction got bigger. When it was a block away, I recognized it as the same jalopy that had just passed. This time it was going a little faster.

Suddenly we found ourselves dodging beer cans, garbage, and a few small rocks. I was never any good at dodge ball in grade school, being skinny my only advantage. I deftly avoided some rotten fruit, but my shoulder smarted when a beer can caught the bone of my shoulder and Peter was bleeding slightly where a rock caught him on his chin.

We looked at each other. We couldn't deny the panic in each other's faces. I looked to the old man for help, pleas for mercy in my eyes. Who else was there to look to? But he just laughed. The jalopy had pulled over about 50 yards down the road and all five of the young men were scavenging around the truck.

"They're reloading!" Peter announced in fear. "What are we gonna do?"

"Call the cops! Please!" I yelled to the old man on the porch. "Please, call them!"

"Go fuck yourselves!" he screamed back and spit off some of the drool hanging from his chaw-filled mouth.

Two of the guys reached into the back of the pickup near the tailgate. One of them pulled out some tire chains. The other a tire iron. Then all five of them walked slowly down the road toward us, taking their time as if they knew there was nowhere we could run or hide and wanted to savor every moment of our fear.

I was so electric I could hardly think. I felt like someone shot me up with speed and I was rushing. Part of me couldn't believe this was really happening, that these guys would really do something *serious*. But as they got closer I could see in their faces they were going to go through with it. They were going to really mess us up. The momentum was too strong, the peer pressure was too great for any one of them to say out loud that this really wasn't fair or right, and to stop what they had started.

Peter was shaking. Literally. An epilepsy of fear was taking over his body and making it useless.

"Maintain, buddy. Maintain," I said encouragingly, though the words sounded ridiculous even to me.

Both of us knew neither of us would put up much of a fight. We could leave the packs behind and make a run for it. But where to? The guy with the chains started swinging them in a circle. The old man across the street laughed harder and louder as they got closer. I tried desperately to change my fear into anger. If I could just get angry enough, I'd at least go down scrapping. But it wasn't working. It didn't have to.

Out of nowhere appeared a brand new, shiny black, '69 Jeep. Top down and black roll bars catching the oranges and reds of the sunset, it swooped down on us and screeched to a halt on the shoulder of the road, directly in front of us. A thirtyish, but boyish looking man kept the clutch engaged while revving the engine.

"Jump in! And I mean now!" he yelled.

I threw my pack in the back, abandoning my precious weed behind the fence post.

Peter just stood there, still in shock, and asked plaintively, "How far are you going?"

The five guys were now running as fast as they could toward us.

"For chrissakes jump the fuck in, Peter!" I said shoving him into the front seat. I grabbed his pack and jumped into the back. The driver released the clutch and we squealed onto the highway just as tire chains came slapping down hard on the rear of the car, leaving a nice big scratch between the two 'E's of 'JEEP.' The five guys getting smaller continued to yell and hurl rocks that would never reach us. The old man had risen to his feet and had his fist in the air. So much for peace on earth. But let's hear it for magic!

The man behind the wheel was a looker. Short black hair. Dark blue eyes. Big white teeth beneath a nicely trimmed black moustache. His tanned and muscular neck bulged through a light blue sweatshirt. When he reached for the clutch or accelerated, I could see the muscles of his upper legs flex through his gray sweatpants. But I was smitten with his smile and friendly eyes.

I tried to get out of my lowest chakra when he introduced himself as *Father* O'Keefe. *Father* Dan O'Keefe.

"Close call, eh guys?" He looked first at Peter, then at me in his rear-view mirror.

I returned his look. But Peter was still blithering.

"Thanks!" I said, feeling the word was far from adequate, but he saw the expression on my face and I knew he knew how grateful we really were. "Sometimes I'm amazed at how lucky we are."

"The Lord does work in mysterious ways, you know."

Uh-oh! We're in for some evangelizing. Well, I guess it's the least we can do. C'mon. Give us your spiel and get it over with.

"You guys must have some really good karma!" he added.

Well, now. 'Karma' is it? Maybe Father Dan is hipper than I think!

Father Dan was an Episcopalian priest. His parish was Elko, Nevada.

"I'm just coming back from a three-day retreat with Alan Watts," he explained.

"Oh, *The Way of Zen*," I said.

"You read it?" He turned briefly to look at me.

"A couple of times," I answered.

His eyes got bright and we launched into a lively chat about Buddhism and mystical Christianity. We were so engrossed in the conversation, I didn't remember switching places with Peter. By the time we got to Elko about midnight, Father Dan and I were getting each other high from the rap.

Peter and I spent the night in a small meditation room in the Rectory. The room was sparse, but comfortable. Icons of every religion ceremoniously decorated the room, but Jesus took center stage.

In the morning, after showering and eating a big bowl of granola, Father Dan drove us back to US 40. He gave us each a big hug. Before he drove away, he turned back to us and said, "Remember. Take no thought for food or shelter… or rides… and all shall be provided unto you." He flashed the peace sign and drove away.

Within 10 minutes of his leaving, a light green van pulled over. It was very conservative looking, inconspicuous. Almost non-descript. But when the side panel door slid back, a lavishly decorated interior appeared, reminiscent of a sultan's tent. The smell of incense rose into the open air. Two young women and one young man sat cross-legged on the carpeted floor. The driver had blond hair down to his shoulders. The guy in the passenger seat was the longhair who went for food back in Sparks. Freaks every one! We were back in our element!

The driver smiled at us through the door, a shit-eating grin on his face.

"Where you headin', brothers?" he asked.

"Woodstock," Peter and I answered simultaneously.

"Woodstock?" he echoed. "Well get your asses in here, because this is the Woodstock Express! Can you drive? Because from here on out it's non-stop!"

Peter and I cheered, "All right!" As we climbed in, we made exaggerated gestures of salaam to show our great appreciation. Inwardly though, I was thanking Father Dan who I was sure had something to do with this.

As soon as we got going, one of the young women lifted up a piece of carpeting in the corner of the van, and under that a piece of floorboard. She pulled out a bag of weed and a pipe. Before passing it around, she lit some incense and changed the tape in the cassette deck. The rest of the trip all the way to Woodstock was pure bliss. As if some guardian angel wanted us to get there. Not one bad vibe for the next 2000 miles.

Our van mates were the best. Good smoke, good food, good company, good conversations. Most of which were speculations about what was going to happen at Woodstock. The more we speculated, the more we believed each other's stories. By the time we got to the New York State border, I succumbed to the crescendo-ing Woodstock energy. I was a convert to the gospel of the impending collective consciousness… of what was to be, heaven on earth, and thought made manifest.

When we got closer to our destination, the traffic got heavier. Soon it was jammed to a near standstill. Miles of cars on the only major road crept along as if they were part of the grueling afternoon commute from Manhattan to Westchester. After three nights and two days of non-stop driving, everyone was wasted and anxious to get out and stretch. Keri and Rich did just that and walked beside the van for a ways. We had a hard time keeping up with them we were moving so slowly.

The excitement was contagious. So many cars. So many people. Unbelievable! What a rush! It was almost unbearable! We were all impatient to get out of the van, including our poor driver Bill, who noticed some cars just pulling over to the edge of the shoulder and parking. He did the same.

"That's it for me! End of the line," Bill said tiredly as he pulled off to the side.

When everyone had their gear together and Bill locked up the van, we joined the parade. The parade became a crowd. The crowd became a throng. It had started. Tomorrow was officially the first day, but it had already started.

Someone in front of Bill passed back a cigar box. Bill dipped a fingertip into it, put something to his tongue, and passed it to Peter. Peter did the same and passed the box to me. I opened it and saw thousands of tiny orange barrels. Orange sunshine! I moistened a fingertip, nabbed one of those little barrels with my magnetic digit, and put it on my tongue. For a moment, I imagined myself an anteater.

By the time we walked through what was supposed to be the fenced entrance, there was no fence and the ticket-takers had given up. The sheer number of people was staggering. Within minutes, Peter and I lost sight of each other. I tried to find him for a little while, but as the acid took effect, I gave up. I never saw him again. Not back in LA or any of the many places I would find myself. His whereabouts have remained a mystery. But I think of him often and I remember the trip that led to Woodstock. The trip that ended in a place that would change my life. A place that affirmed human beings create their own reality. And the reality can be nice if you want it to be. If you will it to be.

Of the concert itself, I remember little.

CHAPTER 4
August 15-17, 1969

I remember clouds and torrential rains and mud. I remember hearing music coming out of speakers hanging in the woods that circled the outskirts of Max Yasgur's farm. It took me a while, probably not until the second day, to realize that the music blaring out of the speakers was happening *live* just a hundred yards away! Was I out of it or what?

I ventured that hundred yards once, completely overwhelmed by the scene. Talk about sensory overload! Smell was the first to overwhelm me. The smell of sweaty half-naked bodies writhing and undulating all over each other. Beautiful! Then the smells became the colors. The colors became the music. The music became the smells. The bodies were pogo-ing up and down. Breasts were bobbing up and down. Cocks were flapping up and down. Hair was tossing everywhere.

I wanted to join in, to meld with my brothers and sisters, but I couldn't make any headway. It was like I was a metal shaving being repelled by the wrong end of a large magnet.

Then again, it may have been the acid. Or the mushrooms. Maybe the mescaline. Who could tell? Who wasn't in a similar condition? So I made my way slowly back into the woods. It took forever. Maybe the sopping wet sleeping bag I was dragging behind me had something to do with it. I wondered how long I had been dragging it. I figured I must want it because my hand was attached to it.

Was there anything else my hand should be attached to? Do I have other possessions I should know about? How about a car? Where were the keys? Wait. I think I hitch-hiked here. I think I... "Think". But who am... "I"? And how long have... "I" been standing... "Here"?

So I started walking again, backwards, talking to my sleeping bag, pondering the Isness, when I bumped into Jon. Or Jon bumped into me.

Startled, we jumped upright and twirled in complete synchronization to see who or what it was. We each took half a step backwards and stared at each other. Eyes into eyes. He was a head taller than me, but we instinctively compensated, Jon scrunching down a few inches, me standing on the balls of my feet. We circled and sized each other up and down. Front and back.

Jon was also dragging a wet sleeping bag behind him. We must've looked like two very strange birds, each sporting the same tail feathers, doing a ritual mating dance. The sight of each other amazed us. But it didn't surprise us. We were too obliterated to be surprised by anything.

There we were. Two freaks. Stoned out of our minds. Soaking wet. Standing on a little knoll in a clearing in the woods. Two brides of Catatonia, wearing bridal gowns of wet skin, damp pants, squishy shoes, and long, flowing trains of North Face's best down sleeping bags.

The clouds parted and a ray of sun shone through, briefly dabbing the spot where we stood. This was almost too much, even for me! Too dramatic! Too Hollywood!

But this was the time of magic, right? How about Father Dan saving us like that from those rednecks! Wasn't he somethin'! Everything happens for a reason. You live your life by the signs. And the signs were everywhere for those who take no thought. Like I wasn't! So shut up already and enjoy the moment!

And I did. As I was saying, we were immersed in light and we looked into each other's eyes.

At the moment of contact, we burst out laughing. We laughed as if laughing were the consummate biological function. Better than farting. Or eating. Or belching. Or cumming. We laughed 'til we had to hang on to each other's shoulders. And that weight became so heavy, we dragged each other to the ground until we were lumps of jello lounging on clumps of soggy down.

Jon, with some effort, raised himself to his elbows, looked at me with a huge, loving grin, and said, "It just doesn't get any better than this!"

For the next two days, we were inseparable. We never got around to normal conversation, the kind where you learn facts about each other. But we shared the same experiences. Jon could turn the most mundane chore into a cosmic event. While we helped Wavy Gravy scoop bulgur and veggies onto paper plates, Jon made references to Ganesh and Milarepa. Into a sentence heavy with hippie jargon, he'd insert a quote from *The Bhagavad Gita*, *The Upanishads*, *The Koran*, or *The Bible*. He could find the cosmic parallel between pulling a booger from your nose and the Jainist principles of *ahimsa*.

The Hog Farm's camp became our headquarters, our haven, our refuge, our retreat from the masses of humanity just beyond the trees. Some listened to the concert from the speakers that were randomly spaced throughout the woods. Many were content to stay put.

We made brief forays to the edge of the 500,000-ring circus. And when we did, I imagined that this is what India must be like. But in our state, we needed the peacefulness of the woods. We listened to would-be folk and rock stars on the Hog Farm's small open-mike stage. We passed chillums and joints with passers-by and patiently listened to them describe inscrutable trips only *they* could understand. We watched and enjoyed the carnival and its outrageous characters and wished our heads were on swivel joints. Everyone was beautiful. And even when they weren't they still were.

One woman really knocked Jon and me for a loop. She seemed totally out of place. She was dressed completely in black. A black sheath clung too tightly to her baby fat body. Around the hips, it hitched up into neat little horizontal pleats making her stomach look like a halfway-opened accordion. From her calves to where her hem started just above the knees, sagging black silk stockings couldn't hide hairy legs. Her large breasts supported the upper half of her low cut dress entirely by themselves and the two thin straps that draped loosely over her square shoulders looked bored with nothing to do. A few wild black hairs crept out of her bosom's sizable valley. Dark hair shaded her upper lip as well, thick enough to be a moustache a young pre-teen boy would be proud to sport.

The hair on her head, a mangled mane of jet-black ringlets, was done up in a sloppy bouffant and held there with black ribbons. Her eyelids were dressed in light blue mascara and outlined with kohl. On top of her eyes were brows that looked painted with India ink. She carried her black, mud-caked, stiletto pumps in one hand. With the other hand, she casually swung a black patent leather purse in a perfectly repeating arc, like the pendulum of a grandfather clock.

Her face itself was wonderfully full and round. The skin was smooth, white, and flawless. Her cheeks were naturally rosy and really didn't need those daubs of gaudy rouge. Her eyes were dark, big, and intense. Her teeth were bright and even. Her lips were painted harlot red and she sashayed through the crowd as if she were one. She constantly smiled a Mona Lisa smile. And despite the garb, the gait, and the make-up, she was completely angelic and at second glance… well, maybe *third*… really very beautiful.

Most people tried to avoid her. She stood out so much from the rest of the tie-dyed crowd, they couldn't help but stare. If she caught someone doing that, she'd stop and stare right back with the challenge, *"Can you handle me?"* She'd wait and if you averted your eyes, she'd move on with a flourish of her hips which said, *"Well! I'm sorry, but if that's the case, I just can't be bothered!"* Then she'd resume her stroll, forth and back, scanning the crowd with a sense of aloof superiority.

Every once in a while someone *wouldn't* look away. Then she'd walk with large, happy, deliberate strides, and pounce on the spot immediately in front of the innocent voyeur. The staring game would continue with renewed intensity. A couple of times, I watched her pounce in front of one of the many zombies who were glued by one drug or another to the damp ground. She and her prey would just sit there, nose to nose, staring at each other. After five minutes or so, she'd stand up, brush the dust off her cocktail dress, adjust it, and smile down on her conquest as if to say, *"It was good for me and I hope it was just as good for you!"* She seemed to know that it was. Then she'd continue walking her beat, like a lady of the night waiting for a good time. But only with the right john at the right price.

When she caught Jon and me staring at her, she gave us no more than a moment to make up our minds. Jon and I looked quickly at each other, then back at her. By then, she was in front of us. Jon quickly sized up the situation and with a tone of decisiveness said, "Better. *Much* better!"

She sat with a graceful and childlike plop in front of us, grinning as big a grin as you can get, her red cheek muscles bursting with glee. Nothing was spoken. Her eyes said everything. We stared for eternity. Somehow she managed to stare at the both of us without darting her eyes forth and back, or even blinking. It took me a while to settle in. To breathe deep and full again. I know because when she first sat down my chest felt constricted, but after a while, I felt perfectly at ease. And the three of us just sat there in a little triangle, leaning in a little, making a minor pyramid, Jon's and my face no more than six inches away from hers.

And then she closed one of her huge eyelids. There on her eyelid she had painted a tropical paradise. A stretch of beach with palm trees and gentle surf. You could tell the sand was warm and the coconut palms were heavy with fruit. A conch shell lay in the sand and a seagull flew in the blue sky just above a wisp of clouds. The breeze was just right. Jon and I were transfixed, then transported. We went for a long swim.

After what seemed like hours but was probably only a couple of minutes, she lifted her eyelid and broke into another enormous *"I told you so"* grin. She stood up and looked at us lovingly, like a mother toward her children. Then she walked away, turning back just once as if to say, *"Now you two boys play nice and be good!"*

She was already out of hearing distance when I found my voice and offered a feeble "Thank you."

Jon looked at me, then toward her, and said, "Better. *Much* better!"

Everything was "better" to Jon. When the clouds got thick and dark and it looked like it was going to dump on us again, Jon would look up and say, "Oh… Better! Really this is *muuuuch* better!" And if the sentence started sarcastically, it always ended convincingly, for himself, and for anyone who happened to be around him. It was all part of his *Better* philosophy.

When you get dumped by your lover, that's *better*! When you find out your lover gave you the clap as a going away present, that's even *better*! When the cops knock on your door only to tell you a neighbor's complaining about the loud music, but you forgot to hide the bong and the cops see it through the open door and you end up busted down at county jail… *BETTER*! No matter what happens, it's better because nothing happened to make it any different. Because at every moment you must choose the positive or negative universe. Because all good hippies pick the positive universe. Because at any particular place, that's where you're supposed to be.

Better is beautiful! For two days, things just got better and better. Until it was so beautiful Jon couldn't take it anymore. He left before Woodstock was officially over. I knew it was hard for him to leave and I knew I would probably leave too rather than face the vacuum that would be left behind. For me Woodstock was Jon and Jon was Woodstock. When he left, he said he promised not to bump into me again until the next time.

He knew I lived somewhere in Laurel Canyon. All I knew about him was that he was from Ridgewood, New Jersey, but was living at a farm in upstate New York. Naturally, it was called *Better Farm*. He left, but not before teaching me how to "walk in the way of the Lord."

According to Jon, everything in nature had a perfect pace and proper gait. The planets revolved around the sun at just the right speed. Birds flew as fast as they're supposed to. Plants grew at just the proper rate.

Jon looked around to make sure no one was eavesdropping. Then he leaned close to my ear and shared the secret. "Walk toe to heel and you join the rhythm of the universe. That's how Jesus walked. Toe to heel. That's how a Lord walks!"

"And just where did you get this information?" I asked him totally intrigued, respecting his confidence.

"Aquarian George in upstate New York told me," Jon answered as if his source were beyond reproach. "And I believe him! He's really into all the mystics and great teachers and the occult and stuff like that. Think about it Giacco! You know something's true the moment you hear it! You just feel it in your bones! Or somewhere in the depths of your being."

I didn't need further convincing, but Jon must have felt it necessary.

"Think about how Indians walk through the woods." Jon said. Then he demonstrated while he explained. "Your weight is on your back foot. The toes of your right foot reach forward for the next step. But if there's a stone to slip you, or a twig to crack, jeopardizing your stalk or whatever's stalking you, there's still time to retract it and try another place. When you walk *heel to toe*, however, take a step and you're committed to it! Your weight is on it! You can't take it back! You're stuck!

"Ever notice how babies take their first steps?" Jon asked excitedly. "Toe to heel!" he continued, not waiting for an answer.

"Next time you see a baby, pay attention! They instinctively point their toes to the next tentative footing. They're in perfect rhythm with the universe. For a while. Until they begin to mimic their parents and start walking heel to toe! What are the results I ask you?" Once again, he didn't wait for an answer.

"They're vulnerable for the rest of their lives. They're forever off guard and completely out of balance!"

Jon stood up and started lordwalking in circles around me. Toe to heel. Toe to heel.

"Imagine all the people in Manhattan walking toe to heel. It would really slow them down," he said with the medical concern of a real doctor on TV.

"Stress levels would drop immediately. And more importantly, when you walk toe to heel you notice everything you're supposed to. That's the human's proper pace in the scheme of things! That's how the Lord walked!"

"Which lord is that again, Jon?" I asked. I don't know why, but he laughed and punched himself in the forehead.

CHAPTER 5
September 1969

The Japanese Trading Company. That's what the sign said above the building. Part of a row of buildings, each one representing a different country. Mine had dragons and Kanji all over it. All the plate glass windows were painted with psychedelic yin yang symbols and flying Sufi eyes. The row of buildings was a facade for the Pacific Ocean Park amusement park. It was built on the pier that separated south Santa Monica beach from the north Venice boardwalk. Anyone could easily wander under the pier and among the pilings. But for security reasons, the owners had made it almost impossible to gain access to the pier itself from the beach. Cyclone fences topped with barbed wire ran the length of each side of the pier. The only easy access to it was from the buildings that fronted it.

I never did see the park when it was operating, but it must've been wonderful. The tiny back door of my studio entered directly onto the pier. I used a madras tablecloth as a wall hanging to hide the door so no one would know it was there. I can't remember a time when I didn't need a secret place. And there were plenty of them out on the pier. I explored them a lot and knew them inside out. Every nook. Every cranny. Every spook in every haunted house.

When I opened my little back door the first sight that greeted me was the carousel. Most all the rides were still intact. The horses and elephants and giraffes on the carousel still retained the depth of their colors despite the salt air. Beyond the carousel was the roller coaster. Enormous. The cars on the loading platform waited to fill up with imaginary daredevils talking excitedly, waiting their turn. None of the rides were functional. All power had been turned off to the pier. Yet on moonlit nights you could easily throw a mental switch and turn everything on.

After rehearsing late into the night and when the last of the dancers had gone, Saul and I would slip out the back door and find a nice ride to sit in. The Tilt-a-Whirl cars had the most comfortable seats, but an old ferris wheelchair had the best view of the ocean and stars. Every now and then you could hear teenagers, girls and boys, running under the pier or smell a waft of whatever they were smoking. Then we'd follow the sounds and smells and when we were directly above them, we'd lay on our stomachs and spy on them through the cracks in the timbers. Watching them trip and fuck and listening to their stories made me realize how sheltered my own teen-age years were, and envious of all the "good times" that were probably right under my nose and that I never took advantage of because I was such a dunce when it came to sex and sin.

One time we spied on a group of five young surfers who frequented the waves next to the pier. I recognized them because they used to meet at dawn in front of my studio and their chatter would wake me up. I'd peek through a postage-stamp-sized scratch in the painted plate glass window and let my early morning hard-on admire them as they passed by, bare-chested in their low slung board shorts.

Yep. It was the same guys. Saul and I could make out some words between the crashes of waves against the pilings. "Fuck the crack of dawn." "Mick Jagger." "How far can you shoot?" "Round pound." One of them started imitating Jimi Hendrix miming a guitar above his head and wailing lines from "Purple Haze." When he got to the part that should go *'Scuse me while I kiss the sky,* he sang *'Scuse me while I kiss this guy.* None of the other kids skipped a beat. Fuck! It was Hendrix! It must be OK!

Saul and I immediately straightened up and cramped our facial muscles trying not to laugh. When we got control of ourselves we resumed our spying.

We could just make out the highlights the moon made on their bodies standing in a circle. Sometimes their faces would fall into a shaft of light. Some had their eyes open, others tightly closed. Some even tilted their heads back and looked directly up at us but never saw us on the other side of the timbers. Their oversized trunks either hung at their knees or had slipped all the way down around their ankles. Some of the stronger waves made it up to where their feet and trunks were sinking into the sand and you could see the foam glowing with phosphorescence, heightening the movement of their hands pumping furiously up and down.

Without saying a word, Saul and I looked up at each other. He rose to his knees, unzipped his pants, and pulled out his "pecker" as Saul liked to call it. "What can I say?" Saul whispered as he stroked. "It's contagious!" He looked up at the sky with the expression of someone whose desire has passed the point of no return.

Saul and I never got it on together, unless you consider voyeurism and masturbation to be sex, which we didn't. There was never any embarrassment and we never talked about it. When he was finished, he chuckled mischievously. I wondered if his pool of cum would drip over the edge of a plank onto the young skin of a surfer. I got my answer when I heard one of the guys below say, "Fuck, some bird just shit on my shoulder!" We stifled a laugh. Saul put his "pecker" away, zipped up, and we headed back to the ferris wheel.

Saul always had the best dope. That night we smoked some Gambian Red. Smuggled in peanut shells that had been slit with a razor, the peanuts replaced with the pot, and the shell meticulously, seamlessly, glued back together. Saul had been given two shells. One was more than enough to send us soaring. Such a treat to have that light, airy, expansive, intelligent smoke fill your lungs rather than the dense, heavy and dopey Mexican bud that had been around the past few weeks and only made you sleepy.

The more stoned we got, the wilder the ideas we'd come up with for my dance troupe. Saul had asked for something very far out that he could market. I intended to give it to him. I needed a black stage with a black cyclorama. The cyc should rise at least twenty feet and have hand and footholds all over it. With proper lighting we would be able to give the audience the illusion of levitation. We would defy gravity and blow their minds.

Saul thought this was great, but his priority was the Free Press concert happening on Saturday. It was supposed to be a love-in/anti-war gathering. Right there on that expanse of beach between Pacific Ocean Park and where Venice proper started. The lineup consisted of Spirit, Nitty Gritty Dirt Band, and Taj Mahal, interspersed with anti-war speeches. For a change, we would be on the stage itself and not on scaffolds. Still, it was just more go-go dancing. And we'd be doing it for free just like all the other entertainers. Saul said the exposure would be good for us and the Free Press would mention our name.

Saturday morning I awoke to the sounds of people walking, running, roller skating past the studio. Hardly unusual except for the numbers of them. I peeked through my window and saw a steady stream of bare chests, tie-dyed halter tops, beach towels, ice-chests, picnic baskets, banners and signs. The concert didn't start til one, but the crowds were arriving early.

My gang arrived around eleven. We warmed up with sun exercises and calisthenics. Then we each took a half a tab of acid and headed for the beach a block away. It wasn't Woodstock, but it was as dense. The stage was about twenty feet from the boardwalk and faced the ocean. A small crew was finishing up and a skinny, balding, bearded guy was doing a sound check. On the far left were the pilings of the pier and the skeleton of the rollercoaster silhouetted by the blazing sun. On the far right was a massive, partially buried pipe. The part that stuck out of the sand was a good three feet high. It ran from god knows where in the bowels of Venice or Santa Monica to spill god knows what into the ocean. In the hundred yards or so between the pipe and the pier, the boardwalk and the ocean, were thousands of people arranging blankets, putting on lotion, smoking pot, tripping out.

It was a real family affair. Nuclear and otherwise. Lots of kids of all ages. Young hippie moms breast-feeding their newborns. Young hippie dads sporting their tots on their shoulders. Lots of short-haired liberals who sympathized with the drop-outs, but hadn't yet dropped out themselves, who maybe wanted to, but couldn't.

They were the people who had complied with two of Leary's suggestions. They had turned on. They had tuned in. But the dropping out was left to the hippies. The clean-cut liberals were the stoned, young, left-wing members of the establishment, who enjoyed the fringe element of the freaks. They counted on them to bring fun, color, and diversity into the culture. And they would fight passionately for their right to express themselves as free spirits. They knew that by securing the rights of the fringe, they were securing their own.

These were the young blue-collar and white-collar workers who relished the uninhibited cavorting but who were too shy to cavort themselves; the modern politicos who wanted the freaks to be the scene, while they worked behind the scenes. These were the peacemakers, environmentalists and civil rights activists who worked within the system. They were the true revolutionaries, the salt of the new earth. They were the pillars of the future society that would bring in the Aquarian Age. The freaks, the hippies, the flower children had already dropped out and were leaving the earth's atmosphere, creating lifestyles, language, fashions and issues that would, they hoped, become part of the mainstream culture in following years.

It was a wonderful day. Everyone was on a high. Spirit really got everyone on their feet. Dancing. Swaying. Gettin' down! The speeches were empowering and solidified the crowd's resolve against the war. They knew that the threat from the outside was now and forever a lie. They knew that the country had better start thinking in a new way. And they knew that these rallies were meant to attract the media and make people pay attention. They needed a venue where their opposition could be clearly seen and loudly heard. So they rose to the occasion and hooted and whistled and hollered at the top of their lungs in response to buzz words that echoed through the loudspeakers. But the crowd was there as much for the music as they were to make a statement. They were there to have a good time and have some fun.

The vibes everywhere were great, and though I and the other dancers had dispersed among the crowd, there was no need to work it. So when the next band walked on stage and began tuning up, I started back toward the stage and hoped the rest of the crew weren't too stoned by now to find their way back. I was flashing my badge at one of the security guys in front of the stage. That's when I saw them.

All along the boardwalk, from the pier to the sewer pipe, stood an impenetrable wall of LA's finest decked out in full riot gear.

Where had they come from? All of a sudden like that? Didn't anyone see them approaching? Was it possible an entire stadium-load of people could collectively be so oblivious to their arrival?

I followed the wall of chest-shielded, head-helmeted, face-masked robots. They just stood there at the ready, most holding clubs, some lightly bouncing them in their open palms. Legs slightly apart, solidly grounded, black leather chaps catching the glare of the sun, they looked like a thick wrought iron fence. I looked to the right and saw the crowd begin to notice the fence extending quickly along the length of the pipe almost all the way to the surf. A wave of bad vibes crashed upon the crowd.

The negative energy was palpable. It cut through the crowd quickly like a scythe through grass. The panic in the air was razor sharp. You could feel people working hard to keep their acts together. Trying to be calm. Buddies continuing to drink their beer and assuming forced poses of macho nonchalance. Boyfriends telling their girlfriends to be calm. Mothers calmly gathering up their kids. Dads calmly, but firmly, persuading them it was time to go. But the kids knew something was wrong. Like a dog sensing an earthquake. Like a gull sensing a hurricane.

One of the anti-war speakers grabbed the microphone. She tried to keep the crowd, now on the very edge, from falling off. She tried reason. She tried humor. She tried sarcasm. Someone from the Free Press was talking with a riot squad honcho. The cop had his arms impatiently akimbo, while the Free Press guy used his hands and arms freely, gesturing first toward the crowd, then to the police, then back to the crowd, trying to communicate reason over mayhem. The colorful shirt he wore made him look like a sailor flagging semaphore. I could tell he wasn't getting anywhere when he threw his hands into the air. In the meantime, the crowd was becoming more anxious and vocal. A verbal assault on the cops was gaining momentum from the braver souls, while others were, as inconspicuously as possible, trying to make their way off the beach. An empty pop bottle soared over my head toward the boardwalk and before it fell short of its mark, I saw the head honcho look toward his men, nod slightly, and yell, "Clear the area. Now!"

Suddenly it was chaos. Clubs cracking skulls. Kids screaming and being trampled by both the cops and the crowd. Some people putting up a fight. Guys trying to rip the masks from the cops' faces to get something to punch at. Feisty women kicking and biting their assailants. Kids trying to hang on to, but then violently bucked off, the bronco legs of police who were trying to pummel their dads. Lots of bleeding. Lots of pleading. Lots of stoned, dazed acid-heads trying to get a grip. People running every which way trying to escape. Many were backed up to the ocean and more than a few began swimming out into the water beyond the reach of the incessant swinging clubs. The rest scrambled blindly trying to reach the pier or zigzag through the police to the boardwalk. A typhoon of colors. A tornado of demons. A torrent of pathetic faces, their expressions disfigured by anger and fear and panic. A tsunami of nightmares in the blazing California sun.

I ducked under the stage and when the first row of cops charged the beach, made a run for the boardwalk and ran as fast as I could toward my studio. I looked behind me. Close at my heels were another forty or so people and a half block behind them about 10 of the storm troopers. I fiddled with the keys and got the door to my studio opened just in time, but not in enough time to prevent the crowd from rushing in behind me. When we were all inside, we locked the door and started piling everything we could against it. As we pushed the piano into place we could see the silhouettes of clubs on the other side of the painted plate glass windows.

The silhouettes got nearer and darker and crashed through the glass sending shards and slivers everywhere. One of the cops lobbed in a canister. The gas quickly permeated the air. People were screaming. The cops batted the remaining glass out of their way and entered through the windows. The people inside were either blindly confused and tearfully running right into their clutches, or lying in a frozen fetal position on the floor.

At the first sound of the breaking glass, I ran to the very rear of the studio, lifted the madras wall hanging and scurried out the little back door onto the pier. I made my way as furtively as I could to the Tilt-a-Whirl. To the car that had the loose seat cushion. The seat was hollow and I used to hide my stash there sometimes when I had a paranoically large amount. I scrunched in and fiddled with the cushion until it fell back into place. About a half hour later, I heard two cops walking around, talking, turning over barrels and crates. Then silence. I stayed in my hiding place until late that night.

I had never before referred to cops as "pigs" even though at the time it was a perfectly politically correct thing to do. We are all divine. I always tried to remind myself of that. I made a habit of saying it to myself when I got mad. The same way other people counted to 10, that's how I said we are all divine.

We are all divine. We are all divine. We are all divine. We are all divine.

I worked hard not to slur anybody. But this night, I learned the meaning of the word "pig" and knew many things would have to change before I stopped using it.

I sneaked back to the studio but was afraid to turn on any lights. I leaned my mattress against the wall and stuffed a narrow piece of foam on the floor. There, in that little cave, I huddled until dawn, wondering how the world would react when it learned of my early retirement from The Dance.

It didn't take much light of day to see that practically everything was destroyed. The piano, the stereo, the few furnishings. All my records lay smashed and strewn across the floor. If I stared at them without blinking, I could imagine they were part of the design of the linoleum. I threw a few pieces of clothing in my backpack, walked to the highway, stuck one thumb north and the other thumb south. That's how I ended up spending the night in Laguna with Josie.

CHAPTER 6
October 1969

Josie reminded me of the perfect California girl. The kind evoked by the Beach Boys. In her dark green Dodge Dart convertible. Her head leaning back against the head rest, her long, sun-streaked, dirty blonde hair hanging over the back of the front seat. Sparkling blue eyes. She was a beach beauty for sure. Actually a woman of 32, she passed easily for a petite bombshell 10 years younger. When she pulled over she said, "I'm only stopping for you because you look completely unintimidating. Hop in."

I said, "Thank you. I think."

She'd heard about the "riot" on the news. But when I told her how the cop-attack had affected me personally, it became more real to her and she felt compelled out of a sense of hippie charity to offer me a place to stay for the night. That would be at the home she shared with her husband Tyler in the Laguna hills overlooking the ocean.

The house was early 60s. Modest. Immaculate. The furnishings, the decor, everything about the house looked straight and middle class. The only decoration that belied anything but a wide-eyed Keene culture was a God's eye hanging over the TV. And that could easily be taken for token folk art. Upstanding and wholesome people lived here. The kind that make good neighbors. The kind that never are the center of attention. That's just the way Josie and Ty wanted it.

Tyler was out of town on business. He was a pilot. Flying a few tons of marijuana from Mexico into the states. They were personal friends of Timothy Leary. In fact, they were at the forefront of the League for Spiritual Discovery and I gathered they traveled in a circle of friends concentric to, but beyond mine. When Josie pulled her hair back into a ponytail to start dinner, I realized this whole scene of the tastefully dressed housewife, living in a respectable subdivision, was a well-planned facade to enable them to perpetrate cosmic conspiracies. I imagined Ty walking in wearing a dark blue captain's uniform with epaulets, upon which were embroidered the Dead's skull and roses, but he wasn't due back until the next afternoon.

Of course I found all of this out much later, after Josie and I had shared an experience that made us completely trusting of one another.

The way she juiced the carrots. The way she checked the steaming rice and veggies. The way she moved. The way she talked. It was as if she were operating on a different plane. She was high, but not on drugs. She never offered me any. And I had nothing to offer. But as we talked I was getting a contact high.

It started off with references to Arjuna, but by the time we finished dinner and the moon was rising, we had covered everything from Joel Goldsmith's *The Infinite Way* to Paramahansa Yogananda's *Autobiography of a Yogi* and *The Sufi Message of Hazrat Inyat Khan*. It excited us that we both had read so many of the same books. And we found our conversation addicting. Everything we said to each other made perfect sense. Her sentences spiraled into mine spiraling back into hers, spiraling back into mine, each time getting a little higher. When we got around to the Evans-Wentz translation of *The Tibetan Book of the Dead*, we were soaring.

I told her about some of the experiences I had had experimenting with breath while tripping on acid. How I would gradually slow my breathing and make the time between exhaling and taking the next inhale, longer and longer. Eventually I'd reach a point where the time between breaths was so long, I wondered if I could accidentally asphyxiate myself. As soon as I began to wonder, it was over. I was back in my mind. And I'd start gasping for air, frightened.

"That's where free will comes in," she said tingling. "I know what you're talking about. I've had the same experience. If I could just choose of my own free will to have the faith to surrender… I'm sure somewhere in that space between the breaths is the answer!"

We were standing when it happened.

The room suddenly darkened like I was about to black out. Without warning, I was thrown across the room and landed at the foot of the sofa. I looked up at Josie and she was immobilized where she stood, inside a blinding aura that was glowing yellow and white. I rubbed my eyes when she started changing, first into an old lady, then into a baby, a child, a young girl, an old woman again. Over and over, faster and faster through all the phases of a human body's life. Like a film run at such a high speed you no longer see frames that make any pictorial sense, she turned into a constant blur of rotating light.

I was paralyzed when a disembodied voice floated across the room. It was distinguishable as Josie's but sounded like it had been run through a sampler and processed. A couple of octaves lower with a reverb.

"I have absolutely nothing to do with what is happening," the voice said. "I have merely been chosen as a channel of grace for you." And then Josie raised her arm and pointed a finger at me. And I was filled with information. Not verbal. Not visual. But the message was total and complete. It was perfect. I had never experienced such direct communication. There was no room for misunderstanding or misinterpretation. It was clear and precise and perfect. And though I can't verbalize it either, it was an affirmation that the truth we'd been skirting around was just that. The truth. And all the books we had talked about were true. And all the intimations of truth we had experienced were true. And the truth was closer than your own breath.

As the room brightened and the aura faded, Josie dropped to the floor and I collapsed against the sofa. Neither of us spoke or moved for at least fifteen minutes. Finally, Josie, looking exhausted, got up and said, "I think I'd better go roll a joint."

When she came back, I said, "Josie, I think I just had an acid flashback. I never did know whether there really was such a thing, but I think I just…"

"No, you didn't just!" she interrupted. "It really happened. I was there too! I can't explain it. I can't account for any of it. But it did happen. We are not going crazy!"

We smoked the joint and came down. We both felt drained.

"I'd like to sleep with you tonight," Josie said quietly. "I mean really just *sleep* with you. Next to you. I love my husband. But I just feel I need to sleep next to you tonight. OK?"

And that was fine with me. But after we got in bed and started cuddling, Josie threw her long hair over my chest and started kissing my stomach. She worked her way down and when she felt my cock getting hard against her body, she worked her way back up until our lips met. She slowly and gently slipped her tongue in between my lips and parted them, reaching in further and further.

I ran my hand along the side of her body, caressing her breast and ribs. When I got to her hip I went to reach under it and she accommodated by lifting and giving me enough clearance to explore her vagina. It was so sweet and moist and comforting. And we comforted each other all night.

Before I left the next day, Josie gave me her copy of *The Aquarian Gospel of Jesus the Christ*. I gave her a brotherly kiss on the lips and neither heard from nor saw her ever again.

I walked down the curving roads to the Pacific Coast Highway. It was time to go home. But I didn't have one. I didn't want to go back to the pier or Suzanne's. So I hitched north a little past Malibu and when one ride told me he was taking Topanga Canyon Boulevard over to the valley, I told him to let me out at the Country Store in Topanga. At the phone booth outside, I called Dean. Collect.

CHAPTER 7
October 1969

When Dean finally pulled into the gravel parking lot of the Country Store, I was beaming like a little kid, happy to see him, my first love, my patron, my big brother, my father. But Dean was just shaking his head.

"Look, Giacco," he said getting out of the car. "It's been almost two years and I just can't keep going on like this. Bailing you out all the time. Putting up with your antics."

"Dean..." I said, ignoring his opening statement. "Last night I had *the* most incredible experience. I got a ride to Laguna with this woman who..."

"Shut up and listen to me for once!" he interrupted sharply. "Lisa and I are thinking of leaving."

"What do you mean, you're leaving?" I asked, taken completely off guard. "This is really out of the blue!"

"No, it's not completely out of the blue! Where have you been?"

"But Dean! It was always me and you! The three-ways with Lisa were just for fun! I thought we all understood that!" I could tell from the resolve on his face, guilt-tripping wasn't going to work, but I continued. "I thought *she* understood that. I thought *you* made that clear to her!"

"Giacco, it hasn't been me and you for a very long time. It's been you and Peter. It's been you and Suzanne. It's been you and every runaway waif you rescue and bring home at my expense!"

My mind was reeling. Dean was waiting for a response. But I was rewinding my life to the few months when I *briefly* became an adult, according to my parents. But then what did they know?

It was the final summer before being conscripted into the "real" world. 1965. I had just graduated from Georgetown's School of Foreign Service and didn't want to jump into any old job. It had to pay well and require extensive international travel. In addition to that, my "unauthorized" junior year abroad in Europe had raised a lot of questions about myself. And I barely managed to make it through my senior year, compulsively looking for sex, not getting any, and hanging out with poets and other weird people down at DuPont Circle.

Even then I feared the trap of the real-world corporate lifestyle I was expected to follow. I just felt it wasn't me. So I went up to New York. I took a job as a soda jerk in an offbeat ice cream parlor in the West Village called The Cliché. Just temporarily. Just to give myself time to find the perfect position. I guess I was just stalling.

Dean arrived in New York with a brand-new MBA in his back pocket. He was in town for job interviews. I had just finished my shift at The Cliché and was already out on the sidewalk when I passed Dean walking into the cafe. As the door closed, we both turned to look at one another, then turned away.

Across the street, I turned to look once more just for the hell of it. Dean, with his short but tousled blonde hair, gray three-piece suit and briefcase, was standing outside the cafe looking back at me like an ad for Gentleman's Quarterly. He started to cross the street.

I looked away and walked up Barrow Street. Before I turned the corner, I looked back again. Dean was at the far corner, quickening his pace. I wanted to believe he was following me, but I could hardly believe it. He was too good looking. Too *WASP* good looking. Too well-bred good looking. It must be a coincidence. What could he possibly want with me?

Before I turned the next corner, I looked back again. He wasn't there. He wasn't following me after all. I was right. He had better things to do. And then when I turned, there he was, out of breath, standing right in front of me. He had run all the way around the block.

"Should I just take it that you don't want to meet me?" Dean asked.

I was flustered and I thought too long about what to say. When I finally opened my mouth, I said, "I don't know what you're talking about," it didn't ring true for either of us. I was busted.

Dean laughed. "Let's go get a coffee or a drink or something. How about it?"

I nodded and smiled, a little uncomfortably. And off we went.

He bought me a few drinks and later, over dinner, we exchanged life stories, or at least the parts that made us look our best. Then we took in a movie, I can't begin to remember what it was because my mind was doing cartwheels. When it was over and we were back on the street, he asked if I wanted to spend the night with him in his hotel room. I thought about it, trying to make the thinking process obvious on my face, trying to play hard to get, and said "OK" like my heart wasn't really into it. The problem was my heart was too much into it. Dean just laughed, quietly, almost politely.

Dean took his clothes off first. His body was as handsomely put together as his face. He got into bed and pulled the sheet up to his navel.

"Well, c'mon. Hop in," he said, screwing up his face.

I was nervous. I had done plenty of mental acrobatics rationalizing the desire to sleep with men. I found plenty of reinforcement in all the philosophies and histories I had chosen to agree with. I had even in my own mind regarded the Classical homosexual experience as somewhat noble. But I was short, very short, on experiences.

I sighed. "The truth is Dean (lying through my teeth,) I've never slept with a man. I've never slept with a woman either. I'm nervous and I feel awkward."

Dean looked at me more than a little askance. "It's true!" I said. "Don't be mad. Don't think I'm weird. But I think I'd rather leave now and have a cup of coffee with you again tomorrow, than to spend the night and never see you again."

An expression of frustration passed across Dean's face. "I think you've been working at the Cliché too long," he said sarcastically.

"Well, I know maybe it sounds corny, but that's the way I feel!" He looked at me with wonder in his eyes. "And I'm a little afraid," I added.

Dean softened and said, "Well maybe you can have both. The night with me *and* coffee in the morning.

So I undressed and climbed in next to him and spent the night. He made love to me so tenderly and sensually, I felt every inch of my body had gone up to heaven. And he never tried anything that might cross boundaries that would scare me off. We did have coffee together the next morning, and I spent the next night with him. And the next. When he flew back to Chicago, I was miserable. But he called often. He's one of the few people I've ever known that could give me a hard-on just talking on the phone. Not that the topics of conversation were erotic... they weren't. It was just the sound of him. If that's not a first love, what is?

During one phone call he told me he was accepting a position with NBC in New York and would be out in a couple of weeks. I liked to think he took the job because of me. A few days after he arrived, we found a basement apartment on Barrow Street, just off Sheridan Square. Deciding to live together was a pretty big commitment, considering it was based only on a three-night stand and a bunch of phone calls. But that's how sure we felt about one another. And we wound up living together for the next few years.

Dean came from money and culture. He was a blue blood. He had gone to the finest prep schools and Ivy League colleges. I came from the opposite. Immigrant parents. A scholarship to a decent university which looked with scorn upon my unapproved year abroad in Europe, though that year proved to be the most enduringly important. Nevertheless there were embarrassingly large gaps in my social education. Dean filled them in. He was only a couple of years older than me, but decades older in understanding the lifestyle of a sophisticate.

He taught me by example how to dress and introduced me to Brooks Brothers. He insisted on letting me buy stuff on his account. He introduced me to New York's finest restaurants and turned me into a gourmand. We went to many plays and musicals. Museums and symphonies. We hobnobbed with his colleagues from NBC, met for oysters after work at the Oyster Bar in Grand Central, and went to upscale Upper West Side parties. And he persuaded his uncle to give me a job writing ad copy for Columbia Records.

In return I gave Dean, with help from Richelle, a glimpse into the "other" worlds, and a lot of trouble.

Delia, Dinah, and Richelle were our best friends. They lived across the street on the second floor, and from our basement window we could yell up to them and they down to us. Delia was a social worker. Dinah and Richelle were flight attendants for Pan Am. Richelle had a boyfriend named Jack.

We spent a lot of time together. Especially with Delia and Dinah. They were great friends to us. And great fun. We did most everything together. We'd take walks through Washington Square Park and listen to beat poets and folk singers. One of them was a guy named Bob Dylan. He had a strange but captivating and passionate voice. A few nights later, we caught his act down at Gerte's Folk City. We'd take in obscure off-off-Broadway plays followed by ferry rides to Staten Island and back. In the summer, you could find us at Rockaway Beach.

We spent wonderful weekends at a 200 year-old farm we rented in Vermont during the ski season. Rick Lavigny was the owner and as it happened, mayor of West Rutland. He always thought we made the nicest foursome, but he could never figure out if Delia was with Dean and I was with Dinah, or vice versa. He'd look for hints, but he was too yankee to ask. It was reassuring to Dean that the right combination never entered his mind as an option.

Back in The City, Dean and I made perfect dates for Delia and Dinah when they didn't have any, but wanted to go somewhere, like the Doors concert at Hunter College or Ramsey Lewis at the Rainbow Room or concerts at Fillmore East. Likewise, although it wasn't premeditated, they were a great cover for us when we needed it. Like when Dean's father came out for a visit. Or my Aunt Cecille and Uncle Carl came up from New Jersey.

One day, not long after we met them, Richelle came over to borrow some exotic spice Dean had picked up in Chinatown. She looked at the book I was reading. It was *Beat Zen, Square Zen, and Zen.*

"How long have you been into Eastern philosophy?" she asked.

"Well, I guess since I was a sophomore at college," I replied.

"What brought it on?" she continued.

"You mean the Eastern stuff?" I asked. "Well, really it was sort of by accident. I went to a Catholic college and if you're Catholic, they make you take Theology. I knew after two semesters of it I couldn't take any more, so when I went back my sophomore year, I registered as a Buddhist so they wouldn't make me take it."

"And they went for that?" Richelle asked, rummaging through our spice rack.

"Well I knew they'd eventually doubt my sudden conversion to Buddhism so I started reading up on it. And one book led to another."

"Giacco, why don't you come over Friday night. I think Jack might have something you'd really like!" Richelle found the spice she was looking for and poured some into a jigger. Dean was going to be entertaining some friends from work Friday night, so I said, "Sure. How can I resist now that you have me so curious?"

I had noticed some recent changes in Richelle. She was letting her hair get frizzy. Dinah was worried because she had reneged on working a couple of flights. If you did that too often, you were gone. But Richelle never seemed to worry and outwardly she seemed more vibrant and cheerful than ever. My curiosity as to what Jack had for me limited itself to the realm of books or at most a secret chant.

Instead, that Friday night in the girls' apartment, he handed me a sugar cube and told me to let it melt in my mouth. Delia and Dinah hovered over me, making faces and telling me I was crazy, but too curious to protest too much. Richelle kept reassuring me, promising me that Jack was an excellent guide.

"Guide?" I gulped. "A guide for what?"

"Just let it melt in your mouth," Jack cajoled. And he and Richelle each popped a cube into their mouths to prove its safety, to lead the way.

500 grams of pure LSD 25 eventually coursed through my brain. I had never had such powerful stuff. When it was scary, Richelle and Jack were there to talk me through it. When it was funny, we laughed so uncontrollably, Delia and Dinah would look completely perplexed and their expressions would make us laugh even harder. When I started getting atomic, Jack read to me from *The Tibetan Book of the Dead*, and said, "to struggle is hell, to relax, divine." Richelle played all the right records at just the right time. And when I peaked I saw God in a bottle of Mazola oil, just standing there next to the red and silver baking soda on the shelf. And then I stood up and began to dance like I've never danced before.

From then on Friday night was trip night. Jack lived on the first floor of an old brownstone two blocks away. On weekend nights, a line would form from his apartment door at the top of the landing, all the way down the stairs and out to the street. In 1966, LSD was still legal. No laws had yet made it contraband.

When you got to the open door, you were greeted by Jack standing behind an ironing board with a bowl of sugar cubes on it. Immediately to his right was the refrigerator. When you forked over your three bucks, he'd take a vial out of the fridge, suck up some of the liquid acid into an eye dropper, hold it over a sugar cube and let it sponge up the 500-milliliter drop as he squeezed the bulb. Then he'd wrap it in aluminum foil and hand it to you.

Sometimes experienced heads would have him drop it directly onto their tongues. Sometimes a real renegade would have him drop it directly into their eyes! And if you were a friend of Jack's, it wasn't unlike him to double the dose. A thousand mics of pure LSD!

When it was my turn at the ironing board, I would smile at Jack and say, "I'll take one on the tongue and three to go." I'd stick out my tongue and Jack would always put two drops on it. Then he'd slip the wrapped cubes into my shirt pocket, pat my chest brotherly-like and I'd leave, hoping to make it the two blocks home before I started coming on. Jack's was the best take out in New York!

One time, Dinah came with me. Just to chaperone. Back then, it was always nice to have someone straight around just to be sure. Acid wasn't for partying. Acid was for ego death. And rebirth. By the time we got to the corner, on our way back to my place, the acid completely overtook me. The sidewalk became soft and spongy and my legs kept falling into it. Dinah had to support me the entire way. She was half scared, half laughing, as she tried to give me instructions on the basics of walking.

Eventually even Dean got into acid. It became a ritual Friday night affair for all of us. During the week, we each put on our workday uniforms and went to work. But when Friday evening arrived, we turned into spacemen and spacewomen. And like astronauts, we were well prepared. All the albums were arranged in order of their ability to induce relaxation or insight. Munchies were stocked for the trip down. And we always kept a couple of caps of Thorazine around in case of a bad trip. Though a lot of times you can learn more from a bad trip than from a good one.

When "Sergeant Pepper's Lonely Hearts Club Band" came out, I bought it on a Monday, but it stayed wrapped in its cellophane until Friday night. We were saving it. And we put it in our play list of albums right after Donovan and the Moody Blues so it would be ready to listen to, to travel with, to learn from, to *become*, just about the time we'd be peaking. It didn't disappoint.

I had been tripping on acid a couple of months before I ever had my first toke of marijuana. That was about the same time I first cheated on Dean. When he found out, he sat me down and calmly lectured me.

"Listen Giacco! Remember those first nights in my hotel room? You've created a history for me based on those nights alone and the ones we've shared since. But you've taken me out of context and no matter what I tell you, you shine it on. You just don't get it!"

I squirmed a little. I didn't like being reprimanded, though that's not what he was doing.

Dean continued. "I am only gay for you," he said slowly, methodically, emphasizing each word. "You're the only reason I'm gay. I don't want to sleep with any other men. If you should leave or give me cause to leave you, I'd go straight. Because the straight world is easier for me. Because I do just fine in the straight world. Because I really like the straight world and I really like women. You are an anomaly in my life. You are unique in my life. Even I don't understand it sometimes. And I think you don't believe me... and I love you very much."

I just sat there. I didn't respond. I loved Dean very much, too. But it was also true that I didn't believe he was gay *only* for me. I didn't believe him for a long time. And when I eventually did, it was too late.

"I love you too," I said and reached over to give him a hug. "It's just that for the first time, I like myself. And for the first time, I feel desirable and attractive. And for the first time, I feel free and want to experience everything."

"And the fact that I desired you and still do isn't enough?" he asked, wincing a little.

He had me there. I didn't have an answer for him. But he must've loved me a great deal to put up with my shenanigans. Dean was dedicated to the double life and succeeded at it. But the more stoned I got, the harder it was to keep up pretenses. I went from one job to another. My circle of friends became more and more radical and extreme. *I* was becoming more and more radical and extreme. I would spend entire acid trips dancing. I couldn't bear having to get dressed in the morning and make believe I was eager to get ahead at some job that, when stoned, seemed ridiculous.

Dean was always there for me. The crazier I got, the more stable he got. When I lost one job, he'd help me find another. When I was broke, he paid the bills. He paid for weekends in the country. He paid for the drugs. It was Dean who allowed me to explore inner space while taking away all the risks. I took it all for granted. And to me there were no risks to be taken.

Until a mid-week party we went to in the East Village. Third story loft in an old warehouse. Some Japanese artist was having a happening. The loft was small and packed. But the only people I knew were the ones I had come with. Dean. Dinah. 15-year-old runaway, Bobby, who turned into an ancient sage when you tripped with him, his 14-year-old mistress, Monique… and Dennis Taylor.

Dennis was a beauty. About three years younger than me. A Midwest country boy from Nebraska. He had a perfectly proportioned body that glowed with health. Dennis had just arrived in the city. He had gotten my address from his dad who had gotten it from my parents. Mr. Taylor had become friends with my folks while vacationing in Florida and wound up buying a condo in the same complex where my folks lived. I was upset when my dad told me he had given them my address. Mom had assured Mr. Taylor I would help Dennis get settled in the big city. My mom and dad didn't have a clue as to how I was putting to work the degree they had sacrificed so much for. And I didn't want any intruders spilling the beans about my lifestyle. But when Dennis finally showed up on my doorstep, I secretly thanked them. The innocence he was so anxious to give up, made *me* anxious to help him.

Bobby, Monique, and Dennis were all tripping, but Dean, Dinah, and I would wait as usual for the weekend. The happening was called "Self-Immolation."

The room and everything in it was painted white. Six or seven people, including the artist were all in white. In a corner was a huge aquarium with 10,000 frogs in it and a couple of microphones whose cables led to an amplifier. When the amp was turned on, the sound of the frogs croaking was deafening and disturbing. Then the lights went off and black lights came on. The artist, a woman of about thirty, started painting green, fluorescent polka dots everywhere. First she started with the walls. Then the furniture. Then the floor. She was scrupulous in not leaving any space untouched. She took forever. The room was getting hot and filled with cigarette smoke. Dennis walked over, opened a window, then walked back and stood next to me.

The frogs were really getting to me and I wasn't getting the message the artist was trying to send. I was tired and I was bored. But when the environment was completely pointillist and after the third person in white was covered with dots, it became clear what she was doing. She was making everything disappear! As she got closer to covering everything and everyone with fluorescent dots, that's all you could see. Glowing green dots. Every direction. Up. Down. All sides. Dots everywhere and only dots. When the last person in white was 'immolated,' she started on herself.

She was almost through putting on the last dot when I noticed that Dennis wasn't watching, but had his back to her. He was just staring out the window, a serene smile on his face. And before it registered what was happening, Dennis took a running start, put his arms in front of him, hands overlapped, and swan-dived out the window to the pavement three stories below.

Monique screamed. But it was only after the artist had completely immolated herself with polka dots that people realized what had happened. Only Dean had the presence of mind to call the cops and an ambulance. Bobby leaned out the window to look. When he turned around he was as white as the walls were when we first arrived. He put a hand to his mouth and ran looking for a bathroom. He only made it to the aquarium. The frogs croaked in amplified horror.

Bobby and Monique, still tripping, were really freaked out. All of us were. And all of us stayed up half the night trying to sort it out. The next day, it was Dean who called Mr. Taylor and helped make arrangements to ship Dennis' body home. Dinah swore she would never trip again. Dean insisted there always be somebody straight around to watch over us when we were tripping. That was a job Delia liked doing. But even Dennis' death didn't deter us from continuing to get high.

Dean decided to take a job in LA. When he asked me if I wanted to stick with him, I said, "Yes." But I had already turned in my Brooks Brothers suits for slacks made out of scarves and neckties. I had turned in my fashionably neat Beatles cut for hair that was just growing itself. And if I were very good and let it grow as long as it wanted to, wonderful markings would appear as it approached the middle of my back. I had turned that back on the entire establishment, but could only do so because Dean hadn't.

"Are you just going to stand there spaced out?" he yelled at me.

I came out of my reverie and looked into Dean's eyes. He always said I had the deepest, saddest and darkest eyes he had ever seen. He took a resigned sigh and lowered his voice.

"I still love you. Lisa loves you. We love you so much that if you want to, you can come back to Chicago and live with us. She's even willing to give it a try as a threesome. But I am primary in her life and I am forcing myself to stop making *you* primary in mine."

I just stood there trying to take it all in. Somehow the significance of what Dean was saying was escaping me. I was viewing this meeting and listening to this conversation from somewhere high above us. I was just watching myself go through the motions and words. Watching myself looking hurt and a little scared. But the one doing the watching was completely detached.

I knew Dean well enough to know he had arrived at this decision after a lot of thought. And I'm the first to admit I was surprised it hadn't happened sooner. I really hadn't spent any time with him since I got back from Woodstock. Which reminded me that I still hadn't paid him back for the money he wired to fly me home.

Dean looked at me, fighting back tears. He knew without my saying it that I wouldn't be taking him and Lisa up on their offer.

"Not that you deserve it," he said, getting down to business, "but when I bought the house in Laurel Canyon I put it in both our names, so as soon as it sells, I'll split any profits with you and that'll be the end of it. OK? In the meantime, I'm sure you're busted so here's some money. I'll pay myself back out of your share from the house."

Dean waited for me to refuse his generous offer. Not that it wasn't sincere, but he held out a chance that I wouldn't accept it as an assertion of my independence. I watched myself thanking him and holding out my hand. I wished him and Lisa all the best. He shook his head sadly.

"Do you want to come back with me to the house? Do you have a place to stay?" He was still looking out for me, even after all this.

"I'll be fine, really," I assured him, though I didn't have a clue as to what would happen next. The witness that was watching assured me everything was perfect. Dean and I hugged and I watched until his car was out of view.

The house sold faster than expected. Lisa moved in with her folks for the few weeks remaining until their trip to Chicago. Dean moved in with Jerry Smythe who owned a house on Appian Way overlooking Laurel Canyon, a few doors down from John Phillips' house. Two other guys lived there as well. Jobraith Jones and Tom McIntyre, both of whom were members of the cast of "Hair." I went there three or four times during the next few weeks to visit Dean.

Jerry and Jobraith were always around, but I never met Tom, though I could hear him playing his guitar in his bedroom. Dean used to kid me that it was just as well, because if I did meet him, I'd only fall in love with him. He wanted nothing to do with being instrumental in providing me with yet another romantic escapade. Not that my infatuation would be reciprocated.

On my last visit Dean gave me a check for $4700, my share of the profits from the Laurel Canyon house. I didn't see Dean and Lisa again until a couple of years later when Dean sent me a round trip ticket to Chicago to visit them at their home in Winnetka. Just for a long weekend. The three of us slept together every night, just for old times' sake.

After that, I never saw nor heard from them ever again. Two more people to add to the list of those who changed my life and disappeared forever from it.

CHAPTER 8
October 1969

I spent the night shivering on the deck of the Moonfire Inn which straddled Topanga Creek. Along toward dawn, a young earth mother woke me up. Her name was Kathy and she was the breakfast cook at the Inn.

After gently interrogating me and deciding I wasn't a threat, she said, "C'mon inside. I'll make you some fresh chamomile tea."

That sounded good and I followed her inside. As she replenished the industrial coffee makers with water, filters, and coffee, she studied me carefully. She was trying to come to some conclusion about me but didn't ask any questions.

When she started mixing eggs in a bowl and dicing garlic and onions, I offered my help. She handed me some pancake mix.

"Think you can handle making enough for twenty servings?"

"If that's the same thing as making enough for myself twenty times over, I think I can handle it."

Kathy laughed. "Go wash up first. But make it fast. These eggs are for you and they're almost done."

Within a week, Kathy and I were the co-breakfast chefs at the Moonfire Inn. She helped me find an old house, in desperate need of repair, at the very top of Observation Drive. The owners across the street were anxious to sell it before the next major mud slide, a quirk of the area I wasn't told about, and I innocently handed over a $4000 down payment on the contract they would carry.

The next eight months or so were idyllic. Kathy and I would meet halfway down the hill at 5:30 every morning. Then we'd walk through the woods sharing a joint and collecting wild chamomile. By six, we had all the burners going and the smells of organic coffee, fresh eggs, herbs, veggies, and whole wheat pancakes filled the Inn. I could never refute arguments for vegetarianism even though I practiced it haphazardly. But when Moonfire himself showed up one morning and asked me to remove my leather belt and get myself some cloth shoes, I apologized for my insensitivity and agreed with him wholeheartedly.

He gave me a copy of Dr. Ehret's *Mucusless Healing Diet System*. It turned me into a Vegan. I eliminated all grains and dairy products from my diet. A handful of almonds each day supplied my protein. I fasted every Sunday and three days at the end of each month. Organic coffee enemas were a weekly ritual. Sometimes I would do a 10-day fast of salt water and lemon juice with honey. I had so much oxygen in my brain, it was like being stoned. And I could get by on five hours of sleep a night and feel well rested.

Once in a while I worked the dinner shift, but breakfast was the most fun. It was laid back and relaxed and the small breakfast crowd was always interesting.

Neil Young was a regular. He'd come in about seven, take a guitar off the wall and start playing soft ballads. Topanga Creek bubbled and gurgled beneath our feet. The sun would finally get high enough to hit the kitchen windows and shafts of light speared the steam rolling up from the boiling potatoes.

Every morning I'd go out to the dining area and ask Neil what he wanted for breakfast and every morning he'd say the same thing. "Surprise me!"

It became a ritual. I conjured up curried tomato omelets. Mushroom and asparagus frittatas. Pecan waffles with loganberry syrup. Fresh figs smeared with almond butter. Poached eggs atop a bed of roasted potatoes and ginger chips. The wilder the combination, the more he liked it.

Sometimes some of the guys from Canned Heat would come in. Or maybe Taj Mahal. Sometimes, Kathy and I would be cooking in the back and we'd hear great jams going on out front. Maybe one of them would pass a joint back to us through the serving window. Then it would take forever to get breakfast together, but no one seemed to care. This was Topanga, where rockers had come to escape the frenetic and crazy life of Hollywood, the Strip, and the Whiskey a Go Go. This was still the country. It was a trip. It just didn't get much better than this!

But country as it was, there was no lack of socializing or adventures, especially sexual. Both the Moonfire Inn and the Corral, the local pub, drew a free-spirited and stoned crowd. Hitchhikers in need of food and shelter were always hanging out at the Moonfire.

Those with some money hung out at the Corral because it had great live music and served alcohol. A lot of well-known musicians enjoyed playing there. It was a perfect place to try out new material.

Both the Inn and the Corral were ideal for picking up strays. Some of them made my evenings memorable. My house was always filled with freaks needing a place to crash. Many stayed for weeks on end.

At the Corral, Tolucca, the large beautiful bouncer, decided to have the hots for me. One night when I took a tab of the Peace pill, she saw I was very vulnerable and persuaded me to go home with her. She shared a house with Taj Mahal. When we got there, he was sitting at the kitchen table over a pile of something he was inspecting with a magnifying glass. I wanted to see what he was doing, but she whisked me up to her room before I could even say "Hi." When I protested, Tolucca told me he was tripping and didn't like being disturbed.

Tolucca was something else. Light brown and incredibly soft skin. Large glistening black eyes. She was exotic, but her big lips could suck your face off and her cavernous vagina could swallow a slight man like me whole. She came on with a vengeance. She just tore at my clothes and threw me down on the bed. She was fucking me, or trying to, before my spinning head could even adjust to the room, much too busy with African weavings and baskets.

What? No foreplay? I'm not that kind of boy! Please be gentle with me!

When I couldn't keep a hard on, I thought she was going to get downright nasty. Instead, she got up, threw on an African robe and stood at the side of the bed looming over me.

"You're useless!" she yelled. "Get out of here so I can be alone. I'd rather do it myself."

I quickly dressed and sheepishly climbed down the stairs. Taj was still at the kitchen table. When he looked up and saw the sorrowful and embarrassed expression on my face, he burst out in deep laughter. Rather than let me leave feeling totally inadequate, he called me over and gestured to a chair.

"Don't fret, bro'," he said still chuckling. "Tolucca is too much for anybody. There's no satisfyin' that big black sister! So don't worry 'bout it! She'll only hold it against you for the rest of your life!"

I must've looked like a scared puppy just hit with a newspaper for peeing all over the rug, because Taj went into a fit of laughter that lasted a full five minutes. Then he took half the pile of African beads he was sorting and pushed them across the table to me.

"I'm looking for all the ones that have these diamond designs on them," he said holding one in his palm as an example. And we spent the hours remaining until dawn in total silence, sorting African beads together. By the time I left my eyes felt like an abused kaleidoscope.

A few days later, just toward the end of our breakfast shift, a young man walked in. When Kathy saw him, she rolled her eyes and said, "Oh, no!"

"Oh, no, what?" I asked looking him over through the serving window.

He was about 25, wearing a robe made out of an army issue blanket. When he took it off, I could see crucifixes and ankhs embroidered on the inside lining. He was lean, with long sandy hair and bright blue eyes. He had a slightly crazy look, but there was something about him I found attractive. Maybe that was it, his craziness, his unpredictableness.

"That's Reverend Trey," Kathy said. "Always causing a scene. Spouting Jesus stuff all the time. A real nuisance! Don't say anything to get him going!"

I walked through the swinging doors into the dining room and took his order. He gave it to me staring intently into my eyes. As I turned to go back into the kitchen, he stopped me.

"What's your name?" he asked.

"My name's Giacco," I replied curtly, but not impolitely.

"I mean your *real* name," he said.

"That is my real name," I replied.

"That's your *given* name," he insisted, "not your *real* name!"

"Well, thanks for setting me straight," I said, "but I've gotta get your order in now, so see you in a few."

"Have it your way. I just thought maybe I was supposed to be a channel of grace for you." At the sound of those words that Josie had uttered not so long ago, I stopped in my tracks and turned back to look at him. He bowed his head over the placemat in what seemed like a monk at prayer.

I avoided any further conversation with him, but when he paid his bill, he said, "Meet me out in front at seven tonight and I'll tell you your real name." Then he flew out the door.

He didn't seem surprised when I showed up. I half-heartedly hoped my humoring him would lead to some kind of sexo-spiritual experience. Those were always the most satisfying. But when he told me to jump in his beater of a car, not much more than a glorified oil pump, I became apprehensive.

"Want to come up to my place?" I asked, thinking if I took the initiative I'd have more control over the situation.

"Can't do that," he said bluntly. "Can't give you your name there. It's got to be in *my* spot."

"Where's your spot?" I asked.

"Just hop in and I'll show you." And I did, throwing caution to the warm wind funneling down the canyon from the San Fernando Valley.

A full moon was coming up. We had driven a couple of hours. Past the sprawl of the valley floor. Past the freeways. Past all signs of civilization. One of his headlights suddenly went out, but as we made a turn the good one cast a brief swath of light on a sign that said "Angeles National Forest."

A mile or two down a paved road that headed into the San Gabriel Mountains, Reverend Trey pulled onto a gravel one. It dead-ended a few miles farther at a trailhead beside a little stream. As we got out I could see the remains of previous campers. The night air was warm and I could still feel the heat of the rocks and pebbles of the desert floor rising through my canvas shoes.

Reverend Trey made a fire with the scraps of wood lying in the circle of stones left by our most recent predecessors. The moon rippled on the surface of the stream. A coyote howled. I fantasized how I would let Reverend Trey seduce me with cosmic revelations. We would make passionate man-love under the desert sky. I also fantasized how Reverend Trey would slit my throat and throw my body on top of the rippling moon. The former fantasy was so compelling I only briefly entertained the latter. Neither happened.

"Stay here," he commanded, and with one big leap, he crossed the stream and ran to the middle of a small grove of scrub pine. The moon cast a pale blue light on his face as he began twirling like a dervish and howling. The howls turned into unintelligible, but syntactically correct sentences, with subjects, verbs and objects. What I thought was gibberish was some strange language I'd never heard.

He kept spinning and spinning, chanting in tongues, until I thought his frenzy would drill his body into the ground. Then he collapsed in a heap. I stood up to see if he was OK. He looked at me and ran energetically back to the campsite. He grabbed me by the shoulders. His eyes were afire. He looked pale. Beads of sweat were still on his brow.

"You're *real* name is... Jeremiah!"

"Jeremiah?" I puzzled.

"Jeremiah," he repeated, emphasizing each syllable. "The poet warrior!" And as soon as he said it, he turned around and ran up the trail and disappeared into a shadow.

I called out a few times, but there was no response. I started out after him, but a few hundred yards up the trail, shadows of trees and boulders turned into rattlesnakes and mountain lions and I tricked myself into being afraid, so I turned around to wait for him at the car.

When I got back down the trail, the fire was almost out, Reverend Trey was nowhere to be seen... and the car was gone!

Better. Much better! I thought of Jon as I stoked the dying embers and looked around for more kindling. I wasn't even sure where I was, but I was sure it was far from everything. I was sure Kathy would be furious with me for not showing up for work. I was sure Moonfire would fire me if he found out. I was sure I didn't like the situation I was in.

The ground and rocks had given up all their heat and the early morning hours were surprisingly cold. But within an hour of sunrise, it got warm, then very warm, then hot. By the light of day, the place seemed peaceful and tame. And I was mesmerized by the desert stream swirling around my shoeless feet.

It was so clear and swift, no more than a foot deep, about four feet wide. You could see every grain of sand that made up its bed. The sand was uniformly fine, dotted every now and then with pebbles and medium sized rocks. It looked like a Zen rock garden, except the rocks sparkled like polished jewels under the constantly glazing veneer of the stream.

I felt my toes sinking deeper into the sand and studied the eddies the obstacles my feet made in the stream. The eddies were faster than the rest of the flow and ate away at the bed, forming a little trench a fraction of an inch deeper than the rest of the bottom. Where the stream was blocked completely by my ankles, the sand built up, making the bed a little higher than the rest.

This is fascinating! If Reverend Trey had murdered me and thrown my body in the stream and no one ever discovered it, I could have been instrumental in shaping the course of this miniature river! I mean we're talking millions of years here, but by my actions, I can alter the course of this stream! For every action there is an equal reaction or something like that. Right?

I looked around for a really big rock. When I found one I thought might have some impact, I placed it strategically in the middle of the stream. I studied the eddies and backups it made and tried to imagine far into the future, based on the visible alterations it was now making in the bed of fine sand, the grand canyon it would eventually form. Geologists of millennia hence would explain to students in universities that, "This wonder of the world, this grandest of grand canyons, was formed over many years by wind and water erosion, glacial activity, and the rock that Giacco put smack dab in the middle. See how the canyon takes a sharp right there and splits into two forks? That was Giacco's doing!"

So this was karma! Geologic karma. Logic karma. Every step you take has a consequence. Every thought you think has a consequence. Every emotion you feel has a consequence. I knew it before. I could explain it to someone else. But now I *understood* it. And once you understand a truth, the real work is in the living of it.

I began to feel guilty about the rock, so I struggled to lift it out of the sucking bed of the stream and tossed it onto the bank. It was stifling hot. I took off the rest of my clothes and sat naked in the middle of the stream, watching my buttocks make what would be great swimming holes 100,000 years in the future. That's when I heard a car coming up the gravel road.

I pulled on my pants just as a park ranger pulled into the campsite. I told him I had been ditched there by some friends as a joke. The truth was too hard to explain. The lie was easier to believe. I hitched a ride with him to the highway.

Once there, I got one ride after another up the valley. By late afternoon I was at the east end of Topanga Canyon. Easy as pie. And then an Impala convertible stopped. The driver was a balding, neatly dressed, well-scrubbed kind of guy. Maybe late twenties, early thirties. A kind of a goody two-shoes, do-the-right-thing kind of guy. Certainly not the kind of guy you'd expect much conversation from, let alone a surprising one.

"Get in," he smiled.

"Hi," I smiled back. "Thanks for stopping. I'm going as far as the…"

"I know where you're going," he said straightforwardly. "I know where you live."

I looked at him carefully, trying to imagine him with long hair or any hair at all. Trying to remember where or when I had met him. Nope. I didn't know him. His face was completely unfamiliar to me.

"How do you know where I live? I don't think we've ever met!"

"We haven't until now," he said, his eyes smilingly glued to the road. "But I know you live at the top of Observation Drive."

"I don't understand. How do you know that?" I said a little nervously.

This time he did take his eyes off the road. He looked directly at me and said, "Your name is Jeremiah, isn't it?" and looked straight ahead again.

I felt myself shake a little. My throat got dry but my hands were wet. "And assuming that is my name, which I'm not sure it is, but if it is… how do you *know* that?"

"Because I'm the Thief on the Cross," he said, turning to me as if it were a stupid question.

I was sure this was a practical joke of some sort. But how could it have been executed so quickly, so premeditatedly? And by whom? And why?

"That's it," I said firmly, "you can let me out here. Right here. Now!"

"No, I can't do that," he said calmly. "I'm supposed to see that you get home. It's OK. Don't worry! I know exactly where it is."

And he did. By the time we traveled the winding roads to the top of Observation Drive, he had told me about a score of other Biblical characters who had recently discovered who they *really* were.

"The Lord is among us," he said seriously and joyfully as I got out of the car. "And as soon as everyone has their real names, he will reveal himself to us!"

He drove off. I caught him looking at me in the rear-view mirror. Just a flash of a smile behind his eyes. I never saw Reverend Trey or the Thief on the Cross ever again.

I was beat. I was dirty. I made my way up the long path to the house and barely acknowledged the people crashing there. Most of them, I'm sure, didn't even know it was my house. Fortunately, no one was in my room and I slept restlessly. When I did get up, I realized I had missed yet another day at work.

I got fired the same day they arrested Charles Manson. Pigs were everywhere. Police, troopers, deputies. People were being hassled up and down the canyon. I got stopped and questioned twice between the Moonfire Inn, where I picked up my last paycheck, and the Country Store.

Everything was getting strange. The vibes were unstable and could go any which way. The Thief on the Cross had weirded me out. Unlike my experience with Josie, I was uncertain of the magic Reverend Trey had performed. It just smacked a little of the satanic. He had weirded me out, too. Were charlatans playing with my mind?

Topanga was losing its charm for me. After all these wonderful months, there were too many signs that it was time to move on. I was fighting hard not to fall into a depression. I felt trapped. I didn't have the energy to create options for myself. I was used to letting things happen to me.

I was standing in front of the Country Store thinking so hard it might have been out loud.

Please, somebody come and take me away from here!

As I turned to walk into the store, I saw a young, bearded, long-hair coming out of the phone booth. His eyes lit up and he ran toward me with arms extended, ready to embrace me. He was halfway there when I recognized him.

"Jon!" I yelled out.

I was beaming as he swooped me up and spun me around and whispered in my ear, "Giacco! It just doesn't get any better than this!"

CHAPTER 9
June 1970

I studied Jon carefully as we loaded his red VW camper with the supplies we needed for the drive to Tucson. His energy was so bright and contagious, it was like the vibration of a tuning fork in the key of A. Perfect pitch. It stood out from him a good foot and preceded him wherever he'd go. That's what made him seem imposing and larger than life. If you got within hugging range, he'd give you one that made you feel stronger, as if you'd become a person of more mass. Not heavier, just more substantial.

Jon was over six feet tall, with nicely muscled long legs and a hairy chest. Straight and fine brown hair framed his square face and solid neck down to the shoulders. His eyes and smile were the most engaging part of his body and most consistent. The rest of him changed depending on whether he was the ascetic or the bacchanalian bum regaling himself on the bounties of the world. Over the years as our paths crossed and meshed and diverted and crossed again, I would watch him go from lithe and lean to paunchy and soft a number of times. Whichever way he went, he was a wonderful sight to behold.

Jon was in the lean body and supple mind as he began organizing all the supplies. Everything had their place. For a guy who could play a commendable game of basketball, he sure was tidy. Not that there's any real correlation between basketball and tidiness. It's just that he was always so physical and large in his movements, I didn't think he was capable of neatness.

But then Jon was always a surprise. And he had a mind few could keep up with, whether it was throwing out sports statistics and trivia with loggers in a town called Twisp, discussing Civil War military strategies with Alabama crackers, arguing foreign policy with beltway bandits or ruminating on the subtleties of Buddhist texts with stupa priests. Jon was in awe of very few. But many of his peers were in awe of him.

No one had had as many part time jobs, had transferred to more colleges, or changed majors as much as Jon. His college transcript looked like a military brat's school records. His resume would have looked like one belonging to a day laborer. But through the gift of a photographic memory he had acquired the most interesting details on many subjects. Through the gift of a quick and analytical mind he could see how they fit into the big picture. Through the gifts of humor and drama he could explain it like a storyteller completely engrossing his audience. And through the gift of philanthropy, he shared it all with me.

While Jon checked the oil, I went inside the house to see if Barb had any more questions before we took off. Barb and Henry were the most recent wanderers the Moonfire had coughed up into my house. They had already been crashing there a couple of weeks but wanted to stay in Topanga through the summer. When they offered to make the mortgage payments for me while I was gone, I took them up on it. It was only $95 a month. And though I still had a couple of hundred bucks left from what Dean gave me, I didn't have any money coming in, so it would work out just fine, as usual.

When I walked back out, Jon was polishing the two white doves on the side of the van's passenger door with the sleeve of his shirt. Then he bent down and gave them little pecks on their cheeks. He turned around, saw me, opened the door and swept me in like a chauffeur does his master and slammed the door shut. Then he slapsticked his way in front of the van. At the driver's door window, he stretched out his arms, gave me a wide-eyed grin, and said, "I can hardly wait 'til right now! Let's go!"

And off we went puttering down the hill. I looked over at Jon and studied him some more. The first night after we met at the phone booth, the adrenalin that flowed from the reunion eventually subsided over a dinner of broiled tofu marinated in soy sauce and mustard, steamed broccoli, and carrot juice with a beer chaser. Jon had eyed the meal curiously, but wiped his plate clean. I think inwardly he'd hoped I was a bacchanalian carnivore. Then over some primo weed, Jon explained how he'd caught up with me.

"When I left you at Woodstock, my dear friend, I really left! I couldn't find any of my stuff. I couldn't remember which bush I hid it under. All the bushes looked the same. The last bush I looked under was right next to the road. And this pickup came tooling along packed with freaks. Almost sideswiped me. When it slowed down, one of them yelled, 'Jump on!'"

Jon jumped out of the kitchen chair into a semi-crouching position, his arms extended upwards, his hands draped slightly forward. He looked like a lean primate about to reach for the limb of a tree.

"So I did, except there was no room at all in the bed of the truck. I had to ride all the way to Marathon hanging on to the tailgate. When we stopped at a truck stop, I went in to take a leak. I had to whizz something fierce. On the wall next to the urinal was this vending machine that I thought was for condoms, ya know. But when I looked closer, I saw that it dispensed these little novelty trinkets. So I reached in my pants and found a quarter. And I also found the inside of a gum wrapper that had your name and 'Laurel Canyon' on it.

"I put in my quarter and out popped a miniature bowling ball bag keychain. If you squeezed it, it opened up to become a change purse. Too perfect! I opened it, carefully rolled up the gum wrapper like a scroll, and stuffed it inside the bowling ball bag. And that was the extent of my belongings after Woodstock. My very first post-Woodstock material acquisition. A miniature bowling ball bag with you inside. It sat on my dresser all year."

Jon reached into his pocket and produced the tiny bowling ball bag. He tossed it on the table and then sat back down. I opened the plastic neon orange container and inside was the silvered gum wrapper, tightly rolled and folded over once. I took it out and carefully unfurled it. You could see that the wrapper had been carefully hand-pressed to free it of creases, perhaps a number of times over the course of the last nine months. On the paper side were scrawled my first name, a phonetically spelled version of my last name, and "Laurel Canyon Calif." The handwriting was that of a person definitely in an altered state.

You could tell it took a great deal of effort to make the inscription, forcing the mind to rule over the fingers and eyes like that. I was touched.

It was Jon's way of saying how much he connected with me at Woodstock. How much he thought of me and cared for me. I looked up at him almost blushing with flattery. His eyes moistened. Our relationship seemed so cosmic and magical, you'd think we were meant to be lovers. And we were. But not physically. We were lovers on a spiritual plane. And it was so fulfilling, I didn't want to entertain libidinous thoughts that might interfere with what we had going.

I will admit that every now and then I tried to conjure up images of us making love, but there were never any visceral longings for that to happen. In fact, in the beginning, our conversations were always so out there in the ethers, we had yet to get around to anything of a mundane nature. Like what we liked and didn't like. I thought I was doing a great job at being a regular Joe and was waiting for just the right time to tell him my most secret desires.

Once during a conversation he mentioned out of nowhere that maybe we should have sex just so we could say we had. As if we were filling in a missing gap.

"I don't know why, but I want to be able to say that I've had sex with you! It's just that I really don't feel any groinal sensations!"

I laughed and said I was flattered and not to worry about it. I wasn't having any groinal attacks either. Nevertheless, I felt a pang of jealousy when Jon mentioned Rose.

"We decided to take a trip and I told Rosie, 'Rosie, we just have to find Giacco! You have to meet this guy. You will fall in love with him!' And it was just supposed to happen I guess. Because just outside of LA we picked up a hitchhiker who thought he knew you. And he took us to a house in Laurel Canyon where this woman Suzanne lived. And Suzanne told us we'd find you in Topanga. And in Topanga, I'm checking the phone book to see if you're in it. And I turn around and there you are!"

I had only gotten as far as "I told Rosie" and didn't hear the rest of the sentence.

Who is this Rosie? Where does she fit in?

"Well then, where's Rosie?" I asked excitedly. But the excitement was forced because I felt threatened by this intrusion into our relationship.

Jon lowered his voice and looked to his left and right as if making sure the coast was clear. "Rosie… well Rosie had to deliver some… *packages*… to friends… in Ridgewood. That's where we both grew up. Just a couple of kilos. A quick trip. Get there, turn around, come back." His voice returned to normal. Which meant a little loud and a little excited with a hint of elation in it.

"Rosie, god bless her beautiful, mouth-watering soul, is going to meet us the day after tomorrow. Wait, no. The day after that. Two days from now. And you two are going to love each other!" Jon's eyes widened. "You and I are gonna pick her up at LAX and then... Tucson!"

For the next two days, Jon and I explored my favorite parts of Topanga Canyon. Mostly by foot. Imbibing and toking at all scenic overlooks. Though just being with him was a high, Rosie was always there, like a cloud preventing me from getting the unadulterated sunshine I thought I deserved. I resented getting only those two days to be alone with Jon in Topanga, but we chatted each other up the entire time and that was about the equivalent of a week with any other person.

Eventually LAX came into view and the time to pick up Rosie was at hand. I jumped into the back seat. Jon kept the VW bus in the slow lane of the freeway all the way to the airport. When we exited on to the "Arriving Flights" ramp, I was a little nervous. But when I saw her waving us down at the Taxis Only parking in front of the baggage claim area, my anxiety, insecurity, resentment, whatever it was I had been feeling, dissipated immediately.

She was quite beautiful. Her smooth olive skin glowed with the healthy bronze of a recent sunbath. Her long, dark brown hair curled slightly at the ends. She was on the skinny side, but somehow the shape of her hips and breasts made her seem voluptuous. Her nose had a slight hook to it. She had eyes whose color I could never quite name. They gave her a Sophia Lorenesque kind of exotica. In her conservative solid yellow day dress cinched around the waste by a flowered scarf, she looked very sophisticated and lady-like. Maybe a fashion model. But when she started jumping up and down, flailing her arms and mugging at us, we cracked up. Our Fair Lady reverted to Eliza Doolittle. My kind of girl!

"Isn't she a wonder?" Jon asked in awe.

"Well, I can tell from here, she's a trip!" I said.

Jon pulled over and Rosie opened the side door and threw in her one piece of luggage, a carpetbag made of an old oriental rug. Then she got in, closed the passenger door, leaned over and gave Jon a big kiss.

"Hiya, Honneee!" she said squirming her lips into a pucker for one more.

"Om Shivaya, my devastating devi, you!" Jon mooned back.

Then she turned around to face me and gave me a big hug and kiss as Jon pulled into the airport traffic.

"Hi Giacco." She pulled back about eight inches and stared at me. "I feel like I already know you. Jon's done nothing but talk about you for months. And now that I see you, there's something strangely familiar about you. I'm not sure what it is."

She shimmied between the front seats, sat down next to me, and started pulling clothes out of her carpetbag. Without a trace of self-consciousness, she took off her dress. She didn't have on a bra or underpants. Out of politeness, I faced forward, but noticed some people in passing cars turning their heads for a second look. Rosie just waved at them as she slipped on some cutoffs and fashioned the scarf that she wore as a belt into a halter top. She recounted to Jon her trip back east and how everything had gone just fine and how she couldn't wait for us to get into the desert.

Then she said, "I know what it is!" She leaned against me and put her cheek next to mine. "Look, Jon."

Jon looked in the rear-view mirror at us, puzzled. Then his eyes brightened.

"You two look just alike!" He exclaimed. "It's uncanny. You look like brother and sister. You could be twins!"

"Yeah! Can you see it?" Rosie said. "The nose, the skin coloring, the hair."

It was true. Rosie and I looked as much alike as two people of the opposite sex can, without one looking effeminate or the other butch. It was even more remarkable when Rosie and I would walk down the street together. Our body types seemed of the same issue. We were the same height and weight. Everywhere we traveled in the months and years to come, people would assume we were brother and sister. And if we introduced ourselves as such, no one ever doubted it. There were times when sitting at the end of a dock silhouetted by a sunset or watching us walk into the distance, even Jon couldn't tell us apart.

Rosie hopped back in the front seat and began interrogating me. "OK, give me the dish!" she ordered. Where was I raised? What brought me out to the west coast? What did I do for money? When she asked if I were involved in any "special" relationships, I was a little apprehensive. I told her "no," then corrected myself and said, "yes, the one I'm having with you two."

That made Jon and Rosie smile and they looked at each other, just for a moment, like two parents pleased with how they had raised their son. Then they looked at me. They liked my answer but they knew I was holding out. I could feel it as they faced forward. So I admitted that at times I preferred men physically, though not by much; and women emotionally, though not by much; and either gender intellectually. It was just that sometimes I got all turned around and didn't know which was most important to me. I wanted to be open to whoever came up with the right combination.

Rosie and Jon both turned to me at the same time with a look of self-satisfaction.

"We knew that!" they said in unison.

"For you, it only makes sense." Rosie added approvingly.

"Do you want me, Giacco?" Jon asked. "If you want me, you can have me, that's how much I love you already! So if you want me, just say so Honneceee!"

I laughed sheepishly, but Jon knew that I knew we had already moved beyond that chakra. When or where was beyond us. But we both knew it. All that mattered was that it didn't matter. Jon and Rosie talked about a person's sexual orientation as if it were no more important than the color of their hair. It was just another adjective. It had nothing to do with important things.

Up ahead was a rare red light. Jon yelled out. "Chinese Fire Drill!" We all got out and ran around the van. "But everybody take a different seat when you get back in. I'm tired of driving."

Jon jumped in the back, Rosie in the front, and I got to drive.

By the time we got to the outskirts of Yuma and three more fire drills, all our egos, ids and libidos were on the table. No thoughts had to go through any censorship on the way out of the mouth. We were completely and pleasurably uninhibited around each other.

We were performing running commentaries about ourselves, each other, people on the street, and people in passing cars. We came upon a construction site busy with tanned and sweaty young workers. Rosie turned to me and asked, "OK, Giacco, which of those workers on the roof do you like the most? I'll take the red-head with the bandana over there."

"Hmmm. I think I'll take the stud with the blond hair and the ripped T-shirt. Looks like he has a great chest."

"But we can't be sure now, can we?" she said with mischief in her eyes.

As we turned the corner around the site, Rosie undid her halter-top and leaned out the front window. Then she yelled as loud as she could to the rooftop.

"Hey you!" The men on the roof all looked down, and then did a double-take. "No, not you. You! Yeah, you! Take off your shirt. I want to see your chest!"

The blond looked over at his co-workers, laughed and peeled off his shirt with one macho crisscross move over his head. Then he puffed out his chest.

Rosie clapped first her hands, then her breasts together, looked at Jon, then at me. Jon was open-mouthed in pretended shock. I gave her two thumbs up. Then she waved back at the worker and yelled up. "You win! Congratulations. You passed the test!"

"Rosie," Jon halfheartedly admonished, "You're going to get us in trouble. Stop attracting attention!" As if that were possible for Rosie.

Rosie looked at Jon with "party pooper" on her face and put her halter top back on. But all the way to Tucson, whenever she saw a good-looking guy on the side of the road, she'd yell out to him to take his shirt off. At a stop light in Casa Grande, she managed to get three young businessmen to lift their shirts up.

"You at the end! Up higher. Past your nipple. That's right. Oooh, nice!" It's amazing we didn't get busted.

I knew she was doing it for me. She was doing all the things she knew I would do if I thought I could get away with it. Rosie was, to say the least, very intuitive, very persuasive, and very unpredictable.

And on top of everything else, she was very holy. Oh, there weren't any trappings of sanctimony or "better-than thou-ness." If anything, all three of us might have been viewed as the anathema to all standards of proper conduct. But each of us saw behind the other's eyes, a fiercely burning light. At least that's what we told each other we saw. And having been told it, we began to believe it. Not in an egotistical way, but rather in a self-effacing way.

Both Jon and Rosie mocked everything good naturedly, including themselves. For being too serious. For being too flippant. For being too courteous. For being too rude. My humor was also based on self-deprecation. It was a defensive tool I learned to use against local bullies as I was growing up. A tool that persuaded them not to beat me to a pulp, which they seemed to want to do often. Like every time I got a 100% on a test or wore my boy scout uniform in public.

In grade school, I was "Professor Bones." In high school, I was "The Nerd." I got so good at putting *myself* down before anyone else could, I used it long after it was really necessary. Now, I sometimes heard people refer to me as "a real *head*," which was a compliment of the highest order among stoners.

Nevertheless, old habits die hard and belittling myself was often effective in diffusing threats. But in the company of Jon and Rosie, it was a personality trait we shared and one that bonded us... this penchant for making fun of ourselves. For debasing each other. For reminding ourselves how insignificant we were.

I don't know how we got on the subject, but Jon started talking about J. Krishnamurti and Annie Besant mentoring him to be the next Christ and how J. told them all to get lost. That he was no avatar. He was just a *Hu Man*. *Man* was the loosely translated Sanskrit word for "mind." *Hu* was the Sanskrit phoneme that represented the most primordial sound known, the sound of breathing... and therefore, the energy which makes breath possible… what people call *God!* To be a true human was to be conscious of god. All you can do is breathe and live!

I told Jon and Rosie about my experience in Laguna with Josie. They quizzed me as if I was a drink of water and they were dying of thirst. But as I tried to answer their questions, I realized what had happened to me was almost impossible to verbalize… and the farther away in time I got from that mystical night, the more I doubted it really happened. The experience we shared seemed so simple and conclusive. Perhaps too conclusive. It took away the incentive to seek. And seeking was half the fun. And if it had happened, why me? And if me, so what? What next? Playing devil's advocate to Jon?

"Do you still make decisions?" Jon asked. I detected just the slightest smell of sour grapes on his breath.

"Well, for better or worse," I answered as candidly as I could, "it seems like decisions are always being made *for* me. Which bothers me sometimes, yet so far everything seems to have worked out OK."

"You know, Giacco… the thing with Josie and all… this transference of *Truth* as you call it?"

Jon looked at me in the rear-view mirror to wait for my nod and said, "Knowing the truth is one thing. Living it is another. That's where the real work is. And as long as you're caught in your mind somewhere between decisions… well, you're really not alive!"

I was confused. But I knew Jon was talking as much for his own benefit as for mine.

"Like, every moment you're confronted with decisions," Jon said. "Should I order the ham and cheese or the pastrami? Should I go to the movies or do the laundry? Should I become a dentist or an actor? It doesn't matter. Krishnamurti would say it doesn't matter. What's important is that the whole time you're making up your mind... well, it's all wasted energy. You're not alive. Just make the damn decision, live with it and move on!"

"Well that sounds kind of easy," I said.

"Well, I gave you sort of an oversimplification. Those examples are OK, but it's more subtle than that. The workings of the mind are so fast and convoluted that most of the time we're not even aware it's constantly weighing options, making comments, talking to itself, separating us from… from just *being!*"

"OK, I see where you're going," I said. "But just to keep things simple, let's keep things simple. I get two options thrown at me. I pick one as fast as I can. And I hate it immediately afterwards and realize it was the wrong choice. What do I do now?"

Rosie turned to me and said, "You punch yourself, of course!"

"You what?" I blurted.

"Punch Thyself!" And she quickly brought her fist up to her forehead and crossed her eyes. "Works for me every time. I should know. I make lots of wrong decisions. But when I start to get mad at myself, I just say 'punch thyself'. Then I give myself a good bop on the head and let it go at that. But be careful. One time I did it in a supermarket and some guy thought I was giving him the Sicilian fuck off move and Jon and him almost got into a fight!"

"That's how Rosie got that beautiful, hooked nose!" Jon chuckled. "Punching herself."

Rosie gently rubbed her fist into Jon's nose and then bent over and kissed it, laughing.

"Giacco. In the back there. There's a box of books. I've got two of Krishnamurti's if you want something to read." Jon gestured to the back corner of the van.

Under some blankets, I found a large box. As I rummaged through it, I saw that every book had something to do with self-realization. In addition to *The Bible*, *The Koran*, *The Bhagavad Gita* and other *normal* sacred books, there were books by mystics about the mysteries at the core of the world's major religions. There were biographies of avatars. Jesus, Buddha, Sri Yukteswar, Meher Baba. Books on all different kinds of yogas. Hatha, Bhakti, Karma, Jnana. Books on all kinds of diets. Macrobiotic, microbiotic, fruitarian, airian. Books by gurus I'd never heard of from cultures I'd never heard of. A path for anyone's foot, no matter how strangely shaped. But when I saw a copy of the *Aquarian Gospel of Jesus the Christ*, my heart raced and I understood why Jon and Rosie had been so excited by my story about Josie. Between the *Aquarian Gospel* and Brother Philip's *Secret of the Andes*, I found a book by Krishnamurti.

When I faced front I asked quietly, "Jon, are we on some sort of quest?"

Jon turned, looked at me and laughed, then turned back again. "Yea, Giacco. We're all on a big, giant, fucking, quest. That's why the three of us are smoking cigarettes. That's why we've eaten nothing but peanuts for a day and a half. So that we get so constipated we don't have to stop until we get to Tucson. We won't have to. We're bound for glory!"

Jon looked over his shoulder at me. "Get it? We're so constipated, we're *bound* for glory?"

Rosie punched Jon in the forehead. "I think your brain is constipated! Punch thyself!"

Jon looked at Rosie with a close-to-tears Stan Laurel face and said, "Better. Much better."

Rosie looked at me and our eyes locked on to one another's. Silently they acknowledged that we were indeed on a quest. And then we laughed out loud because we also knew we had absolutely no idea what it was.

The copy of *The Teachings of Don Juan: A Yaqui Way of Knowledge* sitting beside Jon should have been a clue.

We made it to Tucson just in time to hit the hippie health food co-op before it closed. Our bodies were thirsty for fruits and vegetables. We bought a twenty-pound sack of Valencia oranges, a 10-pound bag of Basmati rice, assorted root vegetables and a case of real ginger ale. Plus some nuts and treats to while away our taste buds. I argued with Jon about the rice. It wasn't exactly in keeping with Dr. Ehret's mucusless healing diet system. I was only a little surprised when Jon said, "Ehret be damned! Let's indulge ourselves!" And then he asked me if I knew how Dr. Ehret died. I shook my head.

"Your dear Dr. Ehret died in Rome after completing a 40-day fast," he said with an irrefutable air.

"You mean he starved to death?" I asked worriedly.

"No. He was just fine. But he was so high and lightheaded, that he tripped on the sidewalk and hit his head on the gutter. Cracked it wide open." Jon looked at me to see if I doubted him. Where he had picked up that tidbit of information, I'll never know. But I knew from Jon's face, it was true.

"So let that be a lesson to you. Don't walk the streets of Rome unless you have some mucus in you."

"You have enough mucus in you to tour all of Italy," Rosie threw in.

"Yes, well that's why we *stick* together, sweetheart," Jon tossed back. "Now you two can put the food away. I've gotta interrogate one of those Indian bros I saw stocking shelves back in the store. Be right back."

Jon was only gone a few minutes. When he jumped back into the driver's seat he said, "We have to make just one little stop and then we're on our way." About three miles east of Tucson, Jon pulled in front of a bunch of rundown buildings surrounded by an adobe fence.

"Stay here," Jon said. "This'll only take a minute."

Rosie and I looked at one another and then our eyes followed Jon as he walked under the arched entrance. Sitting quietly in a chair against the cracked adobe wall of the building nearest us was either a very old, wizened man or a younger man who had had a very hard life. We couldn't tell from that distance. But we could see deep lines in the dark, leathery face that was partially hidden by long straight black hair. Jon approached him and they talked a while. We couldn't hear what they were saying, but we could make out Jon's hearty laugh every so often. Then the old, young man or the young, old man stood up and Jon and he disappeared around the side of the building. When Jon returned, he was holding a small bag in his hand.

"What was that all about, you ask?" he blurted before we could get the same question out of our mouths. "Well, just never you mind. It's a surprise."

"It's drugs," Rosie said assuredly.

"It's a surprise!" Jon insisted.

"It's a surprise drug," Rosie corrected herself.

"It's alive!" Jon said throwing the van into gear. Rosie looked stumped, then shook her head and let it go at that.

We headed toward the Santa Catalina mountains in the Mt. Lemmon watershed. The summer sun cast brilliant oranges and reds behind us as the VW van struggled up the sandy and graveled road of Upper Bear Canyon to the Seven Falls trailhead. At the top of the canyon was a small parking area large enough for about four vehicles. We were the only ones there. It was almost dark. There was just enough light to make camp.

Rosie got out the pup tent while I started setting up the propane stove. Jon was admiring the last rays of light and the darkening shadows of the canyon walls.

"No need for that Giacco," he said when he saw me pumping up the stove. "We won't be eating. I mean you can eat if you want, but it'll be better if you don't."

I stopped pumping. "What'll be better if I don't?"

"These!" And Jon opened the bag he'd gotten from the old, young guy at the run-down dude ranch. Rosie and I walked up to Jon and the three of us stared into the bag.

There were about a dozen grayish-green round martian-looking things with short white fuzz growing out of their centers. I had never seen fresh peyote buttons before, only cleaned, dried, chopped up ones. I picked one from the bag. It felt fleshy. As I stared down at it, I understood why Jon had said it was "alive."

Jon looked up from the bag. "This is why I think we should fast. The less we have in our stomachs to upchuck, the better the trip will be."

Jon and Rosie slept in the van. I tried to sleep in the tent, but every sound I heard became a rattlesnake slipping into my bag or a wildcat clawing at the rip-stop nylon sloping above me. The only reassuring sounds were those of Jon and Rosie making love in the van. I finally fell asleep to the long, drawn-out howls of coyotes, plaintively serenading one another under the nearly full moon.

CHAPTER 10
June 1970

The chilly desert dawn gave way to intense heat as soon as the sun slid over the canyon wall. We went through two quarts of ginger ale before we even reached the path that steeply wended its way past the Seven Falls. The going was rough. Thongs weren't the best choice for footwear. The thongs kept slipping on the sandy stones and our feet kept slipping out of our thongs. But I was more worried about a rattlesnake bite in my Achilles heel than I was about making progress.

As if reading my mind, Jon turned back to look at me and said, "Remember. Walk toe to heel so you can retract your foot if you see something you don't want to step on!" That bit of advice didn't comfort me, but the sound of the first waterfall inspired me on.

There beyond a wind-eroded boulder was the first pool filled with the rushing water of a narrow 20-foot falls from the pool above. The overflow emptied through a smooth V in the lip of the pool's polished stone banks and became a small stream, bordered by thin ribbons of young, light green desert grass as it meandered gently downhill between the rocks. The pool was about four feet at its deepest. The path to the next higher falls and the pool waiting at the top of it, continued on the far side.

Jon, toting a daypack filled with the sack of oranges, walked around the edge. But Rosie and I, holding bottles of ginger ale and our shirts above our heads, slipped gently into the cold, refreshing water and bobbed our way to the other side.

All of the seven falls were beautiful, but each was slightly different. We reached the very top one, rested a bit, then started down again. The third falls from the top was our unanimous favorite. It felt the most inviting. It had a nice pool about three feet deep and fifteen feet across. Its bowl appeared to be one solid smooth stone, like an apothecary's mortar. The water was sparkling clear and rippled gently at the side edges. But at the far end, in front of a tan cliff, a white pestle of rushing water pulverized the pool into froth. At the valley end, the overflow was a good five feet wide and spilled thinly and gently twenty feet to the next pool below.

In the immediate vicinity of the pool, small grasses and bushes grew. One lone, small, but determined mesquite provided a patch of shade. Jon took out the sack of oranges and dumped them all into the pool. Then he took the bottles of ginger ale from Rosie and me and arranged them carefully in the empty sack. He gently placed the sack under the water and secured it to the root of a bush working its way toward the pool.

Jon motioned for us to sit down. He divvied up the buttons after first rinsing them in the pool. They became more alive, the way dry rocks do when you wet them. The withering green-grey suddenly became shiny obsidian black with overtones of Aztec emerald. The white hairs of strychnine perked up from a circular bed of light gold.

Taking turns with the army knife, we fastidiously removed the white hairs of poison and cut the buttons into quarters. Inside, the flesh was greener, almost fluorescent. Jon waded in the pool and retrieved three oranges. When we peeled these we were ready. We looked at each other and gulped with warranted apprehension. Jon reassured us and himself that we had removed those white hairs of poison and all would be well.

Then we each took a quarter of a button and munched on it as quickly as we could, trying not to breathe through our noses. We followed that immediately with a section of orange. Nothing could hide the taste of the peyote. Whoever decided thousands of years ago that these were fit for human consumption must've been truly inspired. They had the texture of dense veal aspic, but the buds of the tongue revolted against a taste they weren't equipped to handle. Forget bitter, sweet, salty, sour. Try moldy, mordant, nasty and styptic.

We each had gotten down two buttons. Jon put his fingers to his lips and blew a kiss into the air. "Ah, what a feast! Somewhat reminiscent of rotten squid stuffed with hard boiled thousand-year-old eggs. Don't you think?"

While Rosie ran to throw up behind a rock, Jon started on his third button. I could feel my stomach spasming. My mouth was pumping saliva like there was no tomorrow. I kept swallowing and breathing deeply.

"Try to keep it down, Giacco. But if you can't, don't fight it. If you can't keep it down, let it out. It's really only *after* you vomit that you get really high anyway. I *can't wait* to throw up!"

Just talking about it and hearing Rosie off behind the rock was all it took. I ran to a bush on the other side of the pool and vomited until I had the dry heaves. But after a slug of ginger ale and another orange, I tried to eat a third button. The aftertaste of bile complemented the peyote perfectly, but I decided I'd had my fill after eating just half of it.

While Rosie and I were composing ourselves by the side of the pool, Jon went off to complete the ritualistic upheaval. When he came back we played and waited to get high. Splashing each other in the pool, making designs in the sand, collecting pebbles. It was in the midst of one of these games that we looked around, then at each other, and realized we were flying.

For a long time, we didn't speak. We were trying to come to terms with what we were experiencing. On peyote those terms would be unique for each of us.

When I closed my eyes, the patterns on the inside of my lids changed rapidly and continuously like a kaleidoscope gone haywire. The designs became thousands of rattlesnakes intertwining. The rattlesnakes turned into scorpions and tarantulas and then back again. They began mutating into vibrantly colorful but nightmarishly frightening creatures who had choreographed a dance of swirling mandalas. They started to attack me and part of me knew I should let them, but I couldn't.

I forced my eyes open and drank in the landscape. The exterior trip was easier than the interior; a distraction from the thoughts which were triggering these unpleasant hallucinations. My eyes kept wanting to close, they were so tired and heavy, but as soon as they did, the morbid patterns would re-emerge and I fought to raise my lids. It was like bench pressing five hundred pounds.

I slipped into the pool and waded to the far end where the water overflowed into the pool below. I sat in the pool up to my neck and gazed out at the desert valley unfolding in front of me. The water felt soft and soothing against my body.

I turned around slowly. The water sparkled like diamonds and for some time I was completely mesmerized by how the light played with it. The green of the lone mesquite became more distinct, and separated it from the now golden cliff. The gentle and fragile grasses swayed gracefully in the warm and delicate breeze. Wisps of clouds wrote holy words on the light blue sky. This place had something downright spiritual about it.

I finished my 360-degree tour when two things occurred to me. The first, that it was already late afternoon. The second, that Jon and Rosie were nowhere to be seen. I panicked for just a moment when from the corner of my eye I saw something waving at me from above. It was Rosie leaning over the falls from the pool above me. She was grinning from ear to ear. She blew me a kiss and pointed over my head to the pool below me. I leaned over the smooth, wide, stone lip of the falls. I imagined I was clinging to the spout of a stoneware teapot filled with cold spring water. I could feel the silky liquid pouring past my neck and over the back of my head. There below me, Jon was sitting in a lotus position facing the valley. I could make out both groans and sighs mingling with the bubbling and gurgling of the falls.

Comforted that everyone was accounted for, I surrendered my body to the water and floated on my back, my feet against the stone rim. I was a surfaced submarine and my sonar ears clearly detected the beat of my heart pulsing little waves through the water. It was slow and steady like a tom-tom. This time when I closed my eyes, I flew out of myself to the top of the canyon and gazed back down. The three of us, each having found a perfect spot, perfect because that's where we were, looked like three anchorites in front of their caves patiently awaiting a bolt of enlightenment.

From far above me, the golds and browns of the canyon, the bronzes of our naked bodies, the greens of the bushes, grasses and trees, the blues of the pools all became like blobs of paint on a slick canvas. I reached down and started finger painting. The colors began swirling together as if I were an alien pastry chef mixing batter for a marble cake. I dipped a finger into the bowl and tasted it. It was delicious.

An old, young Indian stood next to me and started gently massaging my shoulders and hips. I opened my eyes to admire his face, to ask him questions.

Instead, I saw I was surrounded by floating oranges bobbing against my skin. I stared at one and it started laughing at me. But the laugh was coming from behind me. I turned around and there were Rosie and Jon, kneeling side by side at the edge of the pool, laughing. I cracked up, too. We laughed until we cried. Jon and Rosie each stuck out a hand and pulled me to them. I climbed out and the three of us put the crowns of our heads together and hugged and sighed until our sighs were long and deep and one.

We were all still high, but in that pleasurable descent mode. Where everything around you is still intensely sensual but your mind no longer succumbs to its own hallucinations except the one in which you think you and everything around you is real.

Our heads still touching and our hands grasping each other's arms Indian style, Jon spoke softly.

"My dear Don Juan. If everybody has their 'spot,' then this is definitely mine."

Still holding on to each other, we slowly leaned back and tilted our heads toward the sky, stretching our necks and backs like a blossom unfolding. And then we looked at each other. Jon had tears in his eyes. Upon seeing them, Rosie's eyes also moistened. I felt very lucky to be with them.

As the sun descended, the textures of our surroundings became even more intense and interesting. Colors that weren't there at noon now seemed to dominate. Glowing oranges and reds, deepening purple shadows.

"So how did it go, brother Giacco?" Jon asked me.

I stared at him while I thought about it. "Well, whenever I could get my ego out of the picture, it was fine. It was fantastic! One of the best trips I've ever had. Memorable! But I'll tell you Jon, there were times when this sense of self-preservation would come out of nowhere and overwhelm me. I could feel myself frantically scrambling to find an *I*. Really, Jon, I have to admit there were times when I was actually praying 'just let me get out of this one alive and I'll never do drugs again!' Of course, right now, I can't wait until the next time."

Jon laughed. "If you were *really* praying, there would've been no *self* to preserve."

"Come again?" I said.

"Prayer isn't beseeching or asking for anything! Prayer is supposed to be pure meditation. Prayer should bring you to *thoughtlessness*. I mean a place where there are no thoughts. And if there are no thoughts, there is no mind. And if there's no mind, there's no *self* to preserve.

"So what's the prayer, Jon?" I asked.

"Hey! What do I know? I'm just a curious slob. I don't know. That's the big question. Who has the prayer?"

Jon looked distractedly at the lengthening shadow of the tree rippling in the sunset-tinted pool.

"I know one thing. For every person there's a prayer. And for every prayer there's a teacher you learn it from. And every one of them knows there's only *one* truth. But you have to find the teacher who speaks just to you. The one who uses just the right words that make things click. Who uses just the right metaphors and symbols that make things crystal clear to you. Someone who strikes just the right chords in you in every way on every level so when they impart their knowledge, you're hit on the head with it and the light bulb goes on and the ego goes off."

Jon looked just a bit frustrated, more a look of longing, and started doodling in the sand. He made concentric circles around each of a number of small stones that lay in front of him. Rosie and I looked at him as if he were an Aztec priest performing some sacred rite.

He looked up, but rather than meet our gaze, he stared off somewhere beyond us. "I think you can get very, very close to it on your own. But you can't cross to the other side without a teacher. The chasm that separates you from the experience of the truth is probably only a hair's breadth in size," he said bringing his thumb and index finger together in front him, "but it may as well be infinitely wide. I'm convinced you need a teacher. You can't get there without a teacher!"

"Lucy, Groucho, Krishnamurti, Don Juan, I am, aom, amen...."

Rosie leading the way, me in the middle, and Jon bringing up the rear, we chanted our way back down the hill, borrowing from each other's mantras. The full moon had cleared the far rock wall and made the way bright and easy. It bounced in each of the beautiful pools we passed, splashing our eyes with light. At the very bottom pool, Rosie broke into a different melody. The tune sounded familiar, but I couldn't place it. It sounded like the kind of waltz you'd hear coming from the calliope of a merry-go-round.

"The sun is the mother ship
on our journey through space.
If we can be what we know is true,
then there is no need to race.

It takes twelve ages for a one way trip.
The Piscean Age is almost through.
It is said each age has a christ...

Rosie stopped in the path just before it opened upon the parking lot. She turned around and looked at both of us.

...have you checked to see if the christ is you?"

CHAPTER 11
July 1970

The next morning, we broke camp and headed back into Tucson. I had no idea where we were going next. I didn't care as long as I could stay with Jon and Rosie. I couldn't imagine us apart.

Rosie as usual was on my wavelength. "Now where, Mr. Harvey?" she asked with *ready for anything* in her voice.

"Well, where would her ladyship like to go?" Jon inquired.

"How about the Grand Canyon?" Rosie and I said at the same time. We looked at each other. "Stop that!" we both spoke at the same time again, sending the three of us into hysterics.

"Well, let's head north then and just follow the signs." John said turning onto the highway. "But let's stop for breakfast. I'm starving!"

As we entered a diner just outside of Superior, Arizona, Jon noticed the headline on a newspaper behind the clear plastic vending stand. "Protesters Burn More Than Draft Cards" it read. John put in a quarter, lifted the plastic front, and pulled out a paper. We had just sat down in a booth when Jon jumped up, said, "jiminy christ!" and ran for the phone booth at the other end of the diner.

Rosie and I leaned over the newspaper. Under the headline was a photo of a young man standing on the base of a statue. He held aloft a card, partially consumed by flames. A crowd of young people carrying signs surrounded him. The photo caught many of them with their mouths open and it was easy to guess what they were yelling. In the background were police approaching, clubs held high. The story accompanying the picture was datelined Eugene, Oregon.

"Oh, my god!" Rosie yelled and looked up at me, her eyes wide and serious.

"What is it? What's going on?" I asked.

"Look here. That's Rob! Jon's younger brother!"

Jon walked across the diner quickly and bumped the table as he sat down spilling some of the coffee out of their cups.

"I just called my Dad. Rob must've planned this in advance 'cause my father knew all about it and gave me an address and phone number of a house in Vancouver, B.C., where Rob's heading. *If* he can dodge the F.B.I.!"

"Where's Christy?" Rosie asked with concern.

"Who's Christy?" I asked.

Rosie reached into her purse, took out her wallet, and opened it. She held it out for me to see. On the right side, opposite her driving license, was a picture of a young, slender man with light brown hair. Leaning into him with one arm around his waist and the other holding a baby, was a dark-haired woman with big, brown, smiling eyes.

"This is Rob. This is Christy, his wife. And this little angel is Robert. We call him

Robbie," Rosie said, pointing each one out over the top of the wallet.

"We're going to Canada!" Jon announced, looking up from the newspaper.

"What about the Grand Canyon?" I asked.

Jon looked at me intently but not sternly. In a quiet, but decisive voice he reminded us, "I said we'd go north and follow the signs. If this isn't a sign, I don't know what is!"

We drove past signs that showed the way to the Grand Canyon. We drove through the Mohave desert. We drove day and night, taking turns at the wheel, only stopping for take-out food and gas. We drove up 99 through California. I thought of suggesting we stop in Topanga to check on the house, but didn't want to seem inconsiderate, so I kept my mouth shut. Not that the atmosphere had grown heavy or anything. To the contrary. It was as lighthearted as ever. But it was obvious that Jon was anxious to get up north and as a good musketeer, I had already emotionally committed myself to *all for one and one for all*.

The bond between the three of us had been immediately strong. Seven Falls had only made it stronger. And now it grew even more so as the road disappeared under the van. It just felt right. We all agreed it felt right. It was meant to be. Jon was ecstatic.

The three of us could trade anecdotes for hours. I told them about Reverend Trey and my "baptism." Jon confided some titillating stories about his ninth-grade teacher and the "Greek Club." Rosie demonstrated the smuggling capabilities of Tampons. We were a very entertaining trio and our own best fan clubs.

When we had to make a pit stop, Jon would just pull over to the side of the road and the three of us would line up in the bushes. Jon and I would unbutton our flies and drop our pants while Rosie stepped out of her cutoffs to squat. We were like aboriginal children who hadn't been taught urban propriety or etiquette. We were totally comfortable with our bodies and their biologic functions. We were completely at ease expressing our feelings and thoughts, no matter how crazy, weird, morbid or fantastic.

And as we got to know each other better, we made more and more fun of each other and we became more and more alike. Especially Rosie and me. Not that any of us didn't have an original thought. It was just that we were so in tune with one other we found ourselves using each other's phrasing and language and gestures. A mutual admiration society. An osmosis of personalities. It bordered on the telepathic. It was ridiculous. We had so many inside jokes, so many knowing looks, I'm sure some people found us downright impudent, if not intimidating.

The first time we decided to stop for a night was in southern Oregon. We picked up a young freak on his way to the Sunny Valley commune where he lived. He was coming back from San Francisco. Something about ATD or something. Whatever. He had some dynamite sinsemilla he picked up in Garberville and after getting us wasted, he invited us to crash at the commune for the night.

The commune was a trip. Really together. Really organized. Really healthy. Really *structured*! A beautiful hand-built lodge housed the common kitchen and dining area. Small, neat, clapboard cabins dotted the surrounding woods. A cedar building near the lodge was the communal bath and sauna. You could smell the cedar as distinctly as opening a package of incense.

The commune was so well ordered it almost freaked us out. Oh, the people were nice enough. They were civil and hospitable. But we felt a little out of place. An intrusion. Like they'd put up with us because they knew it was the right thing to do but couldn't wait for us to leave so they could get on with their business. I never could find out what their business was. Except they seemed to have a lot of rules.

Even Jon, who could warm up the most frigid crowd, was having trouble getting through their aloofness. Later on we'd learn that they were just suffering from overexposure. They'd been featured in a major magazine and had been inundated with hippies on the run looking for a place to call home, and runaways from what they called home looking for a hippie. And of course the cops who hassled them both, and in turn, the entire Sunny Valley commune.

So in retrospect, it was understandable they were cool to us. And cool to Jon when he asked to use their phone even though he said it was collect. I could see them paying attention as he dialed and they didn't *at ease* until they heard Jon telling the operator he wanted to make a person to person call to a Mr. Robert P. Harvey in Vancouver, B.C. and charge it to his father's home in Connecticut. We all stared at Jon while he waited for operators to perform mumbo jumbo east across the country and then back west. Jon grimaced once. It was probably the sound of his father's voice reluctantly approving the call. Then Jon yelled into the phone at the sound of a stranger's voice. A brief pause and Rob got on the phone. The two of them began a short, but animated conversation.

When Jon got off the phone, he was smiling, then his expression changed to consternation.

"Rob, Christy, and Robbie got into Canada with no problem. But the chances they'll ever get to come back to the States is almost nil."

"That's OK," I said, not understanding why Jon should look so concerned, "Canada is far out! Sometimes I wish I were Canadian! I'd be proud to be Canadian! You can always visit him there. It's not that far!"

"I don't get it," Rosie butted in. "You don't see your brother anyway for years at a time. And when you do all you do is fight!"

"Yea, I know," Jon said chuckling to himself, remembering some distant event. "Well, anyway, they're going to be there for a while so we can take our time from now on getting up there."

That night, the three of us slept on the cold dining room floor. The van would have been more comfortable, but we were too tired to relocate. We were still tired when we woke to the sounds of some communal early birds beginning breakfast. It was hard to believe they were always that noisy. We groggily looked at each other to affirm it was for *our* benefit.

As unobtrusively as possible, we washed up, politely turned down a weak invitation to stay for breakfast, and hit the road. The road was our ocean. The van was our island. I couldn't have been stranded on it with better castaways.

We took a lot of back roads into Portland and stayed a couple of nights in the University district. A freak we met laid some acid on us and we spent a day tripping in the Rose Garden. The acid wasn't very strong, but was very pure, and the trip was remarkably even and relaxed and enjoyable.

In Seattle, we ran into a couple of outrageous hippies who worked at a hole-in-the-wall, organic, vegetarian, gay pizza parlor. Our waiter was a freak named Doug. He was dark and tall. He had long, very straight brown hair and a big, slightly darker beard. His voice was deep and resonant. Were he wearing the traditional northwest costume of a flannel shirt and jeans, he would've looked like a logger to reckon with. But his loose-fitting aqua blouse and chiffon pantaloons dispelled all machismo. The pink veil and jangling earrings didn't hurt either.

By the time he took our order, we were in love with him. He was crazy in just the way we liked. And so was his lover, Don, who was so adept at throwing pizzas he managed to wave at us in between tosses.

We ended up spending almost a week with them at their little house on a hill in Leschi overlooking Lake Washington. The house was filled with love and gentleness. Doug fawned over Rosie. They'd cuddle up on the couch and do each other's hair and nails. Don made some of the most inventive meals a radical faerie could concoct.

On their day off, we took some mushrooms and swam naked in the Arboretum. Later, on our way back to the van, I picked up a flyer lying on the sidewalk. It notified us of a free Yoga class happening that evening. Naturally, Jon took it as a sign that that's what we were supposed to do that night. So off the five of us went to a house on Capitol Hill that doubled as quarters for the Vedanta Society.

The mushrooms must've made us more limber and dexterous than we thought possible, because everyone in the room kept looking at us. Unless it was because they were all wearing Indian whites and we were all in jeans and tank tops. Except for Doug who had on shiny green genie slippers and orange toreador slacks. I also don't think the yoga teacher appreciated Doug swaying forth and back like an Arabian scarf dancer while he was trying to explain the history and therapeutic effects of the next yoga position.

Or maybe it was Rosie, when one of her breasts popped out while doing the Lion. Or Jon when the back of his pants split in the middle of the Plow, revealing by the sight of his hairy asshole, he wasn't wearing any underpants.

Despite the fact they didn't thank us for coming when we left, we felt renewed and invigorated as we drove away. The city's lights were just coming on and five bright floods brought a billboard to our attention.

"Come To The Land Foreign Yet Near. Come to Beautiful British Columbia."

Rosie and I looked at each other and knew we'd be leaving the next day.

Doug cried and gave Rosie one of his many scarves while Jon and Don and I reached toward each other for a group hug. Doug and Rosie came over and joined in. When we drove away, Doug yelled through his tears, "See ya soon!" Then he let out one of those loud, piercing, tongue-contorting warbles only veiled and grieving belly dancers have mastered. We could hear its echo all the way to Blaine.

Although we were prepared for a thorough search at the border, the Canadian authorities just waved us through. It was most unusual not being hassled by someone in a uniform. We weren't used to such civility. When we found the street in the Burnaby district of Vancouver, Jon got a little excited. He started calling house numbers out loud. When he stopped in front of a simple, brown-shingled house, two faces pulled back a curtain and peeked out. A minute later, Rob and Jon were shaking hands and slapping each other on the back and Rosie and Christy were hugging. Little Robbie ran up and tugged at Christy's pants until she was forced to disengage herself and pick him up. Jon introduced me and I followed them into the house.

It was dark inside. The only light came through some partially raised shades above the sink in the kitchen overlooking the back yard. The sky was grey with those depressing northwest clouds that tease a brief and thrilling hard rain but instead only tinkle on you incessantly. The meager light that made its way into the living room added no cheer. The whole place seemed, if not sad, at least serious.

Christy and Rob looked different than they did in Rosie's photograph. Sallow and sullen. It seemed an effort for them to keep their outward spirits up. Little Robbie was the only one who didn't seem haggard. Jon tried to lighten things up with stories of Woodstock and Seven Falls and Better Farm, but the more he spoke of our good times, the more distant Christy and especially Rob, became. It was as if they almost resented us. Resented Jon in particular.

"So what is it Jon?" Rob asked with an edge in his voice. "You think you're special? You think you have some sort of *aura* protecting you from all the shit that's going down?"

"Hold on, bro!" Jon said putting up his hands to hold back what he knew was the beginning of an onslaught of fraternal digs. "I'm just trying to get through this absurdity the best way I know how. Just like everyone else."

"Would anyone like some tea?" Christy offered in an attempt to change the subject. No one answered. "C'mon, Robbie. Help mommy make some tea." Christy walked into the kitchen and put a pot of water on the stove. Robbie looked around the room and then followed her.

"What's your trip, anyway? We came up here to help you guys out."

"How? By running all over the country, getting high, having adventures? Living on scams and drug deals and Mom and Dad? Is that how you're helping?" Rob paced forth and back a couple of times and then headed for a chair in the corner. As he passed Jon he said, "All you're helping is yourself."

"Hell, Rob," Jon defended himself. "You know how I feel about the war! You know how I feel about Nixon and the Gestapo!"

"Then why aren't you out there protesting? Why aren't you out there running away from the law?"

"Hey! If Rosie and I happened upon a rally or a protest, we'd be the first ones to speak our minds, the first ones to be dead weight for the pigs to carry off! We just haven't run into any yet! In the meantime, we're working on ourselves! I think the world could *use* some positive vibrations! Don't chastise us for that!"

"Oh! I get it." Rob snarled. "Go with the *flow* and all that bullshit! You just want the world to *happen* to *you*. But *you* don't want to make anything *happen*!"

"Well, just what the fuck do you want me to make happen, Rob?"

Rob softened somewhat. "I don't know, Jon. You're smart. You've got a brain. Use it.

Do something with it. Go back to school. Get a degree. Teach. Write. Work with the handicapped. Join the Peace Corps! Do something!"

Jon plopped on the lumpy sofa and laughed softly. "Look at us! Here you're my younger brother and you're talking to me like you're my father. I don't get it. How did this happen?"

Rob chuckled and the tension left his scrawny body. "Don't you have any goals, Jon? World peace? An end to world hunger? For Christ's sake, becoming a millionaire, owning a yacht, raising a family? Isn't there anything you want to strive for?"

Christy brought in the tea. Rosie, who had been sitting uncharacteristically quiet the whole time, rose to help her with the cups, honey, and spoons.

"I don't know, Rob. But if I find out, you'll be the first to know."

Rosie and I looked at one another. We both knew Jon had said that to put an end to the conversation. At least that's what we hoped.

Rob poured himself a cup of tea and impatiently coaxed some honey out of the jar with his spoon. As if to minimize the impact, he spoke without looking at Jon.

"Dad wants you to drive Christy, Robbie, and me to Montreal. He's going to meet us there with a lawyer friend of his. Grandma's real sick, too. He wants you to come home for a while."

Jon stiffened at this news and turned sharply toward Rosie. They both spun around to find me. There was a hint of panic in their look, like someone who'd forgotten they'd brought their dog along, and suddenly remembering, worried it had slipped out the front door and was wandering into traffic.

Jon sighed with relief when our eyes locked and he motioned me with his head toward the door. Then he announced to the rest, "Me and Giacco are going to take a walk."

When we were on the street, Jon started walking briskly. I had a hard time keeping up. Neither of us spoke. By the time we covered a few blocks I was out of breath.

"Slow down, Jon! Where do you think we are, New York?"

"Sorry. Rob just knows how to press all my buttons. Gets me uptight. Then I get mad at myself."

Jon slowed down and we entered a small park with a black filigreed wrought iron fence around it. "What do you want to do, Giacco?"

"What do you want me to do?" I answered, avoiding the question, stalling for time to think.

"You can come with us back east if you want, but you should do what you want to do."

"Well, Jon, if there's any signs for me to read, I think this is one of them." We stopped walking and stood facing each other. "I think it would be easier on everyone, including me, if I headed back south for a while. We'll get together soon. I've gotta check on the house and all anyway."

"I just know we need to be around each other," Jon said. "There's something going on. I'm sure you're part of it. Rosie's sure of it too."

"I feel the same way, Jon. Our paths might not be identical, but they're meant to be a braid. We're just going to have to go through one of the twists for a while.

We started back to the house. We did the last block toe to heel.

Very early the next morning, before anyone had woken up, Jon and I quietly slipped out, but not before waking Rosie so I could say goodbye. I leaned over her lying on the mat on the floor. My hovering presence woke her up. When she opened her eyes, they were immediately bright and clear, free of the grogginess you'd get from someone like me. She put her arms around my neck and pulled herself up and gave me a warm and juicy kiss. As her lips left mine, she voiced the "smack" in an effort to reinforce its staying power.

"So long for now, my love! My brother! I will miss you so much!" Tears began to well in her eyes, but her smile showed every confidence we'd be together again.

Jon gave me a ride all the way to the border. He didn't want to push his luck by taking me to the U.S. side and crossing back again, so he let me out in front of Canadian customs.

It was very hard for us to say goodbye, so we did it quickly. I jumped out of the van and ran over to the driver's side. Jon leaned out the window and gave me a big hug and a huge kiss on the forehead. I slowly pulled away, turned around and started walking.

When I was about 10 feet away, Jon called out. "Giacco!"

I spun around. "Whadya want, Juanny?"

"I don't *love* you!" Jon yelled. "Love isn't a strong enough word. I *lorf* you!"

I laughed. "I lorf you too, Jon," and continued walking away.

"Giacco!"

I turned around again. "Now what, O wise one?"

"Remember Lucy and Groucho! They're waiting for you!"

"How could I forget? Every time I vomit, the fondest of memories will come up!"

Jon started laughing and crying at the same time. I continued walking.

"Giacco!"

In mock perturbation, I spun around once more and threw my hands up in the air. "What now?"

Jon put the van in gear and slowly drove in an arc around me before pulling onto the road. As he passed he said, "Giacco. Remember to walk in the way of the Lord."

I yelled back, "Which lord was that again, Jon?"

We both laughed and punched ourselves in the forehead.

CHAPTER 12
October 1970

That's what I was doing as I tried to hitch a ride into San Francisco, otherwise known as The City. Practice my lordwalking. Walking toe to heel is hard to do at first without looking conspicuous, but Jon promised it would be second nature to me after a while. I had the entire length of the Golden Gate Bridge to practice on. Cars sped past me. Some drivers shook their heads in sympathy for the deformity I must've had that caused me to walk so strangely. I didn't mind. I would notice everything I was supposed to while they, in their unnatural transports, would miss out on it all. Besides, no one could stop to pick me up now even if they wanted to, so what could be better than this?

I seemed to be the only pedestrian on the bridge. Then again, I couldn't see very far. Maybe it was the cold and damp fog which was quickly retreating toward the ocean. When it passed me on its way out, I could feel the warming sun and The City brightened and whitened looking like a settlement on a Greek island. Maybe Mykonos.

I watched the fog clear the west walkway of the bridge. It left behind a short figure leaning over the railing. The wind carried the song of a high tenor. It just barely reached my ears but I could tell it was sweet and pure. The young man turned around to look at The City. Though he was eight lanes of traffic away from me, I could tell he was only about five-foot two or three. He was balding prematurely, but the hair he did have grew to his shoulders. His face was round and his eyes were big and bright. A short beard covered his chin. He noticed me and began yodeling. Then he yelled something but I couldn't make it out. Something about "tomato." I smiled and waved as if I'd understood. He waved back and turned around to yodel at the entrance to the bay. The wind blew the yodel my way. It was complex, but sweet.

I continued lordwalking across the bridge. Then down to the Marina, the length of Divisadero, up Haight all the way to the entrance to Golden Gate Park. I didn't realize what a circular route I had taken, never having been in San Francisco before. Just inside the park, I stopped for the first time and suddenly realized how tired I was and how my feet and legs seemed to have muscles I never knew could cramp. I was hungry too, but only had about thirty cents to my name. Not that it mattered. These were the days of magic. As long as you didn't worry about it, everything you needed would be there. Like the night I arrived in Seattle after leaving Jon in B.C.

⁓𝓶𝓶⎯

I had been standing on the freeway, trying to take no thought for food, shelter, or rides, and was pretty much succeeding at it. The rides came one after another. The last ride I got before entering Seattle was from a young hippie fisherman named Eric. I thought it was a very nice seaworthy name. His manner and speech were rough and jagged. As rough as the week-old stubble on his face. As jagged as the sleeves he had cut off his Husky sweatshirt. Eric and his ancient station wagon, "Dolph," smelled of fish and salt water. As he reached to turn on the car radio, I was struck by how large his forearms were. With a little click of the knob, heavy rock music blasted out. It fit his looks perfectly. I was surprised when he turned down the volume and hunted for another station, settling on one that was playing arias from La Boheme.

His house in Alki was one of five cottages nestled into a hillside overlooking Elliot bay. The cottages were connected by a steep wooden staircase off of which led narrow concrete paths. Except for Eric's, all the houses looked neat and trim under the light of their lamp posts. Eric's was basically a one-room shack as funky on the outside as his station wagon. But inside it was as quaintly appointed as Mimi's garret. And it had a wonderful view of Bainbridge Island, Magnolia and Downtown. We smoked some excellent hash which hastened my drifting off into a sleepy reverie. Through drooping eyelids the last image I had of Eric was of him walking to the shower wearing a towel.

When I woke up toward dawn, I was naked in Eric's bed. A thick forearm lay across my chest and a powerful leg across my thighs. His mouth snored softly into my ear. My cock was hard, but trapped uncomfortably beneath his leg, so I gently lifted it so my cock could flap up.

The movement woke Eric. He rolled over and stretched like a satiated animal. Then he turned to me, noticed my hard cock, grabbed it like a baseball player grips a bat, squeezed once and released it, and then jumped out of bed laughing.

"We'll get to *that* later," he said good-naturedly. "But I'm starving!" He started opening and closing cupboards, getting out cereal and bowls and sugar.

"Was I good last night?" I asked sarcastically.

"I only did for you what I would want someone to do for me," he said sincerely, pouring milk over some corn flakes. "Get me out of my dirty duds and put me between some clean sheets so I can get a good night's rest." He sat on the side of the bed and handed me a bowl and spoon. Then he looked at me squarely in the eyes. "And that's all I did! Not that I didn't want to do more. But only with your permission."

His forthrightness gave way to bashfulness. The big lug was disarming.

"You have my permission," I said.

For the next two weeks, Eric was an attentive friend and lover. He took me all over Seattle, introduced me to sailing, taught me some songs on the guitar, fed me, bathed me, massaged me, and bed me. It was like being on a holiday!

But like all holidays, they come to an end. When the Inland Boatman's Union called him up to see if he wanted to work a tug going up to Alaska, Eric couldn't say no. He said I could stay in the house as long as I wanted. He left some food and some weed. He even left me the car, though I only used it the one time to take him to his boat down on Harbor Island. I missed him immediately. But I didn't long for him. I appreciated his naturalness and his kindness.

That very night, as I parked the car below the steep stairs that led to his house, I wondered about all the good fortune that seemed to come my way. Was it really because I was finally in the here and now? Or was it just luck and coincidence?

As I climbed the stairs past some of Eric's neighbors, I had an inexplicable craving for a Snickers bar. I deliberately put the thought out of my mind, knowing there was nothing of the sort in Eric's kitchen and continued up the stairs. It occurred to me that when you're climbing or descending stairs, you always use your toes and never your heels. Did that count? Was there such a thing as *lordclimbing*? I noticed a young girl coming down from the house above Eric's. She was unwrapping something as she skipped lightly down the stairs.

We met on a landing. "Want some Snickers bar?" she asked as friendly as if she knew me.

I was dumbstruck!

Could it be? Did I actually have powers? Like the kind Yogananda talks about?

"Well, do you?" she asked again. "One bite was all I wanted. You can have the rest." And she handed me the bar. I took it, still dumbfounded. "My name's Julie. Julie Oki. What's yours?"

"Jeremiah," I answered with some hesitation.

"You don't seem too sure about it," she said, and then shrugged her shoulders to say it didn't matter.

"Thanks for the candy," I said and started back up the stairs. Julie scowled at my seemingly brusque behavior and headed down the stairs to the road.

Back at the house, I made a pot of tea and practiced the chords Eric had taught me. I was just getting into bed when I heard a rapping at the window over the kitchen sink. It was Julie.

Julie was in high school and couldn't wait to graduate. Her impatience was manifested by rebelling against her old-fashioned Nisei parents. She did everything and anything she wasn't supposed to. She was the first Asian girl I met to dispel forever the stereotype of the demure, shy, coquettish Geisha.

I was older. I should have known better. But she was *so* insistent! Insistent that I take acid with her. Acid she had gotten at school. Insistent that I smoke her pot. Insistent that we screw. And we did. Every afternoon and night for two months. It became a ritual.

When we were through, she'd get herself together, and walk in her house and past her parents as if nothing had happened. Cool as a cucumber. Slippery as an eel. Her parents thought she was at cheerleader practice. Her parents worried she was spending too much time studying every evening down at the library. Her parents were so proud!

After dinner, she'd sneak me leftovers. She'd watch me eat with Akito puppy eyes. Then she would watch me eat *her* with those same Akito puppy eyes. Her eyes were always moist. *She* was always moist… and always in a state of arousal. Foreplay was hardly necessary. In fact, she was eager, if not impatient, to try the new positions she'd heard so much about from her girlfriends. I possibly learned more about sex from Julie than from any other female… or male, for that matter.

I just trusted her when she said her parents didn't have a clue. They were too old-world to be suspicious. She was much too cheerleader to be a suspect. Until one night there was a tapping at my kitchen window and it couldn't be Julie. Julie was in bed with me.

Toe to heel, I crept to the kitchen. Three faces peered in. Mr. and Mrs. Oki and Julie's younger brother, Tommy. Tommy was smiling. Mr. and Mrs. Oki were not.

Toe to heel, I crept back to the corner of the house where I kept my gear, quietly throwing into my pack any clothes I could find.

Toe to heel, I crept to the window Julie had just climbed out of and followed her into the shadows of the laurel bushes behind the house.

"There they are!" cute little Tommy screamed.

Toe to toe, I descended the stairs four at a time, with Mr. Oki right behind me. I jumped the last six steps to the mid-hill landing. The weight of my pack slammed against my back almost knocking the wind out of me. But I couldn't stop.

Toe to toe, *forget the heel*, I set a speed-lordwalking record to the beach across the street. I turned just for a second and got a glimpse of Julie's ear being boxed by Mrs. Oki. Mr. Oki was catching his breath on the landing.

Toe to toe, I ran along the water's edge toward the lights of Seattle, my stride more relaxed now, more grace-full. Feeling the cold air filling my lungs. Feeling free. Feeling alive.

This is better! This is much better!!

Toe to heel, I disappeared into the darkness.

I was excited by the prospect of what would happen next.

I mean, if everything happens for a reason, then what did all this *just happen for? Did I wish it, like I wished for the Snickers bar? Did I make it happen? Did I will it subconsciously? Was I afraid she'd get pregnant? Was I afraid of commitment?*

Not that it mattered. These were the days of magic. As long as you didn't worry about it, everything you needed would be there. So I stuck my thumb out to see where it would take me.

Just outside of Garberville, this guy Andy picked me up in his van. I was taking a leak in the gully. I knew I had missed a sure ride when I saw a blur of wolves howling at the moon. They rushed by me as I climbed back on the roadway. Luckily, the driver saw me in his side-view mirror and pulled over, screeching dust into the wolves' faces and briefly obliterating the moon. When I told him I was heading for San Francisco, he said the next town was as far as he was going, but it would be a better spot to hitch from. I climbed in and he passed me a soapstone pipe filled with hash. A quarter mile later we were brothers. Three miles later, I was at his house to crash for the night. Optimists were everywhere and it didn't take long to know if someone was cool or not. Mi casa, su casa, karma casa.

Andy lived in a friendly looking, ramshackle house on top of a dry hill. A few madronas scattered around. But no other houses in sight. Tie-dyed parachutes on the ceiling, incense, candles, fixtures, and furnishings more appropriate to a yurt. Your basic freak's house. The voices of two women in continuous banter came from the kitchen, interrupted now and then by the sound of a joint being sucked to its conclusion. On the living room floor lay a bib-overalled longhair guy, one strap undone, the bib folded partway back revealing his chest and a Grateful Dead tattoo. The Flying Burrito Brothers were twanging in overmodulated harmony, the stereo much too loud for the little speakers that straddled Rocky's ears. Andy told me that Rocky was tripping on some new Owsley acid. As we stepped over him, he opened his eyes and looked innocently, almost beatifically, at us.

"Rocky, isn't that music too loud? Doesn't it bother you?" Andy asked.

Rocky screwed up his face, paused a long curious moment, and in all childlike earnestness asked, "What's a *bother*?"

It was with Rocky in mind that I arched my shoulders back and let my pack drop to the ground. Then I let my body do the same, settling against the pack. My muscles ached, my tummy growled, my body wanted to sleep. But what's a *bother*?

My eyes stared up at the treetops just now being oranged by streetlamps going on all around the Golden Gate, and inside the park; along the small-curved bridges, and at the entrances of the tunnels beneath them. Precisely on schedule, a hand reached in front of my face holding a glowing, but quickly diminishing roach. We did the thumb and index finger ballet as we transferred custody of the little one. As I toked, I turned to see who the hand belonged to.

CHAPTER 13
October 1970

Eighteen to twenty. Dirty yellow hair. Cropped short, but in such a hodge-podge way, it was probably very recently long. Maybe the work of some redneck cops. I wondered if he had ever been in Boca, Truckee, or Sparks. Maybe Hank's father and his gang had gotten hold of him. I could just see him getting worked over for the sport of it and then sent on his way with his locks butchered by dull scissors in the hands of duller minds. He tries to hitchhike afterwards, which is most likely all he was guilty of in the first place. He sticks out his thumb embarrassed and humiliated like a sheepdog fallen victim to a crazed groomer. And now, to add insult to injury, he is forced to go for a walk in public!

Michael had a corn-bred Nebraska face. It was square and honest. Along with the forthright look came a strong jaw and bright teeth. His top lip was slightly disfigured from what looked like an old cut. A minor imperfection, but important enough to keep him from being on the cover of a teen idol magazine. A bottom lip just full enough to cast a small shadow on his chin. Blue-green eyes just deep-set enough to isolate them from the rest of his face. As he talked, he closed his eyes longer than the usual blink, so that in contrast, when he opened them again I noticed how bright and beautiful they really were, despite the redness from the pot. He licked his lips often trying to overcome the dry-mouth and each time his tongue passed over a lip it left a swath of slick that picked up the light of the streetlamp and glistened. My eyes kept moving up and down from his eyes to his lips, the glimmer in each going on and off like a blinking sign. To me he was very handsome.

He was squatting beside me Indian style, his knees almost hugging his ribs, and I could tell his body did his face justice. Never mind he was wearing baggy pants. Never mind the oversized sweater so big I could see the V of his neck and the plaid of the flannel shirt under it. Another swatch of plaid poked through the elbow of the sweater. A square knee jutted through a hole in the pants. I knew from the knee that it led upwards to a muscular thigh. I knew from the V in his neck that it led to great pecs and probably a hard, concave stomach. I knew from the way the sweater hugged the curve of his back that his shoulders were broad and his lats were wide. Nothing to the extreme, mind you, just enough to fit the mold of a farm-boy high school quarterback whose body is more developed than most, from sports and hard work.

I knew all this because I had become expert at picking out the "sleepers." The ones who don't get noticed immediately upon entering a party. The ones who stand at the edge of the crowd, in the shadows. Who don't bring attention to themselves because they're a bit shy, a bit unsure. Who get relegated to being an observer. When really, with just a little peeling back of their cover, beauty explodes! I observe them. I notice them. I like their shyness. I like their insecurity. I find it appealing. I am attracted to "sleepers." I seek them out. I'm one myself, I think. Or I like to think!

But Michael wasn't relegating me to anything. He was just standing up handing me a banana with one hand and motioning me to follow with the other, as if it were understood we were going to hang out together. We hadn't yet any reason to get into that bad habit of creating histories for one another based on too little information. We simply took each other at face value and liked what we saw.

When he stood up, his body retreated further into his clothing, but it couldn't escape the truth of my X-ray vision. We walked out of the park and headed west. Michael rambled on about Nebraska and the old hemp fields behind his grampa's barn. And how much he had learned in the two months he'd been in The City. It was even farther out than he'd imagined. But he wasn't some no-nothing hick. He knew how to blow glass. And liked to write songs. He could survive in the wilderness. And he loved the country, but knew he had to come to The City because back home he was considered just too odd. His dad thought he was just plain weird. His mom had passed away, and only his brother ever really understood him. Michael didn't talk about him much at all, despite my prodding. He was indeed a sleeper, and a bit mysterious.

But he wasn't naïve. He had already figured out how to use the system. Food stamps, rent vouchers. And no city slicker was gonna take advantage of him. He was gonna take it slow in picking out his friends. Too many times already he had been hit on by men. He wasn't angry. He just didn't know what to make of it. "I mean, yeah, sure, back in Nebraska... locker room stuff... or maybe stag parties out in the woods, too much Jack and all of that... but just coming' up to you on the street and hitting' on ya? I don't know about that!"

That's why he had had the nerve to approach me, or so he said. I was obviously from out of town. The backpack said regular Joe. I was a safe bet. He would rescue me from a cold October night. We would rescue each other from being strangers in a strange town. He was definitely a sleeper. But likely he was still in one closet or another, which put me in an uncomfortable situation. The burden of his trust.

Asleep is what we both pretended to be long after we got into bed. I figured one of us had to make a move. I was four or five years older. I guessed it was up to me. For whatever reasons. The main one being that it might be fun. Everybody's everything anyway. No labels, no categories. We're all one. Everything in nature is part of a continuum. Morality is conventional and has nothing to do with nature.

I propped myself up on a pillow against the wall and looked around the room. Or rather the garage. Michael had sweet-talked the space out of an old, kindly, and very effeminate gentleman named Kyle who owned the Victorian house that faced Page street.

The garage was off the alley behind the house. After he pointed out the bathroom and shower in the basement of Kyle's house, he opened the garage door and the entire room appeared. From the alley it looked like a diorama. All three walls and the ceiling were plastered with posters. Some were of rock stars. Some were of exotic destinations. Others were just the usual psychedelic stuff. The cement floor was quilted with carpet samples a couple of layers thick. On the sides were crates used as dressers and closets, depending on whether they faced up or out.

In the foreground, just off center and at an angle, two school desks with attached chairs butted each other, face to face. A tie-dyed sheet spanned the desktops providing a tablecloth for a breakfast nook without the nook. In the background, raised off the floor slightly by a few extra layers of carpet samples, was a double-bed mattress that was either really lumpy or just looked that way from the colorful blankets and bedspreads strewn all over it.

The room looked cold and vulnerable. If there had been a wall of glass instead of the garage door it would've made a nice storefront. The passersby would have much to scrutinize. When we walked in, I felt we were the two mannequins that would complete the window display. I wondered, what pose should I assume?

Michael pulled the door down behind us and latched it at the bottom. He turned on the space heater which came to life surprisingly fast, shedding waves of toasty air. He lit some candles and turned off the overhead light. The garage became a cozy and secure clubhouse. And I've always had a clubhouse complex, so it was perfect.

I looked down at Michael. He lay there. Sleeping? His eyes were closed, but a gentle snore fluttering with tension made his slumber suspect. The covers had been pulled up only to his navel, the space heater and our two bodies making more than enough heat on this late fall night. He lay there still as a statue, one arm under a pillow, the other across the chest I had seen through his clothes. His pecs were solid and his stomach gently rippled down to his navel. His stomach fluttered in time to his snore.

I adjusted myself as if I were sleeping alone, not concerned about disturbing anyone else, hoping the movement would give me additional information about how deep a sleep, if any, Michael was in. I drew my legs halfway up, lifting the covers partially off Michael's body. With a deep sigh, the kind you use to end a full day's work, *I'm-so-tired-nothing-can-wake-me-up* kind of sigh, I let my right leg slowly relax, slowly fall, and let it fall where it may, which happened to be on top of Michael's leg, just above the knee.

No response. Not the slightest movement. I leaned forward and one by one threw back the covers until only the sheet remained, clinging to his lower body and revealing it to be as lean and as muscled as I had expected. As I leaned back against the wall I tried to discern if he had an erection, but couldn't be sure by the light of the last remaining candle that would extinguish itself in a few minutes. I thought I had seen a brief rise and fall under the sheets and deliberated if it would be safer to assume it was just the imaginings of my wishful mind. A mind that maybe distorted reality to suit its own desires. A mind that interpreted the most innocent body language and references made in simple conversations to mean admissions of hidden desires.

Michael remained motionless. I hoped my rustling would have at least produced one slight physical sign of nervous anticipation. A grunt, a briefly opening eyelid, a little syncopation in the steady fluttering of his snore. Nothing. Not a thing that would allow me to go on with less paranoia; to go on without violating his trust. Either he was truly dead to the world or the greatest Zen master in the neighborhood. The odds were fifty-fifty. I placed my bets and proceeded in slow motion. But not without those infernal internal selves standing around my brain yelling at me.

I wish I could have been more bold, like Eric was with me in Seattle. It worked for him. Instead, all I could do was listen to the Jekyll of my mind and watch the Hyde of my body.

You're crazy. Out of your mind. Don't make such a fool of yourself. Look at you, you're going through with it. I can't believe you're doing this. I can't believe you'd risk a friendship!

On and on I went. And all the time my mind was chastising itself, my body was changing positions... edging my knees along the sheets, like two soldiers creeping on their bellies to the front line, until my left knee was just close enough to feel the hair on his thigh, my right knee just close enough to his waist to feel my own electricity bouncing back off his skin. Or was it his electricity bouncing off mine? The one candle flickered wildly as the flame reached the pool of melted wax at its base, and cast a giant, weaving shadow of my right hand as I brought it down slowly and deliberately on top of his. I watched the shadow, my pulse racing. The candle steadied itself just as I made contact.

This is it! The die is cast! The damage done!

No response.

Don't be cruel, now! Give me a sign! Don't let me continue if this isn't what you want!

I could slide my hand up to the rise of his chest where a few yellow hairs guarded his nipple, or down the curve of his bottom rib into the flat of his stomach. Instead, I put my hand around his wrist and headed for his elbow. Not a light touch. Not the reverent stroke you'd use to touch the Pieta or David, but the kind of pressure you'd use to explore a Henry Moore. My fingers opened with the size of his forearm, contracted slightly around the elbow, broadened again considerably over the bicep and was open-palmed by the time they got to the shoulder. I let my hand drag over his chest to where I could feel his heart. Was it beating fast? Fast enough to mean something? No good. Mine was beating so hard I could hear it in my hand and couldn't distinguish his beat from mine. I hoped they were the same.

My left hand went to his hip. It was a fine maneuver. On the way there I finessed the sheet further south revealing the hip bone itself, and soft, silky hair inches below his navel. I slowly lifted the sheet to take a peek. He wasn't necessarily hard, but what Playboy magazine would have called "enhanced tumescence."

He opened his eyes. I wouldn't have noticed, since mine were elsewhere, but the energy they released when he lifted his lids was so intense, it simply hit me mid-grope and made me look up. As soon as my eyes met his, he closed them again and chuckled. I was busted!

I continued to stare at his closed eyes waiting to read them when they opened again. Trying to come up with something to say if their message wasn't friendly. Maybe he'd just shine it on. A horny brother's night moves. Two soldiers on the battlefield of lust. I wondered what he would think of me. I wondered if I would be embarrassed. I wondered at the gentle speed bumps of his stomach. I wondered why my hand would not stop its southernly advance. Soon it would be too late!

He chuckled, this time a little more deeply. Now *he* was busted! I sighed and waited with a strangely even breath. He laughed outright. From his gut. Not a mocking laugh. Not a nervous laugh. Not a cynical laugh. It was lighthearted and disarming. Guileless and wholesome. The kind of laugh you and your best friend have after you've dared each other to jump off the quarry cliff into the swimming hole and it's really high and really scary, but you both do it and when you both come up for air, you catch your breath, look at each other, and break up laughing. It was that kind of laugh.

It was a laugh that said OK. It was a grateful laugh. It was a laugh of relief. I watched his hand leave his chest and land on my knee. He paused, then ran his hand roughly up my leg to the inside of my thigh. I threw the sheet all the way back and lay on top of him. We just lay there for a while, syncing breaths, breathing deeply, relaxing in each other, getting comfortable. He gently pressed my head down to his and kissed me like a man who had a lot to say but just now found someone to say it to.

He rolled me over to trade places, the kiss uninterrupted. Giant shadows jumped over each other, flickering wildly, then suddenly black. Only the smell of the extinguished candle and the smell of each other remained.

CHAPTER 14
October 1970

In the morning when I woke up, Michael was just lying there, arms behind his head, eyes open staring at the ceiling.

Oh, no. Does he have the post-ejaculatory I just want to sleep alone in my own bed and not wake up to the stranger who'll remind me of what I did the night before blues?

When he saw that I was awake he turned away from me and slithered face down all the way under the covers.

It's worse than I thought. He has the please just get up and go away quietly and close the door behind you. Did your blues turn into yellows? You coward!

He continued slithering until his head was parallel to my hips and his feet dangled on the floor. *Now this is more like it!* I could feel his bristly chin on my skin. He kissed it.

Just as I thought I was about to be ravaged, he slipped out the foot of the bed, and grabbing my ankles, pulled me onto the floor. He had a playful smile on his face. I love a bit of mischief. I tried to grab him and pull him down for a bit of wrasslin', but he was much stronger than me and laughed at my vain attempts to get him on the floor.

"We'll rough house later, Giacco. No time for sex. It's time to get you squared away. Get up and get ready. Don't shower! But I'm gonna take one. Be right back." And he left before I could ask any questions.

When we reached the dirty granite building that housed the Department of Social Services, Michael turned to me and began issuing instructions.

"OK, now here's what you do. Don't say a word, not a word. Just hold my hand and look bewildered. I'll do all the talking."

"Michael," I said, "What are you up to?"

"I told you I'm going to get you squared away," he answered.

"Well, just what does squared away mean anyway?"

"Do you have any money?"

"About thirty cents!" I replied.

"Do you have a place to stay?"

"I don't mind staying with you for a while, if that's OK. And then I have to head back to LA."

Michael grabbed my hand and started pulling me up the stairs.

"Of course it's OK. But what about food? The least you can do for both of us is get food stamps." He opened the door and led me inside. "Now, remember, mum's the word. No matter what happens, just be a mute for a while!"

Michael sat me in a chair in a waiting area and went to speak to a man behind a counter.

Then he came back and sat next to me.

"What did you..."

"Shhh!" Michael snapped. "I told you, not a word. You'll blow it for us!" So I grimaced at him, but held my tongue. Eventually, a young woman stuck her head out of a door and called our names. She was wearing a simple dress with blue flowers on it. Her almost orange hair was thickly braided and pinned up on top of her head. It was probably very long when she wore it down. Her face was small with pale freckles covering her cheeks. Her blue eyes sparkled. She reminded me of a character in a black and white Ingmar Bergman movie, except I had to provide the color.

She introduced herself as Nancy Stein, one of the caseworkers. As she walked, or rather sauntered in front of us to one of the small cubicles that filled the room, her dress swung fro and to, helped by a swinging right arm that brushed the fabric in rhythm to her walk. It looked like the promenade part of a square dance.

At her desk, she pointed to a chair. Michael nudged me into it, still holding my hand. When she offered to get Michael a chair, he declined and said he would stand. Nancy settled into her chair and piled some folders onto a corner of the desk, pushed her purse to the side, and pulled out a clean folder with some blank forms in it. I noticed her purse was partially open. Almost spilling out past the clasp was a black 35mm film canister and a pack of Zig-Zag rolling papers. She saw me staring at her purse.

"OK, Mr. Giordano. What seems to be the problem?" she asked looking directly at me, while closing her purse and putting it on the floor next to her feet. I opened my mouth, but before any sound came out, I felt my hand being squeezed hard and heard Michael answering for me.

"Miss Stein. This guy never talks! Or at least hardly ever! And when he does, it's gibberish! I can't make any sense at all of what he's saying. He's been sleeping on my porch for the past three days and nights. And when I try to find out where he's from or what he's doing, he just stares at me. Like he's in a trance. I've been giving him some food and the other night I gave him a blanket, but I can't have him living on my porch. What am I supposed to do with him?"

I looked up at Michael with a look of alarm and disbelief and a bit of anger. He squeezed my hand harder. I wasn't sure what to do. Speak up and bust him? What a way to end the beginning of a beautiful relationship! I didn't want to be in this situation, but I couldn't think of an easy way to get out of it without both of us looking like jerks, so I gave up and decided to go along with him. After all, I really was broke. It was a bit theatrical, but I did meet some of the conditions for qualifying for General Assistance. And it did embody what I believed to be a true role of government, providing the basic necessities of life for all of its citizens.

Miss Stein stared at me. I looked back with forlorn, slightly scared puppy eyes. She formed a tiny smile with her lips, but a bigger smile with her eyes. For a moment I thought she was on to us. And maybe she was. But before I knew it, she was filling out forms and explaining things to Michael while with every other sentence looking back at me. She asked about assets, savings and stuff. She didn't seem satisfied with the non-answers

Michael gave, but didn't push it.

"Well, I'm gonna need proof of indigence, but for now here's some food stamps and a rent voucher," she said, sliding them across the desk to me. I just looked at them. Michael reached over and picked them up. "It's just enough for a month. Then you'll have to come back in to be re-evaluated."

"Thanks," Michael said, trying not to look too pleased. "At least this'll get him off my back! I've got enough problems of my own, but I couldn't just kick him out into the street." Then Michael looked down at me. "He seems really sweet and harmless. I don't know what his story is, but he sure is messed up!" I glared at Michael, then quickly mutated my expression so Miss Stein could see one of worried perplexity.

We had just turned around to leave when Miss Stein said, "Wait!"

I expected she had found some obstacle in what I knew had been too easy a path. Still holding my hand, Michael turned me around and sat me back down in the chair.

"You know," Miss Stein said, "If Giacco applies for ATD, he wouldn't have to come back every month."

I looked questioningly at Michael. Michael looked solidly at me, then softly at Miss Stein. "What is ATD, Miss Stein? I've never heard of it."

"Please, call me Nancy." Miss Stein looked at Michael as if she knew she were in on a joke. "ATD stands for Aid to the Totally Disabled..." Miss Stein... Nancy... slowly turned her head to me. "...including *mental* disabilities. You get far more in benefits and in some cases it's *permanent!*" She said it with such satisfaction, for a moment I thought she was selling Vegematics.

I jerked my head sharply in Michael's direction. He was already looking at me with a glint in his eyes. I met his mischief with anger. This was going too far!

"Oh, don't get me wrong!" Nancy assured me. "I'm not suggesting you *are* mentally ill. I'm sure your *current* condition is only temporary and you'll get over it *very* soon." She gave me a long, slow wink. I couldn't make eye contact with her. My eyes kept darting forth and back like I was watching a tennis match.

"It's just that... we're *so* busy here... it often takes *nine* or *10 months* before an applicant for ATD can even be *evaluated* by a doctor!" Nancy looked at me with feigned pity for just a moment, then brightened. "But there's this rule... in your case quite convenient... that says all applicants for ATD *automatically* get General Assistance until they can be evaluated... without having to come in every month! And all you have to do is apply for it! Even if you're turned down, which I'm sure you will be, at least you'll get a few months of food stamps and rent to tide you over. So if you don't mind I think I'll apply for ATD for you and..." Nancy looked knowingly at Michael, "...let the system do the rest!"

Michael was looking at her with a steadiness that made me feel like I didn't know what was going on. Like Michael and Nancy were part of a conspiracy I didn't know about. Maybe Nancy was an undercover agent for the League for Spiritual Discovery or something and this was her way of sabotaging the establishment. It had its own morality. In a way, I could get behind it.

Yeah. This was a nice Ghandian way of doing things. Except the saboteur was using me *as the wooden shoe. How dare she suggest I was deranged! But wait! She was just going along with our little act. It was only to get General Assistance without a lot of hassles. It was only temporary, probably a month or two. Just long enough for me to get back on my feet. Back to Topanga. Back to some sort of job. Something would turn up. And the part of me looking down at me sort of liked the theatrics of it all. How well we're all staying in character!*

Michael felt me looking at him. When he turned toward me he had an opium grin on his face. Nancy looked pleased and relaxed as well. I felt her looking at me. I felt them both heaping face after face of kindness upon me. I succumbed like a speed freak suddenly shot up with secanol.

"Thank you very much," Michael said affectionately. "How considerate of you to think of that!"

"Well, that's why we're here. To help. And speaking of helpful, I don't know of many people who would've taken the time to become involved in the plight of a transient. Almost saintly, if you ask me."

"Yeah!" Michael smirked. "I'm so good they call me 'Michael the Archangel.'"

Jeremiah? The Thief on the Cross? And now Michael the Archangel? Oh man!

"And you can call me anytime," Nancy Stein said in a very professional social worker voice and stood up from behind her desk.

Michael tugged at my hand and I stood up. Nancy put both hands together at her chest and said quietly, almost collusively, "Go in peace, boys!" and gave me a big wink.

I kept looking back at Nancy as Michael led me out of the room past other case workers looking up from their desks. I was still a little confused a block away from the building. I wasn't sure what had happened.

"We did it!" Michael blurted, as if he had been holding it in. "You were great!"

"I wasn't great," I demanded. "You were both in on it, weren't you? I saw her blow her cover. She's an agent of the Revolution! Isn't she? Boy, San Francisco really has some far out people in it!"

Michael looked at me like I was a loony tune. "What are you talking about? She fell for it. Hook, line, and sinker! We were great!"

"Whaddya mean?" I insisted. "The winks! The looks! The helpful hints!"

"You're nuts!" Michael laughed. "C'mon, let's go celebrate!"

We stopped at a small grocery store on Market Street and bought some food for dinner. Michael was gloating at his accomplishment all through the Haight. As we walked up the alley to Michael's place, we saw the figure of a man standing in the window of the house overlooking it. He was waving at us. It was Kyle, Michael's landlord. Then he disappeared from view. By the time we reached the garage, he was standing in front of it.

"Michael, could I talk to you for a moment?" he said. His thin, liver-spotted hand gracefully danced forward and waved Michael toward him, like a hula dancer inviting you into her heart. Michael cheerfully walked up to him but lost the bounce in his step when he saw Kyle's light blue eyes were full of seriousness and concern. Kyle put his arm around Michael's shoulder and they talked.

Kyle left and Michael unlocked the garage door and raised it. I followed him inside. When he closed it and turned around I saw his eyes were moist.

"I have to leave," he said. His eyes lowered, and then his head. "I have to go back to Nebraska for a while."

I started to say something, but he stepped on my line and kept going. "My aunt called. My father's dying. He tried to kill himself. Just like my brother."

Michael offered no details. I was reluctant to inquire. We just stood there staring at each other. Michael with a blank, glazed look. Me, trying to reach through his eyes and embrace his pain, if that's what it was. It could have been confusion. It could have been conflict. It could have been anything, he looked so stunned.

And then some semblance of an expression came over his face. The look he was going for was hopeful, but he only got as far as wistful.

"After mom died when I was a kid, dad grew more distant from us. My brother and me. My dad and I aren't even that close," he said, trying to excuse himself of something. "It was my aunt who raised us. But I have to go back. It won't be for long. Don't know how long. Depends on a lot of things. But I'll be back." He tried to sound convincing but he knew he wasn't. I just wanted so much for him to know he could count on me. That I was there for him.

Michael walked up to me and gave me a hard hug. "I've only known you a couple of days and already I know I'm going to miss you a lot, Giacco."

I hugged him back. He pushed me gently away, just far enough to comfortably begin unbuttoning my shirt. While he did that, I reached down and tugged at the buttons of his 501 jeans.

Later, in the middle of the night, I woke up to hear Michael gently crying, trying to stifle the sobs into his pillow. I reached over and kissed his shoulder.

"You thinking about your dad? It's OK. Just let it out."

Michael turned over on his back. "I'm not thinking about my dad," he said quietly through his tears. "I'm thinking about my brother."

"The one who tried to kill himself?" I guessed.

"Yeah. Except he didn't try. He succeeded." Michael rolled over toward me and nestled his head against my chest, his breath warming my neck. "He fuckin' flew out the third story window of some loft in New York a few years ago. The only thing recognizable about his head was the smile on his face!"

This story sounded too familiar. I felt myself tense up and my heart quicken.

Michael continued through his tears, "He was my hero. My buddy. I loved him. He made my life so much easier. And he would've made all this easier too," he said referring to the two of us lying naked together in bed. "Sometimes I hate him for not being here."

Michael rolled back on the pillow, his arms under his head. He looked up at the ceiling and cried out angrily, "Dennis, why did you leave me?"

I gulped so hard, I thought I would choke.

CHAPTER 15
Halloween 1970

There was a damp chill in the night air as I walked up a North Beach side street to the Columbus Theater. Posters on telephone poles announced the Cockettes and the Bride of Frankenstein. Michael had mentioned them. Said I should catch one of their shows if I ever got the chance.

Michael was back in Nebraska. I'd gotten one call from him on Kyle's phone, but I wasn't around at the time. Kyle left the message for me on the window of the garage. All it said was "Michael says Hi. He's OK. Will call again sometime. Not sure from where." He never did. But Kyle had his aunt's address in Nebraska. He gave it to me. At least that was something.

I never did confide in Michael the fact that I knew his brother. That I had some peripheral involvement in his death. I just didn't know how to bring it up. How do you bring up something so ridiculously coincidental? Or was it powerfully cosmic and karmically predestined? I would bring it up when Michael came back. When I'd have more opportunity to find just the right moment. I just hoped he wouldn't figure it out on his own. Before I could come clean. Before I could understand it myself.

I really liked Michael. It felt good making love to him. Good, like in healthy. It was *good* for you. And it felt good living in Michael's little abode. I settled right in. Kyle appreciated the rent voucher and the graceful transition in tenants. In a state of wonder, I appreciated how easily things seemed to come my way. How I really didn't have to think about it. How I didn't really have to make any decisions.

I could see a crowd gathering in front of the theater. It didn't seem that there were that many people, but they sure took up a lot of space. As I got closer, I realized it was because of all the colorful costumes. I'd never seen such original and fanciful creations. They ranged from the pornographic to the monastic, the monstrous to the beauteous. The raiment of Wraiths. The garb of Gargoyles. The habiliments of the Horrible. Fashion commentaries and satires on every issue, political, social and sexual. And a few party poopers like me wearing country-hippie drag.

When the doors opened, everyone streamed in. And like water seeking its own level, costumes sought the seats that could hold them. People with dragon tails, wings, or gargantuan heads, were relegated to the back rows. Siamese twins and four-footed creatures sat in the aisles. Those with simply enormous genitalia, fairies, cave men, the deformed, the demented, and me, made it to the front rows.

The ushers didn't know what to do with one man dressed all in black. Strapped to his feet was the Golden Gate Bridge and the San Francisco skyline. On his extended arms and front and back of his head were enormous clouds. The seat of his pants was cut away revealing a white ass with little craters painted on it. He was supposed to be the "Full Moon Over San Francisco." He ended up standing in the balcony.

I could see in the wings, Cockettes making last minute adjustments to the sets and themselves. One of them walked out on stage and down the four steps to the first row. I have absolutely no idea what period of history his drag was supposed to be, if any. It was all frills and layers of clashing colors, patterns, and fabrics. Crinolines fighting each other. Scarves choking a chintz doll face with brightly rouged cheeks. His long hair, long beard, and huge moustache, glistened with multi-colored glitter. This was no Finnochio's. These were the Cockettes! And as if there were any doubt, he can-canned his dresses forth and back in front of his face, showing us how well-endowed he was.

Then he magically pulled out from somewhere in the depths of his wardrobe, a tin can which he held out in front of each member of the audience. In it were little tabs of acid. I noticed no one who let it pass by without reaching in and taking one. I did the same when it was held out in front of me. The Cockette winked, curtsied, and went on to the next person.

He was working his way through the crowded aisles when the lights dimmed and the music started. The curtains opened and the old movie version of The Bride of Frankenstein was already playing on the screen. The monster lay strapped on his gurney. Igor stood beside him ready to monitor the anticipated horny response the monster would have to the still inanimate female companion lying near him.

Dr. Frankenstein placed electrodes on the head of the bride to be. The lever was slowly pushed down and the juice made her head twitch, her eyes bulge, and her hair stand on end. She creakily stood up and looked around. Then she saw her groom. Obviously she didn't believe in arranged marriages. Just when she started freaking out and screaming, the screams of another, mimicking her, rose over the audio track of the movie.

The screen slowly faded and in its place appeared the Cockettes, outlandishly dressed to capture each of the monstrous characters of the screen. Without warning, they broke into an original musical production number. The singing was loud and off-key. The choreography was sloppy. The Cockettes were obviously stoned. Yet they sold the number through their sheer energy, spirit, freedom, and *you-got-a-problem-with-it?* attitude.

The audience went wild. They hooted and hollered. They bravo-ed and brava-ed. It was just about that time that I realized I was going to have a scary trip. Sometimes there's just no accounting for it. It just happens. Sometimes your mind just gets away with you.

I stumbled out into the lobby. It was filled with a sea of vampires, werewolves, and other monsters climbing and descending stairs to the restrooms on the second floor or buying munchies and thirsties from the snack bar. I could only see the ugly. Only the grotesque were in my foreground. The beautiful fairies and sex gods and goddesses were in the background being quickly absorbed into the beige walls of the lobby. Movie posters that were supposed to be attached to the walls were now floating in mid-air.

I found an empty, cushioned bench between two columns and sat down, clutching the seat with my hands to keep from falling overboard. I don't know how long I stayed there just staring. My eyes were dry from not blinking enough. My body was caramelized into inaction by this entire movie-going experience.

The Cockettes show ended and the creepy crowd streamed into the lobby, filing past me as they left the theater, laughing and carrying on. I pulled my legs under me and sat in a half-lotus position on my Devil's island, trying to pull myself together.

Two humans stood in the middle of the lobby waiting for someone or something. The crowd rushed around them. They stood rock still forcing the flow of the crowd to diverge into two streams. I thought of the stones I had placed in the middle of the creek the day after I met Reverend Trey. I wondered how these two people would alter the landscape in years to come.

They stood out from the crowd. One, because they weren't moving. Two, because they looked fairly normal. The guy wore jeans, a conservative grey plaid cowboy shirt and, around his neck, a red bandana. He was clean-shaven and had long thin dirty-blond hair. His teeth were perfectly straight and white. High prominent cheek bones underscored laughing, energetic eyes set unusually far apart. It was this last facial feature that prevented him from looking like a stereotypical California surfer.

The girl wore a simple, farmer's wife's dress with a flowered apron. In one hand she carried a matching Amish bonnet. She had very long black hair that hung absolutely straight until the last six inches where it got a little wavy. It was her eyes though, so big and bright and blue, that made her stand out. She had that continually amazed and spaced-out look like the bliss-ninnies who are supposed to wait tables in health food restaurants but seem completely unaware they have any customers.

The guy turned and saw me looking at them. Breaking into a crazy smile, he nudged the young girl next to him. When she looked up, he gestured to me with his jaw. They both approached. As they got nearer, I could see their pupils were very dilated and the girl's skin was flushed.

They leaned over, their heads about three feet away and studied me. They started talking about me as if I weren't there.

"Trudy! He is *really* stoned!" The word "really" was as long as the whole rest of the sentence. "Do you think he's OK?"

"Sure! He's just on a trip. He'll be OK." Trudy looked up at the guy she was with and studied him studying me. Then her big eyes got even bigger with some realization. "Lizzie, you sex maniac! You're just looking for an excuse to pick him up! You never quit, do you?"

Trudy sighed as if she had been through this a hundred times before. But there was such drama in the exhale, it made me suspect she was just trying to cement a very new friendship by acting like it was an old one. It was OK. That's what Michael and I did. People do it all the time.

"I think he *wants* to be picked up," Lizzie answered, scrunching up his nose and brow and squinting into my eyes like an old man looking over his reading glasses. "I think he *needs* to be picked up!" Lizzie decided. He reached for my elbow, breaking the invisible bubble of my psycho-prison, and escorted me out the door. Trudy, with reluctance, knowing she should do the sisterly thing, did the same.

I was putty in their hands. I never said a word until we were at the car. It was Trudy's mom's Studebaker Lark. All the windows were open and scrunched in the back seat fanning himself was one of the Cockettes, his feathers and gowns filling up the entire rear of the car. Trudy went around to the driver's side, opened the door and kneeled on the front seat, facing the recumbent, comically ridiculous drag queen.

Lizzie opened the passenger door and stuck his head in. "Bobby, what are you doing here? Aren't you going to the cast party with Sylvester and Cloud?"

Bobby could hardly get out the words. "No, Liz. I don't feel good. I took some mescaline before the show. Then some acid during the show, and then a Quaalude after the show. I don't know why, but I don't feel so good. Maybe all the sweating and running around and everything, but now I've got the chills and the shakes, and all I want to do is go home and relax. I'll be OK. Did you like the show?"

"It was fantastic!" Trudy said. "Everyone went wild. They loved it! You were especially great! Bobby fanned himself more quickly, cooling the blush of the compliment. Then he quickly pointed at me through the window with a multi-ringed finger. "Who's this?" he asked a little jealously.

"Who's this?" Trudy asked Lizzie.

"Who's this?" Lizzie asked me.

"Who's this?" I asked, pointing at myself. "This is Giacco," I answered, and then looked around me to see if anyone else answered to that name. "Yes, I'm sure of it. The name's Giacco. And thanks, Lizzie. I got lost there for a while. I guess I was stuck somewhere I didn't want to be. Thanks for the jump start."

Lizzie turned to Trudy with a self-satisfied look. "I told you he wanted to be picked up! Well, then, pile in everybody, and let's go home!"

Home was a cluttered three-bedroom apartment on the first floor of a four-story building on the corner of Frederick and Arguello. Just opposite the park. Only about four blocks from my garage.

In the living room was a waterbed. Two candles burned on an end table. Two bodies wrapped in sheets turned over in their sleep, oblivious or unconcerned about our entering the room, and sent waves to the sides of the bed and then back to the middle.

At the other end of the room, an old Three Stooges film was on the TV. The volume was off but it would've been easy to add your own sound effects to their face-slapping antics. The light the screen threw on the floor flickered from scene to scene like the light from a fireplace. Except the light was blue and cold instead of warm and orange. In front of the TV was an air mattress. The kind you take backpacking. A tie-dyed sheet was thrown over it.

Trudy reached to Lizzie for a hug. "I gotta go, Lizzie. I've gotta get the car back. I'll see you tomorrow or Monday."

"Thanks, Trude," Lizzie said as he squeezed her and planted a big-brother kiss on her mouth. "Are you OK? Can you drive?"

"Yeah. I'm fine. I only took a taste. I'm mostly on a contact high and once I get away from you guys I'll be fine."

Trudy closed the door behind her and the bodies on the waterbed undulated to the minor disturbance.

"Wait here Giacco. Let me get Bobby into bed and then you and me can… *get to know one another*." Lizzie winked and then steadied Bobby's shaky walk toward the far end of the living room. Bobby limply smiled at me from behind his fan as he turned down the hallway.

I waited long enough to get tired of standing, so I lay down on the air mattress. I turned off the TV just as Larry was bopping Moe and Curly's heads together. I thought of Rosie and Jon and closed my eyes in order to transport myself back to the Seven Falls of Sabino Canyon. I heard water running for a long time, and then gentle splashing and some laughter. I must've dozed off for a few minutes or at least fallen deep into my reverie. What I heard next was water dripping on the floor next to my head.

When I looked up I saw Lizzie and Bobby standing naked above me, still drying themselves. It was a strange perspective. Looking up at their balls and just above that, two erect cocks dangling three feet above my head. Bobby's was more erect than Lizzie's but both were jutting out enough to almost obscure their smiling faces way off in the distance.

At first I thought Lizzie had come into the room with someone I hadn't met yet. Only when Bobby ran a multi-ringed finger down Lizzie's chest did I make the connection. I would've never guessed this good-looking boy was the same Cockette I saw melting into the plaid upholstery of the Studebaker. Without his headdress, gowns, feathered boa and excessive make up, Bobby looked like anybody else. Anybody else, that is, who is an eighteen-year old blond, muscular, Aryan youth archetype. Put some lederhosen on him and he could be an Eagle scout on the cover of Boy's Life, one of the favorite erotic magazines of my prepubescent youth.

Lizzie was obviously his scout master, mentor and guardian, though he was only maybe six or seven years older. He was leaner than Bobby and not as muscular, but very attractive nonetheless. He exhibited a paternalistic dominance which Bobby seemed to adore.

Lizzie must've thought that I wanted to spend the night with him because he sheepishly said, "I hope you aren't disappointed. But Bobby really needs me tonight. He's really shaken up from the drugs. And after all we *are* lovers. You understand, don't you? We'll get together some other time." Then he dropped a blanket down by my side. "In case you get cold." They turned around and walked down the hallway, arms around each other's shoulders, Bobby's cute butt flickering in the candlelight.

I closed my eyes and fell asleep conjuring up images of Bobby earning a few merit badges.

CHAPTER 16
All Saints Day 1970

I was dreaming I had a stomach-ache and I was rubbing my tummy in a counter-clockwise motion just like they teach you in yoga class. Sounds of cupboards opening and closing, and dishes being washed, made my ears start to waken. In between the faucet being turned on and off I could make out something about "tomatoes."

My eyes were trying to open. I yawned and stretched out my arms letting them drop above my head. It was then I realized a hand, obviously not my own, was *still* rubbing my tummy. I forced my eyes open and looked up at one of the most beautiful storybook characters I ever saw. A very young, round face, belonging to someone in his early 20s I guessed. His complexion was flawless. His forehead was perfectly smooth and continued all the way up to the crown of his head. I'd never seen such beautiful baldness. Not a bump. Not a wrinkle. What hair did grow from the sides of his head was black and soft and fine. And his neatly trimmed beard was made of the same stuff.

An iridologist would have used his eyes as examples of perfect health. The whites were absolutely white, the pupils were absolutely black, and the irises were a translucent light brown, without any trace of speckles or other indications of internal impairments. He was full of light.

He was kneeling beside me wearing just his pajama bottoms. Even in that position, I could tell he was diminutive. Maybe five feet-four at the most. His hairy chest was barrel shaped and his stomach was soft without being flabby.

Even after our eyes made contact, he continued rubbing my tummy. I'm not *that* easy and normally I would have at least questioned what he damn well thought he was up to. But there was such an innocence about him, such an elfish quality, such a munchkin goodness, that I just watched him as his hand traced the circular route around my belly button.

"You are really one hot tomato," he said, and aimed a short, but distinctive yodel at the ceiling, like a baby wolf aiming a falsetto howl at the moon. I tried to recall where I had heard it before. Then he bent over and gave me a sweet little kiss on the lips. At that moment, I recognized him as the little man I saw on the Golden Gate Bridge.

Suddenly from behind him a high-pitched voice yelled, "Richard! Leave that poor man alone!"

Richard jumped to his feet. I looked past him to another man who looked like Richard's older brother, though they were not related. He shared a similarly patterned baldness, but his hair and beard seemed hard and bristly and it stuck out from the sides of his head and chin like a bottle brush. He had a mock scolding look on his face and his fists were resting akimbo on his hips like a mother chastising her child.

Richard defended himself. "I'm not bothering him, Duck! I'm not bothering you, am I?" he asked me.

Before I could answer, one of the bodies in the waterbed bolted upright, sending a huge wave toward the foot of the bed and me. Fortunately, the seam of the huge bladder held and sent the wave caroming back under the woman and the mystery person still under the covers.

"Duck! Richard! What the fuck is going on? Can't I ever get to sleep in late, just once?"

Her face held no anger. Instead it pouted just a little, then smiled as if to say, *Kids, what're ya gonna do with 'em!* She looked vaguely familiar but the remembrance remained beyond retrieval. The first thing I noticed was a storm of jet black ringlets around her face. The skin of her round face was smooth and creamy white, accented with a natural blush on her cheeks. Her lips were as red as her eyes were dark, and she had nice breasts that sloped gracefully downwards toward a baby fat stomach. She was Rubenesquely beautiful and as she flung the bedspread to the side, further covering her comatose partner, I imagined the tempestuous love-making that must've gone on before our arrival the previous night.

She stood up completely naked and walked over to Richard and Duck, stood between them and put an arm around each one.

Richard started rubbing her belly and looked up at her with wounded eyes. Duck gently pinched her nipple and said, "Psylvia, you have the nicest titties!"

"Why, thanks Larry! That's sweet!" And she kissed him on the forehead.

The three of them stared down at me. I lowered my eyes and noticed Psylvia's legs were really hairy. I knew that true earth mothers were adopting the European fashion of not shaving, but even so, these were unusually hairy legs. Almost all the way up to her crotch, which verified her femaleness.

"Who's this?" Psylvia asked, looking down at me. "Gosh, I think I know him from somewhere! Who is he?" she asked again.

"We don't know yet," Larry-Duck replied.

"But he sure is one heck of a tomato, isn't he?" said Richard.

Duck put a finger into the side of his cheek and thought about it. "He's a little too skinny to be a tomato!"

"Well, maybe he's one of those imported Italian tomatoes," argued Richard.

"He looks more like a zucchini to me," said Psylvia. "Have you checked to see if he's a zucchini?"

Richard grabbed Duck's nose and gave it a little tweak. "I was just about to when Larry rudely interrupted!"

Behind the trio I heard a young woman coming out of the kitchen. She swung her head and upper torso around the doorway, her tilted head making her straight blond hair seem longer than it really was.

"Coffee's on. And breakfast is almost ready. C'mon in." Then she swung exactly the same way out of view back into the kitchen.

Duck. Larry. Whatever his name was, extended an arm down to me and offered his hand. "C'mon. Let's get some coffee." I grabbed it and he pulled me up. My shirt which was crumpled up around my neck fell back into place where it belonged. My pants were still on and when I surreptitiously checked, my zipper was still up.

I introduced myself and gave the hippie handshake to Duck, Richard, and Psylvia. Each shook my hand limply, not so much out of wimpishness, but more because they seemed to regard my handshake as passé or affected.

"Wait a minute!" Psylvia said grabbing me by the shoulders. "I do know you! We've met before. I'm sure of it. In fact, I know exactly where we met!"

I looked at her carefully, squinting my eyes as if that would squeeze out some memory cloistered in the folds of my gray matter.

"You look familiar," I said, still a little rummy from lack of sleep, "but I can't conjure it up. Tell me. Give me a clue."

"Uhh, uhh," she said. "It'll come to you eventually, though I will admit I was into a different head space at the time. I might get into it again. You never can tell." She then put her face right up to mine and winked an eye ever so slowly. Nothing registered, so she shrugged and just said, "I can wait. When it does come to you, you'll know why you're here!"

Psylvia and Duck turned to go into the kitchen. I started after them. But Richard made a beeline for the waterbed. Psylvia stopped in her tracks, Duck bumped into her, and I stepped on Duck's heel. He let out a little "ow!" Psylvia almost ran Duck and me down trying to get to the waterbed. Duck and I followed her.

"Don't you even think about it!" she harshly stage-whispered to Richard.

"I wasn't going to do anything," Richard protested. "I just wanted to see who you brought home from Yosemite."

"His name is Nick. I call him Nicky. And he's mine! Hands off! Do you understand, you little twerp?" And she shook Richard lovingly and then gave him a big hug. "He's wonderful! Be good to him now. For me. Please. Don't freak him out all at once. Go easy with him. And now, if you'll all just stand back, please! Just a little bit. I think you're violating his space. Let *me* violate it instead!"

Psylvia slowly, carefully, pulled back the covers, revealing an inch or two at a time, the barely-out-of-his-teens mountain boy she had brought home. As the covers unveiled his face and chest and stomach, the three of them let out quiet "Ooohs."

When their "ooohs" ended, I "ooohed" as well. They all looked at me and smiled approvingly.

Psylvia pulled the covers down past his knees. He wore a big stiff cock that trembled almost imperceptibly at the tip.

"Aaaaah!" The four of us sighed in appreciation.

"What a beautiful early morning hard-on!" Psylvia commented as if about a sunrise. "He must be dreaming about me!"

And with that she gently swung one leg over Nicky's waist. When her knee made contact, the mattress rocked like a rowboat. She steadied herself with the foot still on the dock and then gracefully climbed on board.

"Let's let the young'uns have some privacy," I said to Richard and Duck, who would have just as soon stood there and watched. I grabbed Duck's hand who grabbed Richard's hand. They were surprised at how comfortably assertive I was. *I* was surprised at how comfortably assertive I was. I sighed as if I had been through this a hundred times before. As I led them out of the room, I sighed with the same drama that Trudy had sighed at Lizzie. So what did that mean? Was I trying to cement new friendships by acting like they were old ones? Or *were* they old ones?

As we single-filed into the kitchen like three grammar school kids on a field trip, I looked down the long hallway. At the far end was a mattress on the floor. Two bodies lay curled together. I guessed it was Lizzie and Bobby.

At the kitchen table sat the woman with the blond hair and at her side, a big bear of a man with a big face, big hair and big beard. His big blue eyes stared at me from behind big rimless glasses that made him look authoritative, professorial and erudite.

Richard, Duck, and I sat down. On the table was a pot of freshly brewed coffee, a cup of honey, a gallon jar of homemade granola, a creamer of half and half and a pitcher of milk, an oval serving dish with scrambled eggs, and a platter of buttered toast. I was a little surprised at how well-set the table was.

The big man, the man that made me, Duck, and Richard look like three of the seven dwarves in comparison, lay a big arm across the table toward me and said, "And here, we have whom?"

"Baird, may I have the pleasure of introducing Giacco Zucchini?" Duck courteously asked. "Giacco Zucchini, this is Baird... and this is Ellen. This apartment is mine and Ellen's. Or at least it was for a while," Duck mooned wistfully.

"Nice to meet you, Ellen," I said waving hi across the table. She nodded back, her mouth full of toast, but her eyes full of reciprocation. "Nice to meet you, Beard," I said offering my hand.

"Baird! It's Baird! Not Beard!"

"Sorry, Baird," I said, keeping my hand out.

He took it and after a hearty shake, swept his hand above the food. "Eat! Drink! Be Mary! And if you can't be Mary always be a Mensch."

Ellen took a swig of coffee and put down her fork. "Baird, Marys can be mensches, too. Mensch is a state of mind."

"Mind is a state of mind," Baird informed her, and then he looked at each of us, pausing long enough to ensure we had made eye contact with him. "Now I must go paint!"

He pushed himself away from the table and stood up. "By the way," he said, looking down at me, "Are you moving in with us?"

Before I could answer, he announced, "Well, of course you are! Why wouldn't you? We're the universe! Welcome to Hunga Dunga!" And he left the room puffing himself up.

I reached for the eggs and then turned to Richard. "What's Hunga Dunga?"

"You know the Marx Brothers movie, 'Animal Crackers?' Remember the scene where Groucho is dictating a letter to Zeppo for his lawyer?"

Duck took over. "Groucho says, 'Take a letter... care of Hungadunga, Hungadunga,

Hungadunga, Hungadunga, and McCormick...'"

Richard continued. "Well Groucho asks Zeppo to read it back to him and then yells at Zeppo, 'Wait a minute! You left out one of the Hungadungas! The most important one!'" Richard paused and looked at me waiting for some kind of acknowledgment. "Well?"

"Well what?" I asked.

"Well, you're looking at him." Richard replied with self-satisfaction."

"Looking at who?"

"Looking at the most important Hunga Dunga, of course."

"No you're not! I'm the most important Hunga Dunga!" Larry announced.

"Who says?" Richard said combatively.

"You're both full of shit," Ellen interrupted. Her voice was definitive and spoken with a sense of pure objectivity. "Everyone knows that *I'm* the most important Hunga Dunga!"

"Who said!?" Richard and Duck asked sharply.

"I had a dream last night." Ellen confided. "Harpo was in my bed and we made passionate love. When he came, he honked loudly over and over! It was then I knew for sure I was the most important one!"

CHAPTER 17
November 1970

It wasn't until just before Thanksgiving that I realized I wasn't a newcomer to Hunga Dunga. Everyone got on so well with each other, I assumed they'd all been together for a long time, maybe even years. To the contrary, everyone, including me, had converged on Larry and Ellen's apartment only within the space of about the previous three months.

There was Trudy, happy to leave her Mom's house in Berkeley and eager for new experiences, even if she had to force herself into most of them.

There was Nicky, who had become known as the "deer" because he always seemed so wide-eyed and frozen in place, perhaps entranced by the light generated by Psylvia.

There was Psylvia, who seemed more angelic and beautiful with each of the many times I observed her selflessness, simplicity, hard work, and most of all, humor.

There was Richard, whose biting witticisms and sardonic repartee could cut all but Baird down to size.

There was Baird, who was ostensibly opposed to any philosophy that had a name.

There was Lizzie, who would often catch himself using the word "mine" but would correct himself before anyone could yell "shame."

There was Ellen, who was the most politically active and somehow beautifully impatient with people who weren't fighting for a cause.

There was Bobby, who, smitten with the glory of being a Cockette, longed for stardom in Hollywood or on The Great White Way.

There was Larry, who was incapable of telling even the smallest lie and whose thoughts were never censored before escaping his mouth, regardless of the consequences.

And then there was me, who like everyone else to one degree or another, knew there was something very interesting going on.

Ellen and Larry met at San Francisco State. Baird was an old high school chum of Ellen's back in Albuquerque. He quickly seduced Larry with whom he had a three-day affair. Larry picked up Richard at the Stud. Their relationship evolved from lovers to brothers practically overnight. Lizzie used to be Richard's roommate in L.A., and before that, in New York. Lizzie met Bobby at the baths on Folsom Street and Trudy at a Love-in in Golden Gate Park. Psylvia knew Ellen through some anti-war activist friend in Philadelphia and had brought Nicky home after literally bumping into him at the top of Half Dome in Yosemite. And I already explained how I got here.

We were bursting at the seams. Yet no one thought to leave or for a few of us to go off and get an apartment of our own. We all wanted to stay together. It's not that each of us loved all the others equally. But the connectedness with just one or two was so strong and easy, each of us was willing to work at connecting with the others.

Richard disliked Baird's arrogance, but Richard also loved Larry, who respected Baird's integrity immensely. So Richard stayed and was willing to work on it. Ellen thought Nicky was a flake, but Ellen found in Psylvia the sister she always longed for. So Ellen was willing to work on it. I was leery of Trudy, but Lizzie loved Trudy, and Richard and Psylvia loved Lizzie, and Duck loved Richard and Psylvia, and I loved Duck, Richard, Psylvia and Lizzie. So I stayed and was willing to work on it.

There were so many different connections, it was impossible to break one without having to break others. So we were all willing to work on it. To stay together and work on it. Even though the supporting walls in the apartment seemed ready to burst. And we weren't finished yet!

Grateful Dead Concert. At the Winterland. Psylvia, Duck, Lizzie, Nicky, Richard and me were tripping on mescaline. Is there any wonder a Dead-head is loyal? We danced up a storm. I hadn't danced like that since the Free Press concert on Venice Beach. It felt like I was touching a part of a distant past life. I seldom danced anymore. I mean really *danced*. Usually I just stood in place and moved modestly to the music. But this night, I let loose. If any band can get you in touch with some primal force, it's the Dead.

Ripple in still waters, where there is no pebble tossed, nor wind to blow... We were in a circle, our arms over each other's shoulders, our eyes shut, swaying forth and back to the music, singing with Jerry, feeling connected, all on the same beautiful trip. When the song ended, we opened our eyes and tried to stop swaying. But our arms remained on each other's shoulders.

It took about twenty seconds for it to dawn on us that there were two new people in our circle. How they got there was beyond us. But there they were, like magic. Lizzie and Richard knew *one* of them. The other, no one had ever seen before.

"Tom! Tom McIntyre!" Lizzie half-whispered in astonishment. "What are you doing here?"

My memory struggled with the name, trying to place it. All of a sudden I found myself tele-transported via some mescaline frequency to the house on Appian Way in Laurel Canyon. I was with Dean. We were listening to someone playing the guitar behind a closed bedroom door. A flash of light and I was back in the Fillmore. So *this* was the Tom McIntyre that Dean lived with just before he and Lisa moved back east. The one he didn't want me to meet.

Dean was right. I could have fallen for this hippie man. He was macho. He was hot. And he could croon a country tune that would make any cowboy's heart melt. But Dean was also right about another thing. I definitely was not Tom's type, though it was no hindrance to us becoming close friends.

"What happened to 'Hair?'" Richard asked. "Aren't you still in the cast?"

"Great news!" Tom announced to Lizzie and Richard, and then looked at the rest of us. "After the first of the year, they're putting me in the San Francisco cast!"

"That's perfect! It'll be just like old times," Lizzie said, referring to days back in New

York when he and Tom used to audition for the same TV commercials and Richard was known as the "ear" at a small recording studio. "Isn't this great, Richard?"

"Everything is just needless to say," answered Richard with a silly mescaline grin on his face, a phrase for which he would become famous.

Lizzie went around the circle introducing Tom to each of us. Until he got to the mystery intruder.

"And Tom, this is someone. I have absolutely no idea who he is. Who are you?"

"Hi everybody!" the mystery man said. "You must think I'm crazy, but I saw all of you in this circle and the energy was so fantastic that I just knew this is where I wanted to be! I couldn't help myself! I was just pulled into this vortex of love!" He took a deep, contented sigh, as if he were finally home after a long time away. "My name's Chuck. Chuck Cohen."

"You're quite the tomato!" Richard said sidling up to Chuck and rubbing his tummy. Chuck returned the tribal greeting.

"You're a little dramatic about it, but that's OK," Psylvia said. "This is where you *must* belong." And because Psylvia said it, we agreed it was true. Psylvia, of all the people at Hunga Dunga, was loved by everyone. She was so *present tense*, so much the embodiment of what a hippie should be. So natural! Whenever she spoke, we listened. But more often than not, it was her actions, not her words, that influenced us. Baird on the other hand, was all too quick to postulate what was, and was not, proper behavior. He almost had a conniption when he woke up the next morning and found two more people sleeping on the floor.

"OK. That's it! I can't breathe it's so dense in here! Either we get a bigger place or something's gotta give. And I don't want it to be me!" Baird almost exploded with frustration, a rare outburst from one who I fancied was running for resident Buddha.

"Baird, you're such a genius!" Lizzie said. "Why didn't we think of that before? Let's get a bigger place. Big enough for everyone! We've certainly outgrown this pad!"

And that's what we did. At first, all twelve of us would go to visit a place. We must've freaked out the prospective landlords because they always found a reason not to rent to us. So we changed our tactics. Two or three people would go out and scout houses for rent. When they found a likely one, the rest of us would visit it in small, separate, totally unrelated groups. Then we would reconvene and voice our pros and cons. Like everything else at Hunga Dunga, coming to a decision was a major task. But eventually we found just the right house in just the right neighborhood. We knew the landlord might not want to rent to twelve weird looking and acting freaks. So we sent Lizzie to close the deal. Lizzie made the perfect front man. He said he would use his training as an actor to portray the very essence of responsibility and dependability. Actually, it came naturally to him. He was born with it.

I stopped by the little garage apartment to pack up my few belongings and to give Kyle an overdue rent voucher. I sent Michael a postcard telling him of my whereabouts, but I guess he never got it because I never heard from him. I wrote him a number of times from a number of whereabouts, but never received anything back. Nada. Zilch.

I sent a postcard to Jon and Rosie too, in care of Rosie's mom. I included some cryptically glowing lines about Hunga Dunga. Then I went to see Nancy Stein at Social Services to put in a change of address so I could get next month's food stamps.

"Oh, your timing is perfect," she said. "I was just going to send you a notice that your psychiatric evaluation is set for December 28th at 10 AM."

"What psychiatric evaluation?" I asked.

"You know. To determine whether you're... *disabled!*" She smiled. Then she pushed herself back from her desk. "We've recovered our voice, I see... or rather *hear!*"

I stumbled around among a few thalidomide thoughts. All of them were lame. I used what I thought was the least deformed. "I think I had my head up my ass!"

Without so much as a look of admonishment, she said, "Well, The City can do that to you! Especially if you're *new* in town! And you can't very well talk with your head way up *there*!" She snickered and pulled herself back up to her desk. One of the wheels on her chair squeaked, but without skipping a beat, she happily continued. "No matter. Never mind. The wheels are in gear!"

The words hung around me and circled like pictures on the inside of a rotoscope. I went on a brief mini-trip. Somewhere I'd been before. Or somewhere I was going. I couldn't tell. Nancy Stein snapped her fingers in front of me.

"Now don't get all freaked out. It's just a formality. I'm sure the doctor will find you quite normal and unfortunately when he does I'll have to take you off General Assistance. But not to worry! It usually takes months for the evaluation to come through and like I explained before, until then you keep getting food stamps and rent vouchers!"

I thanked her, but couldn't help feeling a bit apprehensive.

CHAPTER 18
December 1970

By Christmas the twelve of us were in the house on 18th Street, between Sanchez and Church, in the Castro. It was a neighborhood just beginning to burgeon into a happening place. The house was a big two-story Victorian with an unfinished attic. It was built in 1904 and had survived the 1906 earthquake and fire. In the back was a nice, terraced yard with a quaint little cabin on the top tier. The house was painted sky blue with white trim. We always referred to it as Big Blue when giving people directions.

It must be a law of physics that no matter how large a space allotted, the human being will fill it to capacity. As if twelve weren't enough, four more were soon added to the roster:

Lizzie picked up Greg hitchhiking and was smitten with his regular Joe mannerisms and deep voice. He had so much facial hair, that were he to shave, I probably wouldn't recognize him. He was a smart cookie and dismissed small talkers by ignoring them.

Tom met Brandon backstage after a performance of "Hair." He had *long, flaxen, waxen* hair. No moustache. No beard. Affable, good-natured, a real "sweetie" in Psylvia's book. He was a former state champion high school gymnast from Colorado. They made a handsome twosome, and acted so normal and natural, they made male-male coupling seem mainstream.

Alvoye. A very tall, very slim, light-skinned West Indian. One of Baird's sexual conquests. He had striking hazel eyes and a wild dark brown Afro that made Angela Davis' seem like a Marine cut. Everyone agreed he was one of the most exotic animals to be seen on the streets of the Castro. Another notch on Baird's big gun.

And Luc. A French Belgian. Into leather and pierced nipples. He lived for backroom escapades. He enjoyed reciting Shakespearean monologues from the landing at the top of the stairs, dressed in nothing but a leather jock and chaps. He was yet another notch on Baird's gun.

After Luc, I stopped counting. Whoever was in the house at any given time was a Hunga Dungan. Who was a core member and who was peripheral was determined by each of us in our own minds. We were all strong-willed anarchists. Yet people gravitated to various little circles of love that intersected each other at different points. Though there were widely divergent life styles, what we held in common could be found in the areas where the circles intersected. A certain unspoken consciousness.

One time I made the mistake of guessing out loud that this consciousness existed among us in varying degrees.

"Consciousness exists in varying degrees? Who are you to guess?" Baird attacked. I surrendered immediately. One: because there's no way to argue with a koan and Baird's mind worked like one. Two: Baird was right. And so was Richard. Everything *was* needless to say. All you had to do was watch Hunga Dunga in action. Everyone loved each other enough to do whatever was necessary to continue living together. We did naturally and through expedience, what others called "communal."

One of the natural and expedient things to do was to pool all our money. *All* our money! It was easy to do for the people who weren't bringing in a dime. It was easy to do for the people who were getting their money from the government, which was most of us. It was less easy for the one or two people who, at any one time, were working for a living. Nevertheless, whether it was food stamps, rent vouchers, or cash, everyone was expected to put it *all* in the communal pot. To hold back a percentage was anathema. It showed a lack of faith, though to use the word "faith" was itself anathema. Baird wouldn't stand for it. Faith. Grace. Take no thought for food or shelter. Desirelessness is moksha. Any and all spiritually encapsulating terms were "needless to say." So we didn't say them. Because it was understood we should be *living* them.

Oh, sure, there were times when we knew life would be easier if everyone were contributing. There were times when Ellen was the only person working. Other times when it was Psylvia, or Duck, or even me, moonlighting to augment my General Assistance. There were times when some of us silently prayed the "deer" would get off his duff and do something. Anything except sit there, putting out positive vibes into the universe, and staring innocently wide-eyed at the cavorting of the seemingly crazed.

Yet we reminded ourselves that putting out positive vibes into the universe was a noble profession and who were we to judge anyway? So we did what was necessary because we all wanted to live together, because we *were* the universe and had to learn how to live in the universe, not run away from it. We had to learn how to live together in harmony and that was quite a feat for a bunch of eccentrics.

Being anarchists, we detested rules. Hunga Dungan self-government was based on traditions and at Hunga Dunga, traditions were often established overnight. Like the "Family Meeting" which anyone could call at any time. Like the one Ellen called the afternoon of Christmas Eve.

"I called this meeting because I'm tired of doing all the cooking," Ellen opened.

Everyone sighed as if they had been through this a hundred times before. And regardless of who called a meeting or why, it would seldom address just one issue. It always mushroomed into a venting session.

"Look, you guys," Lizzie said, completely ignoring Ellen's concern. "I've been putting in every residual check I get from the Almond Joy commercial, but I'm never going to get my dream vacation in Hawaii if I have to cough up everything."

"Well that's a hell of a non-sequitur," Ellen remanded.

"Well, you are all aware of how much I want a loom," Trudy stated matter-of-factly, ignoring Ellen's remark. Ellen let out a sigh of despair.

"I need a piano," Bobby insisted.

"And *I* need a winter coat," Duck sheepishly added.

"Why should Tom and Brandon get to sleep in the cabin?" Baird wanted to know, competing for the right to set the agenda.

Tom and Brandon looked at each other, knowing their love would see them through all tribulations, even that of having the privacy of their hide-a-way threatened.

"First things first. Zwagen needs a tune-up," Richard prioritized. "You can only expect so much from a Beetle before it has a seizure!"

"And I want everybody to be at the rally against the eviction of El Centro de la Raza and to save the International Hotel," Ellen exhorted.

Alvoye, always silent unless pressured to give his opinion, scratched the southwest quadrant of his Afro with a chopstick.

"Well, you know at least three of us eventually want to have a place in the country," I reminded.

"And I'm one of them!" Chuck piped up. "And I think at some future date we should discuss what happens to *lump* sums of money that might come our way!"

Richard turned to Chuck. "Now there's an interesting scenario!" And you could almost hear a number of cranial grist mills grinding that one up.

"Nicky wants land too!" Psylvia said for Nicky. Nicky's eyes got slightly larger, if that were at all possible, when he heard his name. "The most important thing to remember is that everybody's equal and everyone should get whatever they want," insisted Psylvia, simplifying the whole mess. "And if you can't get what you want when you want it, at least we're all getting what we need when we need it." Psylvia turned to Nicky and batted her eyelids at him. "At least *I* am, I'm happy to say!"

Richard yodeled, a signal at a family meeting that something heavy and philosophical had been said. That was treading on dangerous territory. That was elevating the discussion to another level. That was Baird's cue to "elucidate," a service he himself always volunteered.

"May I elucidate?" Baird asked, though really it was not a question, but rather a Hunga Dungan parliamentary procedure by which Baird brought the meeting back to *his* order. Under his breath Richard said, "Oh no! Another Lucy date!"

"I heard that, Richard!" And Baird frowned.

"Baird, please! Continue! You know, I *love* Lucy!"

Duck and Psylvia giggled.

Baird threatened Richard with his eyes. "As I was saying..." Baird looked around to ward off any other snide remarks. "As much as I myself reject the structure of some of the other 'communes' with which we interact, not to suggest that we are one, a commune I mean, like The Friends of Perfection, the Angels of Light, the Golden Aura Commune... I can't refrain from noting some trends that are developing and some lessons to be learned." Baird always made you feel like you were in a college lecture hall.

"Thank god for Flo Airwaves," Larry interjected. Flo Airwaves were the coolest neighbors any commune could have and consisted of Rolli, Travis, Althea, Danny, Joan, and

Glenn. At least I always called him Glenn, much to his chagrin. He insisted on being called "Divine." His friend from Baltimore, John Waters, also liked it when we call him "Divine." Flo Airwaves was one of the few communes whose name really didn't mean anything other than as a reference to the Grateful Dead lyric, *let the airwaves flow.* For Flo Airwaves we were very grateful.

"You may thank whomever you wish, Larry, but please keep god out of it!" Baird requested. "Now then, may I continue?"

"Yes, please do," Ellen said impatiently. "And then let's get back to the cooking problem. OK?"

"I *am* addressing the cooking problem, Ellen. If you'll just bear with me!"

We all adjusted ourselves where we sat on the floor in the living room and settled in for a Baird discourse.

"Anarchy is the label that best describes us, and I know how repulsed everyone is by labels. But if anarchy is to work, it requires a certain level of *consciousness.*"

"Consciousness? Levels?" I threw at Baird. "Why just last week you were putting me down for even bringing it up!"

"My, my, my. Hung up on *time*, are we?" Baird socratized. I just rolled my eyes.

"As I was saying," he continued, "anarchy, if it is to work, requires a certain level of consciousness. Otherwise it degenerates into selfishness and greed, and therefore violence."

We all waited for Baird to say more, but he didn't. There was a half-minute of rare silence. We all looked at each other.

Ellen had had enough. "So does that mean you're going to start cooking? Or doing the dishes?"

"Regard this Big Blue house," Baird started up again ignoring Ellen's question, "as a laboratory. Experiment with yourselves. Trip out on what works and what doesn't. Without any rules. Just because it's happening and we do what we do because we *want* to do it."

"Baird, that really excites me," Richard said. "I'd like to go upstairs right now and experiment with myself."

"Pleez, pleez, pleez… s'il vous plait!" Luc interloped in his Flemish/French accent. "Reeshard. It eez not necessaire to rideecool Baird! Allow me to tranzlate: To *be* or not to *be*. Zat ees ze questione. *Be* nice. *Be* helpful. Someone help weeth ze cookeeng! I, myself, would love to help, but I'm piercing Deevine's nose tonight as a Chreesmas present."

"Thank you, thank you, thank you, Hamlet the Leatherette!" At last, the mighty Greg had spoken. He was standing up, leaning against the wall, the only one who chose not to sit in the circle, though I intend no sociologic implication. It was probably a leftover habit from his one and only job all through and after college. A newspaper reporter for The Lodi Chronicler keeping his emotional distance. *Just the facts, ma'am!*

Greg, ever the pragmatist, forced truth into action with a curtness unusual for one so sedate. "The fact is, people, that it's six o'clock PM. The fact is that it's Chanuka, Christmas Eve, Winter Solstice Paganland, or just another Day in the Life of Hunga Dunga, whichever term you're most comfortable with. The fact is that I'm hungry and I know Ellen planned a special dinner. What I suspect is that she's tired and bit off more than she could chew and she's asking for help. So, Ellen, *I* will help you… and anyone else is invited to participate. But in the future, Ellen, if you don't want to cook, don't cook! Can everyone live with that?"

Everyone looked at each other and then up at Greg. *Can everyone live with that? What? Ellen not cooking if she doesn't want to? That was an easy one!* One by one, each person nodded, mumbled or voiced some kind of "yes."

"Is there anyone who *can't* live with that?" Greg asked with finality.

No one said anything.

"Well, if anyone does, either come up with another solution, or *live* with it!"

And that became a tradition. Of how we made decisions. "Can everyone live with that?" became a call for a Hunga Dungan vote. Either everyone *could* or *would* live with it, or someone *couldn't* or *wouldn't* live with it. Either unanimity or nothing. Well, not quite nothing. And not quite unanimity. A lone veto didn't count unless it was accompanied by an alternative suggestion. Then *that* was bounced around, fondled, embraced, or vivisected. If more than one person objected to whatever was being proposed, the issue was tabled until further notice. Until further notice, things would remain the same.

Greg polled the circle with his eyes. "I hereby call this meeting adjourned! Let's eat!" And with the feeling that, inexplicably, everyone's problems were solved, the circle began to yawn and stretch. Fifteen people stood up and followed Greg into the kitchen. Everyone was so eager to help they were officious. Ellen wound up kicking everyone out yelling she'd rather do it herself.

I held Baird back until everyone else was in the kitchen. I asked him, "Baird, way down deep do you think there really is a *most* important Hunga Dunga?"

"Giacco," he answered, "We are all of us *combined*, the *most* important Hunga Dunga. As individuals we are merely important… and all equals. Equally weak!"

He must have seen my brain at work. Lifting his muumuu so as not to trip, he said, "This is just one big fucking experiment Giacco!" With that he rushed into the kitchen.

In the years to come we experimented with ourselves in our laboratory called Big Blue. We experimented with ways to rid the Self of jealousy, material attachments, greed, selfishness, prejudice, hubris. It was rarely verbalized. It was just done. And done with great humor and a sense of the absurd. Traditions became more refined over time. Communication became more finely tuned. Through hints, innuendos, caucusing and cajoling. Through every means except rules. Anything even resembling a rule was forbidden and even to speak about such matters was an admission of not being *here and now*.

That's why almost no one had their own room. There weren't enough rooms to go around. Some people, through *tradition,* managed to garner the same room for a period of time. But if we ever suspected them of thinking of it as *their* room, we knew it was time, and sometimes, *they* knew it was time, to move them around. At least until the time when *everyone* could have *their* own room.

That's why no one had their own clothes. It wasn't fair that Trudy's mom was always buying her new clothes from fine stores, and Ellen had to patronize Saint Vinnie's. It wasn't right that Lizzie had come with a veritable *wardrobe* and Nicky had come with the shirt on his back. So we simply had closets labeled "Coats," "Dresses," "Pants." And drawers labeled "Underwear," "Socks," "Sweaters." Mismatched socks became our trademark. Whenever there was a gathering of the local tribes, people would come up to us, look down at our feet, and say, "Oh, you must be from Hunga Dunga!"

And though I never could get beyond my self-consciousness to do so, it wasn't unusual to see Baird, Bobby, or Lizzie, coming down the stairs in the morning in a house dress. Or Psylvia, Trudy, or Ellen, wearing bib overalls, for that matter. There was only one negative consequence of our taste in fashion that I can think of. It did take away the surprise and fun of cross-dressing on special occasions like Halloween.

Privacy was the rarest of commodities. Most mornings, you could find Ellen sitting on the toilet, while Bobby shaved, Duck brushed his teeth, and Nicky took a shower. Sharing the same space at the same time was a given. Anyone who may have been shy or squeamish about other people's biological functions, soon got over it or left. We were really into biological functions, especially making sure they functioned happily.

We regarded lust as just another biological function. And making it function happily within the walls of Big Blue was something we struggled with, but succeeded.

By *tradition*, we never competed for the affection of someone a family member may have brought home. Well, at least we were never *aggressive* about it. We would never horn in on anyone's current affair. In fact, we encouraged and respected it. But if the fires of a romance dwindled, if and when *love* transmuted to *kinship*, the "guest" was fair game.

I guess that's one of the reasons why some of us were hesitant to bring "guests" home for the night. We knew that unless we made it very clear beforehand the person was "hands off!" he or she could be subjected to torture by fawning. Hunga Dungans excelled at fawning especially if the "guest" were nice and/or sexy. If both, watch out!

Chores were never assigned, but self-inspired. Or guilt-inspired. We had expectations of each other, but we knew the only way to realize the expectations was to model them ourselves. And if there was any competitiveness at Hunga Dunga, it was to be a good example.

We also knew that to insist on having something of your own more than likely meant someone else would have to go without. So we tried to give everybody what *they* wanted knowing that's the only way we could get what *we* wanted.

We only had one bank account. And no matter how much or how little each person contributed, all were entitled to share in the family's resources. Each of us got a small weekly allowance. Through *tradition* and his knack for working with numbers, Richard became the "accountant." We gave him power of attorney for each of us, so he could cash all our checks. He made all the deposits. He paid all the bills and kept all the books. When the bills were paid, anything left over was divided into "funds." The loom fund, the piano fund, the trip to Hawaii fund, the land fund. It would take time, but everyone would get what they wanted. Even though we knew that wanting *nothing* was the key to success.

And we knew that if we could solve *our* problems, then the rest of the world could solve theirs. It was a self-imposed experiment in non-attachment. It was an experiment in which being a willing participant was a self-test of how evolved you were. We were willing participants because we were part of circles of crazy love. Where the circles didn't intersect, conflict sprouted as often as the alfalfa and mung beans in the middle cupboard. Where they did intersect, there was beauty and laughter. And where they were congruent, magic abounded. And that was enough to keep us together. That was enough to make us all willing to give it a try.

CHAPTER 19
Christmas Eve 1970

Traditionally, dinner was the best time of the day to find everyone together. Christmas was no exception. The only "table" that could accommodate sixteen diners (and typically, a few extra guests,) was the floor. Normally we rolled out straw mats and threw down lots of old cushions we had collected. Upon the straw mats we placed the food and utensils. Upon the cushions we placed ourselves. Nothing fancy, everything utilitarian. Tonight, though, the "table" was appropriately festive with boughs of evergreen and holly. At each end of the mats, and in the middle, burned large Christmas candles that Tom's mother had made herself. Alvoye picked out an album of Christmas carols. How they found their way into *our* house, I'll never know. He placed the needle gently on the first cut.

Baird almost threw a fit and refused to sit until something less overtly religious replaced it. Alvoye frowned, but acquiesced and put on something by the Incredible String Band. It wasn't surprising, therefore, to note the look of disdain on Baird's face when Luc requested we say grace before eating.

All hell broke loose. "Whose grace? Whose god?" Baird yelled. Even a prayer that acknowledged the most generic of supreme beings was offensive to him.

"I will not tolerate the beseeching, pandering, or parley-vous-ing to any power outside of *myself* or any of *yourselves*. I'd rather put Duck on a pedestal and worship him!"

"Why, Baird," Duck fluttered. "Had I but known you held me in such high regard, I wouldn't have used your cock ring as a gasket on Zwagen!"

Baird turned red and bit his tongue.

"Oh this is nice talk on Christmas Eve!" Bobby scoffed. "I feel like saying grace! *Grace, grace, grace, grace, grace!* There, it's too late! What are you gonna do about it?"

Baird sat down with a thump. Everyone was on edge. At that moment on Christmas Eve, everyone wanted to be alone.

"I have an idea." The voice was quiet and calm. "Why don't we just have a quiet time, like the Quakers do before they eat." Everyone turned and gasped in surprise. It was Nicky! The quiet deer had spoken. And no one dared put a sarcastic crimp in this one. No one dared do anything that might put Nicky back into his all American, Orange County, wholesome, mountain boy-meets mondo - bewilderment trance.

The stun wore off our faces.

"I can live with that!" Richard said to Baird across the straw mats. "Can *you*?"

"Yes, Richard. I can. Though one can only wonder what you'll all be thinking!"

So for those who were wishing they were alone, this was about as alone as you ever got at Hunga Dunga. Sitting in a circle around a table of straw mats emulating Quaker quiet time before the evening meal. Who knows what each of us was thinking to ourselves. It didn't matter, but I could guess.

Some had their eyes closed. Mine were still open. I caught Tom reaching for Brandon's hand. And then Brandon made a move toward Ellen's. She took it, and with her free hand reached for Richard's. Like a gentle wave, hands reached for hands, and Baird only shrugged in surrender when Luc took Baird's and Baird took mine. I closed my eyes and I guessed everyone was glad they weren't alone.

After at least two minutes of quiet, someone had the courage to disengage themselves. Of course we couldn't see who it was. We just felt it. Like gently falling dominos, we dropped our hands and in unison yelled, "Let's eat!" From then on, no matter how angry any one faction of Hunga Dunga got at another, we always held hands and observed a moment of silence before the evening meal. It was the one ritual we cherished. It was the tureen that held the jambalaya. It was everyone's door prize.

Christmas dinner consisted of two enormous acorn squashes stuffed with all kinds of veggies, bulgur, walnuts and raisins. Gobs of melted Jack cheese kept it together so that when Duck was given the honor of carving the "turkey," the servings draped barely long enough from the spoon to make it to the plates.

For those who needed some old-fashioned holiday cuisine, there were bowls of mashed potatoes, yams, cranberry sauce, and green beans. And pumpkin pies for dessert! The Friends of Perfection had given us *seven* bottles of their homemade loganberry wine from their farm in Grants Pass. It was yummy. *And* it had a nice kick to it!

While we were still having seconds of the pies and thirds of the wine, Richard got up and went into the kitchen. We could hear the sink filling with water. Then he came back and stood in the doorway.

"I'll do the pots and pans but if each of you would wash your own plate and silverware, that'd be great. The sink's all ready with hot, soapy water."

We all picked up our dishes and filed past Richard into the kitchen. We each gave him a peck on the cheek as we did.

Later that evening, practically all of us were hanging out in the living room, drinking loganberry wine and smoking some great hash Flo Airwaves had laid on us as a Winter Solstice present. Tom strummed on his Martin and serenaded us with Dylan, Roy Orbison, and Bob Wills tunes. Richard could put on a harmony that would give you shivers. And I wasn't half-bad either. Lots of times, when Richard and I were alone, usually in Zwagen doing errands, we'd sing simple folk tunes in harmonic acapella that usually had references to things Baird would hate. Like "Do Lord," and "May the Circle Be Unbroken," and "This Train." It would really get us high.

Everyone was draped around everyone else. On the couch. On pillows on the floor. In the overstuffed chair that could comfortably accommodate three or four people who didn't mind sitting with their appendages wrapped around each other's. No one minded that. When I looked around the room, it reminded me of stories I'd heard about the Tasaday, the lost tribe in the Philippines.

Tom was in the middle of "Louise" when we saw the lower half of a dark figure descending the stairs. Black, patent-leather, stiletto-heeled shoes came first, followed by black silk stockings and the hem of a black cocktail dress. The kind that's ridiculously tight around the knees.

The descent was nonetheless very graceful, like a runway model's. As for the gracefulness, it could have been Alvoye, but the legs weren't thin enough. A few steps more and we could see the hips and waist, a black, evening-gloved arm flanking each side. The tummy was too chubby for it to be Bobby, unless he had padded his washboard stomach. Another step brought the breasts into view. They couldn't be Ellen's. Hers were perfect apples. These were larger, gently sloping, sumptuous eggplants. It must be Psylvia!

Her face entered the light of the lamp in the foyer at the bottom of the stairs. She was heavily made-up.

"Psylvia!" Lizzie said in surprise. "We need money, but really, you don't have to hit the streets for it!"

Lizzie meant it as a joke, but the briefest of hurt expressions came across her face.

"Psylvia, where are you going?" Richard asked with true concern.

"I'm going to Midnight Mass," she answered with an unspoken dare for anyone to give her any flack about it.

"I don't believe it!" Baird said. "You're not even Catholic. You're Jewish!"

"So?" Psylvia wanted to know. "I like the incense and the pageantry. I made my confession while I was in the shower, and now I'm going to give Jesus his Christmas present."

"What's that? A roll in the manger?" Lizzie quipped.

Tom said, "Isn't that a Christmas Carol? 'A Roll In The Manger?'" And Richard and I joined Tom in the first verse as Psylvia smiled and walked out the front door. But before she did, she looked at me and winked. If she were confirming a secret we shared, I didn't get it. Even a few days later, after one of the Sisters of Perpetual Indulgence talked with me, I didn't get it. She had also attended the midnight mass, habit, roller skates and all, and told me what she saw:

At Saint Anthony's, Psylvia waited in line on the far right aisle along with everyone else. She closed her eyes and breathed deeply through her nose, inhaling the frankincense and myrrh. The young altar boy was freshly scrubbed and frocked. He stared at Psylvia as he rhythmically swung his heavy, gilded urn forth and back in a wide arc. Psylvia's black patent leather purse swung forth and back in time with his.

As she knelt down at the railing in front of the altar, she most likely couldn't help but feel the disapproving glances from the two women on either side of her. The priest was three mouths away. He was probably in his 40s, but he had a robust, boyish look about him. Maybe from too much of Jesus' blood that day. When he reached the woman on her right, Psylvia readied her tongue, stretching it out as far as she could as if she were struggling to get as deep as possible into the throat of her lover.

It was her turn next. The priest stood in front of her. Psylvia's shoulders and breasts seemed to melt at the sounds of his soft Latin words. She looked as if she were imagining him naked, whispering sweet nothings in her ear. When she felt the communion wafer on her tongue, she slowly closed one of her eyes and kept it closed.

The priest drew back in surprise, then leaned in to get a better look. He studied her eyelid with longing. After waiting as long as she could, the woman on Psylvia's left glared at the priest and made strange sounds in her throat. The altar boy tugged at the priest's large, embroidered scapula, trying to snap him out of his spell.

CHAPTER 20
December 1970

I was nervous when I got up that morning. A 10 o'clock appointment with the shrink in an office up on Polk. Should I wash my face and brush my teeth, or should I b.o. him to distraction?

What should I wear? I was in a quandary. What I considered neat, others certainly didn't. Who cared? But if I did get dressed up, I'd be doing it to *please* him. Did that mean I wanted something from him? I was confused. What did I want? Did I want his sympathy? Did I want his disdain? Did I want his approval?

No! I just wanted to go as myself. I didn't want *anything* from him. I just wanted to meet him man to man. So what if he realized I was probably more together than he was. If everything happened for a reason, then this was no exception. Obviously he was supposed to learn something from me and I from him. And when they cut me off General Assistance, as I fully expected would happen, I'd get by.

I took a long shower and scrubbed my teeth. I dressed the way I always did. Grabbing a pair of jeans out of the "Jeans" drawer, a tie-dyed undershirt from the "Underwear" drawer, a Mexican peasant pullover from the "International Bucolic Boutique" box, sitting on the shelf in the "Exotica" clothes cupboard, and one blue and one green sock from the "Sock" drawer.

Everyone had secretly taken to hiding their favorite pair of shoes and discovering them each morning with great surprise. "Oh, look what I found under the bathroom sink! A pair of sneakers that fit *me* perfectly!"

It got to the point where we all knew where everyone else's hiding places were, but we never let on. Once Baird caught Richard putting a pair of shoes into a small closet next to the garden tools. Baird went to retrieve what Richard had hidden. Richard blocked the closet with his small body.

"Baird. The name of this closet is 'A Can of Worms.' I beg you. Don't open it!" Baird thought about it, and thought about the chances anyone else would take the size 12 shoes he hid in *his* special place each night. Baird looked at Richard and retreated.

The "Can of Worms" closet came in handy on a number of occasions and was the safest place to put anything you really didn't want to share. Like that special pair of earrings or a piece of hash you'd been saving or even money. The closet was filled with tins and boxes and envelopes of all kinds. No one knew whose they were or what they contained. But no one dared to snoop. Not if anyone wanted to keep their shoes!

I passed by the room where Baird had recently been sleeping. He was sitting on the bed.
"Off to your ATD interview?" inquired Baird.
"Yes," I said without stopping.
"I'm very proud of you, Giacco," Baird called after me.
I stopped at the top of the stairs and turned around.

"Proud of what?"

"This act of revolution!" Baird said, stating what he thought was the obvious. "It sets a good example for the rest of the family."

"Baird," I said with determination in my voice, "I am not physically disabled. I am not mentally disabled. I intend to be as true to myself as I can and to represent myself as honestly as I can: a reasonably mature, intelligent, well-meaning, human being. So don't get your hopes up!"

"Would you step into my study for a moment? Please?" He gestured to the alcove under the bed that was built on a platform halfway up to the twelve-foot coved ceiling. I knew Baird was receiving some kind of government assistance from the Army. The Vietnamese version of shell-shock or something. I figured it must be invisible or unnoticeable, whatever it was, because he didn't look or act disabled to me.

I pulled out the Donald Duck pocket watch that I found in a pocket of the jeans and checked the time. I reluctantly shrugged and walked in. Baird followed. He reached around me to a stack of hardbound "Square Deal" Composition notebooks, and pulled one out. In the pre-printed label on the front, next to "property of," was written *James B. Hiller*. Next to "Subject" was written *Da Nang, 1966*. A thin, blue, bookmark stuck out from somewhere in the middle.

Baird handed me the notebook. "Just something for you to consider."

I walked to the window and sat down in front of an easel that supported a painting Baird was working on. It was thematically Greek with a background of receding hills. In the boulder-strewn foreground were young, beautiful men, women, and children, dressed in togas that revealed perfect physiques. Although all the torsos were facing the hills, their faces looked back over their shoulders, directly into the eyes of the viewer. Some of their faces looked familiar.

At the point of infinity, deep in the hills, you could barely make out a golden thread. The thread got as thick as a rope by the time it passed through each character's hands and reached the foreground. It continued toward the lower right hand corner of the painting. As it approached the edge, it got thicker until the rope's end became exposed. If you got right up to it, you could see the intricate detail of the weave. It was made of intersecting mandalas, each complex, no two alike. The effect was impressive. The golden rope left the canvas just life-size enough for you to grab on to. Where it went after that is anybody's guess.

I positioned myself so the light coming through the window fell on the notebook. I opened it to the marker. On the left-hand page were rough sketches of Vietnamese peasants working in the fields and close-ups of faces and details of almond-shaped eyes. On the right-hand page was this:

July 4, 1966

The existence of leisure time, whether due to technology, the division of labor, or the creation of surplus, allows men and women to put aside the mundane chores required for a subsistence survival. It gives them the time to make music, art, and dance. It gives them the time to create a culture. It gives them the time to think. And to think about thinking. And to think about not *thinking. And then to not think. To just be. And be happy.*

This is the true role of government. To create leisure time. But now I must go to work for my government. Now I must go and destroy neolithic plows. Now I must go and fracture arms of farmers. Now I must go and napalm granaries. Now I must go and kill leisure time. Now I must go and eradicate a culture.

I closed the notebook, stood up, walked over to Baird and gave him a hug. "I'm so sorry," I said. "I'm sorry you had to do all that for your government. But I gotta go now, Baird."

I hurried down the stairs and out the front door.

―――

The doctor's office was nothing like I had imagined. It was a small, two-room office on the second floor above a chiropractor's. On the outer door, a sign said, "Eaton P. Hull, Doctor of Psychiatry." Inside I was greeted by a room whose walls were paneled in fake pine. There was a closed door at the opposite end of the room. Five chairs lined one wall. They were made out of plastic tubing.

On a chintzy and chipped white enamel coffee table was a free-standing sign surrounded by brochures and magazines. The sign said, "Please Be Seated." So I sat on the edge of the table.

I picked up a six-month-old copy of Newsweek and was leafing through it, when I heard muffled voices behind the inner door. They got louder just before it opened.

A man in his late 30s was shooing another man in his late 20s out. The older guy had thinning sandy hair. It was cut very short and his forehead curved forever above his granny glasses. His pants were creased and the sleeves of his white shirt were rolled up to mid-forearm. He was the Shooer.

The Shooee had long, curly blond hair that bounced freely with every movement. He wore patched jeans and a wrinkled yellow short-sleeve shirt. There was a large wet area around his crotch. It was getting larger as the faded jeans turned a darker blue with each wick of the fabric. I thought it was safe to assume the Shooer was the shrink and the Shooee was the patient.

"And don't come back here until you talk to your social worker and get a note from a *doctor* saying you are *clinically* incontinent! *Clinically* incontinent!"

"But, Doc!" explained the guy trying to get through to him. "I don't come from another continent. I'm not a foreigner! I live here! I'm in-state! Right here in The City!"

"Then I suggest you go see someone at the Department of Immigration," he said opening the outer door for him.

"Awww, man!" The freak moaned. "Is it in the same building as this one?"

The doc closed the door in his face, and I heard the freak shuffling down the hall, grumbling.

"The little pisser! I wonder what antic he'll come up with next!" he said, not too much under his breath. In fact, I think he said it for *my* benefit.

He looked up, approached me, mechanically introduced himself, grabbed a file out of a holder that was fastened to the wall next to the door, and escorted me into the inner office. Without being invited, I took the chair in front of his desk. He sat behind it. The desk, that is.

He checked his watch and then started going through the file in front of him. After about three minutes he looked up.

"So what seems to be the problem?"

"What problem?" I asked seriously.

"Well, isn't there something bothering you?"

"What's a bother?" I asked.

The doctor stood up and leaned forward on the desk. "Now look here! Don't get smart with me! They sent you over here for a reason and I want to know what it is!"

"I really don't know what problem you're talking about. I'm fine, really. The planet needs some help and the country isn't doing too well either, but *I'm* doing just fine. I needed some help when I first got into town. But I'm fine now. Really. And thank you. Everyone's been very kind." And I began to stand up to leave.

"Sit down, sit down. I haven't finished my evaluation," Doctor Hull said so calmingly, soothingly. "Ms. Stein has collected some very interesting information on you. I'd like to discuss it. Please."

I sat back down, crossed my legs, and molded my back into the contour of the chair. I was feeling relaxed now that *I* had taken the initiative to disqualify myself. He sat down and bent over my file.

"It says here that you are a graduate of Georgetown University. School of Foreign Service."

I nodded.

"And you worked briefly in New York. A promising job with a major corporation."

I nodded.

"And you left it?"

"Yes," I answered.

"Why?" he asked.

"I began experimenting with other layers of being, other layers of consciousness."

"How?" he asked.

"LSD, mescaline, psilocybin. Mainly LSD," I answered candidly.

"How many trips have you taken?" he asked.

I thought a while. "Oh, I would guess in the hundreds. Maybe two or three."

He just stared at me. Then he went back to the file.

"There's something here from the DMV. Your license is suspended?" He held it up to me. "Ever own a car?"

"Hmmm. Yeah. A few."

"Tell me about them," he asked. I couldn't tell where he was going with this.

"I had an old VW Beetle for a while back in New York."

"What happened to it?"

"The engine seized up on the Long Island Expressway. It was out of oil. I thought you didn't have to put any oil in those things. When I learned it was *water* VW's didn't use, boy, did I feel stupid!"

He didn't laugh. I wasn't trying to make him. "And what became of the VW?"

"I left it there on the side of the road." I tried to make that sound not so unusual. I didn't care to add that I was stoned out of my gourd at the time, but what I did tell him was the truth.

"Cars and me don't get along. I figure if one dies on me, let it rest in peace right where it is."

The doctor slouched a little and thumbed deeper into the file. "You are listed as the former proprietor of a house in Topanga Canyon. Is that true?"

I sat upright. "Former?" I inquired.

"Yes, according to this, the bank foreclosed on it last month. Didn't you know?"

I took a deep sigh and shyly said "no." He glared at me gently like Dean might have. I felt like the son who forgot to take out the garbage.

"How does that make you feel? Losing your house?" he asked.

"Well, I can think of one person who will be very disappointed in me, but what's done is done." I paused a moment, and saw Dean saying goodbye in front of the Country Store. I started thinking I was *apologizing* to *Dean*. *Explaining* to *Dean*.

"I mean, nothing any different happened along the way that would've made it turn out any differently. All I can do is trip out on all the stones in the creek that shaped the canyon."

The doctor prodded me with his eyes to continue.

"One minute you're here, the next you're not." I said. "One minute you have a house, the next you don't. I'm not happy about it. I guess I'll have to take a trip down there and see about stuff. I guess it was just supposed to happen. Like maybe I'm not supposed to be attached to it or something. A karmic lesson."

"That's it? That's all? A karmic lesson? You ruminate over it for thirty seconds and that's it? Isn't there anything you really, really want?" he asked with some interest in his voice. At least that's what I hoped I detected. "Something that if you didn't get it, you'd be unhappy, or if you had it and *lost it*, you'd be distraught?"

"I'm not sure which one of my Selves should answer that," I said, choosing my words carefully, trying to be fastidiously truthful. "There's so many different Giaccos."

"And what does that mean?" Doctor Hull probed.

"I mean, you know. There's the Giacco that smokes cigarettes. There's the Giacco that fasts. There's the Giacco that wants to be perfect. There's the Giacco that knows he isn't. We're all a mass of contradictions. But we do our best. At least *I* try to."

I looked at the doctor to see if he was still with me or not. His face was a little screwed up, but he seemed to nod in agreement.

"So when you ask me a question, I'm answering it from the Self that *knows* the truth, but not necessarily from the Self that's *living* the truth. There is a difference, you know! By the way... what was the question?"

Doctor Hull rolled his eyes. Then he rolled his shirt sleeves further up. Way past the elbows. He leaned back in his chair and played with a pencil. "I asked you what you *really* wanted," he said quietly and seriously.

"Well," I answered just as quietly and seriously, "I guess I want to be self-realized." I thought about it. "God-realized would be better, would be the *best*, but, gee, you're not even supposed to want self-realization, let alone god-realization, or anything else for that matter! God, who the hell do I think I *am*?"

Doc just moved the pencil forth and back in front of his face. It looked like a windshield wiper for his granny glasses. I wondered if he were trying to hypnotize me.

Maybe I was already under hypnosis!

I felt compelled to come down to earth a little and try to put it in everyday terms for the Doc.

"It's this way, Doc. I just figure that as long as you have to be doing something while you're walking around on the planet, you might as well be doing stuff that might make you Self-realized. That is, if that's what's supposed to happen to you. And if that's *not* what's supposed to happen to you then whatever *does* happen to you is what was *supposed* to happen to you all along. And if what happened to you made you happy, then it's better. If what happened to you made you sad, it's *still* better! You just didn't know it. I guess!"

Doctor Hull rose from his chair and walked around the desk to mine. He held out his hand as he said, "Well, Giacco. I see our time is up."

I shook his hand as I stood up. "Is that it? Aren't you going to tell me what *you* think makes the perfect life?"

"I really don't have the time to discuss that now, Giacco."

"But I was really looking forward to talking with you," I said truly disappointed. "It's not every day I get to talk to a psychiatrist and I really wanted to make the most of it. Shit! I always do this! Whenever I meet someone, they always end up learning more about me than I do about them. Not fair!"

And I made a promise to myself right then and there to become the deep, silent type.

"You'll be notified of my findings by Ms. Stein. But if I were you, you might want to check on that *house* in Topanga Canyon." He said the word "house" as if it were a figment of my imagination. Then he placed the palm of his hand on my back and put the slightest pressure on it as he accompanied me to the office door. He opened it and as if in a weightless environment, the pressure of his hand on my back provided enough momentum to prove one of the laws of inertia: A body in motion tends to stay in motion. It got me through the waiting room and all the way out the front door, whether I wanted to go or not. I thought this was a somewhat terse ending to what was just beginning to be a rather mature, articulate, and enjoyable discussion.

A frumpish-looking woman sat on the chair closest to the outer door. She had a fly swatter and kept batting at imaginary fairies she had named. As I closed the door behind me I heard Doctor Hull saying, with an edge in his voice, "Judith, that's not going to work with me! So cut it out!"

CHAPTER 21
February 1971

After checking in with Hunga Dunga, I took the doc's advice and headed south. The few days I spent in southern California reminded me why I didn't belong there. On my way down, as soon as I hit the Ventura County line, I encountered a rare rain storm. The pigs in their patrol cars interfered with my hitchhiking and caused me to become drenched when I might have been dry and warm in any number of cars. I was happy to head east into Topanga Canyon, looking forward to meeting up with old friends.

Before I headed up Observation Drive to my house, or should I say my *former* house, I stopped off at the Moonfire Inn. I didn't recognize anyone. Restaurants in general experience a turnover in employees rather quickly. But when the employees are hippies, the turnover is as fast as a sous-chef dicing celery. Only one of the workers remembered Kathy. He thought she was living somewhere in the valley with a Hell's Angels beer-guzzling, meat-eating biker. Oh, what we do for love! I decided not to try to find her.

I walked all the way up Observation Drive, torrents of muddy rain water cascading over the toes of my shoes. I had never experienced such a downpour in all the time I lived in Topanga. When I reached the very top of Observation Drive, I turned to admire the view I used to have from the living room windows. There was no view to admire. Visibility was practically zero and the house seemed suspended and isolated by the heavily rain-laden clouds dumping their burden on an all too absorbent earth. Dark rivulets swept around the foundation of the house and met halfway down the flagstone walk leading to the front door. From there a small stream of diluted mud ran the rest of the way to the street, diagonally across the road, and down the hillside.

From the outside, the house looked much as it had when Jon and I left it, except for the For Sale sign. I wasn't surprised to find the front door unlocked. It was never locked when I lived there. I don't even recall ever having keys to the place. When I walked inside I found more reason for it to be unlocked. There was nothing to protect. It was completely bare. Everything was gone. The stereo. The books. Hundreds of albums. A chest that contained all my mementos from the past. Trinkets and photos and poems that used to remind me how embarrassingly sentimental I was.

For a moment I felt betrayed by Barb and Henry, the people who were supposed to look after the house for me. For a moment, I felt disappointed in myself. Had I been less spontaneous and more practical, I'd have been able to surprise Hunga Dunga by selling the house and contributing substantially to the land fund. On the other hand, had I been less spontaneous and more practical, I might not have had a Hunga Dunga to surprise. For a moment, I wondered if it had been worth all the adventures.

I immediately got over it. What I'd told Dr. Hull had been the truth. I'd lost a house, but I'd gained a karmic lesson. And no way would I grieve over it. I wanted to think of myself as a person of integrity. Now the test would be not to make the same mistake in the future. If I did, then I didn't learn my lesson. Unless, of course, if it wasn't a mistake to begin with, if I could do it all over again, I doubt I'd have done anything differently. In many ways, what'd happened since leaving Topanga was worth a house. Except right now, it would've come in handy.

I'm quite sure I wasn't just rationalizing, though the joint I was smoking as I toured the house may have helped substantiate my priorities, material possessions being far down the list. After all, *I* wasn't living my life. *It* was living *Its* life through me. All I was responsible for was to watch *It* happen. And marvel at *It*.

It was easy to marvel at, especially when I picked up a manila envelope that was lying on an empty shelf in the empty bookcase and I saw my name scrawled on the outside. Inside were an assortment of bills and notices. Many were from my mortgage bank and utility companies. They changed in color depending on how urgent or threatening the bill was supposed to be. I thought about the person who got to pick out the colors and assign them varying degrees of imminent doom. I felt sorry for some of the colors, feeling they had been unjustly maligned. And I promised them I wouldn't let that be a factor when choosing a color to paint my room, if and when *It* decided I should ever get a room.

There were also 108 postcards. All from Jon and Rosie. Practically one card for every day we had been apart. Before reading them, I put them in the chronological order of their postmarks. They traced practically every burg, village, and roadside attraction Jon and Rosie had traveled through on their way across Canada and back into the states. The last one was from some town in Maine. It was postmarked November 7th, just a few days before I sent Rosie's mom my new address at Hunga Dunga. I wondered why I hadn't gotten any mail from them there. I wondered where they went after Maine.

Only a few of the postcards told any story. Jon's dad and a lawyer met with Rob, Christy and little Robbie at some resort on Lac Megantic in southeastern Quebec. I could only imagine the counsel the lawyer gave Jon's brother, because in the next postcard, Jon and Rosie were traveling alone. Rob, Christy and Robbie were going to northern British Columbia to buy land.

I studied the pictures on the front of each card. I could tell they were picked out with great care for either their beauty or their tackiness. I lingered on the funny and loving messages on their backs. Some of them just one-liners, but I could hear Jon and Rosie speaking them and see them making faces at me and each other. I laughed out loud. It tickled me to know them.

The last item I found in the manila envelope was a letter from Saul Weinstein. It was hurriedly written, but neatly folded and sealed in a plain white envelope with my name on it.

Giacco!

Where are you? Get in touch! Urgent you save next July!
Don't get too high! (without me!)
Your bro, Saul
P.S. New Address: 1261 Wilshire, Suite 750.
525-6700.

There was no date on it and no stamp on the envelope. Saul must've come up here looking for me and just left it. I thanked Barb and Henry for saving my mail for me. How considerate, since I assumed they had ripped me off for everything else or at a minimum, allowed it to happen.

I left the house and walked toe to heel down the walk to the street. Not to emulate some lord, but to keep my heels out of the growing puddles. The whole hilltop seemed spongy. Just the weight of my body on the flagstones caused the ground around them to squirt. A car pulled up. On the driver's door it read, "Canyon Realty." A middle-aged woman carrying a briefcase got out, opened an umbrella and ran around to the passenger door. A younger woman, neatly dressed under a clear plastic slicker, straddled a puddle and huddled next to her escort. They tried to hopscotch simultaneously up the walk so as to avoid the puddles and rivulets without abandoning the shelter of the umbrella.

As they got into earshot, I heard the younger woman say, "This is a hell of a day to go house hunting!"

The realtor tilted the umbrella toward her client, giving her a generous portion of the bumbershoot's protection. "This won't take long because I'm sure you'll immediately see this home's potential. It's a beautiful fixer-upper, previously owned by a very conservative gentleman. And the view is simply spectacular!"

I started down the road, hoping to hitch a ride. There was no traffic at all. I expected the realtor and her prospective buyer to pass me at any moment, but I knew it was unlikely they would stop for me. A half-hour later and I was back on Topanga Canyon Boulevard without the realtor ever having gone by. I guessed the woman must've liked the house to be spending so much time inspecting it.

I walked up to the Country Store and bought a cup of coffee. I borrowed a pen from the longhair behind the counter. Next to Saul's note I wrote "He Lives! Giacco can be found at..." and gave him my address and phone number at Hunga Dunga. I put the note back in the envelope wishing I'd been more careful when I first opened it up. I crossed out my name and replaced it with Saul's and his address. The clerk, though I figured he was wasted, was actually right on top of it. When I looked up, he was handing me some scotch tape and a stamp. I taped the envelope shut, pasted the stamp on with my fist, paid the clerk and flashed him a peace sign. I dropped the note in the mailbox outside the door.

The rain was becoming bothersome. The drops were dense and hard and bit the skin like horseflies. It bothered me that it bothered me. This was a definite sign I was not yet enlightened.

Part of me wanted to visit Saul. I could be there before he ever got the letter. Part of me wanted to look up Suzanne or maybe even Josie. I hadn't had sex with anyone in a while and they were two of my favorite women. So what if they were already "involved." I didn't object to three-ways with the right people. Part of me wanted to see if I could find Peter, my old Woodstock compadre. Now wouldn't that be nice! But that might take some research. Part of me just wanted to get out of the rain. I stood on the side of the road and stuck a thumb out in each direction. I'd let somebody else make the decision for me.

The car that stopped was going to Pacific Ocean Highway and then north. Suzanne, Saul, Josie and Peter would have to wait.

As soon as I hit Monterey, I felt better, despite the incessant rain. Santa Cruz was a delight and encouraged me to believe that the collective consciousness was expanding on schedule. When I reached the San Francisco city limits, my pulse actually quickened with the warm rush a traveler gets when he's almost home, even though I wouldn't have the best of news to share with Hunga Dunga.

I didn't get into San Francisco until mid-morning the next day. The rain had abated into a steady drizzle. I gave up trying to hitch through The City, and caught a bus going to Upper Market. I had been up all night and was as damp and miserable as I could be. And I could make myself pretty miserable. That's probably why it didn't click when I read the headline of the paper the man across from me was reading: "Mudslide in Topanga Kills Two. Homes and Land Washed Away."

As I climbed the front stairs to Big Blue, all I could think of was Home Sweet Hunga Dunga. I knew that as soon as Psylvia and Richard saw what a wet puppy I was, they'd fawn all over me. Psylvia would insist on making me some soup, and Richard would insist on undressing me and putting me into some nice dry, warm clothes. What more did I need to lift my spirits?

I saw the mailbox was full and there was a package on the doormat. I retrieved the mail and bent down to pick up the package. It was about a foot and a half square and three inches thick. It was addressed simply to "Hunga Dunga." It felt heavy and I guessed Ellen's mom had sent us a big box of candy, which she did now and then for no good reason, other than to let us know that she loved us. It was very mutual. Maybe it was Brandon's mom. She sent us care packages of cheeses and salamis on a regular basis, not because she loved us, but because she was convinced we couldn't take care of ourselves and that we were all starving.

Both guesses were wrong. A return address on the back said "Lama Foundation, San Cristobal, NM." I shrugged. I was too tired to be more curious. But I came to life when I looked up from the package and noticed a little trinket hanging from the door knocker. It was a tiny, neon-orange, bowling ball bag.

CHAPTER 22

Valentine's Day 1971

As soon as I entered the room, a bunch of voices in unison yelled out, "Giacco!" Two of them came from Jon and Rosie, sitting on the couch, half hidden by the various appendages of Richard, Duck, Psylvia, and Chuck. Jon and Rosie attempted to disentangle themselves from the human knot, squealing half-hearted threats to the rest. Jon and Rosie ran to me, Jon dragging Richard behind him, Richard refusing to let go of Jon's leg.

Rosie gave me big kisses all over my face. "Happy Valentine's Day," she blew in my ear. Jon hugged me hard. I felt like somebody slipped a body-muff around me. Richard reached up and grabbed my belt using it to hoist himself upright. He practically pulled my pants down.

"Why didn't you tell us about these tomatoes?" Richard admonished.

Jon pushed me away and held me at arm's length. He looked at me with intensely loving eyes and for a moment I thought I was in one of those schmaltzy romantic movies where the lovers on the dance floor are suddenly bathed in a warm spotlight, while the others dance around them in the shadows and the music swells and the rest of the world disappears. A second tug at my belt caused the house lights to ramp up full and forced me to acknowledge Richard humping my leg like a neglected puppy.

"How come we never heard of these angels?" Richard demanded. "Were you keeping them for yourself?"

"Richard," I answered, handing Chuck the package under my arm so I could push Richard off me. "I wasn't trying to keep anything from you. You, of all people, should know how impossible it is to describe really *prize* tomatoes like these! You have to experience them. You have to taste them, touch them, smell them! Words just aren't enough!" I looked up at Rosie. She blushed and laughed. Jon looked around sucking up all the satisfaction in the room and said quietly under his breath, "Better!"

Richard sidled up to Jon and gently rubbed his tummy. "As a connoisseur of vegetables, I understand perfectly. Please, everyone, please excuse my momentary lapse into a supermarket mentality. I should have known I was in the presence of a rare variety."

"You're excused," I said.

"No, *you're* excused," Richard said.

"I'm accused?" Psylvia said. "Of what?"

"You're accused of not excusing Richard," Duck explained.

"Well, excuse you then!" Psylvia threw at Richard.

"No! Excuse me!" said Chuck shoving the opened package across the floor into the middle of us. We all stared down at it. It looked like a large hand-bound book. Brown hemp strings stuck out from the spine. On the cover was a mandala with the title encircling it. Depending on where you were standing, it read either "Be Here Now," "Here Now Be," or "Now Be Here." Beneath it were some smaller books and what looked like a record album.

Jon knelt reverently over it and lifted it carefully out of the box. He opened the book to the table of contents and read aloud. "Journey. The Transformation. Dr. Richard Alpert, Ph.D. into Baba Ram Dass." Jon looked up at the faces staring down at him. "Oh, wow! Do you know what this is? I should have known you people were chosen ones. And on Valentine's Day, no less. *Much* better!"

"What are you talking about?" Duck asked.

Jon didn't reply. He simply sat on the pillow next to the floor lamp in the corner of the room and started to read.

"Do you know what he's talking about?" Duck asked me.

"Jon?" I spoke like trying to wake someone up without startling them. "Jon?"

Jon looked up and gently smiled. "Later, Giacco. Later." Typical. I don't see the guy for months and when I do and have a thousand things I want to find out, he sloughs me off for a paperback book, as if we were never apart and had all the time in the world ahead of us.

The rest of us looked at one another with question marks on our faces. All except Rosie. She seemed to know what was going on. Out of deference to what was possibly a "sacred" moment for Jon, she drew the attention away from him.

"Hey, everybody! Speaking of being the 'chosen' ones, I think I've been *chosen* to show you how to make tofu taste like barbecued chicken. If you'll all just follow me." And all of us followed Rosie into the kitchen leaving Jon bathed in a warm spot of light while the rest of the world faded away.

In the kitchen, Rosie started gathering ingredients. She seemed instinctively to know where everything was. But no one was surprised. Jon and Rosie had only been there three days but were treated as kin by everyone who'd spent any time with them. Ironically they arrived moments after I had left for Topanga.

At first, Jon was stumped by the "bad" timing. It wasn't like us to miss each other by mere minutes. Our relationship was too synchronistic. Cosmic crossings of paths had become the norm. This time there had been a misconnection. But Rosie reminded Jon there must be a reason. Obviously it was so that Hunga Dunga could meet them without me around to skew their impressions. For even if I had never existed, Jon and Rosie would have been completely embraced by Hunga Dunga and Hunga Dunga by Jon and Rosie. All on their own. Which is the way all of us would have wanted it.

Rosie explained that in Maine they had fallen in love with a little farm in North Leeds. Jon borrowed money from his grandmother and bought it for $7000 cash. It took less than an hour for them to move their possessions from the van into the 150 year-old house. Until spring, there was really nothing to do except stay warm and dream.

The dream was they would lead a pure and monastic life. They would try to *live* all the spiritual principles they had learned. They would gain insight from hardship and austerity. The only stimuli they needed would be generated from within. They would create their own little ashram and when *I* would inevitably show up, I would live with them on their little farm and we would all become holy and enlightened.

"Then we got your postcard!" Rosie grimaced at me. "At first we were jealous. It pained us to think that other people had taken our place in your heart. We started thinking that if you were so taken by Hunga Dunga, you must be having a really great time. And when the snow reached the middle of the bedroom window, Jon and I started getting antsy, thinking we were missing out on something. And our little dream started becoming a nightmare until one day we both looked at each other and yelled, 'What the hell are we doing here! Let's go see Giacco! Then when spring comes, we'll abduct him and bring him back to Maine!'"

Rosie was doing this weird thing bathing slices of tofu in a concoction of condiments and tamari. Only Psylvia seemed to know what was going on. She fiddled with the pilot light on the oven and then retrieved some broccoli from the refrigerator. Richard, Psylvia, and Duck showed more than a little apprehension when Rosie mentioned stealing me away to Maine. But they relaxed when she continued.

"Now that we're actually *here*, we understand why Giacco is," Rosie said, tapping me on the chest with the handle of the spatula. "I understood immediately. Especially when Jon told me all about Psylvia and…"

Psylvia shot Rosie a no-no look.

"Oh, I forgot!" Rosie said, looking guilty. "But really now, wouldn't you know?"

I didn't get it. "Wouldn't I know what?" I asked her.

"Never mind. You'll figure it out someday. Unless you've totally fried your brain!" Rosie winked at Psylvia and laughed conspiratorially.

Then she turned back to her marinade. "I guess the only way this is going to work, is for Jon and me to abduct *all* of you," she said sweeping up everyone, slowly and lovingly, into her eyes.

"I'm for that!" Chuck yelled.

"Me, too!" Richard added.

"Or vice-versa." offered Duck. "Now get to the part where you explain what Jon's doing in the living room."

"So we're driving through Arizona. And both Jon and I really like Tucson so we always stop off there for a few days. There's this really neat hole-in-the-wall vegetarian restaurant. It's called 'Buddha Burgers'. Their slogan is 'Let Us Make You One With Everything'. It's really far-out. Anyway Jon gets to talking to one of the cooks and it turns out that Tucson and Santa Fe are all abuzz with this rumor that's going around that Richard Alpert..."

"Stop right there," Duck put up his hand like a traffic cop. "The name sounds familiar, but remind me."

"Shall I *elucidate*," Chuck snooted, making out like he was Baird. "Richard Alpert is Timothy Leary's colleague at Harvard. Remember when they got in trouble for turning their students on to LSD?"

"*Was* Leary's colleague," corrected Rosie. Now they've gone their separate ways. Different paths. Leary went with the chemical, Alpert went with the mystical. He figured LSD got you so high and no higher. He disappeared for a while. Then he showed up in

India, found a teacher, saw the light and became a sadhu. Now he's Ram Dass."

Rosie gestured with her head toward the living room and then back to us. "And that must be what this package is all about. Before Alpert dropped out of sight, he promised that if he found the road to Enlightenment, he'd bring us all along. But no one knew how he would spread the word if he did. This is it! The Package!"

"Yeah, but how did *we* get on the mailing list?" Richard wanted to know. "Anyone here know anything about it?"

Everyone shook their heads.

"That's why Jon said you were *chosen*. You were chosen to be on the mailing list. Why or how doesn't matter. You got The Package. And on Valentine's Day! What could be more perfect?"

Rosie leaned in to us and whispered, "And I know, because I know him so well, that Jon feels really honored to have been here when it arrived. He feels *so* honored he has to give it his full attention *right now*! The rest of us can wait! But The Package can't! It would be blasphemous!" Rosie handed a cookie sheet of patties to Psylvia who slid them in the oven.

"What package?" a voice asked from the doorway.

We all looked up. It was Ellen. By the time we filled her in on Buddha Burgers, The Package and everything else, dinner was almost ready. On top of the stove, staying warm, were two cookie sheets of tofu patties that looked and smelled just like barbecued chicken breasts. A third sheet sizzled in the oven. Next to them on a burner, a kettle of water was just about to boil, just about ready for the corn on the cob.

On the table, an enormous bowl of steamed, heavily seasoned, and heavily buttered broccoli sent oregano and thyme vapors into the air. Richard poured Hunga Dunga Vinaigrette over a fresh garden salad and I could feel my saliva glands activate at the smell of the dominant vinegar. The kitchen smelled exactly like a Fourth of July picnic and we were surprised when we realized how effortlessly it had been prepared.

The smells brought Tom and Brandon out of the cabin in the back yard where they had been fucking all afternoon. The smells brought Luc, Alvoye, and a "friend" from the back bedroom where they had been piercing each other's bodies and getting stoned to bear the pain. The smells brought Bobby and Trudy from the front upstairs bedroom where they had been sorting through a box of clothes they exchanged with Flo Airwaves. The smells brought Nicky, Greg, Lizzie, and a longhaired carpenter complete with tool belt, from the attic where they had been discussing the possibility of bartering the creation of a couple of rooms. The smells brought Baird thundering down the stairs ranting and raving.

"Who has brought meat into this house? I smell meat and I want it out of here, now!"

As he entered the kitchen, his face was all screwed up in righteous indignation but upon seeing the handsome carpenter, it softened some. Nevertheless, he pursued his attack with vigor, took three big steps which brought him all the way across the kitchen floor to the stove, and picked up a barbecued "chicken" breast.

"It's tofu, Baird," said Duck.

"It looks like chicken to me," Baird said suspiciously. He took a miniscule bite off the end but didn't swallow. He just rolled it around in his mouth as if he were tasting wine.

"Tastes like chicken to me," insisted Baird.

"It's tofu, Baird," Richard said.

Baird could hardly meet Rosie's eyes. To cover his embarrassment, Baird started expostulating about the hidden and therefore unexpurgated cravings of certain people who say they're vegetarian, but spend all their time trying to imitate meat, which means they're not vegetarian in their minds, which means they're not vegetarian at all.

No one argued with him.

Baird decided to interpret the lack of debate as a capitulation he was right. Then he cocked an ear toward the living room.

"And what is that dreadful droning noise?" Baird asked with equal grouchiness.

We all listened. Through the wall, the muffled chant sounded like a choral group of apes and buzzing bees warming up. Baird pushed the door to the living room open, and walked in. The rest of us followed.

Jon sat in a full lotus position at the foot of a speaker. Palms up on each knee, thumbs just touching index fingers. On the turntable spun a record, the Hindi script for OM spinning on the label. The album cover leaned against The Package. In a basso profundo, Jon chanted along with the devotees of Baba Ram Dass' guru.

Baird walked directly up to the turntable, and lifted the needle off the record. The silence jarred Jon's eyes open. He looked up at Baird and smiled.

Baird looked down his nose at Jon. "Please! Have you no decency? I mean, in the future would you play this drivel in your van and not here?"

Jon looked confused, but continued smiling.

Richard interceded and tried to explain to Baird about The Package. Baird picked up the book Jon had been reading and leafed through it.

"It's wild!" Jon said seriously, expecting Baird to sense the magic. He didn't. Then Jon looked at Rosie. "Rosie, my tantric maharini, now I know for sure we need a teacher. We just can't get there on our own. We've gotta find a teacher!"

"Nonsense," Baird said sternly. "Everything you need to learn you can learn from observing *nature*! Tell me that *you're* God and I'll buy it. Tell me *Richard's* God, I'll let him be. But don't tell me you need anything other than yourself to discover the truth. And whatever you do, don't bring anything other than yourself into this house! Especially gurus and their evangelical devotees! Please! We should put a sign in the foyer saying, 'No Chanting or Praying Allowed!'"

Duck was outraged. "You mean if I wanted to start praying to Allah five times a day in this house, you wouldn't let me? Who do you think you are?"

"Larry," Baird tried to sound reasonable. "You can believe anything you want. Just leave all the trappings outside and keep it to yourself. Be *It* and don't talk about *It*. Isn't that right?" Baird asked, turning to the carpenter, staring at him intently.

The carpenter looked a little stunned and said nothing. He just fiddled nervously with his tool belt. Richard surveyed the carpenter. Baird surveyed everyone in the room. "Don't we all feel the same way? Or should we have a family meeting?"

Everyone let out a sigh of fatigue. "Never mind," Larry retreated. "When I start practicing Islam, you can call one! First I have to find out which way is east anyway."

Jon stood up. He was almost as tall as Baird, but not as stocky. Jon looked directly into Baird's eyes and said very calmly, "I didn't bring anything into this house. The Package came to *you*. Unsolicited. But you're so sure of yourself, you just want to ignore it. Don't you think it would be safer *not* to be so sure of yourself?"

"You're the one who said he was *sure* he needed a teacher!" Baird countered.

"Yeah, but that's just another way of saying I'm sure that I'm not sure which leaves me a hell of a lot more options than you're leaving yourself!"

Richard wedged himself between Baird and Jon. He came up to their chests. A hand on each tummy, he rubbed gently while pushing them apart. "Gentlemen, gentlemen. I *am* God. And need I remind you that *everything* is needless to say? Now go to your spiritual corners and *don't* chant 'Hunga Dunga' 100 times." Then he looked at Psylvia and said sweetly, "Would you put on some music, my little gurken?"

Psylvia reached for the Wonderwall album that happened to be sitting beside the turntable but then thought the better of it. Throwing George Harrison at Baird right now might be construed as an insult. She needed a musical compromise. Something that would speak to Baird's *nature*, yet acknowledge Jon's penchant for the Chant. She found one in the stack of albums on the book shelf. A collection of Appalachian Blue Grass with lots of yodeling in it.

In the middle of the first fiddle solo, Ellen stuck her head into the room. "Dinner's ready!" Then she cocked an ear and added, "What's all that boo hoo, yodely yodely stuff!"

Trudy pulled a couple of more records from their sleeves and placed them on the spindle of the turntable. Then she ejected the blue grass album right in the middle of a refrain of cascading yodels that sounded almost celestial. The next record fell into place with a quiet flop. The strums of Julian Bream's lute music added a soothing ambience to the candles Luc was lighting. Tom grabbed the stack of mats from a lower cupboard and dealt them out to Alvoye and Brandon who distributed them around the floor to form an oval.

When everyone had their heaping plates in front of them, we held hands for quiet time. Jon broke the silence.

"Happy Valentine's Day, everyone. It's obvious that we are all loved very much."

Baird started to say something, but Ellen elbowed him in the side. The lute music ended and the next record fell. Psylvia roared when Frank Zappa started singing, *call it a vegetable, call it by name.*

Richard, in a calm, normal, dinner-conversation voice, asked the carpenter if after dinner, he could play with his zucchini.

CHAPTER 23
February 1971

Breakfast. Everyone fends for themselves. When I entered the kitchen, Jon and Baird were already at it. Embellishing their bowls of homemade granola with fruit and brown sugar, and embellishing their philosophical opinions with obscure quotes and fanciful anecdotes. Baird was so incensed, yet awed, by Jon's command of literary, historic and spiritual references, his rebuttals were punctuated with spitlets of milk and the occasional flying shard of granola. It was obvious they liked each other. It was obvious they enjoyed their diametric opposition.

Psylvia and Rosie were sipping carrot-celery juice in the backyard. They giggled now and then in response to delightful noises coming from the little cabin where Tom and Brandon spent so much time.

Little Richard came bounding down the stairs. He seemed especially puffed up. Maybe it was the tool belt he sported around his hips. He didn't say anything, but was whistling the tune to "Oh, what a beautiful morning." Just before he started the second verse, a big hunky guy wearing nothing but a hand towel that barely made it around his waist, tentatively descended the stairs. He stopped halfway down. We all bent our heads so we could see who it was. It was Lizzie's carpenter friend from the day before.

"Richard," he yelled toward the open kitchen door. "I have to go to work. Where are my clothes? And give me back my tool belt!" Richard just kept whistling as he pulled a frying pan out of the cabinet.

"How do you like your eggs, Mr. Wonderful?" Richard yelled toward the stairs.

Lizzie rushed down the stairs tying the belt of a bathrobe that most of us associated with Ellen. As he flew by the carpenter, Lizzie's hand caught the carpenter's elbow, causing him to lose the grip he had on the towel. The towel dropped to the stairs. Everyone let out sounds of appreciation. Even Jon. Richard sang *and it looks like it's climbing right up to the sky!* The carpenter grabbed the towel and ran back upstairs.

"Richard!" Lizzie called sternly. "I want to see you in my office immediately. The "office" was the unfinished attic that Lizzie wanted remodeled. We all took offense at his use of the word. That was premature and presumptuous. We hadn't yet decided the attic would become an office, let alone Lizzie's. Most of us wanted a meditation/seduction/orgy room. But Lizzie had no doubt he would get his way and continued using the word as if repeated enough, it would become reality.

Lizzie climbed back up the stairs. When we could hear him climbing the ladder into the attic, Richard rolled his eyes at us and followed.

Rosie and Psylvia were just coming in the back door when Jon called out to me. "Hey, Giacco! Isn't it just incredible about Psylvia? I mean what are the chances..." Rosie stifled the end of Jon's sentence with a big, juicy kiss. I was glad Jon found Psylvia as much of a trip as I did. She *was* incredible!

The phone rang. Psylvia grabbed it off the wall. "Hunga Dunga residence," she sweetly declared. "One moment." She held the phone out to me. "This lady sounds official," she whispered.

I took the phone from her. "Yes, this is *Mister* Giordano." Everyone in the room looked at me. "Department of Social Services? Yes. Yes, I can answer a few questions. Shoot!" I relaxed against the wall but was back at attention before my shoulder had barely touched.

"Can I make my own bed? What kind of question is that? Of course I can make my own bed!" Long pause. "Bodily hygiene? Whaddya mean *bodily hygiene?*" Long pause. "No, I don't need any help taking a bath!" Long pause. "Wash dishes? Cook for myself? Wait a minute. What is going on?" Very long pause.

"You gotta be kidding me? This is ridiculous! I'm coming down there right now! This is absurd!" I slammed the phone into its cradle.

"What was that all about?" Jon asked.

"Aid to the Totally Disabled. ATD. They put me on ATD! The woman said I'd be getting a retroactive check for all the time I was on General Assistance and a monthly check depending on how totally disabled I was."

"That's wonderful news!" Baird exclaimed.

"Congratulations!" said Psylvia. "I hope Lizzie doesn't get too jealous!"

"What? Are you all crazy? This is terrible. I'm not disabled! How dare they classify me as disabled!"

"How much are you going to get?" asked Baird.

"That's what the woman was trying to figure out. You get $240 for your basic, no frills, totally demented social misfit. But for everything you can't do for yourself, like wash yourself, or make your bed, you get extra."

Baird was irate. "You mean you were turning down all that extra cash? Why didn't you tell them you were totally incapacitated when it came to daily chores? You could've cleaned up! I don't know about you, Giacco. Sometimes you can be so inconsiderate!"

"What are you talking about, Baird? Is that *your* little secret? Is that how you're paying your share of the bills? 'Oh, those poor farmers I blew to pieces. I just can't cope anymore. Support me for the rest of my life!'"

Baird looked genuinely angry and turned away.

Jon, much to my surprise, chastised me. "Giacco! Listen to what you're saying! The only ones who come back from Vietnam as healthy as when they went in, are the ones who never had a heart or soul to begin with! Who wouldn't come back from that hell-hole half deranged?"

Baird threw a sharp glance at Jon. None of us, including Baird, knew how to take it. Baird didn't know if he liked being referred to as half-deranged, even if it supported his indignation.

"I'm going right down there and straighten out this whole mess! I said. "This is ridiculous! What could that psychiatrist have been thinking?"

Baird, taking advantage of the rare support from the others, turned to me, and in disciplined calm, said, "Giacco, please think about this for a while. Don't do anything rash."

I went to the jar where we kept trolley tokens and grabbed a few. I knew what I said to Baird was a little harsh and I myself didn't really believe it, but I was too involved with the State's assessment of my mental health to be rational. I took a flannel shirt off the coat rack in the foyer and slipped it on over my tie-dyed T-shirt.

As I slammed the door behind me, I heard Jon saying, "Wait, Giacco, come back here. Let's talk this over!"

I opened the door and stuck my head back in. "Jon, there's nothing to talk about. There's no way that I'm going to be crazy! At least not *officially*!"

Jon said, "Well, whatever you do, remember to walk toe to heel."

―――

When I walked into the Department of Social Services building it was most deliberately *heel* to *toe*. Like normal people. Heel to toe. Except on stairs. Then it was toe to toe. Like normal people.

"Toe to heel! Toe to heel!" I kept muttering to myself. Or maybe it was just slightly audible because I did notice some people looking at me as I passed them by. Maybe they just thought I was trying to beat them to the counter. One woman kept up with me. I pointed to her feet. "See! Heel to toe! You walk heel to toe! Once in a while, maybe, toe to toe! Like when you're walking up stairs. Maybe down stairs too, though I think then it's primarily whole foot to whole foot. But toe to heel? What? Is Jon crazy or something!" The woman slowed suddenly and fell back into the pack of other people making their way to the information desk.

An old man saw me coming and relinquished his spot as I reached the counter. "I demand to see my file," I told the clerk. "Now!"

The clerk cast a glance at a security guard at the far end of the hall leading to the elevators. "Are you a client of ours?" she asked soothingly.

"Is that what you're calling us? Clients?" I screamed at her. "Yeah. I'm a *client* if that's what it takes. Let me see my file!"

"I'm really sorry, Mr...." she paused, waiting with fingers ready at the keyboard of her terminal. "Giordano," I completed. "Giacco! 526-233-7423! File! Now!"

"Yes, Mr. Giordano. Would you like to make an appointment to see your case worker?"

"No... I... Want... To... See... My... File! Iwanttoseemyfile"

"I'm sorry, Mr. Giordano. But we never let our clients see their files. Now if you'd like someone to...."

I tried a different tactic and was effusively sweet. "Yes. It would be so *kind* of you if I could... just for a moment... talk to your supervisor." But I couldn't maintain it for more than a sentence. "And I mean..."

"Can I be of help?" The voice came from a kindly looking elderly man approaching the clerk behind the counter.

"This young man would like to speak to you, sir," said the clerk apologetically. He insists on...."

"I know," interrupted the white-haired gentleman. "Charlie rang me up and told me what was going on. Why don't you just step into my office, Mr. Giordano." He motioned me to the end of the counter where he lifted up a section and guided me through.

On the way to his office, he stopped at a bank of file cabinets. Consulting a slip of paper the clerk had given him, he scanned the labels under the handle of each drawer until he found "G-H". He opened it and thumbed through the folders, deftly separating one from the others. He pulled it out and just as deftly tucked it under his arm. I tried to deftly follow him into his office.

He motioned me to a chair and standing at my side, opened the folder and started thumbing and scanning through the documents. Without taking his eyes from the contents, he sat behind his desk and laid the opened folder in front of him. He pulled out a three-page, stapled document from the back part of the folder, and looking right at me, handed it across the desk. As I read it, I could feel his eyes staring at me, assessing me, trying to anticipate my reactions.

Much of the first two pages were beyond my layman's comprehension. Fortunately, the last paragraph on the last page started with a bold heading entitled "Conclusion." I honed in on it.

Patient exhibits, in my opinion, the classic behaviors of a paranoid schizophrenic accompanied by random and mild delusions of grandeur. In addition, beginning symptoms of Tourette's Syndrome are evident.

The antecedents of patient's condition can easily be traced to massive and abusive ingestion of lysergic acid which has resulted in organic brain damage. He is relatively passive and harmless and I see no need for concern that he will exhibit negative societal interactions. Due to the organic nature of his illness, no rehabilitative interventions are likely to have a salutary effect.

It was signed "Dr. Eaton P. Hull, D.P."

I looked up. The white-haired man whose name I never did get, was still staring at me. My mind covered lots of territory looking for a clue as to how I should be acting, feeling. I really didn't know. If this diagnosis was true, I should be really worried.

I put the document slowly and carefully back into the folder. I looked up to see the supervisor still staring, but this time his eyes were saying, "You asked for it." Not one further word was spoken. I stood up and pushed the folder across the desk to him. He stood, picked up the folder and, once again, deftly tucked it under his arm. His eyes never left mine. I turned around and left, feeling intimidated and vulnerable. But, as I closed his office door behind me, a visceral anger began to well up inside me. By the time I was on the other side of the counter where lines of people waited to be counseled, patronized, condescended to, bureaucrated and manipulated, I was fuming.

The marble floor echoed the snarl in my step as well as my voice. "Those goddam, unenlightened, scum-sucking, shrivel-brained shrinks! Organic brain damage! My ass! Mother-fucking fools! What are you looking at? Didn't you ever see a *paranoid-pissoid-schizoid-fuck me-megalomama* before? You too! What do you find so interesting? Yeah! You! No, don't bother looking away! I'm harmless! They said so. Besides, I'd like to see *your* fucking diagnosis. And what the hell is Tourette's syndrome anyway?"

I elbowed my way out the door onto the street. I was so pent up with rancor, I didn't have the patience to wait for a bus. My feet just headed up Market Street and kept going. They alternated between speed-walking and shuffling, while I mumbled and muttered and swore to no one and everyone in particular.

Back at Hunga Dunga, everyone tried their best to console me, but no one tried harder than Jon and Rosie to provide me with a healthy perspective.

"Don't you see," Rosie implored. "This karma is *good*. This is *very* good karma, Giacco! You're free! You don't have to worry about money anymore! You're free to become Self-realized. God-realized! You can devote every minute to it!"

"But what if it's true? What if it's all true and I'm really crazy?"

"Giacco, don't be ridiculous!" Jon demanded. "Consider the source, for christ's sake! Even if this diagnosis *were* true, you have to take into account the military, industrial, allopathic, capitalistic, classist, racist, sexist, homophobic stew from which it was concocted."

"In fact," Jon continued, "my *favorite* hypothesis, and a likely one at that... is that this Dr. Hull has done you a favor! *And* on purpose!"

"Are you implying he's part of the same Aquarian conspiracy I think my social worker is?" I asked.

"Could be," said Jon.

"You mean Dr. Hull and Miss Stein are undercover hippie revolutionaries?" I inquired.

"Why not?" Rosie asked.

"Besides," Jon added, pushing an index finger into my chest, "Maybe they're playing a role and don't even know it! Maybe they're just manifesting the plan of the supreme intelligence. If they're aware of it, they're part of the plan. If they're *not* aware of it, they're *still* part of the plan. All that's important is that *you're* aware of it."

"The way I see it," Rosie said, removing Jon's finger from my chest, "is that nothing happens by coincidence. Everything happens for a reason. And there's a reason you've been freed from having to think about supporting yourself. You should be smiling."

"You should feel secure," said Richard insecurely.

"You have a right to feel *smug* without feeling *superior*," Baird decided.

"Be happy," Psylvia yelled across the room.

"Don't worry," Jon whispered in my ear while he hugged me close.

Instead, I worried about all of us. Dr. Hull. Nancy Stein. Jon. Rosie. Hunga Dunga. I worried about all the people who had *already* been part of my life. Michael. Dean. Suzanne. Josie. Saul. Peter. Their faces appearing before me in no particular order as if the chronology of events in one's life is less important than their impact.

I worried about all the little forks in the road and all the reasons one was chosen over another. I worried that I had had too little to do with the choices. That everything continued to just *happen* to me rather than me *making* it happen. That I was at the mercy of everyone except myself.

I worried that all these other people had determined *for* me, that at this precise moment in time, I should be standing in a room in a house in San Francisco, surrounded by strange and beautiful beings, rather than standing anywhere else.

And then, I guess because I'm *crazy,* I got a view of myself from way out in the galaxy. I watched myself worrying. And I worried about me worrying so much.

And then I broke up laughing! But not for long!

CHAPTER 24
February 1971

I soon discovered that I wasn't an isolated case of an aberrant social system. I was merely at the forefront of a *craze*. Or should I say *The Craze*. Aptly named, for everyone we knew was clamoring to board the loony bus and get themselves declared ATD! "Aid to the Totally Disabled" soon became "Aid to the Totally Demented." Everyone wanted to be paid for being what Little Richard called "sky farmers."

The schemes they came up with to prove themselves unable to function in society were as creative as the outrageous costumes they made at Halloween.

Travis from Flo Airwaves declared with great histrionics his fear of all shadows, especially his own, to anyone who would listen, especially anyone on the front steps of the Department of Social Services building. A good day for him was a sunny late afternoon, when the shadows were long and distinct. Then he could be frightened out of his wits just as all the social workers were heading home for the day.

Moonglow from the Golden Aura commune absentmindedly twiddled with her twat and fiddled with her nipples on all buses and trolleys, insisting to her case worker that these forms of transportation caused uncontrollable waves of sexual arousal.

Likewise, Lucas from the Friends of Perfection had a sexual problem. He felt compelled to come on to any and all men in uniform. It was a true addiction. This prevented him from holding a steady job. Elevator operators, UPS delivery men, mailmen, even an elderly crossing guard outside his last place of employment, all had filed complaints with whomever his boss was at the time. And god forbid he found himself at a protest march where there were lots of policemen. It was not, he explained to his evaluating psychiatrist, a pretty sight.

Our own Alvoye made an art of looking bewildered. The mastery of his facial muscles and the length of time he could sustain a vacant expression, made even us wonder if maybe we had a problem on our hands.

Richard remained somewhat mysterious as to what his dysfunction was, but I suspect it had something to do with his accosting strangers in grocery stores and rubbing their tummies while calling them a variety of names, some of them vegetables. Sounds innocent enough, but Richard could call someone "Bok Choy" or "Mustard Greens" and make it sound pornographic. Only his dwarfish stature and cherubic face prevented him from being throttled on many an occasion.

More often than not, he'd call them Frank. "Hey Frank!" Richard said to one of them. "Now don't go bruising any of those tomatoes, though you are definitely quite the tomato yourself!"

"My name's not Frank, it's Vince," the guy would reply. Richard would go up to him and rub his tummy and look up at him with dreamy eyes. "Hey Vince, you really are quite the tomato, you know." And Vince would be so taken aback he'd look at his boss for some signal as to what to do. The boss just laughed and Vince just stood there letting Richard rub his stomach.

Richard called all men whose name he didn't know "Frank." "Hey, Frank," he'd say to the attendant at a gas station. "Fill 'er up, and check the oil, OK?"

"Thanks, Frank," he'd say when the ticket taker at a movie would give him back a stub.

Richard calling all strangers Frank got to be such an integral part of his language that the rest of us picked it up. Anyone whose name we had yet to learn was called "Frank." Even Ellen, probably the most "normal" of us all, would say, "That Frank guy up at the sandwich shop sure is a cutey," which meant she didn't know his name. And it was always a shock to the person on those rare occasions when the guy's name really was Frank. He thought we had some psychic powers or something.

And Lizzie. Well, Lizzie was not known for his artistic bent. He had a head more suited to finance and money markets. It wasn't his fault. He was raised on it. So it wasn't surprising to us that his "peanut butter" fixation was a little weak.

What I found a little scary was that most of the freaks who applied for ATD got it! Before anyone knew it, at least half the members of all the communes were on it. In fact, Lizzie was the only one we knew who wanted it, but for the creamy, crunchy life of him, couldn't persuade the shrinks to give it to him. He finally gave up.

As for me, my reaction was twofold. On one hand, this demographic surge in the population of demented San Franciscans supported the notion that indeed the doctors, case workers, and even social services administrators were all in on the conspiracy. It was indeed the Revolution, but a graceful one in which all systems would be transformed from the inside out. With love, peace, harmony, and a lot of yuks to boot.

On the other hand, it created in all of us, to varying degrees, a sense of obligation to justify the money we were getting from kindly Uncle Sam. Our intercommunal cartel, which consisted of about fourteen communes, were already providing a number of free services to the community. We hoped we would become role models for the rest of society. When they saw how much sense it made, they would eventually "catch up."

Friends of Perfection ran a free bakery which produced and distributed wonderful breads and rolls to the communes at hand, and the community at large.

They also published *Kaliflower*, an intercommunal magazine. It contained vegetarian recipes, poetry, stories, political commentary, cartoons and "tools" for dealing with conflict, relationships, the Establishment, etc. Above all it featured articles that focused on self-perfection. Perfection of the body, mind and spirit. Perfection of the environment. Perfection of society. It was such an important part of intercommunal communication that many people referred to The Friends of Perfection as the Kaliflower commune. Eli, the autocratic founder of Friends of perfection, hated that!

Kaliflower's influence cannot be understated. When it ran a series on "asshole consciousness," the sudden drop in the sales of toilet paper must've stymied local businesses. Squatting became the norm. Many communes retrofitted their toilets to accommodate foot stands. And the left hand found itself less used in public but more vigorously washed in private.

Kaliflower was delivered by volunteers to all the communes. Some lucky volunteers might get stoned, fed, or fucked. It was one of the perks that came with the job. They also solicited from the communes, any want ads, art, or articles, they wanted considered for future issues.

The Angels of Light provided the community with free theater, often producing revues that required lavish costumes and elaborate sets. The announcement of a new production was heralded throughout The City and no one ever walked away from one of their performances disappointed. More often than not, they walked away astounded.

The Dolores Street Gang gave us Sylvester, our own disco diva with a five octave voice. Sylvester entertained us for the joy of entertaining us. And Flo Airwaves gave us Divine, the persona of all that is fabulous and outrageous, the diva non pareil, and soon to be a movie star!

Flo Airwaves, conveniently only one house away, also gave up their basement to any and all who needed work space. Within days it was filled with big and whiny woodworking machines that had been stored in communes' garages and basements. At last, the carpenters and furniture makers among us would have a place to practice their craft. Naturally, anyone could use the space. And if they didn't know how to operate a certain machine, someone would teach them. All for free.

Golden Aura was the hotbed of free alternative medicine. From reflexology and shiatsu to iridology and high colonics, "Dr." Moonglow and her staff radiated a contagious holistic health at the bedside of their patients which may account for the fact that so many of them got well. With help from the subsidies provided by ATD, one of them was actually enrolled in pre-med at San Francisco State.

The 2020 Fell Street commune, known as Good Visions to some, distributed used furniture and assisted other communes that needed help, especially Hunga Dunga.

The Good Dog guys were expert auto mechanics. VWs were their specialty but they worked on everything. Most everyone drove beaters that were in regular need of repair and so their free garage was invaluable to us. Thanks to the Good Dog guys, they just kept us *truckin' on down the line.*

And Hunga Dunga would soon be providing everyone with free food. It was a *service* thrust upon us by the Friends of Perfection.

Others might have called it subsistence living, but to us it was luxury. Whether it was food, entertainment, transportation or medical attention, there was more than enough for everyone. The communal economy had an algorithmic effect on the old saying, "Two can live as cheaply as one." Now it was "Sixteen can live as cheaply as four and do it in style."

No one worried about a roof over their head. No one worried about having clothes to wear. No one worried where their next meal was coming from. That made it a lot easier to do *for free* what you were *best* at doing. Especially since what you were best at doing wasn't always a marketable skill in the "real" world. I always thought that was silly. There was *nothing* that a person *liked* to do that wasn't appreciated by someone, somewhere, sometime. There was *nothing* that a person was *best* at that wasn't wanted or needed.

There was the free yoga class, the free modern dance class, the free pottery class, the free guitar, plumbing, woodworking, batiking, you-name-it class.

Individuals at Hunga Dunga were no exception. You could get any part of your body pierced for free by Luc. You could get a hair-cut, though Ellen didn't get many requests for her services. Alvoye would be happy to consult you on your fashions. Baird was a prolific artist and always giving away paintings, drawings, and silk-screens, as well as doing the graphics for posters and program notes. Brandon enthusiastically taught tumbling, a skill revered by the Angels of Light. Little Richard was happy to share his skill with the wok and with embroidery needles. Psylvia was the all-time tie-dye queen. And Larry-Duck was the person to go to for his movie tips and knowledge of film history.

But what would be my pro bono contribution to our micro society?

Jon insisted that becoming Self-realized, and then maybe God-realized, was the greatest contribution anyone could make to the planet. I was a little skeptical. It seemed self-indulgent. It smacked of hubris. Who was I to think enlightenment was waiting for me right around the corner? Besides maybe I was already enlightened, but my mind was getting in the way. What about that extraordinary event I shared with Josie in Laguna? Some people don't even get one glimpse in an entire lifetime. Sometimes, you *do* get a glimpse, but *only* one. One should be enough. That's what I'd been told. I did, though, secretly long for more.

Anyway, I figured out that $240 a month came to $8 a day. I became obsessed in doing something: chores, stuff, anything that I myself could grant was of some service to someone. Anything that I could say at the end of the day, with absolutely no qualms, was worth $8. After all, I was working for the government. They just didn't know it.

Sometimes I worked for the Parks Department picking up litter and broken bottles in Golden Gate Park. Other times I was a horticulturist for the Department of Agriculture, planting marijuana, golden seal, and comfrey seeds on median strips. I worked one graveyard shift for the ASPCA by super-gluing all the locks on Animal Control trucks. As long as I could honestly say to myself at the end of the day that what I had done was worth eight dollars.

"But you're being ridiculous!" Jon argued with me. "You're doing way more than $8 worth of labor. You don't need to do it *hours* at a time."

"I just want to make sure the government's getting their money's worth, Jon!"

"Giacco!" he yelled down into my face. "You are just still fighting the War of the Catholic Guilt!"

"So what! Just let me be!"

"Well, as far as I'm concerned," Jon insisted, "any person just sitting still, centered, whole, healthy, and happy is well worth eight dollars a day! Any government would be stupid not to grab a deal like that. Think of the reduction in crime! Pollution! Violence! Traffic! Not to mention all the positive things thinking positively does to the planet. Please! Give me a break!"

Baird would calmly give the definitive observation. "Giacco. Don't you see? The entire nation is based on *consumption*. If Americans don't consume, the government's in trouble. If Americans don't consume more than they did the year before, well then the sky is falling! Therefore, if you don't have the money with which to consume, the government will *give* you the money. They want you to have it. You're doing them a favor. If you want to be a good American, take the money. Go forth, my son and *consume!* If you want to be a revolutionary, take the money and *don't* consume! Or do what I do. Make art!"

This was the topic of conversation at least once a day, every day. I would try to find things to do that might be construed as more than just simple acts of charity, while Jon and Rosie complained they wanted to spend more time with me before they headed back east. They got to spend lots of time with most everyone else. This was sort of nice, because by the time they left, they were really Hunga Dunga. Or at least Hunga Dunga hoped they thought of themselves as such. That's how enamored everyone was with Jon and Rosie. And Baird was one of their most ardent admirers.

By the end of the month, Jon and Rosie were ready to leave. They wanted to get an early start on preparing for their first spring on their farm in Maine. They begged me to come with them. They cajoled. They sweet-needled. They guilt-tripped.

"Part of the money you get comes from the federal government, doesn't it, Giacco?" Rosie asked. She took my silence as a "yes" and continued. "Well, you can work for the federal government in Maine just as well as you can here."

It was reasonable. It was hard to argue with. I never had a problem recognizing the arbitrariness of political boundaries. I almost went with them. If it wasn't for Larry, in his totally uncalculating way, reminding me of what I had at Hunga Dunga, where we still might go in the future, and how I couldn't leave until we all got there.

Jon and Rosie left for Maine. Chuck took the opportunity to visit his folks for a week and went with them as far as Chicago. We all promised to come and visit Jon and Rosie in the summer. I hoped they wouldn't think I loved them any less for choosing to stay with Hunga Dunga, but Lizzie had come up with something that seemed to more than satisfy my need to be worth at least eight dollars a day. He wanted to call it "Greenleaf."

CHAPTER 25
March 1971

Eli from the Friends of Perfection was delivering *Kaliflower* one day, and cornered Lizzie to harp on the fact that Hunga Dunga had no socially redeeming *raison d'etre*. No *group* karma yoga happening. And there was a need, though it was an ambitious one, that Hunga Dunga could fill. What the community needed was a reliable source of the best and cheapest food.

Not only did Eli plant the seed for Greenleaf in Lizzie's head but fertilized it with detailed instructions of how to bring it to maturity. Lizzie was enthusiastic about taking on a group project and threw himself into it with the gusto of a recently graduated business major starting his own corporation. He was inspiring because this was truly a labor of love. He wouldn't be working directly for Uncle Sam like so many of us were, but indirectly because the rest of us would be subsidizing him with our pooled income, much of which came from the Big Benefactor.

Still, he had to sell the idea to the rest of us. I was easy because it gave me the opportunity to salve my ATD conscience. But others were reluctant to commit to what might end up being a full-time job. In keeping with tradition, only those who really wanted to, had to do it. That included me, Chuck, Greg, Little Richard, Duck, and of course Lizzie.

This is how it worked.

Lizzie applied for and got a wholesale grocery business license and opened a bank account under the name of "Greenleaf" though most of us called it the "Free Food Conspiracy." "'Greenleaf' is a reasonable name for such an enterprise," he said. "'Hunga Dunga' would arouse suspicion methinks!" And because we knew it was really his baby, we let him have his way.

Little Richard would be the bookkeeper. Since he took care of all the money for the house and was always the one behind the scenes making things work, it seemed only natural that Richard would handle the money for Greenleaf. Richard's name was added to Lizzie's on the business license *and* the bank account.

Lizzie's place was in front of the curtain. And rightly so. Lizzie just had that successful look about him, that body language, that relaxed air that seems to come built-in to those born of wealthy and socially positioned parents. Of all of us, no one was more suited to being the front man for a business. Despite his hippie appearance, his breeding crept through. His experience as a New York actor, which gave him training on acting friendly or business-like, also helped considerably.

Having a license as a wholesale grocery allowed us to change food stamps, the *lingua franca* of communes, into real money. Normally, a grocery store would only accept food stamps in exchange for food at the time of purchase. Then they would bring the food stamps to the bank and have them credited to their account. That's the way it was supposed to work. But we didn't think the government would mind if we altered the flow of things a bit. The result would be the same.

Once a month, when the Big Benefactor was at his most magnanimous, Richard would make the rounds of the fourteen or so communal households that made up our "Free Food Conspiracy." Each household gave us all their food stamps. It didn't matter how much or how little. It didn't matter whether the house had three people in it or thirty. The only thing we insisted upon was that they give us *all* the food stamps they had. And because they all understood how and why it worked, they did.

Richard would take the food stamps to the bank. "I must go see 'The Big Benefactor' now. I'll be back soon." Once there, he'd turn the food stamps into hard cash. The next day we'd go shopping:

Crates of organic fruits and vegetables from the Farmers Market. Fifty-five-gallon drums of olive and safflower oil direct from the processor. Forty-pound bags of the best coffee beans from a tiny storefront in North Beach. Ten-gallon containers of freshly made tofu from a small company in Japantown. Gallons of unpasteurized milk and juices from a budding hippie enterprise in Santa Rosa. Grains of all kinds by the bushel from a distributor in the East Bay. Condiments by the box from a wholesaler in the Mission. Seasonings by the pound from a collective in Marin. Luxury items like papayas and mangoes we could only afford by the handfuls, but we'd go as far as Castroville and Salinas to get a great deal on garlic and artichokes.

Households gave us "wish" lists and we kept them in mind. When we could, Golden Aura would get their kiwis or Flo Airwaves their shitake mushrooms. Only once did a commune ask for chicken, but we had Eli quickly inform them that meat was not an option, and would they please scrutinize the philosophy upon which their diet was based. We had to have Eli do it because Hunga Dunga was much too anti-evangelical to take on such a ticklish task.

Our buying habits were ruled by one motto: "The best food at the best price." In time, Lizzie and Richard became well known at all the wholesale outlets. Lizzie would throw the bull with the owners, find out what vegetable or fruit was the deal of the day, bargain incessantly as if he were in some kasbah, while Richard fondled the tummies of guys on the loading docks.

The two of them became part of the "regulars" at the Market. Though a bit more notorious than the usual customers, and I'm sure the topic of many a conversation, they were extremely well liked. At the Farmers Market, when the sons of old Italian produce merchants saw Richard coming, they'd laugh and stick out their stomachs in anticipation of Richard's greeting and yell things in Italian I hoped were friendly.

Lizzie earned nothing short of their outright respect. He became so knowledgeable of products and prices that he could've started playing the commodities market. He even began keeping track of global weather anomalies and how they might affect the futures of a certain crop. If anyone were planning a trip out of the country, they would consult Lizzie about what kind of clothes to pack.

At the Farmers Market, Lizzie would make his choices, Richard would follow behind acting both as quality controller and treasurer. Lizzie always referred to Little Richard as his "Little Comptroller." Richard always referred to Lizzie as *"mon capitan d'industrie."* The phrase was lost on Lizzie until Luc's friend Catherine came to visit from France and explained it to him.

The rest of us were referred to as "the workers." Four of us at a time took turns doing different jobs on two different teams. One team was called "Dunga." This duo went on the buying trip with Lizzie and Richard. Dungas did the grunt work loading the crates and barrels and boxes into Romeo, Duck's microbus. It wasn't all that much fun and you had to get up at four in the morning. And it was hard work.

Romeo only made the maiden run. It was too small. We hadn't quite grasped the concept of "tons of food" until we saw it in real life. And had to load it into a vehicle in real life. And then move it, lift it, pack it, rearrange it and fight with it in real life. After just that first trip, Romeo, the microbus, told us in no uncertain terms that it wanted nothing to do with Greenleaf. It was too old, weak, and decrepit. Some of us were ready to back out of Greenleaf ourselves, claiming the same excuse. At any rate, we needed a truck with more guts and spunk to haul what amounted to a small mountain of food.

The Good Dog guys from the Free Garage gave us an old, but reliable, Dodge step-van, which of course we christened Juliet to be a companion to good old Romeo. Baird and Psylvia painted enormous cornucopias on its sides with fruits and vegetables that spilled over onto the hood and fenders. It gave Greenleaf a visual legitimacy equal to a Pepsi truck and transformed it into the true rolling food market that it was. On the inside were freshly painted shelves and bins. The Dungas were responsible for organizing the food on the shelves and keeping the bins filled with bulk grains and flour and stuff.

When the Dungas returned home around nine-thirty, the two Hungas took over, delivering the food. This was the most fun of all. The hours were great, and we all looked forward to our turn being a Hunga, which more than made up for being a Dunga. You'd get to drive up to a house that invariably stuck out from all the others around it. Whether it was the paint job, the strange decorations in the windows, the people cavorting naked in the doorway, or the blaring music, you could always tell when a house was a communal home.

Whoever the driver was that day would honk Juliet's horn. A face or two would peer out a window, and then the house would empty of its inhabitants, each carrying an empty bag or box. The other Hunga would open the back doors and lower the small wooden stairway that Nicky had made from scraps he found in Flo Airwave's basement.

Every now and then Nicky *did* do something extraordinary. The folding stairway was one of them. Normally he wasn't esteemed for the degree of his participation in the practical day-to-day requirements of communal living. Nicky didn't contribute very much. He had no interest in being on ATD. He had no interest in being employed. He had no interest in being a housekeeper. If he did do something that needed to get done, it was always on *his* timetable. But he was cute. And those eyes did shine fire. And he loved Psylvia. And, after all, he still was very young, just a few months out of his teens.

At family meetings, some suggested that life would be *easier* for *everyone* if Nicky got a job. Or the kitchen would get cleaned faster if Nicky would help. But that's as far as anyone would go. No one would ever tell someone else they had "responsibilities." You had to go to that place willingly, because you wanted to, because you knew how it worked.

But every now and then, Nicky would come across. Without fanfare. Without hoopla. Quietly. As if there were almost no forethought involved. It was always a surprise: A primitive, yet beautifully carved totem pole for the back yard. The downstairs toilet handsomely retrofitted into a squatter. And now, this! This sturdily and finely crafted staircase, complete with smooth, polished banisters, and beautifully tooled balusters. It simply invited you, wooed you, into the truck. And once inside, the rules were simple. Take as much of everything as you need. And no more. It worked perfectly. Well, almost perfectly.

Since we were the last house on the route, Hunga Dunga got stuck with all the leftovers determined by the preceding "shoppers." There might be eighteen bunches of spinach, but only two tomatoes. Or 10 pounds of basmati rice, but only a half-pound of granola and none of the beautiful peaches everyone else had gotten. Even then, after taking stock of what we had the most of, we never came home without dropping something off at Saint Joseph's, the Vallejo Gospel Mission, or the downtown Food Bank. But we endured. We suffered nobly, silently congratulating each other for our selflessness. It was a humility that could easily become arrogance, so we tried to pay attention and bust each other as often as possible.

When we were invited to dinner by other communes, which was fairly often, we tried not to covet the bowl of peaches so ostentatiously displayed in the center of the table. We did this by loudly gushing over them, smacking our lips, and making a scene. And we expressed our surprise over whatever they had cooked for us, even though we pretty much knew what they had to work with since we delivered the food. Unfortunately, most of these communes lacked really good cooks. Either they ended up serving everything raw, offering with it some banter about how brutal it was to boil a vegetable, or they served "goosh" with cheese on top. It was difficult not to be a critic, since I, myself, was a master of goosh.

One of the most imaginative cooks, possibly a culinary genius, was Lana. She was in the kitchen with Psylvia, Ellen, and Duck when Chuck and I, the Hungas that week, walked in. I didn't see her. I was carrying a box of turnips. On top of that a twenty-pound bag of carrots. And on top of that, reaching past the top of my head, a twenty-pound bag of potatoes that I steadied with my nose.

"Can somebody please take some of these things?" I said, probably with a note of irritation in my voice.

"Coming, coming, don't pee in your pants!" a strange female voice said. A voice with a distinctive Philly twang. I felt a tug at the bag of potatoes and watched in cross-eyed slow motion as they left my nose and fell into the arms of Lana. The falling burlap heap revealed a likeable, possibly beautiful face. Creamy skinned with a slight blush at the cheeks. Her light brown eyes were everywhere, looking me over.

"Hi, I'm Lana," she said and began to walk around me, cradling the potatoes like a baby.

"Hi, Lana. I'm Giacco," I said turning my head to follow her, then whipping it back the other way to meet her as she completed the revolution around me.

She put the bag on a chair, stood once again in front of me, and looked directly into my eyes. "It's *'Lahna.'* Not short 'a' *'Lana.' 'Lahh*na!'"

"Pardon me. I stand corrected… *Laaahh*na!"

"What? Did I just hear a smidgen of sarcasm in your voice? Are you accusing me of being pretentious?" She tilted her head slightly and continued without waiting for an answer. "You know, Giacco, you're in a very vulnerable position right now, standing there with all that stuff piled up to your chin. I *could* have my way with you if I wanted to."

My eyes got a little bigger as she took another walk around me, this time feeling my ass along the way. When she reached her starting position, her hands slowly reached under the box of turnips, fingers tiptoeing toward my belt, or so I thought. Instead, her eyes still on mine, she took the carrots and turnips from me and dropped them on the counter. Then she wheeled around and gave me a big hug, putting off the put-on.

"I am *sooo* glad to meet you!" she said, underlining every word. "At last! Psylvia's told me so much about you. About everybody!" she said, spinning around again to encompass everyone else in the room.

Lana knew Psylvia from Philadelphia. They met only a couple of weeks before Psylvia left for the west coast. But both swore that had they known each other longer, they would have been best friends. And since "would have's" don't exist in a "be here now" world, Lana decided to move west and make what might have been, happen.

"So here I am!" she announced. "You don't need to tell me a thing… knowing Psylvia the way I do is all the education I need. And I know right now that we're all going to *love* living together and getting to know one another."

The rest of us cast furtive, questioning glances at one another, but everyone kept an eager smile on their face. Once again, we tried to muster the patience of a diviner, knowing time would reveal to us what the winds of fate had blown on our doorstep… what the cat had brought in… how the dice had rolled… which way the mozzarella would bounce. It only took as long as that night's dinner.

Lana concocted a meal of such delight, we were brain-dead. Our oxygen was imprisoned in our stomachs, sentenced to the unusual, but certainly far from cruel punishment, of digesting the most exquisite eggplant parmigiana we had ever tasted. That had been accompanied by garlic bread and a delicious salad with tiny bits of gorgonzola cheese in it. The *entrée* was followed by a dessert of fresh-from-the-oven pear tarts with Sambuca poured over them. We washed everything down with some fine wines Lana brought with her. By the time the last crumb of homemade crust was gone, we embraced Lana as *famiglia*.

She embraced each of us, but she lingered, practically loitered, at each of the men. She studied them, making direct eye contact. Not harsh, just curious and playful and a little alluring. Even on this first evening, my impression watching her was that she brought out the "Zorba" in men. Like in that scene where Zorba is berating his young English boss for being so shy and naive and says something like... *If there is any great sin, it is when a woman calls a man to her bed, and he does not go.*

Anyway, we felt pretty sure she was just another loose goose. Another intelligent, talented, hippie slut like the rest of us.

She was. The most mundane conversations were sprinkled with sexual innuendo. The simplest gestures emoted erotic possibilities. Her gaze held the potential for lewd behavior. But Lana did not casually engage in sex. When she had sex, it was with an old-fashioned notion of romance. It was a Fred Astaire and Ginger Rogers movie. She planned her seductions carefully and thoughtfully, with great attention paid to where and when sex would happen.

Unlike the rest of us. The rest of us seldom *planned* sex. We looked for it a lot, but we seldom planned it. We had it whenever and wherever we could find it. In the likeliest and unlikeliest places. At the likeliest and unlikeliest times.

CHAPTER 26
March 1971

One of the bennies of being a Hunga and getting to deliver the food was that the interactions sometimes led to erotic trysts. Many a delivery ran late waiting for one Hunga or the other to finish a "quickie" in an upstairs bedroom or a downstairs pantry. Sometimes with a friend, sometimes with a current love interest, sometimes with someone you just met. Sometimes with *two* or *three* or *four* you just met! If that were the case, sometimes the Hunga left behind could wait no longer and went in and joined the crowd. Our intercommunal cartel consisted of men and women who played a rainbow of sexual roles and who, chameleon-like, might change their color at any moment. This always made group sex entertaining if nothing else.

One of the most memorable happened at Dolores Street, the next to the last house on the route. Greg and I were the Hungas that week. When we got there, Sylvester and his backup singers, a few musicians, and a couple of dancers were rehearsing a routine for the upcoming Cockette's show. A few teenage groupies hung out. Sylvester shouted, "Take five." Rita and Benny who lived there came out to the truck along with Sylvester and picked out what they needed for the week.

Sylvester said, "Why don't ya'll come back in the house. You look really thirsty! We'll get high and then…" Sylvester coyly approached Greg, undulating his tongue up and down like a belly-dancer about to let out one of those ear-piercing yelps, "I'll wet your lips for you!" He lunged and sloppily lapped Greg's face. Greg turned red. He was usually very shy once he left the comfort of Hunga Dunga and now he seemed nonplussed. Sylvester, completely unflappable in the presence of anyone, let alone someone like Greg whom he called a "squeamie," turned around and rummaged through one of the cupboards. "Now let's see…"

Although every house we stopped at offered us tea, coffee, snacks, and the usual homegrown weed, Sylvester did everything to the hilt. He brought out whiskey, cognac, hash, and cocaine. He invited everyone in the house to "refresh" themselves before rehearsing some more. Greg and I, Rita and Benny, the groupies and the band, followed Sylvester to an upstairs bedroom. Some of the band members reached into their stashes and contributed to the contraband growing in the middle of the floor. One of the teenage groupies pulled out a chillum. Another was rolling a five-paper Euro-joint. Before long, the room reeked of the herb. Even one of their cats, draped over a pillow, was passed out cold.

The cognac and coke alone had had the desired effect upon Greg, turning him from Jekyll to Hyde. From "Mr. Squeamie" to "Mr. Squirmy." It was Sylvester who instigated it, the *ménage a' vent* that is.

"Just look at little Greggy!" Sylvester teased. "He's just squirming all over he's so pent up with energy! I do believe we are all being called upon, although at a *vibrational* level, mind you, to *ease* his TENSION!"

Sylvester jumped Greg and one of the teenage girls at the same time, his big black arms bridging both their bodies. Another teenager, a boy, started undoing Greg's shoes. Two of the musicians looked at each other, shrugged their shoulders, and began quickly undressing. Rita stood up and calmly undid her halter. The bed was quickly filling up.

I thought about joining in. I even got as far as sitting on the edge of the bed. A few limbs fell in my lap. Another knocked me flat. But I was never any good at group sex. Three was difficult enough. I was always too concerned someone's feelings would get hurt. Possibly mine. And besides, the chances you'd walk off in love with someone were pretty slim. I've always been best at one on one. If there are fireworks, at least you know who they're for.

I disentangled myself and sat on the windowsill watching the laws of sexual chaos at work. Occasionally the randomness disappeared and was replaced by the pleasing designs of synchronous bodies in motion. When everyone was through, they smoked a pack of cigarettes, and each told the others they were the best sex they had ever had.

I reminded Greg we still had one more house to go. It was Friday, after all. Not that it mattered to us. Everyday could be a weekend day if we wanted it to be. But for all the other nine-to-fivers it was the beginning of the weekend, which meant a greater selection at the bar of your choice.

The Stud was my favorite. No bar anywhere could match the Stud. It was a hippie's paradise. It had the best rock and roll and a dance floor that could accommodate any number of dervishes. Most were gay, some straight. Most were men, some women. Most were friendly, unassuming, and unpretentious. There were a few who were not.

From time to time, the Stud's bouncers would pass out acid to the crowd, usually dispensing it as you walked in the door. Those were my favorite nights at the Stud. Usually my most successful, too, if success were determined by going home with someone. Mind-altering drugs let us all cruise one another in a larger historical perspective. The Infinite. The music released a giant collective soul, generous and sensitive enough to let two people fall in love on the basis of nothing more than a vibration. The Stud was one fine place that made all future and past bars pale embarrassingly in comparison. It was more like a Church in which we worshipped Life.

There were other bars, of course, catering to every fetish imaginable. Castro Street, three blocks from Hunga Dunga, was fast becoming the neighborhood of choice. When we first moved into the area, it was a quiet neighborhood with a small business district. It had one movie theater, a grocery store, hardware store, and other small shops, including Harvey Milk's photo lab. It was the only gay-owned business on Castro Street that I knew of. Then, as if overnight, the street and its side streets blossomed with bars, coffee houses, restaurants, clothing stores, leather shops, all of them catering to the gay and lesbian community. Finding a sexual partner was as convenient as picking up a quart of milk at the corner grocery.

If none of the bars worked, or you were just in one of those gluttonous moods, there were always the baths. They were either as decadent and lavish, or decadent and funky as you can imagine. So I will leave it to the imagination.

On the home front, sex of course was as natural as eating or shitting. There wasn't an hour during the day or night when sex wasn't happening somewhere in The Big Blue House that Hunga Dunga lived in.

Tom and Brandon had each other multiple times a day, or so it seemed. To keep their relationship "fresh," they would sometimes bring a "guest" home. Usually he was athletic, handsome, and muscular. Once in a while, just to be nice guys, they'd pick out of a crowd someone shy and plain and who looked in need of an ego boost. Whoever it was, they'd go up to the lucky guy and use the line they used on all their pick-ups. "How would you like to be ravaged by two of San Francisco's hottest lovers?" It always worked. And when the "guest" left near dawn, I'm sure he took a memory he would conjure up many times in the future!

Lizzie had Greg. Greg was never quite convinced he had Lizzie, but hoped for the best by always acting aloof and uncommitted around him, especially since he was the man who replaced Bobby in Lizzie's life and, well… "What goes around, comes around." Nevertheless, Greg should've known that Lizzie was really waiting to be smothered by him, and by playing it cool, Greg was simply foiling his own plot. In the meantime, they each had the other at their sexual disposal, should they want it.

Ellen was carrying on a torrid love affair with a man she met at a tenants' rights rally. His name was David. He had a passion for social, economic, and political justice. His consciousness, his activism, his obvious delirium over Ellen, made his average looks seem ruggedly handsome. His unkempt clothing seemed tailor-made, his scruffy beard and shaggy hair seemed professionally groomed. We were more than a little impressed that David had absolutely no desire to move in with us, though for all practical purposes he *was* living with us.

Baird was a serial lover. Each boyfriend would last about two or three weeks at the most. The time between boyfriends was magically non-existent and there was the constant possibility that one of them might move in for good, as had happened with Alvoye and Luc. I have no idea where all of Baird's consorts came from. Baird seldom went to the bars, seldom went out at all. He usually just stayed in his room painting or making some kind of art. It was one of the great unsolved mysteries.

Nicky was having sex with Psylvia on a regular basis. A testament to his stamina, since he was regularly having sex with two other women from other communes. He was a darling, doe-eyed, Don Juan that women loved to fawn over, and men loved to dream about. Nicky just couldn't say "No." Psylvia knew deep down that he loved her and did her best to take it in hippie stride.

Nicky did have sex with men, often with the blessings of Psylvia. He liked guys flirting with him, and he flirted back. He liked it when we admired his body. He liked being gratified, especially if he wasn't expected to return the gratification. He didn't mind getting "done" and sometimes sought out opportunities. But he'd only let the men of Hunga Dunga "do" him or so he said, as if it were a matter of honor, keeping it in the family. We tried to accept this as a gesture of love. The best he could do. The willingness to be vulnerable. This is what I guessed Psylvia hoped he would learn all along. Some took Nicky up on his "invitations" from time to time. The rest of us made do quite well with the cornucopia of sexual opportunities our San Franciscan lives afforded us. San Francisco and the intercommunal network afforded us a lot! Especially men.

No wonder Lana was so frustrated! It was so unfair, really. She was a delight to look at. A little too big-hipped for my tastes, but in another era, she'd have been the paragon of feminine beauty. A man of legendary machismo, like Paul Bunyan, would have found Lana irresistible. Her incredibly intelligent eyes called out to you, even from a distance. Her breasts were small, but of the comeliest shape. Everyone liked touching them, but she didn't like you to do that unless you intended to go further.

Lana was conservative, compared to the rest of us. She didn't wear evocative clothes. She thought group sex was overrated and antiquated. She wanted to be courted, wooed, and romanced. So did the rest of us, but we were willing to indulge ourselves while biding our time for Mr. or Ms. Right to come along. She was not. She talked about the lack of "Mr. Rights" more than anyone else.

One time, Lana and I were sitting in the living room listening to Carole King's "Tapestry." She was slouched in the overstuffed chair, legs apart, her dress up past her knees.

"How can a woman such as me, so full of passion, who revels so much in the act of making love, survive in a household that's primarily gay, involved with a community that's primarily gay, in a city that's demographically top-heavy with gays! What am I doing here?"

She seemed on the verge of tears. I went to her and bent over her, placing my hands on her knees so I could look her in the eyes. I tried to comfort her. I was unaware I was swinging her knees in and out, in and out, in time to *I feel the earth move under my feet, I feel the sky come tumblin' down.* I didn't realize she found it unbearably arousing.

In the middle of our heart-to-heart, Lana pushed my hands off her knees, grabbed the neck of my t-shirt, and pulled my face up to hers. She glared at me with eyes that conveyed extreme sincerity. She spoke slowly and distinctly.

"Don't you ever do that again unless you mean business, mister!" She pushed me away and left the room.

CHAPTER 27
April 1971

To disperse her sexual energy, Lana revived an interest in pottery. She joined a potter's co-op and before long was bringing home beautiful and unique pieces, some very practical, others fanciful. She said she was "enraptured" by the feel of warm, pliable, moist clay spinning between her fingers. She said she "applauded the clay's power to absorb her."

Soon, her culinary masterpieces were being presented on exquisite dinnerware, enhancing the food as well as the living room floor. But many of us were concerned with the number of penile-shaped vases that started to adorn the mantle and end-tables. Some of them were grotesquely misshapen.

The amount of money she was spending on clay was also of concern to us. Little Richard gave Lana an explanation of how our finances worked by giving her a tour. He took her upstairs and pointed to the "Can of Worms" closet, which Lana sardonically said she'd find very useful.

He opened the little closet's door and pointed to the cigar box that contained each day's "mad money," a perfect euphemism to those of us who were "demented." Every morning, Richard would put anywhere from twenty to fifty, one-dollar bills in it. This was to be used for bus fares and movies, to replace the quart of Half-and-Half you just found empty in the refrigerator and can't drink coffee without, and emergency personal necessities, like a tube of oil paint or a tube of K-Y.

You could take as much money as you wanted. You never had to account for it. It was understood that when the cigar box was empty for that day, it would not be replenished. It was understood you should consider the needs of others when deciding how much to take. Nevertheless, it may have been a major factor in making Hunga Dunga a bunch of early risers. It was the early bird that got the K-Y. It was the early bird that got to go to the movies.

The dipping of Lana's hand into the communal "cookie jar" upset the precarious financial balance we had silently perfected through trial and error over the past six months. Just when people were feeling enough of a financial pinch to want to bring it up at a Family Meeting, Lana got a job teaching pottery at a ceramics studio. This allowed her to use their facilities for free and to embezzle clay for her own projects. She contributed more than enough money to the communal funds to ward off any complaints. In fact, her phallic vases were acquiring a local reputation and were in great demand on Castro Street. A nearby florist displayed some of her vases in front of a sign that read "Give Your Lover a Floral Ejaculation!"

As so often happens when you live closely with other people, you get to know them *too* well. Sometimes the true depth of their talent is obscured. Somehow, seeing them insert a tampon or giving themselves an enema, interferes with the ability to appreciate them as an artist. Baird liked to paint naked in front of the large bay window of the second-floor bedroom that faced the street. His big, but soft body, his hairy shoulders, back, and buttocks, would distract me from seeing what was occurring on the canvas.

At Hunga Dunga, everyone was an artist. We knew them when they were mere beginners at their crafts. We didn't see, right before our very eyes, the journey of their art into mastery. It took outsiders, whose opinions we respected, to make us see the true stature of their talent. Some of us didn't see it for a long time. This was painfully true for the way we regarded Maxime.

Toward the end of April, Luc walked in the house with what looked like two lost souls, friends of his from Paris on a year-long "pilgrimage" of America's "holy" sites. "Holy" sites were any cities in which the antics of "flower children" made the news on French TV. Needless to say, San Francisco was the Lourdes of their itinerary.

Catherine LeForestier was slim and sexy, mid-20s like Luc, and had frizzy, auburn hair. She always looked so radiant and smelled so nice. Every tableau she entered became a Degas painting, softening the edges and warming the light.

Her English was adequate but spoken with a far thicker accent than Luc's. At first, we had to really pay attention to understand her, but soon we got used to it. It was this ability to communicate and her inquisitiveness that made her seem so much more accepted than her brother Maxime. She wanted to know everything. She made it a point to spend time, one on one, with everybody. And each of us, in turn, felt flattered by her interest. She made all the odd things we were starting to do out of habit seem new and fresh. And she wanted to be included in all the daily goings-on, welcoming those days when she took someone's place being either a Hunga or a Dunga on the food run. She was the exact opposite of Maxime who was two years younger but acted like an old fart.

Maxime was an animate object, but barely. He could always be found sitting in the overstuffed chair in the living room. He was like a growth on the upholstery. He spoke absolutely no English and made no attempts, that we were aware of, to learn even simple phrases. He just sat there, hour after hour, day after day, looking amiable, but stunned into immobility. He had very kind eyes and a strikingly sensuous mouth, but the rest of his face was obscured by a big, bushy, reddish-brown beard and long, curly dark brown hair. We could only surmise he was handsome. He may or may not have had a great body. We couldn't tell. Somehow, he managed to always be already dressed, even when *some* people were deliberately trying to catch him naked.

Maybe that's why he stayed in that chair all the time. Maybe he was scared. Maybe just insufferably shy. Maybe it was the language barrier. He just sat there. Like a sponge. He just absorbed. The only time he moved was to take a joint from someone, inhale half of it, and then pass it on. For four months he absorbed. More than just our dope and food. Much more. It was like he was absorbing every facet of Hunga Dungan life on the sly, our antics, our craziness, our hassling, our sexual shenanigans, our humor, our politics, our very being. He was a big French sponge that just sucked up vibes. But he did it so benignly and passively, few barely noticed. What at first may have intrigued us about him, now bored us to the point of ignoring him entirely. I think this is what he wanted, and if so, he was cleverer than anyone gave him credit for.

At one Family Meeting, the subject of Maxime came up. We were all sitting in a circle on the floor of the living room. All of us except Maxime, who gently, but warily, smiled at us from his nest in the overstuffed chair. Bobby was a bit put out.

"I'm sorry you guys, but Maxime is getting on my nerves. He's like some kind of alien being just studying us all the time. He does nothing. He just sits there!"

"He's allowed to just sit there," Ellen stated.

"Really, though, Ellen," said Larry, reaching over and patting Maxime's hand where it lay limply on the chair's arm, as if he were an inanimate object, "He really does do *nothing*. He's a very inoffensive bump on a log."

Catherine translated for Maxime. His eyes brightened and he laughed softly.

"Well, I think Maxime is very nice to look at," Baird spoke endorsingly, "and Catherine *more* than makes up for his lethargy. Look at Nicky!"

Everyone looked at Nicky, then at Maxime, and then back again at Nicky. We made our comparisons to ourselves. Nicky straightened up and looked puzzled.

"Well, I like that they're both here!" Little Richard said. "Of course my fluency in French may have something to do with it."

"Fluency, shmuency, Richard!" scolded Psylvia. "You know as much French as the rest of us… *nada*! You probably know how to say *voulez vouz couchez avec moi* and maybe *Je'ne regrette rien*! You know where liars go, Richard!" warned Psylvia. "They go to Baird's room!"

Maxime was stifling a laugh, but barely succeeding.

"Well, I for one don't care if Maxime doesn't do *anything* around here. That's his god-given right," Nicky said. "Sometimes just thinking is really hard work!" Everyone looked at Nicky and stared incredulously.

Maxime had his hand over his mouth and his cheeks were puffed and red. He and Catherine exchanged looks and made sibling signals only they understood.

Catherine apologized for her brother. "Eet eez not zerious. Eet eez zshoost that he eez suffereeng from *ennui*."

"Onwee? What's Onwee?" Lizzie asked.

Tom spoke up. "I'm not sure, but I think Onwee is French for gonorrhea." His delivery was perfect and he managed to keep a straight face.

Lizzie turned to Maxime but spoke to Catherine. "Well, you just tell Maxime that he is one considerate bastard! *Onwee* can be *extremely* uncomfortable," he said grabbing his cock and twinging from the remembrance of a previous pain. "And we appreciate the way he's quarantined himself like that in the chair, but it won't do him any good. He'd really better go see a doctor!"

Catherine and the rest of us, except Nicky and Bobby who didn't get it, laughed out loud.

Maxime had to get up and leave the room, guffawing. It became clear to us that even though he couldn't *speak* it, he *understood* a whole lot more English than he let on.

When he was gone and the laughter died down, Catherine very seriously confided, "Maxeem eez reely very… you say… zenziteeve? You know? Heez… hmm… very… deep? Like zee… hmm… ocean? You know? …like Luc?"

Until she mentioned Luc's name, we were all ready to believe anything she said. But we considered Luc, as well as Bobby and Alvoye, the "infants" of the group. We liked them, but their priorities included partying, partying, and more partying. We regarded them as a little superficial. To hear Luc characterized as *deep as an ocean* made everyone skeptically stiffen. Luc, in the face of Catherine's compliment, humbly bowed his head.

Catherine looked around her and understood immediately. Nevertheless, she didn't agree.

"The Luc… I theenk you *leev* weeth heem?... but you do not *know* heem?" Catherine looked around to see if she was making sense. "He eez a brilliant actor, you know. He waz very populaire en Brussels et Paree. Een great demand. On heez way to zee top! He gave eet all up to… *comment dit'on*… find heez soul?"

Everyone but Baird and Alvoye looked penitent. Luc looked around and felt the guilt.

"Eet is partly my fault," he said dramatically. "Eet waz zanother lifetime. You zee me on zee outside, because that eez all I have to show you. I am still trying to find out what eez on zee inside. All I know eez that I love all of you."

Luc's confession was short, yet it had the emotional impact of Sarah Bernhardt reciting the Polish alphabet. We tried to regard Luc differently in the future.

As far as Maxime went, Lana wrapped the discussion up when she announced in no uncertain terms, "I want that man!"

CHAPTER 28

May 1971

It wasn't that Lana was shy. Not by any means. But she did have her pride. She would only bat her eyes at Maxime so much and then that's that.

Fortunately, Friends of Perfection had come up with a very useful tool for handling all sorts of ticklish situations. In fact, Eli said we had inspired it when we asked him to tell the Good Dog guys that meat was not on our shopping list. It was called the "third person." To be more precise, it was a verb: to *third person* someone. It could be used to resolve conflicts, but most often it was used as an ersatz Cupid. You could lessen the pangs of being rejected or the discomfort of rejecting someone, simply by asking a friend from a commune, other than your own, to *third person* the object of your desire for you.

It sounded like something out of the previous century, but it worked very nicely. If anyone were approached and said, "I'm here to *third person* you," you couldn't help but be a little flattered, even before discovering who it was that was interested in you. Sometimes you had a fairly good idea who it was. Other times it came as a complete surprise.

I'm sure it didn't come as a surprise to Maxime when Xena from Golden Aura came to visit.

"Hi, Maxime. I've come to *third person* you in the name of Lana."

Maxime shuffled in his chair at hearing Lana's name, feigning total ignorance of the English language. Xena spoke more slowly and a little louder, as if that would help.

"Lana... really... likes... you! Do... you... like... her?"

Maxime's eyes glazed over. He knew it was inevitable. He could only put it off for so long. It would have to happen sooner or later. After all, what would Zorba say? And why wouldn't he? She was beautiful and voluptuous. But would she understand that, to Maxime, this was just a *divertissement*?

"Maxime?" Xena snapped her fingers in front of Maxime's face.

Maxime flinched into consciousness. "Mais oui! Bien sur!"

"Would... you... like... to...... you know?" Then Xena pantomimed the rest by sticking the index finger of one hand in and out of a circle she made with her fingers on the other hand.

"Oui, oui, oui, oui, oui!" replied Maxime gesturing with his hands as if to say *that goes without saying.*

"Great," exclaimed Xena, like all messengers, happy in knowing she would be the bearer of good news. "She's arranged to trade spaces with Tom and Brandon for the night. She'll meet you in the cabin at 11:30. OK?"

It took another half hour for Xena to explain the details of the rendezvous to Maxime. She even had to draw a map of the house and circle the cabin in the back yard. Then she grabbed the clock off the mantle and played with its arms. When she was sure Maxime understood, she gave him a peck on each cheek and went in to visit with Psylvia and Duck.

Maxime thought a moment, and when he was sure no one was watching, pulled a little note pad from the pocket of his oversized sweater. After searching some, he found his ballpoint pen on the cushion between his legs. He hummed two measures of a tune and then wrote furiously in the pad.

The rest of the day, whenever Lana or Maxime passed each other, they would both avert their eyes, playing coy and shy. But by dinnertime, all of us knew why Xena had come over. Around 11:45 that night, if Maxime or Lana had bothered looking out the cabin windows, they might have caught 10 or 11 pairs of eyes peeking out the kitchen windows. They didn't bother. They were completely preoccupied.

Third-personing became an instant tradition. Often people would saunter about the house gloating, "I was *third-personed* yesterday!" or "You'll never guess who *third-personed* me this morning!" The expression almost became a euphemism for "fuck." "Well, did you get *third-personed* last night?"

Of course, there were bound to be those who would sigh deeply and whine, "Always the third person, never *third-personed*!" This included Richard and me. Why we were so often requested to be *yentas* we never could figure out. Or maybe we didn't want to. It made us feel so *neutral*! Is that how others perceived us? As beige and indistinguishable? Psylvia said it was because *we* never asked anyone to *third-person* anyone else and so people thought we were either *above* all that or weren't especially *sexual* beings. Richard and I exchanged looks that confirmed we both thought Psylvia's reasoning was weak at worst, kind at best.

For the next couple of months, using a third person replaced cruising the bars. And deals were made. "I'll *third person* for you, if you'll *third person* for me." I'd say the Third Person and Asshole Consciousness were the two greatest contributions Friends of Perfection made to our community.

Thanks to Asshole Consciousness, Hunga Dunga had the cleanest lower digestive tracts, rectums, and sphincters in San Francisco.

Thanks to the Third Person, Lana's sexual frustrations were placated, and for the time being we were spared her laments. In fact, most of the time she was ebullient. The only concern she ever brought up was the possibility of getting pregnant. She was a strict Catholic. Well at least as strict as a Catholic can be for one who seldom went to mass or confession. And when she did, she couldn't prevent fantasies of defrocking young priests from monopolizing her mind. She did, however, obey papal directives regarding contraception. She'd waltz around the kitchen early mornings singing Cole Porter.

I got music, I got rhythm,
I got my love, who could ask for anything more!
I got Maxime, I got rhythm,
I'm not pregnant, who could ask for anything more!

What she did worry about was being a *mother*, and knowing that the urge to rebel is *inherited*. According to her, we were all rebelling against everything *our* parents stood for and if rebelling in and of itself were just a generational idiosyncrasy, what would prevent any of our kids from growing up to be strait-laced, Christian fundamentalist Republicans!

She didn't mind *others* propagating! "What I do mind," she said, "Is that as a *mother*, I might *bust my butt* filling the kid with *the* most progressive politics, and *he*, because with my luck, it probably would be a *he*, will be a *monster*! No matter what I do or say. He'll want to *undo* all the things that I tried *to do* for the planet, just like I try to *undo* all the damage I think *my* parents did to the place! Maybe the urge to rebel is uncontrollable. It might even be genetic for godsakes. We're stuck! And if *that's* true, well then, what's the point! We'll never be emancipated from our own tyranny!"

Other than that, she was having a pretty good time.

The rest of us were falling into a routine. Greenleaf provided a regular pattern to follow. The house seemed to be working on automatic. Everything always got done. Everyone knew what had to be done to make it work. Since we wanted it to work, everything always got done.

Greenleaf quickly built a reputation for "quality product and excellent customer service." So much so that two businesses asked Lizzie if Greenleaf would buy food for them.

Both were new, small, vegetarian, health food restaurants. The Yin-Yin was in Noe Valley and run by two lesbians with whom Psylvia was friendly. The other, Gardener's Cafe, was right up the block on Castro and the guy that started it was a recent flame of Lizzie's. Both places wanted to turn healthy food into works of art. They both wanted their new age hippie customers to regard their new age cuisine as unique and creative and full of *prana* and their prices *very* "responsible."

They both fully intended to operate as "collectives." Right after they paid themselves back their "capital expenses." Nevertheless, both of them *did* exist to make a profit! They were capitalists, for cryin' out loud! And therefore might possibly taint the good name of Hunga Dunga!

Lizzie knew that like all family decisions, it had to be unanimous. One veto meant complete inaction until the vetoer produced some alternatives. The vetoers could keep you in limbo for weeks depending on how many viable alternatives they could come up with. Each "alternative" had to be thoroughly hacked to death and then voted on. Things would stay the same until a decision was made. Depending on how long that took, the decision may as well have been a "no."

Baird put up the biggest stink. Duck and Ellen felt a little uncomfortable with the idea. More than a few, like Bobby, couldn't care less. Lizzie did make the persuasive point that it would really look good for us to be depositing some checks at the bank along with all the food stamps. Besides, Ellen, Tom, and Psylvia had real jobs. Why shouldn't he? This would be his "job." He'd charge a fair mark up. Everyone would benefit. And it would really add to the "mutual funds" that could be "mutually" enjoyed.

Greenleaf was going to have to file taxes anyway, and a few *legitimate* customers would help. To say nothing about the expenses that could be deducted including *depreciation*, *amortization*, and a bunch of other mumbo jumbo. Lizzie kept reminding us that "collective" was *very* close to "communal" both in spirit *and* economics. Just a smidgen behind us on the socioeconomic continuum. Greenleaf could show the way to economically reformat the society gracefully and peacefully. He gave a wonderful performance.

Baird, surprisingly, gave his approval, with an aside that he didn't want to be "Mister Stymie" on this particular issue.

Richard, who loved the idea of being an "accountant" with real clients, was wholeheartedly behind it. For a little twerp whose yodeling made angels cast their light upon his face, a fascination with numbers and money just didn't seem to jive. But most all of us were used to non-sequiturs.

Duck still had reservations and thought the idea was "quasi-capitalistic." He eventually said "yes... *for the time being!*" The rest of us liked the word "collective" and so Lizzie got his way.

Greenleaf's buying habits changed a little, but not much. Not at first. Just more of everything. The restaurants were happy to serve the same kinds of food we'd been buying all along. We could only assume; they were going to prepare it more tantalizingly than most of the communes did. They'd have to if they expected any customers.

What *was* different was that the price of a vegetable or fruit became less important than the guaranteed *availability* of it in a specified quantity. That certainly was not too much to expect from a supplier. It wasn't necessary for it to be a "deal." The restaurants were just going to pass the costs onto their patrons. For us, meaning all the communal households, it was "the best food at whatever price we could afford." Which meant you got whatever you got and you were happy with it. But for the "collectives" as Lizzie insisted on calling them, the motto was simply, "the best food at whatever price it took to supply it." They got what they *wanted* and were *very* happy with it.

We did pay attention to "wish" lists. But now, Lizzie was more on the lookout for exotic leaf vegetables and fruits than he was for crisp lettuce. Finding, discovering, or introducing specialty items became his forte. Lizzie nurtured the friendships of wholesale food importers down at the Market. In time he earned a reputation as being *the* man to see when you wanted the weirdest in foodstuffs. As for the "run of the mill" items, nothing but the best, but in larger quantities.

This of course made more work for both the Hungas and the Dungas. Lizzie insisted that we keep the "Free Food Conspiracy" food separate from what he now called the "Greenleaf" food. For the most part they were the same, except for the delectable "specialty" items. Nevertheless, this meant loading and sorting more of everything.

In addition, the "Greenleaf" food was always delivered first. Even before the Dungas went home to let the Hungas take over. And instead of the restaurant workers coming out to get their food like the communes did, Lizzie persuaded the Dungas to carry it all in and put it on their shelves in their kitchens and storerooms. It started feeling like a "job" job. Like something we should be getting paid for. When Greg made a sarcastic remark to that effect, Lizzie just reminded us that everything he made in profit went into the communal fund, so the only thing that was different was that we all had more of everything.

Nevertheless, some of us were getting confused. I wasn't sure whether I was still working for the Big Benefactor as an agent for The Bureau of the Consistently Well-Fed, or whether in some indefinable way, I was working exclusively for Lizzie. Richard, whom I trusted with my life, assured me that every penny of profit went into the single communal bank account. Still there was something that just didn't seem kosher.

After a few deliveries, however, Yin-Yin and Gardener's became part of the route and therefore part of the routine. Any discomfort the Dungas and Hungas may have felt in the beginning was quickly forgotten by the time they made their way stonily through the rest of the afternoon. It may have not been so easily dismissed if we had known that while Hungas were delivering food, Lizzie, instead of relaxing at home, was out drumming up more commercial business.

I'm not sure whether it was the structure Greenleaf imposed upon many of us, or whether *third-personing* was the reason, but we all became more homebodies. We had always hung out with each other in smaller groups, but now we did more things as a family. The sexual liaisons within the house were fairly stable, and those of us who were still "eligible" often entertained our dates within the confines of the home.

Food was often used as a form of entertaining your date. Home-made ice cream was especially fun to make. We'd decipher the recipes together in the kitchen while family came and went or joined in. The accompanying discussions and conversations were always so quick-witted and enjoyable. And the pay-off was always scrumptious. Both the ice cream *and* often the date.

We played countless games of monopoly and scrabble. Charades was also a favorite. And we started this game called Lists. The first person gave a noun. Like "orange." The next person would repeat "orange" and add another noun like "chair." The next person would say "orange, chair" and add something else. If you couldn't remember one of the words in order, you were out of the game. Usually, people could keep up for the first 10 to 15 words. After that, they started dropping like flies. But a few people, Richard and Duck especially, could go on for what seemed forever. Sometimes the next morning at breakfast, the first words out of either's mouth would be the list from the night before. Then whoever turn it was, would add yet another word. I believe Richard set a record, never to be broken, of 96 words. He was simply amazing. He tried to teach me his pneumonic "trick" but the train of his associative thought followed a track far too circuitous for me.

More popular than Lists, and much less taxing on the cerebrum, was "Hey, boys and girls, let's put on a show." Since there were a number of actors in the house, assigning roles and reading plays aloud was always a winner. Even being in the "audience" was better than watching TV any day.

One night toward the end of the month, Lizzie distributed copies of "The Importance of Being Earnest" by Oscar Wilde. We really got into it and did such a respectable job for a first-time read-through, that Lizzie suggested we actually perform it for the other communes. We turned our living room into a theater. Alvoye and Greg made the sets under Baird's supervision. The rest of us auditioned for roles. Everyone got one, including some who played the opposite sex. Over the next few weeks, rehearsals took up many evenings. When the big night came, the living room was packed, and it was standing room only. As soon as the lights went down and the blue spot came up on the set, there were oohs and aahs. The audience knew they were in for something special. They were. We were a huge hit!

To many of us, the most enjoyable thing we did to amuse ourselves was to make music. Tom was an accomplished guitarist and had a wonderful baritone voice. Bobby had progressed nicely at the piano. I could keep an interesting beat on the bongos and play badly a small flute called a *kena*. Richard harmonized with Tom and everyone could see it got them both high. And he could embellish any tune with his yodeling. I never knew anyone who could break into a yodel in the middle of "Mack the Knife" and make it sound like it belonged there.

No matter. Being a musician was not... I repeat, was not... a criterion for making music. The house was filled with all kinds of instruments. An old clarinet. Many kinds of recorders and flutes. A variety of percussion instruments from around the world, African finger pianos to Balinese gourds. Many of them adorned the walls or tabletops and substituted as decorative folk art. But when Tom got his guitar out, that was usually the signal that music was going to happen, the decorations reverted to their true natures, that of producing sounds.

Psylvia became quite accomplished with the spoons. Ellen made the Indian cymbals shimmer and tremble like frightened bells. Luc played the tuning fork, but it only sounded good when Tom was playing in the key of A. Luc played it regardless of what key Tom was in. Catherine revealed a hidden talent on the concertina. Nicky screeched out notes on the clarinet that made some of us wince, but we wouldn't have had it any other way. Trudy had traded a weaving for a dulcimer, but her gentle music was often lost in the din made by Lizzie who always got carried away when he got his hands on the large tambourine. Baird on more than one occasion wound up taking it away from him, claiming it was a matter of self-preservation.

We were all pleasantly surprised when Maxime picked up his guitar and joined in. We looked at each other but nobody said anything for fear it might make him self-conscious. We did, however, temper the volume at which we were playing in hopes of hearing the music he was making.

He was good. He was very good. Even those that didn't know the first thing about technique could tell. Maybe they got their cue from Tom when he looked over at Maxime and beamed at hearing the riffs Maxime played between the chords Tom was strumming.

After an unorthodox version of "Uncle John's Band" and an even stranger arrangement of "Stairway to Heaven," Tom played a couple of his own songs. He wrote sentimental ballads that fell somewhere in between folk, country, and western. When he finished, we gave him a nice round of appreciative applause. Then, Catherine asked Maxime to play one of his songs. At first, Maxime flashed a look of anger at Catherine for bringing it up. But Lana and Luc started coaxing him. Soon we were all chanting, "We want Maxime! We want Maxime!"

Maxime finger-picked a beautiful intro, and then started strumming chords in one of those minor keys that sounds haunting, yet not depressing. He started singing. His voice was slightly throaty with a rough masculinity. It had character. It set him apart. It worked well for him. It fit his face. None of us could understand the French lyrics, but the emotion came through. And it became obvious, he was no amateur.

When he finished, we applauded wildly, and Maxime blushed and put his hands over his face. Catherine, however, looked exasperated and chided him gently in French. They exchanged a few words before Catherine dropped the whole thing.

"What's the matter?" Lana asked. "I thought he played and sang like an angel!"

"*Mais oui!* Of course he did," Catherine admitted. "Eet eez zhoost I wanted heem to play one of *heez* songs. Instead, he haz sung for you a childreen's song. From when we were babeez. I theenk you call eet, lullabye-bye? *N'e cest pas*? I wanted heem to play zee song he writes *now*, but he eez so, how you say,... stubhorn!" She shook Maxime gently as if he had misbehaved. Lana's entreaties were to no avail. Tom began another song when the phone rang.

"Giacco, it's for you!" Ellen called from the kitchen. "Long distance. From L.A."

Ellen was crouched forward, ready for the gun to go off for the 400-yard relay. She handed the receiver to me, stiff-armed behind her. I grabbed the "baton."

"That's not how it works, Ellen…" I began to explain. But she ignored me, racing into the living room with her arms held high in front of her, "breaking" the ribbon at the "finish line."

I shook my head and said "Hello," into the mouthpiece.

"Giacco! It's Saul! Saul Weinstein! I'm just calling to tell you to get your dancing shoes on!"

CHAPTER 29

June 1971

I hadn't seen Saul since the Free Press fiasco in Venice, so I was surprised when he called, and happy to learn his production company was thriving. Rock festivals were what he did best, and he wanted nothing but the best for the "Celebration of Life," his latest production, and the event that would humble Woodstock, or so he had confidently declared over the phone.

He wanted me to head up "Vibe Control," the psychological arm of "Crowd Control."

"You'll be more than dancing," he said as if it were a plus. "You'll be entirely responsible for maintaining positive vibes! Hiring dancers and jesters, getting flags and banners made, maybe some roving minstrels! Anything you can come up with."

"Well, that sounds like a *godly* chore!" I quipped into the mouthpiece, "a god-awful amount of work, I mean!"

"Delegate! Delegate!" he admonished. "I want you to do it. It'll be cool, you'll see. July 21st through the 28th. But I want you to come down now. We only have six weeks!"

I thought about it no more than a few seconds. "OK, Saul. You got it!"

We agreed that I would fly out immediately. Nicky, Psylvia and Richard would drive down three weeks later in Zwagen. That would give Richard time to teach Lizzie how to keep the books for both Greenleaf and Hunga Dunga. Lizzie's name was added to Richard's as power of attorney so he could deposit the ATD checks.

Saul flew me down to New Orleans. He put me up in a motel near the festival site, and gave me more than an adequate budget for casting, labor, talent, and materials. In addition, he'd pay me 1500 bucks cash after the concert, which of course would go into the land fund.

I liked the idea of "casting" people. It could provide the stuff sexual fantasies are made of well into the next six weeks and beyond. I liked the idea of being in New Orleans for a while. I liked the idea of working with Saul again.

Saul was staying in the same motel, about 15 miles outside of New Orleans on Interstate 10 West. In fact, he had rented the whole second floor which consisted of about 12 rooms. Two connecting rooms served as Celebration's main office. A couple of days before the concert started, we would all move to the festival site, right on the Atchafalaya River, just south of route 10. The motel rooms would then be used exclusively by the performers.

Although the motel was nice, I couldn't fulfill my tasks from the suburbs. So every day I went into the French Quarter trying to accomplish what was turning out to be more of an undertaking than I thought it would be.

The first thing I did was to post notices in all the health food stores, cafes, clubs...

anywhere a few good hippies could be found. I needed to hire dancers, clowns, jugglers. I had to get all of them costumes. I had to get banners and flags made. I had to arrange for backstage passes and meal tickets. I needed help!

Zwagen and the trio arrived just in the nick of time. But there was *no* time to waste! I immediately began to delegate. Now who would be good at keeping track of the expenses? Someone who was more disciplined and organized than me. Like Richard! He should be able to breeze right through it. If there *were* a breeze, any hint of one was at best, sluggish and heavy. And the hippies I interviewed from my "office" in the courtyard were weighing it further down with the smoke of Caribbean marijuana and Lebanese hashish. Even the local swamp grass was potent. Days just seemed to come and go, go and come, in doldrums of delirium.

The fig leaves dripped with humidity. The air in the little piazza was heavy and stagnant. It was so palpable one almost *swam* rather than walked across the courtyard. At least that's how Little Richard appeared as he approached the table. It was as if he was trying to machete, in slow motion, the invisible, yet almost gelatinous substance surrounding him, impeding his progress.

The iced coffee that waited for him on the small glass-topped table spurred him on. But I could have told him it would do little in terms of quenching his thirst. Richard leaned back in the bamboo chair and daintily dabbed, with a Mardi Gras cocktail napkin, little beads of perspiration off his smooth forehead. Nicky and Psylvia made their entrance, listlessly approaching us. They were fanning each other with plastic menus. Psylvia decided it wasn't worth the effort. "My *sweat* is working up a sweat for godsakes!" All three were struggling with the climate of these humid lowlands. I hoped they would get used to it soon because I was counting on their help.

Richard and Nicky were happy to help. In fact they were thrilled to be working a rock concert as part of the crew. They missed Woodstock and they sure as hell weren't about to miss out on this. Psylvia had taken it all in stride and said she was a veteran of every major rock concert that ever happened. Whether or not she had actually attended didn't matter. She was there in spirit. We took her at her word. Sort of.

"Were you at Monterey?" Nicky asked.

"Yes, silly!" Psylvia answered.

"Were you at the Dead concert in Eugene?"

"Of course, Richard!"

"Were you at Woodstock?" I asked.

"You should know, Giacco!" And she winked slowly at me. "Don't you remember?"

I racked my brain but ended up just smiling at her stupidly. She smiled back, but hers seemed to say, "What a dunce you are!"

As hot and sticky as it was, the arrival of Richard, Psylvia, and Nicky was like an Arctic blast to me. Even though they were melting before my eyes, just having them around made me more confident I could pull this off.

Richard loved sitting in the motel's air-conditioned room sorting the receipts I had so far collected, and noting them in a ledger. He'd treat himself late afternoons to a gin and tonic at poolside and then take a "siesta" before the evening's activities started.

Nicky, so handy with tools, got himself a little gig with the company building the stage, so he spent all his days at the site. By the time of the concert, he was golden brown and convinced he could build something grand on the land we would eventually have.

Psylvia, a no-nonsense kind of gal when she wanted to be, or had to be, rented a sewing machine, and single-handedly made seventy-five large banners, exploding with wild colors. Some were adorned with cosmic symbols. Others with tiny mirrors and bangles. Still others were just fun! Saul loved them! He was happy I gave her all the money I might have spent on three or four people.

And I had a fantastic stroke of... dare I say *luck*? Jon would say there's no such thing. Jon would say *karma is as karma does*. OK. I had an average, ordinary, nothing special stroke of not good nor bad, but perfect, karma.

I met Bruttar! He was standing in the middle of Jackson Square. He was wearing loose-fitting "whites" that had been stamped all over with colorful mandalas. His sun-bleached blond hair was neatly braided into two long pigtails. He tossed three, no five, no... seven golden hoops into the air and kept them hovering around his body. He did it effortlessly while chatting with the small circle of onlookers around him.

When he finished his little act, I waited while he scooped up the change and two-or three-dollar bills that had been dropped into his hat. When the hat was empty, I let two more dollar bills drift into it. As they passed his face, he looked up.

"Hey, thanks man!"

"No. Thank *you*!" I said. "I don't know much about juggling, but I know that whenever someone makes something look simple, it probably requires a lot of skill. And I'm so uncoordinated, anybody that can juggle *two* of anything has my attention!"

Bruttar laughed. "Well, really, it only takes practice. But thanks for noticing."

"You also have a terrific way with people. I saw the way you kept them engaged and laughing. That's like adding another seven hoops to the ones you were actually juggling."

He laughed again. "You know, that's really the most difficult part for me. I've got the timing on the hoops down to where it's automatic. But reading the crowd and playing off them, that's where the challenge is!"

"Well, you did a fine job! Everybody walked away smiling." I paused a moment as if I were just coming up with the idea. "So how would you like to work the Celebration of Life festival?"

"You mean it? You serious?"

"Yeah," I was happy to say, seeing he was so excited by the prospect. "You'll get a backstage pass, free meals, and $100 for three days. All you have to do is walk around keeping people upbeat and positive."

"That is far out! Thanks!" And he brought both hands together as if in prayer and lifted them to his forehead. Bowing slightly to me he said, "Om Shivaya!"

He invited me back to his house for tea and a snack. On the way I told him about the job Saul had given me and what I hoped to accomplish. Crowd control and security would be handled by The Devil's Rovers, a local biker gang, ala Hell's Angels. Bruttar made a face at that bit of information but didn't say anything. I was in charge of Vibe Control, but so far, he was the only person I'd hired. I was getting a little nervous. Time was running out and I needed to get at least another 25 or 30 people together. To dance. To clown. To jest. To minstrel.

I was on one of my motor-mouth road trips and didn't try to interpret the sly grin that was altering his pleasant face into an even more pleasant face. I also failed to realize that we had stopped in front of an old, white-washed, one-story warehouse on the edge of the French Quarter.

"Here we are," Bruttar announced as he walked up the two steps to the large wooden door. As we entered, I noticed a small hand-carved nameplate under the mailbox. It read "Wayside of the Maitreya Buddha." "Giacco," Bruttar said, motioning me past him into the room, "Welcome to the *WOMB!*"

Inside consisted of just one enormous room and two smaller ones on either end. I guessed they were the kitchen and the bathroom. The furnishings were scant. In less than a minute, everything could be removed, leaving a space adequate for a volleyball tournament or widget manufacturing. Everything was white. The table, the chairs, the walls, the wooden floor. The 10 or so people inside were also in white. Except their "pajamas," like Bruttar's, were decorated with colorful mandalas. For a split second I remembered with a pang, Dennis and the Self-Immolation happening in New York. A few mandalas stamped on the walls and furnishings, a few frogs croaking, and the people would have disappeared.

A couple of them looked up at us when we came in, but then went about their business. Bruttar called to a young girl across the room. "Lissam, would you please make us a pot of some ginseng tea? And is there any zucchini bread left?" Lissam, a young girl in her preteens, looked up and smiled. As she left the room for the kitchen, Bruttar added, "Thank you darlin' Lissam."

Though he was polite, I couldn't help thinking that Bruttar held some kind of patriarchal position with this group. His request of Lissam was more of a directive than a sentence that ended in a question mark. I was right.

Bruttar was the head honcho, the founder, the spiritual leader of what I came to regard as more of a cult than a commune. They were followers of Maitreya Buddha, the Buddha to Come. And in their own Bruttar-fabricated way, were as zealous of the Buddha's Second Coming as any born-again Christian was of Jesus.

Fortunately, they followed none of the moral strictures imposed by Fundamentalist Christians on their "weak sinners." In fact, in many ways they were very much like Hunga

Dunga. Ingesting lots of dope and psychedelics, organic vegetables, and sexual secretions. Lissam was Bruttar's daughter, yet it was obvious he had more than a brotherly relationship with a "devotee" he called Sareem.

The Waysiders, as they were known in the neighborhood, followed a path that combined Theravada Buddhism, Cherokee animism, and Creole voodoo. When I remarked that their habitat and clothing seemed spartan in contrast to such a rich blend of spiritual beliefs, Bruttar explained it was the Buddhism that dominated their *external* appearance but warned me that the voodoo and animism was equally influential in their lives. In fact, all their names were combinations of East Indian, American Indian, and African words. When I inquired who gave them their names, Bruttar said matter-of-factly that he did. "Bruttar" he said, leaning over to me and looking deep into my eyes, "means 'the Revealer.'"

As we sipped the hot tea, Bruttar explained that their path was one of discipline, work, and perfection of the physical body. Enlightenment was but a ruse. Only when the Maitreya Buddha returned, could anyone even begin to "pray for redemption." Therefore, there was no need to get all bogged down in austerities and self-flagellating rules and regulations. Just be "ready" when the Buddha returns.

It sounded contradictory, talking about discipline and work in one sentence, and then disparaging conventional codes of conduct in another. That is until I learned the "work" he referred to would be regarded by many as "fun."

The entire family were street performers. They could all tumble and juggle. To varying degrees of expertise, they could all dance and make music. Sareem did a clown act at the Children's Hospital. Now I understood the reason for the grin on Bruttar's face when we were walking to his home. The whole family made their living as performers, on the nearby streets of the French Quarter, at renaissance fairs, county fairs, and civic events. The tourists of Jackson Square were, however, their whole-grain bread and unsalted butter.

Bruttar clapped his hands. "Everyone gather 'round. We're going to have a family meeting." Well, this sounded familiar. But when they were all assembled, I realized their family meetings were far different than ours. There was little discussion. Just dictates from Bruttar, one of which was that his family suggest ideas.

"We are all going to work the Celebration of Life festival," Bruttar announced. "But we need more artists and performers. Sareem, this afternoon I want you to go down to Jackson Square and do some recruiting. You know them all. Just get the good ones… and the *reliable* ones. Make sure you get that bluegrass trio that's always on the corner of St. Ann and Chartres. And the dying swan lady. You know, the one who does farce ballet. She's a riot! Gotta get her!"

Lissam suggested some fortune tellers and magicians. Bruttar concurred enthusiastically. Then Bruttar turned to me. "Can I assume we can offer these people the same deal you offered me? I'm not being too presumptuous, am I? I mean, if it seems like I'm taking over… well, just speak up!"

"That's fine," I said. "I've got a budget left that will handle thirty-five people. So just try to make sure the list you come up with is no more than that. Including yourself."

"Don't worry about a thing," Bruttar said. And I knew without a doubt that I didn't have to.

From then until the day before the concert, I was with the Waysiders every afternoon and often joined them for dinner. In fact, I spent quite a few nights crashing at their place. The main room was turned into a rehearsal hall. Rather more like a circus. There might be as many as five acts going on at the same time. I was more than impressed with the acrobatic routines and the juggling. The bluegrass band was a knock-out. The "wash-board, oil can, cross-cut saw" player was a band unto himself. The crowds would love them.

But I was most touched when one night, Bruttar lowered the lights and turned on some colored spots hung from the rafters. He opened the back door and motioned them in. "This is all Lissam's doing," he stage-whispered to me.

Into the room paraded eleven fairies, elves, and pixies. Boys and girls, friends and neighbors of Lissam's, costumed in joyous creations worthy of a Nutcracker Suite. They all rattled bells or tambourines or blew heartily through kazoos and slide whistles. The kids paraded around us, dancing and skipping and weaving through us. The adults instinctively made a row of arches under which the little parade passed. It gave me goose bumps. How could anyone be bummed out after seeing them? Saul and I were going to get even better than we expected, or for my part, deserved. The Waysiders of the Maitreya Budda had surpassed my expectations.

The day before the festival started, Nicky, Richard, Psylvia, and I went out to the site to find a nice place backstage to set up a camp. Afterwards, I told Richard I had to drive into town and give Bruttar the backstage passes Saul had finally, at the last minute, printed up. Richard, really psyched because of all I had told him about these people, insisted on coming with me.

When Richard met Bruttar, he, with no hesitation whatsoever, went up to him and rubbed his tummy. Richard was an instant hit with everyone, especially Bruttar, who said Richard had such an enormous soul, even a blind person could see it!

The Waysiders had just finished dinner but offered us some anyway. We said we were fine, but a pretty woman called Jhira insisted we have some dessert. Then Sareem took a chillum out of a drawer and loaded it with hash. It only had to make the circle once to do the trick.

"Before I get too wasted," I said to Bruttar, "here's the passes you'll need to get in. Use the backstage gate with the big number 9 on it. Get there early and have your people camp out front, where the action is. Make sure you're in the thick of things. Oh, and here…" I handed him a cashier's check for 3500 dollars. "I'm really not supposed to pay you until after the festival is over. But you know how crazy these things can get. And well… just in case we leave right after the show."

"Brother Giacco," Bruttar said, his eyes red and watery from the hashish, "you trust us."

"Implicitly!" I said.

"You love us," he said, stating it as a fact.

"You got that right!" I said. And they all laughed like the kids they were.

"Now I have something to give *you*, my friend." And Bruttar stood up to leave the room. "This may take a while, so just relax. Sareem, load them up another pipe." And he headed for the back door.

"Where are you going?" I asked.

"I'm going to meditate on your new name!"

"I want one too! I want one too!" Little Richard practically squealed in childlike desire.

Bruttar laughed. "But Richard. Finding people's true names isn't a minor matter. I have to know the person for a while. I have to be connected to them. Only then is the name revealed to me."

Richard looked glum and forced his mouth into a pout.

Bruttar laughed some more. "OK. OK. I'll give it a whirl. Actually, I feel as if I've known you for lifetimes… and there *is* no doubt we're connected somehow." Then he walked out and let the back door slam behind him. We could still see him in the light of the full moon making his way toward a stand of magnolia trees.

"Would you do the honors?" Sareem asked as he passed me the chillum and struck a match.

About a half hour later, Bruttar walked in. He looked exhausted. His shirt was off and sweat poured down his chest. You could see it pounding. He placed his hands upon his knees and rested there bent over, like a runner just finishing a marathon. Then when his breath was more regular, he walked over to us and said, "Richard. Your real name is Zietar!"

Richard looked up at Bruttar. "Zietar?" He pondered it out loud. "Zietar. Zietar." He pronounced it a couple of ways. "Zie*tar*… *Zie*tar! I like it! I like it a lot! Does it mean anything, Bruttar?"

Bruttar, his eyes still glazed from the recent trance or whatever mental state it was that he had entered, said, "Zietar means *he who warbles like a bird*."

Richard took that in, and his face betrayed just a little disappointment. Then after further rumination, he grinned in delight. I thought the name was right on and was a little in awe at its appropriateness. Bruttar had never heard Richard sing… or yodel! That made my anticipation to hear my new name increase.

Bruttar took a few steps closer to me, sat down on his haunches, looked me in the eyes, and said very solemnly, "Giacco. Your real name is… Chazan! And from here on you shall be called by that name!"

"Chazan," I repeated, stretching the "z." "It's beautiful, Bruttar. I like it. I like it. It sounds so hot… yet smooth. Nice! What does it mean?"

When Bruttar answered, I felt like the number one pin, just as the bowling ball strikes.

"Chazan means," he said, pausing theatrically, "The Poet-Warrior."

Winds of Topanga and echoes of Reverend Trey circled my head! This was the second time I'd been told that my real name meant The Poet-Warrior. I was speechless. Maybe it was the second round of hash, but I felt light-headed and dizzy up until the time we left. At the front door, Bruttar, Sareem, Zietar, and myself, now *Chazan*, huddled together in a tight circle, our heads bent touching one another's. Then Bruttar, very calmly and deliberately, gave me a kiss on the lips. I couldn't find the words to express my true emotions. I just looked at Bruttar, hoping he could read my mind.

Richard rolled his eyes, looked back at Sareem and Bruttar as he descended the two steps, and said, "*Everything* is needless to say!"

When we got back to the motel, Psylvia and Nicky were packing for our move the next day to the festival site. Richard told them of our new names. They both laughed, much to Richard's chagrin, but from then on, they often called us *Zietar* and *Chazan*, much to the rest of Hunga Dunga's chagrin.

Later, when Jon and Rosie learned of our names, they always called Richard *Zietar* or *Ziets*. But Jon refused to call me anything other than Giacco. Only when he mocked me for having said something spiritually pretentious, would he call me *Chazan*! But that soon passed, and he used the names interchangeably like everyone else.

The next morning when I looked out the window, there were already four or five buses and about seven semis. I wondered which groups they belonged to. The line-up of performers over the next few days was mind-boggling. An alphabet soup of bands. Neil Young, Canned Heat, Country Joe MacDonald, Pink Floyd, Paul Simon, Taj Mahal, on and on. The swimming pool was full of new arrivals, trying to cool off and waste time until their rooms were vacated and cleaned so they could move in.

We were all packed and ready to leave, but the pool looked inviting, and I knew once the festival began, it was unlikely I'd get any swimming in. I threw on a pair of trunks and ran down the two flights of stairs to the pool and without hesitating, dove in.

When I surfaced, I saw a dark-haired, Mediterranean-looking face, bobbing a few feet away.

"Hey! Don't I know you?" I yelled above the sound of the other guys in the pool having a splashing fest.

"Probably," he answered with a hint of disdain in his voice.

I studied him quickly and then said, "I know you! You're Cat Stevens! I really enjoy some of your..." But before I could finish my compliment, he turned away from me and swam toward the shallow end of the pool. As he pulled himself up, I admired his compact body and the way his baggy trunks clung to his ass. His hair was slicked straight down from the water. I thought he looked better wet than dry. I started swimming toward the shallow end, but by that time he was halfway up the walk to the motel office.

I yelled to him. "Are you leaving?"

He turned brusquely and yelled back, "Am I getting smaller?"

"Well, I guess I'm not on *his* Peace Train," I said to no one in particular.

"Don't mind him," a red-headed face said behind me. I turned around. "I'm his drummer. He's just tense. He always gets this way before a concert. Besides that, he doesn't feel just right about this gig. He keeps insisting something's wrong, but he doesn't say more than that."

"Well, there's nothing to worry about," I said confidently and in-the-know. "I've been working on this festival for six weeks, and I *know* everything's under control. The vibes are going to be the highest!"

I started telling him about Saul's Vibe *Control* and the great people I had hired. But Richard, I mean *Zietar*, was yelling at me to get into Zwagen and "let's get going!" He threw me a towel and my clothes. Then he hustled me into the back seat of the Bug and slid in beside me. Nicky threw the car into gear and Psylvia handed me a cup of coffee and a muffin. It wasn't until we were over Lake Pontchartrain that I slipped out of my damp trunks and slipped on some jeans.

CHAPTER 30

June 1971

The festival site was a wasteland. Maybe "fallow" would be a kinder word, but the 120 acres or so Saul rented from some local agribusiness guy, gave no hint that it was going to rejuvenate itself anytime soon. It stretched, flat, eroded, and dead, but not vacant. Hundreds, maybe thousands of young settlers had already arrived. Some scoped out campsites. Others had already kicked back and were partying. And a good majority just wandered aimlessly, like *I* was doing.

The only natural feature that kept the festival site from being a perfectly boring rectangle was its western boundary which followed the curve of the Atchafalaya River. At least here a few trees and bushes grew with lots of grasses along the water. Here, there was shape and variation and it was easy to look at.

The bluff above the river sloped steeply twenty feet or so to the shore, its flanks redder-brown than they usually were, dampened by the brief but measurable showers earlier in the day. Rains would come and go during the next few days, sometimes so hard the pellets of water hurt the skin. But right now, in just a flash, the sun threw open its cloudy trench coat and lewdly exposed itself in all its Southern glory. The sun began to suck the moist earth dry. You could see it in the aroused breaths of steam that rose a few inches into the air and disappeared.

Sluicing through the steam on their way to the river, two male bodies whizzed by. Small groups of people were gathering to watch them as they greased up the bank with river water, ran to the top, and threw themselves onto the slippery ooze. One was naked. The other in his underpants. Their bodies were streaked with mud. They looked like they were from some primitive jungle tribe in the Amazon basin.

The river was the same color as the embankment. The current was impressively swift. So much so that when one of the guys splashed into the raging tepid water, and swam back to shore, he was at least 40 feet downstream from where he started. Rather than cleanse his body of the mud, the dark brown water seemed to simply gouache it all over him more evenly. All in all, it was one of the ugliest waterways I've ever seen. Yet everything does have its beauty.

The slide into the river provided something close to a teflon coating. And after 10 or 12 slides, the young men had sculpted a ceramic-smooth, very slick body sled course that ramped up just right at the bottom. It would fling stoned and euphoric born-again aborigines far out into the shit-brown rapids. Many of the growing crowd of onlookers stripped down to nothing and tested the ride, whooping and hollering in glee.

I recognized immediately that this satin slide into a swirling river, dense with the run-off of silt, chemicals and cow dung, would likely be one of the highlights over the next few days. This would be a hallowed spot. That should have been an indication of things to come.

I looked behind me. The flat acreage was already sprouting clumps of colorful hippies. The clumps would grow and spread through the night until by mid-morning the next day, there was a luxuriant field of flower children, though the press used words like "bedraggled bums" and "thickets of imaginatively squalid campsites."

After running into Bruttar, we changed our plans and decided to camp out near the Waysiders, smack in the middle of this field that was blooming almost *too* vibrantly. We could always use our backstage passes if we wanted to get away from the crowds. We could abandon the miniature shanty towns for the relative comforts of the trailers and RV's backstage. Or so we thought.

Psylvia recruited some stagehands to help her hang flags and banners. The Waysiders had everything so much under control that I found myself with time on my hands. Saul asked me to work backstage with him, at least for the first day, to help with any last minute snafus.

At 2:30 PM on the 23rd of June, Saul stepped out on stage to welcome the frighteningly large, boisterous, and increasingly impatient crowd. He was glad the height of the stage, the cyclone fence in front of it, and the leathered "security guards" from the Devil's Rovers lined up in front of that, separated him from the huddled masses.

Gatherings such as these, even if well-organized, had a way of taking on a life of their own. Saul knew better than most that the mood set on the first day of a rock festival was all important, and this one was already starting two days late! He had been trying to secure a site, was refused, and hassled with permits, licenses, insurance, and the IRS. These were the last things he needed to deal with right now! The crowd had approached fifty thousand! If they weren't constantly entertained, they could turn mean.

When he took the microphone out of its stand, they settled… well, certainly not *down*… but enough to cue Saul to start speaking. After taking care of some practical business (where the toilets were, drinking water, *pick up your litter!* etc.) Saul explained the "house rules." The ones absolutely no one follows. The ones meant more for the ears of local authorities than the tens of thousands of young, psychedelicized bodies jockeying for position as far up front as possible.

Saul tried to adopt a voice that sounded nonchalant, the voice of someone who, because he just trusted everyone to be reasonable and well-behaved, expected the rules to be obeyed and their importance appreciated. Like… "And remember kids! *Absolutely* no drugs or alcohol of any kind, shape, or form! And *absolutely* no nudity or lewd conduct."

A collective snicker tumble-weeded toward the stage. Saul had expected it and just let it roll by. He had only put so much emphasis on the "absolutely" because he noticed the Martin County Sheriff shooting looks at him. The looks said in a very southern drawl… *You know if it were up to me, bubba, no way would you be here in this goddam field!*

The crowd was getting antsy again. Saul motioned to someone offstage. Music started blaring through the loudspeakers. The crowd jumped and roared. Then they realized it was just a recording. Saul tried to enthuse the crowd by screaming out at the top of his lungs the lineup for the coming days.

The list contained a few bands of national recognition interspersed evenly with the "others." The others included a few groups that had gotten songs on the charts, but not very high, and some regionally popular groups. There was no mention of the really *big* names that were rumored to be showing up. The Stones. The Dead. For the two weeks before the festival, word on the street was that even the Beatles were going to drop in unannounced. No one officially connected with the festival did anything to quash the rumors. I myself believed them. After all, Saul had promised this would top Woodstock.

Even though Saul spiked the VU meters when he called out the few well-known names, it became increasingly clear to the crowd that the bulk of the music they were going to hear would be made by big fish in a small pond. Some people take that personally.

As if reading their collective thoughts, Saul started emphasizing the "true spirit" of the gathering and often invoked the name of *Woodstock*, almost challenging the crowd to rise to the consciousness of that occasion. This was not just a "celebration of music." Oh no, it was far more substantial than *that!* It was a "Celebration of *Life*!" and he urged people to "trip out" on the beauty that is their neighbor.

Nevertheless, Saul would have been smarter to open the festival with one of the few headliners he'd booked rather than with a local bluegrass band. When he announced them, there was only scant applause.

They weren't bad. At least there was music, and they kept the crowd amused. When Saul climbed down the metal stairs at the far end of the stage, I was waiting for him. His forehead was wet with sweat. When he crinkled his forehead, drops fell past his eyes onto his cheeks as if he were wringing out the washcloth of his mind. He seemed on the verge of a breakdown.

"What was that all about?" I asked him.

"It's worse than you think," he said. "Everyone's backing out. You know that list I just screamed out?" I nodded yes. "Well, I'm not even sure about some of *them*!" And he let himself grab the railing for support.

"But I thought all these groups were already booked! A done deal! Contracts! How can they do that?" I said in disbelief.

"Well, ya know, Giacco," Saul said with a little *I've been a bad boy* guilt in his voice, "a lot of these groups sign intent contracts, but their lawyers write them up so they're not really binding. They put in these contingency clauses that they can invoke whenever they want. They see how things are going and depending on that, sometimes the decision to appear or not is really a last-minute thing."

Saul continued explaining and making excuses. I let him ramble. I looked at him with real concern and I could see what really happened. Saul bit off more than he could chew. This would be the biggest production he had ever done. And to keep his confidence up, he turned a *maybe* into a *yes*. *We'll think about it* and *sounds great* into *you've got a deal!*

No wonder he'd been frantic the past week. Phone calls to L.A. and New York all hours of the night and day. Lawyers. Managers. Promoters. So much *schmoozin'* trying to finalize things. The week before that it was all County Commissioners, Sheriffs, and Police Chiefs and the haranguing from a multi-level scam of bureaucrats that made Amway seem one-dimensional. Hassles to be sure, especially when they came at the last minute, but nothing that having your money hobnob with the right folks couldn't fix.

But the rock groups. They were different. They were fucking temperamental *artists*. Half the time they wanted to be the vanguard into the new age, where principles were more important than money, and their fans would follow them to the ends of the earth because they were so in the "know." Those times you had to prove you were "one righteous dude" before they'd allow their name to be associated with yours, a scuzzy businessman.

The rest of the time they wanted to be treated like prima donnas... with deference and respect... and tested you to see how much you *really* wanted them to play at your *little* festival by making you cater to their every whim and run a gauntlet of petty, demeaning, and servile errands to prove your desire. Of course, you always picked up the tab! "Allow me!"

On the phone, Saul always sounded and looked so composed and together. But *now* I could see right through his skin, and it wasn't a pretty sight. There as plain as day, was a seething, boiling, globulating mass of viscera. Spumes of gases erupted continually while rivulets of carnivorous acids, roller-coasted around his throbbing innards. Poor Saul!

I felt especially bad because I knew that there wasn't a speck of greed motivating Saul. He wasn't doing all this for the money. It wasn't a con. He believed in the Magic. He thought by a sheer act of will, he could get the wheels spinning and magic would take over. Everything would just come together. Even at the last moment. Just as it always had before. Just as it had at Woodstock. Just believe it, act as if it's going to happen... and it will!

When I stepped out of Saul's shoes back into my own, he was still jabbering. Something about not enough toilets and the river being dangerous. A *whump, whump, whump* from up above was drowning out his words. It was the helicopter Saul had hired to ferry the "headliners" from the Motel to the site.

Saul looked up, shielding his eyes from the intense afternoon sun. "Thank God! It's Cat Stevens!" Then he turned to me. "If we can just get through tonight... I'm sure everything will work out. If I can just get Cat to play a really long set. I'm going to see what I can work out." He about-faced and headed toward the heli-pad just beyond where the trucks were parked. He had only taken a few hurried strides when he turned around and yelled to me. "You can check back with me later. Go on. Go out there and enjoy yourself while you can!"

CHAPTER 31

June, 1971

I left the relative security of backstage and made my way around the edges of the crowd. I could feel a huge organism taking on a life of its own, a life that was different from the one at Woodstock.

Why? What is it that influences the psyche of a mob? What kind of progeny springs from the womb of a throng inseminated with sex, drugs, rock 'n' roll... and alcohol!

Lots and lots of alcohol!

That's what was different. Or at least one of the things. Every other blanket and straw mat had a bottle of something on it. Cheap wine in gallon jugs. Expensive Bordeaux in long, thin, delicate bottles. A golden fifth of Tequila guarding a paper plate with lemon wedges circling a mound of salt. Southern Comfort and Jack Daniels seemed to give even hippies from the north a southern drawl. If you could view the scene from one of the helicopters hovering above, it would look like a Pollock patchwork quilt of bright blankets, tie-dyed sheets, and lots and lots of bottles!

As I passed the group squatting around the Tequila, a young boy, no more than fifteen or so, looked up at me as he licked salt off the side of his thumb. We stared at each other just briefly, though for him the moment may have been timeless. His face was thin and his cheeks sallow, but his blue eyes shone brightly around his very dilated pupils. For a split-second, he melted into my young friend Bobby from New York, and I wondered about him and Monique and other friends I hadn't seen or heard from for so long.

The skinny teen broke into a big, stupid grin and raised his fist in a power-to-the-people salute. He brought it down into my dangling hand and I felt his fist open and leave something behind in my palm. It was tiny, brown, and barrel-shaped. Acid, I presumed. Without hesitation, I threw it in my mouth. As I nodded thanks and walked on, I could taste the bitterness as it dissolved under my tongue. I wondered what it had been cut with.

I walked the periphery of the site, just at the edges where you didn't have to step over anyone to make progress. Once, I glimpsed Lissam and her elves snake-dancing through the crowd. They were maneuvering around sheaves of swaying bodies. You might think the crowd was inebriated with the music, but I've never known bluegrass to do that. I hoped it was the music and not the drink. One of the swaying bodies, a beer-bellied, scraggly-haired man, stumbled and bumped into Lissam. She fell into three pairs of outstretched hands that caught and righted her. The drunken lout who tripped her, for that's what I decided he was, threw her a dirty grin and I could sense Lissam's nervousness. He laughed. She led her parade away at a slightly faster clip.

I was starting to come on to the acid. I took a deep breath and tried to relax my walk. Then I thought of Jon and took the next few steps toe to heel. That immediately put me into a more manageable frame of mind. I took a sharp right and headed for the river.

The banks were now completely dry except for the sluice where one wet naked body after another swiftly catapulted into the rain-gorged river. The brown rapids in the middle seemed ravenous, yet each body tried to outdo the previous one by catching more air at the bottom and hurling themselves farther out. I sat about twenty feet away and went on a trip.

The procession of bodies shooting by hypnotized me until they were almost a blur, an action photo taken at a low f stop. I would have been totally mesmerized except it seemed every five or six bodies that streaked by caused a spark of recognition. It happened every time this one particular guy slid by. I tried to focus my eyes and my brain. The next time he came around I latched on and followed him as he drifted downstream.

Mud sucked up to his calves as he tried to climb back onto the bank. A beautiful hishi necklace of red coral and white clam shell was his only adornment. The water dripped off his hair. It was dirty blond. Either that or it was very blond but really dirty. I couldn't tell.

As he scrambled up the bank and approached the top, I carefully and methodically looked him over. I couldn't decide if I was zeroing in on this guy because I actually knew him, or because he was just striking the right sexual chords in me, and I wanted to believe I knew him. Or did it matter? The acid alone was excuse enough to be staring so hard. I didn't need any others.

He felt the stare. He looked around trying to find where it was coming from. He must be tripping, I thought. Could he really be so sensitive on the natch? I decided his ESP was the result of acid in the antennae. When he looked in my direction, the sun caught him full on his face so there were no shadows on it at all. Except one. Above the hishis, above the chin. A tiny shadow fell across his upper lip. A dent in the flesh? A cut? A small but disfiguring scar?

He caught my gaze and his face dissolved from perplexity into disbelief and finally, elation. Or was that my face?

I stood up and called out, "Michael!"

"Giacco!" He yelled back over the crowd at the top of the chute. While he made his way toward me, I could hear him talking out loud... "Far fucking out! Very, very, far... distant... remote... out in space... light years fucking out. Too much! Too fucking much!"

By that time, he grabbed me and pressed me to his chest, and didn't lessen the tightness of the hug for a good two minutes or however long eternity is. And I hugged back just as tight. We just stood there, very close. We felt each other's hearts beat against our chests. The beat was fast. We slowed our breaths, deepening and lengthening them. I knew he was tripping. I could tell because we were breathing in precise synchronization and we both *knew* we were doing it. We were consciously enjoying it. A consciousness too rare to attain without the help of a catalyst. In this case a chemical. Feeling each other's chests rise and fall in unison, we enjoyed letting our breaths slow down, and our hearts relax, and our grips on each other loosen, and we even let out a long sigh at exactly the same time as we stepped away from each other.

I was flattered when I saw his erection. But then, I had clothes on and mine could be taken for a big fold in my baggy pants. I could afford the luxury of being flattered without being embarrassed. He didn't realize he was standing at attention until he followed my eyes to see what I was looking at.

"Uh-oh!" he said as his eyes met mine and he let me know he fully understood the situation: that he was completely naked and had this beautiful boner that just would not go down. People were staring at it, yet he didn't panic. He wasn't even embarrassed! Far from it. Instead, he started laughing, turned on his heels, waved his arms in the air, tossed his shaggy mane and yelled, "C'mon. Follow me!" He reminded me of Trigger, rearing up and pawing the air before taking off for the chase.

He galloped a few yards past the slide and then started to trot in a spiral pattern. I thought he was tripping out again until I realized he was honing in on where he thought he had left his clothes. A great strategy I had to admit. Without breaking stride, he targeted an old, beat-up rucksack with the heels of some sneakers poking through, snagged one strap as neatly as the brass ring on a carousel, and made a bee-line for the sluice.

My feet were practically on top of his head as we schussed into the Atchafalaya. When our heads bobbed to the surface, we were already twenty feet downstream. The swirling currents were as strong as they looked from the top of the bluff. The water, though not really refreshing, was cool enough to take the heat out of our groins and shrink our genitals. But instead of immediately swimming for shore, Michael motioned me to keep going. We were thirty yards or so past the place where most people disembarked before Michael headed toward the bank. We swam as hard as we could directly for the shore, me with my clothes still on, Michael holding his pack in one hand. We were another hundred feet downstream before we climbed out.

I plopped down on my back in what was the closest thing to a clearing in the middle of some light green bushes. The sudden warmth of the sun made me shiver. Michael dragged himself on top of me and just rested there, breathing heavily, catching his breath. The weight of him felt good but then the tiny stones and twigs under my back asserted their presence. I wriggled trying to accommodate them.

"Why didn't you ever answer my letters and postcards?" I asked while his wonderful body slithered around mine.

"What letters? I never got any!"

"The ones I sent to your aunt's address," I said.

"Aunt Pearl died last summer. Maybe they cancelled her post office box," he answered. "I should've checked into that," Michael said. "I was thinking maybe after telling you about my suicidal family, you didn't want anything to do with me!"

"Oh brother, the exact opposite! I want everything to do with you!" And then I worried that that kind of talk might scare him off.

Instead, he kissed me deep and long, letting me know he liked hearing that kind of talk. "I'm sorry I didn't try harder to get in touch. Don't really have an address to give you. My life is a mess, Giacco."

Then he sat astride me and pulled off my shirt. "But we're here together now. That's all that matters!"

He untied the drawstring and loosened my pants. I lifted my hips an inch or two as he pulled them off me. Then he hovered over me, holding his body a few inches above mine, as if about to do a pushup. The isometric pose presented the same well-defined, buffed body I remembered. I would have been as thrilled had he gotten soft and acquired a spare tire. It was the look in his eyes and his smile and who he was that pressed my buttons.

By the time he lowered himself and covered the length of my body with his own, his cock was in the same position it was when he was last seen on top of the bluff. Only this time there were no admirers standing by except me. I was equally excited. A few gyrations and we were both at the brink. He interlocked his fingers with mine and extended my arms above my head. The bottoms of his feet pushed hard against the tops of mine. He kissed me deeply, and we fought each other to see who could probe the deepest. I opened my eyes and saw that his were open as well. Suddenly I could feel the muscles in his thighs tighten and his breath quicken. A look of surprise flashed across his eyes just before he squeezed them shut, followed by a spasm and a moan.

"Oh, man!" he said lifting himself up, parting our chests, but leaving the rest of us intact. "Phew! That was intense!" And then somewhat apologetically, "even if it was pretty quick!"

"Listen, man," I said, rubbing his chest and pinching a nipple, "When you gotta shoot, you gotta shoot! And wow, that was some load!"

Michael laughed, sat on his haunches, and studied me. Then he leaned back on his elbows, spun himself around, and scooted like a nine-year-old in a crab race to the river's edge. He slid in up to his waist and watched the ripples he made join the current. I joined him.

We splashed water on each other and scrubbed each other with handfuls of mud we scooped from the bank. We didn't say a word. We took our time. I'm not sure about Michael, but I felt I was starting to peak on the acid. I could feel the water rushing around my buttocks, breaking its flow into little swirling eddies. Michael navigated the wake of my body like a kayaker trying to paddle upstream. My thoughts left me entirely until I became aware that Michael had turned us around 180 degrees, and I found myself standing in *his* wake.

"You turn me on!" Michael seemed genuinely embarrassed and laughed.

"Michael," I said a little embarrassed myself, "I just have to *think* about you, and I get hard! Look ma, no hands!"

"Well then, I hope you don't think about me too much in public!" We both cracked up. Michael let himself drift into me. He wrapped his legs around my waist. I helped him remain buoyant by cradling his butt. I confessed, "When we made love those few days in San Francisco, there were times I worried I would be too quick. I was so excited, and I wanted to make it last as long as possible! I used to have to think of weird things or words, make up absurd mantras, repeating them over and over trying to control myself."

"I *know*," Michael said. "I was just *doing* the same thing before, trying to control myself, by thinking of other things."

"Like what kinds of things?" I asked him. "Give me an example."

He paused and then said candidly but nervously, "Usually I think of my brother Dennis." Michael looked at me and must've decided *I* needed support. He unwrapped his legs, planted his feet firmly in the river bottom, and this time kept *me* buoyant.

The mention of the name was like a cue to fall under a hypnotic spell. I de-atomized instantaneously and materialized in the East Village loft. I heard the croaking of frogs. I saw the smile on Dennis' face just before he turned and flew out the window. Michael knew where I had gone and brought me back with a snap of his fingers and a voice barely audible above the sound of the river.

"I know you knew him. I know you were with him when he killed himself. I found out a few weeks after I got back to Nebraska. I was going through a box of my father's stuff and came across a postcard Dennis had sent him. He mentioned a 'Giacco' he was staying with. Don't ask me how I knew... but I *knew*... I knew for certain that it was *you*! And that *you* were probably with him when he died.

"At first it got me mad. Maybe I was jealous. I know it sounds crazy or something, but I picture you and him getting it on. I know you two must've done it. Anyway, that's what I was thinking about when I was trying not to cum. Because it gets me so jealous. But you know what? It only excited me more. Now figure that one out!"

"I don't want to figure it out," I told him, trying not to let the acid impede my ability to communicate. "But for the record, your brother and I never got it on. And I didn't give him the acid… though it very well could've been me if he'd waited 'til the weekend. And I didn't tell you in San Francisco because you were such a mess, what with your dad committing suicide and all. I was still trying to come to grips with what all this meant... the feelings I had for you… the strange connection… and…"

"It's OK. It's OK," Michael said squeezing me a little tighter to him. "And for the record, Pop didn't commit suicide. He tried, but he failed. Like he did at everything else. Especially trying to raise his sons to be like him… or at least the him *he* wanted to be, but never was. He died six weeks later. From a heart attack. If he'd had a clue, he wouldn't have made it *that* long!"

I didn't really know what to say.

Clue? A clue to what?

It's very difficult to carry on a conversation when you're on LSD. It's hard to remember what someone's said from one sentence to the next. Or even what you *yourself* last said. Eventually I spoke, hoping that the words coming out of my mouth might fall somewhere in the neighborhood of what we were talking about. It wouldn't have been important to me except this was Michael waiting for me to say something and I really liked this guy.

"Still, I should've told you as soon as I realized..."

"Forget it!" Michael insisted. "Besides, I meant it literally when I said, 'now go figure that one out!' Now that I know you two didn't get it on, it makes things even more complicated!"

I dropped my feet to the river bottom but kept my hands on his shoulders. "I'm sorry Michael, but I'm lost. What is it I'm supposed to figure out?"

"Now I don't know who I'm really jealous of. You… or Dennis."

I was losing it. "One more time, Michael. Run that by me again"

"Don't you get it? Are you really going to make me spit it out?"

I waited for the spit. It flew at me. A big wad of it.

"Dennis is the one who brought me out. More than *out*. We were *lovers*, for chris'sake!

My own brother! Not just fuck buddies. *Lovers*!"

I accepted the information without surprise, shock, judgment, or disbelief. I simply took it at face value. I don't think Michael would have told me if he'd expected anything less. He got a lot more. I felt something very deep and molecular. It may have been unconditional love. If so, it's a nice feeling. But I just stared at him and said nothing.

I imagined Michael and Dennis sharing the upstairs bedroom of an old frame farmhouse. It's 10:00 PM. Pop is watching TV. He's already sent Michael to bed. It's a school night. Dennis is two years older and a junior in high school. He gets to stay up later. But he leaves when Pop picks up a photo of Mom and pours another drink.

When Dennis walks into the bedroom, the lights are out, but he knows Michael is feigning a restless sleep. Dennis takes off his clothes, pulls back the covers, and gently slides in next to his brother. They lie still for a while, and then they make love. What was rough and rivaled wrestling a couple of years ago, is now practiced and athletic sex. By the time Dennis leaves for college, the sex matures into a love much richer than brotherly.

"Giacco! Michael to Giacco! Still with me?"

The reverie lasted but a moment, yet I saw it in great detail. "That's incredible!" I said when I came to. "The whole idea of it! It's incredibly beautiful!"

"You really think so? You don't think it's sick or perverted?"

"No way, man! I think it's wonderful. I think it's perfect. And don't let anyone tell you differently, Michael! What you and Dennis had is rare and… I don't know… like the consummate love or something. I'm too stoned to try to explain it but I know it's good. You loved each other. It was *right*. And it was *supposed* to happen. And fuck society!"

Michael still didn't look convinced. He sank under the water and took me with him. When we came back up, we both shook our heads, my longer hair slapping him in the face. "I needed that!" he laughed.

"So did I." I made a move for the shore. "C'mon, we'd better get out of here before we turn into prunes."

Michael took his clothes out of the daypack. Surprisingly they were just damp although the sneakers would squish for a few hours more. We spread out our clothes over the surrounding bushes. While we waited for them to dry, we crouched Indian style and rocked forth and back, and talked without speaking, and rocked, and listened to the river… and rocked.

CHAPTER 32

June 1971

The sun was setting behind us when we finally climbed back up the bank near the slide. A few diehards were still schussing. Their splashes interrupted the sheen of the rolling river, now a strange burnt brown color from the reddening sun.

Those that frolicked and those that watched were having a good time and you could feel it. Their laughter was light and free. But as we made our way to where I guessed the Waysiders' campsite was, what laughter we did hear seemed burdened and incarcerated. People were not having a good time.

On the stage there were a lot of people milling around, some on their knees, fiddling with cables and such. But none of them was holding a musical instrument. Not a good sign. I turned toward the most dense part of the crowd and then looked back to see if Michael was still behind me. He was, studying the assortment of mishaps queuing outside the First Aid station.

The Flying Eye banner which I knew marked the spot, waved at me when it was caught by a bright spotlight sweeping the crowd. A few more shafts of light, this time all different colors, speared the darkening sky. They crossed with the first and crissed with each other. I could feel an increased activity in the adrenal glands of the crowd as they anticipated that *finally* something other than obscure bluegrass was going to happen.

"Giacco! Over here!"

I looked around. There was Nicky's head bobbing above the crowd, doing jumping jacks. When he was sure I saw him, his head submerged beneath the sea of faces. I grabbed Michael's hand and led him in the direction of Nicky's last known whereabouts. We came upon them huddled together in front of one of the tents like three chimpanzees.

"There you are!" I shouted and knelt down to try to embrace all three of them at the same time.

"Hear no evil, see no evil, speak no evil. Hear no evil, see no evil, speak no evil. Hear no evil, see no evil, speak no evil."

I released them and stepped back, directing my question at Little Richard. "What's wrong with Psylvia?"

Richard slowly looked up at me. He was so high, the energy coming from his eyes fuel-injected my own trip which I thought was leveling off. "Everything is needless to say," he recited. And then once again with a bit more feeling, "*Everything* is just *needless* to say!"

"I get the point, Richard," and then turned to Nicky.

"Psylvia is not getting a good *read* from this place," Nicky explained. "I told her it was just because she was tripping, but she insists there's something negative going on."

Psylvia interrupted her mantra and pulled me down in front of her. She looked at me earnestly. "Giacco, there *is* something wrong here."

I held her hands in mine. They were clammy and cold. I felt I was being called upon to be the comforting, fatherly type. "There's nothing to be scared of, Psylvy. I'm here now. We're all here together. You, me, Nicky, Little Richard... oh, and Michael," I said pointing behind me. "Michael, this is everyone. Everyone, this is Michael."

Michael said "Hi."

Nicky said "Hi."

Little Richard said, "I'd love to come over there and rub your tummy but I'm afraid I'm too stoned to get up."

And Psylvia said "Hi," but it was pretty feeble.

"Really, Psylvia," I said as reassuringly as possible, "there's nothing to be afraid of."

Psylvia's eyes got big and alert and she squeezed my hands. "Giacco, I'm not *scared*," she asserted. "I'm *working*! *Somebody* around here must fight off these dark forces!" And then she released my hands, closed her eyes, and returned to her chant. "Hear no evil, see no evil, speak no evil. Hear no evil, see no evil, speak no evil." This time, though, instead of hearing it as a mantra, I heard it as an exhortation... almost as an order to the thousands of souls that surrounded her waiting for *something* to happen.

A crackling from the PA system and a more frenzied crisscrossing of the spotlights got everyone's attention. I stood up.

"Ladies and gentlemen! Brothers and sisters! Freaks and freakettes! Why beat around the bush when we can have... CAT STEVENS!" Even at this distance I could see a genuine smile on Saul's face as he exited the stage.

To tumultuous applause, hoots, whistles, and rebel yells, Cat sauntered on stage, positioned himself on a stool, then looked around giving a silent count to his band. A one and a two and a three and a ...

Oooooo baby, baby it's a wild world...
and it's hard to get by just upon a smile, girl...

The cheers from the crowd got even louder, as if that were possible. And considering they had been holding it in since early that morning, it was.

I turned to Psylvia and said, "See?"

She looked up and said, "Wait." Then she lowered her head and continued ordering the fates around. "Hear no evil, see no evil, speak no evil. Hear no evil, see no evil, speak no evil."

The rest of us grooved on Cat Stevens and tried to ignore the incantation behind us. Cat played for a good hour, and then, whether upon Saul's beseeching or whether he was always so generous, he played one encore after another, stepping briefly offstage in between. The crowd loved it. The crowd was happy. People were having a good time.

Until Saul walked on stage just before Cat was about to start another song. They talked less than a minute, and then Saul walked to the front of the stage and lifted a mic out of its stand. The crowd started booing and chanting, "We want Cat! We want Cat!"

"Settle down, settle down," Saul urged, pressing columns of air down with his palms. "You can have Cat back just as soon as I give you this message." Saul waited until the PA's echo finished reverberating and he had at least enough of the crowd's attention to make sure the message would get out.

"The First Aid station is reporting an awful lot of people who are very sick or on bad trips. If anyone offers you *brown* acid... they're little pills, like those little saccharine-shaped things, but they're *brown*... stay away from them! I repeat, do not take the brown acid going around! It's bad! Bad! Thanks for your attention. And now, once again, Cat Stevens!"

The crowd broke into scattered thunderstorms of applause. But not loud enough to overpower "Hear no evil, see no evil, speak no evil."

I squatted in front of Psylvia. "Psylvia... where did you get the acid?"

"From Bruttar. Why? Do you want some? I think he has some more."

"What color was it?"

"It was on a sheet of yellow paper... and it's *yummy!* You should try some! That's what Nicky and Richard are on too! Except I'm on *more* of it!"

Relieved, I turned to Michael. "And you?

No answer. I tugged at his shirt tail.

"Huh! What!" Michael said ripping his face from the stage where it had been glued and, in the process, leaving part of his expression behind.

"Ow! Hope that didn't hurt!" I said apologetically. "I was just wonderin' what kind of acid you took."

"Oh. Some clear, plastic stuff. Tiny squares. I picked it up in Lincoln before I hitched down. Why? What kind did you take?"

Now that's an interesting question! Why didn't I think of it?

Then I conjured up the skinny teen who turned me on.

Bummer!

I forgot Michael was waiting for an answer. So did he, so it didn't matter. Still in a crouch, I swiveled on one heel and wedged myself between Psylvia and Richard. I turned to Psylvia and she looked into and around my eyes intently, diagnosing my condition. She broke into a sneaky grin. *That must mean good news!* I thought. Then she started chanting into my face. "Hear no evil, see no evil, speak no evil." The tone in her voice was that of a school marm. "*Hear* no evil, *see* no evil, *speak* no evil."

Uh-oh! I thought. So, I joined her.

I guess I can't account for the next few hours, because when I woke up, I was lying next to Michael. It was so dark, I didn't know who it was at first, but after I brailled the face, I figured it out. We were in a pup tent. My stomach felt a little odd and I had a massive headache, but other than that, I was fine. I vaguely remembered Psylvia playing with my head. Some kind of mind over body voodoo. She's *so* funny! I remember laughing so hard, it was like purging, which I think I may have done.

A strange sound caught my ear. Like a train chugging up a hill and then slipping backwards a few yards before climbing again. It was coming from Michael. I must've still been high on the acid for it to sound so loud and grating. Then it went away. Then it came back again, louder and closer.

It wasn't Michael snoring. It wasn't a train. It was a motorcycle revving up. And then another. And another. In the distance I could hear people swearing and threatening. And then other voices yelling at them to stop swearing and threatening and to go back the fuck to sleep. And then a scream. And more yelling and swearing and threatening.

I reached over and shook Michael. "Wake up, Michael. C'mon, man, wake up. There's something going on."

"Who? What?" Michael struggled to say as he tried to get his bearings. "What's going on? What time is it?"

"I don't know," I answered, zipping down a triangular flap and looking out the back screen of the pup tent. "It's pitch-black outside. No moon. Nothing."

I turned around and felt for Michael. He was sitting up. I put my hands on his shoulders and leaned my chest against his back. Behind us, the sounds of anger and fear were getting louder, spreading from the outskirts inward. But just outside the front of the tent, we heard two voices singing softly, almost in a whisper. They were terrible.

While I'm away from you my baby…
I know it's hard for you my baby…
Because it's hard for me my baby…

The front flap opened, and Psylvia and Richard stuck their flashlighted faces into the tent.

…And the darkest hour is just before dawn.

"Psylvia, you couldn't carry a tune if your life depended on it!" Richard said with exasperation. The flashlight made the expression on his face grotesque. "How can you expect me to harmonize with you if you keep changing keys every other measure?"

"Oh, Zietar!" Psylvia said, dismissing his remark, "don't be a twerp!" And then to us, "Time to get up boys. It's time to go!"

"What time is it?" asked Michael.

"And the darkest hour is *just before dawn*," Psylvia sang off key. "Now don't ask any more questions. Just pack up everything. We're getting out of here."

"Where are we going. What about Saul?" I asked.

"We're going away from here, right now. After that, I don't know. You can check in… or rather check *out*… with Saul on our way to get Zwagen."

Nicky poked his head into the tent resting it above Psylvia and Richard's. "Hi, guys! Ready?"

"Hi, Nicky!" I said. "What're we doing?"

"We're getting out of here. Hurry up! Bruttar's gang just left. He told me to tell you that if we wanted to hang out with them in New Orleans, we were welcome."

The sound of motorcycles got closer. Nicky, Psylvia and Richard retracted their heads at the same time. Then Richard stuck his back in once more. He was all seriousness. "Now hurry up you guys!"

As we made our way to the backstage gate, we could see single headlights circling tents and sleeping bags. In the light of one I caught a glimpse of a bottle being thrown. The roar of engines and the squeal of tires kicking up dirt and gravel dominated the air.

Just before we reached the gate, one of the headlights caught us in its beam and headed for us. As it got closer, the biker swerved around some people in their sleeping bags and knocked down a couple of makeshift tents. Somebody swore at the Devil's Rover, and he spun the bike around. I could make out the glint of something metal swinging in his right hand. Then a lot of commotion. In the distance we could hear the sirens of either the police or an ambulance... or both.

Backstage, while Nicky, Richard, Psylvia and Michael packed Zwagen, I went to see if I could find Saul.

The lights in his trailer were on. Three men stood on the steps leading up to it. One of them was Saul. One was the Martin County Sheriff. The other was a State Trooper. I stood a respectable distance away and listened.

"I don't care who the fuck you are! You better get this fiasco under control as fast as a jack rabbit or we'll bring in the National Guard!" said the trooper.

"What the fuck were you thinking, hiring the Rovers for security. I told you this was gonna happen!" yelled the sheriff.

"Two drownings! Three knifings!" said the trooper.

"Three cases of alcohol poisoning! People O.D.'ing all over the place!" said the sheriff.

"I just hope you got liability insurance up the *asshole*, asshole." said the trooper.

"We got the entire police departments of three towns on the way! You gonna pick up the tab, bubba?" said the sheriff.

Saul finally spoke. "I know it looks bad, officers, but if you bring in the police, it's just going to get worse!" Then Saul noticed me in the shadows. "Look, I have an emergency to attend to. Please excuse me. If you want to wait in the trailer... fine. If not, I'll be back in half an hour. If you want things to get better, let me do my job!" He took all three of the stairs in one bound and rushed toward me.

He grabbed me by the elbow and led me away from the trailer, speaking quietly and quickly.

"Giacco, your timing is perfect. I couldn't get away from those guys. Listen... get your people out of here!"

"We're all ready to go," I said.

Saul looked at me a little surprised, but then realized there was no need to be.

"I don't know what to say. Things just didn't work out. It's all that fucking alcohol!" I let Saul rant and rave a few minutes and list one reason after another for the quickly degenerating scene, the contagious hysteria. By that time, we were at the heli-pad. The pilot was in his seat. I noticed a couple of pieces of luggage and a brief case set beside one of the skids of the chopper.

Saul picked up the brief case and opened it. He pulled a check out of its book and started filling it in. As he handed it over, he said, "Giacco, cash this as soon as you can. When the funds are gone, they're gone. If it bounces, all I can do is say I'm sorry… for now."

I looked at the check. It was for $750. Half of what I was supposed to get. I decided not to mention it. We had never counted on Psylvia or Nicky making any money off this thing, so we were really in better shape than expected. I figured Saul had enough problems to deal with.

"I'd better get to the car, Saul. Everybody's waiting on me." I gave him a big hug and promised to stay in touch.

As I climbed into the back seat between Michael and Nicky, I heard the *whump, whump, whump* of the rotors. We were on the dirt road leading off the site to the paved county road when I looked back. The chopper was rising and moving forward at the same time, its nose slightly aimed groundward. Sirens got ear-piercingly loud as the police cars converged at the heli-pad. The last thing I saw was the silhouette of the chunky Martin County Sheriff waving his fist at the metal dragonfly disappearing into the Atchafalayan dawn.

I never saw nor heard from Saul ever again.

CHAPTER 33
August 1971

The tomato plants were on crutches. Without them they would have sagged to their knees they were so heavy with fruit. All the vegetables in Jon and Rosie's Garden were county fair contenders. And Jon and Rosie were the first to admit it was because of Zietar, who of course would never have subjected any of his "children" to the trauma of a competition.

He sat there in the middle of the row, grooming the ground around each plant, patiently, meticulously. A few sunflowers towered above him and attentively listened to the little melody he was sweetly singing. Jon and Rosie and I sat among the snow peas eating one for every three we threw into a colander. The serenade rippled across the furrows, and we smiled knowingly at each other, a little envious of all the love Richard was bestowing on his charges.

Nicky was on the side of the house tinkering with the solar shower he improvised using coils of black PVC pipe. Psylvia was in the kitchen making a "surprise," though we suspected it had something to do with dessert.

I thought about Michael. He would have really loved it here. But he left us at the beginning of July when we got to St. Louis. He didn't make up his mind to head back home until we were already a few miles east of St. Louis on Interstate 70.

"Quick! Which way do you want to go?" Richard asked as we approached the interchange. "Left to the Pacific, or right to the Atlantic?"

"What happened to north? You got something against north, Zietar?" Psylvia poked him in the ribs.

"What! You want to go to Chicago?" Richard queried in a way that meant Chicago was not an option and then looked over his shoulder at us. "How about you guys? Any ideas?"

"Well," Michael said, "I really should be heading home I guess." And then I caught him stealing a glance at me.

"Are you kidding? I blurted. "You're not getting away *that* easy!" I could already see how this was going to end but I insisted anyway. "We're stickin' together, brother!"

Michael smiled as if thanking me that I still wanted him around. But then he turned to me, whispering confessionally, "Giacco, I have to get back. I hate to leave, but I have to, man!"

He leaned forward over Richard's shoulder. "Zietar, you can let me out at the interchange. OK?

"Oh, this is *better*... this is *much* better!" I said, failing to hide my disappointment.

"Eureka! That's it!" shouted Psylvia. "Let's go see Jon and Rosie!"

Little Richard looked approvingly at Psylvia and said, "A simply splendid idea, my little petunia! Now why didn't I think of that?"

Nicky finally perked up and announced, "Yeah! Let's go visit Jon and Rosie! That's a great idea! They'll love it!" He draped himself over the back of Psylvia's seat. "This is so exciting! I've never been to the east coast before!"

"East coast!" Michael yelled. "No, really, you guys. It sounds great, but I can't do that. You'd better let me out at the next on-ramp going west."

I stared at Michael trying to get inside his head. I needed to let him know how much I wanted him to stay. He knew. But for the next three miles he avoided my gaze. When Richard pulled over, I reached into the back and retrieved Michael's pack for him. Everyone got out of the car to stretch. I nudged Michael a few yards away.

"What's going on, Michael? Why do you have to go home? We won't be gone more than a few weeks. Or is it me?"

"Naw, Giacco!" Michael said punching me affectionately on the shoulder, "How can you say that? Of course it's not you! I wish we could stay together! Really!"

"OK. Me too! How about this? Why don't I go back to Lincoln with you? Take care of whatever shit you have to take care of, and then we'll boogie for San Francisco! Sound good?"

"Aw, man! Giacco, don't make this harder for me than it is."

"Hey, Michael… just say it. Whatever it is. Just spit it out. It's only me."

"Giacco. I'm married! And she's six months pregnant!"

I just stood there. I didn't say anything.

"She's really sweet. It just sort of happened."

I just stood there. I didn't say anything.

"Well… it didn't *just sort of happen*… but it's a long story and well… well, I just have to go back… and you can't come with me. At least not yet. Not until I sort everything out. I'll let you know, OK?"

I just stood there. I didn't say anything.

"Giacco, I really love you. You must know that!" He reached behind his neck and unclasped the hishi bead necklace I had admired at the "Celebration" fiasco. He put it around my neck, made sure the clasp was tight, and gave me a bear hug. He whispered in my ear, "I really, really, hope we come full circle, brother."

I whispered in his ear, "That's what I want, Michael. You know where I am. I'll leave the ball in your court. Take care of yourself." He pulled out a scrap of paper and a pen, scribbled something on it, and handed it to me. He hugged me again as hard as he could, and I hugged him back not wanting to let him go.

But I did. I just turned around and walked back to the car and hopped into the front passenger seat of Zwagen. Richard and Psylvia were in the back. Nicky pulled out onto the road and except for me, they all waved at Michael when he flashed the peace sign at us. It didn't make up for what I thought was a look of distress on his face, which made me screw up mine.

I unfolded the scrap of paper. It read, Michael Taylor, General Delivery, Lincoln, Nebraska, 68588.

"Oh, this is just great! This is an address?" and I went into my sulking mode.

Everyone was quiet, I assumed out of deference to some pain they thought I was feeling. I wasn't sure what I was feeling. A little hollow, maybe? Like the way your stomach feels an hour after Chinese, only in my heart. In my mind, I was busy listening to an assortment of voices commenting on the situation.

Psylvia leaned over my shoulder and said, "It just doesn't get any better than this!" And Nicky followed with, "Wagons, ho! Next stop… North Leeds, Maine!"

When we walked into the kitchen of Jon and Rosie's little farmhouse, Nicky was already scrubbing up for dinner. Rosie put the colander of peas on the counter along with a head of bok choy and some carrots. Jon and I sidled up next to Psylvia who was hovering over a big bowl she'd just taken out of the refrigerator. It looked like it contained a light green custard, but when Psylvia broke the surface with a wooden spoon, we realized it was a bowl of cloudy water with a hardened crust of lard or grease on top.

"Green butter!" she informed us. "I used the trimmings from your plants down by the creek, Jon. Hope that was all right. Weren't much good for smoking, anyway. Oh, and I threw in all the roaches that were lying around just for good luck!"

"What're you going to do with it?" Jon asked.

"Oh, you'll see. Wait til after dinner. Now go get Zietar. Tell him Psylvia's starving and to get his butt in here."

Jon turned for the screen door just as it swung open. Richard walked in, his arms full of tomatoes, radishes, and romaine. His whole body was a rich tan. Even his smooth scalp had the healthy glow of polished copper. His eyes shone especially brightly above his satin cheeks.

Psylvia tested one of the potatoes baking in the oven with a fork, directing her question to Jon and Rosie. "Are you sure you two don't want any baked potatoes?"

Jon and Rosie looked at one another to check each other's resolve. "No, thanks Psylvy. We've been raw all summer and we're going to stay raw." Psylvia closed the oven door and went back to stirring the mystery batter, intermittently adding walnuts and raisins.

"Boring. Very boring," Nicky critiqued.

"Look at you two," Richard added. "You're so skinny you're turning from tomatoes into string beans!"

"We just want to get our bodies as clean as possible," Jon defended. "The life of the ascetic is sustained by *other* nutrients."

"But look at Rosie's complexion!" Psylvia said. "It used to be so creamy and smooth. Now she's breaking out all over. What're you reverting to... teenagers or something?"

Rosie looked in the little mirror next to the spice rack. "It's only temporary, Psylvia. It's just all the toxins coming out, that's all. It'll clear up eventually." Then, placing a hand above one eye and the other hand beneath it, she stretched the lids apart and leaned into the mirror studying her iris. "The spot on my liver is almost gone, and my colon is clean as a whistle! A few more weeks and I'm sure these pimples will clear up."

I leaned against the counter and turned to Jon. "How come you're not breaking out, Jon?"

"Nicotine, my friend. Nicotine is the secret to beautiful skin!" Jon stated authoritatively. "It keeps the toxins from erupting out of our most extensive organ." And having prescribed the antidote, he reached for a pack of bare ass Camels, hardly hiding behind a tin of Baking Soda, gently pulled one from the pack and fired it up.

"Don't you think that's a little hypocritical?" I asked. "I mean if one of the keys is the *breath*, then isn't that what you should be working on the most?"

"Everything in moderation, Giacco," he replied. "Everything in moderation. Or at least, one vice at a time. OK?" Jon saw I wasn't convinced and added, "I'll get around to it eventually, *Chazan!*"

I let it ride. I hadn't made any progress in overcoming that addiction myself, so I knew better than to pursue it.

Rosie was still looking in the mirror. "Mirror, mirror, on the wall... who is the purest of them all?" she said facetiously and then struck a pose.

"I am!" Richard said, pushing Rosie aside and letting his image replace hers.

"No, I am!" said Psylvia, bumping Richard's hip with her own causing him to lose his balance and relinquish his spot to her.

"Well, beauty *is* in the eye of the beholder, and I for one, love every volcano on her chinny chin chin," Jon said in fealty to his mistress. He took Rosie's chin between his thumb and index finger, lifted it, and gave her a luscious kiss on the mouth. "As long as they don't erupt on me!"

Psylvia forked the potatoes out of the oven onto a platter, lowered the temperature slightly, and replaced them with a rectangular baking tray filled with dark brown batter. "Let's eat!" she ordered.

We took our places. A large salad, corn on the cob (two cobs raw, the others cooked), one bowl of lightly steamed snow peas, one bowl of raw snow peas, the steaming potatoes, a crock of butter, a small dish of sour cream, a custard dish filled with chopped chives, and some hard peasant bread, adorned the table.

We held hands for quiet time. We felt the collective beta waves smoothing out from the biofeedback of each other's touch. When the waves seemed as gentle as the Gulf of Mexico at dawn, I opened my eyes just enough to survey my friends, my family. I caught Jon coveting the potatoes, sour cream, and butter. Then he caught me catching him, snickered to rebuff his capture, and said, "Shut up, Giacco, and let's eat!"

Later that evening, as we did every evening since we arrived, we passed the time in our own special way.

Zietar worked on an embroidery. In the foreground, a magic duck paddled across a pond. Its eye was encrusted with red, gold, and black sequins. Grasses grew along the bank and on the small hill in the background, the apples on a tree were ready for picking.

Jon curled up in the window seat of the small living room, reading about the Kargyupta lineage of gurus.

Rosie sat cross-legged on the floor, making notes as she studied a book on medicinal herbs.

Nicky and I sat back-to-back listening to a Ravi Shankar album.

Psylvia walked in with a heaping plate of fresh-from-the-oven brownies. They smelled seductively good, but Rosie waved them away without looking up when the plate was lowered in front of her face.

Psylvia just said, "Sorry."

Jon shooed them aside as well. But Psylvia said, "Now don't be a twerp, Jon. If you're going to smoke cigarettes, one or two brownies aren't going to hurt! Trust me! You'll like them!"

Jon took one, and then checking to see if Rosie were still engrossed in her book, took another. The rest of us didn't need cajoling. They were the best marijuana brownies ever. Isolated tastes of walnuts and raisins, uncontaminated by even the slightest essence of reefer, and completely void of anything the tongue might detect as resembling grit or sand. Those kinds were the work of amateurs. Psylvia was a pro. They were worthy of a Blue Ribbon at the upcoming Androscoggin County Fair, if only they weren't illegal. They were smooth and creamy. They were so delicious, they were irresistible. They were also extremely potent, but we wouldn't know that until after we had already scarfed up every last one and it was too late.

I got off two fairly coherent notes to Michael. I sent one to him in care of his Aunt Pearl even though that address had proved useless, and the other to General Delivery, probably equally useless, but I had to try. I put Hunga Dunga's return address on the backs of the envelopes and licked them with love. Then I closed my eyes and fell into the music of George Harrison.

Rosie chuckled good-naturedly when Richard slurred "Good night" and zombie-like, made for his little foam bed out on the front porch. Nicky and Psylvia were already in the midst of an amorous prelude, oblivious to Jon sports-casting their foreplay, play by play. Only when Jon threw a napkin in the air and excitedly called "Foul!" for illegal holding, did they blush in false modesty and head for their tent down by the creek.

The three of us were alone. Jon read a few more pages in his book and then closed it with a heavy sigh. Rosie looked up and felt his frustration. "What is it, Jon?"

Jon looked at Rosie and didn't speak for a few minutes. He just looked at her. His eyes were moist. The beginning of a tear was forming in the corner of his left eye. Finally, he spoke.

"Rosie, Oh Rosie, my beloved Devi. Milarepa had Marpa. Marpa had Naropa. Naropa had Tilopa. Yogananda had Sri Yukteswar. Sri Yukteswar had Lahiri Mahasaya…"

"And?" I said, bringing myself into the conversation.

"And when are *we* going to have somebody? When are *we* going to meet *our* teacher? How long are we supposed to wait? Don't I want it enough? How could I want it any more than I do?"

Very gently, Rosie said, "My tortured, crazed sadhu. Maybe you want it too much! Did you ever think of that?"

"Maybe you should try self-flagellation," I said, trying to lighten things up. But as soon as the words left my mouth, I was sorry I'd said them. Jon simply let his head slump into his hands. I couldn't end the evening on this note, so I tried once more. I lit two Camels and threw one of them to him. "Here, let's flagellate our lungs with these."

Jon took a deep drag, exhaling slowly, evening his breath. "Ah! Now this is *really* much better!"

Rosie rolled her eyes up to the ceiling and said, "Punch thyself! You too, Giacco. Both of you! Right now! Punch thyselves or I'll come over and do it for you!" And with that she jumped Jon and with little, tiny punches, pummeled his stomach. I scooted over on my knees and joined in, practicing my noogie technique on his head. Then Rosie and Jon started in on me. Before long, everybody was pummeling everybody else.

The pummels turned into kneadings, turned into a mild Shiatsu, turned into broad, sweeping, Swedish strokes, turned into platonic but affectionate petting. The solace of human touch, and I'm sure, the brownies, helped Jon and me fall asleep where we were on the floor. Just before I dozed off, I saw Rosie reach for the green afghan on the sofa. She cuddled close to Jon and spread it out to cover all of us. Just like three raw, but tender, snow peas in a pod.

One glorious Maine summer day glided into another, and before anyone knew it, August was halfway gone. Richard had written Hunga Dunga such gushing magical things about the farm that Larry insisted on flying out to see for himself and to help with the harvest.

Everyone was thrilled. We loved Duck. Especially Ziets. After a short tour of the farmhouse, Larry followed Richard out the back screen door. We followed. Richard swept his arm grandly over the large colorful field. "My garden doth bear too much fruit of my loins!"

Larry was impressed. "Thy loins are indeed splendid to have fathered so vast and varietous a field abloom!" Need I say more about what a fun addition it was to have Larry around the house?

However, Larry had never been in such close quarters with Jon for any extended periods of time. He was about to find out how possessed a man can be! The only music we listened to was George Harrison's "My Sweet Lord." It's the only album Jon would play. We'd get to slip in one of our favorites now and then, but for the most part it was "My Sweet Lord." Over and over. Larry didn't know how we could take it. He was starting to crack.

At one dinner, just after quiet time when we were supposed to not be quiet, Duck said brightly, "Well, what topic shall we discuss over dinner tonight?"

Jon looked up and said, "The only thing worth talking about is god!"

Larry laughed until he realized Jon was serious! Then he was stunned. I was happy that so many of my family were getting to know Jon and Rose the way I knew them. As total loony bins.

The five of us found that month idyllic and seeing the silhouettes of Duck and Ziets on a log in front of the garden made my heart swell. But all good things come to an end.

Psylvia, Nicky, and I had made more than enough money from the festival to fly three people home, which is what we ended up doing, because Richard refused to leave "his" garden until it was completely harvested, and he refused to give us Zwagen reasoning that only he knew its eccentricities well enough to handle a mid-continental breakdown. Larry looked forward to the road trip with Ziets.

Jon and Rosie begged, pleaded, and literally stood on their heads trying to get us to stay, but Nicky and Psylvia, as good a time as they were having, knew it was time to get back to Hunga Dunga.

I, predictably, couldn't make up my mind whether to stay or to go, but the decision was made for me when Ellen called one evening and lectured me about my responsibilities to the Free Food Conspiracy. At that moment, I decided that when I got back to The City, I was going to tell Miss Nancy Stein I wanted off ATD so I could do whatever I wanted to do without feeling guilty about it.

Psylvia slept through almost the entire flight. But Nicky was locked into the pages of the *Whole Earth Catalog* he borrowed from Jon. He furiously scribbled down titles of books and the addresses of any organization that could provide information on alternative energy systems, composting, gardening, hand-made houses, yurts, domes, semi-subterranean dwellings… anything that might prove a valuable resource in attaining self-sufficiency.

For Nicky, Jon and Rosie's little farm had provided a vision of the Holy Grail. He wouldn't be happy until it sat upon a table of his own making, inside a house of his own making, on land of his own scaping.

Psylvia wouldn't be happy until Nicky was.

Richard wouldn't be happy until he could watch little tomato plants reach for the sky.

Larry was doing his best to make everyone happy.

And I couldn't be happier. I guess. Until I got home and found two letters waiting for me. The same ones I sent Michael from Maine. "Addressee Unknown." "No Forwarding Address." The red letters may as well have spelled out "Left the Planet!"

I felt so helpless. That feeling you get when your puppy is stolen or wanders off and you never know if it's OK or not. And maybe never will. All I could do was hope Michael wouldn't give up on me and would write again.

CHAPTER 34

October 1971

"Now really," Miss Nancy Stein said, and stood up from behind her desk. She leaned forward, and straight-armed, placed her palms flat on the desk pad for support, "and don't take this personally, Giacco... but *that* idea is absolutely half-baked!"

"But Nancy," I implored, using her first name, hoping by now we were friends, "I know of people on ATD who are learning a trade, and the State is paying for it! If I could learn how to blow glass or something, then I could make things and sell them and get off ATD. Here, look, I brought you a catalog. The Oakland School of Arts and Crafts." I pushed it in front of her.

Miss Stein continued leaning over, looked down at the catalog, and just shook her head. "Giacco, what you don't understand is that those people are just *temporarily* disabled. They can be rehabilitated. They attend therapy sessions regularly. They can *take* classes. We *want* to help them get off welfare."

"So?" I said, unwilling to think my request was unreasonable in the light of this further information.

"So... you have *organic* brain damage," she reminded me. "You're *incurable!*" Those words really stung. She knew it too. I could tell by the way she tried to make me see the bright side of complete irreversible insanity. "You're not capable of taking a class or learning a trade or anything like that. That's why you've never had to undergo therapy! That's why there've never been any conditions placed upon your ATD! Go home... relax... enjoy!"

"Well, if that's the case," I said indignantly, "just take me off the stupid thing. I don't want to be on it anymore. I don't want any of your precious money. Just cancel the whole thing right now!"

"Now that *is* really crazy, Giacco! And the more you talk that way, the crazier the shrinks... I mean the doctors... are going to think you are! You're going to open a can of worms that might cause more problems than you know!"

I had images of straight-jackets and padded cells. We were both silent while we visited our separate scenarios, though they may have been the same. She cocked her head to one side and wrinkled her brow as if to say *trust me, take my advice, that's the way it is, don't push a good thing.*

She sat down and folded her hands in front of her. I retrieved the catalog and without looking at it, threw it in the wastepaper basket at the side of her desk. I turned around and walked out.

When I opened the door to Big Blue, I heard a guitar being played falteringly. Still, I could discern the intended rhythm. It sounded like a tango. Like something Maxime would play. I thought maybe it *was* Maxime, but he and Catherine had left for Paris a couple of weeks before.

We were sorry to see Catherine go. She would be missed. Richard was totally bummed when he got home and found out she was gone. We didn't think we'd miss Maxime, since we spent so much time ignoring him. Or rather copping to his desire to be ignored. The opposite happened and his absence left a noticeable void. We would've been happy to have them both back.

I hung up my coat in the foyer and walked into the living room. It was Tom playing the guitar. He sat on the floor with his back resting against the sofa. Brandon sat across from him reading a magazine.

"Giacco's here!" Brandon yelled toward the stairwell. Then to me he cupped his hands around his mouth and stage-whispered, "Family meeting!"

At first I thought *Oh no,* but then looked forward to it. I was feeling a little sorry for myself about the ATD thing and all, and a family meeting was a good place to get things off your chest. I sat on the back of the couch, my knee coming to rest against Tom's shoulder. I reached over to pat Tom on the head but couldn't resist mussing up his hair. "Whatcha playing?"

Tom tilted his head back toward me, but his fingers continued plucking. "Something I heard Maxime working on. I'm trying to figure out the chords before I lose it in my head."

"I like it," I said.

"Yeah, me too!" Tom agreed. "When he played it, it sounded so simple, but really nice and moody." Tom released the neck of the guitar and fixed his hair where he felt I'd messed it up. "Now that I'm trying to piece it together, I'm finding out it's very tricky! A lot of major sevenths and augmented chords. I wish he would've let me tape him!"

"What's the meeting about?" I asked.

"Zietar called it," Brandon told me. "I think he's going to lobby us to increase the amount we put into the Land Fund each month."

What sounded like a small herd of cloven-hooved bovines rumbled down the stairs. Thudding and thumping into the living room, Zietar, Psylvia, Trudy, Lana, Nicky, Chuck and Lizzie circled the sofa and overstuffed chair deciding where on the floor they wanted to sit. They were followed by those ever-vigilant cowpokes, Ellen, Greg, and Baird. Ellen's Birkenstocks clomp-clomped like a stumbling pony on the last few steps and Greg, who almost bumped into her, raised his hands in front of himself, reining in his steed.

Baird sauntered through the living room and kitchen into the back yard, neighing commandingly as he rounded up the strays.

"Git along little dogies!" Psylvia smiled up at Baird as he corralled Bobby, Luc and Alvoye into the circle. Baird didn't get it, but I chuckled contentedly to myself, seeing how *simpatico* Psylvia and I were in picking up on the same imagery.

"I want to sit next to Trudy," Lizzie pouted. Trudy, already comfortable on the sofa, scooted to the left as Lizzie forced himself between her and Tom, who still had his guitar in his lap. "Hey, watch out for the guitar!" Tom yelled. He put the guitar tenderly between his legs, the neck straight up. He slid his hand up and down the frets. It was very sexual. I could tell Brandon was aroused.

"Can't you move your big fat ass over a few more inches?" Bobby complained to Alvoye. Alvoye obliged but appeared to measure his butt with his left hand. "Oh, Alvoye, it's just an expression!" Bobby rolled his eyes.

Richard leafed through a ledger, then closed it with his middle finger marking the page and slapped the book against his leg. "Will this meeting *puleeze* come to order!" he more than requested.

"Thank you," he said, though a few people were still elbowing each other. "First thing... let's go around the room and set the agenda. "Greg... you got anything?"

"*Nada*... and you may all thank me anytime!"

"Psylvia?" Richard rotated his head 20 degrees to the right.

"Maybe... but first I want to make an announcement." Everyone waited for her to continue. "Unless there are any objections, I am going to become one of the purveyors of fine food at the Yin-Yin!"

Nicky turned to Psylvia with a surprised look on his face. "When did this happen?"

"Yesterday," she replied. "Lynn and Estelle needed some help in the restaurant, and they asked me if I was interested and I said 'yes.'" She sounded just a bit defiant as if expecting some flack and to further her cause added, "and to all of you who were skeptical about the Yin-Yin, they really are a collective. After expenses, everything the Yin-Yin makes is split evenly." She looked around the circle. No one said anything. "Well, can everybody live with that?" No one said anything so she ended with, "Good!"

Lizzie piped up kiddingly with one addendum. "Now you just watch out, Psylvy, that you don't let those girls seduce you! They can be pretty determined is what I hear!"

"Oh, Lizzie!" Psylvia said a little too sweetly. "Did it ever occur to you that I took the job so I could seduce them!"

Lizzie just laughed, but Nicky was thinking about it with his brow furrowed. Like somebody just gave him an algebra problem.

Richard looked anxious and shifted from one buttock to the other. "All right now. Are we through with the announcements? Can we please get on with it? Does anyone else have an agenda item?" He looked at Nicky.

"Nicky?"

The sound of his name startled him out of his calculations. "Land!" he said without hesitation.

"We've already heard from Psylvia, so we'll go on to Baird," Richard said, but Psylvia spoke up anyway. "*Land* is the word I hear coming' across the south forty."

Richard made a face and ignored her. "Baird?"

"Well, I have been ruminating on the plausibility and possibly beneficent effects that a rural retreat might have on the spiritual maturation of a collective consciousness."

Richard paused and then said, "Huh?"

Luc said, "I say whatever Baird said."

Duck interrupted. "Richard, wouldn't it be easier to ask if there's anyone who doesn't want to discuss land?"

"Oh, Duck!" Richard said, "You are just so… so… *je ne sais quoi!*"

"Well, if that means I'm very queer, what else is new? You're very *quoi* yourself, you know?"

Richard ignored him, but asked, "Is there anyone here who doesn't want to discuss land?"

"Look, you guys." It was Bobby. "I'm not interested in living in the country, but as long as you don't dip into the other funds, I'll go along with whatever you come up with."

"Ditto for me," said Alvoye.

"Omigod," said Trudy. "Alvoye said three words in a row!"

"Be nice, Trudy," chided Psylvia.

Ellen spoke up. "Let's cut all the crap! We all know what's going on! Some people here want land. I don't know why they want it, but they feel they *must* have it. I, for one, will probably never use it. Oh, well maybe for a visit, but I can't imagine living out in the country."

Richard looked to me to cancel out this less than enthusiastic pronouncement. "Giacco, how about you?"

I tried to be the great compromiser. "Well, you all know that I really want to get out of The City, but it's not *completely* self-motivated. I mean we're buying food wholesale now, and distributing it for free… well, at least to the communes, if not the restaurants… and it just seems the next logical step is to start growing it. Something. Anything. Apples, corn, soybeans. Something we can give away for free."

"Let's be realistic, Giacco," Baird said. "That's a few eons down the road, don't you think?"

Trudy didn't let Baird's remark dissuade her from futuristic thinking. "What I want to do is start a school. Can you imagine it? A school in the country? Maybe for arts and crafts or even a real alternative school with classes and everything?"

"Wait a minute, you guys!" Lizzie said. "Don't you think we're all getting a little ahead of ourselves? We don't even have the money to buy land and already we've got a school and three crops growing! I think we're talking through our hats. How much does land cost anyway? Does anybody know?"

"And where do we want to buy land?" asked Lana.

"And how much land are we talking about?" asked Greg.

"Lizzie," Richard said, opening the ledger and addressing his question, "we already have $2600 in the Land Fund. With a 10 percent down payment, we could buy something for $26,000."

Everyone seemed surprised we'd accumulated that much money in so short a time. With that one sentence we realized doing something *grand* like starting a farm was actually a possibility. And at the rate we were going, an imminent possibility.

"I have something to say." We all waited for Trudy to speak. She fidgeted with her coveralls as an excuse to stall until she could find just the right phrasing. "I don't want you to think that I've been holding out on you guys, but… well, when my father died, he left me a trust fund… and… well, when I turned eighteen, I was allowed to tap into it… and…

well..." Trudy hesitated, looked around the circle, took a deep breath, and spoke quickly through its exhale, "as of this moment I will contribute $2000 to Hunga Dunga... but *only* if it goes into the Land Fund!" Trudy beamed, thinking she'd reap tons of accolades for her magnanimity. It backfired.

"I *can't* live with that!" screamed Baird. "You either give it to the family with no strings attached or keep it!"

"How much more are you holding out on us?" asked Greg.

Trudy turned red and turned defensive. "I'm not holding out on anything. I get a small lump sum every year. That's all. Really! I just came into this!"

It was evident from the skeptical expressions on Richard, Greg, and Chuck's faces, that they weren't going for it, but they remained silent. After all, this wasn't a cult. We wanted everyone to contribute everything because they wanted to, not because it was a rule. Still, there had never been any reason to believe someone had a private stash of money sequestered somewhere... for *just in case*. Now, Trudy presented the hardly likely, but slightly possible scenario in which someone was watching out for *him or herself* rather than for the whole family... *just in case*.

It lasted no more than a few moments, but there was a sense that everyone was sizing everyone else up. Did Lizzie have a secret bank account? Was Greg the son of old-money blue bloods, just out slumming with the hippies for a temporary good time? Lana's father had died a few years earlier. Did she have an inheritance we didn't know about? And how about Chuck? His folks were rolling in dough!

The moments passed. The questions were beside the point. We weren't hurting financially, so any other monies that fell into the communal pot would just be gravy anyway. Those that knew deep within themselves they were contributing every penny they had, happily and faithfully looked to the family to provide for their well-being. Those that were holding out... well, they just hadn't come around yet. We trusted they would in time and would do so voluntarily... when they were ready. And when they were ready, they would understand how and why it worked to everyone's advantage. And they would understand how silly it was to hold anything out in the first place. That is, if anyone were holding out. And we wanted to believe no one was. So, no one was. And what could we have done about it anyway?

"Well, now that you know I have it, I guess I'm stuck, huh?" Trudy said, her voice trapped in a truth. All eyes were on her, not coldly, but challengingly, though I saw what could only be called sympathy in Lizzie's gaze.

"OK! OK!" Trudy gave in. She turned to Richard and said, "Zietar, tomorrow I'll write you a check for the two thou!" Then she panned the circle. "Is everybody happy now?"

"Trudy, that is really generous of you," Psylvia said without the slightest hint of sarcasm. And there was none. She said it in absolute sincerity and in so doing, subtly informed the rest of us that she expected the tone in any of our subsequent speeches to be equally loving and trusting and genuine. Then Psylvia made a motion.

"I make a motion that *all* the money Trudy just contributed to Hunga Dunga go into the Land Fund. Is there anyone who can't live with that?" She looked around taking a visual poll and listening for the first objection. There were none. "The motion carries! Now what?"

Trudy seemed relieved, yet a little embarrassed at what she thought may have only been a conciliatory gesture on our part. She got what she originally wanted, *and* without compromising the true spirit of Hunga Dunga. But did Psylvia's influence skew our vote as a way of teaching Trudy a lesson? Or did everyone *really* agree? Second-guessing at this point was too tiring.

The attention spans of Alvoye and Bobby were being stretched to their limits. Ellen sensed the need to wrap up the meeting. "It's obvious to me that we don't have enough information for us to continue talking about land. So, this is a ridiculous waste of time. I think we need to start looking around. At least to get an idea of what's available."

"We could have a meeting with Friends of Perfection and ask them how they found their land in Grant's Pass," Nicky suggested.

"There's always the real estate section in the Chronicle," offered Duck.

"There are also such personages who specialize in the selling and buying of real property," said Baird. "I believe they are called… Realtors!"

No one appreciated his sarcasm.

"I'd like something close by, you know, a weekend retreat," said Ellen.

"Yeah," agreed Lizzie. "If we're going to grow food to give away through the Free Food Conspiracy, it's gotta be within driving distance to The City."

"Well, south is out," Nicky determined, "because land is too expensive between here and LA and… I don't know… too deserty if you go inland!"

"Besides, it's all humongous corporate agribusiness," added Greg.

Psylvia got up and went to the bookcase. A stack of road maps was lodged between the Scrabble game and an old dictionary. She pulled the entire stack out and thumbed through it. Retrieving a map of the western United States, she rejoined the circle, unfolded it, and spread it out across Nicky, Ellen, and Chuck's laps.

Everyone bent over it to see where Psylvia was pointing. "Someplace around Santa Rosa might be nice." Everyone straightened up. "It's close and there's lots of small farms around there and it's really sunny a lot… not like here!"

Another index finger slid across the creases of the map. It was a big finger. It could only belong to Baird. When it stopped it covered a 12-square mile area of Humboldt County. He lifted his finger to reveal the towns of Benbow, Garberville, and Miranda. Everyone hunched over to study the square inch. "This is where the big trees are. And it's lush. And I bet you get more for the money, the farther north you go!" Everyone straightened up.

"If we go that far north," I contributed, "we may as well investigate southern Oregon." I started to point, but quickly retracted my finger for fear we would start doing the hand jive.

"Look," Duck suggested, "why don't we just start exploring. Whenever somebody gets a hankering to…"

Richard stopped him in his tracks. "*Hankering? Hankering?* God Duck, you sound like you're out in the boonies already!"

Duck threw Richard a few daggers and then shook him off. "As I was saying, if anyone *feels* the need to get out of The City, they can go on a land trip. In fact, I'd like to head up to Mount Tam this weekend. It'd be just as easy to keep going north a bit and see what's for sale. Anybody wanna join me?"

"I wouldn't mind going with you, Larry," said Ellen. "I really need to get out of The City for a couple of days."

"I'll go too, Duck!" said Zietar. "It'll be fun!"

"Oh! I see!" Duck smirked. "Well, you know you have to have a sincere *hankering* to come along… you little dogie!"

"OK! OK!... I have a *hankering* if that's what it takes!"

That weekend, Duck, Ellen, and Richard hankered on the first of many "land trips." No one ever went alone, but no more than three ever went in search of the perfect rural setting. That first trip, like the many that followed, ended in nothing more than a camping trip. They always had fun and always returned healthier looking. But it didn't bring us any closer to the valley of our dreams, to our Shangri-la, to our Eldorado, to… at least for me… our *Bali Hai*.

That was part of the problem. The land had to be everything to everybody. Maine had had a profound effect upon Nicky. And Psylvia and Richard weren't unfamiliar with the beauty of New England. So, the three of them had a vision of gentle hardwood forests, bubbling creeks, and the sensual variety of four distinct seasons, especially flamboyant autumn.

In *my* wildest dreams, the land would have been a tropical island, replete with mucusless food for the picking. From the trees, from the sea. Gardening would be optional. So would shelter and clothing. My land was surrounded by a womb-warm ocean and gently buffeting trade winds. And it lounged under an enormous umbrella made of sunshine and whose ribs were rainbows. We would live the Essene science of life according to the Essene Gospel of Peace, and the angels of the Air, Sun, and Water would bathe our bronzed, naked bodies while we swam in lagoons.

Of course, I knew that my dream was the most far-fetched of all, so I never even verbalized it. But if I had a runner-up fantasy, it was the one Richard, Psylvia and Nicky shared, so I exchanged my monocle for their wrap-around windshield.

Baird saw himself as a Gentleman Farmer slash Meditative Hermit. He did expect the hermitage to offer every amenity, including a solarium/studio in which to make his art. It would also be nice if eventually there were formal gardens with extensive statuary… some quiet and beautiful place where he could play Plato to some Aristotle he picked up.

I think Bobby, Luc, and Alvoye didn't quite understand the physical implications of creating a rural habitat conducive to a Hunga Dungan lifestyle. The concept of hard labor was alien to them. All they talked about was hot tubs and saunas and the outrageous parties they were going to throw. To quote Bobby, "As long as it has a great sound system, I don't care where it is!"

The only thing we all agreed upon was that it had to have a spectacular view. Too bad we didn't realize at the time that some of our criteria should have included... oh, inconsequential things... you know, like access to water, sun exposure, drainage, soil fertility, easements, and accessibility. But to the person, we were all city slickers. And if the land had a picture postcard view... well... we would be smitten. Fortunately, the decision-making process at Hunga Dunga was cumbersome enough to prevent us from making any rash decisions. But so many communes were getting in on the back-to-the-country act, there was some pressure to find something before all the best postcards were out of print.

Friends of Perfection already had a thriving community up at their farm atop a mountain in Grants Pass in southern Oregon. Flo Airwaves was also bitten by the bug and had just put some money down on twenty acres outside of Willits, a few hours drive north of The City.

At the very end of October, Tom, Brandon, and I spent a weekend with Rolli and Travis camping on their new land. They talked about it as some people do about a new puppy. How cute it was. How full of life. They promised to be patient while they trained it to behave obediently. And they expected, in return, for it to give them unconditional love. We were politely enthused as we walked their boundaries, but the looks Tom, Brandon and I exchanged said... *Boring! Not spectacular enough for Hunga Dunga!*

When we pulled up in front of Big Blue, Richard and Psylvia were sitting on the front steps. Richard had a manila envelope in his hand which he kept slapping against his thigh. As we climbed the stairs, Richard held it out to me.

It was bordered with red, white, and blue diagonal stripes and had the words *First Class* stamped on it. "It's for you, Giacco," Richard said. "Hurry and open it up!"

"I will, Ziets," I said tiredly, "as soon as I take a shower. I'm feeling really grubby."

"No, Chazan!" Richard insisted. "I can't wait! I want you to open it now!"

"OK! OK!" I said, roughly taking the envelope from him and plopping down on the next to the top step. Richard sat down next to me. If he were any more next to me, he would have been on top of me. At least Psylvia had the courtesy to sit on the top step looking down between our shoulders.

I ripped open the top of the envelope and reached inside. There was a short letter and another envelope. The letter read:

Giacco/Jeremiah/Chazan,

We lorf you so very very. We absolutely harf being by our twosome alonely. The son of Better Farm now belongs to another. But we lorf the moocho moola.

Now's the time for all good men (and Rosie) to come to the aid of their hula hula. By the time you get this, we are on our way. We'll pick you up at the airport. Don't ask questions. Don't even try to come up with a "no." Money is no problemo. It's time to hunt and so a-hunting we will go!

Lorfing you like crazy,
J and R
P.S. Say Bali Hai to everyone for us!

I stuck a corner of the letter under my leg so it wouldn't blow away and opened the envelope. It had a big logo on the back. A globe with thick longitudes and latitudes. Across it in large letters read Pan Am. Inside was a ticket.

"My god!" I exclaimed. "It's a ticket to Hawaii!"

"Here, let me see that!" Psylvia said reaching down, plucking the ticket from between my fingers.

"What are they up to? Where did they get the money?" I asked, not expecting an answer.

Richard pulled the letter from under my leg and read it a few times over. Then he looked up pronouncing his decipher of the cryptogram. "They sold the farm in Maine! How could they do that? How dare they do that!" Richard was as upset as if he'd been swindled of his life savings.

"Wait a minute," said Psylvia. "This isn't a ticket to Hawaii."

I turned around and reached up for the ticket, but she just laughed and held it above her head. "What do you mean? It says San Francisco-Honolulu right there on the first line."

"This…" Psylvia said standing up and shuffling a bad soft shoe, "…this is a ticket…" then she bent over, alternately slapping her legs just above the knees, and extending one palm to me as if turning over the dance floor, "*this* is a ticket… around the world!"

"What the…?" Richard and I said simultaneously. Psylvia jumped down a step and sat next to me. The three of us studied the packet of coupons stapled together. The first said San Francisco-Honolulu. But the next coupon said Honolulu-Bangkok, then Bangkok-Colombo. The rest of the coupons provided a connect-the-dots itinerary that circled the globe in a sewing machine zigzag stitch gone amok. Next to the San Francisco-Honolulu leg, it said 10:15AM, 14 Nov 71. But only the word "Open" was listed as the date for the other legs. The very last coupon said, "This ticket is valid for one year from the date of issuance or twenty-four thousand miles, whichever occurs first. Travel is restricted to the Northern Hemisphere."

Before I could catch my breath, Richard jumped up and ran into the house, broadcasting the news into every room and up the stairwell and out the kitchen door and into the back yard. As Psylvia and I walked into the foyer, she asked me, "Well, are you going to go?"

Before I could answer, Baird, descending the stairs stately attired in a kaftan, looked down pompously and asked, "Is it true, Giacco?"

"I think so, Baird. As far as we can tell. The ticket looks legit."

"Are you going to go?" he asked me. And Psylvia turned to wait for the answer to both their questions.

My brain was overloaded with conflicting thoughts. What about the land? What about Hunga Dunga? What about ATD? "I… I don't know. I… I think so!"

Baird just kept staring down the banister at me. He sighed, and seemed decisive, yet reluctant, when he said, "Giacco… I think not!"

BOOK TWO

Orbiting the Planet

CHAPTER 35
November 1971

Diamond Head and the Ko'olau Range beyond caught the late morning sun and tucked its rays into the pali's folds of green suede. When the plane banked, I could look directly down into the ocean. A spectrum of blues and greens that undulated like a lava lamp made the subtlest of currents distinguishable.

As the wings righted for the final approach, I felt my heart quicken at the prospect of seeing Jon and Rosie again. I also felt a little dismayed that I did not have all of Hunga Dunga's blessings packed in my small knapsack. I had a shirt from Lizzie. And a paper heart from Trudy. And a fabric rainbow from Lana. And Zietar gave me his embroidery of the cosmic duck. But from Baird I had only the looks of one who'd been betrayed.

Baird was furious that I had even considered leaving on such a trip without the consent of the family. Just the idea of someone making a unilateral decision bugged him to no end. Lizzie was also upset, but he admitted that what he was feeling was spawned from jealousy, and not from anything I'd done. The four people I would miss the most, Psylvia, Chuck, Richard, and Duck, were my greatest supporters. They were the ones who pleaded my case at the Family Meeting, the one that Baird called immediately after learning of the ticket.

"He's got to go," argued Psylvia. "How can he not go? How can he not take advantage of this?"

"But *why* is he going?" insisted Baird. "What does he hope to accomplish?" he asked as if I weren't sitting right there next to him.

"Baird, it's an adventure," Richard stated the obvious.

"There's more to it than that," Baird said. "Jon and Rosie are guru groupies!" Then he turned to me. "Giacco, you don't need a guru. You have your Self."

Chuck spoke up. "Is that what this is all about, Baird? What does it matter to you if Giacco finds a teacher? What? Are you afraid you'll no longer be master of all you survey?"

Everyone could see the blood climb up Baird's neck to the top of his head as he turned to face me. "You're going to force me to resort to the divinity game. The very teachings you seek are the teachings that tell *me* to tell *you* not to go!"

"And what does that mean?" I inquired.

"Giacco," Baird answered with concern, "Wanting enlightenment is as much a desire as anything else. Maybe it's the last desire... the ultimate desire... but eventually, you have to give that one up too. So, you may as well give it up now."

"Look Baird," I tried to explain, and I hoped it was true, "I'm not going with any expectations whatsoever. You've got it all wrong. In the first place, *I* didn't make the decision to go on this trip. The ticket *was* the decision. I would've never come up with it on my own. I mean... I really don't have much choice in the matter. It's a sign. I have to go. I just *have* to go because... well, because it's just too far out *not* to go."

"A ticket around the world for christ's sake!" Richard chimed in. "Baird, really, how can you expect Giacco to turn it down? Besides, you know Jon and Rosie. With their karma, all he has to do is hang onto their coattails!"

"And what about money?" Baird asked.

"What about it?" Duck said. "Jon's paying for everything. We'll still be getting Giacco's checks. Don't worry. Richard will take care of everything."

Baird tried a different approach, completely atypical for him. "Well, Giacco, the truth is that I don't want you to go because... well, because I'll miss you too much."

That took everyone off guard, especially me. Not that anyone believed him. It was obviously a tactic of last resort, but at Family Meetings, when all else failed, you went for the heart.

"Gosh, Baird!" I finally said, "That makes me feel really good. But it's not like I'm leaving forever. It'll only be a few months at most," even though I knew the ticket was good for a year. "And not only will I miss you... and everyone else... but I really *will* think about what you've said... really."

That seemed to placate Baird, or so I thought. But when the vote was taken, Baird said *no*. I guess he felt obliged to be consistent. Fortunately, he was the only one who objected despite the fact that he'd lobbied Bobby and Alvoye to vote with him. And Luc was very recently defying Baird and becoming more independently-minded every day. Baird cast them all an angry and then disappointed look when they voted *yes,* and Baird could not come up with a reasonable alternative.

I really don't know what would've happened if the family *had* decided I shouldn't go. It would mean *I* would have to make a decision, and everyone knew how hard that was! I'd have to decide whether to abide by the wishes of the group, or to strike out on my own again. That's what it would come down to. That would be the bottom line. Maybe that's what Baird was up to. Maybe he was trying to force my hand. To choose commitment over commentary. Action over observation. To strive toward achieving a shared vision rather than watching the movie of my life from some plush seat in the ethereal loge.

With the usual exceptions, everyone knew that Baird regarded this whole affair as a philosophical conflict. As far as he was concerned, we may as well have been playing out roles from the *Bhagavad Gita*. With the usual exceptions, everyone understood why I had to go and encouraged it. For them there was no conflict. It was just what was happening. And they were happy and excited for me. The usual exceptions shined me on and thought of me as no more than a person who has to collect experiences the way some people have to collect stamps. To them it was just a hobby. To me, it was becoming an unchosen career.

Nevertheless, on the day I was to leave, I found my body loitering in different rooms of the house and my mind lingering on Baird's words. I couldn't argue the fact that it was all the same. Whether your external world was familiar and mundane or exotic and new. It was all the same. You took your mind with you wherever you went. So why go anywhere? In such a mood I could've talked myself into chronic immobility. Upon Baird's words I could have lingered indefinitely. Just because it's all the same.

Psylvia saw the vortex I was falling into and gave me a stage-slap across the face to snap me out of it. Richard picked up my pack. Each of them grabbed an elbow and escorted me out the door. The rest of the family, except Baird, was gathered on the front steps. They threw confetti at me and yelled *"bon voyage!"* and "be sure to write!" and "only drink boiled water!" The three of us climbed into Zwagen. I saw Baird standing in the upstairs bedroom window as we drove away.

When the flight attendant opened the door, a rush of tropical air flooded in. As I made my way down the stairs to the tarmac, it engulfed me. First around my face, then up my sleeves and pants. I felt the contentment of that little boy hiding in his sofa cave next to the heating vent. But that was nothing to the contentment I felt when I saw Jon and Rosie standing in the open door of the terminal.

Rosie started running toward me and I made a move in her direction but an attractive, dark-skinned, nubile woman in a grass skirt stepped in front of me. At first, I thought she was topless but it was an illusion made by the way the necklace of flowers rested against her breasts. Other necklaces hung in the gentle crook of one arm. She jiggled one free and placed it over my head, kissing me on each cheek. "A-lo-ha!" she said. The *ha* was the most energetic syllable, as if it needed a little push through the hot air in order to reach my ears. Hearing a word in the language of vowels, the languid air, the smell of the frangipani around my neck, the tops of palm trees swaying just beyond the security fence, and the figures of Jon and Rosie, now almost upon me, made my soul swoon.

Rosie threw her arms around me and kissed me. She fondled my hishi necklace and said how nice it looked against my Sicilian complexion. I took it off and as I put it around her neck, I said it looked even better against her exquisite tan. I told her I would love for her to wear it for a while, to absorb her beautiful self, but as much as I would like to, I couldn't let her keep it because it had a very special significance to me. When she pried, I believe it was the one and only time I didn't tell her the whole story. Not because she wouldn't understand, but because I myself didn't know what the whole story was. Michael had been a quandary for me, and I didn't have the energy to try to unravel the knot I felt in my stomach every time I thought about him.

Rosie looked wonderful. Her skin glowed. Her face beamed. She was toxin free. Jon nuzzled her aside and gave me a loud and wet smackeroo on the lips. He was thinner than I'd ever seen him, but his eyes were brilliant.

"You guys look wonderful!" I said. "Are you still all raw?"

"Well, I'm still raw," Rosie answered. "Probably from punching myself too often. But Jon here… "

"I…," Jon took over, "I like to think of myself as *basically* fresh, but highly seasoned."

"Oh, in other words, you're off the diet?" I concluded.

"Well, let's just say I'm on a culinary sabbatical… but I'm making up for it by smoking many, many, more cigarettes!"

"Much better, Jon. *Much* better!"

We got off the bus on Kalakaua Avenue a block from the International Market and walked toward Queen Kapiolani Park.

"Where are we going?" I asked.

"To the Jungle!" Jon answered mysteriously and made a face like an African mask.

I screwed up my face with ignorance.

Rosie explained. "The 'Jungle' is what the locals call the neighborhood behind the park, Giacco. Jon is just trying to be cute. Ignore him. That's where we're staying. We got us a small apartment. You'll hate it, I'm sure."

"Why would I hate it?

"It's tacky," Rosie said, "but it's the best we could do. We had a hard time finding someone willing to rent to us by the month."

"Well, how long are we planning on staying here?"

"Who knows?" said Jon. "Time is relative. Why, you got an appointment to be somewhere?"

"The only appointment I have is to be with you," I said. "My engagement book is in your hands."

"Well, let's scope out Hawaii for a bit and just play it by ear," Jon said. "After all, we have a whole year ahead of us." I gulped silently wondering how Hunga Dunga would take that news. I guessed if I wanted to, I could always cut my trip short and go back to The City early, depending on how things worked out. But I really couldn't imagine leaving Jon and Rosie in mid-journey.

A half-block away, coming toward us, was what looked like a purple popsicle stick. As it got closer, we realized it was an old, wizened woman wearing a muumuu. She was walking briskly, but slowed when she noticed us, almost to the pace that seemed more appropriate for an emaciated octogenarian. When we moved to the side to let her pass, she sidestepped in the same direction. She held out her hands, blocking our way with a wall of paisley.

We stopped and she lowered her arms. Then she crossed them, leaned back on one leg, and scrutinized us. She looked all around our bodies, squinting her eyes trying to see something. We looked more carefully at her. Though she looked ancient, she was really just middle-aged, maybe early 50s or so. It was her skin and bones that made her look so old. She was so skinny she was hard to look at. Like a holocaust victim. She displaced so little space; it was curious that the energy she emitted seemed large.

Her voice was powerful and young. "Look at you three! It's about time you got here!"

Jon, Rosie, and I looked at one another and then smiled, humoring her.

"Now *you*..." she said grabbing Rosie by the forearm, "You are a beauty. Just look at your aura, would you? It's just the most glorious blue!" She released Rosie's arms and crossed hers again, pressing the purple fabric flat against her chest.

"But you two!" she said looking at Jon and me. "Tsk, tsk, tsk. Your auras are a nice shade of blue too, except for that ugly, shitty-brown fringe all around it! *When oh when*, I ask you, are you going to stop smoking cigarettes?"

Jon and I shrunk to about two feet tall and looked glumly penitent.

"By the way," she said, reaching into the neck of her muumuu and pulling out a little cloth purse, "I'm Florence." She undid the large safety pin that substituted for a clasp and opened the purse. She peered into it and explored its contents. Then she retrieved a small pair of scissors and a pack of bare-ass Pall Malls. When she coaxed one of them out, she cut it in half with the scissors and worked the remaining half back into the pack. She put the cigarettes and the scissors back in her purse, redid the safety pin, and dropped the purse back under her dress. I guessed from the length of the thin cord around her neck, that the purse must've come to rest somewhere around her belly button.

In a gesture reminiscent of Bette Davis, she held the half-cigarette between her fingers and raised it to her lips. "Gotta light?" she asked Jon.

"Uh, yeah… sure." And he fiddled in a pants pocket for a book of matches. As he lit her cigarette, Jon introduced himself, Rosie, and me. Jon blew the match out. She inhaled deeply with great satisfaction. Though she didn't cough when she blew the smoke into our faces, her chest did convulse slightly. Then she rested the elbow of the arm holding the cigarette in the palm of her other hand and stood there for a minute just looking at us.

"Well, thank you very much. It was nice to make your acquaintance." She started to walk by us, then turned. "I'll see you tonight, OK?"

"Tonight?" Jon asked. "Well, I don't know if we can…"

"Queen's Surf Beach," she ignored him. "Sunset. Every night. That's where I am." She turned again and walked briskly away. The three of us watched her. Then she turned to see if we were watching. She smiled and continued walking, but this time her gait seemed different. It was because she was walking *toe to heel*!

Jon's jaw dropped to his Adam's apple. Then he turned to us, but our wide eyes said more than our voices could have, so none of us said anything and we continued on our way.

Rosie was right. I hated the apartment. It was one half of a small duplex. It was clean enough. It was big enough. But I wouldn't say it was tacky! There wasn't enough there to be tacky.

What did the ad say? For rent. Freshly painted, two-room, sensory deprivation chamber?

The eye thirsted for something… anything… interesting or colorful to look at. The only things that broke the monotony were a pile of Rosie's clothing in the middle of a mattress on the floor, and some books spilling out of Jon's backpack. Most colorful were the papayas, bananas, and mangoes in a large wooden bowl sitting on the counter next to the sink.

I made for the fruit. That's when I noticed the porch… I mean the *lanai*… off the kitchen. Just a small screened-in patio, maybe eight by four. It made up for everything else. There were a couple of weathered rattan chairs on either side of a small bamboo table with a glass top. A vinyl covered foam pad lay unfolded off to the side. It looked like it belonged to a lawn chair. It did. To the one that was in a sitting position just outside the lanai in the tiny backyard. But what a backyard! An old guava tree. A lime. Two papaya trees. Three young bananas. All fenced in by hibiscus bushes.

"This is your room if you want it," Rosie said. "What do you think?"

I turned from our miniature Eden and announced, "I love it! It's great!"

Rosie and Jon were very pleased. It really was the best room in the place and the lanai was where, for all practical purposes, we all wound up spending our time. The rest of the apartment became merely a storage area for three backpacks and a place where Jon and Rosie could go to be by themselves.

Rosie squeezed one of the papayas in the bowl and took it out. "Want some papaya, Giacco?"

"Sure. Sounds good!" I answered. She sliced it in half long ways and scraped the black seeds out into a plastic bowl. "How about you, Jonny?"

"No thanks, honnee!" Jon called from the area to be known as the bedroom. He was rummaging through a paper bag next to his pack. Rosie went to the refrigerator and pulled out a quart of yoghurt. She scooped tablespoons of it into the papaya halves until they were filled. Then she placed a cumquat on top of each one. She guided me back to the lanai and handed me one of the sundaes and a spoon. We each sat in a rattan chair.

Jon came in and dragged the foam pad closer to us. There was a whoosh of air as he plopped down on it. "Ahh! Excuse me," he said widening his eyes and raising his brows as if he'd just let go a big one. "Really!" Rosie said. "Have you no manners?" He put one joint on the glass top of the table and lit the other one. As he passed it to Rosie, the wind picked up and the sky cast over. The sudden rain was refreshing. The wind remained warm as it blew steadily through the lanai. The papaya was sweet as candy. The yoghurt provided the pretense it was health food. The entire digestive system, from the palate to the colon, welcomed the whole concoction. The rain lasted no longer than it took to finish the one joint of what Jon claimed was Maui Zowie. His claim was probably correct because by the time the sun once again flooded the back yard, the afternoon was utterly transcendental.

"Now this is the life to which I can easily become accustomed." I informed them. Jon and Rosie laughed in agreement and the three of us drifted off into private thoughts.

I thought about how fast a person's perspective can change. How now, just a half-day away, it's as if it never was… Hunga Dunga, that is. I thought about comings and goings. About couples and uncouplings. About how readily the mind can visit one cosmos and then another… from micro to mac. And know that neither is grander than the other, but simply concentric.

CHAPTER 36
November 1971

As the sun began its descent, we walked the five blocks to Queen's Surf Beach. As if we knew where we were going, we arrived at exactly that strip of beach where someone was obviously the center of attention. We approached and the circle of people reminded me of petitioners eagerly awaiting whoever was holding court to dispense favors and grant requests.

It was Florence. The strange woman we met earlier in the day. She sat cross-legged on a thin blanket. Her knobby knees did to my eyes the same thing that fingernails on a blackboard do to the ears. To one side of her, a pack of Pall Malls lay open with four cigarettes spilling out. They pointed to the small pair of scissors. A half-cigarette, almost all ash, dangled from her lips. She reached for one of the loose cigarettes and cut it in two with the scissors. Then, rather than put the cigarette she was smoking out, she used it to light one of the fresh halves. The only time a half-cigarette left her lips was to pick flecks of tobacco from the sticky corners of her mouth. She smoked while she talked. She smoked while she read a palm. She smoked while she threw yarrow stalks for the I Ching. She smoked while she read Tarot cards. In between sentences, she exhaled smoke from the side of her mouth. She never flicked an ash, but let it grow as long as it wanted to until gravity made it fall onto her muumuu. Then she'd brush it off haphazardly, unconcerned, though I did notice a few burn holes in her dress. I never did understand why Florence chain-smoked half a cigarette at time, but it was the least of her eccentricities.

When she saw us in silhouette standing in front of the setting sun, she gestured with some breaststrokes for her groupies to spread out and make room for us.

"All of you… move over… make space for Jon and Rosie!" she ordered. Then, as if an afterthought, "Oh and… what's your name again… Gino? Marco? Something mafia like that!"

"Giacco," I corrected her.

"Yes, that's it! Let Giacco in too!"

Faces of all ages looked up, but most of them were young. They shifted their butts in the sand and the circle widened. They hadn't quite decided what to make of me, but they immediately seemed to regard Jon and Rosie as celebrities. Maybe it was because Florence hadn't forgotten their names. Or the way she said them. Their regard was heightened by the interest Florence showed in them. She behaved as if they *were* special. She obviously liked their company. She obviously connected with them on a vibrational level. She asked them perceptive questions. She offered to answer theirs. Florence was polite to me, but she made me feel like I was a vestigial appendage of the dynamic duo.

"Are *you* our teacher?" were the first words out of Jon's mouth after Florence finished her background investigation.

She laughed though it sounded more like barking. "My Lord, no! "Whatever makes you think that?"

Jon looked embarrassed. "Just asking."

And that one question promoted Jon and Rosie to the top of her short list of illuminati innamorati. Florence motioned Jon and Rosie to sit in front of her. There were unintelligible whisperings around the circle. I was conspicuously ignored.

"What about Giacco?" Jon asked.

Florence fanned the cards with their faces down and slid one out onto the blanket. Then she closed the fan and shuffled the cards while gazing from Rosie to Jon to the cards and back again.

"Giacco? I'll do him separately, some other time," she offered casually.

Even at my angle to them, I could see a look of distress come over Jon and Rosie's faces. Every mystical signal was momentous, and every spiritual nuance was of great importance to seekers such as us… or perhaps from Florence's point of view… seekers such as *them*. Maybe Florence didn't regard me as being in the same league. Maybe she didn't see me as a true seeker. Maybe I'd already forfeited my claim to being one when I told Baird I was just "tagging along to bask in the afterglow of Jon and Rosie's karma!" This was a convenient way of shirking the responsibilities of an apprentice sadhu. Florence felt Jon and Rosie's discomfort at my exclusion.

"Giacco has his own karma," she said softly, reassuringly. "It is very much connected to both of yours… especially Jon's… but not entirely. Giacco is…" She tilted her head in thought but the sagging flesh around her neck stayed where it was. "Giacco is incomplete!" She said it quickly to get it over with. "The two of you are the most complementary Yin and Yang I've seen in years, or maybe ever. So, I can read *your* cards… at least at this point in time… as if you were one entity. But Giacco, I'll have to do alone."

Everything she said made sense even though I worried some kind of precedent was being set. Some self-fulfilling prophecy that would always put me in Jon and Rosie's shadow. I didn't mind if I had to walk behind them. I just hoped it was on the same path.

"Now," Florence said to Rosie, "Give me something on your person that you cherish." Rosie thought for a moment and then undid the hishi necklace and handed it to Florence. She dusted the card with it slowly forth and back imbuing it with its energy. Then she placed it next to the card. She turned the card over. It was The Lovers. "This is the Significator," she explained, indicating The Lovers card in front of her. "This is you!" Then she cut the remaining cards in three stacks and asked Rosie to pick them up in any order and hand them to her.

"I want you both to breathe deeply. Meditate. Focus your energy on your breath." She did the same. After a minute, she placed the deck in the palm of one skeletal hand, and with the other, drew the first card from the top. She laid it face down, covering The Lovers with it. She crossed that card with another. Then, very swiftly, she dealt eight more cards; all face down, arranging them in a spread resembling a Celtic cross.

The reading lasted about a half hour. As she turned over each card, heads in the circle craned to see what it was. The pictures were fun to look at though I would not have noticed all the details within them if Florence hadn't pointed them out. Despite her interpreting the cards for Jon and Rosie, the words also seemed to apply to me, though that was not her intent. How she came up with their meanings was lost on me, I assumed she was tapping an intuitive wellspring rather than channeling some invisible messenger. What was not lost on any of us were the salient instructions, admonishments, cautions, and predictions. Some were very specific, others more general:

Jon and Rose were embarking on a trip of great consequence, but we were still carrying too much "baggage." We were not to bring anything we had packed, except necessary documents and money. She instructed us to give everything away, including our backpacks. She commanded Rosie to make each of us a small, zippered, cloth bag that we could carry over one shoulder. We were told never to accumulate more than the bag could comfortably hold.

"There is an *infinite* supply to those who keep themselves empty," she said to the entire gathering, not joyfully or inspirationally, but rather as if it were a law of physics and she were Archimedes teaching his students how to use the lever and fulcrum. "So, keep yourselves *empty* and everything you need will come to you in abundance."

She focused her attention back to Jon and Rosie. "Your numbers are nine and twenty-two. Nine is the number for love. Twenty-two is the key to the universe." Then she once more visually swept the circle and gave everyone a brief refresher course in numerology. "Whether you're shopping or deciding which bus to take, pay attention to any numbers that come your way. Add up the digits. She panned the circle of faces mesmerized by her words and spoke to them. "If you know which numbers are auspicious for you, great. If you don't... find out!"

Her eyes went back to Jon and Rosie and her voice got softer and less didactic. "If the digits of any numbers you run into add up to nine or twenty-two... that's a sign. Follow it!"

Her voice got even softer, almost intimate. "You will meet a Swami. However, he is not dark-skinned. He is fair."

"Is that our teacher?" Jon asked excitedly.

"I'm not sure," Florence replied. "You will definitely learn from him. He may be your teacher. He may not be. But you'll know when you meet him."

The last thing I remember about what Florence said that evening sticks in my mind because it was difficult for her to say. It was the only moment during the reading she looked, first surprised, then uncomfortable.

"Like the perfect circle you are," she prefaced, placing one hand on Jon's shoulder and the other on Rosie's knee, "complete and sustainable unto yourselves, your circle cannot encompass a larger universe until it is torn asunder... until the circle is broken!"

Rosie and Jon looked horrified. "What does that mean in real life?" Jon asked.

"Well, this is hard for me to say, but I think the cards mean you and Rosie must go your separate ways!"

Rosie audibly gasped. Jon squeezed her hand.

"Oh, not immediately," Florence quickly added. "But within the next year I would say, the two of you must, for your own spiritual growth, follow different destinies."

This came as a big blow to the three of us. I, for one, could barely think of Jon without thinking of Rosie, and vice-versa. It was almost enough for me to want to declare Florence a charlatan. However, she ameliorated the bad news with one last sentiment.

"Look, you two. I've been around long enough to know most everything comes full circle. Maybe not in one lifetime, but usually. I *feel* it's very likely that, should this come to pass, should you two find yourselves going your separate ways, it will only be temporary."

A big look of relief came over Jon and Rosie's faces. Until she continued.

"Mind you, *temporary* may mean years! Maybe even decades! But before you leave this earthly world for good, both of you will come full circle back into each other's arms."

Rose put the hishi necklace back around her neck and she and Jon rejoined the circle, looking glum and confused. Almost as a conciliatory gesture, Florence beckoned me to the spot they had vacated.

"I guess this is as good a time as any to see what the cards hold for you, Giacco," she said.

I liked the picture of the Fool most of all and I hoped that the card would come up, but to my great disappointment, she carefully placed her Tarot cards in a purple silk scarf and wrapped them in a ritualistic manner with the same sanctimony that Marines fold the American flag. From a large straw bag, she produced a different deck of cards. The kind you play poker with. Regular playing cards. I felt demeaned and especially common. She was going to read *my* fortune according to Hoyle! I was obviously not worth the deference with which she had read Jon and Rosie's future.

After cutting the cards with her left hand, she discarded the top card and then dealt sixteen cards face down, four across by four down. The backs of the cards all had the same logo on them… an eagle with its wings spread and the words, "Compliments of American Airlines." This, of course, did nothing to further my self-esteem. The next two cards she placed off to the side, again face down.

Pointing to them she said, "These are your Wish cards, but we'll get to them later." Sweeping the back of her hand just above the top row of four cards, she said, "This is the Far Past." She turned each one over, left to right, and studied them. Then she looked up and pronounced their meanings.

Nothing she said could be refuted because it was so general. It could have been true of anyone: I had conflicts with my parents. I suffered from feelings of inadequacy. I had a traumatic experience, probably in high school.

She passed her hand above the next row of cards… the Near Past. She turned all of them over and smiled in relief. I guessed things were looking up. The card which seemed to catch her attention the most was the King of Clubs.

"This is very, very good," she said brightly. "Yes, very nice, indeed! Not too long ago you came under the influence of a protector! A mighty protector! One to be reckoned with! Male. Paternal. God-like!" She looked past me at someone sitting in the circle of onlookers. I suspected it was Jon. "Yes, this is most comforting!" she concluded.

She came to the third row while her ghoulishly skinny hand swept gracefully once more over the cards. I tried to remember the traumatic experience in high school to which she must've been referring. There were so many to choose from! Her voice snapped me out of it.

"The Present!" Florence announced as if unveiling the latest sedan out of Detroit. Considering the gusto with which she introduced this part of my life, the cards themselves revealed little.

"Curious," said Florence. "If I didn't know you were sitting here in front of me… if there were a curtain between us… I would have to swear there was no one on the other side! I've rarely seen a Present with so little presence! It's as if you're not even here! Like you're one of the shadows made by the fire in Plato's cave!" She looked up at me and stared hard, trying to find me. I felt others in the circle doing the same. It was embarrassing, which surprised me because I always thought it would be really cool to be invisible. "Oh well," she said casually. "This should make the Future all the more interesting!"

Two of the four cards in that bottom row really excited her. "This is most telling! How perfect!" she said very pleased with herself. "Look, Giacco! The Ace of Clubs!" My eyes widened in anticipation. "The Ace of Clubs foretells of a great journey. A journey over water!" My eyes remained wide out of politeness. Everyone there had learned not an hour ago of our plans to go to India. So what else was new?

"And right next to the Ace of Clubs is the Eight of Spades!"

"And…," I prompted.

"And… well… the Eight of Spades represents a journey, too. *A hazardous journey!*"

She summed it all up. "The journey will be over water. And it will be very hazardous. That's what the cards say. In fact, I would be very careful every time you find yourself near a large body of water, if I were you!"

Oh, better. That's much better! How very comforting! I snuck a look at the expanse of ocean not more than thirty feet behind me and felt a little shiver from a spray of foam that misted my face.

"Now I want you to concentrate very hard. I want you to wish!" Florence instructed me. "Wish for anything. Wish for as much as you want. Wish. Wish." Her voice got softer. "Wish… wish!" The word became a violet crystal hanging from a piece of fishing line, swinging before my eyes. I closed them and tried to sort through my desires.

I pictured a road. It was much like the yellow brick road in the Land of Oz. *I wish to see the Wizard, the wonderful Wizard of Oz*, I heard myself singing to myself over and over. The Emerald City beckoned in the distance, a brilliant light shining behind it. I clicked the lobes of my brain together three times and repeated silently, "There's no place like Om! There's no place like Om!" I was cracking myself up! I felt like I was in a sitcom, but you had to have my sense of humor to get the jokes. I just couldn't focus. I opened my eyes just a little, and saw the crystal was still swinging forth and back. *Now that's a quartz of a different color!* I yelled silently at myself to get serious.

I closed my eyes tighter and thought about what I really wanted.

The first thing that entered my mind was the blond, hunky surfer sitting next to Rosie. I wished he would steal into my lanai that night and have his way with me. When I realized what I was thinking, I got even angrier at myself. I kicked and scratched and forcefully pushed that thought out of the way, feeling it was inappropriate for one seeking enlightenment, but understandable considering I hadn't had sex in what seemed like forever.

I commanded my mind to sit on a passing cloud, tried to imagine what it would be like to know and see everything, possess complete understanding of the cosmos, and wished to be the embodiment of Love and Peace. To my extreme chagrin, images of the surfer slowly pulling down his wet trunks as he approached my foam pad kept yanking me away from such noble thoughts. I tried my best to haul my ass back to the cloud and keep it there.

"Ready?" Florence asked, snipping the rope of my cerebral tug of war. Both my wishes went splattering into mind-mud.

"Uh, yeah, I guess so." I said.

She turned over the first Wish card. "The King of Spades! Now that's what I like to see! The Seeker! *You*! Can't you see the resemblance?"

I bent over the card and squinted. Long black hair, dark and shifty eyes, a distorted angular face with a cubist nose. Yep, that was me all right! No wonder I wasn't scoring!

She turned over the second Wish card. It was the Queen of Spades.

"Oh, no!" She backed away from the card like it was a black widow spider. "And it's facing the King!" Her eyes darted around the circle and refused to meet mine except in passing. The young woman sitting immediately to Florence's right, sucked in a short, sharp breath.

"Well, that's enough for today," Florence said, throwing her cards, the crystal, her Pall Malls and little scissors into the straw bag. Her knobby knees creaked as she stood up. "See you all tomorrow… bye!" And she toe-to-heeled it across the beach, her little bony feet leaving claw marks in the sand.

Everyone stood up. No one knew what to do or how to be. It was like a cocktail party for the extremely introverted. We just stood there like dunes in the wind, unable or unwilling to make conversation. Jon and Rosie shifted over to me, while all the others, except for the woman who gasped, shifted in the direction of the neon signs of Kalakaua Avenue.

"What was that all about?" I asked them worriedly. More worried about having somehow insulted Florence than what the cards may have said.

Jon and Rosie just shrugged.

"Death!" A breathy voice said almost deliberately trying to sound foreboding.

We turned to the woman, now pulling a sweatshirt from her daypack. She slipped it over her head and wriggled her arms through the sleeves. Her voice was muffled through the soft grey fabric. "The Queen of Spades. Not necessarily evil or bad. But when it's facing another face card… I mean *especially* when it's facing the card that represents *you*…" Her head popped out the knit collar and she shook her long brown hair loose. Her voice, unfiltered by the cloth, finished the sentence with shocking clarity. "Well, it means… Death!"

CHAPTER 37
December 1971

A strange kind of ennui descended upon the three of us with the swiftness of a tropical storm. Could it have been Florence's readings? She definitely touched a nerve in all of us, from the very first day we met her.

Rosie believed that whatever Florence had said to us, lending any mental energy at all to her words would only reinforce their actualization. The only thing to do was to get it out of our minds. She took off the hishi necklace and handed it back to me. "This is beautiful, Giacco, but I don't think it's a good luck charm… at least not for me." I took it from her and put it back on. I never took it off again.

Jon pointed out that the Queen of Spades would've shown up regardless of what I was thinking. We all create our own reality with our thoughts. But that's exactly what it was that bothered me.

If I couldn't control my mind, as evidenced by my ability to *not* think about sex when I didn't want to think about it, then I *couldn't* create my own reality. I could only create the ones dictated by my desires. And if that was true, was it possible I didn't desire enlightenment enough for *it* to become my reality? Everything would be just fine if I could get rid of my mind once and for all.

On subsequent evenings with Florence and her entourage, eavesdropping on other people's destinies, we realized that Florence had a predilection for dire consequences. She would play upon your weaknesses. She could fuck cabalically with your mind.

The three of us decided not to think about any of it any longer and renewed our vows to submit to everything that crossed our path without internal commentary. We would just let the universe happen to us. In the Islands, that is particularly easy to accomplish.

If Hawaii were a verb, it would be used in the passive voice. We languidly surrendered to all it had in tropical store for us. We didn't have to do anything! Well… maybe allow ourselves to be fondled by ticklish warm breezes; or be playfully manhandled by the surf; our noses seduced by exotic fragrances and our oiled skins bronzed by the therapeutic sun. We had to permit our palates to be surprised by strange and elegantly tasting fruits. And since it was futile to resist, we had to let our minds be altered by mythically potent herbs. Other than that, Hawaii did all the work. She was so kind and bountiful it was easy to live in the ever-passive tense.

Inaction seemed to come so easily, and the senses seemed perfectly satisfied even when we were doing absolutely nothing. We weren't lazy or unimaginative. We were just being Hawaii'd and were too weak-willed to fight it! I thought this is what it might be like to be a heroin addict.

It was with the greatest effort that we finally kicked ourselves in the collective butt and decided to do something. Something unique. Something physically challenging. Like hiking across the moonscape of Mt. Haleakala.

It was hardly a challenge. Not for space travelers like us. We did the whole thing toe to heel and even then, we had to loiter around craters and blooming silversword plants to make the trip last a weekend. As Jon pointed out in bottomless understatement, "Let's face it guys. Once you've seen a silversword plant in bloom, you've seen them all!"

It's a good thing we'd gotten a hold of some acid. It made the loitering much less boring. We discovered, much to our delight, that we'd become weightless. And we realized in triplicate, that we really *were* space beings. And when the real full moon rose that night, shining its light onto the lunar landscape under our feet, we danced a slow-motion, gravity-free, bunny hop all the way to the Kaupo Gap.

The next morning, just before dawn, we stumbled euphorically down the crater side, descending through a couple of climates and a few mezzanines of clouds. Eventually the sea separated from the sky as their blues hued differently under the rising sun. The horizon hazily appeared but became more defined as the solar protractor began to circumscribe the far edge of the world.

We made our way toward the sea. Koa trees graced the broadening slope. Then wild blackberries. The sun was getting higher and hotter. The foliage was greening and thickening. Wild papayas offered us breakfast and another hundred feet down, ripe bananas, caused us to loiter once again.

By noon, we were at Wailua Falls. By three, we had dipped in all seven of its pools. By five-thirty, we were at the airport in Kahului. By six-thirty, we were back in Waikiki, sharing an inspirational sunset with Florence and her regulars and all those in the world similarly occupied.

Life was so laconic and self-indulgent I felt a little guilty. The only times I felt I warranted such a lifestyle was when I found myself talking about god stuff. Or more often than not, listening about god stuff. Usually, the spiritual repartee occurred between Jon and any one or more of the many hippies who had decided that if they were going to pursue enlightenment, they might as well start in the Garden of Eden.

It was only at those times when I listened to bright-eyed, innocent, inquisitive hippie angels; or long-, short-, or no-haired zealots who proselytized about one path or another, that I felt somewhat redeemed. That I was doing something worthwhile. Passively absorbing holiness, the same way my skin was passively absorbing the sun. Combing the cosmic beach for spiritual driftwood without even having to leave my towel.

It didn't matter what the words were. Or what language they were in. As long as they had something to do with peace, contentment, light, bliss… my ears hung onto every word said by these visitors to our blanket. But my eyes and mind inevitably found themselves hanging onto the lips that were speaking the words. And then the throat. And the chest. And the concave stomach. And finally, the holy of holies! That's where my eyes and mind always ended up.

I would like to, but can't account for, the correlation between physical beauty and the desire to know god. It seemed the more a person yearned for the light, the more attractive they were. At least to me. The more they teased my mind with cosmic insights, the greater the rumblings in my groin. I fell in love with all of them.

That included Caleb, a devotee of Kirpal Singh. He was from New Zealand. His surfer body was so tanned that his sun-bleached blond hair and eyebrows seemed artificial in contrast to his skin. He had just been initiated on the big island. He couldn't tell me anything about what went on, but he seemed afire with an energy that really excited me.

Then there was Sarah. From Arizona. She strolled the beach every afternoon around four o'clock. She always wore a very modest, white chenille robe that covered her up to her neck. She may or may not have known that when she came up to our blanket, which she invariably did when she spied us in our usual place, the sun behind her revealed a slender, almost boyish figure. It was obvious she was naked underneath, and it took very little imagination to see in detail how inviting she was. Rosie always chuckled, but Jon always had to work at keeping his eyes from wandering.

When Sarah looked down at me and her long-hennaed hair fell forward and her light blue eyes got a faraway look as she spoke of B'Hai… well, she struck chords down in my lower abdomen I wasn't sure were there anymore.

But as attracted as I was to both of them… and a few others as well… I guess I was only supposed to get my *spiritual* rocks off. Caleb was a practicing celibate, or so he said. *How convenient!* But he did intimate he might otherwise be interested. *How nice!* And Sarah always talked about sex as if it were definitely many rungs down the ladder from where she knew the fruit called "bliss" was just waiting to be picked by her. *How delicious!*

I guess for me, sex just wasn't in the cards. But I hated the idea that sex and enlightenment were mutually exclusive, so I decided not to think about it. I only hoped this dry spell wasn't yet another precedent of things to come. Or in my case, of things *not* to come. It didn't last that long. It's just that I had hoped my next sexual partner would be a human.

CHAPTER 38
Christmas Eve 1971

"Bartender! Hit me again!" Rosie demanded after she slurped through a flexi-straw the last drops of her electric tropical fruit punch. She held her glass up to Jon. "And pass me that bowl of macadamia nuts."

Jon opened the refrigerator and took out a clear plastic pitcher three-quarters full of a neon orange liquid. He refilled her glass, and then topped off his own. John looked at the bowl on the counter but left it there. "Those are the mushrooms, sweetie… the ones Caleb gave us. I'd let the acid kick in a little more before I do any."

"Oh! Right!" Rosie agreed. "Well then, just in case I get the munchies you'd better put them out of sight." She took the glass from Jon, pursed her lips around the straw, and daintily sucked. "This is really good, Jon!"

Jon walked out the screen door of the lanai, the pitcher still in his hand, and stood under the banyan tree.

"Yoo-hoo. Giacco. Where are you?"

"I'm right over here, honnee!" I answered through a smile I couldn't wipe off my face. Jon looked through the branches.

"Not that high. Lower down," I directed.

"Oh, there you are!" he said when he spied my shadowy form melting into the sagging curve of a broad limb. "Want some more punch?"

"No thanks, Jonnie. I'm doing just fine. But you can take this glass in for me, OK?"

Jon walked toward my voice and swung one leg over the branch that was just beneath mine. It was so low to the ground, he looked like he was mounting a child's hobbyhorse. Once he straddled it, he bounced up and down, and the wood steed cantered in place.

"You doin' OK, Chazan?"

"I'm doing fine! How about you?"

"I'm starting to feel a ripple up my spine. But Rosie's already flying! She hasn't figured that out yet, but I can tell!"

"Did you do any of the mushrooms?" I asked.

"No, not yet. We want to wait a while. See what the acid does. Is this the first time you've done mushrooms and acid together?"

"Probably not," I said, noticing it was getting more difficult to form my words, "but it may as well be!"

"Are you OK out here by yourself?" Jon, the Protector, asked.

"But I'm not out here by myself," I chuckled.

"Well, you soon will be! Jon said. "Here, hand me your glass. I'm going back inside with Rosie." Before he closed the screen door behind him, he looked back at me. "Come on in soon, OK?"

I relaxed the length of my body against the limb and took two or three deep breaths.

The first three tiers of the main branches of the banyan were so wide you could walk on them. They stretched out almost horizontally from the trunk. The one that invited me to lounge upon it dipped downward before curving back skywards at its extremity.

I heard some undecipherable conversation coming from Jon and Rosie through the screens of the lanai, but the recognition of their voices alone was soothing. Jon clicked on the radio, and music filtered into the backyard.

Stevie Winwood was singing, *God is your vision of Heaven, and Heaven is in your mind.*

I looked around me. The limbs of the banyan reminded me of muscular arms. At times they began to move and writhe like thick pythons. The bark under my back began to undulate... slowly, but with an undercurrent of great strength, like the massage of a powerful Samoan.

I closed my eyes so as not to detract from the tactile sensations. My skin noticed that the breeze was picking up before my ears did. There was a consciousness that my body was operating at a molecular level, each molecule hypersensitive to my arboreal environment.

I melted deeper into the tree. The molecules of the banyan began flirting with the molecules of my skin. As if sensing how amorous I was feeling, the banyan undressed my molecules until they stood there naked, cells and all.

It was futile to resist. I let the banyan absorb my atomic structure and felt the exchange of electrons as I became the tree.

There was a very deep rumbling emanating from somewhere deep in the trunk. An earthquake about to happen. I could feel it coursing through every limb. And the limb I was now a part of seemed to engorge itself with power, making us both tremble.

The wind steadily increased titillating all the leaves, caressing them, not gently, yet not recklessly either. They twisted, they rustled, excited now by the increasing pleasure. The stroking fingers of air left no leaf untouched. They swirled in ecstasy as the fingers played with their topsides and undersides, no erogenous zone too taboo for exploration, and every zone an erogenous one.

Even the larger limbs swayed euphorically, like hips too aroused and begging for more, unwilling to slake for a moment the seduction. The banyan started to groan in unfathomable satisfaction when a gust of wind brought it to a state of frenzied passion.

We couldn't prolong the rapture. We were beyond control. The sexual cyclotron scattered multi-colored universes of atoms into multi-colored universes of stars. Each one exploded with the intensity of the grand finale of a Fourth of July fireworks display, showering humanity with shimmering rainbow sparklers. The crowd sings *oohs* and *aahs* and gasps in delight. They applaud wildly with gratitude and appreciation.

The wind died down. I opened my eyes. I felt wonderfully satiated, but fatigued. I pushed myself up until I was leaning on my elbows. Somehow unsurprised, I found myself naked. I let my legs dangle around the branch and surveyed my body as if it were something separate from me. I watched my cock reluctantly subside to a less rigid position, stiffening momentarily now and then on its way down.

The inside of my thighs, my lower abdomen, my cock, and my groin were sweetly sticky from what could only have been banyan sap. Too bad I had to end up in the hospital.

Equestrian judges would not have regarded highly, the dismount from my wooden steed. I assumed I had achieved oneness with the banyan, but we parted company unexpectedly and I hit my head on the terrazzo floor of the patio.

Jon and Rosie were far more freaked than I, though my vision was very blurred, and my head was pounding with excruciating pain. I think it was all the blood that got to them. At the small, one-story hospital, Jon provided no useful information whatsoever. He avoided with indignation the questions the admitting nurse asked regarding payment for services, and instead lashed back at her about the hospital's obvious lack of adequate personnel to attend to my immediate needs. These were mere formalities that could be dealt with later.

She didn't pursue the questioning any further but pointed out that it was three o'clock in the morning and now Christmas Day. We waited a long time. A doctor eventually arrived and looked me over. A concussion was his diagnosis and a two to three day stay in the hospital was in order plus a full battery of tests and X-rays. I resisted as best I could, but everyone, including Jon and Rosie, thought I should stay. I wonder if the doctor noticed that the three of us were still tripping.

While visiting me late that afternoon, Jon picked up a magazine. One of those expensive rags meant for a very select demographic group, in this case, nutritionists. In it was an article about a group of researchers seeking the one place on the planet with the most perfect diet.

Their consensus was a little island named Puka Puka. The team of doctors who wrote the article began on a scientific note, studying the diet of the native population. They itemized the foods, their preparation, and caloric intake, putting to use their scientific methods. Those methods obviously didn't last for long, because the article turned into a more personal recounting of their experiences. This included the lack of clothing worn by the women, and the morality that was equally scant. More than once, they referred to the local "mead" that seemed essential to their culture. By the time the scientists were midway through their study, the mead seemed equally essential to them. The article made Jon's wanderlust increase with an intensity of which only he was capable. However, it was not the perfect diet that he searched for.

The morning of my third and last day in the hospital, Jon announced it was time to move on. We had learned all we would learn in Hawaii, and it was time to cross the "great waters" as Florence had predicted. An administrative looking guy came in, handed me a bill, and then left. When Jon and I looked at it, we nearly shit in our pants. This was certainly a time to speak up against the corporate health care system! What ever happened to the Hippocratic Oath? We ranted and raved a score of socio-philosophic arguments that rationalized running out on the bill. The most persuasive was that if Jon spent his money on the hospital bill, then we wouldn't have enough to do any traveling at all.

I can't explain why that administrative guy seemed to distrust us, but we could see he was loitering in the hall within eyesight of my room a little too long for comfort.

Jon very assuredly and calmly strolled about the room, admiring the few wall decorations that didn't have tubes coming out of them. As he did so, he gathered up my clothes. Or rather, cloth. There wasn't much to gather since Jon and Rosie had brought me to the hospital virtually naked except for one of Rosie's sarongs that she had hastily tied around me.

Following Jon's eye movements and mouthing *one, two, three,* we bolted for the window and jumped out of it into a hibiscus bush. The administrator ran immediately into the room and leaned out the window. He yelled for security.

Jon and I ran toe to heel as fast as we could. Me with my hospital gown flapping in the tropical breeze, unintentionally mooning the poor man. Jon, giggling and waving Rosie's sarong above him like Isadora Duncan, we ran toe to heel down the street. We ran toe to heel through people's yards. We ran toe to heel through dirt paths walled on both sides by sugar cane. We ran toe to heel all the way down to the sea. We ran toe to heel until we were back at Queen's Surf beach, and, of course, our Rosie. We felt like embassy staff with diplomatic immunity. We could do no harm; we could get into no trouble.

Nevertheless, we decided to leave the next day, just in case.

CHAPTER 39

Good Friday, March 31, 1972

Now where was I? I had a temperature of 104+ degrees. My bedding was soaked with sweat. I was delirious. I love delirium! If you're going to have a fever, it may as well be fun! What could be more fun than drifting in and out of dreams while bathing in the luxury of hot springs?

When I drifted in, which was briefer than my drifting outs, I noticed Jon tending a fire in the freestanding stove in the middle of a squat hut. The dwelling was poorly sided and uninsulated. Daylight filtered through cracks in the wood.

Rosie leaned over me and dabbed my forehead every so often. She tried to get me to drink some tea but was unsuccessful. Drifting out was so comforting, I required nothing.

During a moment of drifting in, I heard Jon and Rosie talking. Though I couldn't really understand the literal conversation, the gist came through: It was Good Friday. I was the Poet-warrior, Chazan. If not enlightened, I had at least done the most spiritually honorable thing to do, "Accept all, deny nothing." Jon and Rose also seemed to be saying it was fitting that I should die here in Kathmandu.

Kathmandu? It was fitting that I should die here in Kathmandu? On Good Friday? Wait a minute! What the hell are they talking about? Die? Just so it will sound profound or something to say I died on the same day that Jesus was crucified?

It was an easy date to remember, that's for sure! Just like people who remember their friends and relatives whose births or deaths fall on Christmas or New Year's. Valentine's Day or the Fourth of July. The others are so easy to forget. But they'll remember mine! Because it will be easy! I was just so damned accommodating!

I drifted back out. I would have liked to stay out a while longer.

But there was this young, handsome Englishman. He was a traveling hippie like us, but a nurse by trade. He very reluctantly gave up some magic potions he'd been hoarding should he ever find himself in similar circumstances.

I was completely better in two days. Completely! Not a sign of illness. I was feeling as good as the Ascension itself!

All who knew what had happened hailed the English nurse as an angel and his magic potion, Lomotil, as a gift from his god. Lomotil, a name that was very conducive to a chant.

Many travelers in Kathmandu chanted "Lo-mo-til, lo-mo-til" over and over and with great feeling, and the English nurse became very popular and revered along with anyone else who had any of the magic potion. And the company that made the magic potion was removed from our "industrial/military complex" bashings list.

"The Resurrection," as Jon and Rosie kept calling it. They admitted to me that they truly thought I was going to leave my body. Jon had been preparing by rereading portions of the Tibetan Book of the Dead. He showed me the passages he had dog-eared. Rosie was wondering how she would break the news to my parents, especially when she would tell them how she and Jon had taken the liberty to have me cremated atop a burning ghat along the Bagmati River.

Nepal was virtually the end of the road for Jon and Rosie. The journey had taken its toll on all of us, but most of all on them. They had bet that Florence's predictions were wrong, but they were starting to get on each other's nerves and drift apart. They had bet that they would find their teacher in the lands famous for them. And they almost did. Several times.

If Nepal was the virtual end of the road for Jon and Rose, the literal beginning for all three of us was at the Pan Am office in Honolulu. The morning after my abrupt self-discharge from the hospital, we spruced ourselves up to look as respectable as possible and took a bus downtown. A nice Pan Am ticket agent, whose nametag said Mary Ellen, looked over our around-the-world tickets. Everything seemed in order for a change. "It just doesn't get much better than this!" Jon concluded.

On the 29th of December, we were on a flight destined for Bangkok, which would just be our diving board into South Asia. Jon wasn't all that interested in Thailand and didn't want to "waste" much time there. He wasn't quite sure why, but he felt Thailand was merely on the fringes of the cosmic sarong. He wanted to be in Colombo by New Year's Day. He was anxious to get entangled in the fabric, not the fringes.

Not at all to his delight, however, flights from Bangkok to Colombo had been suspended. Something about civil unrest and uprisings. Maybe we weren't very politically astute at the time, or considered politics beneath us, or just assumed that ignorance *was* really bliss. I don't know for sure which applied to us, but we were obliged, despite the ants in Jon's pants, to spend a week or so in Bangkok awaiting the resumption of flights to Ceylon.

Jon and Rosie spent every day visiting temples and monasteries. Sometimes they would spend a whole day in a temple trying their best to "sit" cross-legged in silent bliss watching their thoughts pass by. A few times, Rosie, much more limber than Jon, would have to help him out of his lotus position, gently undoing one locked leg at a time and massaging his knees.

They sought out every Buddhist monk, holy man, or anyone who looked holy, though most of them were just homeless, wandering, and seeking food and shelter. Often, they would corner one of them, and quiz them incessantly for some gem of truth or clue as to where they could find a teacher who would immediately recognize them as the genuine seekers they were and give them the truth they sought.

I tagged along as usual, but tired quickly of the silence and meditating, too curious about the hubbub that blasted us every time we were out on the streets again. I decided to go solo and stopped tagging. I visited the floating market and the sex side of Bangkok, though I never had any. Sex that is. I walked for miles every day getting lost on purpose and savoring the unsavory and hectic hurry-up and clanging of Bangkok traffic and hawkers.

I took buses to the outskirts of town and spent hours watching women tending terraced paddy fields and vegetable gardens. I made my way to the delta of the Chao Praya River, which I found disappointingly polluted, though the reflection of the sky, in the sheen of oil and waste, was psychedelic!

When I stayed in town, I inevitably ended up relaxing in the gardens of upscale hotels. The noise of Bangkok gave me a thirst for quiet and serenity that only these places seemed to provide. The best were the gardens and zoo of the Siam Intercontinental Hotel. It was there that I met Jerry and Linda, a seductively interesting couple.

They were from San Francisco. Linda was on the plump side with wild hair and wilder eyes. I could imagine her clearly on the back of a Harley, clinging to her old man's waist with one hand; her other squeezing his chest.

Jerry, on the other hand, was something to behold, while I was holding back the something that was tickling my libido. He was a visually striking man; easy to recognize even from afar. He had a totally shaved, perfectly shaped head, a face whose features would stun anyone with its radiance and manliness, and a body he reveled in revealing and that I reveled in surreptitiously regarding as flawless.

More importantly, and probably this is what enhanced his other attributes, was the constant serenity and surety that made him a candidate for infatuation.

So, of course, I was infatuated with him. I had only known him a few hours and already I was smitten! As I spent the following days with them, I realized my schoolgirl crush wasn't unwarranted. And by the time we left for Ceylon, I understood Linda's devotion to him.

They were devout Buddhists. At least Jerry was. Linda was Buddhist by contagion and determination. Determined not to let this man get away from her. She also had a trust that he was her teacher, in much the same way Rosie and I regarded Jon. She knew all too well what a find Jerry was. A spiritual man trapped in an exquisite physical vessel.

They were seasoned travelers and had already hitchhiked through places other seekers would not have dared. Like war-torn Cambodia and Laos, getting rides from insurgents and counterinsurgents, and sharing the wrath of mortars and land mines with both sides, somehow protected by their aura of non-partisanship and their oblivion to what was happening around them. The oblivion was perhaps the result of shell shock, but it was a device that worked to their benefit.

Despite maintaining this demeanor, the travels had taken their toll and they made their way to Thailand for a bit of R&R. Their high and hair-raising tales entranced me as we sat cross-legged in an equilateral triangle amidst the weaving salas and zoo of the hotel.

When Jerry talked, I never let my eyes leave his nor did his ever leave mine. They were so clear and blue and riveting, which was a good thing because my eyes desperately wanted to wander and explore the landscape of his body. But I worried that Linda would notice if my eyes wandered. So, I didn't let them.

I worked at being attentive to Linda and showed great interest in her, because after all, it was the right thing to do and she was interesting and she was a sister on the path and I wanted to earn her trust, though I must admit the motives for all this may have been somewhat ulterior.

The connection we felt was strong, mutual, and almost magical. Jerry suggested I join them when they continued their journey. Linda seconded the motion.

"Next stop, India!" Jerry announced enthusiastically. And Linda followed with, "Please Giacco, become part of our family!" Her use of the word "family" made me feel polygamous. It was a strange feeling.

And it was tempting. Merely considering it made me feel like a traitor to Jon and Rosie. But at the same time, I realized how all of us are interchangeable. That when left alone or abandoned, we will by nature gravitate to those who will fulfill our needs.

They were leaving the next day and were hoping for a "yes" from me. That's when I told them about John and Rosie. In a way, they *were* Jon and Rosie, which made deciding even harder. But in the end, loyalty won out, maybe because of history or momentum. Nevertheless, as difficult as it was to do, I resolved to stick to the plan and stick with Jon and Rosie. Jerry and Linda were disappointed to say the least but understood.

Jerry, Linda, and I parted at sunset that last day, certain our paths would cross again. I conjured them up often in my mind, especially Jerry, partly as an exercise in keeping fresh an image I might need when whacking off. My way of meditating on sex.

Linda and I hugged each other as the neon lights of the hotel came on. It was then, as our bodies touched, that I realized the plumpness I had attributed to Linda, was not a plump. It was a baby in the making! That explained a lot. That gave a more comprehensive explanation of Linda's use of the word "family" and it made me understand more completely Linda's emotional and physical clinginess to Jerry.

Did he know? How could he not? Why had they never mentioned it? Not for me to say, but if there had been the slightest bit of envy toward Linda, it dissipated immediately, and I felt guilty for finding myself more drawn to Jerry than to Linda. Suddenly I saw her pre-pregnant. Slim and sexy. For the first time, visions of a three-way seemed tasty. And the thought of being party to a birthing made me feel very special. All those suppressed libidinous thoughts turned paternal and I felt purged.

Jerry hugged me tight and long until, through his strong will, he made our chests breathe in rhythm. Then he gently pulled away, his hands on my shoulders. He looked right at me and through me. His eyes misted over as he said, "Giacco, we know our relationship is permanent because it is infinite."

He dropped his arms to his side, resigned but trusting we'd bump into one another somewhere along the line. He walked over to Linda, draped an arm around her shoulder, and without looking back, walked away. I watched as they got smaller and smaller. Then I sat back down on the grass and looked at the slip of paper on which Jerry had written his address. There was something else in his handwriting on the other side:

A little zoo
Where gibbons playly free,
And weavers in a sala
Weave patterns so
Intricately

The movements and
The colors make you
Wonder
Who's the thread and
Who's the weaver?
And when I haven't the
Faintest idea,
It is still too much

When I hooked up with Jon and Rosie later that night, I told them about Jerry and Linda, but in the most casual and insignificant way. Jerry and Linda were going to be mine, and mine alone. The day after they left, we learned that flights to Colombo had resumed. Rosie, Jon, and I booked a flight for the next day. Jon was ecstatic. Ceylon! Now that was where it would really begin. That was a country that held promise! Far from the more traveled paths of seekers, that's where the holiest would hide out.

On the plane, a stewardess passed out newspapers and magazines. When she came to me, I took that day's copy of THE SUN, which all in caps, dominated the banner. To the right of the banner was a picture of an orb, with the obligatory flashing shards of light shooting out from a perfect circle. In the middle was a face, neither smiling nor pouting, just non-committal. To the left of the banner was a spotted lion. It held a defiant sword high in the air. Under the lion, in small print, it said, "Registered as a newspaper in Ceylon." Above THE SUN, it read WEDNESDAY. Below THE SUN, it read January 12, 1972.

I leafed through it, and one column caught my eye. It ran the length of the page with HOROSCOPE in bold letters at the top. Since I was only interested in mine, I ran my finger down the page to CANCER, where I was ordered: *You will attend to matters with enthusiasm. Extensive travel is indicated.*

I liked that! A good omen. I needed one! If I had any doubts about continuing my journey with Jon and Rosie, they were dashed by those two simple sentences.

CHAPTER 40
January 1972

A smooth landing. We waited for the stairs to be wheeled up to the door. Just as when I landed in Honolulu, as soon as the door opened, I was bombarded by olfactory delights, but the air tasted different, more exotic, indefinable, and less benign. Once we were out of the airport, we got other tastes of this strange new life which would become common flavors throughout our travels.

Beggars! Some were young, some were old. Some were healthy, but most were frail, infirm, and decrepit. Little boys with big dark eyes implored, "baksheesh, sa'ab," over and over again. Relentless. Clinging. Gently frisking our jeans. Coveting all we wore and represented. Brazen enough to reach up and touch Rosie's hair. Even though we were just *"Heepees,"* white oddities to be stared at and made fun of, we were worthy enough to hound for a rupee, a piece of clothing, a scrap of food, a book of matches.

Conspicuous! We felt ridiculously outstanding. Standing out is something we did not want. If we couldn't be completely inconspicuous, we wanted at least not to be thrown in with the wealthy tourists going to Galle and other resort towns where the white man is rich only because the natives are so poor.

Colors! A 360-degree survey of our surroundings provided a palette that shocked our eyes. Gaudy, vibrant, and clashing. They must've been picked out by a blind interior decorator. Yet somehow, they worked.

Noise! People loudly hawking their wares. Vehicles honking incessantly as they swerved in and out and around each other, vying for a piece of cracked pavement on which to further their way to who knows where. Many swerved at us. Taxi drivers not wanting to give us just a ride, but a ride to their cousin's hotel, the best in town, and guarantees in broken English of their encyclopedic knowledge of everything we might be interested in. Only later in India, would I regard the mayhem of Colombo to be tame in comparison. If I knew then what was in store for us, I would have more quickly accustomed myself to the smells, the colors, and the din. I would have more quickly accustomed myself to sensory overload!

We found a guesthouse in the center of town. The Lakni Wesa. Jon immediately struck up a conversation with the English-speaking owner and learned a few phrases in Sinhalese he thought might come in handy. I was overwhelmed and just wanted to rest. Rosie, as soon as she had settled her belongings in the room, disappeared into the market down the street.

I must have slept the entire afternoon. When I awoke, there was a white cloth bag on my bed. It was zippered closed. Carefully arranged around it were a thin blanket and a pair of pajamas made of lightweight white muslin. "Pajama whites" as we called them were de rigueur for the well-dressed man and we saved them for special occasions.

Next to the pajama whites was a small stack of colorful rupees, my passport and plane ticket, and a couple of long, colorfully striped pieces of cloth, hemmed on one side, forming a huge cylinder. This last item was called a *lungi,* the sarong-like piece of clothing most working-class men, wore for pants.

It took me a while to master the lungi. Skinny as I was, I never could step into it and wrap it tightly enough around my waist so it wouldn't slide off my hips every few minutes. Yet the young men I would watch wrapping it around them after bathing or swimming were so adept at it, they could wrap it in a way that was not only secure but had built in pockets in the folds to hold what we would usually hold in wallets.

I did eventually get the knack of the lungi and learned to love it. The climate here was so deliciously hot and humid, even skin was too heavy a garment. The lungi was the next best thing to being naked. Why men back home didn't wear skirts was beyond me. How did we get to the point where men wore the pants, and women, the skirts? The opposite is obviously more comfortable anatomically speaking. Isn't there any common sense left anymore?

The lungi! The ease of dressing. The freedom the cock and balls yearned for in this sweltering and almost debilitating heat. Pants! I never wanted to wear pants again!

And conveniently, I was also a natural squatter. All the men would sit on their haunches when it came time to rest, to talk, to socialize, to eat, and, of course, to shit. Well! I'd been sitting on my haunches since I was a kid! Always did sit like that, even as an adult! So, I was a natural, and I sometimes thought that in a previous life, I was Ceylonese. How refreshing to squat and let my cock and balls dangle in peace.

One item was missing, however, which I didn't realize was required until a few weeks later when a young girl, effortlessly balancing a basket of rotti on her head, passed me by and giggled. Then I caught the glance of a wizened old man who rolled his eyes and shook his head as he squatted across the road in front of his open-air thatched hut that was his store but also doubled as his home.

What was missing was the length of cloth you're supposed to wrap around your privates under your lungi! A diaper of sorts. A *lungoti*. When I was hanging out, squatting, I was literally hanging out!

I should have been too embarrassed *not* to wear one, but I refused to smother my privates. Once they had felt the air of freedom, they would never go back. After all, *it don't mean a thing if it ain't got that swing.* So, I simply learned to squat in such a way that I could tuck my lungi under my crotch and thought how nice it would be to have someone fluff my balls in the suspiring tropical breeze.

But this was all tangential to the most important items I found at the foot of my bed that afternoon. Or rather the items that were missing! My jeans. My T-shirts, all my clothes. I had been robbed!

I yelled and cursed. Jon and Rosie rushed into the room. Jon was wearing a lungi and Rosie a sarong. She was topless. What a vision she was. Oh my god, she was so beautiful in those yards of burgundy fabric wrapped around her slim waist and long legs. She wrapped a yard or so of light orange cloth around her breasts and tied it behind her. The orange halter-top complemented the burgundy sarong perfectly. Very classy! It screamed, "I'm not a tourist!" Or so she thought. With her dark hair falling straight down to her waist and her beautifully tanned skin and alluring looks, she was a goddess.

On the other hand, Jon, in his lungi, looked ridiculous. But who was I to talk after wrestling with mine, getting all tangled in it, trying to get it to stay in place for a minute before it would drop down around my ankles?

Rosie informed me she had taken the liberty of giving away all our clothes! We were going native! Everything we needed would fit in our white cloth bags which hung comfortably over our shoulders. It was just as Florence had ordered Rosie to do on Queens Surf Beach. We would give up our Western ways. We would bring no cameras or anything that would hint we were mere tourists. No, not us! We were sadhus on a quest. If we needed anything more than Rosie allowed, whatever it was would be provided unto us. Her one concession was that I could carry a pen and a notebook, and Little Richard's embroidered duck. Traveling light took on a whole new meaning.

※

We stayed in Colombo just a few days. Then we were off in search of The Teacher.

Jon had heard rumors of a well-regarded guru on the east coast of the island. But there were ruins and temples as well that we didn't want to miss. We knew that wherever worshippers flocked, there would always be the chance of catching on to some gossip that would lead us to the guru.

We took a very colorful train out of Colombo heading east toward Trincomalee. The old steam engine alone was a trip to the past, and the cars were multi-colored. Narrowly gauged, it could have been a circus train from the Depression replicated by Lionel. If a train could be called "cute," then this was it.

It was cute. It was charming. It was dirty. It was a cute, charming, and dirty little train. The seats were amenable only to the softest-rumped which left me out. But my eyes were amazed at the landscape. It didn't take long to leave the bustle of Colombo behind and find ourselves chugging rickety rick through lush jungles, our journey interrupted by stops in every village, large and small. At each stop, masses of people charged the train, some to board as passengers, others to make quick sales. We were regarded as a potentially lucrative source of income and given much, too much attention. Children stared at us from the platform in wide-eyed amazement as if they had never seen a white person before. Their mothers pushed them to beg from us, but we feigned ignorance as best we could.

Vendors walked down the aisle with baskets of luscious looking papayas, mangoes, bananas, and avocados. Other vendors conducted their business through the windows. Their hands and those of their customers reaching in and out, exchanging food, beedies, and sweets for a few rupees and running beside the train as it pulled out trying to make that one last sale which might mean the difference between feeding their family that night or not. The vendors on board hastily did the same and jumped off the train just in time.

The train became so crowded that people rode on top of the cars along with their chickens and goats and broken suitcases, likely used decades ago by their English masters. Everything that may have been Western seemed a hand-me-down and down, and down again.

The man sitting across from me wore a loose white shirt and pajama whites, which distinguished him somehow as being of a different class than the bare-chested men in lungis and the women in saris of inferior quality.

Next to me was a young man with very long hair wearing a less than fresh lungi. He regarded my long hair and decided we had something in common. Then he placed his forearm next to mine to compare skin color. My healthy looking tan from Hawaii was turning into a dark matte brown. This did not compute with their image of a Westerner, which was fine by me. By the time we left Ceylon, I might have passed for a native had it not been for my sometimes indiscreet way of squatting. The young man kept his arm next to mine. His skin was smooth and beautiful. His body was sinewy and lean, I would imagine not by choice, but by his undernourishment. His face had very fine features with a smear of sacred ash called *vibhuti* on his forehead. And though his teeth were stained, they were easy to disregard because his smile was broad and genuine.

The man in white lit up a real cigarette, not the customary *beedi*. The young man in the lungi kept smiling at me as he lit up a chillum, which brought a look of scorn from the gentleman, but a gleam to my eye.

"Ayubowan! Kohomadha?" He asked. I looked at him twisting my face into "I'm sorry, I don't understand." Jon leaned over from the booth behind me where he and Rosie were sitting, and responded for me, *"Ayubowan! Bohama hondai! Stuthi!"*

The young man laughed and said, *"Ayubowan! Bohama hondai!"* Then he passed the chillum to me. *"Rasai!"*

I could see he was impressed by the way I held it between my fingers and sucked in through the circle made by my thumb and index finger. The hash was primo! I passed it back to him, but he said no in that yes-like manner all South Asians seem to have, and pointed to Jon. So, I passed the chillum to Jon who took a long drag. "Better, much better," He sighed through the exhaling smoke. Then Jon relit the chillum for Rosie. Watching a woman smoke a chillum made our friend with the matted hair laugh uproariously. He said softly, *"Lassanai!"*

The man in white now looked at the four of us with disdain. But I think he was just jealous. I thought that, because he opened his English language newspaper with such flair and fanfare. He wanted to let us know that he was educated and anxious to use his English on us. He was bothered we were not responding appropriately. But we were too busy passing the chillum around. After all, this was the first time we had gotten stoned since Hawaii. Well at least for Jon and Rosie. Jerry, Linda, and I had shared some nice Thai bud the days we spent together, but I never let on. Besides, that was among the manicured gardens of the Siam Hilton. This was an entirely new setting. And getting newer with every puff I took.

I looked forward now to every village we came to, taking in stride the hundreds of arms reaching in and out and the entreaties of the vendors and begging children. The noise, the hard wood seats of the train bouncing my bony ass up and down, the man in white now on the verge of outrage. They all could have been a bother to me. But the never-ending chillums did away with all the bothers.

Even when the train slowed to a crawl as it chugged over a river and we noticed six bloated bodies floating downstream, it was not a bother. It just was. The man in white looked at me and said, "The Troubles." I just stared back. Where was I, Northern Ireland?

Pointing at the bloated corpses, Jon said, "Oh that is better, much better." The man in white gave Jon the most curious look. The young man stared at the bodies too, but the expression on his face was void of meaning. He said something in Sinhala, or maybe it was Tamil, and that gave the man in white his opening.

Jon and Rosie turned around to listen in. "Your young friend here says this is why he is going to Trincomalee. To free himself from the illusions of this world by making a pilgrimage on foot to Jaffna to see Guaribala." Jon's eyes widened. He heard that name back in Colombo. The rumor of the guru. Jon turned to Rosie and said, "It just doesn't get much better than this!"

"But he is crazy, this man you smoke with. Pay him no mind." To his chagrin, Jon paid the man in white no mind and started rummaging through our scant belongings.

"Rosie. Where's that map?" He asked. Rosie retrieved a map of Ceylon out of her bag. I knew what was coming. So did Rosie. Jon studied the map, and I felt a detour about to be announced.

While Jon traced a finger from Trincomalee north to Jaffna, Rosie kept stabbing a few other places on the map with her fingernail and looked at Jon as if he had done something wrong and if he kept it up, he'd get punished! She did all the talking with her fingers. But her message was loud and clear. Jon's impulsive detour would be gratefully postponed for a while.

I don't recall a day since that train ride that we weren't stoned. And I regard that loco motive to be the first time I really felt I was being pulled on a journey that would transform my life.

CHAPTER 41
January 1972

We arrived in Trincomalee to a sliver of sun setting into the Indian Ocean. We were in a trance as we walked through town in search of a place to stay. Maybe it was all the hash. Maybe it was the smells and colors of the market, the people eyeing us as we passed, staring unabashedly as if we were oddities from a carnival placed on a sideshow display for their scrutiny and amusement.

We inquired about a place to stay from a man who was squatting in front of his store sipping chai. We went in the direction of his bobbing head toward a dirt road that paralleled the beach. It was getting dark as glittering stars filled the sky. Just south of town, which transitioned somewhat abruptly from hustle and bustle to quiet and calm, we came upon the Chinese Guest House. Though quite late, the owner was still up. His name was Mr. Yo and he greeted us with glee. The guesthouse seemed virtually empty of lodgers. Mr. Yo showed us to a spotlessly clean, but sparsely furnished large room with four beds in it. One wall of windows looked out at the ocean which we could clearly hear, but only see when the shallow moon brought out the phosphorescence in the waves that lapped at the sand.

The guesthouse had only one common bathroom used by all the lodgers. The toilet was a cement hole with footrests on either side, ribbed to keep your feet from slipping when you squatted to take a shit or pee. The price of the room was absurdly cheap, at least for us, and even more absurdly cheap if we stayed a week or more. And that's what we wound up doing.

The Chinese Guest House was perfect. Mr. Yo spoke excellent English, which made life easier. And in all the subsequent places we would stay on our journeys, we would look back at the Chinese Guest House as the cleanest and most comfortable of them all. What a great way to start a sojourn!

Early the first couple of mornings, Rosie went to the market and brought back small clay pots of buffalo curd and an assortment of tropical fruits. Our breakfasts were the best! Fresh curd with papaya and bananas! Just looking at it made my mouth water.

This became the morning ritual, taking turns returning the empty clay pots for new ones filled with creamy curd and choosing the most luscious looking of the many fruits. Some were very unusual looking, and we briefly experimented with them. We ended up sticking with the ones we knew.

The Chinese Guest House became our refuge. And Trinco, as we began to call this town, became home and headquarters for trips to different parts of the island.

One morning we woke up to find we were not the sole residents of the Guest House anymore. A young hippie man named Henry, from Shepherd's Cross in England, greeted us with a bright smile and brighter eyes. His skin was so white we did not think it possible. He wasn't an albino or anything. He was just very, very white, as if being English prevented him from tanning. He approached us as we were finishing our breakfast. Henry may not have had the ability to tan, but shy was not a trait he possessed.

"Hey, mates!" he said, squatting next to Jon. "Henry's my name. Yours?"

"Jon here. And this is Rose and Chazan." I liked hearing Jon use that name for me, but it wasn't meant for the public. So, I added, "But you can call me Giacco."

"Nah, mate! Chazan is a bloody good tag. I like it heaps."

I surrendered, while giving Jon a chiding look.

After a few more exchanges of small talk, Henry withdrew from his lungi a huge spliff, lit it, and passed it to Rosie. Jon took it off Rosie's hands while she was in the middle of a coughing fit. Then I did the same to Jon and passed it back to Henry. We were very impressed.

"So, my friend, where did you come upon this excellent herb?" Jon asked.

Henry called over a little boy, seven or eight years old, and said something to him in a mixture of mime and words, the magic word being "ganja." The young boy's eyes lit up with understanding, and off he ran.

Jon, Rosie, and Henry discussed philosophy and spirituality for hours. Henry would include me every so often by asking, "So, Chazan, what do you think of that?" I knew he really didn't care, and I usually answered with inane phrases like "Cool. Very far out! Sounds right to me!"

"Too right, sport!" was Henry's usual retort, regarding me as if I were in a minor league compared to Jon and Rosie, and then having made the lame effort to include me, would return to his jabbering with Jon and Rose.

Henry ended up hanging out with us a lot. He was as totally enamored with Jon and Rosie as they were with him. They thought Henry was a perfect addition. I was not as smitten and didn't like people who talked too much. And maybe, just maybe, I was a little jealous.

He seemed to invite trouble with his loud voice and arrogantly fearless ways. I did not like attracting attention to ourselves. As nice as he was to me, I felt he did so out of deference to Jon and Rosie, not because he truly liked me, just as I did not truly like him. This, of course, violated the rules of being a flower child. So, we hid as best we could our antipathy for one another beneath superficial expressions of brotherly love.

I did secretly thank him, however, because once he had sent that young boy off for ganja, other kids would stop by and open their cupped hands from which would fall beautiful buds and for which we gave them a few rupees. We were never without dope. We were swimming in it! These kids were contributing to the delinquency of adults! This was a curious reversal from stateside morality. I felt sorry for all the "felons" who got caught buying beer for their local high school football teams.

A few days later, an Australian couple arrived. Both were very pleasing to look at. "Debra and Peter," they both said simultaneously pointing at each other, and then again in unison, "G'day mate!"

I laughed at them. Their accents were so friendly.

"Giacco," I said. "But if you hear someone calling "Chazan," well that's me too. Guess I have multiple personalities! But all of them are harmless!" I said kidding around.

"Now don't go getting' us up a gum tree!" Peter laughed. Though I didn't get the metaphor, I laughed with them.

They must have been no older than 19 and 20 respectively. And when they told me they were on their honeymoon, I was so surprised I lost my fine-tuned squatting form. I fell over and exposed my genitals to their handsome, young faces. It should have been very embarrassing! But Debra spoke before I could turn red.

"Looks like you lost your nappy!" she said, giggling.

"You look good arse over tit, mate! Peter added with good-natured sarcasm. "A dazzler, you are! You do that trick often?"

And they both chuckled. I liked them already, but still had a hard time believing they were married. They just looked too young! And Peter's remark and Debra's nonchalance at my being a flasher, made me feel they were open to all experiences that came their way.

I tried to push myself up but rolled over again. The three of us got the giggle fits and Peter extended a hand and pulled me up. His firm grip made me feel a strong bond with them and I hoped they felt it too.

They both had an outback athleticism about them, a healthiness and innocence that made them seem the essence of purity and naiveté, which I learned later was totally off the mark.

Debra had bright blue eyes and long dirty blond hair. Her skin glowed with health. She always looked beautiful and could wrap a sari around her with the deftness of a native. She only had a few saris; all were very tasteful. In her white one, she was pure. In blue, she was pure. And in the colors galore of her assortment of sarongs and tops, she was still pure, with a gold ring on her toe and a gold bracelet around her ankle and a gold ring pierced through her nose. When she was naked, she looked like Botticelli's Birth of Venus. As she stepped off her shell to slip into her one pair of jeans, she still had the pure glowing look of a virgin, though I assumed that was unlikely.

Peter was what I called a "sleeper." That his face was handsome was obvious. But there was an unpretentiousness about it, as if he had never looked in a mirror before. He had an exotic look about him. His dark brown hair dangled in tight kinky curls. His eyes were a deep hazel. His skin was tanned to the brown of a man with an aboriginal gene. Maybe that was the allure. Maybe that's what made him so exciting. He preferred baggy clothes and wore his pajama whites rolled up to just above the knees. His calves were muscular which gave the rest of his body away to my x-ray vision. And he could roll "fair dinkum beauties" with the best of them!

It was only after sharing a particularly tasty joint that Debra and I were able to persuade Peter to try on one of my lungis. He unabashedly took off his clothes and stood there naked while stonily contemplating this new apparel. I stonily contemplated his perfect body. He turned to model the garment and Debra and I applauded in approval. She ran up to him and they embraced. I was sorry we had brought no cameras. I would have to rely on my ganja-seared mind to remember how wonderful they looked, which was asking a lot of myself. I did my best to imprint them on my brain.

For a moment I wondered why all the men and women I befriended or who befriended me were real beauties. Could that be true? Or was there some axiom which stated, "the hornier you are, the better looking people get?" No! I decided that was not the case. All of them *were* beautiful in their own way. And that was as it should be.

To top it off, things were once again in balance. Rosie, Jon, and Henry. Peter, Debra, and me. Not that this was a permanent arrangement. It was just part of the cosmic dance spent in the arms of brothers and sisters who recognized they were, indeed, related.

Every evening after dinner, all of us would dance our way through the old Dutch fort to Swami Rock at the northeast end of the bay. There, perched on a high cliff overlooking the Bay of Bengal, stood Koneswaram, an impressive temple dedicated to Lord Siva with shrines honoring Lord Muruga, Shakti, and Ganapathi as well. It was the only place in town for a worshipper to be. I always ended up hanging out around the shrine honoring Ganapathi, or Ganesh as I soon began to call him. Ganesh was my kind of guy. He required only fervor of worship and it didn't matter how a devotee displayed that fervor. Decorum to Ganesh was unnecessary. I always had the feeling that the less decorum and the more feverish the fervor, the more Ganesh liked it! Needless to say, this encouraged madness and magic!

Offerings of food, flowers, and money were the most sedate ways of worshipping Ganesh. But it was not uncommon to see a man rolling on the hard rock around the shrine like the hand of a clock, or banging his head against the stone. Maybe it was the Hindu version of "Punch Thyself."

Men and women danced in a trance, which entranced us. They wore the most dazzling garb and moved so delicately and flowingly, especially their hands and fingers, which seemed to strum invisible lyres. The sounds of strange stringed instruments, drums, and flutes played and collided because each musician was seemingly playing a different song.

Singers sang. Chanters chanted. Incense of every kind filled the nostrils with dizzying smells that mingled with the odors of the food cooking on makeshift grills. But as redolent as they were, the smell of hashish and ganja dominated the air and wafted their way to the nose, easily distinguishable from the other aromas.

The small colorful statue of Ganesh was decorated every night with flowers and other offerings at his feet. He stood on one foot, the other raised as if in mid-step of a dance. His trunk curled to the left, and under his tusks it looked like he was smiling. He just stood there inanimate and yet on the verge of coming to life on top of this dome of rock. Crazy people were everywhere. The carnival-like atmosphere was so powerful it transformed the demurest and introverted into the kind of people you crossed the street to avoid back in the States.

Worshipping Ganesh was so different from the reverence demanded by Christianity.

It was so far removed from the standing, kneeling, and perfunctory responsorials of the Catholic Mass. It was at the other end of the spectrum from the Chinese doing Tai Chi in unison like synchronized swimmers. This was spontaneous and improvisational worship, each individual worshipped Ganesh in his or her own special and sometimes insane way.

God of prosperity, health and knowledge, Ganesh played the guardian of all the temples to other gods. I fell in love with him. It was a love that would last a lifetime; a love anyone could express anyway they wanted. And any *way* was accepted unconditionally.

Though Jon was still eager to travel north to Jaffna to find Swami Guaribala, we cajoled him to explore sites in the vicinity. Eventually we needed to be in Talaimannar where we would take the ferry to Dhanushkodi, our portal to India. Why backtrack, when there was so much more to be experienced in the rest of the island? He reluctantly agreed, especially when Rosie said, "But Jon, it just doesn't get much better than this!"

"Touché," Jon replied. "Or as they say in Australia, 'Touchy,'" teasing Debra and Peter with an affectionate glance. And so, we would dance our way to well-known and not-so-well-known places. Sometimes all six of us, sometimes in pairs, sometimes alone. Mix and match, change your partners, do-si-do and, depending on what we had eaten that day, skip to the loo.

But most of the time, we traveled as a sextet.

CHAPTER 42
February 1972

The first pilgrimage we made was to Parakrama Samudra, its three ancient lakes mirroring trees of every shade of green. In the distance, clouds rested on two flat-topped mountains, the closer, purple gray; the farther grayer blue. Men in their lungis and women in their saris bathed in the cool waters. Young boys slid down a mud sluice and splashed each other as they flew airborne into the lake. We watched them and they stared at us. The boys mirrored our curious smiles or whatever other expressions were bouncing off our innermost thoughts.

Suddenly, I had a flashback of Michael, sliding down the sluice at the Celebration of Life. I got goose bumps thinking about him. Where he might be, what he was doing, what kind of husband and father he was, and why he hadn't written?

And of course, I thought of my Hunga Dunga. I thought of them all with such a deep longing, it almost ached. I realized I hadn't thought of them at all since Bangkok. And I was a bit unnerved by how quickly one can forget his past by being in the present of another culture, one in which all your previous frames of reference are destroyed, allowing you to become a child again where everything is for the first time.

We visited Anuradhapura, the most ancient of Ceylon's many ancient cities dating back to the 4th century B.C. It had boasted nine-story dagobas and ostentatious palaces and mansions. Now it was all rubble, the most enchanting rubble I had ever seen.

At Polonnaruwa, the ancient ruins and sleeping Buddha were more wondrous than we had imagined. We were overwhelmed and out of respect, we got ruined in the ruins, and two white-bearded monkeys stared back at me for what seemed an eternity. Mesmerizing mantras whispered through the trees and grasses, and how exquisitely peaceful it was in comparison to nothing else.

Outings to such places as these seemed to quiet our constant chattering. They put us in very reflective, meditative moods. Seldom had I seen us so silent. That is, except for Henry, who never shut up. I once overheard Peter quietly telling Debra, "What an ear basher!" I took that to be a derogatory remark but what a colorfully apt one.

From Polonnaruwa we took a train to Batticaloa, only to find all the guesthouses full. So, we took a taxi twenty miles up the coast to a small town called Kalkudah. There, too, The Rest House, the only "hotel" in town was filled, so we had to sleep on the beach.

The beach was beautiful, curving off into jutting peninsulas on both sides. It sloped gently upwards to small dunes. Beyond them, the land was thick with coconut palms. So thick that from the air, it must have looked like a huge lawn that needed mowing. These trees, whose trunks were taller and more graceful than a giraffe's neck, not only satisfied me aesthetically, but satisfied so many of the needs of the locals. Cooking oil, food, milk, mattress stuffing, fuel, candy, and liquor were just some of their gifts. And since then, the coconut palm has always been my favorite tree. Merely seeing one on a calendar brings my tropical nature to the surface. I felt this place was where I truly belonged.

We camped on the far end of the scalloped beach that faced northwest. That evening, we witnessed a sunset only the most eloquent of the many gods could describe. It was possibly the inspiration for the wild pastels used everywhere in the temples, huts, clothing and even the cosmetics the natives so generously applied to their bodies. The colors were so luscious they looked fake. And if we had had a camera and took the most accurate photograph, people would still think it had been touched up if they hadn't seen it for themselves.

The days were always hot, but I guess temperature is relative because that night felt downright cold. We made a small fire and tried to fall asleep. Our thin blankets seemed totally inadequate. Jon and Rosie clung to each other for warmth and possibly sex. Henry shivered by himself, inching his way closer to the fire, and keeping it going with coconut husks and twigs. Though my soul was being kept warm by Peter and Debra, my body was not. The three of us inched closer and closer to one another, trying to get that little bit of extra body heat. I froze my ass off as did everyone else. Just as I was about to drift off, I heard Jon quietly say to Rose, "Punch thyself!"

The village of Kalkudah was small and from the unending stares we received, we were sure we were the first white people they had ever seen. But when we woke up the next day, we noticed a few other campsites scattered down the beach. How jealous we were of their tents. We walked toward them and met these other foreigners who had found their way here, attracted I assumed, by the incredible setting and the peacefulness. But it was the surf and not the setting that attracted them. Two Germans, one Dane, a very shy French boy, and three freaks from Laguna Beach had already set up camp. Their boards were either standing tall in the sand or strewn around their campsites.

Surfers were truly the new Magellans and Cooks. They were always the first to discover hidden gems, that no one would have thought to visit before. The notoriety that followed, would eventually ruin the pristine beauty of their discoveries. That's why it's always dangerous to revisit a place that was once special to you. I would not be surprised to go back someday and find the beach littered with T-shirt and hamburger stands.

It wasn't the surfers' fault. It's just that they were there to find the perfect wave, and we were there to find the perfect way. Embarrassing in retrospect, we felt our reasons for being on this beach took priority over theirs. How egotistical of us!

Nevertheless, we all got along fine because in addition to the perfect wave they were also in search of the most primo dope. We had *that* in common and smoked together on the beach in perfect harmony, despite some language barriers. The Dane, as one would expect, was the translator for everyone.

The boardheads found the weed and hash so fine, they had trouble rousing themselves off their blankets to test the waters. Even someone like me who had never surfed before could recognize this exceptional find of beautifully consistent, but scarily enormous waves, curling and cresting just beyond the reef.

For me, the most exceptional finds were the shells that made beach combing much too easy. Huge conch shells dotted the beach every few steps. I amused myself for hours just walking the fine sand, letting the sudsing surf tickle my ankles, while admiring the most amazing shells an ocean had ever tossed ashore. While I walked, local children joined me and filled my hands and arms with them. Their dark, sparkling eyes and sweet smiles beseeched me to take them as gestures of friendship to the strange white man in a lungi. Either that or the greater likelihood was they were hoping for some rupees!

The next day, we played in the surf and on the beach, and just relaxed. I read from J. Krishnamurti's "First and Last Freedom," which I borrowed from some left-behind paperbacks at the Chinese Guest House. Oh, J.! Why did you deny you were the new Christ for the Aquarian Age? You deserved the title!

I read him slowly, the words once again striking chords within me. Sometimes I drifted off into a reverie that included Bruttar from the "Wayside of the Maitreya Buddha" commune and the Celebration of Life debacle. Not surprisingly, I thought again of Michael and the two of us drifting downstream through the muddy waters of the Atchafalaya River.

I was still drifting when Jon's shadow blocked me from the last rays of the sun. "Chazan," he said, "I think it's time for us to move on."

"Move on! I am in heaven! How can I move on?" I replied, my face full of disappointment.

Jon admitted that he, Rose, and I had been experiencing a weird, subtle form of alienation from each other. Maybe it was the injection of Jerry and Linda or Peter and Debra or Henry into our insular threesome. It had happened so gradually, neither of us was sure it was true. It was hard to verbalize because its roots lay in the heart. But we both knew something was amiss. I stood up and Jon and I walked along the beach. We reached the end of the bay where the glow from lanterns on small fishing boats bobbed up and down; distant, yet they provided a feeling of warmth from the cooling air.

We sat down and got loaded. I was quiet and inward. Jon started talking god talk. When he did that, I was always turned into mush. I knew he was just laying a cosmic groundwork so that I might keep everything in perspective when he suggested that we split up for a while.

"Split up?" I asked like a kid whose dad has just told him he and mom were getting a divorce. "Did I do something wrong? Is it my fault?"

"Chazan, we love you and this is just for the time being. Rose and I need to be alone for a while. Henry's going to continue solo. We want to go north to Jaffna and find Swami Guaribala. You can join us if you wish, but I think you're happy here and aren't ready to move on."

Oh, better. Muuuuch better, I said to myself. *Not ready to move on? What the hell did that mean? Not evolved enough to appreciate the wisdom of a teacher? Not eager enough to give up this idyllic setting, my beloved palm trees, my beachcombing, my Debra and Peter? Not ready?*

He was right. And maybe so was Florence. I felt a little badly. Maybe my subliminal libidinal passions were preventing me from staying on the path I thought I had chosen. As

Florence had intimated, I guess it just wasn't in the cards.

Despite Jon's invitation, once having said he and Rosie needed to be alone for a while, I felt I had no choice but to decline. I didn't want to be an albatross around their necks, which were stretching for the guru. So, I reluctantly agreed. At the same time, I anticipated the adventures I could have on my own or with Debra and Peter, should they want me around. After all, they were on their honeymoon. A very strange honeymoon, but a honeymoon all the same. If anyone had wanted to be alone for a while, it should have been them!

CHAPTER 43

February 1972

When I woke up the next morning, I carefully lifted Peter's hand off my shoulder. His arm had spanned both Debra and me. He must have done it unconsciously, pulling us all closer together in the middle of the night for added warmth against the coolest hour before dawn.

I quietly disentangled myself and walked over to where Jon and Rosie were sleeping, rearranging my lungi on the way. They were gone! The only thing they left behind was the depression in the sand where they had slept and a note under a conch shell.

Meet us at the Lakni Wesa Guest House in Colombo
Beginning of March.
Lorf you immensely,

JonPon and the Rose

I dropped to the sand, their note in hand, looking at the outline of their bodies. I started getting all choked up, though I wasn't sure why. A feeling of abandonment? Who abandoned whom? Did it matter? The choked up turned into some tears, and before I knew it, the tears turned into a purge and then into a detachment. Wasn't that Buddha's answer to suffering? Detachment?

The tears were already falling when I realized Peter and Debra were at my side. They also said it was time to move on. For all *three* of us to move on. Together. I declined their invitation as well.

"You guys are on your honeymoon!" I said looking up at them. "You're due for some alone time don't you think? I never heard of anything so ridiculous, wanting a third wheel on your honeymoon! Have ya gone completely troppo on me?"

Peter and Debra looked at each other with amazement and a touch of pride that I had picked up some of their slang. They burst into laughter.

"You're a good bloke, you are," said Peter still laughing, "and a bloody funny one at that!"

"And we've been doin' this 'honeymoon' thing for over a year now!" Debra added. "It's been yonks since we did the 'honeymoon' thing! It's no big fuckin' deal, Giacco! Just think of us as three bloody good friends!"

"And right now, if you didn't hang with us, we'd go wonky in the noggin! You wouldn't want to be responsible for that, eh mate?" Peter said, trying to guilt trip me with disarming, if somewhat notorious Australian slang.

"Are you absolutely sure?" I asked. Don't you want to think it over?"

"She'll be apples, she will!" Peter said with confidence.

"Beg yours?" I questioned, trying to outdo Peter at his own slang game.

"No worries, mate!" And Peter started laughing all over again.

"It's a dead cert!" Debra said. "I can feel it in me little toe. And me little toe is never wrong!"

"Dinkum? I asked.

With that, they both looked at each other and fell to the sand laughing. They scooted on their "arses" over to me and gave me big hugs.

"Dinkum!" they reassured me and then laughed some more. Their embrace was all the reassurance I needed. To this day, the sound of an Australian accent brings me great comfort, for no matter what the content of the conversation, I always think of them.

When we had pulled ourselves together, Peter suggested we go back to Batticaloa and with luck we would find a room where we could really get a few nights of sound and comfortable sleep.

We took a bus to Batticaloa and on it, a very nice looking, and gentle-mannered man named Rudramoorthy timidly approached us. He was inquisitive. He was educated. He spoke fairly good English and was anxious to put it to use. He had many questions for us, and he spoke of wondrous places we should visit. He had such a warmth about him, we became fast friends. And he invited us to stay at his house.

His wife, Jasmin, and their two beautiful children, a boy and a girl, greeted us. The kids stared at us in wide-eyed amazement, as if their father had brought home some exotic souvenirs from his trip. His wife's gaze kept changing from a welcoming smile at us to a mild, "Now what have you done?" glare directed at her husband. But once Rudramoorthy said something in a mixture of Tamil and Sinhala, their chins swinging like pendulums, she opened the door wide and invited us in, wondering where she would get the extra food she needed to host us adequately.

The house was modest to say the least. They seemed poor to me, but from what I saw of the town as we entered it, they probably were considered middle class to some. We talked awhile and Rudramoorthy explained that he was Hindu and his wife, Sinhalese. He was Hindu, and in this part of Ceylon, a first-class citizen in an area controlled by Tamil Hindus. She was Buddhist, as were most of the people in other parts of the island.

By all rights, she was in dangerous territory. Even more so for having married a Hindu. But who can explain love, Rudramoorthy happily lamented. He told us of the seemingly never-ending uprisings of the well-educated, but disenfranchised youth in Ceylon and the repressive government killing them. Rudramoorthy's eyes were moist and sad before they changed to reluctant acceptance of both his family's fate and that of his country.

I could think only of Krishnamurti: "The threat from the outside is now and forever a lie!" If only everyone would look inward. If only they would realize they're all made of the same stuff. If they chose not to, why couldn't they just throw whipped cream pies at each other, instead of using bullets. Again, where were Larry, Moe, and Curly when we needed them!

It was late, and we were very tired. Jasmin offered to cook us a meal, but we politely refused saying we had already eaten along the way. Nonetheless, she made a pot of chai and brought out a plate of sweetmeats and we all fell in love with Rudramoorthy and his wonderfully shy family as we shared tea, ate delicious treats, and spoke of our native lands.

The kids slept with them, and they let us sleep on the kids' mats in a corner of the one-room house. They gave us extra blankets and we slept well for a change.

In the morning, we had more tea and some rotti with buffalo butter and jam. Then Rudramoorthy, Peter, Debra, and I were off to see the sights of Batticaloa. Rudramoorthy was an excellent guide and when we found ourselves alone at the town's old fort, he pulled out some hash, wrapping a dampened handkerchief around the narrow part of the chillum. We all got very high. Rudramoorthy warned us not to tell his wife! We found that amusing and assured him, "No worries." He had none, so he said. He was the perfect person to get stoned with. Always gentle, always centered.

We spent two days in Batticaloa. Each day, we'd stop at a market, and Peter, Debra, and I would buy fruit, vegetables, rice, sweetmeats and teas to bring back to his house. The second day, we also brought gifts for his wife, including a gold earring Debra had picked out, and toys for the kids. Though he wouldn't find it until after we left, we hid a bunch of rupees under Rudramoorthy's pillow, enough to make his life relatively easy for a couple of months we hoped. We were so happy to be able to do it. Rudramoorthy proved to be such a very good and generous friend.

Five-thirty in the morning, Rudramoorthy roused us from a sound sleep so that we wouldn't miss the 6:30 bus to Nuwara Eliya. At the station, he sheepishly offered a hand to Debra, who rushed him with a big hug. Peter and I did the same. He was flush with emotion, and I never met a man who cried so readily. Then again, given his situation, he may have had many good reasons to cry.

Peter, Debra, and I boarded the bus. It was full to the brim with people. It was full above the brim with baggage and boxes tethered to the roof. The bus looked so top-heavy I thought it would fall over before we even left the station. The 10-and-a-half-hour, bumpy, dusty, dirty, wonderfully horrific ride, would take us to the 6,000-foot-high city of Nuwara Eliya which sat on the top of the Hatton plateau in the high country I had seen in the distance from Parakrama Samudra.

We drove through dense jungle for a while, passing frond-roofed mud huts, thickets of banana trees and palms, fields of sugarcane, fantastically colorful flowers, and the lushest of vegetation.

The bus struggled around curves and lurched us higher and higher. It lurched so often, I was tempted to pinball my way to the front and teach the driver how to use the clutch. But I restrained myself, and Peter, Debra and I merely laughed anxiously with each missed gear.

As we gained elevation, the vegetation looked similar to that of the mountains in Northern California. As we entered the city, the potholed, worn, and dusty road gradually became better maintained and therefore more comfortable. The road turned into a smoothly paved boulevard lined with trees. Where mud huts had dominated the landscape, suddenly, or so it seemed, enormous Tudor mansions appeared. They once belonged to British and German land barons. Now they were gone. The memory of them lingers, as do the artifacts of their occupation.

There were sidewalks for chrissakes! The locals walking them wore overcoats and carried umbrellas! I noticed a Catholic church and a small movie theater whose marquee read "Easy Rider." Well! That explained a lot about the looks we were getting from passersby on the street! What must they think of us?

We exited the bus at a very nice station. As soon as an older man, whose curiosity got the better of him asked us a question, others gathered round; some joined in. All of those that did speak English, spoke it very well, and with a decidedly British accent that was softened by their native tongue. It had a very pleasing lilt to it. A dark-skinned man, obviously a gentleman, offered to escort us to a nice hotel in town, the Pedro.

The Pedro Hotel was old and beautiful in that prudish Tudor way, with large windows and heavy furniture. It had a snooker table! And the menu in the dining room even featured fried eggs with bacon!

And this is still Ceylon? What happened to the tropical beaches? How could the tea plantations, the terraced rice paddies, the water buffalo, the monkeys, all have given way to this hotel, which could be any popular resort in any number of alpine settings around the world!

The pure air and chilling altitude reminded me how good it felt to be in the high country. And the journey from the beaches to the mountain-top retreats explained why this place is rightly known as the "resplendent isle."

We were shown to a ground-floor room, which had a great view of Mount Pedro. But there was only one bed and a small settee that could be slept on if you didn't mind your legs dangling over its edge. I felt a twinge of discomfort for the first time since the three of us started hanging out together.

Cuddling together for warmth on the beach, still in our clothes, was one thing. It seemed natural, innocent, and necessary. Cramped on the kids' mats on the floor of Rudramoorthy's home was another. You'd often see three or four men taking a nap together on one small mat. No one was shy about it. No one raised an eyebrow.

If this had been a thatched hut in the middle of the jungle, it would be a no-brainer. If this had been cold sand under swaying palms, no one would think twice about doing whatever it took to stay warm. But this place was so Western it brought out the Motel 6 in me!

Despite the fact that the room was as cold as sleeping outdoors, despite the fact that I often jumped into bed with any number of people at Hunga Dunga with absolutely no reservations, we were now faced with options and therefore conscious decisions. But I was thinking for the three of us and once again underestimated Pete and Deb.

I offered to take the settee and threw my bag on it. They looked at each other, and then me, and threw their "dilly bags" on the settee as well.

"Looks like this will do us just fine! Plenty of room for three!" Debra said easily as she looked at the bed and then up at Peter.

"So why you throwin' that squizz at me?" Peter said. "It's an easy go!" he agreed.

I just shrugged with no objections. Who was I to be the prude? I shivered, not from the cold of the room, but from thinking about how much self-control I would be able to muster.

After settling in, we went downstairs to the restaurant and had a delicious meal. Debra and I had a few bottles of the local brew, but when Peter noticed they had Guinness Stout, he ordered a schooner. Then another. Then another.

After dinner, Peter invited me to play a game of snooker and stood up a bit tentatively. He was inspecting cue sticks and rolling them on the table to test for the straightest.

Debra whispered in my ear, "I think ol' Petey is a bit plonked!"

I was a lightweight when it came to alcohol and my tongue was already getting a bit thick.

"I think he has company." I slurred.

Debra laughed at the both of us as I made my way to the table. Peter racked the balls and ordered another schooner.

I loved to shoot pool, but I never even tried to play snooker. Peter was very good. Maybe better than usual because of the condition he was in. He sank one ball after another, and I thought I would never get a turn. He took each shot with such studiousness I thought maybe there was money on the line or something. That is until he stretched his torso over the table to make a difficult shot and as he stroked the stick forth and back in preparation to launch the cue ball, his lungi got caught on a backstroke, came undone and fell around his ankles.

He turned beet red. Debra, a few onlookers, and I, burst out laughing.

"That's it!" Peter said with an embarrassed smile on his face. He pulled the lungi up and tightened it around his waist. "You win. I hereby forfeit this game."

Tired, a bit tipsy, and with Debra and me on either side of Peter, steadying him, we went back to our room. The bed stared at me once again as we let loose of Peter and let him fall on the bed, his lungi partially unfurling. I rolled him to the middle of the bed.

Debra, without the slighted hint of self-consciousness, started to undress.

"We are going to sleep in the altogether, aren't we?"

I thought she meant we were all going to sleep together. But then she asked, "So why do you still have your clothes on?" I guess I still had a long way to go before mastering Australian. But following her lead, I took off my shirt and my lungi and lay as close to the edge of the bed as I could. Debra crawled in on the other side of Peter, pulling the light blanket over the three of us.

In the middle of the night, it got so cold, Debra and I awoke shivering, while Peter seemed to be in a dead sleep, sprawled all over the bed, hogging most of it. Debra rolled him over on his side toward me. Without a smidgen of the nervousness *I* would have had, she reached over Peter, put her hand on my chest, drew us all together, skin to skin. Debra spooning Peter spooning me. It was a good thing that was the order. If I had been in Debra's place, Peter might have felt something hard against his 'arse!' I might have found myself very embarrassed if a poke were enough to bring Peter out of his stupor.

Surprisingly, it was Peter whom I felt getting hard against *my* 'arse.' I tried to ignore it giving Peter the benefit of the doubt that his oblivion was for real. But then in that oblivion, he threw his hand around my body, and it came to rest on my stomach just under Debra's hand on my chest. I hoped my loudly pounding heart would not keep Debra awake. I hoped Peter's hand would not slip further south. I did not trust myself. I thought of dead puppies.

Eventually we all fell asleep and, in the morning when we woke up, Peter and I both had 'morning wood.' Or was it the remnants of a brotherly love unconsummated? Since we were strangers in a strange land, no one found it strange, including Debra, whose perfect breasts were taut from the cold and to me, absolutely taunting! She merely laughed and said, "Oh you men are all alike! Just 'ave a gander at those beautiful willies!"

Once dressed, we rushed into the large kitchen, surprising the hell out of the cooks, and hurried to huddle over the wood stove. The cooks laughed at us; our attire totally unsuited to this climate. They made us breakfast. Fried eggs over easy, bacon, toast of freshly baked bread, jam, juice, and coffee. Coffee? What a treat! They tried to show us to a table in the dining room, but we were so cold, we chose to eat in the kitchen with the cooks.

After breakfast, we "borrowed" a blanket from the room next to ours and threw it on our bed, hoping it would fend off the cold that night. Then we ventured out into the streets. We may as well have been in England. Nicely landscaped city parks, a library, Christian churches, well-maintained cars, old as they were; even a garbage truck. Nuwara Eliya, you are one spiffy town!

People stared at us in our lowland garments. "Have you no decorum or common sense?" they seemed to ask as they passed us, so "fashionably dressed" in the well-worn wool pants and double-breasted jackets left behind by the British. We just assumed they had seen "Easy Rider" and ignored them, though we wanted to yell, "We're hippies, not Hell's Angels!" But when we did get a chance to engage any of them in conversation, we found them to be very polite and helpful and I think we dispelled any notion that they should fear us.

In a market, we found some very nice red bananas, big avocadoes or "alligator pears," as Debra called them, and juicy red tomatoes. The day was warming up to a comfortable temperature, and that afternoon we hiked halfway up Mount Pedro, or what the locals call Pidurutalagala, The Rock of Peter. It's the highest point in Ceylon, and we had a very nice picnic with a panoramic view. Then we meandered back to the hotel.

It was a Poya day, the monthly celebration of the full moon and therefore a public holiday. Maybe there'd be a party. We didn't care. We were too tired to be festive, especially me having had little sleep the night before. We were completely content to sit in the overstuffed chairs in the lobby, just being quiet; each of us immersed in our own thoughts. It was nice.

We had an early dinner in the hotel and once again, Peter could not stop himself from sampling the many different beers that were available. He started with a stubbie of Three Coins. After one sip, he declared it was piss! So he ordered a second bottle, this time Lion

Lager. Much better. He had a few of those when he noticed a bottle of XXXX on the shelf. Pure nostalgia in an alcoholic liquid. Peter walked up to the beautiful and highly polished bar. The bartender, poised in his white shirt and black-suspendered slacks, walked over to Peter and said, "May I be of service to you, sir?"

"Toss me over a nice cold Four X, mate, would ya please? And maybe a shot of Mendis." Mendis was the best arrack around. Triple-distilled whiskey made from the coconut palm.

Debra looked annoyed. "You OK?" I asked.

"I'm a bit cheesed off right now," she said quietly. "Peter never drinks like this! He's going to be completely off his face if he doesn't stop! Men! What *they* will do to get up their courage!"

I didn't understand what she meant, but once again we had to help Peter to the room. Once again, we flopped him on the bed, but this time pushed him over to the edge. Debra and I undressed and fell on the bed in the "nick" and pulled the blankets over us. She reached across, shook Peter a bit, and said, "Peter. Peter, you OK? You're not going to chuck up or anything, are you?"

Peter just mumbled something and drifted off. Debra removed her hand from Peter's back and turned toward me. She slid her hand across my chest, and let it loiter there a bit too long. It felt good but tickled a little when she started exploring my chest and stomach. I could feel her breasts at my side and a nipple caressing a rib. Her hand slid down and found me more than ready. She slithered on top of me and leaned down to kiss me. We were getting into a very sweet rhythm, me lifting her up slightly with my hips and she gently pushing against me. The rhythm was accelerating when we felt something move that wasn't us and noticed Peter sitting upright staring at us.

I couldn't read the expression on Peter's face. Debra was all smiles.

"Well, you look pretty wrapped!" he said to Debra.

That didn't help me at all. Then he looked me right in the eyes, his face a magnet that wouldn't let me look away and said, "Fair go mate?" He said it in such a way, I didn't know if it was a question, a statement, or a threat.

I looked at him quizzically, not knowing what to expect. I looked at Debra for a clue. She just laughed and said, "Aw, Pete's just feeling' a bit left out, Giacco. No worries!" Nevertheless, my woody started changing back into a willie.

Before I could change the expression on my face, I felt one of Peter's hands reaching under Debra's ass toward my crotch. By the time he was jostling my balls, Debra and I were at it again. Suddenly, Peter changed positions and stood behind my head, looking down at both of us. He slowly kneeled down, straddling my head, his knees pushing into my shoulders. His inner thighs hugged my ears. He leaned over my head toward Debra, and I appreciated this new perspective of his wonderful body.

Debra took Peter in her mouth and must have had a most talented tongue because he was moaning in ecstasy. His hands were all over her breasts and my chest. My hands didn't know where to go first. They wanted to be everywhere at once. It was so exciting! Debra and I were going at it in a frenzy now. Peter was arching his back. Debra was working him over good. I roughly explored his hard stomach and worked my way up to his pecs. I grabbed them hard enough to leave fingerprints and twisted a nipple.

As soon as I did that, he exploded without warning. I could feel the "explosion" dribbling out of Debra's mouth and onto my chest. It felt hot.

Puffing and sweating, Peter slowly withdrew from Debra's mouth. Debra and I were just about there too, groaning and gyrating, and Peter quickly moved to our sides, wrestling us into some sort of obscure hold that made me penetrate her even deeper, if that were at all possible.

When Peter felt we were getting very close, he jumped behind Debra, his chest against her back, his ass on my legs. His arms were around both of us. He squeezed us together so tightly, I thought we were in a vice grip! I'm sure all of Nura Eliya could hear our moans when we climaxed! Debra collapsed upon me, and Peter upon her. I could hardly breathe from the weight of both of them, but it felt good!

Peter rolled off to one side. Debra rolled off to the other. I lay in the middle, waiting for the usual post coitus tension. There was none. The only tension was that of the blankets Peter was drawing tightly around us as he tucked us in. He leaned over Debra, gave her a kiss, and said softly, "That was spot on, eh? You maniac."

"And you didn't need all that beer after all now, did ya?" she said, just as softly but knowingly.

Then he leaned over me. "You are legend, mate!" And he gave me a kiss. "Now hit the sack!"

We all lay there quietly, trying to breathe normally. It was too quiet. Our breathing was so normal it was abnormal. That's when we simultaneously burst out laughing. It was a lighthearted, happy, from-the-gut-laughter. A laughter that said we had conquered awkwardness and satisfied the desires we were repressing all along. A laughter that felt even better than the sex!

The chill of dawn arrived. It is always sleep's thief, and we woke up with a shiver that we chased into the ash-blackened kitchen. The shiver disappeared into the flames of the wood stove. We rubbed cold hands over it and exchanged warm smiles. Everything was right. Everything was sweet. Everything was apples.

The calm face of our soft-spoken waiter entered and greeted us with a smile. He made us milk tea to warm our bellies and we began another day. We left the hotel through the kitchen door and discovered back streets we didn't know were there, back streets that were hiding from the colonial pretentiousness of the paved avenues.

We walked past the maintenance shed of a golf course. The manicured greens seemed totally out of place. But the dilapidated shed blended in perfectly with the sordidness of the alley. Dirty, disheveled, bleary-eyed, and gaunt men huddled in the shadows. Their "home" seemed to fit them to a tee. As we passed, they were too weak to beg and simply held out their hands in hope of a rupee. We gave them some.

Once word got out that we had given money away, other beggars besieged us where we had noticed none before. Word travels fast when there is a soft touch around. You must give rupees judiciously otherwise you will be surrounded with children, invalids, the deformed and the demented, circling you, clinging to your garments, pleading incessantly until you feel so guilty, either you make yourself a pauper or you learn to make *them* invisible. It was a battle of self-scrutiny, and always an unpleasant investigation.

A fortune-teller at the end of the alley stood up from her little table and tried to seduce us as we approached by singing that she could see all and know all. We had great luck coming our way. But she changed her tune as we passed her by, shouting dire predictions at us for not giving her money.

We made our way as quickly as possible to the boulevard lined with beautiful trees and the beautiful buildings once enjoyed by rich plantation owners and merchants. Now, they were merely facades of civility that hid the dirt, noise and squalor lining the alleys behind the back door kitchens of grand hotels.

Speaking of grand. Nothing was quite as grand as The Grand Hotel. It was so grand it was a joke. A doorman, wearing what looked like a costume an organ grinder's monkey would wear, opened the door for us with a flourish. We walked in and could not believe our eyes. There were at least 10 tuxedoed waiters standing at attention, waiting for someone to wait on. They looked simply grand! And since it was still morning, we had breakfast there. It too, was simply grand. When we finished, we rubbed our bellies and walked out grandly, and promised never to speak of The Grand again!

Obviously, we were beginning to forget where we were. We needed to get back to the humid and humble, the tropical and topical, the present, not the past. We rambled back to our room where the rest of the day we spent consuming our morning, afternoon, and evening rations of "beauties."

I loved watching Peter roll joints. He would sit tall, cross-legged on the bed. His vibrations were so constant and even; his fingers so steady as he wrapped a paper cocoon around the ganja. When he was very stoned, he would close his eyes and sway forth and back and swells of warm air seemed to move across the space. I was having a love affair with them both. I don't think it would have worked out with either of them as individuals. But as a duo, it was definitely love, especially at times like this, when we were thoroughly wasted.

We listened to our thoughts. We wrote letters and postcards to friends, or to ourselves in our diaries. We asked questions like "Whose hand is this doing the writing and why?" And our soft-spoken waiter came knockin' at our window with a smile on his face and hot, fresh, coconut cakes for no good reason at all.

As soon as he was gone, I noticed Debra trying to get Peter's attention by making strange movements with her eyes and chin. Peter finally noticed while I played dumb. They were up to something. And I think Debra was behind it.

He said to Debra, "I dunno if I'm any gun at it, but I think I'd like to 'ave a go. If it's OK with you, that is."

Debra replied, "Onya then!"

Peter stood up and approached me. He grabbed me under the arms and lifted me into the air. I came crashing down on the bed, the springs squeaking in surprise. Peter ripped off my lungi and sat on my legs while he ripped off his own. Then he pinned me down with his whole body. He shoved his tongue in my mouth and kissed me almost violently. He worked his way down my body with his tongue, his hard cock dragging along my inner thigh and then my calf. His tongue was at the head of my cock and he looked up briefly to watch me watching him. Then he glanced at Debra looking for approval. She had her feet up on the chair, legs spread, and her fingers up her sarong. "Do it Peter! Watch them ivories though!"

Peter got back to work. He tongued the head of my cock for a while building up his nerve, then slowly engulfed me, one hand on my chest, the other grabbing my balls. His technique wasn't perfect, but it *is* the thought that counts! I figured I should show him how it's done.

I twisted him over on his back, my cock still halfway down his throat. I felt him gag some, so I retreated a bit. Then I did a clever 180-degree spin and licked him all the way down his fine body until I had his cock in my mouth as well. I roughly grabbed his ass and pushed him in deeper. We finally got into sync. I peered over at Debra who was fingering herself into a sweat, her head tossed back, and her eyes fluttering. I could tell she was close.

So was I. So was Peter. He was uncontrollable now. I could feel the head of his cock swell inside my mouth and a muffled scream came from deep within his chest. As soon as I felt his first fiery squirt, I came too. Each of us, rivers!

As we lay there exhausted, still in our sixty-nine position, Debra joined us on the bed and gave both of us hugs.

"You guys are bloody hot! I thoroughly enjoyed that I did. From go to whoa. And Peter! You are bloody full of surprises."

"I surprised myself, Deb. I didn't know I had it in me."

Debra laughed, "Yeah, but I did. That's why I fell in love with ya, ya bum."

I scrambled over him and sat on his stomach. I stared down at his face. He met my eyes and said, "Mate! That was bloody terrific! Was it good for you too?"

I couldn't help but laugh. I wondered how many times in how many beds those words of insecurity were spoken. I answered his concerned look with a deep kiss giving him a taste of his own cum. "You are a bloody legend you are," I said. "And so's your old lady!" I added smiling at Debra. She beamed back at me.

Peter looked at Debra. "OK, Deb. I did it. You satisfied now?"

"More than, sweets. Are you?" she asked with just the faintest look of wonder and concern"

"I am!" Peter replied emphatically. "It was a hum dinger!"

Then maybe to reassure her, he added, "But ya bloody well know I ain't ever gonna do this again with anyone else besides me mate here, don't ya? So, give us some truth."

Debra looked unconvinced, but lightheartedly said, "Well, as far as male bonding goes,

I think you were both bloody amazin'! But if this were a gymnastics event at the Olympics, I'd give you boys about an eight point five."

"Eight point five!" we both protested. "We were bloody gun, Deb!" Peter insisted.

"Maybe dinkum, but not gun. There's always room for improvement, Peter. Remember, practice makes perfect." She gave me a wink.

And practice we did. Throughout the rest of our trip, the three of us practiced until we knew each other's bodies intimately and they knew each other's bodies better than ever. Not a centimeter of flesh was ignored. I hoped they learned a few new tricks in the process that would serve their marriage well. In every guesthouse and hut, on every riverbank and beach, we practiced. And when we weren't practicing, we were cuddling and keeping each other warm and close to our hearts.

CHAPTER 44
February 1972

The next day we left the West that was.

We took a bus to Nanu-oya. Then a train to Hatton. Then a twenty-three-mile blood-curdling bus ride past beautiful, deep-cleavaged mountains to Sri Pada or Adam's Peak. On top was a footprint embedded in the stone. Though Buddhists believed it to be the footprint of Buddha, Hindus believed it to be that of Shiva. Muslims revered this site as the place where Adam landed after being tossed out of Eden, while Christians prayed to an indentation in stone, they believed was made by the foot of Thomas the Apostle.

I didn't believe or disbelieve these claims. What I couldn't believe was the constant stream of pilgrims coming down and going up the peak. They lent this mountain so much spiritual energy; the peak really was all that it is believed to be.

They all flocked to worship. Buddhists, Hindus, Muslims, and Christians. And except for us, they all came without the slightest doubt that the footprint belonged to the source of their particular belief. All worshipped at this shrine on top of a 7,300-foot peak, yet nobody showed any sign that one God was superior to another's. Sri Pada gave refuge to people of all beliefs. How nice for a change.

Joyful chanting and Spartan cheers gave strength of will to everyone who climbed the six miles to the base of the mountain and then the extremely vertical 9,000 steps to the summit.

The steps were chiseled into the stone more than a thousand years ago. At one time, the treads must've been flat, but over the centuries, innumerable pairs of feet wore them down into nearly forty-five degree sloping angles. It's a good thing there were ropes and chains on either side to hold on to. Without them to help pull us up, climbing them would've been almost impossible.

It was the middle of the night and should have been pitch black, but lanterns lighted the stairs. Every so often, we'd reach a small landing, a natural flat area of rock. Here the obsessively faithful had built little huts, where entire families permanently lived. They served food and tea and provided a place for us to catch our breaths. We didn't rest long because we had to get to the top before dawn, where we would see not one, but two sunrises, the only place in the world where this miracle occurred.

So, we scrambled with the hundreds upon hundreds of people eager to reach the summit; trying to gain altitude while excusing ourselves from jostling those making their way down and they excusing themselves for jostling us on our way up. Our feet and legs were exhausted; our arms ached from constantly pulling on the ropes and chains. It was not a race against each other, but a race against the spinning of the earth.

We made it with time to spare. Time to watch each other's sweat pouring down our faces by the light of torches surrounding the small and beautiful temple that housed the footprint. Debra, Peter, and I cuddled each other against the cold of pre-dawn and thought of revelations, and then thought some more of how *not* to think about them.

The "footprint" was a large indentation in the rock, larger than a human footprint. It didn't look like a foot at all. Where were the toes? They may have been worn away over the centuries by the millions of hands of millions of pilgrims rubbing, groping, and fondling them until the toes blended in with the foot which became just a shallow, irregular hollow that was smooth as marble.

We, too, couldn't resist touching it, sensually of course, as you might a Calder sculpture in a fine museum. We added six hands more of imperceptible, but definite, erosion.

The sun rose above the horizon. Everyone was quiet out of reverence. It climbed higher in the sky and began to warm us. As predicted, a second sun followed! This second orb was less orange, and without heat. It was amazing. But only as a phenomenon of the atmosphere, I concluded. I kept that conclusion to myself though, because the vibrations of these pilgrims of so many different faiths, staring in awe at the two sunrises, were so peaceful, harmonious, and synchronous, who was I to burst anyone's bubble?

After the phantom sun had blended in with the real one, we began the descent along with hundreds of others. Most everyone took the stairs toe to heel, the same way we had climbed them. Not intentionally, but naturally. And at that pace, we noticed everything we were supposed to notice.

When we reached one of the lower landings, we could look over the village at the base of the mountain. It was a village with no name. It existed only to serve the needs of the pilgrims. A steady stream of them kept arriving. By bus, foot, oxen, and makeshift stretchers and carts for the handicapped and disabled. They too would crawl their way to the top on their hands and knees if they had to, drag their lifeless legs behind them if they had to, take a week to do it if they had to. But they would reach the top, arriving with bloodied knees and battered fingers. They didn't care. It wasn't a bother. And they would touch the place where Buddha, Shiva, Adam, or the doubting Thomas had briefly stepped while walking the sky.

―――

We had been up for more than 24 hours, and we were getting rummy from sleep deprivation and exhaustion. Somehow, we managed to find a bus back to Hatton. We fell asleep immediately and what should have been another blood-curdling ride was merely a rocking chair. It was lucky the driver woke us up just in time to make a connecting bus to Butalla. We drove through the night and slept the whole way on that ride too.

We were still in a daze, when the next morning, we found ourselves on the outskirts of Butalla on the banks of the Menik Ganja, the "river of gems." None of us could remember how we got there. We each made up a different story, and they all seemed true. The water looked clean, and we were anxious to "rise and shine." We could think of no better place to "shine" than in this river of gems.

While we splashed each other, we noticed a trickle of people walking downstream along a jeep trail that followed the river. They passed us in groups of anywhere from five to 30 at a time. How many had passed before we got there? How many more were coming? Where did they come from? Where were they going? They paid us little mind, and walked unhurried yet determined along the trail, chanting, singing, praying. Straight lines, forget it! Walking in circles, weaving in and out, strolling diagonally, of course! Much better!

We thought they must be going to a local festival, and it must be close by. A young man broke "ranks" if you could call it that, to cool himself in the river. He spoke a bit of English and that's how we found out this was part of a major pilgrimage, The Pada Yatra, that started near Jaffna and ended 300 miles and 40 days later in Kataragama, Ceylon's most holy and notorious destination resort for the spiritually afflicted.

It was only later we found out that this was an alternative route. The primary route and the safer one, was along the coast. Only at Okanda would the majority of these "bhakta" enter the jungle. We were, however, going to go straight through it.

There were twenty-five to thirty miles left for them. For us, as well, if we chose to follow suit. Or should I say chose to follow lungi? Or sari? Or pajama whites? Or bare butt-naked butts? Or bodies somersaulting, rolling, skipping backwards, or crawling?

"'Ave a gander at that wouldja now! Looks like a walkabout to a woop woop!" said Peter

"It looks bonzer!" Debra exclaimed.

"Should we?" I asked them.

Peter stroked his chin, dripping with gems, and said, "Well, it looks like there's a few kangaroos loose in the upper paddocks, but I say 'abso-bloody-lutely!'"

I only understood a part of what he said, but I took it as a "yes!"

We dried off and threaded our way into the parade that seemed to have no beginning and no end. But the jeep trail did. It ended about a mile later, when the trail narrowed and split into multiple, meandering smaller trails. Only occasionally did it widen enough to allow a vehicle to maneuver through the encroaching brush and trees. The Menik Ganja had disappeared somewhere to our west, about a mile away, though the path followed its course due south.

Passing joints forth and back, we entered the Yala Sanctuary, which I expected to be a jungle full of Tarzan vines hanging from tall canopies of dense trees, and brush that would require a machete. It wasn't. It was a dry jungle, with little brush, and trees whose leaves were delicate and did little to shade us from the hot sun.

Nevertheless, it was still a jungle and home to elephants, water buffalo, crocodiles, leopards, monkeys, seven varieties of deadly snakes, and a host of other beasts, large and small. I tried to convince myself that the steady stream of singing and chanting pilgrims would keep them at bay, but I guess I wasn't very convincing. I found myself on constant sentry duty for any predators that might enjoy the hors d'oeuvre of a skinny Sicilian. Debra and Peter seemed totally at ease, so I felt obliged to be nervous for the three of us, and was that the hiss of a snake inches from my foot, or just a pilgrim rolling by?

I noticed men walking heavily now and then, purposely making loud thuds with their feet. I caught one man's attention. With the largest vocabulary of body language ever exhibited, he told me they walked that way to keep the cobras and vipers away.

Better! Oh, so much better!

We were just a half mile or so outside Galge, the only place between Buttala and Kataragama where a bhakta could rest and bathe, and except for the few who were fasting, bargain for food. A small shrine, just off the trail, yet appearing to be in the middle of nowhere, caught my attention. I easily persuaded Deb and Pete to leave the path and check it out.

It was a shrine to Ganesh, and I felt I had been drawn to it as if personally invited. It was so simple, but so beautiful. The gray of the lovingly hewn stone blocks, intricately meshed, embraced a small statue of Ganesh sculpted out of the same gray rock. The gray was interrupted only by the colors of flower garlands placed around his neck and assorted fruit at his feet. We walked all the way around it before noticing a swami sitting in a lotus position, meditating at the side of the shrine.

His skin was completely covered with sacred ash. He blended in perfectly with the stone of the shrine. He sat so motionless he could have been mistaken for a sculpture. He paid us no mind whatsoever as we studied him. He was in another world, peaceful and sublime. He made me wonder whether Jon was right when he said, "I wasn't ready." Did he mean that I didn't want enlightenment enough? I asked Ganesh to teach me supplication, to teach me how to wear the sacred ash on my forehead without knowing it's there. And I suddenly missed Jon and Rosie terribly.

The tableau of the shrine and the swami was so soothing, we decided to make camp there for the night, and we felt sure that Ganesh and the vibrations of the swami would keep us from harm. But just to play it safe, we thunderously stamped out a clearing for ourselves to frighten off the predators. The swami still paid us no mind, and the devotees passing by must have thought we were performing a ritual dance because they looked at us with approval. We smoothed out two thin blankets on the flattened grass and covered ourselves with the third and last. We lay down close to one another and tried to catch some Zs.

We didn't catch many that night. We hardly slept at all. At least one of us, throughout the night, sat up to have a look around. We scouted the area with squinted eyes. There were howling monkeys. They seemed to be right above us in the tops of the trees. We could hear them gossiping about us. One of them was piercingly loud and obnoxious.

"Rack off!" Peter yelled at him. The monkey yelled back louder. As did some of his buddies. Peter gave up immediately.

There were so many different kinds of frogs, croaking incessantly in so many different languages, it drove us crazy. At first, they were just background singers for the Monkees. As it got darker, the frogs got louder. I had a brief flashback to that awful day in New York when Dennis dove out the third-story window to his death.

How many lifetimes ago was that!

"What a bloody kafuffle!" Debra cried out wildly flailing her arms about her, "but it's these bloody mozzies driving me loony!"

An elderly woman, wearing a thin saffron-colored sari, left the stream of pilgrims and trickled her way slowly, but deliberately, to Debra. The end of the sari was loosely wrapped about her head and face. She was barefoot and her feet were large and flat from having gone that way all her life. Mosquitoes were all over her as well, but the muslin sari was her natural mosquito netting. She kneeled and pulled a container made of hammered tin out of her basket.

She placed it on the ground and opened it. A silvery white goop was inside. It looked beautifully alien and smelled just as unearthly. It smelled of herbs, some familiar and recognizable, others exotic and unknowable. The scent carried me away and for a split second I was in an episode of Star Trek, and she was a kindly alien that had beamed herself aboard the Enterprise.

The old woman pretended to scoop a dollop out of the can and rub it all over her body. Then she pushed the can toward Debra. Debra put two fingers in the can and shoveled out a small mound, about the size of an ounce of temple hash, and following the old woman's example, rubbed it all over herself.

The wrinkled hands then pushed the can toward Peter and me. We scooped some of it out. It had the texture of gritty mud. We rubbed it vigorously up and down our arms and legs, necks, and faces, and took turns doing each other's backs. Then we both did Debra's. We were starting to look like the gray swami.

Swinging her chin forth and back, she capped the tin. She replaced it in her basket and pulled out a few bundles of small twigs, each tightly wrapped with a wide flat ribbon. She stuck the bundles in the ground around our clearing. As she did so, she lingered for a moment in front of each of us and put her face close to ours. She studied our eyes carefully and pulled the saffron cloth down from her face so we could see hers. They were cloudy, yet deep. They seemed to have so much pity for us in them, as if we were the oddest of the odd, the most vulnerable, and the neediest.

Then she reached into Peter's bag and pulled out a pack of matches. How did she know they were there? It didn't matter anymore. We were already hypnotized. She lit each of the bundles and after she was sure they were smoldering properly, she gently replaced the matches in Peter's bag. She bowed her head to us, and as she stood up, bowed to Ganesh. Then she hobbled backwards a few feet before joining the other pilgrims.

We wanted to thank her, but by the time we snapped out of our spell she had disappeared. So had the mosquitoes. And the ointment salved the bites we'd already gotten. "No more mozzies!" Debra cheered. Even the monkeys and frogs had turned down the volume. Debra started croaking, Peter started howling, and I howled and croaked with them, mocking our animal neighbors and ourselves.

We laughed and slept a bit and hoped the mosquito repellant worked on snakes and spiders, too.

A few hours later, I sat up abruptly awakened by a horrible sound. I had goose bumps. I thought it was a panther. It was only Debra loudly yawning, sitting up and stretching her arms wide. The strange noise woke Peter up too.

He forced his eyes open, looked up at us, and asked matter of factly, "Should I be scared of anything?"

We smiled. "Only us my dear." she said, "Only us."

There was a tank of water near the shrine. The water was cool, clear, and refreshing. We splashed our faces and washed the sleep out of our eyes. The rays of the morning sun caught the ripples we had made and the water sparkled stars of sapphires, rubies, and emeralds.

We were now feeling fit for public consumption, so we joined the pilgrims on the path once again.

"You a bit peckish, Pete?" asked Debra. "'ow 'bout you, Giacco?"

"Oh yeah, Deb, I'm starving!" answered Peter. "What ya got?"

"Not a bloody thing, sweets."

"I think we're fasting," I offered, "but we have to pretend we're doing it on purpose. Otherwise, it doesn't work."

"Oh, better! Much better!" mocked Peter. I was flattered that he was using my expression. Well, actually it was the expression I picked up from Jon and which had worked its way into my repertoire of sarcastic remarks. I supposed that others would pick it up from Peter and Debra during their travels, and when they were back home in Australia. It would be passed on and multiplied. And though the source might never be known, it would make Jon a legend in his own time!

We had walked for a day and a half. It would be two full days in a few hours. Peter grabbed my elbow. "I think Deb's a bit puffed. Can we rest a bit?"

"I think it's just a few more miles, sport, but we can take a break."

"Nah. I'm good, guys," Debra said. "Let's keep going. I don't want to be pushing up zeds in the middle of the jungle one more night."

"We'll get there soon. I can feel the anticipation in the others. Just take it one step at a time. Walk in the way of the lord."

"And whose lord might that be Giacco?" Peter asked in all seriousness.

"Any lord you like, mate. Any lord at all!" And I taught them how to walk toe to heel.

After about half an hour, we noticed we were no longer passing people, as was usually the case. No. Now we seemed to walk at precisely the same pace as everyone else. Everyone seemed to be walking in the way of the lord. And suddenly we saw how beautiful the people were, how amazing the landscape was, how wondrous the whole world was, and how lucky we were to be sharing it together.

CHAPTER 45
February 1972

We were lordwalking when the trail widened quickly. There were now large open spaces ringed with ancient rock outcroppings. The trees thinned. The earth was nude. Trails merged to become a road. Streams of pilgrims merged to become a river. We were lordwalking, toe to heel, toe to heel, as the road gently angled downhill. We were lordwalking when just around a bend we saw the sun beginning its descent over the long-awaited vista of the temples and shrines of Kataragama.

The road spilled us out onto the northeastern corner of the sacred grounds. We had seen so many strange, beautiful, and dreamlike places, but this topped them all for homespun simplicity! We were a bit dumbfounded as to what made this unpretentious site such an auspicious one. By that evening, we understood.

Seven distinct hills dominated the southern horizon. A perfectly flat plain dominated the foreground. It was divided by the Kirivehera Road, a boulevard of dirt, which ran the length of the plain. Countless other dusty roads branched off in wild directions, some taking to the hills. Between the roads were fields of light green grass that looked like little parks. The Menik Ganja shimmered not far away, cupping the western side of the temple grounds, separating them from the town of Kataragama itself.

The temples and shrines that dotted the area seemed organic, as if they had emerged slowly over the ages from the dirt itself, and belonged where they stood, deeply rooted. Their inelaborate architecture lent them an aura of mystery. We were sure each of them concealed a brilliant gem of truth inside to make up for the homeliness of their exteriors.

The largest and most intriguing, was the temple to Lord Murugan at the north end of the Kirivehera Road. At the southern end of the road was the temple to the Goddess Valli-amma, Lord Murugan's consort. Both structures were rectangular and exceedingly plain. Both had porches made of tree branches. They looked like they could be forest dwellings. The lesser shrines were randomly scattered about the grounds, along with ashrams and shops that catered to the needs of the pilgrims. Behind the temple to Lord Murugan was an ancient Buddhist dagoba. Nearby was a great Bodhi tree said to have been planted in the third century BC. To the west of the temple to Valli-amma grew a huge Kohomba tree, and in the southwest corner of the grounds, a mosque, whose weathered and worn dome still retained enough gilding to bounce the sun's light onto the backdrop of golden hills.

Pilgrims worshipped at all the shrines, coming and going in brilliantly colored garb. But the vast majority was here to worship Lord Murugan. He was the main man. The main act. In comparison, the others were just side shows, opening acts for the rock star. Groupies of the Lord rolled forth and back on the hard stone entrance to the temple, vying for his attention.

The late afternoon turned into evening. Torches, lanterns, and candles were lit, filling the air with columns of smoke. Smells of many kinds tickled our noses, but camphor and coconut seemed to overpower the rest. Music, chanting, singing or praying, continually bombarded our eardrums. Vendors lined the roads, each selling their specialty: flowers, fruits, incense, herbs, beads, fabrics, powdered dyes, feathers, various sizes of needles and hooks, and oddities I had never seen before in my life. I had no idea what they were used for, but they were presented with great artistry on tables that fronted their rickety stalls.

The service industries were not lacking either. There were men and women who could cook you up a delicious meal, stir you up a refreshing drink, give you a massage your muscle memory would never forget, pierce any part of your body, braid your hair, tell your fortune, read your mind.

Some in the crowd turned to wonder and admire Debra, all aglow with her golden skin and her pierced nose and ears. Peter and I had to dissuade her from getting anything else pierced! We used hygiene as our primary reason. She didn't need much dissuasion when we came upon a high wooden swing with a man dangling from wire cables whose ends had hooks pierced through his back. He willed himself painless. He divorced his mind from his body as the man at the bottom of the swing pushed him higher and higher.

Another man was pushing a long and thick needle through his mouth. First, he pushed it through one cheek, and then, his mouth open with the needle visible for all to see, he pushed it through the other side. Still others walked around dragging heavy objects tied to dozens of hooks in their backs. These acts of self-mutilation were one way to perform *kavadi* to the Lord, the spiritual rewards a thousand-fold greater than the pain, or so they believed.

Ceylon's three main religions were here. Every sect of every religion had shown up. Every cult of every sect titillated the mind and body with their own unique rituals, rites and ceremonies. Some of them were beautiful and contemplative. Others were monotonous and hypnotic. Still others were just plain weird and sadomasochistic. We couldn't comprehend such diversity of worship on such a grand scale as this. Yet a vendor who spoke very good English said that this was only a precursor to *the* festival. The Esala Festival would occur during the height of summer, under a full moon. He went on and on, describing the festival in detail and with more adjectives than I knew existed. He enthralled and entertained us for a long time.

He beseeched us to come back again in a few months. If we did, we would see Kataragama at the height of religious intensity and madness. If we didn't, we would miss the devotees who worked themselves into a trance before walking paths of red-hot coals. We would miss the grand mayhem and beauty of the water-cutting ceremony. We would miss the horns blaring and the bells ringing, announcing the epic myth of a prince-like deity who falls in love with a local girl.

A grand elephant procession parades through the crowds. The elephants are adorned with large brocades made of silver and gold threads, and beaded with gems and baubles. The elephant who is the "chosen one" waits with thrill in his big eyes when he reaches Lord Murugan's temple. Tonight, on this last day of the festival, he will get to be the bearer of the Lord as manifested into the Kataragama yantram, a six-sided star. No one, except a few priests, has ever actually seen the yantram, but it is said to be made of bronze and gold leaf.

The priest reverently places the casketed yantram in an ornate carriage on the elephant's back. The elephant knows his Lord goes to his love who awaits him across the universe, though in this case it was just down the street.

The bulky beast lumbers around the shrines in the vicinity of Lord Murugan's temple and then down the length of the boulevard. Devotees, three and four deep, line the road, throwing flowers and chanting. When the elephant reaches the Temple to Valli-amma, the yantram is placed inside where it spends the night. In the wee hours of the morning, it is returned to Lord Murugan's temple.

I asked the vendor what happens inside Valli's temple once the yantram is placed there.

He stage-whispered, "It is too powerful to talk about. You must be here to feel it. Then you will understand the expressions of ecstasy on the faces of the devotees. But if you do not return, all of this you will miss."

He told his story with such passion and color, we felt we were there, under that full moon during the height of summer. We felt the climax of climaxes. Just thinking about what must go on in Valli's temple made me hard. If the religious intensity were any more mad than what we were experiencing now, we might go mad ourselves. But it was true. Except for our imaginations, we would miss out on this most sacred ritual.

What we didn't miss out on were the swamis. There were so many swamis I thought maybe it was a convention. The International Association of Swamis. Local 108! Some just sat quietly. Others had small groups around them listening attentively as they spoke, their chins tick-tocking a timeless clock.

There were so many damn holy guys here, I thought there must be at least one or two for me. But that didn't do me any good, strolling among the hundreds of them. I wouldn't have known where to start. How to cull the pros from the cons, the real from the false, the illusion from the disillusion. But I reminded myself that I didn't have to look for a teacher. If I were meant to have one, he would find me.

Oh damn! Wasn't I always saying that?

Our ears were ringing, our eyes were rolling, and our heads were spinning. It was too much. We couldn't absorb one more bit of color, taste, sound, smell, or touch, except maybe the touch of one another. So, we began to head for town. We drifted past the mosque, past the Goddess Valli, past the huge Kohomba tree, and were half-way across the bridge that spanned the Menik Ganja where we stopped to take a break.

I looked down into the shallow water and tried to imagine the water-cutting ceremony that was the finale of the big summer festival. It was a ceremony shared by both Buddhists and Hindus. I tried to imagine men standing half-naked, body to body in the shallow water, some genuflecting in it, others drinking it or filling vessels to take home, while sacred elephants guarded the banks. I tried to imagine all this but was sure my imagination could not come close to the reality of it. How could the summer festival be any grander or crazier than what we had already experienced? What we had already witnessed was enough to last a lifetime.

We crossed the bridge over the Menik Ganja into town. It was hard to find a place to stay. It took a couple of hours of asking directions. Hardly anyone knew how to say, "I don't know." Instead, they always gave an answer that often brought us to dead-end, darkened streets. We were more tired than ever.

Eventually, we did find a decent guesthouse near the center of town, close to the bus station. We stayed there a few nights, exploring each day the wonders of the temple grounds and its visitors. But the guesthouse was noisy. And each night, odd smells drifted through our window. Flares of dancing light brushed the walls. It was only the smell and touch of each other that brought us any peace.

Rising earlier than desired the last morning, I suggested we perform our own water-cutting ceremony by taking a dip in the river. We walked down to the Menik Ganja and slipped into the water. It was only waist deep. We splashed and let the holy water rush past our bodies. But because Peter and I were wearing no lungotis, our improvised water-cutting ceremony turned into a cock and balls nibbling ritual for small fish with little sharp teeth!

"Ouch! Peter cried, grabbing his balls. "What we got here mate?" he asked, "bloody piranha?"

"Ouch! Ouch! Ouch!" I blurted as the two of us made for the bank. "Yikes! That one hurt bad!" I yelled.

Debra was in hysterics. "Well, you sports have such bloody tasty bait dangling, what'd ya expect?"

To end our stay in Kataragama on a positive note, I yelled across the river to Lord Murugan, "*That* was our kavadi to you, and you'd better give us a million-fold back in good karma for all the pain, you bastard!"

Debra could not keep from cracking up as Peter and I sat on the bank, lifting our lungis to inspect the damage. It was minor, but enough to be a "bother" as we walked bow-legged toward the station.

We boarded a bus going to Hambantota on the coast where native men in their lungis fished on stilts in the shallow bays. Then we took another bus to Matara. Along the way we saw some of the best beaches yet. They weren't as thick with coconut palms, like those in Kalkudah, but were scalloped gracefully with pure white sand. The green-blue ocean crested in perfect waves, which I was sure our surfer friends would find "awesome, dude!" The beaches were so stunning I was tempted to get out each time the coastline came into view, and spend the rest of my life there.

In Matara, we took a taxi to Dondra Head, the rocky promontory that is the southernmost point of Ceylon. We stared into the vastness of the Indian Ocean. From here, we could have watched the sun rise, scribe a semi-circle in the sky, and set. All three, without ever moving. But we would only get to watch the sunrise. It was getting late and there was just enough light left to clear some rocks and set up a campsite of hand-smoothed dirt. We spent a blissfully peaceful night and slept as if we had been smoking opium.

In the morning, I thought of Little Richard as we awoke to vistas east and west that made "everything needless to say." The needlessness to say anything lasted only as long as it took to shake off the last remnants of sleep. I didn't know it then, but this would be the culmination of my time with Debra and Peter. This would be the end of an adventure that would keep them forever close to my heart. And how fitting it should end at the southern-most tip of this resplendent island.

Debra looked at Peter, her eyes a bit moist, and Peter looked at me. He shuffled over on his butt and draped his arm around my shoulder.

"Giacco," he said, and paused having trouble getting the words out. "Once we get to Colombo, Deb and I are flying to Bali for a couple of months and from there back home."

I knew this couldn't last forever, but I was in denial it would ever end.

"We want you to come with us. Please! You're a good mate you are, and we are rapt with you. We love you! 'Strewth mate!"

Tears flowed freely from my eyes, partly because I wanted to stay with them, partly because I already knew what I was going to say.

"I can't."

"But why?" Debra asked, a tear rolling down her cheek.

There were many reasons. Some practical, others emotional. I stood up, trying to compose myself.

"Jon paid for my ticket around the world. I'd feel like a heel if I didn't go on with them to India."

"He'll understand," Debra assured me.

"The ticket's only good as long as I stay above the equator. If I dip below it, I have to pay cash."

"Well, that bloody well sucks." Peter proclaimed. "How much ya got on ya then?"

"I left San Francisco with four hundred bucks. I have two hundred left."

"You're bloody killin' me mate," Peter replied. "You really are travelin' on the cheap, ain't ya."

"Well, there should be another four hundred waiting for me in Madras."

"Mate, you're making us feel like shags on a rock." Peter said in frustration, while Debra tried to stifle her tears. "You're gonna turn us fruity, you are!"

I looked down at them. They were so beautiful, even now in this, the first unpleasant moment we were sharing.

"I need to be with Jon and Rose," I confessed. "They're like my real brother and sister. I feel like our fates are bound together."

Peter wouldn't accept it. "What's the real reason mate?"

"Aw, Pete! Don't ya know I don't want this to end? Don't ya know I want my life to be tangled up with yours? I just feel my life is already tangled up with theirs."

Peter and Debra looked crushed. They wouldn't face me. Peter merely said, "Well that's a bloody wake up!"

I looked earnestly at both of them. "If only you knew how many times I thought you two were my teachers. You are the very essence of being in the here and now. If only you knew how in love with both of you I am! Do you hear me loud and clear?" I said, trying to get them to look at me. "I'm in love with you! There I said it, and it's done!"

"And ya haven't figured out by now that we feel the same way mate?" Debra said through her tears.

"Oh, you're making this so hard for me," my own tears now flowing freely. "Think of it. Think of us back in Australia. Think of your families and friends. Here in the jungle is one thing. There, back in your home, well that's something completely different. The truth is I'm afraid that if we try to make a go of it as a threesome, it will eventually get a bit sticky!"

A pause.

Debra looked up and laughed through her tears. "This is no time to be making puns, Giacco!"

Peter tried to stifle a chortle, looked up at me, shielding his eyes from the sun. "Don't ya know by now mate that we like it sticky?" He flashed me a huge grin that the sun caught just right.

Until then, I didn't even know what I had said that made them laugh, but then I got it. "Sorry," I said, my delayed laughter mingling with theirs. Our conversation immediately dissolved into bittersweet giggles. They stood up and drew me close, and we hugged hard and long.

"It'll be totally gonzo without ya, mate, but we understand," Peter whispered in my ear.

Nevertheless, they kept taunting me as we made our way back to town.

"You're just a gutless wonder, you are! You should at least give it a go!" Debra chided.

"Maybe when ya get back to San Francisco, you could get some bucks together and come visit us in Sydney sometime, eh?" Peter asked.

"Ya gotta make it soon!" Debra demanded. "Forget your bloody 'sometime.' I know if we can get you to Sydney, you'll never leave!"

"Or maybe we can come visit you in San Francisco! Peter said enthusiastically. "And then we'll never leave!"

"Or maybe we could meet in the middle!" Debra suggested.

We all paused to conjure up a map of the world in our minds.

Damn!

CHAPTER 46

March 1972

It was slow going back to Colombo. On purpose. We took only local buses so we could get off whenever we saw an inviting village or tempting beach. We all knew we were stalling, trying somehow to lengthen our remaining time together. I was full of doubts that I had made the right decision, but why express it now, only to give us all false hope.

We slept on a sublime beach every night. Our lovemaking was no longer frenzied. The rough housing and athletic sex turned tender. We savored each other. We took our time, wanting to make the most of it, but if flesh can show sadness, then that's what we felt as our bodies roamed around each other. We knew that in a couple of days, it would all end.

One village was running into the next, but as we approached Weligama, the thatched huts slowly, but inexorably, transformed into "civilization," with modest buildings and houses. By the time we reached Galle, there were, relatively speaking, five-star hotels, and others of lesser stars, and outdoor cafes where Western tourists sipped imported beers and lassi.

The beaches were polka-dotted with umbrellas shading lounge chairs. Dark-skinned men in white uniforms brought food and drink to visitors from all over the world. White skin seemed to dominate, with dark skin scurrying forth and back between hotel bars and restaurants.

Wandering vendors tried to sell the tourists gems and jewelry, coconut cakes, and papayas ripened to perfection. Despite being ridiculously inexpensive, the tourists haggled over prices as if it were the polite thing to do. Either that or they were just plain cheap!

Women lay topless on the beach and waiters averted their eyes while serving them their shrimp cocktails and gin and tonics. Locals, especially young men, squatted on the edge of the promenade, transfixed and bewildered.

There were no hotels that fit our budgets. No hotels in which we wanted to stay. However, there were enough policemen pounding the pavement and the sand, to eliminate the possibility of sleeping on the beach. They were there to make sure the riff-raff did nothing to disturb the privileged. Riff-raff included hippies, which meant us.

After a couple of hours in Galle, we caught an express bus to Colombo and arrived there four hours later. We checked into the Lakni Wesa Hotel, but the manager at the front desk insisted we get two rooms. No matter. They were just down the hall from each other, but it did not prevent us from sleeping together, which we assumed was the manager's intent.

That night was the last we spent together. We didn't have sex. We just slept quietly, cuddling as close as our skin would allow.

Debra and Peter were leaving late in the afternoon. We could not bring ourselves to talk about it. I was sitting in front of the hotel when they came down with their few belongings.

"You comin' to the airport with us?" asked Peter.

I looked up at them. Debra was already sobbing. I could already feel such a vacuum inside me, I thought I would implode.

"Peter, I can't!" I finally spit out. "It's too final. Watching a plane take you off like that. I just can't."

Peter reached down for my hand, pulled me out of the chair, and pulled me to him. He gave me a big hug and slipped a piece of paper in my hand. It was their address and phone number.

"Please. Come see us. Promise?" And he hugged me again.

"I promise!" I said, beating my fist mea-culpa like on my chest but really trying to say they would always be in my heart. "Sooner or later, I'll see you again. No worries mate!"

Then I went up to Debra, hugged her and kissed her on her forehead, then on her lips, her tears now mixing with my own. We were still hugging and kissing when I heard Peter call, "Taxi!" followed by a two-fingered whistle.

A taxi immediately left the bumper-car traffic and screeched to a halt in front of us. The driver got out and opened the door for them. They got in.

Peter leaned out the window, looked me hard in the eyes, and said, "You're a good bloke, you are. We love you, Giacco. Take care mate, and thanks."

"For what?" I asked

"For being someone we'll never forget."

"And there's no way I'm ever gonna forget you two!" I said, trying to suck back the tears. "*Abso-bloody-lutely* no way! How could I ever forget two of the finest loonies I've ever come across!" We tried a laugh, but it was a bloody weak one.

I watched them drive off as they watched me from the rear window. I could see Debra mouthing, "We love you," and waving. I waved back and blew kisses until they were out of sight. Back in my room, I lay on my bed and cried. I wished Jon and Rosie would show up. I wished Michael were here. I wished Little Richard were here. I wished Psylvia were here. For that matter, I wished all of Hunga Dunga were here. But they weren't.

I never saw nor heard from Debra or Peter ever again.

I sat at the window and smoked one of the many joints Peter left me and I gazed out at the intense crowds of people and cars. Colombo was not my kind of town.

It is Trincomalee that I think of as home tonight. I was so comfortable there and so used to the ways of your people. If I were to describe the best of you, I would tell of the young bicycling baker who shyly shook his pendulum chin while he circled me a few times and then gave me a butter cake for free.

Or the little boy who serenaded me while I mended a rip in my lungi.

Or the dark-eyed woman who cast me an entrancing glance, then quickly looked away when she was caught in the act, and smiled shyly, just a hint of mischief.

And the old man of the fortress rocks. You were much more of a child than your children were. Thanks for the beedies.

But the coin spins around, Trinco, and there were some unsettling stares and cunning money-thirsty cons. I know a bit about both sides of you now, but I didn't get to know all of you. Even so, when I was in the present, I loved you.

Colombo, I feel as if I have already left you. I am ready to move on. You are a perverted little city, you are. You are incongruous with your mix of healthy colonial gentry, and the hungry and poor in rags, who have left their villages in hopes of finding work in the big city.

You are beautiful in a perverse way. Women walk in self-imposed isolation, their heads beneath baskets filled with fruit, breads, cakes, and kindling. Their pace has a rhythm so mellow; the harmony permeates the air and evens out the lunacy of the traffic and throngs through which they navigate.

Your shrines offer salvation, but your streets offer sin. Men whose eyes are hidden by dark sunglasses corner me and open bags or briefcases filled with third-rate gems. Sapphires and rubies among them, all poorly cut, but presented as precious. You insult me with your presumption that I can't tell the good from the bad. And you swear at me when I turn away.

Young handsome peasants turned hustlers, with sinewy, sleek bodies, stare with feigned lust, hoping for an easy 50 rupees. I have no choice but to remain uninvolved, though who knows, if I were braver maybe I'd take you up on your sins.

Colombo, your days are swelteringly hot and it's worth the extra five rupees for a fan that's strong enough to stir the air in my room and create a bit of turmoil for the eager mosquitoes.

Each sunset barely tempers the air with a sea breeze, and your frying-pan streets are finally once again bearable.

I am anxious now to get to India and I hope you haven't been just a precursor to more madness.

I woke up early, and unwashed, went down to the front desk. There was still no word from Jon and Rose, the manager informed me reluctantly as if it were a bother. He regarded me with disdain. He probably suspected me of being a drug dealer or something. I ignored him.

I also ignored all the beggars and sidewalk vendors as I walked to the American Express office. Still no mail from home. I had sent postcards to them regularly and that was no small feat. People here had absolutely no concept of standing in a line. Only brute force could get you to the front to buy a stamp.

I walked to the harbor and wrote in my notebook. Can I capture the truth in words? It's all just images in my mind, which turns into Giacco tripping on Giacco tripping on Giacco tripping.

The S.S. France, docked in the bay, caught my attention, and brought me back to what some called reality, but I called insanity. The ship was beautiful and immense. Launches ferried passengers back to the ship, their arms filled with bags of goodies from their afternoon shopping spree. All the children and young men crowded the promenade to watch. What a sight it must have been to them, tempting their deep desires to sail away on the foam. I felt the same way. I felt it in my gut like when you drive over a bump or down a hill too fast.

As I walked back to the hotel, I could hear a radio blasting *Penny Lane is in your ears and in your eyes and in your mind.* The strains of the Beatles were carried on waves of heat so oppressively humid, everyone was nearing a breaking point, which never seemed to arrive.

The natives seemed especially restless today, and the continual staring, emboldened by the stifling air, voiced itself in jeers and comments. The intonations alone hinted at derogatory remarks.

I stared back dispassionately, which almost balanced out the bad vibes, but maintaining such dispassion is the art of the yogis. For me, it was an exhausting psychological tactic and I wondered if this air I moved through was really a gas. It felt so heavy.

There was an isolated raindrop or two that teased the dusty ground and its passersby with hopes of release. And then it arrived with a fury. The clouds burst and everyone relished the drenching. I returned to the Lakni Wesa completely soaked and the manager handed me a note with a sour look on his face.

The note had a hand-drawn picture of an Om sign surrounded by the rays of a sun setting into wavy lines of an ocean.

"Beautiful Giacco," it read. "We are in room 209 and we love you and miss you very much!" Signed, "Jon and Rosie."

They're back. And they're only a flight of stairs away! I took the steps two at a time and rushed into their room. They looked tired, yet somehow aglow. We hugged each other as if we were long lost-relatives reunited after many years apart.

They had found the swami called Guaribala, the German Swami. He took to them both immediately, but especially to Rosie, Jon said, trying not to display the slightest sign of envy. At first, I sensed a kind of estrangement between them, but it dissipated as they talked excitedly.

Jon and Rosie kept stepping on each other's lines trying to convince me of how impressed they were with this man. He was the ultimate bohemian iconoclast. He was funny and full of life. He loved his drink, and his mischievous face was usually in a haze of smoke from the cigar sticking out the corner of his mouth. They extolled so many of his virtues and eccentricities, I chuckled when Rosie said, "And to top it off, he's gay!" as if that trait clinched the deal for her!

While trying to catch their breath in the excitement of telling me their story, I tried to tell them about the double sunrises and the footprint of Buddha at the top of Adam's Peak and the wonder that was Kataragama.

But I could tell they hadn't heard anything I said, their minds too busy diving into a pool of words, searching for just the right adjectives to communicate the impact Guaribala had had on them. It wasn't necessary. It was all too obvious!

They regaled me with dominoes of stories about German Swami. They told me of his many devotees throughout the island and as far away as Tamil Nadu. They parroted his "one-liners" until they were just one step ahead of tedium.

"No mind, never matter. No matter, never mind."

"Summu Iru! Summu iru! Simply be! Simply be!"

Oh, yeah, they were true and all of that, but I guess I was feeling insecure and that I had missed out on a golden opportunity. That I had veered away from the same path as theirs.

I coveted their experience, though mine was one never to forget as well. And since Jon had told me I wasn't ready, I assumed that had I gone with them, I wouldn't have been as capable to be as smitten as they were. Especially Rosie, who, more than Jon, thought Guaribala might be the one they were searching for. I sensed that Guaribala and Rosie had telepathically bonded, that he had touched Rosie in a way he hadn't Jon. It sounded as if he had been waiting years just for her. And she didn't need to look any further. But Jon did.

My take was that Jon wanted to find a teacher who fancied *him* as the preferred disciple. A guru who would immediately recognize the zealotry in *him*, touch *his* forehead, and bestow upon *him* the enlightenment he deserved. It would be a guru with just a few devotees, handpicked, which to me sounded a bit elitist.

Jon was looking for reasonable excuses to move on. Rosie was reluctant to leave but Jon reminded her that Guaribala was going to Germany for several months and wouldn't be around anyway. Another convincing reason to leave was that the number of corpses floating down the rivers was increasing. This seemed more unsettling to Jon than to Rosie or me. Jon said he felt a tenseness in the air that made him think we should revisit Ceylon at a later date and go to India as soon as possible.

We went down to the Pan Am office and booked seats to Madras for noon the next day.

CHAPTER 47
March 1972

Ayobowan Ceylon! *Namaste* India!

A taxi driver took us to a nice Brahmin hotel and restaurant owned by the uncle of a cousin's mother-in law. It was a two-story, U-shaped, run down and unassuming little place. All the rooms opened to an inner courtyard whose plants were in need of watering. We settled into a room on the second floor and after throwing our bags in a corner, went down to the restaurant where we feasted on badjis, puris, and dosas. What a treat to the tongue!

Jon went back upstairs to rest a while, but I went to the American Express office. Good ol' Little Richard! There was 400 dollars and a short note waiting for me.

"Frank! (only kidding, we haven't forgotten you.)
Make this moola last. Come home soon!
Psylvia is pregnant and we all miss and love you."

Zietar

Oh, how my heart hurt. I missed them so much and now, finally, we were going to have a baby! I hoped Nicky was the father, but it didn't really matter. I still had about seventy-five dollars left which meant I had to live on four hundred seventy-five for the rest of our trip. At the rate I was going, I should be able to make it last. But now I needed to change the wired money into rupees and at a better rate than American Express would have given me. I took the money in dollars and went back to the hotel.

Rosie, in the meantime, had insisted on exploring the neighborhood. She had a penchant for solo adventures, and she could connive with the best of them, using her sensual charms to get her way. When she came back, she was not alone.

Aslam and Shajahan followed her into our room as if they were following some exotic smell they had never sniffed before. She had the two young brothers under some sort of spell, or maybe it was their expectation of promiscuity, which was a common stereotype of Western hippie women. Even meeting Jon and me did not dissuade them from fantasizing their evening would end with a sexual experience of the tantalizing Rosie. They were eager to satisfy her most off-handed wishes.

The most important one for all of us was to change some money and to score some ganja.

Late that night the five of us, led by Aslam and Shajahan, ventured into dark and twisting alleyways where the brothers knew black-market money changers hung out. There were many. Lucky for us, Aslam and Shajahan bargained in stage whispers with a few of them. They got us a good exchange rate for Jon's traveler's checks, and some of my dollars.

Soon after we had made the transaction, we felt the presence of three men following us. We quickened our pace and turned around to find they had quickened theirs.

The brothers started running and we followed as best we could. They must have known this neighborhood well, because they led us into a tiny alley none of us would have noticed on our own. We huddled there in silence trying to muffle our heavy breathing and watched the three men run by. When we felt the coast was clear, we followed the tiny alley until it met up with a busy street.

Aslam and Shajahan laughed. The rest of us were somewhat shaken up. This made the brothers laugh even more. It was obvious they were intrigued by the whole idea of intrigue. Intrigue for intrigue's sake and perhaps the opportunity to impress Rose. First mission accomplished. Now for the ganja.

I was against it, but in an act of faith, Jon gave Aslam some money. He approached a cabbie, and a conversation took place through the driver's window that was comprised of quiet negotiations, outbursts of loud bickering, wildly gesticulating hands, swinging chins, and finally mutual nodding agreement. All of this, while every few minutes the cabbie looked through the rear window at the four of us with curiosity and disdain.

Aslam stepped back and the cabbie sped off. We waited. And we waited some more. After an hour of waiting, Jon's anger began to show. Despite Shajahan's assurances that his brother knew what he was doing, Jon was convinced we had gotten ripped off. If we did, it served us right for trusting these two young men whom we hardly knew.

Yet much to our surprise, the cabbie returned and without really stopping, held out a bag, which Aslam took without even looking inside it. When he brought the bag over to us, he opened it up. The unmistakable aroma of fine ganja leapt out. Inside were a healthy couple of ounces of it. Jon was stunned and a bit embarrassed he had mistrusted them. He offered them some money for their efforts, but they refused with a hurt look on their faces. Rosie, on the other hand, knew all along that the brothers would do nothing to earn her disfavor.

We all walked back to the hotel and on the way, Jon stopped to pick up a bottle of arrack. Back in our room, we drank and smoked into the late hours. At first, Aslam and Shajahan refused the weed saying it was against their principles. But after a few shots of arrack, they said what amounted to, "What the hell!" and joined us.

They say ganja puts wings on prayers and it must put wings on songs as well. Shajahan started singing. His Tamil songs were accompanied by graceful hands forming delicate mudras which sensitively and poignantly enhanced the mood of his voice. The melody flowed in between and around the spaces of notes we were more accustomed to, creating a subtle music that needed no other instruments. His eyes stayed opened, yet adrift, honest, pure, and even. It was beautiful. He was the song.

They left early in the morning, still enamored of Rose, but gracefully accepting the fact that there would be no sexual shenanigans and satisfied to be our friends. They visited us almost every day we were in Madras.

We fell into a well-deserved sleep near dawn. It was almost noon when Jon woke us up, all bright-eyed and ready to boogie. He had gone downstairs to the restaurant, and there on the little table outside our room were tea and coconut cakes. As we sat in the small rattan chairs on the balcony, a man sitting outside his room across the atrium from us, smiled and waved. We waved back and beckoned him to join us.

Like Aslam and Shajahan, he spoke excellent English. Govindam was a very shy and gentle man. Within a few minutes of pleasantries, Jon and he started talking about teachers and our quest.

Govindam was a devotee of Ramana Maharshi and had lived with him for 20 years. He did not try to persuade us that this was *our* path or *our* teacher. Yet he strongly suggested we visit Tiruvannamalai, the site of the largest Shiva temple in India. He also wrote a letter introducing us to the Ramana Maharshi ashram there. We felt we had to go.

The next day we took the earliest bus to Tiruvannamalai. There we found a sprawling campus of shrines and temples. But our timing was off. It was a new moon and only on the full moon does the site draw hundreds of thousands of pilgrims. Perhaps that was for the best, because we got to sit and meditate on the sacred mountain near the temple that is considered a manifestation of Shiva, the destroyer of illusions.

We, or should I say Jon, got to spend time discussing the teachings of Ramana Maharshi with one of his disciples at the ashram. As usual, Rosie and I merely listened attentively as Jon's discourse became more passionate and the disciple more surprised at Jon's knowledge. After a couple of hours, we left, the devotee wishing us good fortune.

Rose and I felt uplifted by the conversation. But Jon seemed unsatisfied and frustrated. Nevertheless, just being in the midst of so many astounding temples that cloaked us in spiritual energy, made us feel we were closer to our goal. We could feel the five elements of water, fire, earth, wind, and space invading our beings. We returned to Madras with a conviction we were mere atoms floating aimlessly, but soon to become one with everything.

After a day of rest back in Madras, we took a bus to Pondicherry to visit the Sri Aurobindo ashram. It was, like most ashrams, quiet. Too quiet. I thought I had entered a church. Few people were there. I missed the madness of Kataragama. I missed "being here now" with Peter and Debra.

We read pamphlets about the teachings of Sri Aurobindo and The Mother, who was believed to be almost as holy as Sri Aurobindo himself. But as peaceful as the place was, Jon was once again not impressed. He was respectful, but not impressed. Both Sri Aurobindo and Ramana Maharshi had too many disciples. They both had the trappings of a religion. Perhaps it was not a religion, as we in the West know it, but a religion, nonetheless. Anything that smacked of religion was eliminated as a contender for our devotion. Or should I say Jon's devotion. But since Jon was our "secret" teacher, if he gave the nay, so did Rose and I, even though at some point we had to decide for ourselves.

On the bus ride along the coast back to Madras, I saw in the distance nicely manicured grounds upon which stood a simple white building devoid of the usual ornateness of Hindu temples. I'm not sure why I felt so strongly about getting off the bus, but Jon and Rosie humored me, and we all got off when the bus stopped at a place called Adyar.

We found ourselves at the delta of the Adyar River and followed its current as it met the Bay of Bengal. Wide, white, sandy beaches and blue surf were within walking distance and looked very inviting. But I was too curious about this unpretentious but obviously special building just a short walk up the river road.

It led us directly to the building. An engraving on the top of the front portal read, "The Theosophical Society." My heart beat faster. This was the home of Jiddu Krishnamurti, raised under the tutelage of Annie Besant and C. W. Leadbeater, who regarded him as the one prophesied to be the world's next great spiritual savant.

Jon seemed impatient and as soon as he read the sign, he turned around and said he would meet us on the beach. He had no use for what he considered a totally Western approach to enlightenment; a trendy, pseudo, psycho-spiritual organization to his way of thinking. His dismissal of The Theosophical Society, Annie Besant, and Krishnamurti surprised me, especially since Jon was the one who had turned me on to him when we were on our way to Sabino Canyon and later, quoting him extensively when we were stoned on peyote. I was also hurt when Rose decided to join Jon on the beach instead of indulging me for a change.

I entered the building alone while they made their trek to the ocean. Other than a curator, there was no one inside. There were, however, rows upon rows of books. And the walls were adorned with pictures of Annie and C. W. and J. The curator asked if he could be of help, but I said no, I would just like to look around.

I pulled a chair from a row of desks and sat in the middle of the large main room. I had already read many of his books and I immediately felt comfortable. I tried to refresh my memory with words of his I had been reading not so very long ago back in Kalkudah. What were they? I tried so hard to remember.

I breathed in and out slowly, trying to absorb through osmosis the words of wisdom within all the many books, articles and treatises surrounding me. Krishnamurti was such a prolific writer, it seemed a futile exercise, but I tried. I knew better than to think the words were the wisdom, or wisdom, the words. I knew better than to think.

I contented myself by observing on the walls some of his quotations printed in large letters on big, framed posters. There they were! Right there in front of me! The words I was trying to remember! Like road signs!

"Truth is a pathless land."

"Freedom is always at the beginning and not at the end."

These were words worthy of meditation. And that's what I did as I walked along the banks of the river to the beach, repeating to myself, "Truth is a pathless land." "Truth is a pathless land." "Truth is a pathless land."

And here we were, the three stooges, looking for a path. Not any path. But *the* path. I wisely kept Krishnamurti's words to myself as I approached Jon and Rosie. As I had promised myself at the outset of this journey, I would not seek, but just tag along in case they stumbled onto something big.

Up at 5 AM, coffee and rice cakes for breakfast, a cordial farewell from Govindam, and off we were to Bangalore!

Well, it wasn't quite that simple. We had decided against taking a First-Class Express Bus in favor of all local buses. This way we would intentionally multiply our adventures. "Brilliant!" as Debra might have said.

The first bus, with the required amount of three times the people and baggage a bus can carry, made it about two blocks before it broke down. Everyone stepped off, climbed off, slid off, and men on top threw down baggage and cargo.

When a second bus came along already packed with people, those stranded by the first bus simply stormed it with no rhyme or reason, as is customary in India. Jon, Rosie, and I just shrugged our shoulders and barely managed to find a spot on the rear bumper, our fingers hanging on for dear life to the open rear window, people's heads peering at us nose to nose.

This could have been fun. We quickly learned to keep our knees loose to absorb the bumps and potholes. This could work.

"Is this much better, or what?" Jon yelled over Rosie.

"This is so much fucking better, I can't find the words!" I yelled back.

"Would you please stop staring at me and back off!" Rosie yelled at an old lady with a prune face and a wayward eye.

"Think of it this way," yelled Jon. "We only have to do this for another 12 hours!"

"Stop touching my fucking hair!" Rosie yelled at a little girl leaning out the window.

We'd stop every few miles to let off some and take on others. People and baggage. Sometimes a chicken or two. We'd step off the bumper to rest our feet and stretch our legs, but we wouldn't relinquish our handholds on the window. Space was at a premium and we needed to protect it. Then the bus would start up again and we'd jump on the bumper and stare back at new faces just inches from ours.

We did this for about 20 miles, when the bus started sputtering and choking, and eventually died.

There were enough people, baggage, and animals taken off the dead bus to form an entire village. Some passengers loudly berated the bus driver, while others took it in stride, squatting on the dry, dusty road next to their baggage. Some began taking out makeshift stoves and food and started cooking.

Jon was not taking it in stride. "My god!" he screamed. "Isn't it bad enough people live shoulder to shoulder along the rivers? Now they've taken over the fucking highways!"

Rosie made it worse. "We got up at 5 AM to catch a fuckin' 6 AM bus, it's now noon, and we've only gone 21 fuckin' miles!"

I was on edge too, but I hadn't seen Jon and Rose so irritated since we started this trip.

Finally, a third bus approached. The stranded all stood up at the sight of it. They were waving and hollering for it to stop, but it looked like it wasn't slowing down. It was already packed to capacity. The throng blocked the road. The bus came to a stop.

The bus driver got out and was obviously trying to explain to the crowd that it was impossible for him to take two busloads of people and baggage on his already overcrowded bus. That did not deter many from throwing their bags on the roof and starting to climb up on top. The bus driver was yelling and pulling on people's legs trying to get them off, trying to make them understand. It was once again pure madness. India, your contorted face is so big, you really do make Ceylon look like a teardrop.

The three of us just stood there, unable to join in the fray.

"This is too much!" Jon lamented. "I give up. This is just too berserk!"

"Look!" Rosie cried out. "Here comes another bus going back to Madras!"

Jon ran to the other side of the road and waved frantically. The bus pulled over and it was only carrying 20 people or so more than it was able to. Plenty of room!

We managed to wrestle our way into the middle of the aisle, where we would stand the entire way back to where we could start all over again.

Except that didn't happen. We had only gone about seven miles when Jon's eye caught a sign that said, "Madras International Airport."

"Stop the bus!" Jon yelled at the top of his voice. "Please, stop the bus!"

A couple of people on board must have understood English and they started yelling at the bus driver too. I assumed they were translating for Jon and telling the bus driver in Teluga to stop the bus. For all I know they were yelling, "Get rid of these dirty hippies. They smell of soap and water! Stop the bus now!"

Whatever they were yelling, the bus pulled over and stopped. Leading the way, Jon shoved through the crowd like a speedboat cutting through choppy water, leaving a wake large enough for Rosie and me to get through.

The bus slowly got up to speed and left us in its dust. We were glad to walk the two miles to the airport. Though we had wanted to travel by ground whenever we could, we were glad we had our round-the-world tickets. They did come in handy!

We had to wait a few hours, but there was a flight to Bangalore and by sunset, we were walking past signs of Satya Sai Baba on our way to The Only Place.

"Ya know," Jon said softly and calmly to me, "Life is just one big fucking dream!"

CHAPTER 48
March 1972

The Only Place was a Western-style hamburger and breakfast joint with a small hotel attached to it. It was filled with freaks from all over the world, especially the UK, Germany, and Australia. Longhaired scruffy men and Earth Mother goddesses had all gone native. It was almost overwhelming to see so many of our kind gathered here in this town. It was very reminiscent of Tucson in climate and landscape. That alone made us feel at home.

But I will admit it was also a bit disconcerting to find so many Western freaks in one place, The Only Place. It felt very much Out of Place. It was as if we had had Ceylon pretty much all to ourselves and we liked it that way. Now we were lost in the crowd. The locals seemed used to us. No more blatant staring. No more curiosity. They had become desensitized to hippies. What was going on?

We struck up a conversation with a couple from Ohio, Bob and Kathy. They were both very thin, looked travel-worn and beat up. They told us that most travelers to India, except for the Australians, took the overland route from Europe. By the time they made it to Northern India, they were either too sick or too tired to travel farther south, and invariably started the journey home. If anyone made it this far, they were indeed troopers of an extraordinary kind. What spurred them on through the dysentery and infected cuts, and all the other germs for which most Westerners had no immunity, was the longing to be with their master, Sathya Sai Baba.

Sai Baba! We knew of him from the States. He had a huge following. It was said he could produce a mound of gems before your very eyes. He could levitate. He could change the color of his gown at will. Yogi Bhajan and Swami Satchitananda had testified that Sai Baba had, in their presence, materialized a human being from nothing. For all seekers who felt they needed material proof of a guru's powers, Sathya Sai Baba had no competition.

It felt like the entire town of Bangalore existed purely for Sai Baba and his ashram. All life centered around him. A friendly Brit, Basil, joined Bob, Kathy and us at our table. Bob, as it turned out, was a very spiritual guy. He had spent a considerable amount of time with Baba Ram Dass, and regaled us with stories of Ram Dass' search for a guru, and his own experiences with trying to be mindless. I liked him. He seemed genuinely desperate for the truth. He got us so high with his talk that I began to think the safest thing to do was to regard every single person I met as The Guru. That was a lot easier than seeking one out, no matter how subtle the search might be in one's mind!

As if just talking about it weren't enough of a high, he pulled some temple hash he had gotten up north out of his fanny pack. It was potent to say the least and a wonderfully different taste from the ganja we had been smoking.

A few tokes and we were blithering idiots. Bob reached for a guitar, and we all sang some of the simpler songs of Neil Young, Dylan, and the Beatles. Basil looked at the clock on the wall. He stood up suddenly and entreated, "Hurry, hurry! We have just enough time to make it!"

Basil acted like a border collie, first snapping us out of our musical stupor and rounding us up, barking from behind as he scurried us out the door. Once outside, he led the way with long strides just short of running. We did our best to keep up.

When we got to Brindavan, Sai Baba's ashram in Whitefield just outside Bangalore, we saw a huge pergola covered with colorful fabric and shading a circular deck of hard wood. It was already packed with mostly Indians, but it was easy to spot the Western hippies intermingled among them. They all chanted and sang as they sat cross-legged on the floor, many of them holding pieces of paper or handkerchiefs. Though they tried to act contented and serene, the anticipation was obvious.

It was too crowded to sit together, but we managed to squeeze ourselves in among the crowd within eyeshot of one another. Some people were a bit aggressive, trying to squirm their way to the innermost circle in preparation to hear His evening bhajan and hopefully to receive His darshan.

I looked around to find Jon. I expected him to be totally annoyed by this onslaught of devotees. This was not the exclusive venue he was looking for. Yet when I did find him in the crowd, he was sitting in a lotus position, thumb touching the middle finger on each hand as they rested on his knees. His eyes were closed, and he looked blissed out. This confused me. But maybe he was just succumbing to peer pressure. Maybe he was going to give this guy the benefit of his doubt since everyone around him seemed to be acting like this guy was *the* one. I took his lead and did the same.

Suddenly a strangely cool breeze blew through the dry desert heat. I felt that Sai Baba had sent it. The breeze made its way through the crowd and without noticing an entrance, Sathya Sai Baba was suddenly standing under the middle of the pergola. He wore a simple white cotton robe. His skin was very dark and his hair kind of afro style. He could have easily been from Harlem. The whites of his eyes were very white, and his pupils very black and intense. Yet as he surveyed the crowd, his look was extremely kind and compassionate.

He turned slowly, taking in the worshipping eyes of at least a thousand people. You could tell some were vying to get his attention by trying to make their eyes look more worshipful than others. Every now and then, he would pause and look at a person intensely. They would swoon and fall backwards or to the side, only to be righted by the people next to them.

He began to speak, and a more pronounced hush fell over the already meditative crowd. He spoke in Teluga for a while. All I could understand was the tone in which he spoke. It was very soothing. But then he would spy a Westerner, and speak in English, or German or whatever language was appropriate for that individual. How did he know?

Sai Baba seemed to be anything and everything you wanted him to be, no more, no less. Perhaps I should have wanted him to be more. But I didn't. Revolutions of thought circled in my mind.

Why do I have such a hard time not thinking!

People started holding out their handkerchiefs and pieces of paper, imploring him with their eyes to notice them. He went up to one old woman and leaned over her little piece of paper. He held up the palm of his hand so all could see there was nothing there. Then the miracle all had been waiting for, happened. A small stream of vibhuti, the sacred ash, poured from his open palm onto the sheet of paper. The woman started crying and mumbling words of praise and thanks, or at least that's what I translated them to be. She quickly folded up the holy ash into the paper, trying not to get it wet with her tears.

Then a gong sounded somewhere off to the right of the pergola. My ears instinctively turned in that direction. When I turned back, Sai Baba was gone. That was the end of the darshan. I was totally bewildered.

We went back to The Only Place. This time, the restaurant, though filled with people, was very quiet. We took a table and the five of us sat down without saying a word. Bob reached for his guitar and the silence was broken only by his tuning it to an open A chord. Then he started strumming it and making tabla-like sounds with the heel of his palm on the wood of the guitar. He slid his fingers up and down the neck, improvising a sitar-like raga, coloring our minds with the rapture we were all assumed to have experienced.

In the middle of all this, Jon ordered a hamburger with everything on it! Pretty bold I thought, since he was a devout vegetarian. Well, most of the time. I think this was his way of letting us know he hadn't been taken in.

Bob put the guitar down and the rest of us ordered food, and except for Rosie and me, it was hamburgers all around. We went up to our room early. Jon was restless and out of sorts. But after a joint or two, he settled down, eventually falling into a deep snoring sleep. Rose crawled in next to him, and I plopped on my bed and fell fast asleep too. But not before asking myself, "Did all this happen in just one day?" I shouldn't have been surprised. A day in India is like two weeks anywhere else in the world.

Basil knocked on our door early in the morning. Too early, but now we were awake, and whatever dreams we were dreaming, whatever messages they held, they were lost in the sudden drumming on our door.

"Hurry up mates! We'll be late for morning darshan!"

Jon rubbed his eyes and looked a bit miffed. "Darshan, smarshan," I heard Jon mumble under his breath, but he rose to the occasion. Rosy staggered to the washbasin and splashed water on her face. I stepped into my lungi and wrapped it tight around my waste. And off we went.

But I stopped in my tracks when I noticed just outside the hotel, a snake charmer, or so I guessed by the beautifully woven basket at his feet. The man was genuinely entertaining with his little magic tricks and antics, and then he pulled the top off the straw basket. A cobra slowly emerged. Most of the small crowd that had gathered to be dazzled stepped back in caution, while a few leaned in closer, an act of faith.

The cobra, now aware of his audience, strikes at them with a frightening intent. It opens its jaws wide and bares its fangs, slimy saliva-goo dripping from its mouth. It strikes again with a horrible hissing sound. The charmer starts talking to it in a repetitive, melodic way. He approaches the cobra, singing to it quietly, beautifully. He carefully removes a flute from the back of his sash and slowly brings it to his lips, singing all the while. He starts playing. It is so lilting and buoyant, yet haunting and soothing at the same time. Hypnotic. He renders the mesmerized cobra harmless as he touches the viper's head and pushes it gently back into the basket.

The crowd is quiet. They too are mesmerized, hypnotized, and hopefully generous. The charmer quietly puts the top of the basket in place and runs a stick through two loops to lock it. Only then do the "oohs" and "aahs" and clapping come, and thankfully, the tossing of some coins.

I feel a hand grab mine and pull it hard. It was Basil's. "What the hell ya doin' mate? Get your arse in gear! C'mon!" He drags me quickly through the hundreds of people all walking in the same direction, my flip-flops kicking up clouds of dust.

"Damn!" he says. "We're gonna miss out on the best seats!" His exasperation had no effect on me as he pushed me into the back seat of a taxi. I was still hearing the flute in my head. I understood his frustration when we arrived at the pergola.

Even more people had gathered for darshan this morning. Probably twice that of the night before. You'd think it would've been disorderly and chaotic, the standard method of assembling in India. But everyone was orderly and congenial as they carefully picked out their place on the floor. It was hard to find a spot of wood to call your seat, but we managed to pour our bodies into some openings. It was body-to-body, skin-to-skin, and when anyone found a spec of floor to sit on, the whole crowd had to adjust. But they did, and waited with a contagious suspension of disbelief for The Man.

There is a blast of a horn, and devotees carrying banners and strewing flowers enter the arena. Music blares and a man leading a beautiful cow with gilded horns walks in. More flowers are thrown. A boy tethered to a huge elephant flamboyantly bedecked in sequins and jewels follows him. Flowers rain from nowhere and soak the beast. They all come to a standstill. There is a long pause. Then to thunderous chanting, Sai Baba makes his entrance, picking up flowers as he goes and throwing them at his devotees. The crowd goes wild!

He is wearing a silky white robe with gold trim. He floats through the crowd, self-composed, self-assured, and serenely powerful. As I see the looks of reverence on so many faces, I ask myself if I should be feeling what they must be feeling, and if not, why not? Would I have these feelings if this were Jesus, Buddha, or Mohamed in my midst? Or would I remain the observer and not a participant?

Sai Baba lingers longer than usual over groups of people reaching out, trying to touch his robe. He speaks softly to them, reads their minds, and tells them their innermost conflicts. Three times he holds up his bare palm, and from it flows sparkling *vibuthi* that the faithful try desperately to catch in their handkerchiefs or scraps of paper.

I brought no paper. I brought no handkerchief. I thought maybe I should have some of that dust. For a cure-all for whatever spiritually ails you, for a souvenir, if nothing else.

I decided to test him. I waited until he was at the far end of the circle, out of the range of any chicanery. I simply ordered him repeatedly in my mind to come to me. *Come to me. Come to me.* My mantra. *Come to me. Come to me.*

He raised his head and looked over the crowd. He started to walk around the circle, still stopping now and then to speak and to let the devout touch his feet, touch his robe; just a brush of the fabric would do. He kept scanning the faces glued to his and made his way slowly in my direction. It seemed he was honing in on me. Lo and behold, he stopped directly in front of me. His feet were inches from my knees. I looked up at him. He gazed inquisitively into my eyes. He broke into a huge smile that I knew was just for me. I will admit it felt very, very good.

Then he moved on. But he looked back once and the smile on his face was so mischievous, I laughed and slapped my knee!

Later, back in town, Jon, Rose, and I spent the rest of the day window-shopping, or should I say windowless shopping, in a couple of different bazaars. We shopped, we got stoned, we ate, we got more stoned, we sang and laughed, we just were being together, stoned.

Which was a good thing because it seemed like it took a long time to do the simplest tasks. Not because we were stoned, but because the pace in Bangalore, though a city of some size, was so very slow. It is a quiet town. The people even walk quietly. The only noticeable sounds came from the bells ringing on the three-wheeled rickshaws sauntering down the middle of the road.

Other than walking, the rickshaw was the favored mode of transportation. Anywhere one goes of any distance, one goes by rickshaw. There are so many rickshaws, this place is turning into an amusement park because you think you are on a bumpy, jostling, fun ride. Fun for the passengers at least.

Jon told the "driver" to take us to the Rama Krishna Math. Fortunately, like cab drivers all over the world that speak little English, the rickshaw drivers do recognize the names of familiar places. So off he cycled, pulling the weight of the rickshaw and three bodies. I felt a pang of guilt, as if I were mistreating an animal. I was relieved to find the trip a relatively short one. We tipped the driver handsomely, and he grinned from ear to ear, changing the course of the rivulets of sweat pouring down his face.

We were just in time for bhajan when we reached the Rama Krishna Math. The ashram was very beautiful. A large photo of the great Bengali saint, Paramahansa Rama Krishna, dominated the expansive room. At times it seemed as if the photo sprang to life and vibrated. Perhaps it was the delicious food. Perhaps it was the devotees, all so happy and content. Perhaps it was my recollection of Paramahansa Yogananda, whose book, *The Autobiography of a Yogi,* had had an enormous influence on all those interested in expanding their consciousness, including myself. Perhaps no book, other than *Be Here Now*, motivated more hippies to travel to India in search of a guru.

Bangalore was dotted with the ashrams of many different teachers, all of whom took a back seat to Sai Baba. I could tell Jon was much more at ease here in the company of familiar and more credentialed teachers, than sitting among the mob at Brindavan.

On the way back, Jon said he did his best to believe, to give up his doubts, to have faith in Sai Baba. But he was convinced it was all tricks. Very good tricks, but tricks all the same. Only trickery could entice such a horde of worshippers. Once again, the amount of devotees a guru had garnered, seemed to be a criterion for the credibility of that teacher. Once again, Jon believed if there were too many followers, it was a sign it was a cult on the verge of becoming a religion. That in itself, was a sign he wasn't The One.

CHAPTER 49
March 1972

It was Jon's birthday. He treated himself to a breakfast of bacon and eggs. Rosie moved the bacon to the side of the dish with a candle. She lit it and we sang "Happy Birthday." The rest of the freaks having breakfast joined in. Jon closed his eyes tight and made a wish. Rose and I knew what the wish was. We didn't have to ask.

When he blew out the candle and opened his eyes, a young freak walked over from his table.

"Happy Birthday, brother!" he said.

"Thanks, bro!" Jon answered, looking up at a skinny guy with dirty blond hair down to his waist, unwashed and matted in the style worn by so many native saddhus and Jamaican Rastafarians.

"Are you here for Sai Baba?" he asked with a Scottish accent. "Are you as smitten as all these other wandering blokes?" he asked curiously, as he swung his arm in a wide stroke that brushed most of the people in the room.

"No," replied Jon. "I'm not smitten. But I wish I were. I wish I could be. Believe me brother, I wish I could be!"

"Neither am I, mate. Neither am I." He pulled up a chair, leaned over, and spoke softly, almost in a whisper. "I could tell he wasn't for you. Takes some balls not to get swept up by all this Baba energy!" he laughed somewhat condescendingly. "Have you ever heard of Krishnamurti?" he questioned.

My eyes lit up! "Krishnamurti!" I exclaimed. "What about him? Is he here?"

The Scot looked at me, tossing back some dreads that were in his eye. "Sorry to disappoint you mate, but I think you're thinking of J. Krishnamurti. This is U.G. Krishnamurti. No relation except cosmic, bro." I looked disappointed.

He turned back to Jon. "Check him out, mate. It may be worth your while!"

Jon was beside himself with excitement. This is the way it should happen. A loner who could assess Jon's mind from afar. Someone who, like Jon, sought the Special One, the one with just a handful of disciples. The one who didn't advertise his powers, who didn't seek devotees. The One, who if found, would only choose the most ready, the most desperate, the ones who had exhausted everything else, who had proved themselves worthy. Or so Jon thought.

"How do we meet him? Where do we find him? What's he like?" Questions drooled out of Jon's mouth, hungry for all the information he could get.

"It's a ways out of town," the Rasta-Scot told him. "But just mention his name to any cabbie. They'll know the place."

He pushed himself away from the table, stood up, walked over to his own table on the far side of the room and put his hand on his traveling partner's shoulder. She was a female version of him, thin as a rail, hair all in knots, wearing a well-worn sarong and a sheer blouse that did little to hide her small breasts. She stood up and the two of them began to walk out of The Only Place. He looked back at Jon and spoke across the room.

"Check him out mate! Don't leave Bangalore without seeing him!" He turned his back toward us, holding up one hand in the V-fingered peace sign as they walked out the door.

Jon gobbled the rest of his breakfast. He rushed Rosie and me to do the same. He was very impatient with us. Very impatient to get going.

He hailed a taxi and we piled in the back seat. "Krishnamurti's," was all Jon said to the cabbie.

"Very far," the cabbie said looking back at us, swinging his chin. "Very expensive, many rupees."

Jon nodded and gestured with his chin to go. "Krishnamurti's," he said again.

The cabbie shrugged and faced front, put the car in drive and sped off, weaving in and out of people and rickshaws. We were heading almost due south, and after about 30 kilometers or so, the arid desert turned into arid selva. The dirt road was just a cloud of dust behind us. In front of us, light-green, delicately leaved trees provided some shade and made unusual designs of light and dark on the windshield as we drove under their canopy.

We had only passed a few huts and small groups of people once we were out of town. This surprised us. There was seldom a stretch of road that was not populated. It felt refreshing for once to find ourselves in an area we could actually call bucolic.

The cabbie took a right onto a dirt driveway that led to one of the strangest houses I have ever seen. It was built out of bamboo and wood and was two stories high, the first story just posts and open air for storage and such. The second story was configured around the trunk of the enormous tree, which shaded the house from the intense sun.

A gardener ardently tended a grove of banana trees, but when he saw us approaching, he ran up the wooden stairs to the main floor. As we got out of the taxi, a young woman, neatly dressed in a simple sari, gracefully descended the stairs to meet us.

Jon had a good feeling about this guy. A lesser-known teacher was right up his alley. Certainly, he would give us the enlightenment Jon felt we deserved. Had not our pursuit been pure? For Jon and Rose, the stakes were high. For me? I had always said I was just along for the ride. I was just hanging onto their lungis in case anything miraculous happened.

"May I help you?" she said in perfect English.

"We would like to speak with Sri Krishnamurti," Jon replied anxiously.

"I'm sorry," she said. "Sri Krishnamurti accepts no visitors without an appointment."

"But we have traveled many miles to see him," Rosie implored. "Please, can't you make an exception in our case? Please, just ask him. Please!"

The young woman ascended the stairs. We waited. She descended a few minutes later and beckoned us to follow her. We told the cabbie to wait and he agreed. He knew we would have no way back to Bangalore from this remote spot, and a large tip would likely be coming his way.

She escorted us up the stairs. She pointed to some cushions on a clean wooden floor. Beautiful rugs were strategically placed around the spacious room. We each sat on a cushion and waited, trying to control our breathing so it was even and meditative. But my heart would not stop beating faster than usual.

We looked around the room and realized it was amazing. It was obvious that master craftsmen had built this place. The hand carved sills of the windows, the finely lacquered beams, the flower arrangements, and lighting fixtures, all reflected a superb taste. Tapestries, wooden sculptures, and colorful paintings adorned the walls. Many open windows let in a refreshing breeze and made us feel we were on a large veranda. The room was spotlessly clean. We felt wealth resided here.

The young woman stood in front of us. She explained that she was Krishnamurti's housekeeper and asked us how we had found out about his country retreat.

"His country retreat?" I asked.

"Yes," she answered. "Usually, he is living in Delhi. There he receives visitors. But here he comes to be alone, to write and to meditate. And he seldom allows visitors." She scanned us slowly, letting it sink in that she found it unlikely Krishnamurti would grant us an audience. Then when she felt we understood how lucky we were, she disappeared behind a louvered door that I guessed led to the kitchen area.

After a few moments, Krishnamurti entered the room and took a cushion in front of us. He was fastidiously dressed in white, and as he sat, he positioned himself in a half lotus, carefully arranging his robe around his knees.

He simply looked at us. No greeting, no small talk. No talk at all. He was completely silent and gazed at us. From the outset, his eyes seemed to be watering. He seemed sad. The silence lasted too long to be comfortable. He was waiting for one of us to speak.

"Namaskar," Jon said, bowing his head slightly. "Thank you for receiving us with no warning, but we didn't know what else to do."

"Namaste," Krishnamurti replied, bowing his head to us. "What is it you want from me?" His English was excellent and from the many books in cases beneath the windows, we could tell he was very well educated; an intellectual.

Jon was suddenly overcome with a grief that was easily heard in his words. He leaned, almost lurched forward, as words tumbled from his lips. "I… *we*… have read most every scripture of every religion and have tried our best to understand their truths. We have practiced yoga. We have fasted for weeks at a time. We have tried every form of meditation that has come our way. We have traveled all over in search of a teacher who will give us the gift of pure light and consciousness. Pure love. Mindlessness. Samadhi." Jon paused for the real question. "Are you the one?"

By the time Jon finished his speech, his eyes were watering. And there was a sincerity in his voice that made Krishnamurti respond in kind, yet not kindly.

"You speak of mindlessness, of samadhi." He said harshly. "It is a void. A nothing!"

"But isn't it full of light? Isn't it a becoming part of everything, one with everything?" Jon insisted.

"I told you," Krishnamurti said more sternly, "It is nothing! It is a void, and the Void is black and cold and frightening in its nothingness! Why do you insist on going there? You can't begin to imagine the feeling of total absence! You do not want to go there!"

"It can't be!" Jon argued. And he began to extract and recite from his photographic memory, passages from the Bhagavad-Gita and Mahabharata, the Vedas, and the Upanishads. Jon was on the verge of babbling when Krishnamurti interrupted him.

He was obviously impressed with Jon's knowledge. It set him apart from so many others. He knew he was dealing with a true seeker, and his eyes watered even more, tears starting to flow.

"I tell you these are just stories. They are just words. Words that are merely objects in themselves, but empty of content. There is no blinding light, no pure love or pure energy." He emphatically continued. "There is only a barren wasteland. It is The Void, and it is blacker than the blackest black, colder than the coldest cold. There is nothing there. Nothing!" he repeated. "I beg you not to go there! Live! Enjoy life! Just be!"

The words reverberated in Rosie's ears. "Just be. Summu iru." The words of Swami Guaribala. The look in her eyes told me she felt vindicated by them.

Jon was devastated. He was openly crying. So was Krishnamurti. He dabbed his eyes with a handkerchief and stood up. The interview was over. We turned to watch him walk toward the louvered door. Jon's eyes were all baggy and bloodshot from crying. Krishnamurti turned to face us. His was also weeping.

He looked at us as a father might his children, after disciplining them for their own good, with unconditional love and compassion. As if it had hurt him more than it did us.

He said, "Summu iru, summu iru!" And then, with a deep bow, as if he were obliged to us instead of the other way around, "Namaste." He disappeared behind the swinging door.

Rosie's eyes brightened again, but Jon was a mess. Rosy and I had to lift him up by his armpits. He was wobbly and shaken. We made our way down the stairs and into the taxi. Jon was completely silent the whole way back. Rosie and I were too timid to make any comments on the visit. But as we approached Bangalore, Jon mustered up his ego, sat tall, and looked ready for the coach to call upon him to get his ass back in the game.

"He's wrong!" Jon shouted. "He's just one person! What gives him the right to declare what's true and what's not? He's just one goddam human being! He's just a B-movie version of the real thing!" We didn't argue with him. "Summu iru," I told myself.

The next morning, while I waited outside our room at The Only Place, I could make out the chafing sounds of bickering coming from Jon and Rosie as they gathered up their belongings. I ascribed it to our visit to Krishnamurti, but only later would discover the real reason.

CHAPTER 50
March 1972

A 15-hour, spring-less wonder of a bus ride left us fatigued and wasted in Panjim, Goa's largest city.

Goa is one of the smallest states in India and to say that its once Portuguese colonization is evident, is an understatement. Its papal influence was a shock to us. Cathedrals were everywhere and schoolchildren wore clean and pressed uniforms. The entire city seemed clean and pressed. It had a democratically elected Communist government. That was a real eye-opener for us. There were few of the homeless beggars we experienced elsewhere. Relatively speaking, everyone seemed well fed and middle class. It was a testament to the best of communism. And I admired the Indian government for regarding Goa as a social experiment from which they might learn, rather than trying to quash it.

I'd always thought that should've been our view of Cuba and Castro. Instead of considering them a threat to the superpower we were, we should've regarded Cuba as a social experiment and borrowed from them the programs that worked. We should have helped them, befriended them. What was there to fear?

Instead, through our embargo and belligerent stance, we drove them into the hands of the Soviet Union. Yet, here in Goa, where most people did not go without their basic needs being met, we glimpsed what might have been the answer to the problems of Third World countries. We were impressed.

We didn't stay more than a couple of hours in Panjim, but took a bus to Calangute Beach, nine miles north of the city. Some freaks we ran into in Bangalore told us this was the place to go. And when we arrived, we understood why. It was overflowing with hippies from all over the world. It was almost too much.

But there's a reason why a place becomes so popular. The beach was exquisite. And we began to walk along it, when only after a few steps, we found the sand so incredibly hot, it burned our feet. Our flip-flops were of little use as protection. The sand snuck in and felt like hot coals. Firewalkers we weren't. We had no towels. So, Jon and I used our shirts, and Rosie, her thin blanket, to hop our way on them down to the water's edge, sighing in relief as the surf cooled our soles. Then we'd hop back toward the shade of huts, houses, and small hotels that lined the beach, always on the lookout for a respite from the relentless Indian sun.

When our feet were ready for more torture, we'd hop at an angle across the sand back to the water, making our cruise down the beach a traversing and tiring affair. Sweat was pouring down us as we zigzagged, hopping on our pogo-shirts to a low-slung house with a large peace sign on it.

Three young men, sunbathing in their lounge chairs, all in the skimpiest of thongs, laughed as we barely made it to the shade of their patio. They were Spanish, but only Luis spoke some English. Minimal at that. They invited us inside where we smoked a mammoth chillum of excellent hash. It was *so* excellent, and we got *so* stoned, not even eating the nice lunch they made for us could bring us down.

There is no language barrier when it comes to humor and Luis and his friends were outrageously funny. The way they cavorted around with each other was hysterical. They broke into song every now and then, trying to harmonize and then laughing when one of them hit a sour note. It must have been the hash. They smoked incessantly. We smoked with them even after we had reached the point of an acid high. In that frame of mind, we regarded their home with wonder. It was filled with artwork and fine furniture carved with intricate designs. I was especially intrigued by a framed photograph of two naked men in an erotic pose.

We also regarded with wonder how touchy-feely they were with each other, and later with us. At least Jon and me. Rosie was somewhat ignored, which surprised me because she was usually the one who received the most attention. Jon didn't pick up on it right away, but the light bulb went on in my head immediately. They were all gay! I looked at the photo on the wall again and realized it was Luis and one of the other guys. No wonder I felt so at home. No wonder I secretly wished I had stumbled upon them alone, because I could have been easily seduced by any one of them.

We ended up spending the night there. I practically resented the presence of Jon and Rose, silently and irrationally accusing them of stifling my libido. We gleaned from a few English words and lots of body language, that many travelers rented houses along the beach for months at a time. It may have been the hash that made them so immobile. Or maybe it was just that continental style of touring I envied so much, and so unlike the *Europe-in-ten-days* approach to travel, so common among Americans. But their hospitality overwhelmed us, and I knew Spain must be a country not to be missed, basing this judgment solely on these three Spanish stoners, *adictos de picadillo y marihuana*, who happened to be gay and seemed proud of it.

We woke up early in the morning, said *hasta la vista* to our brothers, and walked along the beach, the sand now tolerable, but not for long. Westerners occupied every house and hut along the beach. We could make out early morning conversations in French, German, Italian, Spanish, and other languages we didn't recognize, but sounded Scandinavian of some sort. We also noticed hypodermic needles littering the fronts of some huts. Some freaks that had spent the night on their verandas in hammocks turned their heads to watch as we passed by, eyes glazed, a weak, but euphoric smile on their faces. It was only then, relying on my limited vocabulary of a few Romance languages, that I managed to translate what Luis had asked the night before. He had sat next to me on my mat, one hand on my thigh, the other holding a syringe. *"¿Le gusta azúcar marrón?"* I shook my head but only because I was trying to say I didn't understand. No wonder he had a disappointed look on his face as he walked unsteadily back to his bed. I was lucky I didn't wake up with a needle in my forearm and hooked on heroin.

A 15-minute walk north took us to Baga Beach. At the far end of the little bay was a small fishing village. There was only a smattering of freaks to be seen, which was refreshing after the madness of Calangute. It felt as if something clandestine were happening. There were so many curious trips going on. I picked up more gay vibes, but if there were such a scene here in Baga, it wasn't obvious. Certainly not as obvious as behind the closed doors of Luis' home.

It is understandable to me now why this place is such a magnet for weary hippies to get some R&R. The locals are extremely tolerant, the food is great, the drugs flow freely and the scenery is some of the most beautiful I've seen since Ceylon. The people are a delight to the eye with their mixture of Indian and Portuguese blood. Their faces are exquisite with their high cheekbones, dark eyebrows and eyes, and thick black hair. Their skin is so smooth and brown. It teased to be touched and I wished I could do just that. Reach out and touch them. Make love to them.

The women are graceful and swing their hips in a sultry manner. The men are slim, sleek, and muscular. They don't have that gaunt look of the perennially underfed, but rather that of well-nourished bodies, so defined from simply doing hard work. They looked like they belonged to those of competitive swimmers or long distance runners.

All along the beach, villagers seemed unfazed by the antics of their strange foreign visitors. Nudity and drugs were sloughed off as unimportant, and even in the cafes, chillums were prepared without the slightest worry that anyone would mind. It is like a tropical island paradise, except it's not an island.

This part of Goa is made up of slim-fingered lands reaching into the wide estuary of the Mandovi River. Each finger is covered with coconut palms and banana trees. Between the fingers are canals, some shallow enough to wade across when the tide is out. When the tide is in, you'd better be a strong swimmer. We were lucky enough to find the canals at low tide, and holding our bags on top of our heads, managed to cross, chest deep, from one finger to another. With each canal we crossed, there were less and less people, and almost no hippies. That suited us fine.

But when we reached Anjuna and walked around the monastery on the hill, we ran into a random gathering of freaks, who like us, must have longed for a respite from their own kind. They weren't unfriendly, but there was an unspoken understanding that they were weary of the scene and needed some down time, both physically and mentally. We learned none of their names, and they didn't learn ours. Everyone, including us, was quiet and introverted.

For Rosie and me, it was truly spiritual R&R. Jon made no attempt, for the first time since we arrived in India, to find a temple, shrine, holy man, or holy-looking man. He made no inquiries if any were to be found. Our stay in Goa was truly a restful time. And it was one of the only times we would really get to rest.

I will admit that the bungalow we rented on the beach seemed like a holy place. It had simple whitewashed walls, hand-hewn beams, and an exposed tile roof. If we ran quickly across the hot white sand, we could jump into the cerulean waters of the Arabian Sea before we scorched our feet. And we played in the water until the sun was on its way down, and the barefoot trip back to the bungalow was a breeze.

Evening time and we lit the single candle, which highlighted the geometric shapes, so basic, clean, and pure. The beams turned golden, while all else was black and white.

We retired early and I lay awake allowing myself to be mesmerized by the flickering shapes on the ceiling and the sound of the sea gently massaging the shore. A hundred yards down the beach was another bungalow. A very pregnant German girl and her boyfriend were staying there.

We sat up in our beds when we heard the tropical breeze carry her shrieks of pain to our ears. Her boyfriend was frantically wailing in a German dialect I couldn't understand. But the calm and sweet encouragements of a Goan midwife smoothed the rough edges of their guttural mutterings. After a fortunately brief period, there were cries of relief from all of them, followed by ecstatic laughter and the small cries of the whimpering newborn. What a confluence of forces must've been at work to have that child born here in this idyllic place! I got up and wrote in my journal an admittedly trite but sincere sentiment:

If I must die
Then let it be tonight.
Because everything's so perfect,
Everything's so right.

The light of dawn woke me, feeling well rested despite the early hour. I rolled over and the first view I focused on was a placid blue sea against an azure sky. Fishermen in waist deep waters flung their nets in wide arcs, like cowboys lassoing the air. I sat at the window thoroughly engrossed by the scene waiting for Jon and Rosie to wake up.

When they did, and tried to make themselves presentable, we walked up to a Baga chai shop and ate a hearty breakfast, after which we returned to the bungalow for a bowl of ganja. We smoked one chillum after another, making it understandable how easy it was to get hung up here.

We went for a swim. The water had not yet reached bath temperature and was refreshing, though the Arabian Sea was very salty and when we sat on the beach to dry, our skin was covered with a layer of the crystalline substance.

Freaks in various degrees of wakefulness passed by, some stopping to share a joint. They and we had given up on exchanging names. These brief relationships were recognized as transient, and there is nothing more to do than just trip out together. Now and then, I felt a pang of frustration because so many unique beings wandered into and out of my life, and I didn't have arms long enough to embrace them all and hold them close, even if just for a moment.

We lost track of how long we sat there, but knew at some point, probably when our perspiration started to percolate, that the broiling sun, the beautiful Arabian Sea, and the sensitive vibrations of so many stoned people, satiated us. We were completely full.

The morning passed quickly in our stupor, but by the time the sun had passed its zenith, we were back in Panjim, not sure of how we got there, but sanguinely awaiting tomorrow's ferry to Bombay. I was looking forward to a mellow ocean voyage, but just as the ferry ride from Ceylon to India never happened, neither did the one from Panjim to Bombay.

As we walked through town, we passed an Indian Airlines ticket office. Why the pace of our journey was quickening was beyond me for I was enjoying every minute, but day by day, Jon seemed to be more in a hurry. Within a few minutes he had booked us on a flight to Delhi with a stop-over in Agra.

"Delhi!" I protested. "What's the big rush? I thought we were going to Bombay and then to Benares?"

"Change of plans, Chazan!" Jon said unapologetically. "I think I've had enough of India but can't leave without seeing some of the north. Then I want out of here!"

"But Benares," I cajoled, "Is one of those places teeming with gurus and teachers!"

"Maybe so, Chazan, but not as much as at the headwaters of the Ganges!"

I didn't know enough about that to rebut him. I wanted to see Benares with a passion. Now that passion was being dispassionately dismissed by Jon.

"Look Chazan," Jon said, seeing the dismayed look on my face, "You have a ticket. You can change your flight if you want. I didn't put any conditions on it when I bought it for you."

That was fine and dandy. But why did he have to remind me that he was the one who bought it! He knew I was a recovering Catholic! He knew I would be guilt-ridden. How could I in good conscience go off on my own? If I had gone off on my own, it would have been with Peter and Debra. If I went off on my own now, I'd be by myself. My wanderings with Peter and Debra had been a brief separation from Jon and Rose. And that separation was supposedly mutual. This was different. I wished I could backtrack, but our tickets were good for one direction only. You could zigzag a bit if you traveled in generally the same direction. But you could never backtrack without paying a sizeable fee, a sum more than I could afford.

I knew that once we were in Delhi there would be no turning back. It was only a few weeks later that I learned what was really behind his increasingly hurried pace. And when I did, it pissed me off! But in the end, I succumbed to his plan and tried not to dwell on the fact that I would miss out on Benares and did my best to put on the face of an eager team player.

The flight was supposed to leave at 4 PM, but the agent advised us to check back before we took the bus out to the airport. It was still intensely hot, so we cooled ourselves on the veranda of a tourist hotel, sipping Cokes, overlooking the beautiful Panjim inlet, and marveling at the beauty of the local people ambling by.

After an hour or so, Jon went to check the status of our flight, leaving Rosie and I to relish the scenery. When Jon returned, we learned there was at least a three-hour delay, so we whiled away the time by sunning ourselves some more on a small strip of beach near the Indian Airlines office.

Unfortunately, men who used the beach as an open-air outhouse, regularly interrupted our solar respite, and as the tide slowly rose, small turds quietly lapped at the beach. It was a rude reminder that though Goa was indeed special, it was still India. We got up to leave, the envious eyes of men leering at Rosie while their squatting continued. Thankfully, we would not leave Goa with this as our last image.

The bus ride to the airport was the visual redemption. Goa is a sumptuous tropical paradise and a sensory feast. And I would get my ferry ride after all. It crossed one of the many wide inlets meandering through the lush terrain. Were these watery barriers there to detain us, trying to prevent us from leaving? Trying to seduce us into staying? We were such easy prey we had to be strong. And we had to wait for three roundtrip crossings before there was room for our bus! Jon was annoyed at all these delays. Rose was resigned to Jon being annoyed. And I was tempted to remain trapped, to go back to the bungalow in Baga, and stay there forever.

At the airport, we were told the plane was delayed. I took this as a sign we should have stuck to our original itinerary. I guess there's no looking back, though I always was. We talked with a hippie girl who called herself Shashonah. She had been in Bangalore to bathe in the warmth of Sai Baba. So what else was new! She talked of the *now* and the *light* and the *all* and the *everywhere*. I was getting to the point where I believed, without cynicism, in the *nothing* and the *nowhere*. And maybe that was the point.

We finally boarded the well-worn DC-10 and took off on Flight 21 bound for Dehli via Agra. Too bad it wasn't Flight 22 or better yet, 922. That would have made me feel better. Not that I was taking Florence's divinations to heart, but why take a chance. Workers were still packing the potholes in the tarmac with gravel and mud as we taxied down the runway but moved to the edges of the strip as we sped by them.

I was relieved when the wheels left the ground. It was a rough ride, more like a chicken flying from one fence post to another, the posts in this case being clouds. Fortunately, the Indian Airlines flight was a quick one. But it lasted long enough for the hippie sitting across the aisle to fill us in on the stateside guru binge.

Baba Ram Dass was in London on his way to Connecticut. Hari Dass Baba was in Davis, California, at the same time as Trungpa Rinpoche was at Berkeley, cigar in one hand, bottle of scotch in the other. Maharaj Ji, the new kid on the block, and I mean that literally, was in New Jersey, probably waiting for us to come home and rub his little kid feet and give him apples and candy.

Maybe this meant we didn't need to see anyone, here or back in the States. Weren't we already perfect? Weren't we already pure spirit? Weren't we already everything? I mean nothing?

These musings were interrupted by the thought entering my mind that we were making a forced landing. We had only reached some semblance of an altitude, when we were already descending to what was a one-wheel, then the other, then both wheels, making contact with the ground. The nose wheel touched, and we quickly came to a stop.

Twilight was about to turn into darkness. I turned around and through the window of the plane saw lights go on in the distance. What was illuminated was the Taj Mahal. My heart sank. It was too far to walk, and too short a stopover to take a cab and spend any quality time there. All I could do was admire it from afar. It was so dazzling it made the desire I had for seeing it up close and in detail, all the more bitter.

I guess I wasn't in the best space. I passed the time watching passing thoughts. "Realization" is a noun made up of eleven letters. I know because I counted them. *Twice*!

A lovely stewardess told us to board the plane and shortly we were airborne again. The flight was no less nerve jangling, but we arrived in Delhi in one piece.

When we finally were outside the terminal, Jon hailed a taxi.

"The Palace Heights Hotel," he said authoritatively.

"How do you know about this place?" I asked Jon.

"That's the hotel where Ram Dass stays when he's in town. Didn't you hear that guy on the plane?"

"My mind must've been somewhere else," I said.

"Figures!" replied Jon. I didn't know what to make of that. I just said *whatever* under my breath.

CHAPTER 51

March 1972

There were no vacancies at the Palace Heights, which, from its lobby, looked very posh. We were somewhat summarily escorted across the street to a funky hotel whose rooms were really a large hall with dividers. It was very late, but we smoked a lot of ganja before retiring, totally unconcerned that its smell must be wafting throughout the place.

I got very stoned. Just as I was drifting off, a sound entered that lost-in-space place, between being conscious and not. It was the rhythmic snoring of a guy in the next room. Soon the sound of my breathing added a new refrain to the darkness, and slowly all the sounds of the city and the hotel found their place, until what I was hearing was like a fully arranged orchestration. I finally went beyond the strange music to the place called sleep, though I didn't get there until practically dawn.

We were rudely awakened by our next-door neighbors. It was much too early to be gracious to anyone and that included each other. With few words, we packed our paltry belongings and left. We walked back across the street to the Palace Heights. This time they did have a room for us. Especially when the clerk behind the counter eyed the stack of traveler's checks Jon had unfolded. The room was very expensive, but Jon didn't seem to care.

Without undressing, we flopped down on the first-class beds, and enjoyed a first-class sleep. Though we were so tired from the night before; we could have zonked out on a straw mat.

A few hours later, we awoke famished. Jon put on his pajama whites.

"Why are you wearing those?" I asked.

"We're in a fine hotel, Chazan!" he said, as if that were a no brainer.

"Well, I'm sticking to my lungi!" I announced.

Jon gave me a look of chagrin, but I was too groggy to argue. We went down to the hotel's restaurant, and without looking at the prices, ordered omelets, filled with mushrooms and cheese and all sorts of good stuff. The bill arrived and it was as expensive as in the States. Once again, Jon didn't seem to care. A few cups of strong coffee and we were ready to discover what Delhi had to offer.

We went back upstairs to get the hash Jon had bought from the hippie man on the flight to Agra. On the door to our room was an engraved invitation. It said, "Mackroo and Son invite you to view their specialties. Your presence is most welcome." The card looked very professional and somehow exclusive. At the bottom of the card, handwritten, it read, "Please come to Room 409."

I did a quick numerological calculation in my mind. It didn't come out to a number Florence would have wished for us, but I didn't say anything.

Jon unlocked the door and took the note off it. He threw it on the bed.

"I wonder what that's all about," Rosie said.

"I haven't the slightest idea," Jon said, filling the chillum.

"Well, aren't you the least bit curious?" Rosie asked.

"No," said Jon. "Maybe I will be after this." And he fired up the bowl, took a deep toke, and passed it to Rosie. She took an equally long drag and then passed it to me. I inhaled slowly and deeply. It was definitely one-toke hash. I passed it back to Jon, and he refused it, shaking his head, and holding up his hand in a gesture that said, "enough for me," because he couldn't get the words out through his hacking. We were obliterated. It was very good hash.

"Mmmm," said Jon in a more cheerful tone. "Much better!"

We stumbled out of the room, closing the door quickly behind us to keep the fumes inside, and walked to the elevator at the end of the hall. Once inside, Jon went to press L for the lobby, but Rosie's finger got to the 4 button first.

"What are you doing?" he chided.

"I want to see what's in that room!" she answered decidedly, stoned out of her mind and adjusting her halter-top.

Jon just made a face and shrugged. We got out of the elevator and followed the hall to Room 409. Jon pulled himself up tall and combed his fingers through his beard. He was about to knock on the door, when once again Rosie beat him to it.

Mackroo opened the door. "Welcome my friends."

He was dressed in loose-fitting pants and a very fine shirt, tastefully embroidered with little flowers and vines. He gestured us in with a sweep of his hand. The room was more than just a room. It was a suite. A very *large* suite. It must have cost him a bundle to rent it. He said he lived here. This was his apartment though we could see no kitchen or other furnishings that made it look like a place where a person lived. However, it did give Jon and Rose a sense that he was wealthy, and therefore a credible businessman.

The room was overflowing with Kashmiri rugs, tablecloths, tapestries, saris, and hand carved furniture of every kind, from armoires to coffee tables. I will admit, they seemed to be of the highest quality. The finest of the fine. Truly beautiful and stunning. To even attempt to describe each piece of cloth, carpeting or furniture would be futile. Everything was exquisite!

Jon and Rosie were equally as stunned, and immediately started looking around. I plopped on a stack of small carpets.

"Why did you put an invitation on our door?" I asked.

Mackroo regarded me as if I were inconsequential, and seemed to intuit I was the hanger-on, no one to bother with.

"The Palace Heights is very popular among Western tourists," he politely replied, "and because this hotel has such a fine reputation, the management asked me to provide a showroom of the very best that India has to offer. They wanted tourists to have an alternative to the bazaars of Old Delhi where so many Westerners have been sold inferior merchandise at unfairly high prices."

His English was too perfect, too smooth, and almost mellifluous. He turned his attention to Jon, while Rosie was already deeply engrossed in the mounds of cloth and carpets.

"Your card said 'Mackroo and Son,'" I said. "Where is your son?"

Mackroo turned back to me, flashing a look of annoyance that I was deterring him from his appointed task, though answering in a most genteel manner.

"My son is in Kashmir, seeking only the finest merchandise from weavers and woodworkers whom we know and trust."

"Now then," he continued, "please, this is merely a service the hotel has contracted with me to provide. Simply take your time to admire the handiwork of these pieces. If for nothing else, your aesthetic enjoyment."

"Oh boy!" I said to myself. "This guy is a shark!"

I will admit that the rooms were filled with mind-blowing stuff. The kind of stuff with which people of taste would want to cover their walls and floors and bodies. I could not help but inspect some of his offerings. I scrutinized the workmanship carefully. The carpets were tightly woven and securely seamed. The designs were spectacularly intricate with not the slightest hint of gaudiness. The pieces of furniture were my favorites. Tables, large and small, some with elephant heads carved at each corner, others with bas-reliefs of scenes from the Ramayana and other famous stories.

But I wasn't ready for Jon and Rosie's enthusiasm.

"This stuff is awesome!" Jon pronounced. "It's the finest stuff we've come across. Everything's absolutely beautiful!"

"Jon," Rosie said, "we really have to bring some souvenirs back to our families."

Mackroo's expression remained indifferent and composed. The items, he knew, would sell themselves.

I wondered if the desk clerk, who saw Jon's wad of traveler's checks, was in cahoots with this Mackroo guy.

Whenever Jon or Rosie was struck by a certain carpet or tapestry or carving, Mackroo would give a history of the piece and point out the painstaking detail and workmanship that distinguished it from "knock-offs" we were likely to find on the streets.

Jon and Rose were soon rifling through stacks of carpets, waddling in yards of embroidered cloths, testing out the comfort of chairs.

Mackroo remained a very low-key, low-pressure salesman. I found his sales pitch to be too sweet, almost gluey. Something inside told me Mackroo (and Son) was an *artiste extraordinaire* of a con game, but his style and finesse were working well on Jon, and especially Rose, whom Jon seemed too anxious to please.

By the time we left, Jon and Rose were ready to buy a shit load of stuff that they had culled from the piles of items.

"But how will we carry it all?" asked Jon. "We can only buy some tablecloths or pieces we can easily travel with."

"Oh," said Mackroo, all ready for that one, "Of course we provide shipping services. If you pick out pieces now, I can have them shipped first class this afternoon. No need to worry at all. We use only the most reliable transport."

All in all, Jon handed over what must have been a couple of thousand dollars to Mackroo. I couldn't believe it. And though I did not like Mackroo, I was a bit envious of all the wonderful things they had picked out.

As a gesture of generosity, Jon said that I could pick out a small carpet or something to add to the pile.

"I have some money, Jon," I said. "You have been too generous already and if I really want something, I will pay for it myself. But thanks Jonny. That's nice. Now let's get out of here before the whole day is gone."

"OK Chazan! Hold on to your lungi! We're almost finished."

Jon asked Mackroo if he could have a receipt and some sort of verification the items were shipped. This late in the game, he was trying to hedge any mishaps.

"Of course, my friends," Mackroo answered as he fished out a receipt book. It had his name, Mackroo (and Son) on it, along with an authentic sounding address, and a couple of phone numbers. It looked entirely official and above board.

"I will personally bring your selections to my shipping company," he said confidently. "Come back this evening and I will give you the shipping information and redemption stud which you will need when you pick them up in New Jersey. They will, of course, have to go through customs and perhaps you must pay an import fee. But since these are all gifts, the fee will be nominal. I assure you."

It was all too perfect. His knowledge of how carpets are made, the woods used in the furniture, the intricacies of shipping, importing and exporting, all of it, too perfect, yet undeniably persuasive of his good intentions. How could someone so refined, well educated, and nonchalant regarding whether they bought anything or not, be less than upstanding?

We left to his words of gratitude and with reminders to stop by later that evening to pick up the paperwork. Jon and Rosie were all smiles and talked excitedly about how impressed their friends and families would be with their gifts, to say nothing about all the best of the stuff they would naturally keep for themselves.

We hit the streets, Jon in a jovial mood, once again cracking the jokes and making the puns I loved to hear. My ol' Jon was back! But we seemed to be walking in circles. And we were. Around Cannaught Circus, the center of New Delhi. All the surrounding buildings looked relatively modern, most of them a blinding white, and it reminded me of Washington, D.C.

After Mackroo (and Son), the shopping bug, once let loose, burrowed deeper under their skin. Rosie wanted to look at some jewelry. I was simply amazed that we had gone from the pursuit of enlightenment to the pursuit of rugs and jewelry. From the desirelessness of moksha to the acquisition of material goods. It baffled me how quickly the transition occurred.

Jon went off with Rosie, but I really didn't want to go along, knowing I couldn't afford anything anyway. I was still stoned and content to people-watch. After all, there were so many people. And perhaps subconsciously this was my way of passively cruising.

Connaught Circus was aptly named. It was a roundabout with a large park in the middle and surrounded by the most bustling part of a bustling city. Never had I seen such a crazed mass of humanity darting in and out of cars and trucks driven insanely and with sadomasochistic abandon, or so it seemed. Only those with heightened acrobatic skills could cross to the other side in one piece, yet my deduction was that everyone had these skills, for no one got run over.

As hard as I tried, however, I never made it to the other side. I was constantly jumping backwards or sideways to avoid being hit. Horns blared at me, and cabbies yelled and gave me hand gestures I supposed were the equivalent of giving someone the finger.

What happened to the gentleness and timidity of the south? Had we taken our time getting from Panjim to Delhi, we might have noticed the demarcation line between the soft-spoken people of Southern India, and the aggressive, loud, and rude behavior of the North. Would the transition in culture and attitude have been more gradual and easier to adapt to? I guess I will never know. All I knew was that this change in vibrations was abrupt and disheartening.

Few people were dressed as I in my lungi and flip-flops. Most men wore the pajama whites of a professional, or better yet, the suits and ties of the West, though most of these men also sported turbans. The women, fewer in number on the streets, wore fine saris and stylish shoes. I decided that New Delhi was simply another metropolis, which in any country would naturally be more aligned with Western ways. I forgave the impolite, ill-mannered and surly treatment I was often subjected to.

Unwilling to risk my life crossing this traffic circle, I decided to take a long walk. After a few miles from that center of urbane impertinence, I still found myself being looked at with open disdain, accompanied by words I didn't understand, but was confident were slurs. I began a quickened pace back toward the hotel. At an intersection, there was so much traffic of cars and pedestrians, I needed to take a break and squatted on the corner, adjusting my lungi to cover my privates. I hadn't washed my hair or shaved in a couple of days and was sure I looked pretty scruffy. Along with my matte brown skin, I must've looked like a young sadhu lost in the middle of a concrete conundrum.

I was squatting there, my neck on a ball joint, trying to take in the madness around me, when a well-dressed tourist couple approached. The moment they opened their mouths, I knew they were Americans. They spoke very loudly and distinctively, using the simplest words in their vocabulary. They asked for directions, pointing to a place on a city map. I didn't know where the place was, but I mimicked the native they assumed I was. I bobbed and swung my chin, did a pretty good impersonation of a Hindu who spoke a few words of English with a thick accent, and pointed in a direction.

They said, "Thank you," not entirely sure they had accomplished anything. But before they walked away in the direction I had pointed, I looked up at them and, putting on a puppy dog face, asked, "Baksheesh, sahib?"

The man reluctantly reached into his pocket and gave me a dollar. Memories of pre-Hunga Dungan panhandling on the streets of San Francisco came flooding back. It's not that I was in dire need of money. It was just that this was fun!

I walked over to the entrance of an obviously expensive hotel, like a Hilton or something, and sat unobtrusively against the wall in a lotus position, my open hands resting on my knees, my lungi tucked under my balls, my eyes half-closed as if in deep meditation.

One tourist after another came out of the hotel, and at least half of them put coins or bills in my hand. Even some well-heeled locals surrendered a few rupees, which spilled out of my palm onto the pavement. I made no attempt to retrieve them, maintaining my meditative state until they were out of sight. Within a couple of hours, I had collected nearly 10 dollars! Un-fucking-believable.

I returned to the Palace Heights Hotel, to find Jon and Rosie resting, but not asleep.

"Chazan!" said Jon in a most friendly voice. "Where have you been?" He didn't wait for an answer. "You are just in time. I have a surprise for you!"

"A surprise? For me?" I said obsequiously, my tone a leftover from the recent discovery I could beg with the best of them.

"I have been a grouch!" Jon admitted. "And I have taken it out on you and Rose."

"Well, that's an understatement!" Rosie said. Jon glared at her, but his newly resurrected graciousness could not be perturbed.

"The clerk at the front desk recommended a wonderful masseur, a friend of Mackroo's, and he's due here any moment."

"Jonny that is so cool of you!" I genuinely replied. And at that very moment there was a knock on our door.

An elderly man entered, a bag over his shoulder, and handed Jon his card. It read, "J. G. Mera, Masseur and Palmist."

His English was not nearly as good as Mackroo's, and I was a bit suspicious that he was one of his cronies. Nevertheless, I put my hands together in the traditional Indian greeting, bowed slightly, and said "Namaste."

Mr. Mera responded similarly and then gestured for me to lie down on the mat he unrolled on the floor.

"Wait!" said Jon. "Let's do this right." And he handed me a freshly packed chillum. He lit it for me. I took a couple of tokes, and then passed it to Mr. Mera, who refused it, but without passing judgment. I passed it to Rosie and she and Jon finished off the bowl. Those two tokes were more than enough to give me that wonderful phenomenon of floating.

I lay on my stomach on the mat. Mr. Mera lit some incense, rubbed his hands together, dripped some strange-smelling oil on my back and loosened my lungi, giving him access to my lower back and ass. He gave me a most excellent rub down, kneading my muscles expertly.

Then he rolled me over on my back. He played my body like a well-tuned sitar, and as he reached into my lungi to massage pressure points in my groin, he twice struck chords that might have become climaxes had they been sustained. My lungi was a tent that would not wilt. When he noticed, and how could he *not* notice that I was as stiff as an iron lingam, he rolled me back on my stomach and returned to a more subdued motif. Just in the nick of time, I might add!

When he roughly dragged his hands down my back a few times, flinging the bad energy off his fingertips, I knew he was through. It was probably the most memorable massage I've ever had. But I'm grateful it happened in the privacy of our room. I just lay there totally slack, except for the tightening of my aching balls, which were now completely blue with unfulfillment. I knew then that I would be terrible at tantric sex, or so I thought.

Mr. Mera stood up and wiped his hands on a small, frayed cloth. Rosie got on her hands and knees and crawled over to me. She put her mouth to my ear trying so hard to stifle her laughter. She whispered, "Chazan! You simply must have some sex, and I mean soon!"

Oh, where were Peter and Debra when I needed them!

Mr. Mera asked Jon if he could read the palms of his hands and feet. His deciphering of the lines in Jon's hands and calloused feet gave him away as just another smoothie. He was totally off base. He was so immersed in his own duplicity that we could only regard him as very entertaining. Rather than disagree with his diagnoses and prognostications, we merely nodded in thankful wonderment, hoping he would not sense that we were mocking him. Jon paid him generously and he left. I thanked Jon for the massage and felt good about us again, the way I had always felt good about him, though it had been a while.

Jon kept his ebullient mood all through dinner, and Rosie's usual beguiling charm, which had also been missing for a while, was infectious. We laughed and lovingly mocked each other, and I realized I had been missing that as well. It all felt so nice.

It was in the same mood that we returned to the hotel and went up to the fourth floor. We walked down the hall to Room 409. The door was slightly ajar and when Jon lightly knocked, it swung open. It was empty. It was just another nice room in a nice hotel, but no carpets nor rugs nor saris nor tablecloths nor hand-carved furniture, and needless to say, no Mackroo (and Son). There wasn't the slightest evidence that there had been a showroom here just hours before.

The shiver that went down Jon's spine was so strong, I'm sure it showed up on a Richter scale somewhere in the world. Anyone up or down the hall could feel it for sure. Jon took the stairs three at a time down to the lobby, Rosie and I trying to keep up.

"Where did Mr. Mackroo go?" Jon yelled at the clerk behind the desk. "When did he check out?"

The clerk looked at Jon innocently, yet I could discern the slightest look of complicity in his well-practiced smile.

He looked at his ledger, finger scrolling down the list of guests. Then he looked up at Jon.

"I am so sorry, Mr. Harvey, but we have had no guests registered by that name."

Jon was pissed. "What do you mean? He had a whole suite filled to the ceiling with stuff! It was his apartment and his showroom, given to him by this hotel! You are lying, you little piece of shit!"

The clerk was completely composed, while Jon became more exasperated.

"Once again I must tell you sir that we have had no Mackroo registered at this hotel, nor do we allow anyone to conduct business out of our rooms."

Jon pulled Mackroo's card out of his wallet and handed it to the clerk.

"You have never seen this card?" Jon asked.

"I have told you sir; this card is completely unfamiliar to me," he said, barely looking at it.

Jon was beside himself. "Call these phone numbers!" Jon ordered stabbing the card with his index finger.

The clerk clicked his jaw, swung his chin, picked up the phone and dialed. Jon could hear an operator's voice speaking.

"These phone numbers are out of service," the clerk replied, this time a bit shakily.

"And this address?" Jon asked. "I suppose it is out of service too?"

The clerk studied it and looked behind him at a stack of phone books. "Many apologies, sir, but this is a Kashmiri address and I have no phone book for Kashmir. I do not know."

Jon's briefly good mood shattered into a thousand pieces of bad. Rosie and I knew better than to say anything at all. We knew words of placation, words of outrage, any words at all would blow up in our faces.

Jon raced up the stairs. He was ballistic! Rose and I took the elevator. We found Jon in our room packing furiously.

"Jon," Rose asked courageously, "What are you doing? Where do you think you're going?"

"We're getting out of this goddam place," he shouted at Rosie. "Get your things together, Chazan. You too, Rose! We're out of here!"

Only Rose had the talent to charm the cobra out of Jon's basket-case mind. She swore up and down at Mackroo (and Son) and Delhi in general, underscoring Jon's outrage. But among the epithets she sprinkled words like *karma* and *puja* ever so diplomatically reminding Jon why we were here in the first place.

Jon settled down, but not until he recited, "Punch thyself," over and over, and in an act of self-flagellation hit himself hard in the head every time he said the phrase. When his forehead was red, he fell back on his pillow and lay there staring at the ceiling fan. His eyes were watering when he rolled over on his side. His last words before falling asleep were, "My kavadi to you, Lord Muruga. Om Muruga!"

Rose very quietly pulled the covers over him and crawled in beside him, spooning, and holding him tightly. I took to my bed feeling a bit guilty that I hadn't shared my suspicions about Mackroo with Jon and Rose. I just guessed that Jon wouldn't have listened to me anyway. He'd just ignore my warnings as readily as he ignored my suggestions or ideas. And Rose wouldn't have wanted to burst any of his bubbles.

Christ! Surely, it must get better than this!

CHAPTER 52
March 1972

We were at Asmiri Gate in Old Delhi very early in the morning. My immediate unvoiced question was why the hell we had spent any time at all in New Delhi, when Old Delhi was so much more interesting!" At last, back to a cacophony of colors, sounds, smells, and most importantly, squalor. My kind of India!

Merchants were just opening their stores, arranging foods, beads, clothes, incense, and assorted strange and curious items in their stalls. Vendors sold cheap trinkets and T-shirts, most with Western logos or popular sayings on them, many of them quotes from Guru Snoopy and Swami Mickey Mouse.

Women filled baskets with sweets, treats, and breads, placed them on their heads and meandered around the square quietly peddling their goods.

Rosie, still groggy, was leaning against a wall, while Jon went from one taxi to another trying to secure a ride north but having little luck. Begging children pulled at his lungi and shirt, probably having slept on the streets, huddled in some filthy corner or alleyway.

And I surveyed the site with nostalgia. These were the images of the Delhi I had always imagined, now come to life with the lunacy of this part of town.

While doing a 360-degree scan of the frenetic scene, I noticed a man opening a door to his store. It was an antique shop, and when I entered, I found it long and narrow, barely wider than the door itself. It was filled with all kinds of old treasures, but totally disorganized, with lamps next to necklaces, bronze statues of the gods next to baskets filled with exotic hand-crafted beads, and large ostentatious jewelry and baubles.

The confusion of the place made my mind reel, but a sliver of sun bounced off a familiar face that seemed to beckon me. It was a small pendant of Ganesh hanging on a chain. Both the chain and Ganesh were made of pure silver. His face was worn, likely from former owners who rubbed it often, yet it was easily recognized as my beloved friend and guardian. I had to have it. And I was thrilled when the merchant told me it was only two dollars!

I was never a good haggler over price, and simply handed him the money. He started to remove my hishi necklace, but I stopped him. He smiled paternally at me as if he knew it held a special meaning. If only he knew how special. I would do anything or go anywhere to see Michael again. I wished I knew where in the hell he was. The merchant undid the clasp of the silver chain and slipped it around my neck, sliding it under the hishis. I pretended that it was Michael lifting my ponytail and securing the clasp, but when I turned around, it was the approving and tick-tocking head of the merchant. Nevertheless, Ganesh now rested comfortably and securely against my heart chakra.

I immediately felt secure and confident that this silver Ganesh would keep me from harm. It was more than just a talisman; it was a bright neon sign on my chest that told everyone to approach me with deference. Or so I liked to think. Regardless, to this day it has never left my neck, nor have the hishis.

Jon was calling, "Chazan! Chazan! Where the hell are you?"

"Coming," I yelled back. "Be right there."

When Jon and Rosie saw me coming out of the store, they immediately noticed Ganesh hanging from my neck. Rosie fondled it and Jon said it was a beauty, but I felt badly in a way that it was I who would leave Delhi with the smallest and most unpretentious of souvenirs, while they had just been ripped off and had nothing. Nevertheless, they seemed very happy for me as Jon hurried us to a waiting taxi for the ride to Hardwar.

Jon sat up front with the driver. Rose and I took the back seat. It was getting hot fast. There was no air conditioning. The cabbie kept the windows open. We ate dust for five hours.

I thought once we were out of the city, we would be able to relax and simply take in the scenery. I should have known better by now. Traveling in India is a numbing experience. The rivers of people flowing by on either side of the road, their impoverished living conditions, children peeking out of cardboard huts, the slightly more affluent out of corrugated tin shelters, the looks of fatigue and futility on their mothers' faces were unnerving.

The cabbie drove so fast, I thought it was impossible not to run someone over. He refused to slow down for anything, even when Jon yelled at him to do so. Rose and I were as tightly wound up as we could be, constantly pressing a foot on a brake that wasn't there. The traffic was insane.

At one point, a team of oxen pulling an enormous load covered with a dark tarp came into view. The oxen looked like a mutant giant sea turtle, straining beneath the weight of an enormous shell. I was sure this was a head-on collision about to happen. But the cabbie swerved to the shoulder of the road just in time, forcing a dozen or more people to jump out of the way. He seemed to have no concern at all for their safety or ours.

He stopped once, in a small village, to allow us to have lunch. We were immediately surrounded by begging children, and legless men scooting rapidly on their hands, and armless women beseeching us for baksheesh, holding up twisted feet to catch a rupee or two. We were being mobbed and all three of us at one time or another heard ourselves screaming at people and throwing our hands up in disgust at their incoherent and almost belligerent behavior. Had we lost all compassion, all sympathy?

We jumped back in the taxi, trying to close the doors without dismembering any of the arms that insisted on reaching inside. Who knows how many of the already dismembered had become that way at the hands of our driver, who was totally nuts!

He must have been doing 80 miles per hour on a road that should have been taken at no more than 25. He zigged and zagged, throwing Rosie and me from one side of the cab to the other. He drove straight through a "road crew" of at least a few hundred men, some sledge-hammering large rocks in two, others splitting those pieces into smaller ones, and still others chipping away at the small ones until they were the size of gravel, which the final group of men shoveled onto the road.

We had to roll up the windows to avoid being hit by the gravel that the wheels spit up and cringed every time a stone scarred the underside of the taxi. His driving was so reckless that all I could do was cling to Ganesh, my nerves totally frayed. I was having a nervous breakdown.

Suddenly, I was as serene and calm as could be. I had gone over the edge. It was the only way to survive. All my frames of reference from the West were destroyed. There was absolutely, positively no way I could make some order out of this chaos. It was like a bad acid trip where once you decide to surrender your ego, all is peaceful and perfect. I realized that only in this state could one mentally endure a trip to India. I realized why so many Westerners who made this trip overland from Europe never got farther south than Delhi. They were too sick, too tired, too tortured by trying to maintain their sanity to venture deeper south. Northern India was enough. If they made it to Delhi, they often hopped on the next plane home. Thank god we had entered India from the south. If we hadn't, we would have never made it to Goa or Tamil Nadu, let alone Ceylon, and we would have missed out on some of the most wondrous sights and experiences India had to offer.

We continued north in our racecar, hitting bumps or plummeting into potholes that made us hit our heads on the roof of the car. We were certain that in the next village or the village after that, there would be a refuge of quiet and coolness, where we could pull our severed parts together.

But no! The refuge never came. Only more dust, more heat and more fucking humanity. Where was the India of the Vedas, the India of the sitar? Ravi Shankar, your music lied to us! However, when we reached Hardwar, some of his music rang true.

Hardwar was like a renaissance fair. Bazaars as far as the eye could see. Sadhus and sannyasis everywhere. Musicians sat on raised platforms and played their sitars, sarods, tablas and bansuris.

We wandered in a maze of colors and scents and sounds for hours, no longer bothered by the constant pushing and shoving. When we had stuffed ourselves on an assortment of foods from an assortment of booths, we went in search of lodging.

On the way, we passed what looked like a fortress, with tall, thick, and closed gates. A small bronze sign on the gate told us this was the ashram of the child guru, Maharaj Ji. He was the most tasteless of all the gurus we had seen or heard about. He was on tour back in the States, doing the talk show circuit and buying spots on TV. A comprehensive campaign advertised that no one should have an excuse for not having heard about him.

I will forever regret what I did, and I don't know what came over me, but when we passed the gates, I spit on them, my way of saying I could never abide by that kind of blatant spiritual commercialism. Jon and Rosie watched me with approval. I had done for them what they would have liked to do themselves.

We found a very nice tourist bungalow just outside of town. We were physically and mentally exhausted and couldn't wait to go to bed. It was relatively quiet and peaceful, at least relative to what we had been through, and for that we were extremely grateful.

From the bungalow, we could see the sun setting over the Ganges, swift, green, clear, and banked on either side by stone stairways dipping into the current, allowing people easy access to its waters, to bathe or be bathed by its holiness. The first foothills of the Himalayas rose around us, teasing us with the breathtaking peaks which lay beyond.

I lay on my cot feeling like I was finally in the India of my dreams. I listened to the flow of the river, so swift and soothing.

Shiva is breathing tonight. I can see him breathing. His body straight, hands at his sides. Up and down his chest moves, less and less discernible as his breathing becomes slower.

Shiva is breathing tonight. I can hear him breathing. As his breath becomes softer, it mingles with the sound of the overhead fan whirring liquidly with each revolution. Shiva's breath becomes the sound of the river ceaselessly sliding over the rocks, and that too becomes the breath of someone sleeping in another part of our room. When I look for that someone, he is nowhere to be found. Just the breath. In and out. In and out. Encompassing all sounds until there are no more.

CHAPTER 53
March 1972

After a meager breakfast of chai and fruit, we hailed a taxi to Rishikesh. Thankfully, it was a short ride, but we decided not to drive all the way into town. We asked the cabbie to let us off just on the outskirts. We preferred to walk the rest of the way.

We could see the town and the Ganges in the distance. This is where the river flows out of the mountains, and it is one of the holiest places in India. On one side of the river, our side, were ashrams of well-known and not-so-well known gurus lining the banks. Some ashrams were simple, others elaborate. Though the ashrams were open to all the Western "seekers," they were closed to the poor and hungry of their own kind. I thought that was somewhat hypocritical, but hadn't we also inured ourselves against the hordes of beggars just to keep our psyches in a survival mode?

On our walk, we passed many sadhus, each one more outrageous than the next. Here, on the banks of the Ganges, they lived out their lives practicing tapasya, austerities and great meditations meant to please Lord Shiva or his many manifestations. They gave up all their comforts and remained in deep meditation for months. We chanced upon a baba and his friends, who happened *not* to be in deep meditation. If anything, they were in deep partying! They invited us into their hut where they shared some hash with us.

"Om Shivaya!" the baba bellowed before each toke, which he inhaled with gusto. He said he knew Baba Ram Dass, which we doubted until he told us that Ram Dass had given him some acid to try. We hung out there until totally obliterated. Baba was quite the character, but we got along famously. When we left, one of his sidekicks resumed his position standing on his head in a hole, which his buddies filled in with sand. We were amazed. Another trick? Or mind over matter? His ash-smeared body remained motionless, and he looked like an upside-down totem pole.

We continued our walk, only to be suddenly accosted by lepers who insisted on hugging us and rubbing up against us, their flesh on our flesh.

Rosie was a little freaked. "Is this safe?" she asked us. If it wasn't, it was too late.

Jon called to Rose over the partial shoulder of the leper hugging him, "No mind, never matter. No matter, never mind. Summu Iru!" And it seemed ironic to me, or maybe it was sarcasm, that he should quote the very first guru they had met, though we had traveled so long and hard to find others more suitable to Jon's taste.

A nose-less woman grabbed me and kissed each cheek rubbing her face against mine. I reached for my Ganesh and asked for faith I would not return to Hunga Dunga with flesh falling off my body. She backed off just far enough to extend a hand with half-eaten fingers into which I dropped a few rupees. The lepers followed us, clinging to our clothes, begging, and crying. But they stopped when they reached some unmarked boundary, only they knew existed.

Over the Laxman Jhula Bridge we walked, the swift Ganges beneath us, the foothills of the Himalayas on our left. There were ascetics and renunciates everywhere we looked. Some were obviously out of their bodies. Others were merely panhandling.

One of the panhandlers was a beautiful young boy, maybe a teenager, maybe a young adult. It was hard to tell. But he had a look in his eyes we couldn't pass by. Jon gave him some rupees and off he ran to the nearest shop where he could buy something to eat.

We stopped to watch a sculptor working diligently on a statue of Hanuman. The young panhandler scurried through the crowds and found us. He merely squatted next to us as we followed the deft movements of the sculptor's hammer and chisel. But his eyes gazed longingly only at Jon.

Jon was a bit disconcerted by his staring. Rosie and I could only giggle at his chagrin.

"What're you gonna do now, oh great benefactor?" Rosie teased.

"Shoo, go away!" Jon said sternly to the boy. The boy seemed hurt and looked down at the ground.

"Oh, this is better, much better!" Jon said with guilt in his voice. When we stood up to continue our walk, the boy stayed behind. But when we stopped at an open-air chai shop to have a cup and smoke another chillum, we noticed him standing a few feet away staring at Jon like a forlorn puppy.

"Oh, he is very good at this," Jon said. "A real pro!"

Nevertheless, Jon tossed a few coins in his direction. The boy scrambled for them, fighting off other kids trying to steal his booty.

"Now you've really done it!" I said. "Don't you know by now that will only make it worse?"

"Nah!" Jon replied. "We've seen the last of him."

We left the chai shop totally OD'd and incapable of clear thinking. We continued in a daze past a yogi suspended on a two-foot-high bed of inch-long thorns, his body gray with ashes, adding to the lifelessness of being in one state of samadhi or another. The boy had followed us, keeping what he thought was a comfortable distance behind. Jon didn't think it comfortable enough and yelled at the boy to disappear. The longhaired boy in his ratty lungi stopped in his tracks. We thought that was the end of him. But we had walked only a few yards along the Ganges when we heard loud yelling.

We turned to see our young beggar engaged in a row with a merchant who clutched his cigar box of money to his chest while our new "friend" continued to hold out his cupped hand. Though we spoke only a few words of Hindi, we could make out what was going on.

The merchant was berating the boy, practically screaming at him. The boy was yelling back, and he often repeated the word *brahmacharya*. Even I knew what that meant from hatha yoga classes I had taken. It was someone who had taken a vow of celibacy. The merchant kept pointing at the boy, and then much to our surprise, pointed at us, picking us out of the crowd like a sniper. He was trying to say we supposed, that he was just another dirty hippie like us! He was no better than a crazed Western freak and certainly *not* a sadhu, let alone one practicing *brahmacharya*!

The boy was outraged. He lifted his lungi high above his waist and exposed his cock. The shaft was pierced just below the head by a huge silver ring from which hung a heavy amulet. His penis hung between his legs, the weight of the amulet stretching the shaft until it was long and thin, and the head of his cock almost reached his knees. It was such a mind-fucking sight, I thought I had imagined the entire incident.

The boy burst into tears and dropped his lungi. The merchant, his jaw opened wide and his eyes popping out, opened the cigar box and threw a handful of money at him. Jon ran up to the boy and put his arm around his shoulder. The boy buried his face in Jon's chest and sobbed.

We adopted Anupam for the rest of the day, feeding him, buying him a new lungi, and even letting him sleep on the floor of our room in an ashram that provided lodging for tourists. That was easier said than done. The ashram welcomed the three of us but refused to let Anupam stay there. Jon was irate, going on and on about charity and compassion and so on. But the caretaker of the ashram was adamant.

Jon took the boy by the hand and hid him in some bushes on the side of the ashram. We knocked on the door and when the caretaker saw it was just the three of us, he let us in and showed us to a sparse but clean room. It was hours before quiet fell throughout the building. Only then, did Jon tip toe down the stairs and open the front door, leaving a flip-flop behind to keep the door ajar. He went around to the side of the building. Our young friend was still there in the bushes, all these hours later, waiting patiently.

Jon gestured to him to be very quiet. Anupam seemed skittish about entering the building, looking all around him in awe at the furnishings and artwork. He was even more nervous when he entered the room. He acted as if he had never seen the inside of a room, let alone beds, ever before in his life.

Rosie flattened out a couple of our thin blankets on the floor next to their bed and gestured to it. The boy studied the three of us. We studied him back. He was a beautiful youngster, and we could discern beneath the dirt and matted hair, a very handsome face, wide-eyed with disbelief at our kindness. I doubt he had ever slept with a roof over his head.

We smiled at him, but it was difficult for him to smile back. He just stared at us in wonder. We all got back into bed, and sheepishly, he lay on the blankets. He curled up in a fetal position and held the new lungi Jon bought for him close to his chest.

We got up early in the morning and tried to slip out quietly. Just as we opened the door, the caretaker came around a corner. When he saw Anupam, he freaked out and yelled at all of us. But we just walked away ignoring his outbursts, and proud that in some way we forced the ashram to give shelter to the neediest of us.

We walked back toward the main square and had a big breakfast, and for the first time, Anupam seemed at ease and gobbled his food. Jon slipped him some money. Then we went to a taxi stand to find one to take us back to Hardwar.

It was only when we had climbed in the cab that Anupam realized he wasn't coming with us. Leaving this boy behind was one of the most difficult things we had done. We had to put on determined faces to not look him in the eyes as the taxi drove off. We just stared straight ahead. But when we had gone a dozen blocks or so, I looked behind. There he was running as fast as he could to catch up to us. The taxi picked up speed, and the boy gave up and just stood there until we were out of sight. I will never forget the incredibly forlorn look on his face.

I wondered if we had done the right thing. I wondered if maybe, when all was said and done, we had done him a disservice. We had shown him a slice of life that would be forever out of his reach. We had given him one day of security, a full stomach, a clean lungi, a bit of money, shelter, and a sense of belonging. Then we abandoned him to hopelessness. I, for one, hoped that his celibacy would indeed lead him to peace and enlightenment. In truth, that quest was the only thing we had in common.

At this point, we were hungrier than ever for a cool mountain stream, and hungrier than ever for sensory deprivation. Though we should have known better by now, we listened to the promises of our driver that if only we had gone farther north through Dehra Dun to Mussorie, we would have found the isolation we were looking for, with spectacular Himalayan peaks as our backdrop.

The driver made a U-turn in the road, and we headed north again, retracing our steps. Every mile was a test of our nerves and emotional stamina. When we finally reached what we thought would be some sort of retreat, the throngs of rip-off artists and hustlers attacked again. And the peaks were still not to be found. Again, Jon was pissed. Rosie was pissed that Jon was pissed. And I was pissed that Rosie was pissed at Jon being pissed. What a lovely three-some we made.

After harsh words with the driver, back down the mountain we went to Dehra Dun. Back through Rishikesh. Back through Hardwar. Back to Delhi, the most absurd effort at intelligent city life ever attempted.

This time, we spent the night in a funky hotel in Old Delhi. The next day, after breakfast, we arranged for an afternoon flight out of town. As we made our way to the airport, Jon yelled out the window, "This is the most unholy place in the world!"

CHAPTER 54
April 1972

Royal Nepali Airlines, "The only airline where even the stewardesses throw up." On the side of the twin-engine prop plane was a large dotted oval line. Above it read, "In case of emergency, chop here." Really. I'm not kidding. I loved it. I noticed that we were on Flight 11, which made it somewhat auspicious. That is until we were airborne.

It was one of the wildest plane rides we'd had. It was so turbulent that the cockpit door kept flying open and the copilot had to keep getting out of his chair to close it, hesitant to look any of the passengers in the eye. It was so bumpy; we left our seats beneath us often as we hit our heads on the overhead bins. I clung even tighter to my Ganesh.

As we flew into the Kathmandu valley, the majestic peaks rose high above the clouds, certainly higher than any elevation the plane could maintain. I felt the possibility of crashing into a glacier very likely. Below us, terraces of green textured the hills. The mountains got closer and larger, and I was just about to yell, "Take 'er down!" when the captain did just that. It was a surprisingly smooth landing, but after all the crazy bus, taxi, and plane rides we'd taken, I just couldn't handle another roller coaster.

After disembarking, we had to go through customs. It was a most unfortunate oversight on Jon's part that he forgot about the sizeable chunk of hash he had in the bottom of his cloth bag. Rosie and I were in line behind Jon when the Nepalese agent found the stash.

The three of us tensed up, nervously imagining what life would be like in a Nepalese jail. The customs agent looked up at Jon with a serious look on his face, and then at Rosie and me, who were obviously complicit in the smuggling operation. This did not bode well. Then he brought the chunk of hash up to his nose and circled it slowly around his nostrils, smelling it as discriminately as a sommelier testing the quality of a wine.

"Inferior stuff!" he snidely pronounced and threw the chunk of hash back into Jon's bag. It took a while for the sweat on our faces to dry, but once it had, we knew this was a cool country and that Flight 11 had been meant for us.

We found the valley to be the home of polite, smiling Nepalese people and many Tibetan refugees who were the living intimations of the mystery and beauty of the Shangri-la usurped by the Chinese. What a refreshing change this was from northern India, even if the sanitation conditions were worse than ever.

Open sewers carried shit and piss down almost every street. Goats and pigs ate garbage while blocking our path. The smell was too much, but all this was so easily forgotten when we saw the warm smiles on the children and their seemingly ageless parents.

There were lots of Western freaks. Lots and lots of Western freaks. All continually stoned, of course. There were so many freaks that several restaurants catered exclusively to their diet, namely hamburgers, fries and shakes. I didn't dare inquire as to where the meat came from, nor did I really care, since I had stuck religiously to my vegetarian diet. As did Rosie. Jon was the only one of us who now and then fell off the wagon and treated himself to the protein he craved.

We rented a small hut, part of a row of huts, like row houses in London or New York, but dilapidated and askew, each barely holding the other somewhat upright. Our hut was uninsulated, and we could see light sneaking in through the slats of the wooden walls and holes in the sheet metal roof. The floor was dirt, and the only heat came from a small fire pit in the center of the room, which we fueled with small bundles of sticks, or sometimes pancakes of dung, sold by young boys whose sole job it was to deliver them to "subscribers" much like I delivered newspapers to my neighbors when I was a boy.

Unfortunately, our timing was completely off, and we had arrived in Kathmandu just at the beginning of monsoon season. It didn't rain the day we arrived nor the day we left. But the rest of the time, it was always raining. Sometimes just a drizzle, sometimes a downpour, but it rained nevertheless. Our hut was always damp and cold. We were always huddling around the scrawny flames of the Nepalese version of central heating. Staying stoned helped a lot.

The clothing we had was totally insufficient. We went to Tashi's Trek Shop and bought some worn flannel shirts and torn jeans from a hippie guy who was making Kathmandu his permanent home and working here in this backpacker's thrift shop.

Monsoon season, of course, deprived us of the opportunity to do any trekking and witness up close the highest peaks in the world. We would have to be content with the views we got from the plane ride. We would have to be content with scouring the city itself for adventures.

After only a couple of days in Kathmandu, I started feeling ill. None of us had gotten sick the entire time we'd been traveling, and I didn't want to break our record. But I did. I woke up on Easter Sunday and looked up at Rosie, who was crying. So was Jon. But they both were smiling at me lovingly through their tears.

When Jon and Rosie explained how sick I had been, I didn't believe them until they told me the date. I had been out of it for three days but could have sworn I was just waking up from a short nap. I was feeling great and ready to boogie! Jon was most suspicious that I had gone delirious on Good Friday and had resurrected on Sunday. He accused me of doing it on purpose just to piss him off.

Outside, I could hear people chanting, "Lomotil! Lomotil!" and thought it was just a local mantra. Through the tiny window of the hut, I saw some hippies carrying a young man on their shoulders as if he were a deity. He kept cajoling, "Stop it now! Enough! Really, mates, put me down!" His accent was distinctly British.

The days just seemed to slide by effortlessly. No hassles, no aggressive vendors, no clinging quadriplegic beggars, though I guess it would be difficult for one of them to cling to you. Despite their runny noses and ragged clothing, the children were charming, shy, and happy, with round faces, red cheeks, and sparkling eyes. The adults just seemed to be bigger children, and many of them appeared to be equally as stoned as the vast number of hippies who had good reason to choose this city as a place of refuge. We felt safe here. Though lacking in the sanitation department, it was as civilized as San Francisco, but with an overt flair for the spiritual.

Every day, we tried to explore a different part of the city, but usually ended up on the main drag. Stupas rose from the valley floor. At least once a day, we'd climb the stairs of one of these stupas, and smoke excellent hash with a priest or two. Many of them spoke English. Jon, as usual, impressed them with his knowledge and his zeal. He never descended the stairs without inquiring if one of them was his teacher. They usually smiled and said something mystic like "but my friend, I thought you were *my* teacher."

Though he was polite, this infuriated Jon. And Rosie and I made a point of keeping him as stoned as possible. In Kathmandu, this was very easy to do.

CHAPTER 55
April 1972

The freedom of San Francisco was one-upped by Kathmandu, especially when it came to drugs. Everything was legal! Opium, hash, ganja. On almost every corner there was a ganja shop. They were as common as drug stores. They were drug stores. Our favorite was The Inn Eden. When we entered, we saw before us shelves stocked to capacity with gallon-sized glass jars, each filled with a different variety of hash or weed. Brown, tan, yellow, and black hash filled the jars. Others contained ganja from all over the country, pretty buds that sparkled with stickiness. Some were dark green, others had a reddish tinge, and still others were almost iridescent.

"What are those golden chunks?" Rosie asked. "The ones on the top shelf, near the left."

"Oh, that is hashish from the north, miss," the merchant answered. "Would you care to try some?"

"That would be so kind of you," Rosie smiled back. The man took the jar down from the shelf, removed a small piece and placed it in a chillum. He handed it to Rose and lit it for her.

"Mmmmmm," said Rosie, exhaling the smoke while trying to contain a cough. "That is very nice, but a bit on the harsh side." She passed it to me and after sampling it, I passed it on to Jon.

"That brown stuff next to the yellow," Jon pointed. "What's that?"

"Oh, that is finer hash. Very good. Very good. Would you care to try it?"

"No," said Jon, "that's OK." Jon scanned the shelves. "What's the black stuff in the jar behind you?"

"Oh, my friend, you have excellent taste!" the merchant said. "Those are temple balls. The best we have to offer. Here, try some." He took the chillum from Jon, emptied it, and refilled it with a small chunk of the black gooey stuff.

He handed it to me and fired it up. Man! It was smooth! And not too far off from being psychedelic! I passed it to Jon, who took a puff and passed it to Rosie. She finished it off. The three of us did a slow turn of the head to each other, trying to keep a straight face. We were flying! We were already totally stoned just from these samples. We felt obliged to buy something.

"How much for the black temple hash," inquired Jon.

"It is one dollar for 30 grams," he answered.

The three of us again looked at one another in slow motion, trying our best not to get into a giggle fit, which was difficult to do given the odd expression on Rosie's face; she was still trying to exhale the remainder of her recent toke.

Jon said in the most casual manner he could, "OK, we'll take 30 grams," and looked at me as if we were ripping the guy off.

"Can I interest you in some excellent opium?" the merchant asked.

"No, the temple hash will be fine, thanks," I said, remembering the one time we tried some opium at the Chinese Guest House in Trincomalee. We knew we would be sick but didn't quite expect the extent of the vomiting involved. We were at the dry heave stages and could only lie down, trying our best to will our stomachs into behaving. We waited for the high. I guess it came, but we only lay there semi-comatose in weird dream states. We didn't like it at all and had wasted a whole day. It was a bad enough experience that we never wanted to try it again.

Completely satisfied with the temple hash, we left the shop stumbling out onto the street, turning our exit into a Three Stooges act where all of them are trying to get out the door at the same time. When we were outside, we burst into laughter and joined the parade of other stoned hippies, and young, hip stoned Nepalese men, of whom there were many.

No wonder this was such a mellow town. Everyone was stoned all the time. When we were ready for more, we simply stopped into a ganja shop and sampled the goodies. The hash was so cheap and so strong that when we found just a small chunk left in our stash, we simply threw it out as we walked around the neighborhoods, knowing we could pick up another ounce for a song.

Svyambunath was in the neighborhood where many of the Tibetan refugees lived. A wide and long stone stairway led up to an imposing temple. At the bottom of the stairs, guards warned visitors to completely ignore the thousands of monkeys running wildly everywhere, like little bikers taking over an unsuspecting town. One guard told us in very good English, "Whatever you do, do not make eye contact with any of them!"

We climbed the stairs while monkeys darted in between our legs with each step. They were as numerous as roaches in a Florida flophouse but through our peripheral vision, we found them to be cute in their own way.

By the time we reached the top, most of the monkeys had disappeared. To the left of the landing was a stone wall with a bench in front of it. We rested there catching our breath when I made the mistake of peering over the wall.

At the bottom were hundreds of monkeys, and though I dared steal only an inadvertent glance, it was almost impossible not to acknowledge their stares. Big mistake. Suddenly they were baring their teeth and hissing and leaping high trying to grab me and drag me down to their lairs where they would summarily eat me alive! Thankfully, the wall was too high, and they failed in their attempts. But all the way back down the stairs, I thought I was in a horror movie and my knees shook like maracas until we were well beyond the temple grounds.

Before we left the neighborhood, we went to the open-air market where we saw an energetic old man reverently rolling up prints of some kind and tying them up with colorful ribbons. Jon walked over, Rosie and I behind him.

"What do we have here my friend?" Jon asked.

The little man untied a set and curled them out for Jon to see. Jon leafed through a few and then found the thread, the meaning.

"This is the entire Kargyu lineage of gurus!" John exclaimed excitedly.

Rosie and I looked at him in a fog.

"You know! "Tibetan saints. Like Milarepa, Naropa, Gampopa."

The wiry man's eyes lit up when he heard those names coming from Jon's mouth. After complimenting Jon on his knowledge, he explained as best he could. There were so many Tibetan refugees fleeing Chinese occupation, that the Dhalai Lama called for ancient woodblocks to be brought out of reliquaries and that the invaluable carvings be used once again. This time not out of homage to the saints and deities, but to help refugees make money.

There were 70 of them in a set. Though they were only twenty-five dollars, that was a lot for me. But they were so beautiful, even though I didn't understand them to the depth Jon did, I decided I had to have them. Besides, being all on rice paper, they rolled up very tightly and were easy to carry. Jon bought a set, too.

Another day, we came upon an unusual stupa, this one echoing the repetitious chants of devout Buddhists. It was Bodnath. How we had missed it before I'll never know because it was so obvious to the eye and the ear. It was a circular building with a giant hemispheric dome on top. Around the perimeter were large prayer wheels, metal cylinders engraved with Buddhist prayers and set on well-oiled spindles. By spinning the wheels, one set the prayers in motion and out into the universe.

In a constant stupor, we visited shrines and museums, always amazed at the tankas on the walls, some very old, all of them amazing. Jon was always the tour guide and deciphered the tankas for us. He identified which god or guru was depicted and what the colors and the hand gestures meant. He was a delight to be with, a walking, talking encyclopedia. But this was in part due to the hash, which kept him in the ever-present state of *Now*, where all was new and beautiful and full of wonder.

CHAPTER 56
April 1972

While running around the Bodnath spinning prayer wheels, I noticed a couple waving wildly at me and yelling. It was Jerry and Linda, my Bangkok buddies!

They ran toward me with open arms, all smiles and flushed with affection. Linda, hugely pregnant now, hugged me with delight. Jerry picked me up and swung me around, set me down on my feet and hugged me so hard I thought he would break a rib.

Jon and Rose stared at them and then at me, as if surprised I was capable of making friends without them. I introduced them to Jerry and Linda. Jerry was a bit thinner, looking more ascetic than ever. With his shining bald head, he could easily be taken for a young Buddhist initiate. Linda had that ineffable glow imminent motherhood always radiated.

I gave Jon and Rosie some history about our get-togethers in Bangkok and Rose shot me an inquisitive glance, one that asked why I hadn't shared my meeting them. I didn't have a good answer, so I sloughed it off and Jon and Rose didn't probe when I marveled how cosmic it was running into them here. I pretended it was just another one of those magical meetings that were becoming commonplace. Western wanna-be-saddhus bumping into each other along the established routes to potential enlightenment.

Jerry gave me directions to where they were living. Linda insisted I come by as soon as possible. They were anxious to fill me in on their adventures and wanted updates on mine. They didn't extend the invitation to Jon and Rosie. As they left, waving to all of us, Jon gave me another disturbed look as if Jerry, Linda, or both, were ex-lovers whom I conveniently neglected to reveal.

"Let's fire up a bowl!" I said. And after a couple of hits, Jon forgot why he was disturbed.

mm

The next day, I visited Jerry and Linda in their one-room apartment above a ganja shop. I could tell as soon as I walked in that they had been here for a while and intended to be here for some time to come.

The room was spotless. Tibetan rugs on the floor. Tankas on the walls. A little alter in one corner of the room. Candles flickered on a small statue of the Buddha. Linda lit some incense and checked the teapot on their wood stove.

She served tea and cakes and sat on the floor, legs under her butt, hands behind her propping her up, her belly extended like a large balloon. Jerry sat in full-lotus position, looking as content and serene as when I first met him.

They were amazed at how quickly I had traversed the sub-continent, especially since they were the kind to find one village and stay there for a couple of months. They had left Bangkok for Delhi but were as disappointed as we had been with the vibes of the city. So off they went, overland, to Kathmandu. They had been here ever since.

Linda was due in mid-September. I had barely finished telling them some of my adventures when Jerry said, "So, Giacco, are you ready to spend some time with us?"

I knew that by "time" he probably meant an extended period of time. I had to contain my impulsiveness to say "yes." Instead, I said, "Well, of course, while I am in Kathmandu."

Jerry looked a bit disappointed and asked, "And how long will that be?"

"Well, that depends on Jon and Rosie," I stuttered.

"Why on them?" he persisted.

"I told you in Bangkok that Jon and Rosie were the ones who sold their farm in Maine and bought the tickets around the world. I feel a bit morally obligated to stick it out with them. I love them. They are my dearest friends."

Linda was the one who looked disappointed now. "But don't you like Kathmandu?" she asked.

"I love Kathmandu!" I told her. "I love it as much as Ceylon, maybe more!"

"Then what's the hang-up?" Jerry asked.

"It's not a hang-up Jer," I said. "It's just that… oh, shit, I am so confused."

"What's this obligation to Jon and Rose? What's that all about?

"It's not just the plane ticket, Jerry. We share a long and deep history."

"So? That history will still be there when you get back home. Besides, it's History. We are *Here!* We are *Now!*"

Linda interrupted. "We want a history with you too, Giacco."

"You can stay with us, Giacco," said Jerry. "I know it's small, but we can make room. And when the baby comes, maybe we'll find someplace larger."

They obviously wanted their child born in Nepal. I was a little baffled. Why were they so enamored of me? What were they seeing that I couldn't? In the time it took to take a toke off the chillum Jerry handed me, I imagined the two of us watching Linda give birth. Of Jerry and me laughing as we changed diapers. Of learning from Jerry to be like him, to learn from him. Of wonderful intimacies. I reminded myself I was stoned.

I already had a family. Hunga Dunga. And Jon and Rosie. But I really did like Kathmandu so much, I could easily have stayed indefinitely. And they were from San Francisco, so eventually we would all end up back there.

"Let me mull this over for a bit, OK?" I asked, not wanting to give them too much hope and trying to hide any excitement I may have felt at the thought of living with this beautiful and high couple.

"You know where we are, Giacco. Let us know. Talk to Jon and Rose about it," Jerry said as he and I stood up. "They'll understand."

I flashed on Peter and Debra speaking those same words. I shivered with deja vu. I leaned over to kiss Linda. Jerry held the door for me, his arm around my shoulder as I said, "See ya Linda! Later brother!" Linda looked up at me with a hopeful smile on her face.

CHAPTER 57
April 1972

I walked back to our little ramshackle hut, my brain undergoing a minor schizo attack. Jon and Rosie weren't there so I traipsed clumsily to one of their favorite haunts, Aunt Jane's Pie Shop. Sure enough, there they were, Rosy sitting at one table by herself, Jon in animated conversation at another table of freaks.

As soon as she saw me, she flashed me a giant hashish grin and gestured for me to come sit with her in the traditional Hindu fashion of extending her arm, palm down, fingers pulling me toward her. Her smile was heavenly and the moment I saw how cute she looked, beckoning me, I melted. How could I leave her? I sat down in the hard wooden chair.

"And what have you been up to this afternoon, my sweet Chazan?" She asked in a hash-raspy voice.

"I've been sipping chai with Linda and Jerry," I said as nonchalantly as possible.

"Are they going to steal you away from us?" She teased, knowing that was not an impossibility.

"They did invite me to stay with them," I answered honestly.

"Are you going to? A look of real concern came over her face.

"I truly don't know. Right now, I'm just flattered they extended the invitation." And then to change the conversation, "So what's our Jonny up to?" I pointed my chin in his direction.

"He's getting the latest scoop on the guru scene," she answered sarcastically.

Jon had taken to using the hippies living in Kathmandu for his resources. Many of them had become devotees of different teachers. They had found their guru. His longing for one was surfacing again after a brief respite of just traveling and getting stoned.

In every café and hippie haunt, he would make inquiries. Though less obsessed by now, no tale of a holy man went dismissed. He would've tracked him down no matter where it would lead him, even if it meant hacking his way through a jungle or climbing a steep cliff to a cave filled with nettles and roots. Luckily, no one sent him to any of those places.

However, he did visit many priests who had been highly recommended, and fortunately, Kathmandu was teeming with them. He talked with hippie disciples, who with some condescension, would say, "But Jon, you already know the truth. It is already inside you." Jon would just barely be able to keep from punching the guy out.

Or sometimes, a devotee would say, "I have been initiated by so and so, but I can't reveal the secret mantra without jeopardizing my own soul." That one really busted his nuts! And every now and then, someone would actually show him a meditation technique or the proper position to sit while breathing, at which times Jon was gracious, but not grateful. No teachings or mantras nor tantras or yogas or meditation techniques could satisfy Jon. And if Jon went unsatisfied, we all suffered.

Jon returned to our table with a new friend in tow. The new friend was radiantly beautiful with long flowing hair, a perfect complexion, a naturally confident but modest air about him. A real sweetie.

He looked at me and screwed up his forehead. Before Jon could introduce us, he said, "Giacco? Is that you?"

I was scrambling to place him. I did just in time before he had to tell me. "Carlos? Carlos from Laurel Canyon?"

Jon stood there, his mouth open, as I jumped up and Carlos and I hugged and swung each other around.

"Oh, this is better. Much better!" Jon mocked. "First Jerry and Linda, and now Carlos. Explain, please!"

"Oh Jon!" I said, ecstatic at my luck. "You have just met a very famous person." Carlos turned red and pooh-poohed the idea.

"Yeah, famous for being infamous!" he said, "and silly!"

Carlos and I went way back to Laurel Canyon. He, Miss Lucy, Miss Mercy, Obie, and I, were somewhat of a gang on that boulevard called Sunset. "The Gang of Five." We were the craziest of the crazed and dressed appropriately to our reputations.

We always hung out together and were a scene unto ourselves. We were so outrageous that we always got into the Whiskey A Go-Go for free just for the background color we provided. And we always got invited to the parties of the rich and famous so their guests would have something whimsical to look at. We were so notorious, that sometimes we were invited on stage during a concert. So notorious, a promoter once asked if we'd be interested in forming a group of our own.

But we refused. We weren't interested in fame or fortune. Celebrity impressed none of us, and we wanted nothing to do with it. We just wanted to party, take psychedelics and trip out. Miss Mercy and Miss Lucy were the first lesbians I had ever met. Obie was gay. And I was always straddling the fence. But Carlos was straight. Nevertheless, there were times we three guys all ended up in a bed together and snuggled like true brothers, waiting to come down off a trip. Carlos was the youngest of us, only a teen. We always called him cutie-pie because he was just so damned cute. That was undeniable. And the sweetest guy you ever did meet.

The memories came flooding back. Now here he was standing next to me. Not crazy. Not outrageous. Not even stoned! But as cute as ever.

"What in hell are you doing here?" I asked.

"I've been here almost a year now. I was in India for two. I'll probably stay until trekking season, and maybe then head back to the States."

Shit! Another reason to stay here!

Jon and Rose must have read my mind because they both looked as if they were about to lose something.

Jon interrupted our reunion. "Carlos tells me he is a disciple of Neem Karoli Baba, Ram Dass' guru. And he's spent a lot of time with Ram Dass." Jon seemed to regard Carlos as someone special, but Carlos regarded himself otherwise. I could tell from his eyes, he was a true disciple of the Dharma, a most beautiful disciple at that.

The three of us had dinner together, Jon quizzing Carlos incessantly, barely giving the poor guy time to eat his food. But Carlos did not doubt Jon's unquenchable thirst for a teacher, someone before whom he could throw himself down in dunda pranam.

Jon suggested that meeting Carlos was a sign. That maybe he and Rose were meant to be disciples of Baba's as well.

"That may be," said Carlos, "but I never sought him out. It just happened."

"But can you introduce us to Neem Karoli Baba?" Jon said hopefully, pleadingly.

"I can and I would, but he and Ram Dass are in the States."

Jon was freaking out. So close yet so far. "You can't imagine what we've been through!"

"Yes, I can," Carlos said. "And I can give you Ram Dass' address in Boston. Use the name Vineeta. He knows me by that name. Remember, Jon, and I don't mean to be trite or a smart ass or anything like that, but the teacher finds you, not the other way around."

Jon looked despondent. "You'll still give me Ram Dass's address, though?"

"Yes, of course," Carlos said, and then and there pulled out a little book, thumbed through it, and wrote the address on a napkin. Jon folded it up so very carefully, as if it contained the sacred ash that had flowed from Sai Baba's palm.

"I must go now," he said looking at a clock on the wall. "Jon, Rose, a wonderful meeting. Namaste." Then he turned to me. "Giacco, I hope to see you again soon. Will you be staying in Kathmandu for a while?"

I looked at Jon and Rosie for some hint as to what my answer would be. "Carlos, I truly do not have a clue!"

"If it's meant to be, I'll see you again," he said. We all stood up and he hugged each of us. When it was my turn, he held me tightly with his eyes closed. "What a long, strange trip it's been!" he laughed in my ear. And then he left through the side door.

I never heard from nor saw Carlos ever again.

CHAPTER 58
April 1972

When we returned to our little hut, Jon made a small fire in the pit, Rosy handing him small sticks that he arranged carefully like a good Boy Scout. They were whispering to each other. There was an edginess to the murmuring.

Jon looked at me across the room, sitting on my mat, writing in my little book. "Chazan," Jon said, "Rose and I are ready to move on."

I looked at Rosie who merely shrugged her shoulders as if too tired to debate this any longer with Jon. I wished secretly that she were more assertive about what she wanted to do. But she acquiesced to Jon's wishes.

"But Jon," I protested, "We've only been here two weeks! Don't you like it here? Don't you want to stay until we can do some trekking? Is Kathmandu all we are going to see of Nepal?"

"I've had it!" Jon replied definitively. "Rose and I are flying to Tel Aviv to see my buddy Dan and his wife Laura."

"Tel Aviv!" I exclaimed. "That's it? That's the end of our trip!"

"Chazan," Rosie said sympathetically, "You have three good reasons to stay here. If that's what you want to do, do it!"

"And after Tel Aviv? What?" I asked Jon a bit caustically.

"Well after a visit with Dan and Laura, I guess back to New York. There's nothing left for us here. We're ready to call it quits!"

"Jon," I argued, "We have tickets around the world. We would be wasting them to call it quits! When are we ever going to get another opportunity like this?"

"Rosie said you can stay here!" Jon sharply replied. "Do whatever you want, but I am through!"

Our entire trip from the time we left Hawaii flashed before me like a life flashing through a person's mind on his deathbed. I had to be careful. I knew as much as I tried to be in the Here and Now, that I was often guilty of thoughts that included "should have," "would have," "could have," and "if only." I was prone to entertaining my mind with fantasies I thought might come true but were unlikely to happen. Still, I always tried to create a physical and emotional environment which left a window open for that rare breeze of opportunity. The truth is, in my mind I was stalling.

What were the chances that Jerry, Linda, the baby, and I could actually live together for any length of time in the total harmony I imagined? What were the chances that the affection they showered upon me would turn into something sexual, as it had with Debra and Peter? If it didn't, would I be satisfied to sublimate my desires and transform them into the asceticism that Jerry seemed so easily to maintain?

And Carlos. Once I was on my own, alone, could I count on him to be the sidekick I wanted him to be? Would he introduce me to experiences more exciting and fulfilling than those I had already had? Or at least equal to them? Or would he disappear into some remote monastery for which I didn't feel ready? In the absence of Carlos, how about all the beautiful hippies, so stoned, so susceptible to adventures of the heart. Would they be susceptible to mine?

I had always maintained that everyone was interchangeable. That you always gravitated to those who could fulfill your needs. Was I ready to take the chance that what I maintained in my mind could become reality?

I loved Jon and Rosie more than the Himalayas, more than Kathmandu. I knew the very best of Jon. And on this trip, I had seen the worst of him, too. As for Rosie, my love for her never wavered. She was like my twin. I thought of Sabino Canyon and our mystical experiences on peyote. I thought of all the adventures we had had together, Jon's constant jokes that kept me in hysterics, and the incredible inner warmth that passed from Rose to me every time she hugged me.

I was so confused. My head was swarming with options. I had to make a decision fast!

"OK," I said. "How about this?" Jon and Rose listened attentively. "We go to Tel Aviv to see your friends. But only if you agree to travel through Europe at a fairly relaxed pace. No rushing around. Just for a couple of months. It'll be spring and there's so much to see. Sure, it won't be gurus, temples, and shrines, but it's Europe! The Greek islands, the Costa Brava, Paris, Berlin, Amsterdam! It's the West! It'll be fun, clean, good food, sun, and more beaches. It'll be...."

Jon interrupted me. "Are you through with your monologue?"

"Yes," I replied. "You get the drift, don't you?"

"OK, Chazan. You win. If we take our time touring Europe, will you stay with us?"

I hadn't expected this response. I had expected Jon to stick to his plan of flying from Tel Aviv back to New York. I knew he wasn't giving up on the guru quest. He just wanted to get back to New England to seek out Ram Dass. I was really in a quandary now, really had dug myself into a hole that would be hard to crawl out of.

"OK," I said. "We started this together and we'll finish it together!"

Rosie jumped up and gave me a big hug. "Oh Chazan! I love you so much!"

Jon made the arrangements as usual. We gave away our jeans and flannel shirts. We threw away what was left of our hash because we knew that no other country would be as mellow, and we didn't want to take the chance on getting busted when we went through India on our way to Israel. Rose had a strange Mona Lisa smile on her face. We wouldn't find out until we had gone through Israeli customs that Rose had hidden an ounce of black temple hash in her hair! We walked the short distance to town, flagged down a taxi, and hopped in.

"The airport," Jon told the driver.

"Wait!" I said. "Jon, please can't we stop by Jerry and Linda's place, just for a sec? I really want to say goodbye."

Jon gave in. I leaned over the front seat and gave directions to the ganja shop over which Jerry and Linda lived. They were just coming down the stairs as we pulled up.

"What's this?" a startled Jerry asked.

I got out of the cab. "We're off. We're leaving. But I'll see you in San Francisco, OK? Promise?"

"What about us, Giacco? We said you could stay with us. Don't you want to stay with us?" Linda asked plaintively.

"This is the right thing for me to do," I said, trying to convince myself that it was. "I just stopped by because I didn't want to leave without seeing you one more time. I love both of you so much and I'm going to miss you more than I can say. And I hope you take care of each other. That baby is going to be one of the most special babies in the world. And I promise to be the best uncle you ever saw when we're back to San Francisco. I promise!"

I got back in the taxi. Jon and Rosie could barely look at Jerry and Linda and offered a weak, "It was great to meet you guys, really. Take care. We're bound to run into you again somewhere on this planet!"

The taxi slowly made its way through the now crowded street. Jerry and Linda walked alongside the taxi, hands on mine on the rolled down window.

"Are you sure you're doing the right thing, Giacco?" Jerry asked, hoping I'd change my mind.

Linda added, "Please Giacco. Think about it. It's not too late. You can just get out now. You can meet up with Jon and Rose later."

The taxi had turned onto the main drag and traffic flowed more easily and picked up a little speed. Linda couldn't keep up and fell behind, puffing hard. Jerry clung to my hand running faster and faster alongside the car.

"Please Giacco! You don't know what you're doing! You have a place to stay with us. You don't know what you're missing!"

I looked up at Jerry, sweat pouring down his bald head and dripping onto his chest. "You're right, Jer, I don't know what I'm doing. I'm not doing *It*. *It's* doing me!"

The taxi was going faster now, and Jerry lost his grip on the door but was still running behind. I stuck my head out the window and looked at him hard. I tried to turn all I was feeling into a facial expression. I was trying to beseech him without using words to forgive me, to try to understand.

I looked through the rear window. Jerry just stood there stunned. I could still see Linda way off in the distance. I waved spastically to them, tears now streaming down my face. I kept waving until the taxi took a turn and they were out of sight. I turned around and faced forward.

Jon and Rose were silent, staring ahead, not knowing what to say and unwilling to face me.

Oh my god, what have I done? You are an asshole, Giacco! This is a big mistake!

But the die was cast. The taxi was going too fast now to jump out and I just couldn't bring myself to scream, "Stop! Let me out!" The best I could do was try to conjure up the three of us relaxing on the south coast of Crete, laughing together again as we ate souvlaki and drank ouzo.

I silently bade more farewells to Linda and Jerry and Carlos and Nepal and the Himalayas and all the people I would have fallen in love with and all the rhapsodic scenery I would have trekked through. I was unable to stop the inertia of my decision.

In a trance, seeming to have no control over my own destiny, I joined Jon and Rose on the stairs to the Indian Airlines plane that would fly us in their usual bucking-bronco style to Bombay. From there, a red-eye TWA flight whisked us out of the subcontinent in the most wonderfully boring American fashion to Tel Aviv.

CHAPTER 59
April 1972

We arrived early the next morning. Jon called Dan and Laura. While we waited for them to pick us up, I changed into my clean pajama whites, trying to look as respectable as possible.

When they arrived, hugs went all around, big bear hugs between Jon and Dan, gentler ones for Rosie and Laura. For me there were just introductions and handshakes.

Driving through Tel Aviv depressed me. I thought that maybe I was in Queens. The culture shock was probably worse than had I arrived in New York itself.

When we got to their very nice apartment, Fred and Stanley were waiting. Fred, Stanley, and Dan were all old high school chums of Jon's. They were outrageous looking freaks and they all played pro basketball for the Haifa team.

After we settled in, Rose retrieved the temple hash from her hair, and we were very happy she didn't tell us about it until now. What a brazen thing to do! But we were glad she did it. The girls chitchatted and the boys talked baseball, football and of course, basketball. And though the temple hash is supposed to put "wings on prayer," it put wings on sports, sports, and more sports. The testosterone level in the room was ceiling high and the guys were trying to outdo each other in the macho department. No one was more macho than Jon. The conversations were insipid as far as I was concerned, not being a sportsman, and yes, they were fine "brothers and sisters," but what a waste of hash!

If it weren't sports, they talked about, it was reliving their high school days, a shared past which naturally excluded me. Everything beautiful, aesthetic, and spiritual that Jon, Rose, and I had shared, suddenly seemed to disappear. The constantly blasting stereo playing hard rock music only exacerbated the situation.

Though everyone's energy level seemed to be high, we were overly tired from our traveling marathon. Instead of resting as we should have done, Dan insisted we all go to the Tel Aviv country club. There we could have a swim and take a sauna. Rosie and I were not thrilled with the idea, but we forced ourselves to be social and accompanied them. Maybe it was the hash that was making me feel weak. Maybe it was jumping forth and back between the cold water of the swimming pool and the dry heat of the sauna. It was too much of a shock to my body's barely resistant immune system. I fell ill.

We went back to the apartment and Laura, a very sweet woman, put me to bed. I had a high fever and constantly coughed and hacked until I thought my ribs would break. It was pneumonia. I remained in bed for the next few days, while Jon, Rose, Dan, and Laura went to basketball games and hit the bars. The boys guzzled beer while the girls sipped mixed drinks. I was happy with my bedside orange juice.

One day, Dan and Laura were out doing chores and the three of us were left alone in the apartment, me in a half-sleep, the other half trying to shut out the blaring stereo. Jon's vibes had been getting heavier and weirder by the minute. He was reaching a breaking point.

Through the pounding of the bass, I could make out the conversation they were having.

"There's nothing left Rose! Nothing! I just have no tolerance left for any cultures other than American!"

"I've had it with you, Jon!" Rosie said in hardly a whisper. "Greece will be great. And once we're in the north, it will practically *be* the States!"

"There is nothing left Rose!" Jon repeated more sternly. "If you don't want to come you can go back to Jaffna and find your *Australian* John!"

I did my best to keep my eyes three-quarters closed and my breath gurglingly steady and deep. Rosie looked over at me and then back at Jon. Her voice was truly a stage whisper now, but angry.

"How many times have I told you it was a meaningless fling? You were wandering around Jaffna, disinterested in Guaribala. John and I were totally swept up by Guaribala! We went into John's hut to talk and got stoned. We were on a mutual high from Guaribala… and the hash. One thing led to another. It just happened. How many times do I have to say I'm sorry?"

"If it was so meaningless, then why did you take his address?"

"Because I wanted to, Jon, I wanted to! I admit it! John was a beautiful man. He was centered. I was attracted to him. You were acting like a jerk, asking Guaribala all those questions. You tried to discredit him with the vast knowledge you're always so anxious for others to see! Do you want me to rip up his address? Is that what you want? Sometimes I think you aren't as jealous of John as you are of Guaribala! Because he liked me better!" Jon's face contorted into a silent "ouch!"

"That's ridiculous, Rose! Wasn't it me who came back to Colombo all 'summu iru' and 'never mind, no matter?"

"Words, all words! Rosie lashed back. "You are so good at words and so bad at living them!" Jon was stung. "Never mind, no matter," Rosie continued. "Never mind!" she emphasized. "And that's where you are all the time. In your mind! It's fucking you up! I'm gonna rip up John's address right now, you bastard. Because it's *so* fucking important to you, this little scrap of paper. He is just a friend. A ship passing in the night!"

Rosie reached for her bag and started rummaging through it.

"That's it, Rose. Rummage! Rip it up! Have you written him yet telling him how wonderful it was to feel his hands on your body? Did you give him your address?"

"Jon, look at me. Am I in Jaffna, or am I here next to you? So what if we had sex? What the fuck. So what? Big deal. As if you didn't stick it in a few pussies during the last couple of years."

"That was in the past, damn it! Why do you always bring that up? We had a deal! We made a promise! You broke it practically under my nose!"

"If I didn't love you, would I have put up with all your hop-scotching around India? Dragging us all over the place? Never asking me or Giacco if there were someplace *we* wanted to go. No, never! The great leader, our great teacher! We followed you wherever *you* wanted to go. Did it ever occur to you that maybe Giacco or me would've had better luck just going with the flow, and you following *us* for a change? Letting things just happen, instead of always running after a hunch? Damn, you are stubborn!"

"Don't you understand Rose? Every time we made love, every time you called 'Jon' out loud while we were doing it, I never knew if it was me or your *Aussie* John you were thinking of!"

"Oh, that's ridiculous Jon!" Rosie said, pacing forth and back.

Now it all made sense to me, these wild fluctuations in Jon's moods. The time he encouraged me to go off with Peter and Debra, saying I wasn't "ready" and that he and Rose needed some time alone."

Oh sure, he put Rosie's indiscretion aside when he was in the presence of a teacher or seeking out that guru just across the next river. But in between times, he could be incorrigible.

His jealousy blinded him and almost out of spite, he desired *not* to be here now! Rosie and I had been blinded by our desire to regard Jon as our "secret" teacher. We were too timid to stand up to him. But what Jon said next made me sit up in the bed.

"Look, Rose! Tomorrow or the day after, I am flying back to New York. If you want to come with me, cool. If not, that's cool, too."

They were startled when I yelled, "May I put in my three cents?"

They both shut up and stared at me, half-contrite, half-embarrassed.

"I've had it, too! I've had it with the both of you! First of all, I thought we were best friends! I thought you loved me like a brother! Yet neither one of you bothered to confide in me. Neither one of you explained why Jon was acting like a manic-depressive so often. Some best friend I am!"

"We didn't want to ruin your trip!" Jon fired back. "And besides, I thought Rose and I could figure this out by now."

"Still no reason to exclude me! I thought we always shared our innermost feelings with each other!"

"Chazan," Rosie said sweetly, "You *are* our best friend. We lorf you so much." Rosie came over to the bed and gave me a big hug, her tears wetting my face.

"The two of you," Jon said caustically, "Always in cahoots! The twins! Reading each other's minds behind my back!"

"What?" I yelled at Jon. "Now you're turning into a paranoid schizo case! Are you listening to yourself?"

"Chazan, I love you too, believe it or not. I love you so much! But I'm going back to New York and if you or Rose don't want to come along, that's fine! But I'm outta here!"

"Jon," I reminded him, "You promised when we left Kathmandu we'd go to Europe. Chill out in Greece, Spain, wherever. If I knew you were going to just pick up and leave for New York, I would've stayed with Jerry and Linda. I loved Nepal. I could've stayed there. I would've stayed there! And now it's too late. Now I can't backtrack. Thanks a lot!"

"Hey Chazan! It was me who bought the tickets! Without me, you would've never seen anything!"

"Damn you Jon! I knew you would play that card! In your not-so-subtle way, you've been playing that card all along!"

Rosie chimed in. "And where the fuck do you get the notion that *you* bought the tickets?

It was *our* farm. Ours! With you it's always 'I.' It's never 'we!'"

Jon got quiet. He just shook his head. "This is too tiring for me. I am just tired. Tired of everything. We're leaving as soon as possible. Chazan, start packing your bag."

"Damn!" I yelled. "Man, after all this, you're still assuming you're in control. Well now, *I've* had it! This is it! I'm staying! I'm going to Europe. I'm gonna take my sweet time, too! And I'm gonna have fun!"

Rose and Jon were quiet, sullen. We could barely look at each other. "Some hippies we turned out to be!" I said sadly.

Just then, Laura and Dan walked in. The three of us tried to look natural, as if nothing had happened. It didn't work.

"What's going on?" asked Laura. "Giacco, how are you feeling?"

Jon told Dan and Laura about leaving for New York. "I'm going back," he said. "I don't know about Rose and Giacco."

"But Jon," Dan said, "all you've seen of Israel is a country club and a basketball court!"

"I want to go home, too," said Rosie putting a hand on Jon's shoulder. But I think Giacco wants to stay. Can he stay with you until he's better?"

"Of course!" Laura replied. She looked at me, lying prone again, exhausted from the arguments and words which had just minutes before been flying around the room, crashing into each other. "You can stay as long as you like, Giacco. Have you been drinking lots of liquids?" she asked with concern as she put her hand on my forehead. She didn't wait for an answer, went to the fridge, poured me a glass of juice, and grabbed a bottle of water.

"Thanks," said Jon, "for looking after Giacco. He's a very special guy to us."

"We know that Jon," said Dan. We'd take care of him just like we'd take care of you or Rose."

Jon and Rose left late the next afternoon. I didn't go to the airport with them. But before they left, I told them how much I really loved them, and that all this bullshit between us was just that, bullshit. Nothing could separate us. We were inextricably bound to one another by a deep love.

Jon was crying when he hugged me goodbye. Rosie leaned over my bed, and with tears in her eyes as well, said softly, "Remember Chazan, we love you immensely. We always will. No matter what!"

And while I was drifting off into another one of my deliria, they were taking off on a non-stop El Al flight to New York.

Another four days in bed. Dan and Laura took great care of me. I was so grateful for their kindness that I couldn't bring myself to ask Dan to stop playing his music so loudly, especially when his friends came over to drink beer and watch sports, which was every day.

As soon as I could walk without getting weak, and breathe without hacking my lungs up, I thanked them for all they had done, said goodbye, and split.

CHAPTER 60

April 1972

I was alone on the top of a mountain overlooking Ein Gedi, a kibbutz on the Dead Sea. Naked, I sat in the crevice of a smooth rock in the middle of a stream that formed clear pools as it snaked down the narrow valley to the desert below. King David used to hang out here when he was hiding from the government. The series of falls that flowed from one pool into the next were named after him.

I could have very well been in Sabino Canyon, and if King David were as high on peyote as we were, his head would have been in a pretty good space. I thought of all the beautiful freaks who have likewise hidden themselves from the blasphemies of the world. They usually chose to hide in similarly remote and naturally beautiful settings. I thought of Florence back in Hawaii telling Jon and Rose that they would part for a long time before coming together again, and that I would not be part of their plan. Was it serendipity, a self-fulfilling prophecy, or truly an ability to see into the future? Whatever it was, it seemed to be unfolding just as she had predicted.

It was very peaceful and incredibly hot. It was just what I needed to quiet the turmoil I had been through the past few weeks. I took one last splash under the waterfall and retraced my steps back to the kibbutz.

When I left Dan and Laura's I was still a bit under the weather, my lungs were congested but starting to break up. I guess I wasn't completely over my pneumonia. Laura had washed my pajama whites; I had washed my hair and even used conditioner on it. For a brief moment, I thought maybe I should cut it. But fortunately, *Déjà Vu was* playing, and David Crosby was belting out "Almost Cut My Hair," which was all I had to hear. I pulled my waist-length hair back and tied it tight in a ponytail. I couldn't have looked better groomed!

I walked confidently into the commotion of Tel Aviv's busy downtown district. It was pretty nice for a big city. I noticed a policeman at one intersection who was slightly over-armed for my taste, since he was just a walk-don't-walk kind of cop.

Lots of open-air cafes added some color to the bases of high-rise office buildings and hotels, all of them packed with people having lunch or coffee and talking loudly. Only thing was they all seemed to have pneumonia, too. Their combined conversations sounded like everyone was hacking and coughing up phlegm. Hebrew was not my favorite language.

I was crossing at a narrow side street. A group of teenagers crossed from the opposite side. I passed them, but they stopped midway and turned around. Before I knew it, I was surrounded. There were five or six of them. All trying to act like thugs. They started pushing me forth and back yelling at me in Hebrew, their pronunciation so good, every word ended in a spit. One or two delivered their lines with such guttural gusto I thought they'd throw up on me.

Finally, one of them, their leader I presumed, grabbed me by the collar. He asked me a question in what I guessed was broken Arabic. He probably thought I spoke it because I looked like a Palestinian. I shook my head. Then in a thick accent, he asked in English, "You a Jew?"

"No, I'm not Jewish," I said, trying not to sound ruffled.

"Then go back to your side and stay there!" he screamed, pushing me roughly to the other side of the circle where his buddy caught me by my neck. His hand slid under my chain and yanked it pulling my face into his.

"What's this?" he asked, holding my Ganesh in his hand.

"It's a souvenir from India," I explained, "That's where I just came from." My explanation didn't help diffuse the situation. I could feel the tension escalating, the machismo spreading like a contagious disease. Once they had it in their minds to hassle me, they couldn't stop themselves. They were sick with the hate bug.

The kid pushed me back into the circle, which tightened around me. One was pulling at my hair, another at my cloth bag. One was trying to pull down my pants, while the other kid was trying to rip Ganesh from my neck, but I said, "No fuckin' way, man!" and elbowed him in the face.

That's when it got fisty. And they got in some pretty good blows before that traffic cop came over and busted it up. He was totally unsympathetic, merely doing his job, "keeping the peace." Fact is I saw him out of the corner of my eye when he first noticed there was a fracas, and he sure took his sweet time walking over to us.

"You a Jew?" were the first words out of the cop's mouth.

"Jesus Christ!" I exploded. "What's with all this 'Jew' stuff? I'm a Catholic Buddhist American!" I reached into my bag and pulled out my passport.

"How long you plan to stay here in Israel?" he asked, looking over my passport and all the many stamps it had in it.

"I'm not sure, but probably not long," I replied.

"You from United States, but Palestinian, correct." He stated it rather than asked it, but I set him straight.

"With a name like Giordano? Palestinian? I am Sicilian! Italian!"

The policeman glared at me. "You look Arab! Your mother, she is Arab!"

I remained silent. Ganesh told me to shut up.

"So go already then," the cop ordered. "And you, too," he said, looking at the teens.

As I turned to leave, he shouted, "And get some real pants and cut your hair!" He added something else in Hebrew which just allowed him to return to his normal phlegmatic self.

OK. Now what? That was not a good sign. Now I noticed both men and women with machine guns everywhere. What a militaristic little town this was! Soldiers on every other corner. Military vehicles scattered among the traffic. I found my way to the terminal where I could get a bus to Jerusalem. I was totally alone in a country I didn't want to be in, without the company of Jon and Rose, Jerry and Linda, or Debra and Peter. Alone, but defiantly determined to have the "fun" I threatened Jon I would have, the bastard! Damn him!

I boarded the bus. I figured Jerusalem was a major tourist city. I'd blend in more. The bus was crowded with mostly Israelis but there were a few Palestinians as well, mostly older women and a few young children. I could tell the Palestinian women by the shawls they wore over their heads and their children were not as nicely dressed as the Israeli kids.

The only empty seat I could find was next to a young female soldier, a machine gun across her lap, and rounds of ammo across her chest. She was pretty. But she didn't smile back, when I said, "Shalom."

She shuffled over a bit, raised her gun, and I sat down. She looked me up and down carefully and replaced the gun in her lap, the barrel directly facing my stomach. I prayed her safety was on as we rode toward Jerusalem. I tried to make small talk with her, but she ignored me completely, keeping her finger near the trigger. I shut up.

I was very happy to get off the bus and happy to find that Jerusalem seemed like a very interesting town. I did a quick "sightseeing" thing just to say I'd been at all the important places but found the markets more to my liking. Wherever I went, I endured harangues and ugly stare-downs. It was not pleasant. But as I got lost in the small alleys and side streets, as the buildings became less well kept, and as the clothes became more like my own, if not white, at least baggy and more ragged, the people became friendlier.

I now found myself greeting merchants and shoppers with "salaam alaikum" and hearing "alaikum salaam" in return, with curious smiles instead of belligerent glares. A few were actually friendly and though maybe just wanting to make a sale or something, at least they displayed some interest and warmth. I was much more at home among the Palestinians. I guessed that maybe being poor and harassed creates some sort of bond.

But what I really wanted was to float in the Dead Sea and get into the countryside, so I took a bus that dropped me off in Ein Gedi.

CHAPTER 61
April 1972

I thought Ein Gedi was a resort town. There was nothing there. There was, however, the Dead Sea right across the street from where the bus let me out. I walked up the beach for a short distance, but didn't see a soul anywhere, so I just stopped, stripped, and dove in. I felt like the world's best swimmer. Oh, how effortlessly my Australian crawl made headway through the waveless sea. The foam from the salt and minerals floated like icebergs not too far away.

I rolled over on my back and just floated there, letting the sun return my skin to the dark brown it was before being cooped up in an apartment for days. I tried holding my breath and floating on my stomach to give my back an equal opportunity, but the water was so salty, it stung my eyes even though they were tightly shut and I had to spit out the taste it left on my lips.

The Dead Sea was so salty, that when I got out to dry, I was caked in it. My skin itched and stung a bit and it longed for fresh water. I looked around and from the beach, I could look up and down the range of ancient mountains.

On the lower slopes near me, there were well-organized fields of green. I started walking toward them in search of a spigot. When I reached the green and looked beyond, my eyes opened wide. There were row upon row of all kinds of vegetables. There were orchards, all very tidy; mainly of figs and olives and apricots. I could see people in the distance working in the gardens. I walked toward them. As I got closer, I saw that many of them were freaks, or at least there were lots of ponytails, which was always a good sign! I approached a group of about nine or 10 who were very conscientiously weeding rows of lettuce. They were all smiles and very friendly. Most of them were Americans but there were other nationalities as well. Except for one couple from Sweden, all were Jewish. This was the kibbutz at Ein Gedi and what a funky, mellow kibbutz it was. It was really just a well-organized commune, ala Friends of Perfection in San Francisco, with lots of rules and an ideology that all bought into.

It was the kind of farm I envisioned for Hunga Dunga, with the exception that I wanted to preserve the anarchy that made Hunga Dunga so special. Since more than half of Hunga Dunga came from Jewish backgrounds, and since I had grown up with many kids from Jewish families back in New Jersey, and since I had lived in Manhattan, I felt right at home. This made me even angrier for the way I had been treated in Tel Aviv and parts of Jerusalem. Those places were *meshugenah*! But these people seemed as friendly and positive as utopian communists.

Two of them, Mark and Eileen, introduced themselves and then their friends. I told them enough about me to explain my appearance, though that was unnecessary because they really *were* all hippies and couldn't care less. They did cling to their Jewish roots, to experience a kibbutz and do their part helping out, and to reaffirm their ancestry. The difference was they were just Jewish. Not Zionist. And that made all the difference in the world. They considered their Judaism to be a religion first and foremost, not a nation, though Eileen told me that this attitude was anathema at some kibbutzim.

The Swedish couple was hanging out trading work for room and board on their extended journey around the world. All of them were interested in my adventures in South Asia and displayed an academic, if not genuinely spiritual interest, in the many paths there were to God.

Mark and Eileen laughed and apologized when they saw me scratching and fidgeting in discomfort from the salt on my skin.

"Yeah, we know!" Mark grinned. "We all find out the hard way. First thing everyone does when they get here is dive into the sea, and then pray for rain to wash off the salt!"

We walked past some chicken coops and a small stable and corral. There were two kid goats inside the fence, precious and loveable as puppies. A donkey wandered over to see if we had any treats. And its foal, outside the fence, came over to check everything out. I guess they figured the baby donkey would not wander off out of sight of its mother. Just beyond the corral was a very nice, but simple building that had rows of dining tables and an industrial kitchen in the back.

Eileen called out, "Sylvia, are you here?"

"Yes, I'm in the back. I'll be right out," answered a young-sounding voice with an Eastern European accent.

"Sylvia is in charge of all visiting guest workers and temporary residents," explained Mark.

I loved it that this farm I liked so much also had a Sylvia, though she didn't spell it with a "P" at the beginning. That made it seem even homier.

Sylvia Malka was one of the most beautiful women I've ever met. She was petite, but athletic, with long, dark-brown hair and wild green eyes. Her skin was a Tahitian brown, though she originally emigrated from Bulgaria. That was it! There was something "gypsy" about her. And I was once again the fence straddler, aroused by her, and falling in lust.

I could tell immediately there was a chemistry between us. We both knew it but put it aside for the time being as best we could. After I explained my situation, she had to explain hers.

"I'm sorry Giacco, but the dorm is completely full, and we have no extra beds. I am responsible for all visitors, their comfort and our comfort, their security, and our security. We seldom allow visitors who just happen to drop by. Usually this is all planned out in advance. You must apply for a position here, even though it's voluntary work like cleaning, cooking, gardening, building, whatever. You just can't show up unannounced!"

As she spoke, she would look at me, and then quickly look away, afraid to meet my gaze.

I told her about how rudely I'd been treated on my trip here, and how it was too late to get a bus back to Jerusalem now, and that I didn't want to go back anyway.

"Can't you make an exception this time? I pleaded.

"I can and I would, but where will I put you? And I have to let the leader of the kibbutz know you are here, and I know him. He will not like it."

Her accent, her voice, her eyes, her movements, all gave me that twinge below the belt that only one out of a couple of hundred women gives me.

She stopped before we got to the main office.

"I've got an idea," she said, "but remember, my job is on the line. I am trusting you."

"No worries," I said happily, knowing she wasn't going to send me back to the city.

We went back to the fields, where she found Mark and Eileen and consulted with them. They nodded in agreement but felt I was totally unprepared for camping out. *If only they knew how many times I had camped out on the ground with just a couple of light blankets!* Mark and Eileen went up to the dorm where visitors stayed.

In the meantime, Sylvia pointed to an outhouse and an outdoor shower behind the stable. As we walked by a large, sturdily built stone fire pit, she pointed to a flat barren spot between two hillocks just above the fire pit and out of sight of the buildings.

"You can camp here. You'll have to fend for yourself and be, what's your word, discreet?"

"That's the word," I said, "and I will be. I promise!"

Eileen and Mark came trudging down the hill. They brought everything I would need. Blankets, a small pot, a blackened frying pan, utensils, a little jar of olive oil, and some rice.

Mark pointed to a spigot where I could tap into fresh, clean water. Eileen gave me a quick tour of the garden, pointing out where different vegetables grew. Sylvia pointed to some fruit trees not far off. Then she looked at me a bit startled.

"Oh, I forgot to ask you the most important question!"

My heart sank. If she were going to ask if I were Jewish, I would scream. *Et tu Brute?*

"I hope you are a vegetarian because Ein Gedi is completely vegetarian."

I laughed. "Perfect. Too perfect."

She sighed in relief. "Now listen, Giacco. You can help yourself to anything in the garden or the orchard, but please take so little no one will suspect, OK?"

"OK!" I said.

"And you can use the fire pit, but keep the fire small and be finished cooking before anyone notices, OK?"

"They'll never know I was here; I swear!"

"Well," she said, "Many of the foreigners already know you are here, but they will be cool." She said "cool" as if there were five "o"s in the word. I laughed.

"Besides, every night, all of them come down here and build a fire and sing and talk and dance. We have so many, and there is so much long hair here, you will fit right in." She laughed.

"Cooool," I said, "Sounds fun!"

When I was alone, I carefully walked through the rows of vegetables and picked out a nice green pepper, a small eggplant and a couple of tomatoes. I found an herb garden and pulled just a few leaves off some thyme and oregano. I took them back to the fire pit and, relying on my extensive knowledge of the Boy Scout Handbook, built a small fire.

I steamed some rice and while it was cooking, poured just a few drops of oil in the frying pan. I sprinkled a few torn leaves of the herbs and watched while the oil bubbled softly, extracting the essence from the leaves. Then I added the vegetables I had sliced, diced, cut, or cubed.

The sun was starting to descend behind the mountain. The Dead Sea glimmered gold and orange. The smell of the sautéing veggies hit my nose and made my stomach growl. I spooned some rice onto a plate and poured the entire contents of the frying pan on top of it. I chowed down. It was delicious!

I made sure there were no signs that anyone had been cooking in the pit. I went up to the spigot to wash the dishes. While I scrubbed the pan, I saw people walking down the hill to the fire pit. Before long, a big fire was blazing and about 50 people had gathered around it. Most of them were orthodox hippies with a passion for life. Some of them were just extremely liberal Jews. And in some ways, that was the same. Guitars appeared, followed by a makeshift drum.

By the time it was dark, they were singing "My Sweet Lord" and "Here Comes the Sun."

There were a few Hebrew folk songs thrown in. People got up and danced, men with men, women with women, men with women, all waving scarves behind them. Many didn't know the traditional steps and others were eager to show them. They caught on quickly and so did the pace. At some point, they became a blur running forth and back in circles, tripping over each other, laughing. It was a happy scene. There was a free-spiritedness within their tradition, and I wondered if that were oxymoronic.

Then it was back to some Dylan, Neil Young, Judy Collins, and a few Country Joe anti-war songs. A guitarist began singing a Joni Mitchell tune. Her songs are difficult to pull off. I was impressed. It was then I noticed Mark and Eileen looking around. They spied me and I waved from my perch on the hill above them. Sitting next to them was Sylvia. Eileen motioned for her to follow and the three of them climbed the hill in my direction.

When they reached me, they pulled up some ground and took a seat. We all looked at each other and smiled. The view from up here and the acoustics were great!

Without thinking twice, Mark pulled out a chillum and packed it tightly. He lit it and, with a few intense puffs, got it going nicely. Then he passed it to Eileen who took a careful toke, knowing it was strong stuff. Eileen passed it to Sylvia.

She was just about to take it, when she thought better of it and said, "Oh, no, I really shouldn't." But she did sniff some of the smoke before passing it to me. I inhaled as much as I could without getting into a coughing fit. Then I reached across and returned the chillum to Mark, who emptied it out and immediately refilled it.

This time when Eileen passed it to Sylvia, she shook her head, but then said, "What the hell," and took a big puff. I was pleasantly surprised. Holding it in, she passed the chillum to me, and I finished off the bowl while she exhaled a perfect stream of smoke.

Now that we were wasted, the gathering below looked more like a pagan ritual to fiery love. Kosher, of course. We noticed a few people walking away from the circle and distancing themselves enough to do just what we had been doing. Getting stoned. It all felt very right. I wondered how the leader of the kibbutz would react if he knew what these diligent workers were doing when day was done!

The crowd began to thin as small groups of people dispersed, most walking back to the dorm, while some couples scattered into the privacy of vegetables, where I'm sure they were going to fertilize the garden.

I could tell Eileen and Mark wanted to do the same, and with a *shalom* and a peace sign, they said good night. Sylvia lingered just a few minutes, asking me if I would be all right and if I had everything I needed, showing great concern. Then reluctantly, or so it seemed, she added a *shalom* of her own and gracefully retreated up the hill to a trail that led to the main complex. She left behind a delicate scent of desire. The aroma aroused mine.

I went back to my campsite in the hollow between the two small berms and laid out one blanket as a ground cloth. The other blankets I wrapped around me. I looked up at the stars briefly and then fell into a sound and secure sleep.

The sun rising over the Dead Sea woke me up. I was a bit startled to see Sylvia kneeling beside me. On a tray in her lap was a bowl of granola and milk, and some orange juice. I sat up, slightly embarrassed. There was still sleep in my eyes, but what a lovely sight she was. She had such a sweet smile on her face.

"Good morning! Here. Have some breakfast. I have to go." That's all she said. That was it. And she disappeared up the hill. That became a routine. Every morning she'd bring me a bowl of cereal before her day began. I'm sure she was getting herself up earlier than usual to make that happen. She was wonderful to me.

I spent my days wandering through the mountains of the Judean desert, discovering exhilarating waterfalls splashing into streams that took the scenic way down to the Dead Sea, which was always in view from these heights. This uncultivated, unirrigated land was full of cacti and other desert plants. It reminded me a little of the Coachella Valley and the Salton Sea. Without the imposition of human engineering, that California valley could not produce the abundance of fine fruits and vegetables it did, and neither would the kibbutz at Ein Gedi.

The farthest south I ventured was Masada, where I gave myself a personal tour of Herod The Great's fortress. From this height, I could see north into the Jordan Valley. It looked so peaceful. Yet, unfortunately, I knew that wasn't the case. I wondered what those "world leaders" were thinking when they decided that plopping a few hundred thousand European Jews in the middle of Arab lands was a good idea. But politics took a back seat to my enjoyment of the landscape.

Every night, the young Yahweh hippies gathered around the bonfire. Every night, Eileen, Mark, Sylvia, and I got stoned at our vantage point above the partying. I mentioned that I thought I'd take a trip to Eilat, which I knew was a popular seaside resort at the southern tip of Israel, but Mark dissuaded me from doing that.

"We were there, Giacco. You won't like it. It's not friendly at all. It's very *unfriendly*!" I took his advice and remained in the congenial embrace of Ein Gedi and its surroundings, but only for a couple more days.

When Sylvia brought me breakfast the next morning, I told her of my plans to leave. She seemed disappointed but put on a stoic face. Several other "guest" workers were also leaving. They were part of a program that gave American Jews the opportunity to experience life on a kibbutz, but their month-long stay was ending. A shuttle bus would take them the next day to Tel Aviv, where they would fly home. Sylvia said there was room on the small bus, and I could probably catch a ride with them, unless I changed my mind and wanted to stay a while longer. Things were working out well, didn't I think? Didn't I want to stay?

I had a hard time coming up with an answer that wouldn't make her feel badly. Yes, Ein Gedi was a special place. In a way it was like an island. And I was getting island fever. Only in Ein Gedi and only because of Sylvia, Mark, and Eileen, did I feel at home. But the communal atmosphere had stirred the feelings I had for my Hunga Dunga. It was time to move on.

That night I lay in my little trench and stared at the stars thinking about Jesus and his buddies who had stared at these same stars long before me, and King David and the Old Testament prophets who had stared at these same stars long before them.

The stars were displaced by the appearance of Sylvia's face looking down at mine. She looked serious, but then curled her lips into a small smile. I started to say something, but she placed a finger against my lips. Without saying a word, she crawled under the blankets next to me and snuggled close. We lay on our sides facing each other, me stroking her hair and falling into those green eyes. She nuzzled her nose against my neck and chin and placed a hand on my shirtless chest.

When her lips brushed mine, I rolled over on top of her and kissed her gently, moving my mouth across hers from side to side and then slowly parting her lips with my tongue. We kissed deeply for a long time. I kissed her forehead, her eyes, her cheeks, and followed the hollow of her neck down to her bare breasts.

I stood on my knees and began to pull her blouse up over her head. She stretched her arms in the air, arching her back a little, and I easily slipped it off and lay it down neatly on the ground. A few helpful wriggles of her hips and her baggy jeans and panties were at her knees. I pulled them off slowly, while caressing her smooth skin from her pelvis to her feet.

Then I loosened the waist of my pants, which fell to form ruffles around my knees. Lifting one leg at a time, I reached behind me and pulled them off, kicking them into a puddle of cloth.

I stared down at her, the half-moon and stars bathing her body in a wondrous light. I ran my hands gently up her legs and her inner thighs, feeling her skin tremble beneath my fingertips. She reached up for me, but I gently pushed her down and positioned her hands above her head letting her know that I wanted to relish her… *slowly*.

My fingers continued their journey up her stomach and then slowly circled her firm breasts, moving teasingly toward her now stiff nipples. She was delicately squirming and moving her head from side to side. Though I was fully erect, I wanted this to last as long as possible.

I hovered inches above her, my cock quivering, barely touching her stomach. I ran my tongue across her bottom lip, over her chin, then wandered around the valley of her bosom. As my body slid down hers, I felt her nipples brushing the hair on my chest. I grabbed her by the hips and pulled her aromatic crotch into my face. I explored her with my tongue and fingers. It was still a place of some mystery to me, but I was in the mood for discovery, like a spelunker intent on not missing a detail of his descent into a cave.

As I slid back up her body, my cock entered her in slow motion. I felt her pushing back asking me to go deeper and faster, but I was too thrilled by the feel of her to rush. Little by little, I entered with nuanced gyrations. Her body responded with subtle, synchronic twists. She moaned softly.

We paused for a moment, my cock throbbing, my brain telling it to stay in control. We just looked into each other's eyes and enjoyed that moment of oneness. We kissed each other passionately and the writhing, the gyrations, the little thrusts became less subdued. I stayed as still as possible, letting her ride my cock, letting her use me. Then it was too much, and we made love with abandon.

The desert night was cool, but we were sweating from the heat of our bodies. Maybe it was because having sex with women was such a rarity for me that I had such staying power, but I was still iron hard when I felt those unmistakable tremors and stifled screams that let me know she was climaxing. When I was certain her orgasms had subsided, I let myself lose control. It was one of those infrequent, but delicious orgasms, that are totally mindfucking, the kind that drains your whole being.

I fell upon her gently and we rested. We clung to each other tightly, knowing this would be a one-time thing, and an unforgettable farewell. I rolled over on my back and looked up at her while she reached for her clothes and got dressed.

She leaned over and gave me a sweet kiss, stood up and walked away into the dark. Not a single word had been exchanged. Everything was needless to say.

The next morning, she brought me breakfast and coffee. I got up and dressed and ate while she looked at me with smiling eyes. Nothing was said about the night before. But when I put down the empty bowl, she reached into her pocket and pulled out a wallet size photo of herself. On the back were her address and a Hebrew phrase. It was only upon returning home that I bothered to have someone translate it.

It said, "You are a lover of the truth and a lover of kindness. Our relationship is permanent because we are infinite."

I never heard from nor saw Sylvia ever again.

I arrived in Tel Aviv early in the afternoon. Abruptly, Israel returned to its normal arrogant and belligerent self. I felt no need to endure any more of its hostility. I wanted Ein Gedi to be my only memory of this country. Forget your Dome of the Rock, the Haram Al-Sharif, the Wailing Wall, the Church of the Holy Sepulcher. The kibbutz at Ein Gedi was the only holy place I found. I went directly to the airport and as I boarded the plane to Athens, I relegated Israel to the past.

CHAPTER 62
May 1972

As soon as I arrived, I wished I could relegate Athens to the past as well! The reception I received as I walked familiar streets was less than inviting, though not as belligerent as in Tel Aviv.

I loved Greece. Its history. Its ruins. Its hills plastered with houses and buildings all Mediterranean white. Its souvlaki and moussaka. Its swarthy men and thick-browed women. I loved Greece, especially the islands. And Greece had always loved me. So, what was wrong?

Everyone scowled at me, rolled their eyes, shook their heads, or simply stared with disgust as if I were dirt or had a horrible disease. The least offended of them simply ignored me and looked the other way. I couldn't understand how I was offending them. I knew a bit of Greek from two previous extended trips, the last one only eight years before. But everything seemed different now. Before, the air was rare and had that ephemeral mystique for which artists always search. But now the air was heavy with negativity, and it was blowing in my direction. Even my smiling *yia sou*s and *kali spera*s invited no replies except the occasional *a gamisou* or *poustis*, words I didn't understand and that was probably just as well.

As I passed by a bench occupied by four middle-aged men, I felt a hand grab my arm tightly and pull me hard. I spun around and the hand pulled me so close we were looking into each other's eyes, and his weren't friendly. He said something in Greek, his tone harsh. I shook my head. Then he asked in broken English, "You Turk?"

I answered, "No! I am not a Turk! I am American!"

He insisted, "You father, he is Turkey?"

"No!" I said, "I am Sicilian, Italian, Italiano, capisce!"

"You Turkey Sufi," he said insultingly. "Long hair, Sufi hippie Turk!"

I pulled my arm away, already red from his tight hold. "Jesus Christ!" I blurted. "What's with all this Turk stuff?" and walked away.

He yelled, "Turk. *Skata*! *Skata* Turk!" And he and his buddies all laughed. *Skata* was a word I did know, and that was enough for me.

I went in search of my favorite hotel, favorite because it was the cheapest I knew of, and attracted either young travelers or quirky characters. It was still there, looking a bit more beat up than I remembered, but standing. I walked into the small lobby and went up to the desk. The man leaning over a magazine looked up and reluctantly said, "*Kali spera,*" after which he mumbled a few sentences beyond my vocabulary.

I told him I wanted a room for one. He turned around, looked at the keys remaining on their hooks, and turned back. He held up two fingers.

"*Ohi*, just me," I said.

He looked at me in frustration and said a whole bunch of things I couldn't make sense of. After his monologue, I handed over two bucks in American money and he shoved the key across the counter. I said, "*Efharisto*," and turned to leave. He called me, and when I turned around, he gave me the peace sign with unnecessary emphasis, as if he were throwing it across the lobby at my face. Nevertheless, I took it as a good sign and went up to my room.

It was a room. But not much of one. It wasn't very clean, and I checked the sheets on the sagging double bed to see if they had been changed. I couldn't tell, but I didn't find any stains, hairs, or bedbugs. I lay down and the springs of the mattress squeaked, but other than that, it would do.

By now I was famished and walked quickly down the stairs to the very busy streets. People were everywhere, going nowhere, walking around the nearby plaza to see, and be seen. Women walked holding hands, while men on benches went through their obligatory routines of leering and making lewd sounds and gestures. Others gathered at cafes and restaurants. The night was brimming with life. I went from one sidewalk vendor to another, feasting on souvlaki, spanakopita, yiaprakia and finishing off with a big slice of baklava.

I was full. The evening air was a perfect temperature. Life was good. It was already around 10, but the streets just seemed to get even busier. I hung out around the nearby *plaka* for a while but got very bad vibes from the guys hanging out there. I was tired anyway and decided to go back to my room. I took off my clothes, got into the bed with a squeak, and promptly fell asleep.

Two or three hours later, more squeaking woke me up. It wasn't me, however. I lay still and opened one eye to see who was robbing me. There by the light of the neon signs outside the window, I saw a young man sitting on the edge of the bed reaching down to untie his shoelaces.

He'd already removed his shirt, his back was smooth, and his lats winged out as he struggled with his shoes and socks. His biceps and big forearms flexed naturally, with ease and modesty. His hands looked rough, and I could tell he was a man muscled by manual labor.

"*Signomi parakalo*," I said sitting up, "But who the hell are you? I think you are in the wrong room!"

Startled, he turned to me. What a great chest! What a nice face! It was difficult to be rude. He looked to be in his early 20s and grinned widely.

"I speak the English," he said proudly. "This my room. We share, yes?"

"We share no!" I answered. He looked confused and reached for his key and looked at the number on it.

"Yes," he said again, "we share. Number nine, no?"

"Number nine, yes," I said, "but no share."

"A room for two," he said. "Save money! You ask man downstairs."

Then it hit me. That peace sign the clerk flashed at me was not a peace sign at all. He was trying to tell me that this was a room for two people. Moreover, as I knew from my previous trip here, it wasn't all that uncommon, especially among the poorer travelers, to have to spend a whole night in a double bed with a stranger. The only thing you knew you both had in common was poverty.

I relaxed when I understood what was going on. But I tensed up again when he stood up and took off his pants. The rest of him was as nice to look at as what I had already admired. How would I get any sleep with that next to me?

He said his name was Kostas. I told him mine. Though I was tired, he was all too ready for conversation. He got under the covers and we both sat up leaning against the headboard, pillows propped behind our backs.

"Giacco, you are hippie?" he asked.

"I have long hair, yes." I replied. "I am just a guy with long hair."

"That's what I say, you are hippie."

I didn't argue. We moved on to other things. My trip through South Asia; life in San Francisco with Hunga Dunga. He had no stories at all, except about his family and his home. I found that sad. He had just turned 20 and was from the island of Samos. This was his first trip to the big city. I only believed he had never left his island when I saw the excitement in his eyes, like a junior-high student on his first field trip, eager with desire for an adventure to remember.

He had studied English in school for six years but had never once had a chance to use it outside of the classroom. I could see him struggling to find words, but he found enough for us to understand each other.

He lived with his family, who owned a small farm. They grew tobacco and grapes. He was the youngest of three children, but when his two older brothers became fishermen, he had to quit high school to help his parents, who were already old. He did most of the work on the farm. He had never left the island. Now they had allowed him a weekend for himself. It was a birthday present.

"Well, then, happy birthday!" I said.

"Efharisto!" he said smiling. "Giacco," he continued, "you, you," he paused searching for the word and then walked his fingers across the bedspread… alone?"

"Walked?" I tried to fill in the blank.

"Ohi!" he shook his head.

"Ran? Fingers? Blanket? Travel?"

"Yes!" Kostas laughed. "Travel! Oh, my English is so bad!"

"Hey, it's a lot better than my Greek!" I said, laughing back.

"Giacco, you travel alone?" he finished the original sentence.

"Yes, Kostas, I travel alone."

He touched my chest with his finger, then his own. "You, me, good friends, yes? We see city you and me, yes?"

"Sure," I said, though I really didn't know how long I wanted to be in Athens. "Tomorrow, you and me," I said, this time me doing the chest pointing. "We see the city together."

"*Entaksi*! OK!" And he slid down the pillows, rearranged them under his head and pulled the blanket up to his chest. I did the same.

"Now we sleep, yes?" Kostas asked or rather said.

"Yes, I am tired. We sleep now. Tomorrow, we see the city."

"Good night my new friend."

"*Kali nichta*, Kostas," I said, but thinking, "It just doesn't get much better than this."

I was almost asleep when I felt a slightly bristled cheek against my shoulder, a restless arm across my chest and a leg fall heavily over my mid-section. I turned my head and peeked at Kostas. He was snoring loudly. I was hoping he was faking it, but no, he was sound asleep.

I tried to adjust his leg so it wasn't right on top of my hardening cock but figured if he were that sound asleep it didn't matter. I wasn't about to try anything that would make him change his mind that, "You, me, good friends, yes?" So I simply lay there as still as I could, enjoying the weight of his leg on me and the smell of his body.

I woke up before he did. He had not moved. The only thing that was different was a hard appendage pressed through his briefs against my hip. The damned Greeks! Such horny bastards! Even though Kostas was a grown man, his insular life seemed to give him the naiveté of a teenager. An innocence about him disarmed me. I would have loved to be his mentor, but I had to give him the benefit of the doubt that he only had a normal early-morning hard-on, and I tried to ignore it.

When the room filled with light, he stirred and rolled over, his head in the crook of my elbow and his legs pushing the covers below his knees. He stretched his entire body, an arm hitting me in the face. I took the bruise gladly. I studied him scrupulously with my eyes. He was classic. He could have been pried off an ancient Greek frieze depicting a warrior or athlete and brought to life. He was a work of art. I closed my eyes and tried to memorize him.

CHAPTER 63

May 1972

"Giacco, Giacco," he said gently pushing me. "Wake up! It is late!"

I opened my eyes acting as if I were trying to get my bearings. I looked up at Kostas and smiled. We took turns taking a dump and a shower in the bathroom down the hall, only wearing towels wrapped around us. I went first. When he came back, he looked at me curiously wearing my pajama whites. He didn't know what to make of them.

I told him that's what I wore a lot in India, but to Kostas that seemed no good reason for my wearing them here. He shrugged it off after a few minutes. We went outside in search of breakfast, and after some thick slices of bread with jam and strong Greek coffee, we headed off to see the sights, using the wrinkled tourist guide that Kostas pulled from his back pocket.

We spent most of the day wandering around the Acropolis and the Plaka. I wished I had some weed or hash on me. These were places where it would be very cool to get stoned. I thought I would literally get stoned when macho men cast me angry looks and threw out words I didn't understand. But Kostas did.

"Giacco, I buy you real pants, OK? I pay, OK?"

"I can afford to buy my own pants," I said defensively. "Why do you want to buy me new pants?"

"You, me, good friends," is all he said. "Good friends wear same pants, OK?"

"But I like these pants," I said.

He just looked down, crinkling his brow trying to formulate a convincing response.

"You, me, very good friends, yes?"

Again, I assured him we were.

"Problem here." He said. "I do not like it when people call my friend names. I will get into fight with them!"

I saw the feisty side of Kostas and was touched. He didn't have to say more. I realized the words men were calling me must've been mighty harsh. Either Kostas was concerned for my well-being, or I was embarrassing him. This was a dilemma for him. But his allegiance to me took precedence over his own feelings. Though I wore my pajama whites and my long hair almost as a badge of courage, Kostas' loyalty impressed me enough not to want to see him get into a fight because of my stubbornness.

We stopped in a store, and he rummaged through a pile of jeans. After unfurling a couple, he held them against my waist and said, "This."

I rolled my eyes and stepped behind a curtain in the back of the store. The jeans were baggy, which I liked, but were too long. I picked out a belt and cinched the waist just tight enough to keep them up. Kostas got on his knees and rolled up the cuffs.

"Very good!" he said happily, turning me around. "Now a shirt!"

I rolled my eyes again, but we picked out a shirt. It wasn't much different from the one

I already had on, collarless and blousy. But it was colorfully striped and made of heavier cotton.

As we went up to the counter, I saw a denim jacket I liked. I tried it on, and it fit perfectly. I threw it on the counter along with the tags from the other stuff we'd picked out.

He reached into his pocket and pulled out some drachmas to pay the shopkeeper. I stood in front of him, folded his hand over his money, and shook my head. I couldn't allow him to pay. What we spent could easily have been a few months' salary for him. For me, though it was an unexpected expense, it was affordable. I reached into my bag and fumbled around for some money. Kostas just shook his head. I paid the shopkeeper and we walked out of the store. Kostas' gait seemed much more confident than before.

"Now we cut your hair," he said, as if I were Eliza Dolittle.

I looked at him grimly. "Now we *don't* cut my hair!" I said. "No hair cutting! The pants and shirt, OK. No hair cutting!"

It was his turn to roll his eyes, but he looked at me and his smile broke into a laugh, and he said, "OK! No cut hair!" And he threw his hands in the air as a gesture of giving up.

We explored the city some more. There were still some isolated jeers, which we both ignored. Strange as it was, this island country boy was all puffed up, hanging out with a real American hippie, a world traveler. In my company, he was modern, almost "cosmopolitan." That put him way above those doing the jeering. Kostas was acting very cool.

We went to a small restaurant and Kostas did all the ordering. Calamari, stuffed grape leaves, lamb kabobs, and glass after glass of retsina. Ugh! I hated retsina. And I do not take well to alcohol. But I did my best to drink each one down.

After dinner, he ordered some ouzo. That suited my taste much better, being familiar since childhood with the anisette mom used to give me when I had a toothache. Now I was getting tipsy. Still, I managed to match him jigger for jigger for the first two. When he ordered a third, I refused, but he didn't refuse himself. After he downed it, he called for the check. I reached into my bag, but he put up a big Greek stink and insisted on paying. I didn't argue.

We walked out of the restaurant, arms around each other's shoulders, laughing and ribbing each other as if we were the oldest of friends. Every once in a while, he reached up and gave my ponytail a yank and I responded by sliding my hand down his back, reaching into his pants and pulling up hard on his underwear, trying to give him a wedgie. We were being very familiar with one another, but that's the Greek way and I'm sure passersby thought nothing of it. The harder he pulled on my hair, the harder I yanked on the white waistband. It became sort of a sport, walking along, just waiting for one or the other to tug hair or pull a wedgie. Like we were two kids playing flinch.

It was getting late, and we decided to make our way back to the hotel. We stopped at an outdoor café and Kostas ordered two glasses of Metaxa. Fortunately, this was another drink my taste buds could handle, but not necessarily my stomach. I was still sipping mine, as Kostas downed his in one gulp and ordered another.

After he gulped that down, we continued home, this time with a definite drunkenness to our strides, weaving, stumbling, and holding each other up. I felt a beautiful, if somewhat giggly, rapport between us.

He fell onto the bed, the springs squeaking madly. He was sprawled out arms to the side, legs spread wide taking up the entire mattress. The retsina, ouzo, and Metaxa had finally hit him hard. I undid the buttons on his shirt and lifted him up by his neck. His head fell backwards but he managed to slur, "You, me, good friends, OK?"

"You, me, very good friends!" I said, and he did his best to assist me getting his arms out of the sleeves. I threw the shirt on a chair. Then I unbuckled his belt and unzipped his pants. He made no protest but wriggled accommodatingly as I grabbed the cuffs of his pants and pulled them off.

I dragged the bed covers from underneath him and threw them over him. I remembered to pull the window shade down so dawn wouldn't wake us up. I shut out the lights, got undressed, and crawled into bed. He made little effort to make room for me. I shoved him over a bit with my hip, but only managed to secure a few more inches of mattress, barely enough to keep from rolling off. The sagging mattress helped prevent that, however, with its tendency to maneuver both of us toward the center. I closed my eyes hoping the liquor would be my opiate and I would quickly drift off to sleep.

Within minutes he assumed almost the same position he had the night before. His chin against my shoulder. One leg straddling both of mine, his other leg alongside me, skin pushing into skin. His arm across my chest.

I had always been very good at creating just the right environment for a seduction, but very bad at initiating anything once my *prey* and I were alone. I was always hesitant to make the first move. First, I didn't relish the idea of getting beaten up. More importantly, I would never jeopardize a burgeoning friendship for a one-time, seconds-long ejaculation. Usually. This time the situation had been created *for* me. This time it was just *too* much. And if that meant an angry and disappointed face staring up at me, I would take the chance. I was no longer in control.

Simply sliding my hand on top of his gave me a huge rush. The feel of the hairs on the top of his hand. My smooth fingers slipping between his calloused ones. It was a hardworking man's hand, big and broad, thick-fingered and rough. And arousing! I felt waves of love. Not lust, but love. I felt it throughout my whole body. I wanted to stop right there and then, but I couldn't.

My body had a mind all its own and I was merely playing The Witness to what was happening. I felt my hand guiding his, very slowly down my chest. I wished my heart would stop pounding so loudly. Every five minutes or so my hand moved his no more than an inch farther south. It took a good half hour just to travel from the hollow of my chest to the flat of my stomach, just below my belly button. There we took a rest stop. The love was turning to lust.

Kostas' leg was resting heavily over both of mine, just under my balls. My free hand reached down and fell on his knee. It worked its way slowly up his leg, admiring the relaxed but defined muscles. I was trying to see if I could get a touch of the flesh just beneath the fabric of his briefs without getting busted. He stirred; so I stopped. When his snoring told me it was safe, I continued my travels. I reached under his knee, pulling his leg up enough to press firmly against my balls.

My other hand was still resting on top of his, where we had taken a breather. I gathered up courage and slid both of our hands, mine on top of his, further down until he was touching the very swollen head of my cock.

My hand persuaded his to slide down the shaft making sure his thumb slid over the slippery head. My cock was unusually thick. It fit in his big fist just right. I found my fingers tightening his grip.

Without warning, The Witness looking down from the ceiling saw a look of horror on my face. I suddenly realized what *I* was doing! I was filled with guilt and remorse for taking advantage of this innocent and trusting guy who just happened to be drunk out of his gourd.

I released his hand from the prison of my fingers. With a discipline I didn't know I had, I let my arms fall above my head and I lay there motionless but nervous.

The Witness mocked me as I lay there trying to breathe evenly. He was smirking. I wasn't sure what to do so I did nothing. I just looked at The Witness looking at me looking back at him looking back at me.

In the meantime, Kostas' hand was still holding onto my cock, instinctively tightening its grip around it, occasionally relaxing, and then tightening again. No rhythm to it. Totally random. Sometimes he held onto it almost desperately, like a toddler who's learning to walk and instinctively grabs your finger and holds onto it for dear life. Was he dreaming? Should I move his hand away?

I was about to explode. The veins in my cock felt like they were going to burst. But the thought of a toddler clinging to a finger made me feel like a pedophile. Kostas was just a kid at heart. What had I done? Had I gone too far? Did I come to my senses in time? I was prepared to accept the consequences for better or worse. The Witness disappeared. Paranoia struck.

Kostas' hand stayed where I had left it, every now and then making a tight fist, but sporadically. I could feel his cock against my leg. It was stiff. Was that an instinctual and unconscious reaction as well? I believed that it was, and that Kostas had no idea what he was doing. He was an innocent. He was in a drunken stupor. Though I let his hand remain where it was, I arrested the hot flow of my blood, and let my desire subside. I was content to feel his hand on me and his body close to mine. That was more than I could ask for. That alone felt satisfying and if more were to happen, Kostas would have to give me a clear sign. I started to drift off hoping that would happen. I briefly looked up at the ceiling and realized I had the whirlies from too much alcohol. Though his hand still grabbed me tighter now and then, I became less and less aware of it as I fell into a deep sleep.

CHAPTER 64

May 1972

I felt the mattress ripple waves under my body and saw light on the other side of my eyelids. I opened my eyes very slowly, feeling unusually well rested. Kostas didn't notice yet that I was awake. He was standing at the side of the bed, completely naked, rubbing some dried crusty stuff off his stomach and pubic hairs. After getting rid of most of it, he reached into the bottom of the sheets and after some searching, found his underpants.

While doing that, he noticed a sizeable stain on the sheet very near my leg. He drooled as much saliva as he could onto his fingers and quietly leaned over the spot. He braced his knees on the side of the bed and very gently tried to rub the stain off or spread it around or do something so that it wasn't so noticeable. That's when he noticed me staring at him.

Kostas lost his balance and fell. His face landed in my crotch. He immediately pushed himself up, elbows straight. For a split second we made eye contact and then just as quickly he looked away. He stood up and frantically put on his underwear. Backwards! Kostas was overcome with embarrassment as he took off his briefs, twisted them around, and pulled them up again. He was mumbling something in Greek. It was obviously an explanation of some sort. He was almost on the verge of tears.

He pointed to the stain on the sheet and chastised himself in a deep Greek voice. Then he said in English, "I am sorry, I am so sorry." Seldom had I seen a guiltier face. I wasn't sure what had happened in the middle of the night, but for once, the tables were turned. I wasn't sure what expression to put on my face. Just for fun, I stared, hurt and disappointed. But that lasted only a few seconds. I wanted to put him at ease, so my lips turned up into a big smile. When I thought about it, I burst out laughing. He kept berating himself. The more he yelled, the more I laughed. He was bewildered. I jumped up and threw an arm around his shoulder.

"You had a wet dream, Kostas. It's cool. We all have them. It's what men do! Especially when we haven't gotten our rocks off in a while! I'm jealous!"

"Wet dream?" he sheepishly asked. "Rocks? No understand."

"It was just a dream, Kostas. You were dreaming something sexy." I said as offhandedly as I could. He liked that explanation. It gave him a nice out.

"So you not angry? You don't think me bad?"

I laughed some more. "Kostas, it's cool! It's OK! It's normal! It's nothing. Your body just needed a release." I couldn't stop laughing. I'm not sure he understood everything I said, but eventually Kostas smiled and started laughing, too. He seemed relieved I wasn't freaked; that I didn't give it a second thought. What he didn't know was that my laughter was also a feeling of relief, too, though I wish I had had a release as well.

He wrapped a towel around himself and headed for the bathroom. I did the same and used the shower on the floor above us. That's when I noticed there was some dried sticky stuff on my leg. I washed it off. I was sure it wasn't mine.

Over a breakfast of fried eggs and toast, I asked him what we were going to do today. He looked sullen.

"I go home today," he said sadly.

"Home? Today?" I exclaimed with surprise. "You just got here!"

"Today is Sunday. No more weekend," he answered. "I must go home."

"No, you can't! It's not fair! Twenty years on an island and only a weekend in the big city? Your *first* time in the big city?"

"But I must. There is work to do. It will take all day to be in Samos."

"Then I will leave, too," I said. "I have no reason to stay here if you go home."

"Where you go, Giacco?" he asked.

"I want to go to Crete and then to Rodos. I love those islands. You come with me. I will pay for everything."

"I have never go to Kriti or Rodos," he said dejectedly.

I was amazed at his limited experiences. He had never even been to another island! I wanted so much to enlarge his life. How odd it would be for me, the tourist, to be showing a native his own country: the Palace at Knossos, the fortress at Rodos and the beautiful village of Lindos. A country so incredibly rich with history and yet so unknown to this sheltered young man. I felt sorry for him. I felt sorry he was so obligated to his family, that his brothers had left him almost solely responsible for the farm. It seemed so unfair.

"Please," I begged. "Please come with me."

"I cannot!" he said. "They wait for me!"

We both just sat there staring into our coffee. Then he brightened up.

"Giacco! You cut your hair, yes?"

He continued without letting me answer. This was his grand plan.

"You cut your hair and you come to Samos with me. It will be very fine. You live with me. We make a room in the barn. You help me just a little. My family feeds you. We be best friends, OK? For me you cut your hair?"

His grand plan was a life-altering plan for me. This was a big deal. This was one of those forks in the road.

One-alligator, two-alligator. Oh Krishnamurti! Where are you hiding?

I did not expect a reply.

I could live with Kostas but only avoid an insular uproar if I arrived with short hair, sneakers, and looking totally clean, respectable, and Western. Like a grad student from BYU. The people of Athens were about five years behind the times. The people of Samos must be 20 years behind the times! Their image of a Westerner was not who I was, who I wanted to be, or could be. Or could I? Would I?

Ninety-nine alligator, one hundred alligator.

Kostas stared at me, begging me with his eyes.

What has happened to the world? Where can a person go and just be himself? Feel safe and not labeled as weird? Not subjected to any conditional morality?

I wanted to be someplace where there were no conditions at all. The only place that came to mind was Hunga Dunga. There, the length of your hair didn't define morality, that's for sure!

Krishnamurti! Ready or not, here I come!

And Kostas! Live together? What did that mean? Working in the fields only to come home to brotherly love? Or have dinner with the folks and sneak away to our lair where we would get drunk and do things that only our drunken selves dared to do, and would never acknowledge by the light of day?

I reached behind the large rock that was my brain and touched Krishnamurti on the shoulder.

Gotcha! You're it!

"Kostas my brother, no, I can't go with you. I am going to Crete."

He closed his eyes and sank his head. Then he leaned over and, becoming more animated, did his very hot-blooded Greek best to persuade me one last time. It was tempting, seeing him so emotional.

"Maybe *some time*, but not now. OK?" I said.

"Maybe after Kriti and Rodos, you come?"

"Maybe," I replied.

He told me how to find him on the island. I took careful mental notes. That wasn't enough for him.

"Where is black book you have?"

"Right here," I said, reaching into my bag.

He took it, opened it to the back page, and wrote his name and address in Greek.

"You show this to someone when you come, OK? They show you my house, OK?"

"OK! OK!" I laughed. "Now let's get going! Pame, pame!"

He laughed.

We took the underground to Piraeus and by early afternoon, Kostas was on a boat to Samos. We hugged and he cried when we said goodbye, and through the tears he said, "You, me, very good friends, yes?"

I hugged him harder and said, "Yes, you, me very good friends always! Best friends always!"

And he waved to me from the stern of the boat until he was a speck on the water.

I took the underground back to Athens. I went to a city park not far from the hotel. It was the same park where eight years before I sat on a bench, watching fluffy swans glide across the pond. I realized I was sitting on the very same bench now, though I can't swear the gliding swans were the same ones.

As I sat there, no one tried to start a conversation as I half-heartedly hoped, and no one confronted me except to curse. I was in essence the same person, but they only seemed to see the long hair, the cause of much amusement and idle gossip.

I suppose I am conspicuous because of it, and no one can approach me without attracting attention and idle gossip to themselves. It was much easier the last time I was here when

I looked like a young native Greek whose hookup with a stranger would go unnoticed. Has this hair of mine become a barrier to meeting very wonderful people? Or is it a blessing in disguise that automatically culls the spiritual wheat from the worldly chaff? I reminded myself that I was not growing it. Rather it was just growing on its own. *I* had nothing to do with it. Yet how nice it would be in this lovely place for someone of a transcendental nature to sit beside me and say, "Yia sou!"

It had been an intensely emotional day for me. I knew that I had hurt Kostas a lot by declining his invitation. It was always easier for me to be the one getting hurt, than the one doing the hurting. I hated that role.

On the way back to the hotel, I bought some thread and a needle from an old woman darning socks. I wasn't hungry and skipped dinner. I gave the clerk at the front desk enough money for two people and made it clear I wanted the room for myself. No more strangers! I went upstairs and sat on the edge of the bed. A spring went sproing underneath me.

As I carefully sewed Little Richard's cosmic, embroidered duck on the back of my new denim jacket, I reviewed the past few days. It was hard to believe such a brief time with a person could produce so many feelings. But there were more questions than there were feelings and if I'd had the answers maybe my decision would have been different.

Why had Kostas made such a big stink about my pants and hair, but never said anything about the fact that I slept in the nude and never wore underwear? Why was there dried cum on the sheet? Why was there dried cum on both of us? Why was he naked when he got up? Why were his briefs tucked in the bottom of the bed? What was the real reason he was sorry? Did he know from the beginning what was going on?

Or in some mysteriously ironic way, were we equally guilty of involuntary manhandling? Were we trying to express our affection for one another through the instinctual urges of sudden, uncontrollable desires? Were we taking advantage of each other while we thought the other lay there in a drunken sleep, totally unaware and out of it? If the latter were true, Kostas may have taken a lot more advantage of me than I did of him. I chuckled to myself and said, "Bravo!"

But I needed answers to these questions, and I knew then and there I would someday travel to Samos in search of them. The next day, however, the sleek 10,000-ton ship, the Kydon, would take me to Crete.

CHAPTER 65
May 1972

Deck class is the only way to go. Not only is it cheap, but it's where the most interesting people hang out. Most were couples but there were a few traveling solo.

When we arrived in Khania on the northwest end of Crete, I took a bus to the little town of Rethimnon where I had a mediocre meal in a restaurant whose waitress served me as if she were under duress. I was the subject of derisive scrutiny as I walked around the plaka, but it was getting late, and I wound up spending the night there in a flea bag hotel. I'd soon discover that Rethimnon was pretty much representative of the whole island. All except Ierapetra on the southern coast, where I'd been told freaks, by their sheer numbers, had taken over the beautiful beaches and its many caves. They were like squatters taking over abandoned buildings. That's where I wanted to be. On a sunny, clothing optional beach, stoned on hash. Where nudity and long hair were not looked at twice. Well, maybe the nudity, but not the long hair.

Crete is mostly barren yet ruggedly beautiful. When the weather is nice, there is no finer air or fresher smell. But when I woke up, I found the skies drizzling steadily. I took buses past villages once dear to my heart, but now they had all become tourist havens. Or rather havens for tourists with money. The friendliness of the people seemed directly proportional to the amount of money they thought you would spend. Their smiles were superficial. The merchants once wearing blousy shirts, and pants held up by colorful sashes, now wore European suits and ties. They considered themselves stylish businessmen. But chic they were not! I couldn't wait to get to Ierapetra.

The weather got worse. It was rainy, cold, and awful. It poured incessantly. I decided to forego the Palace at Knossos, the ancient relics and the smell of hashish pouring out of the caves at Ierapetra. I tried to remind myself I was still going to have "fun" if it killed me, just to spite Jon. But the weather dampened everything, including my mood. After all, I rationalized, Ierapetra was an oasis in the same way Ein Gedi had been. Once you left its benevolence, you were again in a desert of ignorance and bigotry. I took what may have been the fastest tour of a Greek island ever attempted. I was as foul as the weather, and I was certainly not in my glide!

I took a bus to Ayios Nikolaos and booked passage on the next boat to my most favorite island, Rodos. I was sure that the vibes would get better, the sun would shine, and so would I.

A horde of hippies filled the deck. Of them, the most impressive person I met was the least conspicuous. Had he not initiated it, we would have never spent time together. He was a very young, shorthaired Austrian who singled me out because he overheard me speaking a little Greek to a deckhand and German to a girl from Munich. He spoke no Greek and no

English. The former was not a surprise, the latter was.

At first, I thought he was a dullard, only interested in fucking and being a pseudo-hippie. As it turned out, Freddie was a man of god in a boy's body. On his own, without the help of scriptures or teachers, but a lot of drugs, he lived the truths others only talked about. He seemed to accept the maya around him with equanimity. He had that ability to surrender to what Is and an unwavering faith in the Now. I understood everything he said, but even though I spoke German well, it taxed my brain to discuss esoteric things in a foreign language.

No matter. It's gotten so I can say nothing about anything. My life seems a dream of such magnitude and complexity I can't express an opinion without later chastising myself for not having negated it at the same time. I was a man adrift in the ocean with absolutely no idea in which direction I should paddle. Freddie was a reassuring life preserver. He couldn't tell me in which direction to paddle, but he did keep me afloat.

The crossing was incredibly rough. Rain poured down and I never realized the Mediterranean could be so fierce. Waves crashed over the bow and the boat rocked side to side. People were scared. Many tried to go below deck, but the first mate wouldn't let them in and locked the doors. People were sliding across the deck grabbing onto anything that was bolted down.

One guy took off his belt and lashed his girlfriend to a bench that was bolted down. Others guys noticed, and in acts of chivalry, also took off their belts to make sure all the women were lashed to something. Backpacks and belongings were secured, a few having already gone overboard. Then groups of guys sat in circles around the smokestacks, forming a chain of interlocking elbows and legs. Freddie and I were among one of those circles. The bow of the boat would go high in the air cresting a huge wave and then come slamming down in the trough. The circles of men slid one way, slamming some of them into the smokestack, and then slid the other way, slamming those on the opposite side. People were bruised, wet and cold. Many got sick and threw up into the middle of the circle. But we never broke the chain. We clung to each other for hours throughout the night.

Finally near dawn, the sea calmed, and we saw the minarets of Rodos in the distance. No sooner had the boat docked, than an old Italian woman, "Mama," pied-pipered about 20 of us back to her house. She invited us to spend the restful night that we were supposed to have spent on the deck. We thought her old-lady charm and warm-mannered invitation was an act of sympathetic generosity in the face of our adversity. Instead, she turned out to be a very clever woman who tried to extort large sums of money from us for her minimal efforts.

Freddie and I decided that our sleep deprivation shouldn't let us succumb to her wiles and we shared a room in a cheaper guesthouse. We slept the rest of the day and that night. The next morning, we did a very brief tour of the town. I was anxious to go to Lindos, the village of my dreams. I had spent two blissful months there not so very long ago. I persuaded Freddie to come with me. As we rode the bus, the island of Rodos seemed to highlight the immense changes Greece had gone through in the past few years. Most of the physical changes were tasteful and I was impressed with the way the locals had brought to the surface, their villages' innate beauty. It's amazing what a little stucco and paint can do! Pity it was done only to lure more tourist dollars and that "progress" was measured in monetary gain. "Progress," therefore, also brought to the surface intolerance and incivility to those who didn't have the big bucks.

I raved about Lindos to Freddie, but when we got there, I found it to be my biggest disappointment yet. When I noticed that the ancient well in the town square had been paved over, I should've known better than to even get off the bus. The well was where I used to get my daily supply of water. And now, three Swedish tour buses were lined up, their drivers waiting for the guides and visitors to return.

To the eye, Lindos was as beautiful as ever, but it had become a rich, snooty, spoiled child of the hundreds of moneyed tourists who visited her each day. I took Freddie to my favorite restaurant for lunch. Freshly painted, it still had charm, though I preferred it when the colors were faded, and the stucco was chipping off. I used to have breakfast there every morning, but now, though they would let Freddie in, they refused to serve me. Freddie said something in German to them, and unfortunately the owner understood, and a fight almost broke out. I grabbed Freddie by the arm and pulled him out of the restaurant, the owner following us to the door yelling at us in broken English, "No hippies! No Turkish!" I stopped in my tracks and turned around, bewildered. "What the hell?" I screamed. This time Freddie was the one to grab my arm and pull me away. "Ja, es ist OK, Giacco," he said, trying to mellow me out. "Nur geh' wir langsam weg!"

We took the next bus back to Rodos and I took some solace in believing that no tour guide could take his charges down the extremely steep and rocky slope to the hidden lagoon only very few people knew about. I was one of them and I was sorry I didn't get to turn Freddie on to it. He was a very decent guy.

When we arrived back in Rodos, Freddie and I parted ways. He was off to Mykonos. I waited for a small boat going to Marmaris, Turkey. "*Vielen Gluck und sei vorsichtig Giacco*," Freddie said. I hugged him and gave him the universal hippie handshake. "*Du auch Bruder, du auch.*"

I never saw nor heard from Freddie ever again.

CHAPTER 66
May 1972

When I disembarked, a man in a uniform asked for my passport, first in Turkish, then in Greek, and finally in English, even though I knew what he wanted when he asked in Turkish. At first, I thought he was going to hassle me, but I had always made it a point to have my plane ticket between the pages of my passport. I handed both of them over.

"You Greek?" he asked.

"It's an American passport," I said.

"Yes, I know! I asked if you were Greek!" He gave me a look of warning. His eyes said, "Don't get smart with me," while his voice asked, "but your father, he is Greek?"

"With a name like Giordano?" I said. He gave me another warning glance.

"Then your mother, she is Greek?"

I calmly replied, "No, both my parents are Italian. I am an Italian-American."

He leafed through my passport carefully looking at all the places I had been. Fortunately, the Israelis issue tourist visas on a separate slip of paper because they know an Israeli stamp on a passport can cause problems in this neck of the woods. He opened my plane ticket. The ticket around the world was almost more of a passport than the passport. If a country knows you already have a way out, then it more readily lets you in.

He stamped my passport, but his inkpad had gotten dry, and the stamp was barely visible unless you looked very closely. I was disappointed at first, but later would be thankful. He handed me back my passport and my ticket and for the time being, I was "in."

The beauty of southern Turkey impressed me with its green mountains, fertile plains, unspoiled coves of emerald green waters, and white sand beaches. However, people's attitudes were much like those in Crete or Rodos.

Only in Mugla did I find what I thought was the best of the miniscule amount of Turkey I got to see. The bazaars reminded me of India and for the most part the people were curious but interested and kind. Maybe it was because it was off the beaten track, at least for the time being. Maybe it was that the poverty was more noticeable than in Greece. Maybe it was just that I had a bit of luck. Nevertheless, the food was great, and I found a nice room and the next day explored some archeological sites before heading north.

My plan, and I should have known better than to make one, was to travel slowly north through Izmir and then to Istanbul. From there I would make my way overland through Eastern Europe, with Vienna as my tentative destination for some extended R&R. Then I'd head for lowland country.

As I got closer to Izmir, the vibes got worse and worse. In Izmir itself, I was almost stoned to death. And I don't mean with a chillum, either.

I was looking to take an authentic Turkish bath as my one souvenir from Turkey. I asked a cabbie for directions to a *hamam,* and he said he knew of one close by. I hopped in, but the ride wasn't short, and I suspected we were driving in circles. I could see the driver sneering at me in the rear-view mirror. He let me off in what I thought was a strange part of town, but what did I know? I asked where the bathhouse was. He just gestured with his chin to a dirty building across the street. An arrow on a sign above the entrance pointed to the basement.

I looked around me. It was late. This neighborhood was too quiet for comfort. I was getting bad vibes. I decided I should bag the Turkish bath and get out of there. I picked a direction completely at random and began to walk. I'd only taken a few steps when I heard a small stone hit the pavement beside me. I turned around. There was a group of about 15 teenagers just starting to leave the corner where they were hanging out in the shadows. They were heading my way, about 50 feet behind me.

My urban antennae perked up and I quickened my pace. They quickened theirs, picking up pebbles and small stones along the way. My flip-flops were flopping faster, but I could hear shoes catching up. They started cursing at me. Funny how even in languages you can't speak, you can tell if someone is cursing you. However, cursing is one thing. Rocks are another and one hit me squarely in the back.

The gang was getting in very good firing range. I knew the flip-flops wouldn't do the trick, so I kicked them off in front of me and scooped them up like a runner in a relay race grabbing the baton from his teammate.

I broke into a sprint running toe to toe trying to stay on parts of the street that were flat and free of debris. Oh, how I wished I could be in the Yala Sanctuary walking toe to heel toward Kataragama with Debra and Peter. My long hair cushioned the blow of a stone to my head, but I knew there would be a lump there the next day. I ran like a puma, surprising myself what energy fear can provide. In front of me, a few blocks away, I saw a busy street with lots of lights and traffic. The stones that were whizzing past my ears now just fell short of my feet. I was outrunning them. When I reached the boulevard, they slowed and I turned around to see them making all sorts of lewd gestures and shouting at me, followed by lots of laughter. Now on the main street, I felt safe and dared to look at them, knowing they were no longer a real threat.

"You think you're so tough!" I shouted. "You!" I said pointing to the ringleader. "Come here by yourself you little twerp! Let's see how tough you are!"

He was stunned when he heard English and a couple of them knew just enough English phrases to be obnoxious.

"You fucking Greek!" one of them yelled. "You, Greek hippie!" shouted the other.

"I'm an American hippie!" I shouted back proudly.

"Then you Papa Greek! He like it in ass too!"

The ringleader grabbed his friend, bent him over, and made out as if he was fucking him. "You like Greek fuck, yes? I fuck you up ass Greek way, OK Greek hippie?" They laughed loudly and were still miming the act when I turned around. "Jesus Christ!" I yelled, throwing my arms in the air. "What's with all the Greek stuff?"

A bus was just pulling over to pick up passengers. I had no idea where it was going, but I jumped on it and nearly out of breath, gasped, "Hotel!" hoping that was a universally understood word. The driver just looked at me and pulled away from the bus stop without saying anything.

Fortunately, we were heading into a busier part of town. In fact, it turned out to be the very center of Izmir. I got off when I saw neon signs on large buildings circling a roundabout. I scanned the signs looking for one that might belong to a hotel. I saw three of them, but they all looked pricey. Nevertheless, I went to each one. I was turned away at the first two with a flick of the desk clerks' hands. But the third one treated me, if not with an iota of respect, at least with genuine apathy. To my relief, it was not as expensive as it looked from the outside. When I saw my room, I realized why. No matter. It was a place to be, a safe haven. But I decided that in the morning I would move on.

The next morning when I returned my key to the desk clerk, I noticed a stand with pamphlets neatly arranged in it. One said "Club Mediterranee." I picked it up and the photos were of a nice resort with a pool and beautiful beaches with beautiful people sunbathing. It was in the town of Kusadasi. I knew very well that the Club Mediterranee was off limits to me, but the beaches of Kusadasi bode of a tourist town that was probably more sophisticated and used to strange looking foreigners. The pamphlet also had a small map showing its relationship to Izmir. It wasn't too far away and though I'd be backtracking, I'd temporarily lost my nerve to continue north. Istanbul was only 380 miles from Izmir and a mere 10-hour bus ride. I wasn't ready for that. I desperately needed to regroup. My wits were strained. I thought maybe in Kusadasi I could get my act together. It was less than 80 miles away and maybe, just maybe, after mellowing out, I'd continue north as I had planned. I found the bus terminal and bought a ticket.

Kusadasi was quaint and beautiful, a favorite beach resort for the wealthy jet-setting members of the Club Mediteranee. I wandered through its streets feeling comfortable, the sun and salty air therapeutic to my soul. But when I asked where the resorts were, I was merely directed to a small road which traversed down through the barren hills to a destination out of sight.

I followed it until I came to a guarded gate. There I was stopped and told in no uncertain terms to turn around. When I was halfway back up the road and out of sight of the guard, I saw a path that skirted the boundaries of the exclusive complex. I followed it to a very nice cove, which I thought I had all to myself. But as soon as I got comfortable, a young Turkish boy saw me as he rounded some rocks jutting into the sea. He waved "hi" and I called him over.

He was skinny, wearing some shorts and a Mickey Mouse T-shirt. Unlike most everyone else, he believed me when I told him I was an American, though he eyed my clothes suspiciously. He spoke simple but understandable English, so I tried to carry on a conversation with him using a third-grade vocabulary.

Across the bay, not too far off in the distance, was a big island. I asked him if he knew what it was.

He said, "Oh, that's the island of Samos. Greek! No good!" I fondled my Ganesh gratefully and wondered aloud how I could get there.

CHAPTER 67
May 1972

My young friend was all smiles and eager to please. At the small Kusadasi harbor, we walked from one fisherman to another and just as I was about to give up hope, we found one who was willing to take me to Samos for the exorbitant sum of 15 American dollars. I always carried a few bucks with me and handed him a 10 and a fiver. I gave the boy a handful of liras and thanked him many times.

It wasn't the fishing boat behind him that the wiry old Turk took me to, but a small skiff with an outboard motor. I sat in the bow and after a few tugs on the cord, the engine sputtered to life. Once we were away from the shore, he opened up the throttle to full speed and closely followed the Turkish coastline.

It was a rough ride, the aluminum seat bouncing hard against my ass, and I had to cling to the sides of the boat to keep from being broncoed into the water. Agean foam sprayed me, but it felt great!

The fisherman was very nervous. I would have taken a more direct route to the island I saw in the distance, but he hugged the huge curve of the Kusadasi bay as close as he could without getting into the surf. I kept turning around and yelling above the roar of the engine, pointing to the island in the distance.

He kept yelling back, "Turkey, Turkey!" and was always on the lookout for something, turning his head left and right and looking behind him. I didn't know what was going on. Then after a few minutes, he yelled and pointed toward the horizon. There, not too far away, were two large boats with guns on them. They looked like Coast Guard boats. One was flying a Turkish flag, the other a Greek one. A light bulb went on in my head!

What we were doing was completely illegal and dangerous! He did not want to leave Turkish waters until the last moment. He put an innocent look on his face as he slowed the engines and followed the desolate beaches of the huge barren promontory that defined the southern tip of the bay.

As we approached the tip, he slowed the engines even more and threw out some fishing lines as if we were merely trolling for dinner, spending a leisurely afternoon on the water. He kept the propellers churning just enough to compensate for the current that otherwise would have pushed us into the rocks. He handed me a fishing line and pantomimed that I should imitate him. There we sat, feeling the waves rocking us, our eyes following the fishing lines where they entered the water, and looking intent on catching something. He would furtively glance up now and then to check things out.

Samos was in clear view. It was no more than a mile away. I could easily make out its beaches, farms, hills, and peaks. My heart quickened at the thought of the reunion I would have with Kostas and how surprised he would be.

Samos was the birthplace of Pythagoras. Certainly, even after all these centuries, the people would have wanted to maintain the inquisitive and intellectual tradition that had put Samos on the map. Certainly, they would want to be regaled with stories by a strange but friendly world traveler. And most certainly they would be able to tell that, despite the isolated racist epithets of their countrymen, I still held them high on my list as one of the most spirited and affectionate people in the world.

When the coast was clear, the fisherman pushed the throttle and we lurched forward so quickly that I fell backwards into the bottom of the boat, which had taken on some water. Now my back as well as my front was thoroughly soaked. I righted myself and hung on tightly. We covered that mile in no time at all, and just as quickly as he had thrust the throttle forward, he backed it off and made a sharp turn behind an outcropping of rocks to a hidden cove. There the water was calm, and I waded to the beach and watched as the fisherman slowly guided his skiff around the outcropping and then gunned it back across the strait.

I looked left and right. It was desolate. Nothing in sight. I hiked up to the top of the cliff and walked westward, enjoying the late afternoon sun, and feeling warmer with each step as my clothes dried. I followed a trail above the cliffs, admiring the isolated beaches below me. Eventually I saw a small town in the distance. It was built on hills dotted with blinding white houses cascading down to the beach, which are the signatures of the Greek islands.

It was the town of Pythagorion, named after the $a^2+b^2=c^2$ guy, the one I had just been thinking of. I regarded it as a very good omen and felt optimistic.

As I approached, women in black stared, calling to their husbands to come have a look. An older man seemed to dominate the crowd that was gathering, and he waited for me to arrive, his posture stiff.

"*Yia sou!*" I waved when I was within easy hearing distance.

"*Yia sou,*" he replied but in a less enthusiastic tone than mine.

"*Milas iglezika?*" I asked. That I spoke even a smidgin of Greek softened his stern look.

"*Ohi,*" he replied. "*Milate elenika?*"

"*Signomi, ala,*" then "*milao elinika,*" I said using up most everything I knew of Greek. "Kostas?" I inquired.

They all laughed. The old man pointed to a young boy. "Kostas?" he said smiling. Then he pointed to a man in the back of the crowd and said, "Kostas." He spread his arms as if encompassing the island, repeating "Kostas, Kostas, Kostas."

I got the idea. "Kostas" was about as common a Greek name as you can have. There were men named "Kostas" everywhere. Then he asked, "Kostas Kateris? Samos?"

I opened my black book to the last page and showed him what Kostas had written.

His eyes brightened with understanding.

"*Entaksi!* Kostas Vlaxos!"

The last name murmured throughout the crowd. They looked at me wondering what a person of my appearance would have to do with the Vlaxos family.

"Kostas Vlaxos. Mytilini!" he said. He gestured for me to follow him. We walked side by side, the small crowd following behind. When we reached a badly paved road that winded way up a hill, he pointed. "Mytilini," he said.

"Efharisto!" I thanked him with a smile. They all watched as I trudged up the road. I hadn't walked far when I heard a small bus coming up behind me. I flagged it down and it stopped. I took a seat amid many stares and quiet grumbling. Most of the passengers were old women, but there were a few men and children as well. I'm sure I would be the source of much scuttlebutt for days to come. I wished I were some comic book action hero, with the power to liberate and enlarge narrow minds with a single piercing look.

As we got higher, the barren coast turned into fertile green fields with grazing goats and sheep. In the distance, I could see a peak I'd guess was about 3,500 feet high. The green fields turned into swaths of bushy tobacco. Further up were rows upon rows of grapes.

We came to a junction. To the left was the town of Chora. More than half the passengers got off, still staring at me as the bus took a right and continued up the road, which was getting less paved and more gravelly. Finally, after a few miles, I saw a village in the distance. It was Mytilini. The views were so beautiful I asked the driver to let me off just outside of town so I could walk the rest of the way.

Workers in the fields stopped to look up. Children started to follow me. When I reached the main square, people stared again. I waved and said, *"yia sou"* to everyone, but only a few returned my hello, unsure of whether they should be talking to me at all.

I walked up to a man sitting on a chair outside a *taberna* and asked, "Kostas Vlaxos?"

He looked at my long hair, following it down to my waist, and then looked up at me very curiously. He pointed to a dirt road and waved a hand telling me it was higher up.

"Efharisto," I said, and took the dirt road, getting a bit excited now that soon I would see Kostas. At the end of the road was a small farm. It was very modest; a small white house directly ahead and a barn sitting in the middle of tobacco fields, and many rows of grapes bathing on a sunny slope.

There was a lone body bent over in the field of tobacco. I immediately saw it was Kostas.

"Kostas!" I yelled, *"Yia sou!"*

Kostas stood up shielding his eyes from the setting sun. His face broke into such a happy smile it made my heart beat fast. He ran through the fields and jumped over a fence; his arms spread wide.

"Giacco!" he shouted.

But at the same time an old man and woman had come out of the house and Kostas saw them just before he reached me. His open arms ready to give me a hug turned into an awkwardly formal handshake. I was disappointed but understood his reluctance to greet me too enthusiastically.

His parents yelled something to him in Greek and he yelled back.

"You stay here, Giacco. One minute. Yes?"

"OK," I said.

He went up to his parents and I could hear the many questions and Kostas trying to explain. Mama and Papa kept looking at me over his shoulders. They were trying to keep their voices low, but I could sense their disapproval.

Kostas walked back to me, his head down. "Giacco, why you not cut your hair?"

"It is so important, Kostas?" I asked in return.

"My mama and papa, they do not understand. You are different. You are, how you say?"

"Strange? Weird?" I offered.

"*Ne*, you are weird to them."

"But you tell them, "You, me, very good friends. Best friends," I reminded him, parroting his own words exactly as he had said them.

"Oh, Giacco, why you do this to me?"

"You asked me to come to Samos. Now I am here!"

He just shook his head. He looked at his parents and then back at me. Then he walked back to his parents, and they talked some more. When he returned, he grabbed my elbow, walking me up to meet his parents. On the way, he said, "We have meal together, OK?"

I said, "Yes, that would be very nice, but only if you have enough."

"In Greece, we have always enough for one more people," he said somewhat perfunctorily, a saying peculiar to no one country. But despite the hospitable words, I was already disheartened by the look on Kostas' face.

"*Kali spera*," I said in my friendliest way, and shook his father's hand, though his mother had hers crossed inside the long sleeves of her black blouse and kept them there. Even though her face was wrinkled and her tired eyes full of worry, I could see that she was once very beautiful.

His father turned around and walked back into the house, followed by his wife, then me and Kostas bringing up the rear.

The kitchen was simple, with a wooden table and four chairs in the middle. A Greek Orthodox cross hung on the far wall. In fact, upon further scrutiny, I realized a cross hung on every wall.

"You sit here," Kostas said.

I sat down, as did the father and then Kostas. His mother brought a carafe of wine to the table and the father poured four glasses. He raised his glass and toasted without any of the usual Greek conviviality, rather with complete indifference.

Mama served a simple meal of goat meat, feta, a tomato salad, and homemade bread. Then she took her seat. Papa bowed his head and made the sign of the cross. We did the same. He said a prayer, occasionally glancing up at Kostas, who shied away from his look and kept his head bowed. When he finished saying grace, we blessed ourselves again and began to eat.

We ate in almost complete silence. There was so much tension in the room, I could hardly swallow. Toward the end of the meal, his father started talking in Greek to his son. His mother interjected questions, looking at Kostas, then at me, then back at Kostas. When she looked at us, I felt she knew more than was safe to discuss.

Kostas spoke timidly. Papa's voice got louder. Kostas answered just once, in an almost indiscernibly defiant tone. His father slammed his glass of wine on the table and stood up. His mother just kept shaking her head and tisking with her tongue. I just sat there, frozen. The young man I met in Athens was now a 12-year-old child. The man that was willing to fight a stranger on my behalf now seemed either unwilling or incapable of defending himself, or me, against his father.

"We go outside now," he said sadly.

I stood up, and as sincerely as I could, thanked them for the meal. I told Kostas to tell them how nice it was to meet them and how kind they were to feed me.

Kostas translated, but his father only said, *"Fige!"* as he shooed us out the door, his obligatory Greek hospitality to feed a stranger now completed.

We walked to the barn, and as Kostas hitched a donkey to a wagon, words exploded in a combination of exacerbation, anger, sorrow, and frustration.

"Why you do this to me? Why? I ask you cut your hair and you do not!"

I just stood there. He knew he was wrong. He was embarrassed I had seen him cower before his father. His voice was cracking when he spoke softly.

"I ask Papa you can stay here. He say no! I say I invite you, and Mama say, 'Why? Why you bring this trash into our house? Why you bring shame?' They not understand, Giacco!"

I asked rhetorically, "And if I cut my hair now it will be better?"

Kostas said, "Too late! Too late you cut hair! I tell you cut your hair, but you still have hair," he said, pulling my ponytail.

CHAPTER 68
May 1972

Kostas led the donkey and the wagon onto the road, and he climbed in, gesturing me to do the same. He snapped a small whip on the donkey's back, and we started down the hill.

"I take you to hotel in Samos."

"Can you stay there with me?" I asked hopefully.

He looked at me as if I were crazy. "No! Impossible! Everyone know me, I know everyone!"

"Well, then," I suggested, "if I stay in Samos, can we go to a quiet beach together. You and me, good friends Kostas, I reminded him. We just play and talk on a beach."

He was in anguish. He said nothing. No more words were spoken. When we reached the town of Samos, he stopped the wagon in front of the only hotel in town. "Now you get out, OK?"

He looked very nervous when people gathered near the wagon. Looking left and right at faces he had known all his life, his demeanor suddenly changed.

"*Fige katheki! Parakalo, aseme!*" he yelled at me, making angry gestures as if he were about to punch me out. I knew he was denouncing me in Greek for the sake of the onlookers, trying to save face. Then in the softest of whispers, but without changing the expression on his face, he said, "Please Giacco, leave now. Please!"

A man probably in his late forties stepped out of the hotel. "*Ti yinete?*" he called to Kostas. Kostas was too choked up to answer and ignored him. I jumped out of the wagon. Kostas turned it around and headed back up the road. Every pair of Greek eyes was on me. But I was looking at Kostas leaving. I saw him look back. He was crying. And when he faced forward again, I could see his strong back convulsing in sobs.

I was crushed. But I think Kostas was even more so. Although I would've never guessed it, I actually *did* see him again. Very, very briefly.

The man who had come out of the hotel was the owner. He walked up to me, chasing away the spectators like a police officer at a crime scene, ordering them to "move on folks, nothing more to see here."

He put a comforting arm around my shoulder and led me into the hotel.

"My name is Kostas Kateris. I own this hotel. What is your name? Where are you from?" His English was perfect. So was his German, French and Italian, as I would later discover. He was the Kostas the patriarch in Pythagorion had mentioned, which made me think he was a man of some reputation. I answered his questions and told him the short version of my travels.

He invited me into his living quarters, an apartment in the back of the hotel with a splendid view of the little harbor and adjacent beaches. There were bookcases on every wall and colorful folk art and fine paintings. Though he was starting to show signs of his age, I could tell that when he was younger, he must have been very good looking. While taking in all the mementos lying around, I saw some framed photographs on a hutch. I immediately recognized one of him as a young man. The likeness was unmistakable. He was in a bathing suit holding up a swordfish. The photograph proved me incorrect. He wasn't just nice looking. He was a stud! I felt as if I knew him! I studied the other photographs. One was of a stunning young woman, demure and delicate, and very sexy! She had mischief in her eyes.

He offered me a seat while he went to a small side table and poured two glasses of wine. He handed me one and said, "Cheers," clinking my glass. I was afraid it would be retsina, but it was a nice Cabernet. He pulled up a chair close to mine. "Now then, tell me what happened."

I didn't want to get Kostas in trouble, so I disclosed our meeting and subsequent friendship only in the most general and innocent terms.

He chuckled while he refilled our glasses, as if he had already filled in the blanks, though he may have filled in more than were required. Then, in what I thought was a bold move just having met me, he said, "Are you not curious that I am not married?"

"No," I said matter-of-factly. "Should I be?"

"Surprisingly, it is only because of your long hair that I feel comfortable in telling you this. I am the resident homosexual on the island, the "Poustis of Samos!" He laughed at himself, though he was a man of no affectations. "At least I'm the only one who admits it."

"There are others?" I asked, understanding now that he was a man with a reputation!

"How can there not be?" he retorted. "Homosexuality has been rampant throughout history. Look carefully next time you visit one of our museums, especially the vases that depict Erastes and Eromenos, the male lover and his beloved. In Greece, as long as the man gets married and has children, he has fulfilled his obligations. What he does with his friends in the fields or when he goes to the city is not an issue. We Greeks are famous for that duplicity."

"So why did you never marry? Wouldn't it have made your life easier?"

"When I was 19, I was engaged to the most beautiful woman in Samos. We had known each other all our lives. She was my best friend. Our families had known each other for generations. Everyone expected we would marry someday. But a few weeks before the wedding, I asked myself, 'It will be easier for *me* if I marry, but will it be easier for *her*?' I loved her too much. I did not want to be a man who leaves his wife to keep house and raise the children while he goes off and carouses with his friends. I knew even then that was not the man I wanted to be.

"I brought great shame to my family. The only one who understood was Alida, my fiancée. My father asked me to leave his house. I went to live with an uncle in Athens. There I worked and went to school. When I finished my studies and saved some money, I traveled for a couple of years through Europe, doing odd jobs, honing the languages I had studied by living for a while in France and England. But I returned to Athens when my uncle sent the bad news my parents had drowned when a ferry to a nearby island capsized."

"Oh my god, I am so sorry," I said.

"It's OK, Giacco. It was many, many years ago."

He continued. "I returned to Samos. I was 26 and I have run this hotel ever since. Of course, it wasn't as nice then as it is now," he said proudly.

"And you weren't ostracized?" I asked.

"Giacco, my friend, if you stayed here long enough you would learn that Greeks get used to everything and eventually accept what is. Yes, it was difficult, but I stood my ground and I stood tall. Greeks respect those who are well to do and educated, but most of all they respect those who live their lives with kindness and integrity."

"But wasn't it, isn't it a lonely existence?"

He laughed. "Now the season is just beginning. Only a couple of my rooms are occupied. They will be full in another month. I have many friends from many different countries. When summer comes, they visit. When it is winter, I close the hotel and visit them. It has turned out very nicely. Samos is my home. This is where I belong. And I have some secret reasons for staying."

I didn't pry. I changed the subject for him. "And what about Kostas?"

"Ah, Kostas!" he smiled, leaving a look of melancholy behind. "I have known him since he was a baby. He is one of the handsomest and nicest men on the island," he said with pride. "He can have any woman he chooses. Now he is of the age when the people here expect him to marry. But he doesn't even have a girlfriend. He never has. He just works hard. And he is a good son."

"I can tell that, and I respect him for it." I said. "But certainly, there must come a time for him to act like a man and not just an obedient child."

"You ask too much of him, Giacco. My beautiful Alida is his mother."

I gulped, almost spilling my wine.

As he refilled my glass, he said, "And I am his father."

"What?" I exclaimed. I don't get it. How did that happen?"

"When I returned to Samos after my parents died, Alida had already married Georgios and had two boys barely a year apart. One night she came to me. Her body was bruised, and her eye was black. I held her and comforted her, and one thing led to another. Ah, Giacco, you with the long hair, you must understand how that goes."

"Does Kostas know? Does Georgios know?"

"Georgios is an ignoramus and, what is the English word, a 'creep'? He suspects nothing and never has. Only I know, Alida knows, and now *you* know. Now you can ruin many lives. But I trust you and tell you only so you understand better the situation. In my own way, I try to help her out as much as I can. I slip her money, sometimes to pass on to Kostas." He chuckled. "Do you really think Kostas could have saved enough money to go to Athens on his own?"

He looked at me begging that I be as candid and truthful as he had, and asked, "So tell me now what really happened between you and Kostas?"

I told him the truth. That nothing happened that would define either of us. Just a suspicion on my part and a deep longing that I fantasized I could make come true.

"Then why did you not cut your hair?" he asked.

That was a hard one. I had to think a minute.

"I suppose for the same reason you broke off your engagement and left the island. You needed to be true to yourself. You wanted to be accepted for who you were on the inside, and not on the outside."

"But perhaps if you let people know who you are on the inside first, and then grow your hair? Then maybe it matters less how the outside looks?"

Oh, he was a wise this man, this one. I felt like we were in ancient Greece, and I was Plato to his Socrates. He scrutinized my face and could tell my mind was working overtime.

"Come," he said, "It is late. I will show you your room."

I reached in my bag for some money. He looked paternally at me and said, "Put your money away. You are my guest."

As we walked to the room I asked, "What do you think will happen to Kostas?"

"What will be will be. Probably he will force himself to marry and have children to please his parents. Then, he will satisfy his need for men with brief encounters in the dark corners of the wharves."

"That makes me sad," I said.

"It makes me sad too, Giacco. I pray that when the feelings make him crazy, he will come to me for advice. And I will do my best to advise him well."

He opened the door to the room. It was spotlessly clean with a view of the sea. Its white walls were decorated with art only someone like Kostas could have picked out.

"Tomorrow, you come to my apartment. We will breakfast together. Pick out some of my books. Sit in the sun on the patio where passersby can see you reading a book. Let the people stare. Be friendly. I promise you within a matter of days, you will no longer be an object of curiosity or rumors."

"And do you think word will get back to Alida and Georgios that I am a nice guy?" I asked hopefully.

"Word will get to Alida. I know her. She would like you eventually if she were widowed. But Georgios, never! And Alida, she dares not contest him. She is completely under his control."

"And Kostas?" I inquired.

"Word will reach Kostas as well. But he is too scared by his own desires to let them reignite, especially under the tyrant eyes of his father."

It was presumptuous and daring of me to ask, but I asked anyway. "Couldn't Kostas and I meet here in your hotel?"

"Giacco, Georgious hates me! He forbids Kostas even to speak to me! If Georgious ever found out Kostas were here, he'd kill the two of us! Not because he knows anything about Alida and me. Just because I am the person I am. In a town this small, on an island not so large, it would get back to Georgious. It would be impossible for Kostas to take the chance!"

After that was said and done, he added, "As for me, I would allow it."

I hung my head and sat on the bed. He sat next to me and held my hand. "Giacco, you may not know it, and Kostas may not realize it for some time, but he has learned a great deal from your brief friendship. Let it go. Learn from it. The moment has passed. But if it helps at all, let me say that you are a man I would approve of for my dear son, Kostas."

He kissed me on top of my head and left, quietly closing the door behind him. I thought to myself how sometimes just one good person can make an entire island bearable, allowing its beauty to shine through. Kostas Kateris was certainly that person.

Every morning for the next two weeks we had breakfast together. We talked about so many things, from politics and philosophy to San Francisco communes and the psychedelic music coming out of England and the States. He was very interested in my travels and the pursuit of enlightenment and prodded me for every detail.

After breakfast, I usually read on the patio or on one of the many beautiful little beaches around town. The first day, townsfolk passing the hotel gave me rude looks, but I always responded with steady positive vibrations and a hearty *"Yia sou," "Kali mera"* and *"Ti kanis."* I learned enough Greek pleasantries to be the most pleasant person in town. And it worked, just as Kostas had said it would.

After a few days, my cheerful greetings elicited the same in return, tentative at first, but unrestrained by the time I left. I took my time exploring this eastern side of the island. People recognized me and called me by name. I had learned some of theirs as well. Calling someone by their name has amazing results. Asking someone their name is an immediately disarming tactic. It was one of the more important lessons I would take away with me.

I had become somewhat of a fixture, an odd but benign decoration. I encountered no more hassling or hurtful words. And I hope that maybe I had made it easier for the freaks that would follow.

The night before I planned to leave, I hardly knew how to thank Kostas for his incredible kindness, but he could feel my gratitude and said that he enjoyed my company immensely. I gave him a slip of white paper with my address on it and told him to come visit me in San Francisco sometime. I also said I'd appreciate it if somehow, he could get my address to his son. I saw in his face that he liked my acknowledgment of the truth. Besides Alida, I would be the only one who could ever give him the sigh of relief that comes when there are no more secrets.

I climbed the gangplank to a boat that had seen better days. There were a handful of freaks on deck and the rest of the passengers were crazed Greeks. I went to the stern of the boat to take one last look at Samos. I felt the idling engines slip into gear and we began to move.

Many people gathered at the dock, waving goodbye to relatives and friends. I looked for Kostas senior and found him sitting in the window of his apartment, waving a yellow handkerchief. I waved back with big sweeps of my arm.

I was about to turn around when I saw a man racing down the hill to the harbor. He was wildly waving a white slip of paper and yelling. He reached the dock when the boat was about 100 feet away, picking up speed gradually. It was Kostas. Even from this far away, I could see he was crying and smiling at the same time. He made a fist over the slip of paper and pressed it to his heart. I pressed my fist to my heart as well. We stood there the entire time; fists pressed to our hearts until we disappeared from each other's sight. I never heard from nor saw either Kostas ever again.

All I could see now was the island itself as the boat followed the coastline for a while. Samos was one of the most beautiful islands I had visited in the Aegean. It is unique because it is so lush and green. Clouds hovered among the higher peaks. From this vantage point, I could see where freshwater streams made their way to the sea. The rocky coastline was indented with magic coves and white sandy beaches. It was half Hawaii and half Lost Kingdom. I could imagine it unpopulated and just waiting for Robinson Crusoe and his man Friday. If only Kostas and I could have had it all to ourselves.

I went up to the front, watched the bow slice through the choppy waters, and cried. When I had no more salty tears to add to the sea, I found a nook to call my own. Some Greeks traveling deck class were drunk and getting drunker. The freaks tried to make themselves as inconspicuous as possible. Two of the Greeks got into a fistfight and some of the crew had to break it up.

The seas got rougher, and many people got sick. Fortunately, I never suffered from seasickness. The trip was a tediously slow one, about 23 hours in all, but I managed to sleep surprisingly well and woke up to find I had had a wet dream. It was very satisfying. I wondered who it was about.

CHAPTER 69

June 1972

I was literally going in circles. This was not good. Arriving in Athens had completed one circle. My heart doing loop-the-loops with emotions was another. My head spinning with travel options made up the rest. I could travel by train through Albania and Yugoslavia to Vienna, taking my time and getting off whenever some place piqued my interest. I could explore more of eastern Greece, visit Corfu and from there take a ferry to Brindisi and travel north through Italy to Vienna. I could do so many things, go so many ways. I was dizzy with options.

Now, I realized I was simply traveling for the sake of traveling, with no real purpose except to indulge myself. As long as I was on a "quest," traveling at the expense of San Francisco's Social Services Department, which had "freed me from financial burdens to pursue enlightenment," as Jon had rationalized for me, I felt OK. Now that quest seemed to have disappeared. I had minor pangs of guilt, major pangs of bad karma. I promised to work extra hard for the United States government when I got back, using their stipends for the good of all Americans.

I spent more money than I'd wanted to circling the Aegean, and now I was almost broke. At the American Express Office in Athens, I wired Little Richard asking if Hunga Dunga could spare one more chunk of $400. After all, he'd been cashing my ATD checks, which were going into the communal fund, so I didn't think I was overstepping my bounds. I knew there was a direct flight to San Francisco from Amsterdam, so I asked Richard to send the money there.

I dispensed with the more scenic ways of traveling and booked a direct flight. I sat in the Athens airport six hours waiting for it, but I used the time to recuperate and reflect. I took comfort in knowing that when I got to Amsterdam, I'd be in my element, and maybe find my glide again. I guess I could have gone directly to San Francisco and saved $400. A 17-hour flight wasn't so bad. At least I'd be well fed. But by now I was obsessed with having the fun I threatened Jon I would have. I needed to have one last stab at some extraordinary fun with large doses of magic to throw in his face. "Hah, Jon! See what you missed!"

The KLM flight from Athens to Amsterdam was uneventful. That in itself was a surprise. No one gave me a second look. The flight attendants were unfazed, as if long hair were normal. When we arrived and I walked through the airport, I understood why.

There were hippies everywhere. Interspersed among the business travelers and the middle-class tourists, were freaks galore. Too many of them not to take notice and yet no one seemed to take notice! What kind of strange and weird city was this anyway, where a hippie man with pierced ears, colorful bandana, and dread locks, could not turn a face? Either something was very wrong, or something was very right.

Amsterdam was very right. When the bus dropped me off in the center of town, the assortment of hippies was as colorful and varied as the prostitutes in the red-light district, where I immediately headed. That's where the cheap hotels were.

In one block alone, storefront windows offered horny men their choice of a nurse, a librarian, a maid, a dominatrix, and a demurely innocent Bo Peep waiting for her lost sheep to come knocking on the window, wagging their tails in front of them. Unlike most countries, prostitution was legal. This alone was a testament to the progressive nature, common sense, and tolerance of the Dutch. The women of the streets or behind storefront windows were treated with the same respect that Jesus treated Mary Magdalene. It was nice for a change to see a "Christian" society living Christ's teachings and not just mouthing them for political capital.

The Kabul Student Hotel was in the heart of this small neighborhood where all fantasies are played out. The Kabul had accommodations for every one of every means. Cheapest was the dormitory. If you could spare a few more guilders, you could share a room. And for those that could afford it, there were even some private rooms.

The first floor was a cafeteria that stayed open until midnight. But most people caroused until three in the morning or later. For them, there were a variety of vending machines, one of which even dispensed Heineken in bottles. The hotel was overflowing with this summer's longhaired students. They stayed up late clubbing or wandering the streets on acid, and mingled easily with the men window-shopping for a nice role-play lay.

A lack of funds forced me to stay in the dormitory. Though it was great fun hanging out with freaks from all over the civilized world, I hoped Little Richard remembered to send the money I asked for so I could move up the scale to a room for two, or better yet, one. It was hard to get any sleep in the dorm. Especially when acid or mescaline was passed around and people ended up tripping all night, either expansively praising the beauty of the universe, or huddling in a corner with a blanket over them to keep the demons away.

There was a police station right next to the hotel. But the VW bugs they drove seemed harmless and the policemen eyed both the men window shopping and the freaks wandering in circles with equally polite curiosity. They were always eager to help the man who couldn't remember which storefront had the plump but salacious babysitter, or escort a stoned and staggering hippie to the front door of the hotel. This city was just so damned civilized I could barely handle it. Somehow, I managed.

Within the first few days, I quickly fell into a routine. How odd it felt even to have one. Every day, I would go to the American Express office only to find nothing waiting for me. Then I would walk through Vondelpark, where anything and everything was allowed. It was like being in Heaven and shopping at the Paradise Mall. Hashish, ganja, acid, heroin. Jewelry, trinkets, and clothing from India and Nepal. People shooting up in broad daylight. Circles of hippies passing chillums. Men and women making music and dancing, while others were passed out cold from the previous night of merry-making. I would spend most of the day in the park, my nose directing me from one brand of hash smoke to another. I was always invited to join a circle, where we exchanged stories of our travels and discussed god in all its manifestations.

This of course always got me horny, and though I guessed some of the people I fancied, fancied me back, nothing ever happened. Here I was in one of the most uninhibited countries in the world, and I couldn't find a meaningful trick. And if I did, where would we go? Back to the dorm?

To make matters worse, I was almost completely out of money. Maybe I had enough for one more night at the Kabul and a simple meal. It was time for drastic measures. It was time to panhandle.

Using the talents I'd acquired in New Dehli, and to distinguish myself from the garden variety freak, I hung out in the more affluent areas of Amsterdam and in front of sites, buildings and museums that were de riguer destinations for the mainstream tourist, as well as in front of their posh hotels. I would smooth out one of my light blankets on the sidewalk and sit in a lotus position, hands on my knees, my eyes rolled far back into my head, and my eyelids partially closed like one who is a fugitive from the material world. I was especially pleased with the chipped ceramic bowl I found in someone's trash. It chimed so nicely whenever someone dropped change in it, and it lent a touch of sincerity to my plight.

In my pajama whites and dark brown skin, I could pass for the real thing. I could and would play this role to the hilt. I made sure never to open my eyes to see how much had been donated until I was ready to move on. It was always so rewarding to find a few paper bills that had missed the attention of my ear, but now caught my eye. Once again, I was so successful at this pathetic occupation that I made enough money to sustain myself, but not enough to move up to a double or single room at the Kabul.

Every day I went to the American Express office and every day there was nothing waiting for me. I sent a letter to Richard by regular mail because I couldn't afford to wire him again. That likely meant more weeks of playing the sadhu. It was getting old, and I was getting really antsy to be home, though I had honed my trade quite well. After a couple of weeks, I learned all the most lucrative spots to panhandle. It's true what they say. Location, location, location! Amsterdam was in so many ways like San Francisco, it seemed unnecessary to be here. I was homesick and what I was doing seemed so irrelevant.

Sure, I got to hear Joni Mitchell perform in a small jazz club one night and Ravi Shankar in a free concert in the park. I borrowed one of the yellow bikes the city provided for anyone's use and spent a weekend cycling from Amsterdam to Groningen and back, enjoying the exercise and the scenery. But I seemed to be losing myself in entertainment and recreation that could be found in any major city.

I was also losing track of time. How long had I been here? Four weeks? Six weeks? More? The days tumbled over each other, and as with all routines, they did not lend themselves to too much thought. On a day when I had absolutely no expectations, I went into the American Express office and one of the clerks who by now knew me by name, smiled broadly, as he handed over a large manila envelope. I was surprised and delighted! Inside was an American Express check for 400 dollars! Phew! In the big money again!

But just as enriching to my coffers, was a copy of a photo we Hunga Dungans had taken in the backyard of Big Blue. The sight of us cramped together to fit in the photo made me even more eager to get Stateside. And most exciting of all was the letter from Richard.

My dear Frank... I mean Chazan! We miss you! We miss you so much that this will be the last penny you get! Come home soon, please. The Land Funders, or "Landers" as we are now known, need your support! We got the moola, but no one wants to go land hunting anymore! We went as far north as Grant's Pass and still couldn't find anything that felt like us.

Santa Rosa, Willits, Garberville, Medford, Wolf Creek... nothing. Too many hippies. Goddam! They are everywhere! And everyone's burned out on looking for land. You seem to be the one that finds the juicy places around the world... get your tiny ass and chicken lips back here, now!

Though everything is needless to say, I'll say it. I love you. Ziets.

I couldn't get back to the Kabul fast enough to pack up my few belongings and head for the airport. I was going to complete the big circle after all. Right back where I started from, California here I come!

CHAPTER 70
August 1972

There was a two-hour lay over in New York. This was perfect. The flight had been full of crying babies, and college students who insisted on carrying on conversations with their friends who were seated rows away. Kids! When will they ever grow up! Despite the annoyances, I had managed to rehearse the conversation I would have with Jon and Rosie during my stopover.

I had properly worked myself up, thinking about how Jon had misled me regarding our planned trip together through Europe, and how I could have easily stayed in Kathmandu had I known they would freak on me and skedaddle out of Tel Aviv. They had certainly thrown a kibosh in my wash. I was just as much to blame. If I'd been more assertive and felt less beholden to Jon, I would've simply announced that I was not leaving Nepal with them. The conversation I was practicing would require some delicacy. The last thing I wanted Jon to know was that I had anything but the most fantastic time… without them.

I called Jon at his father's house. Mr. Harvey answered the phone and after the pleasantries, I asked to speak with Jon if he were around.

Mr. Harvey left me speechless when he told me that shortly after Jon and Rosie returned home, Rosie turned right around and flew back to Sri Lanka to find some German guy. No more than a week later, Jon followed in pursuit. Jon warned his father that I might call and said Jon would write as soon as he had an address to give me where I could reach him. Mr. Harvey was waiting for one, too!

All I could say was, "Thanks. If you hear from either of them, give them my regards." Then I hung up.

I was fuming! The nerve! I could hardly believe it! Was this simply irony or some devilishly expensive scheme to get me out of the picture? Oh, this was better! This was so much better! It was the first time I felt something other than love for those two rascals. I didn't want to name the feeling, but it wasn't a pleasant one. My stomach was churning from the most acidic thoughts. I almost felt I could throw up, especially if I had Jon standing in front of me to catch my projectile vomit.

Before I could become more crazed, the PA system blared something almost indecipherable as usual, except for the contorted phonetics of "San Francisco." I checked the gate and sure enough, people were boarding the plane, some continuing this next and final leg from Amsterdam, others boarding for the first time in New York.

I had left Amsterdam at 11 in the morning. I arrived almost 18 hours later in San Francisco. I waited just five minutes for the bus into The City. When it got there, I walked a couple of blocks and hopped on the Market Street bus. I pulled the stop cord just before Church Street and jumped off. My daypack on my back with the rolled up Tibetan prints sticking out one corner, I walked the rest of the way, my heart beating faster as I neared Big Blue. It was beating so fast, I had to sit on a bench in Dolores Park to try to collect myself.

I took a few deep breaths and walked slowly, toe to heel, up 18th Street and then toe to toe up the stairs to the house. I wondered who would be the one to greet me. I was hoping it would be Little Richard or Psylvia, but just as I approached the open front door and was about to hoot out my arrival to whomever was inside, a big man lumbered down the stairs from the second floor. He spied me just as I was about to open the screen door. It was Baird, more formidable looking than ever with his long, bushy hair, and longer than ever beard, making his big face look enormous, like the giant who guards the castle.

"Well, well, well. Who do we have here?" he smugly asked. "The prodigal son returns."

"Hi Baird," I said as enthusiastically as I could. "I'm home."

"Home is it then? You live here?"

"I think so," I said, trying not to be baited by his question. "Can I come in?"

"That depends. Are you non-sectarian or did you join a cult?"

"No Baird," I replied, a bit perturbed, "I did not join a cult. Now can I come in?"

"Who's at the door, Baird?" I heard Psylvia's voice.

"A non-sectarian!" Baird yelled back.

"What's he selling? Tell him we already subscribed!" Psylvia shouted back.

"He says he lives here but I can't seem to place him." Baird answered with a perfectly straight face.

"What's his name?" Psylvia asked, sticking her head out of the kitchen, and starting to walk through the living room.

"His name is Frank."

Oh great! Frank, the name we called anyone we didn't know. I hoped he was just kidding.

"Ya know... Frank... the skinny guy with the dark tan. The one who Richard likes a lot."

Psylvia ran over to the door. "You mean the tomato from the Farmer's Market?"

Before Baird could offer a sarcastic retort, Psylvia was at the door. "Chazan! You're back!" She pushed open the screen door, grabbed me and hugged me hard. I could feel her big belly pushing into mine. I dropped to my knees, lifted her smock, and kissed her tummy all over. She stroked my hair sweetly. I looked up at her and met her eyes. She gave me a long wink as if to say, "Have you figured it out yet?"

The wink didn't register, though she made me feel as if it were supposed to. With feigned disgust, she threw me backwards and I landed with a thud.

With that sound, Richard and Duck ran into the living room yelling, "Psylvia, are you alright? Is the baby alright?"

But upon seeing me on the floor, they pounced on top and locked me in the embrace of long-lost siblings, the three of us rolling forth and back on the floor kissing and hugging. I caught Baird staring down at us, arms akimbo, tapping his foot.

So much attention. So many questions. So much love. Except from Baird. I disentangled myself and stood up. I grabbed my pack, pulled out the rolled-up Tibetan prints, and handed them to Baird.

"Baird, these are for you. I think of all the people here, you will make the best curator."

Baird looked at me suspiciously as he took the roll. When he pulled off the rubber band and flattened them out, his eyes got big. He leafed through them quickly, and immediately recognized their beauty and value. He rolled them back up and stole off to a corner of the living room where he could spread them out and study them.

"Have you picked out a name for the baby? Do you know if it's a girl or a boy?" I asked Psylvia.

"Nope, don't know what it will be, but as for the name, we think it will be Frank McCormick."

"Frank McCormick?" I questioned dubiously.

"Yeah," said Richard. "Ya know, Frank!"

"OK," I said, "I get it already! But McCormick? Where did that come from?"

"Oh, Chazan," Larry said, disappointed at my memory. "Hungadunga, Hungadunga, Hungadunga, Hungadunga... and McCormick?"

"Sorry Larry, how stupid of me! I left out the most important Hunga Dunga! Forgive me!"

Then the three of them started hurling so many questions at me I didn't know which ones to answer first.

"One at a time guys," I pleaded. While I was doing my best to answer their questions without turning them into longwinded stories, I saw Baird kneeling down, hovering over each Tibetan print with amazement.

He looked over his shoulder at me and reluctantly said, "Welcome home, Chazan!" I could swear for the first time, I saw a tear fall from his eye.

I was home.

BOOK THREE

Down to Earth

CHAPTER 71
September 1972

To go where no hippie had gone before! That was our goal. We had decided that this would be our last land trip of the year. Nicky was behind the wheel, I was in the passenger seat, and Trudy was in the back seat as Zwagen left I-5 to head east on I-84, following the rambunctious Columbia River upstream.

There had been a few feeble attempts at land-tripping during my absence, but my return had resurrected what seemed like a fading dream. My zeal to be in the country reignited Nicky's land lust and that of Richard's and Trudy's, as well.

Within a few days of coming home, I was treated as if I'd never been away, and nothing had changed. Yet I could tell little changes *had* taken place. It's natural to click better with some people than with others. It was no different at Hunga Dunga. But what we did try to discourage were cliques. Now I noticed more distinctly different circles of people hanging out together because of what they had in common. They were beginning to define and assert themselves. I guess that was OK as long as they all stayed within the larger circle of Hunga Dunga. We weren't the melting pot we used to be. We were turning into a colloidal suspension. I felt uneasy.

Tom and Brandon were in a world of their own. They only had eyes for each other. However, some were getting restless with this "tradition" that they got to sleep in the cabin in the back yard all the time.

Luc, Alvoye, and Bobby were on a non-stop partying spree that found them getting home just as the rest of us were getting up. We suspected they were bringing strange drugs into the house. Drugs that had unfamiliar names but sounded like euphemisms for uppers and downers. On the plus side, it was the first time I had ever overheard the three of them philosophizing. That was a strangely optimistic development. The Cockettes were starting to succumb to fame and fortune. The Angels of Light, led by Hibiscus, a former Kaliflower-child, did not want his "gender-fuck" theater to be tainted by the root of all evil. We were proud that our gender-fuckers followed Hibiscus. Free theater or nothing!

Ironically, Lizzie was heading the opposite direction. He was completely absorbed in expanding Greenleaf as a purveyor of fine foods, to not only the communes and collectives, but commercial businesses as well. This development annoyed most of Hunga Dunga. To us Lizzie was using the Free Food Conspiracy as leverage into the world of the capitalists. Most treated it as a joke that would eventually go away, but a couple of us saw it as the first tentative grasp for personal gain and power.

We really didn't know what to do about it. Our non-philosophy was that everyone did what they did because they wanted to do it and hopefully within the "traditions" of Hunga Dunga. If traditions weren't strong enough to bring about the desired effect, there wasn't much you could do about it. Just the fact that Lizzie would only use the name Greenleaf Produce and not Free Food Conspiracy was indicative of how he saw his world unfolding.

Ellen and David were more involved in activist politics than ever. We rarely saw them except to meet at pre-assigned places to protest this, that, or whatever. Not that they weren't doing important and noble stuff. Not that we didn't agree and support all their causes. Not that we weren't proud of them. It's just that their circle of interest was being more boldly drawn.

Nevertheless, we all tried to stick to the values that had been the original glue. The stuff that made us want to stay together. Even the "partyers" still roused themselves when it was their turn to be a Hunga or a Dunga for the Free Food Conspiracy. Except now, Lizzie felt compelled to pay them something. Many of us found this disconcerting, although everyone who was being paid just handed the money over to Richard to put into the communal pot. As Lizzie would say, "Who can argue with that?"

Family meetings went smoother and quicker than ever. Our "traditions" were becoming institutionalized rather than an instrument for initiating change. Lana and Greg had an uncanny talent for being all things to all people, yet they usually abstained from voting on anything and just went with the flow. Only when the topic of Greenleaf came up would Greg stick his two cents in, and then it was always in support of whatever Lizzie wanted.

Those of us that wanted land, or the "Landers," included Larry, Chuck, Richard, Lizzie, Baird, Psylvia, Nicky, Trudy, and me. We held the majority, but majority didn't count when it came to making decisions. We bent over backwards to accommodate everyone else's requests and tried never to put roadblocks in anyone's way.

In return for the "Landers" being so incredibly easy to live with, we got the permission and the required money for this one last land trip.

While Nicky drove, I passed the time leafing through the packet of mail that was waiting for me upon my return. Most of it was junk. One was a letter from the Department of Social Services simply telling me that my monthly stipend would increase according to the cost-of-living index. Great! More money. More guilt. I assuaged my conscience by promising that if we bought land I would till it, sow it, and grow food with the diligence of a federal employee.

The only other letter of interest was from Michael, my long-lost buddy. I thought back to our days sharing a garage, and the wild time we had at the Celebration of Life. No one had ever given me a twinge from my heart to below my belt like he did. I ripped the letter open, tearing part of it, but just a little.

Giacco, buddy!

Long time no hear from you. Why? You still like me, don't you? Guess what? I got my teaching degree! Go Cornhuskers! Oh, and I got a divorce and permanent custody of my son. The wife turned out to be a loony bin! Yippee! The kid and I are heading up north. Won't write more until I hear from you and know you got this. I miss you and think of you a lot! Hope you and those great pals of yours are OK. Write soon.

Love, Michael

I instinctively put my hand to Michael's hishi necklace, stroking the beads while I flipped the envelope over. The return address was his aunt's, the same address I mailed my last letter to, only to have it returned "undeliverable." Still, it was the only address I had, and I wanted to reply quickly. The postmark on his letter was six months ago! He probably thought I didn't care about him anymore. Who knew where he was now? Where up north was he heading? And what about this kid of his? I hated not knowing but promised myself I would write again soon or figure something else out.

We passed Multnomah Falls, slowing down just a bit to catch a glimpse, but too possessed by our mission to actually stop and bathe our eyes in its sight. Soon after that, the lush landscape of the Oregon side of the Columbia started looking more and more like that of the Washington side, golden, but dusty and barren, a few irrigated orchards here and there, and fields of dry wheat. When we arrived at the junction of Highway 97, we turned north across the river, thinking the road would skirt the eastern slopes of the Cascades and therefore get greener and more like Maine or Vermont.

Not so. As we drove north up the Columbia Basin it became more like an Arizona desert minus the cacti. The Cascades far off to our left teased us with its peaks and promises of forests, but this part of the Columbia basin was just plain bleak. So many dams had tamed the river and we felt sad for it and wished it could return to its natural cascading self. The mighty river was no longer rambunctious. It was Nicky's turn to be.

"What the fucking hell is this?" Nicky cried. "This is no man's land!"

"Don't get so worked up," Trudy said in that irritably soothing voice of hers. "We've come this far, let's just keep going and trip out on what is!"

Oh my god, I said to myself. If Trudy keeps talking that way, Nicky will lose it completely!

"I agree with you Nicky," I said. "The mountains are to the west. Next road that goes west, let's take it, OK?"

Nicky nodded. His nods became more exaggerated when no road going west appeared for too long a time. He shot me a glance that was not pretty. We drove north for a few hours, when Trudy spotted a junction with a bunch of green signs up ahead. We slowed to read them carefully.

One sign read, "Pateros 2 miles, Okanogan, 6 miles," with an arrow pointing straight ahead.

Another sign pointed to a narrow road going west read, "Methow 20 miles, Carlton 28 miles, Twisp 32 miles, Winthrop 40 miles, Mazama and the North Cascades Highway 46 miles."

Before it could register, Nicky took a hard left and headed west on Highway 153. Just as he finished the turn, I remembered something.

"Hey Nicky! When I was travelin' I met these guys from Washington who were heavy into backpacking. They told me of a couple of places I should check out. Twisp was one of them."

Trudy repeated the name a few times. "Twisp. Twisp. Twisp. Hey, I like that name. I like it a lot!"

As we followed the narrow road that snaked alongside the Methow River and the valley of the same name, the scenery became more to our liking. Rushing water, grasslands on the west, but still the dry hills to the east. One curve revealed snow-capped peaks not too distant behind the hills. Small, neat farms and some orchards were sprinkled spaciously on either side of the river. And as we made our way further into the narrow valley, the North Cascades got closer, forested not in the dense way the west slopes of the Cascades were, but more park-like, with large stands of trees separated by swaths of green meadows.

I could see the wrinkled frowns of Nicky's face dissolving into open-mouthed awe. The excitement the three of us felt filled Zwagen with euphoria.

"Now this is more like it!" Nicky exclaimed.

"This is postcard country!" Trudy added.

"And if my sense of direction isn't all screwed up, I bet this road will take us over the mountains back to I-5! A perfect circle. How convenient is that?" Nicky predicted.

And I, trying to restrain my ego, gloated to myself that maybe my traveling karma would pay off in some unexpected way.

If we had blinked an eye, we would have passed right by the tiny town of Methow, the only eye-catcher a beautiful old home made entirely of river rock. Then the town of Carlton, with one large wood-frame building that was the post office, gas station and general store. A few miles down the road, we came to an intersection. The sign read, "Highway 20," accompanied by an arrow pointing west to Winthrop and Mazama. We drove under a large, wooden, hand-carved sign atop two upright logs that straddled the road, the kind of entrance you might find upon entering the ranch of a rich man. Across the top it announced, "Gateway to the North Cascades." No need to turn. Highway 153 just melded into Highway 20. The farther west we traveled, the more our excitement increased. Land turned greener and the mountains seemed to approach us rather than the other way around. They were majestic. Jagged, snow-capped peaks rose high in the sky. It looked like the Alps.

We arrived in the small town of Twisp. A nothing sort of town. Two bars, both doubling as restaurants, the Mercantile store, a small supermarket. No streetlights, no stop signs. Quiet and delightfully funky.

It was mid-afternoon when we spied a "For Sale" sign where Twisp River Road abutted Highway 20. Nicky instinctively turned left, and we followed an even smaller road while we scanned each side for more "For Sale" signs. Twisp River Road split in two and one of the forks said, "Poorman Creek." There were no more "For Sale" signs. But the three of us agreed that "Poorman Creek" sounded like us, so we took the left fork. Sure enough, about two miles farther was another "For Sale" sign with an arrow pointing to a dirt road whose access was denied us by a large gate. On the gate was a sign. "For further information on this land, contact Slim Fredrickson." There was a Post Office box number and a phone number.

Upon further scrutiny, we noticed that there was no lock on the gate. Nicky pulled up to it and got out, looking around to see if anyone had noticed us. He pulled the latch out of the ground and swung the gate open and then got back in the car. After we drove through, he got out and closed the gate. Country protocol, he figured. The road was rough and bumpy, but Zwagen was a real trooper. We drove just a few hundred yards, stopped, and got out.

We found ourselves in a bowl with green meadows and vine maples surrounding it, hinting at a good supply of water from somewhere or another. The sides of the bowl climbed steeply, and in this late afternoon sun, we could see how the hills in the foreground seamlessly joined the almost perpendicular ridges of forest surrounding us. We all gasped at the same time.

"This is it!" squealed Trudy.

"I think maybe you're right!" I agreed.

"Slow down," Nicky said. "We haven't even seen the rest of the valley. There might be something even sweeter."

And because he used the word "sweeter," Trudy and I knew this piece of land was a contender for sure.

There was a dirt road that switch-backed up the steep hills. It was so rutted we didn't want to put Zwagen through the ordeal, so we climbed back in the car and Nicky did a U-turn. When we reached the gate, I hopped out and opened it. Nicky drove through. I closed the gate, and Zwagen idled, while Trudy wrote down Slim's phone number.

Zwagen was happy to be on a paved road again and took us merrily down Poorman Creek Road, down Twisp River Road and then west again on Highway 20 to Winthrop.

Winthrop was a surprise. Someone had had the bright idea of remodeling the entire town to replicate the Old West, complete with wooden sidewalks and hitching posts. We hated it. It looked so fake. It was a theme park waiting for tourists to discover. We wondered why it was so quiet and why there were no tourists. We nicknamed it Winthrowup and kept heading west to Mazama. Now we seemed a bit too far from civilization, especially when we saw a sign that read, "You are now entering the Okanogan National Forest."

Nicky insisted on continuing, but not for long. A couple of miles more and there was a barricade. On the other side were big land movers, graders, and dump trucks filled with huge boulders. A sign on the barricade read, "The North Cascades Highway." And under that in smaller, optimistic letters, "To be completed by Fall, 1972." We were at a dead end. We'd have to go back to The City the way we came.

That was a bummer. Crossing the Cascades here was much easier. Too bad we weren't more patient. The road opened a few days later. We didn't find that out until it was too late. However, Winthrop would get her tourists. Maybe that would be their destination and they would stay there. Maybe they wouldn't travel any farther. Maybe we'd better act fast!

We drove back to Twisp and called home, collect. Richard answered the phone and accepted the call. When we told him we thought we might have found our land, Richard called Lizzie to come downstairs. Psylvia and Larry followed Lizzie.

"How much is it?" Richard asked.

"How many acres is it?" Lizzie yelled into the phone over Richard's ear.

"Does it have palm trees? Psylvia queried.

"And lots of water?" Larry added.

"Is there a clothing-optional swimming hole?" someone in the background yelled. It sounded like Bobby, but we weren't sure.

The three of us looked at one another. The only question we could accurately answer was Psylvia's and that was only adding to the cost of the phone bill.

"We'll get the details tomorrow," Nicky assured. "But all three of us think this might be it!"

Lizzie grabbed the phone from Richard. "Get all the info you can and call us tomorrow. And if all three of you still feel the same and the price is right, Richard and I will drive up after you get back."

Goodbyes and good lucks were yelled, and Nicky hung up. He was smiling from ear to ear. "Let's get something to eat. I'm starving!"

—mm—

With that command from macho man, we strode smiling into The Antlers tavern. Friday night and it was packed! Packed with drunk rednecks, some with their wives, but most of the men looking for a lady for the night. Jostling each other. Pool players yelling not to get in their way. A three-piece band scrunched up against the wall. The piano player was great, the woman playing the banjo was great, and the third was good at everything else. Drums, sax, guitar, you name it. The music was classic Western with a hint of blue grass. They put on a good harmony but when they played songs everyone knew, the loud voices of the sloshed, beer-drooling, off-key rednecks singing along was a shame. It was a waste of perfectly good air as far as I was concerned and a lack of appreciation for the musicianship I was hearing. A real insult.

But to the patrons of The Antlers, *we* were the real insult. A few men turned when we walked in. Before we knew it, their turn had a ripple effect on the inebriated crowd, and just like watching a wave approach, a crest of red-necked, red-cheeked, weathered-faced drunks crashed upon us. Even the band stopped playing, one musician at a time, until only the banjo made a last feeble strum that resonated quickly into the dead silence.

A couple of the men moved toward us. The crowd pushed in along with them. One man wore a cowboy hat half over one eye. His high leather boots outlined themselves through his jeans, and he had on his Friday night dress-up cowboy shirt, white pearl snaps everywhere. His red neck was as weathered and wrinkled as his face. He was probably in his late

40s and he looked like one tough dude. This was no Halloween costume. This was the real thing. I didn't know it still existed. Spurs and chaw and bowed legs? He went up to Nicky and started playing with his hair, curling it around his index finger.

"Well, hoo hoo, lookee what we got here! Now ain't you a cute thing."

The crowd laughed at Nicky's misery. He seemed paralyzed but managed to glance at me and I just returned an "oh shit" look.

Some of the crowd started filtering behind us, blocking a quick exit. Another guy went up to Trudy and pulled on a strap of her coveralls.

"Now don't you look plain, missy. No makeup. Dirty hair. Don't you want one of us toppin' you tonight? You think you're gonna get any, lookin' like that? Or maybe it's not a man you're after. Hell! I might be talking to a guy!"

The crowd goes wild!

Another cowboy rambled up to me. A young guy. A real stud. A guy trying to show off. The worst kind, though I have to admit he was sort of hunky. I threw that thought out of my brain immediately. Shit. We were in deep shit I had to remind myself. The crowd seemed to be really in the mood for something out of the ordinary. He pulled hard on the rubber band holding my ponytail in place until it broke, letting my hair fall full length to the middle of my back. He whistled.

Then he came around front of me and looked me up and down. "Hey, ya know Francine," he yelled to a plump woman at the back of the crowd, "we could take him up to your salon and give him one of those… whatcha call em? Make ups? Make-overs, yeah that's it!"

I was frozen. He kept rearranging my hair, pulling on it harder and harder. Then he fondled my hishi necklace and pulled on my Ganesh. He had one hand around my forearm and squeezed it tight. A handful of other guys came up and joined in the taunt, pulling on Trudy's coveralls, pushing her from one guy to another. One of them started twirling Nicky's golden locks while he stared like a deer into oncoming headlights.

The crowd got boisterous, yelling for blood, or so it seemed. A Twispilvanian nightmare.

"A little mascara, some lipstick, a nice square-dancin' dress. Hey, Francine! Ya got your make up kit on ya?"

"On my way, Duke!" yelled Francine, the crowd pushing her up to the front, laughing and downing more pitchers of frothy piss-ale.

"Hey you!" Duke slurred to the band. "We need some dancin' music! Strike 'er up! This little sweetie is gonna show us some fine hippie transvesterite dance steps!"

The three members of the band shot us a look of sympathy and helplessness. They started an upbeat song on a slow, sour chord and tried hard to make their music rise to Duke's expectations.

Duke was just about to throw me into the middle of the crowd, when from out of nowhere, a towering, big-shouldered, broad-backed man jumped out and stood in front of us. He spread his arms wide. They must've stretched six feet across.

The crowd, especially Duke, didn't like it at all. Things were really getting out of hand, and I could tell any second someone was going to throw a punch. There would be a brawl and we three, or make that four with our big guy, would be the primary targets. The crowd pushed toward us. Paul Bunyan, or whoever he was, kept them at bay, trying to calm them down while he swept us like a broom toward the exit, pushing so hard he made the few people behind us move aside. Nicky, Trudy, and I took little steps backwards, toe to heel, as he fought harder to hold back the crowd, their displeasure getting more vocal.

It was the first time I ever lordwalked backwards. I found it much easier to do than lordwalking forwards. I went a lot faster. Perhaps there was just more incentive to do so. Our hero turning his head sideways to me, his eyes not leaving the crowd, interrupted these thoughts and others.

"What the fuckin' hell do you people think your doin'!" he whispered to me. "You come in here on purpose just to cause trouble?"

"We just wanted to get something to eat," I whispered back. For some reason I thought maybe he was a reincarnation of Father Dan, the Good Samaritan who saved Peter and me when we were hitching to Woodstock. I even hoped he'd have a Jeep revved up outside waiting to whisk us away to safety.

"Well why didn't you go to the where the farmers go, up the street, the Broken Spoke? They won't like ya, but they won't mess with ya neither. This here's the rancher's bar. Ya don't mess with ranchers! Now grab your friends and make a run for it!"

He was losing ground. The dam would burst any second. I grabbed Trudy by the back of the coveralls where the straps cross, and I barely managed to grab Nicky's elbow and swung him around out of his stupor. We ran out the door just as drunken men and women burst through our friend's tired arms, breached by one or two at a time running after us.

We made it to Zwagen way ahead of them. We had sobriety on our side. We jumped inside, Nicky turned on the ignition, and Zwagen's wheels left some dervish of dust as Nicky got us out of there. We heard other ignitions starting. Like those on four-wheel-drive pickup trucks. We didn't turn on the headlights and since we didn't know our way around, we made a beeline for that Twisp River Road just a block or two away. We raced up it in the dark and almost missed the Poorman Creek fork and Nicky had to skid into the turn. We found the gate to the land we had looked at, unbolted it, drove in, got out and closed the gate, drove to the far side of the large meadow behind a clump of vine maples, and stopped.

Nicky turned off the ignition and we sat there in silence, listening intently for the sounds of trucks that might have caught our trail. We stayed silent for a long time. We felt pretty sure we had lost them. Nicky pulled a joint from somewhere under his seat and lit it. He passed it to me as he got out of the car and started unloading camping gear. I passed it to Trudy and got out to help Nicky.

The three of us walked up the hillside for a while until we came to a small bench of land. We thought setting up the tent would attract attention, so we settled for sleeping under the stars. None of us slept well. We were all taking turns pushing ourselves up on our elbows throughout the night, an instinctive need to be on sentry duty, to have a look around, to sense danger if there were any.

But there was none. I thanked Ganesh once again for keeping the snakes in the grass and other wild beasts away from our impromptu sanctuary.

CHAPTER 72

September 1972

We woke up covered with a sheen of frozen dew. All around us the land sparkled with a fine layer of crystals. The firs, thick at the top of the high ridge above us, glistened. It was beautiful, but we were shivering. And we were starving! We never did get our dinner the night before.

The night before! Suddenly, we all remembered The Antlers. We packed up our sleeping bags and ground cloth, stuffing them in the back seat of Zwagen and leaving just enough room for Trudy. We were more amazed than ever with the landscape. The way the light played on the snow-capped peaks of the Sawtooth Range above us and the Pasayten Wilderness far off in the distance. With great apprehension, we drove into town.

Unwashed and grubby, we timidly opened the doors to the Broken Spoke. Only a handful of people were inside, and they were all sitting at the bar. Some were already drinking. One man was pouring tomato juice into a beer. A few heads turned. Nicky said, "Good morning," and much to our surprise, we got a few reluctant "good mornings" back.

We took a booth near the exit. Just in case. The bartender came from behind the bar and walked over to us. "What'll it be?" he asked.

Trudy answered for all of us. "Coffee! Two eggs over easy, hash browns and whole wheat toast. All around." She looked at Nicky and me. "That OK with you guys?"

"Yeah, that's fine," we both answered.

"Bacon? Sausage? Links?" asked the bartender.

"No thanks," Trudy answered, "just the eggs and stuff."

"No meat, eh?" the bartender asked curiously, sizing us up. And as he walked away, we heard him muttering, "More damn vegetarians!"

More damn vegetarians? Does that mean there are more hippies in this valley? If so, where the hell are they?

Our breakfasts arrived and we ate them with gusto. We felt much better. If only we could take showers.

When the bartender came with the check, he said, "By the way, there are pay showers in the laundromat just at the end of the block." We must have looked and smelled like vagrants. But as Nicky finished the last drops of his second cup of coffee, he could no longer contain himself.

He looked at the bartender and retold the story of what happened at the Antlers so all could hear. Everyone swiveled around on their bar stools, including the man at the very end who was dressed in a police uniform.

Nicky was turning into a man in front of my eyes. It must have been the country air. Or maybe he had just found his element.

"Look," he said fearlessly, "we're thinking about buying that land up Poorman Creek. The piece Slim Fredrickson has for sale. We want to start a farm. We want to live here. But if you don't want us around, just say so and we'll leave."

"Did you talk to Slim yet?" The voice belonged to the policeman.

"No, not yet," Nicky answered. "We're going to call him after breakfast."

"Well, then," the officer said, as if speaking for everyone, "can't say that we like your kind around here, but we abide by the law. And the law protects everyone whether we like 'em or not, and I am here to protect and to serve!"

"Aw, git off yer protect-and-serve bullshit, Ferlin!" said the shaggy farmer drinking the tomato beer. And then to Nicky, "Just stay away from the Antlers. Do yer thing without makin' a fuss. It'll be fine."

Ferlin looked insulted. "Slim won't sell to just anyone. There's no more respected man in the valley than Slim. He can size a fella up and down, inside and out! He's gonna grill ya good. But if he decides to sell it to ya, then yer OK by him. And if it's OK by him, it's OK with us."

It wasn't the warmest welcome, needless to say, but it was enough to keep our hopes up. Nicky thanked them without a doubt in his voice that he was their equal. It was at that moment that I decided never to call him "Nicky" again. Only "Nick."

He went up to the bar and paid the bill. Then we went outside to the only phone booth in town. Well, there wasn't a booth, but there was a phone. Trudy pulled out the scrap of paper with Slim's phone number. Nick dialed it.

We rendezvous-ed at the gate to the dirt road.

Slim was an elderly man, maybe in his mid-80s. But he was tall and strong and full of vitality. His eyes were clear and bright. I never met anyone who talked so slowly and deliberately. Though when he first saw us, he looked a bit annoyed. He softened to an almost grandfatherly demeanor by the time we started our tour. He made it clear he went by "Slim" and not "Mr. Fredrickson."

We tried to hide our excitement as we walked into the beautiful meadow. Slim was so long-legged we had trouble maintaining a suitable stride. The "grilling" we were supposed to get came in the form of questions interspersed among comments about the land.

"Yup," he said with the humility of a simple farmer, "this here 120 acres is damn fine land. Starts here at the edge of the meadow and goes clear up to the ridge, 'cept the ridge itself is Forest Service land. On the east and west ya got yer State Game land. So's you can see ya got yerself lots of buffer."

Then he'd throw in a question. "From San Francisco, eh? Was there once back in the Depression. Nice town. Crazy town, don'tcha know. Tell me again what it is ya do there?"

Except for trying to make sure we had all our questions about the land answered, we let Nick do most of the talking. We had sized Slim up pretty well ourselves. He didn't take to pretention. When anyone uses the phrase "salt of the earth" I think of Slim. The best chance we had of getting Slim to sell the land to us, was just to be salt.

Nick had that look of an innocent fawn. Now here he was in a meadow any fawn would crave. Slim could see that in him. Trudy had on the same bib overalls that caused so much trouble at The Antlers. They made Slim smile. "Ya remind me of my wife Hannah when she was a girl. Hard working. Could keep up with a man any day! But now she has all sorts of troubles." He looked away from us for a moment, up at the hills.

When he looked at me, he simply laughed. "I'll tell ya right now. Two months working this land and you'll trade that stick of a body you have for one that's as strong as a log!" He laughed again. "I should talk! Gotta be a reason everyone calls me Slim!" I guess we had skinny in common and he could relate to me on a purely ectomorphic level.

"We just have odd jobs Slim, Nick said." "I do a bit of carpentry. Trudy weaves. Giacco is a substitute teacher. A couple others back home, work full time."

Oh, is that what I am? Guess I'm gonna have to make that come true so I can say it wasn't a lie. Whatever it takes!

"Teacher, eh?" Slim asked turning to me.

"Yessir. Inner-city kids. Social Studies," I replied casually, as if I had been doing it for years.

"Hannah spent her whole life teachin'! Right here in this valley. One-room schoolhouse back then."

"So, here's the gate where the land starts," Slim said, unbolting a gate at the edge of the meadow and swinging it open.

We were disappointed the nice meadows weren't part of the parcel, especially when he swept both his hands upwards, prayer-like, to the top of the steep ridge, and then spread them wide to trace the ridge as it curved inward on each side embracing the meadow. A beautiful and private bowl of hills and trees, and the meadows that didn't go with it.

"Watch out for li'l rattlers," he said nonchalantly.

I'm sure that was something we all agreed upon silently we would never bring up to the rest of the family.

Slim took the rough, gouged, bumpy road in stride, and we trudged behind. Two miles of switchbacks going up a steep mountain. As we got higher, we could look across the Twisp River to the other side. The peaks of the Pasayten Wilderness were there to behold in all their jagged beauty. We could see upriver the Sawtooth Range and Oval Peak, Buttermilk Butte, and Hoodoo Mountain. The concave side of Oval Peak was filled with a deep snowfield that seemed so close you could lick it.

The mountains rising on the east side of the valley were glowing. With its slow descent, the sun's light enhanced in greater detail the crags, rock formations, pockets of snow and the constantly changing shadows.

But we knew that views were not enough. Maybe for Baird. But not for Little Richard or any serious gardener. Suddenly the dusty road emptied onto a bench of land that was totally invisible from down below. It was mostly flat with a few little knolls that were downright charming.

Slim took us on a tour from one end to the other. "Whatcha got here is 40 acres of bench-land. Fertile and tillable after you get rid of the boulders and tree stumps."

Each of us was picking out a building site. There were so many. We started fantasizing out loud where the garden might go and Trudy's alternative school and Baird's art studio, and maybe we could build little cabins and not have to live together anymore!

Yikes! Is that what was really motivating this land thing all along? Is that what was going on in the recesses of our minds? The words a true Hunga Dungan dare not speak out loud! The idea of a community, and not a commune?

Slim walked the boundaries of the upper 40 with us. In the far corner was a spring. Slim drank out of it as proof the water was potable. Nick whispered to us that this was a great bonus, the potential to have a gravity-fed water supply.

Then Slim took us past "our" land, as we already were regarding it, to the Saddle Pass, the gentle ridge that separated us from the community in the neighboring valley. From it we could look down into the bowl-shaped mountains parallel to ours. We could see where Poorman Creek Road ended and turned into this last cul de sac. It was already somewhat developed, with a huge garden and three or four houses. It was like looking down at an Alpine village. It was the picture-postcard view we had been searching for. It was a postcard we could make for ourselves, right here on Slim's land.

"That there's the Second Mile Ranch," Slim said. "Nice folk, good Christian folk. Some good musicians, too."

I got worried for a minute. Fundamentalist Christians as our neighbors? This could be interesting.

Then Slim pointed to the very top of the ridge. "This side's so steep, Forest Service will never allow logging on it. Ya got Game Land on the far side. And this ridge separates ya from the Second Milers. If it's privacy ya want, don't get much more private than this."

We huddled. One hundred twenty acres. Forty very usable. The rest just a huge privacy fence. How sweet! Though you'd think it was the first question we would've asked, it was the last.

"How much?" we turned to Slim and asked in unison.

"Three hundred fifty an acre."

"Would you consider selling just the forty-acre bench?" asked Trudy.

"Heck!" Slim seemed surprised by the question. "Who's gonna want to buy steep hillside? Nope! All or nothing!"

Slim must've seen Trudy and me calculating in our heads. He was chuckling. Three hundred fifty times 120. Drop the zero. Two times zero is zero. Two times five is 10, carry the one.

Nick did the calculating by dropping to his knees, picking up a stick and writing in the dirt. "Forty-two thousand dollars, guys!"

Our previous expressions of delight turned into sour pusses. Trudy said, "Ten percent down? We don't have that much in the land fund."

I said, "Let's go back to town and call home. We need to discuss this with everyone."

Nick agreed. We all walked the two miles down to the meadow and the hundred yards or so to the gate. We thanked Slim for taking so much time with us and hopped in Zwagen, but not before looking back for one more glimpse of what all three of us wanted to be ours.

CHAPTER 73
October 18, 1972

The phone rang just twice. Nick got to it first. Baird, Trudy, Lana, Psylvia, Ellen, Larry, and I gathered 'round.

"Hey guys, we're callin from Slim's. It's ours!" We heard Lizzie and Richard yelling on their end. Even though they were so loud we could all hear them, Nick turned to us and yelled, "It's ours!"

"It's ours!" we all chimed in, announcing the news to each other. It sounded more like New Year's Eve at midnight. "Happy New Year," with handshakes and kissing going on all over.

"Just a couple of sticky things," Lizzie continued.

"Wait guys." Nick stopped the celebrating to warn us. "Here it comes."

"Slim's lawyer doesn't know how to go about selling the land to us as a group, so we thought…"

Richard grabbed the phone from Lizzie. "Not true! *We* didn't think! Only Lizzie thought it! I only said I wouldn't veto it!"

Lizzie grabbed the phone back. "I thought we could put the land in *my* name and work out some sort of agreement between all of us later. You cool with that?"

We all looked at each other. We weren't used to making time-critical decisions.

Lana said, "I'm fine with it. I really don't care that much one way or the other."

Ellen said, "Me, too. I don't intend on going up there at all. And if I do it would be just for a couple of weeks at a time."

Nick said, "I trust Lizzie. We can work something out after we get the land."

Psylvia felt obliged to go along with Nick.

But I said, "Definitely not!"

And Larry said, "I'm with Giacco!"

And Baird said, "Absolutely, positively not! It's against everything we're about. Either we come up with a way that we all own the land in common or forget it!"

The rest of Hunga Dunga would be polled later when they were around, which was less and less often. It didn't matter. We had enough people against it to stop it from happening.

Lizzie must have been pissed. Richard must have been gloating because he knew who would say what.

"OK, make life difficult!" snapped Lizzie.

Richard grabbed the phone. "Slim's lawyer says if we form a corporation, then he can sell it to the corporation and all of us can be trustees. This way no one person owns the land."

When Nick passed on this information, we all shook our heads at Lizzie. Just like him. He should have given us this information first. It did not speak well for the Hunga Dungan principles he'd been brought up with.

"What're the other sticky things, Liz," Nick asked.

"We got Slim down five thou in return for us tearing down his old house and barn so he can build a new one in the same place."

"Wow!" exclaimed Nick. "That's a lot of work! We wanna be spending our time building our own house, not tearing down someone else's"

"Look Nicky, that's the deal. Can we commit or not?"

Richard grabbed the phone again. "Nicky, we have to do this. We don't have enough money for a down payment unless we get this break in price. Ellen has a lawyer friend. Maybe she can help us get a corporation together."

"One minute," Nick said and put his hand over the receiver at his side. "Whadya think guys? Can we do it?"

"We can do anything!" Larry yelled, though he would be the least likely ever to climb a ladder to a roof to tear it apart. Nick displayed his ever-increasing business acumen when he said, "OK, tell Slim we'll do it. On one condition. We get to keep what we tear down." We waited while Richard and Lizzie conferred with Slim.

Slim agreed. There and then, we had the promise of our first building materials, recycled and all.

We waited until Chuck came back from visiting his folks in Chicago to hold a family meeting. It turned out to be a real doozy. Alvoye, Bobby, and Luc didn't care what we did as long as it didn't deprive them of money to party with.

Tom and Brandon were on a different planet, as usual, and recused themselves from any decision making. They were making plans, so we discovered soon afterwards, to find an apartment for themselves. They were tired of living in a crowd and sharing clothes and such. We found this a little ungrateful since we had tried to accommodate them by letting them live in the little cabin in the back yard. But our philosophy was that people should do whatever it is they do because they want to do it, not because they are forced to do it.

Lana and Greg seemed characteristically disinterested at first, but then brought up some items for consideration. "We don't have enough money," and "What if the winters are unbearable?" and "Won't we need a vehicle that can haul stuff and handle that road?" Oh, those *practical* people! They can be so annoying at times. But it was difficult to burst the bubbles of those who had seen the land, stood on it, looked at its vistas, and envisioned what it could become.

It seemed so antithetical to our way of life that we should be requiring the services of a lawyer, but thanks to Ellen's notoriety as a political and social activist, and her many contacts, we ended up being represented by no less than the president of the law school at the University of San Francisco. And she did it all pro bono.

She persuaded us to incorporate as a church so we would be tax-exempt. With our input, she wrote up articles of incorporation that truly reflected who we were or who we wanted to be. The final document almost intimidated Slim's lawyer, who now felt he was dealing with a group of some substance. Only someone who understood legalese could appreciate the beauty of the document. For the rest of us she had to translate:

1. The church had to have a name. The family meeting that took place to come up with one was lighthearted and at times hysterical, but with persuasive arguments from a few, especially Baird, we finally chose The Church of Manna, which sounded much more legit than The Church of Hunga Dunga or The Church of the Totally Disabled.

2. The church had to publish a creed. Two or three of us tried our hands at writing one, but no one could disagree that Baird's was the most eloquent. It was simple, yet broadly written to accommodate everyone's eccentricities. It read:

"We, the members of the Church of Manna, believe that all truths can be learned through the observation of Nature. That all of Nature is inherently Divine, albeit without the avowal of a Prime Mover. That to be human is to be part of nature and not separate from it. That through reflection and introspection of Nature, all morality, and all paths to self-realization is disclosed."

That was it. Even the lawyer loved it and upon insertion into the document, it became dogma.

3. Officers needed to be elected. This caused some consternation among the family since certain people seemed too eager to be candidates. Especially Lizzie, who pleaded with us to let him be president. It was his over-eagerness that made us choose one of the more disinterested people, namely Greg. We chose Larry for vice president just because he was so damned sweet. Richard was unanimously elected treasurer. It was a natural extension of his existing role at Hunga Dunga. Trudy, secretary, because her penmanship was so good and she dotted her "i"s with smiley faces.

4. Names of trustees were to be submitted. When all was said and done, only 10 of us wanted to be trustees. A couple were afraid of putting their names to any legal document and the remainder wanted nothing to do with anything that might take time away from partying or pursuing their individual "careers."

5. All decisions were to be by unanimous vote. This was the killer. Hunga Dunga had learned the hard way that to get anything done, unanimity seldom worked. One dissent without a viable alternative meant nothing. But two dissents meant keeping the status quo until further discussion and compromise ended in a decision to move forward. Now that this was to be a legal and binding document with a lot of money at stake, we decided all the trustees had to be in absolute agreement in order for anything to happen. To me, it hinted at a bit of distrust, especially since the "motion" carried so easily.

6. And finally, upon the insistence of Baird, who once again argued brilliantly, a caveat was inserted which stated that should the land ever be sold, it could only be sold to another non-profit organization. We unanimously passed all the articles of incorporation, but later, when we had time to digest what we had done, two or three feared this last rule might come back to haunt us. Others felt this was the one article of incorporation that would keep us pure.

On the 18th of November, 1972, 10 of us put our signatures to a deed of trust. Richard wrote Slim a check for the down payment. Slim wanted to carry the mortgage, which was fine with us. He needed the money to supplement his income. He warned us that should we miss one payment, he had the right to foreclose. But we felt sure we could come up with a hundred twenty-five bucks a month. Damn, divided by 10, that was only pocket money from the petty-cash cigar box!

The land was now officially the property of the Church of Manna, the legal entity superimposed upon the far from legal, downright anarchical entity of Hunga Dunga. How yin-yang was that?

CHAPTER 74
November 1972

Nick and I drove Larry to the airport. Among all of us, Larry had been the closest to Catherine. He received a letter from her which included an airline ticket and an invitation for him to come visit her and Maxime at the le Forestier family chateau outside of Paris.

Luc, who had been responsible for Catherine and Maxime's extended stay with Hunga Dunga, was furiously jealous. As were Bobby, Alvoye and a few others. But none took it so personally as Luc. He walked about the house ranting in French, but we ignored him.

At a family meeting concerning Larry's trip, little was said to discourage it. After all, I had set a precedent of being gone a year. How could anyone deprive Larry of a month in Paris? Especially after we learned that Catherine and he had made love! Larry! Of all people! Not the most flamboyant, but certainly one of the most steadfast standard-bearers of Gay! The world of defined sexual orientations was in upheaval! But Larry assured us that he would always be gay as he broke into the song, "It Was Just One of Those Things!" Psylvia joined him, though a bit off key, and so did the rest of us who knew the song. The meeting ended up quite musical, with people foxtrotting off to different parts of the house.

The day after we said *"bon voyage"* to Larry; Nick, Zietar and I packed Zwagen with camping gear and headed for Twisp. We were so anxious to get there, we drove non-stop, taking turns at the wheel. Our excitement reached its peak when we finally took the left off Highway 20 up Twisp River Road. We stopped off at Slim's to say hello. He seemed surprised to see us.

"Ain't you guys maybe a bit too early? Hannah and I didn't expect to see ya for a few months yet," Slim chuckled.

Nick answered for us. "We're missin' our land so much already, we had to stick in one last visit before the snow starts flying!"

"That's smart of ya, but I think you might be too late! We've already had a few flurries." And then in a more serious voice, Slim reminded us that next spring he'd be expecting us to begin tearing down the house and barn.

We went to look them over. The barn was already falling apart and looked like a pretty straightforward job. But the house was quasi-Victorian, with steep gabled roofs and two chimneys. We looked at each other and rolled our eyes. Jesus! This is going to be a job! The State of California was not paying us enough to do this kind of labor! But we decided we would worry about it later.

We drove through the gate, but Zietar was reluctant to take Zwagen much farther. Zwagen was very good to us and had taken us down many a strange, unpaved road, but this road was auto-suicide. He parked her on a flat not far from the edge of the meadow where our land began.

It was already late afternoon, but instead of setting up camp right away, we began the trek up to the bench of land. Even walking was sometimes difficult. We could easily twist an ankle in any one of the innumerable ruts. The road switched forth and back like the iconic snake found wherever there's something Hippocratic.

The curving bank looked like an archeological dig. Roots of trees and brush and parts of round boulders and rocks stuck out of the light-brown, dusty earth. We weren't archeologists for godsakes! We didn't know then how to read the earth. But the earth knew how to read us, and the road made us stumble until we finally made it to the top of the bench where we stopped to catch our breath.

When I turned around and looked west up the Twisp River, the peaks of the Sawtooth Range comforted me. When I looked north, across the valley floor to the Pasayten Wilderness, I could see all the way to Canada. That was comforting, too. For a moment, I imagined I was back in Sabino Canyon, the way the afternoon light constantly changed the expressions on the faces of the young and ragged cliffs. That was comforting, too. I could never be bored by those faces. I found myself breathing easy. I felt good here. I belonged here. I was comfortable here.

I think Nick and Zietar were, too.

We began walking to the other end of the bench, which was impossible to see from the valley. And of course, being surrounded by National Forest, no one could see us from above either, unless someone were making it a mission of some sort. All in all, these 40 acres were definitely clothing optional!

Butted up against the bottom of the steep slope that ran to the top of the ridge was a seasonal pond, dry now, but promising that come spring, it would be a shallow lake. Vine maples completely ringed the lake and I thought what a beautiful landscape this would be for Baird to capture on canvas.

In the middle of the bench was a knoll. Even from a distance, Richard immediately fell in love with it. We all did, but Richard called dibs on it as if we were platting the land among us. Nick and I let Richard call dibs without discussion. Without saying so, we knew there was room for all to find his or her little nook of my-me-mine on this land. Even though that was anathema, we knew deep down we all wanted someplace to go where we could be alone, with no one to see us or hear us.

The knoll indeed looked special. I hadn't imagined what the view was going to be like before we got there but Richard seemed to have projected himself ahead of us and already knew what was in store. For me the knoll was too exposed. But as we walked in that direction, we took note of other potential building sites, and Nick and I chatted away about the hand-made, architecturally ingenious dwellings we could build on them.

When we reached the knoll and climbed to the top, we saw what Richard had seen in his premonition. It had the most amazing view of the Twisp River mirroring the last rays of the sun through the trees on its banks. A river of sequins. That should have given Bobby, Luc, and Alvoye some pleasure. The mountains across the river caught the descending sunlight, turning what was flat and bland during the height of the day into the depths and textures of the crags and stony folds, now all red and orange.

We squatted on our haunches and with silent reverence, took in the spectacular view. Richard was adamant that this little hill was his. He named it Zietar's Knoll and through our constant usage of that name for what would become a landmark, it stuck. "Oh, there's some wild roses just on the other side of Zietar's Knoll. The rose hips are huge!" or "Hey, if you need some yarrow, there are clumps of it. Just walk past Zietar's Knoll and veer to the right."

The sun was getting lower and we headed back. But instead of walking down the road, we kept going up toward the Saddle Pass that overlooked the Second Mile Ranch. On the way, we found the perfect building site for a temporary communal dwelling. Perfect because it was reasonably flat and behind some tall firs, and because it was the closest to the gravity-fed spring.

There was also a little area between the spring and the site that would serve as a fine outdoor kitchen while we constructed something to shelter us. And best of all, a small hill smothered in tall mullen, whose leaves were so soft to the skin, they would make excellent toilet paper. We named this little hill Shitter's Hill.

The rest of the 80 acres was remarkably beautiful even if it was fairly unusable. But it would serve, Slim had said, as the greatest buffer to curiosity seekers we could have ever found.

Almost sunset, so we made our way back down the rutted road to where we had left Zwagen and our gear. We didn't talk much as we set up camp, but knew that, like explorers, we were mapping the land in our heads and assigning names to everything from weirdly shaped trees to uniquely shaped boulders. We were laying claim on behalf of the great empire of Hunga Dunga, to the land that would become its colony. Each of our minds was abuzz with all the ways we were going to make the Church of Manna land the pride of the valley. We would become valued residents of Twisp.

Our flurries of ideas turned into flurries of snow. Our dreams would have to be put on hold. A major storm was on its way. It was time to head south.

CHAPTER 75
December 1972

Nick was on the other side of the Golden Gate Bridge continuing an affair with the daughter of a wealthy Marin County developer. Her name was Chelsea, and she owned a flower shop in San Rafael.

Nick had always been a womanizer. It wasn't entirely his fault. He had that dreamy, innocent look that women cannot resist. Many young women from other communes who didn't fully understand the relationship between Psylvia and Nick, would take the initiative to "third person" him. Once in a while, a guy would. He never refused.

But this was different. Chelsea was from a background that Nick, perhaps unconsciously, always wanted. Old money and refined, but on the wild side. She was playing the role of a hippie but unwilling to give up the life to which she was accustomed. Therefore, she used her trust fund to work within the establishment by starting business establishments. She was another "straddler." We were worried Nick wouldn't be able to resist the material temptations of Marin County. That he would go over to the other side. The dark side.

But even though he'd been missing for days, Nick came through! On the ninth of December, he walked into the bedroom, just as Psylvia was going into labor. We were relieved to see him but still a little angry that he had put us through so much worry. The midwife from the Golden Aura commune had no idea why we were glaring at the father, but she was too busy to care. The baby was coming. Breathe. Push. Scream. Breathe. Push. Scream. Over and over. It was like fingernails on a blackboard. But suddenly, a perfect, beautiful, goo-covered baby came out. It was too cool! The love Nick instantly felt took the form of tears spilling onto his daughter's face and splashing on Psylvia. If she *had* been angry with Nick, she instantly forgave him. So the rest of us did too.

He picked up the infant and cradled her in his arms. And the tears poured. He rocked her and spoke softly to her. We couldn't hear what he was saying, but it sounded reassuring. When he handed her back to Psylvia, he kissed her on the forehead and then on the lips, pressing his into hers intently, as if to say, "Thank you. I love you."

Ellen broke the tender moment, and through her own tears asked, "So do you have a name for her? I saw you making lists the other day."

Psylvia and Nick looked at one another, then at their baby, then back at us. Psylvia said with her beatific smile, "Actually no! We do not know! We figured we'd let you guys decide."

Richard raced out of the room, went to the nearest phone, and called Western Union. The wire he sent to Larry in Paris read: "FRANK MCCORMICK IS A GIRL! STOP. SEND NEW NAME AND A DRESS! STOP."

Larry sent a dress, but not a name. Baby went nameless for a long time. Names for her flew around the house while we passed her from one cradle of arms to another. I never knew any baby could be so loved, nurtured, and cared for by so many people. Obviously, seeing our Psylvia give birth before our very eyes left an indelibly wondrous impression. Everyone vied for the right to hold her, talk to her, sing to her, read to her. Psylvia gave a class in changing diapers. Almost everyone attended and took on the chore with delight, raising their hands in the air like fifth-graders, hoping to be the one chosen to do it. Our baby was staring into a different face every half hour or so. But the face of Little Richard made her squeal with glee. He seemed the most naturally paternal. More so than Nick, who was a good, dependable, and loving father. He just didn't have the innate, intuitive skills that Richard did.

When Larry came home, he and I often wondered if she would grow up as a precocious, secure, self-confident young woman, or full of psychoses and neuroses from the carousel of so many different personalities swirling past her face.

By the beginning of the New Year, we had agreed on a name. She was no longer "Baby" or "Sweetheart" or "Smuggims." She was now the delightful Lily, the pride of Hunga Dunga and the object of all our affection.

There was another young person, a teenaged boy, who would enter our lives and entwine himself around us one by one, like a slow-creeping, but stubborn vine. But for now, it was only Lily who had smitten us, changed our lives, and brought out the best in us.

CHAPTER 76
Winter 1973

"The Whole Earth Catalog." Nick brought it home one day excited to share all the wonderful, earth-friendly products it contained, and the ways to find instructions and tools to create an environment on the Twisp land that would be in keeping with our mission for the Church of Manna.

Sitting side by side on the couch, Nick and I leafed through the thick, heavy catalog, jotting down notes of books we wanted to buy, places we wanted to visit, and people we felt it would be good to contact. The catalog became a reference book we were never without. It was as useful as a thesaurus is to a writer, a cookbook to a newlywed.

It was jam-packed with information on where to acquire old-fashioned tools for those who preferred to do *everything* by hand. Or who had no access to power. Or who just wanted to return to a pre-industrial America. It told where to find books on ingenious technologies like solar and methane. And it provided access to the designs and detailed instructions for building an array of different dwellings.

Many were legacies from our ancestors. Yurts, tipis, and semi-subterranean dwellings. Brilliant architects like Buckminster Fuller more recently devised others. The excerpts from "The Dome Book" and the accompanying graphics were enough to get us both enthused. A dome!

It was something we could pre-fab in The City and haul up to Twisp. It would be an efficient use of time. We showed pictures of finished domes to the rest of Hunga Dunga, but no one was as enthusiastic as Nick and me. In fact, some seemed disappointed that we were only building another corral for the herd of us. The questions flew fast and furious. "Will there be rooms?" "What about acoustics?" "We've heard domes are notorious for their echoey acoustics!" "Will we have to take turns speaking in order not to go crazy?" "How can you hang anything on a curved wall?" These were just some of the nay-saying questions we had to counter.

"Temporary headquarters!" was our constant rebuttal. "Easy and quick shelter for all of us while we decide what to build next, where, and for whom."

The last one was the winner. The idea that someday each of us might have our own little cabin to trick out, or a love nest where we could take our tricks, appealed to everyone. To me it was another sign of the conundrum beginning to surface. We still wanted to be together, but we wanted to drift apart. To have more breathing room, our own spaces, our own clothes. We were maturing and tiring of socks that didn't match. We learned a lot with our experiments in voluntary non-attachment, and strict adherence to pooling all our money. But there was something in the air. Something that had to do with those circles of interests.

The circles, for the time being, still intersected, and though it was probably more out of apathy than anything else, or maybe just a way to make us stop talking about it, we were given the go-ahead to, "Build the fucking dome, already!"

Our own self-imposed rule was that we would build the dome entirely from recycled materials whenever possible. The Friends of Perfection, under the masterful tutelage of Eli, their benevolent despot, had learned how to use The System better than any other person we knew. Eli approved of our desire to evolve from a distributor of free food to a grower of free food. So, he was uncharacteristically helpful. He hired Nick, Chuck, and me as subcontractors to work on a neighborhood redevelopment program. Our pay was to be, as usual, not in dollars but in kind. In this case, building materials… for Twisp!

Kaliflower, I mean Friends of Perfection, had scored a contract with The City to prepare for the redevelopment of certain neighborhoods. Redevelopment of course meant tearing down. In most places, this would have meant a quick demolition with bulldozers and wrecking balls. But we were here to recycle, not demolish. Not tear down, but deconstruct.

We painstakingly deconstructed two old Victorians in the Mission, putting aside every possible reusable piece of material. First, was a quick scan for the most obvious and often most coveted. Mirrors, mantels, stained-glass windows, that kind of stuff.

Lath and plaster generally got tossed but under them were the two by fours, sixes, eights, 10s and 12s. We also kept all the big beams and timbers. We patiently denailed them and piled them carefully in stacks according to their length or size. We would retrieve them later that night and sequester them in the bowels of one communal house or another.

Windows, doors, toilets, and sinks, we salvaged them all with the greatest of care. We knew these could be readily re-used, and with a little cleaning and refinishing, looked very fine and boasted Victorian class.

Light fixtures, outlets, switches, electric panels, and the wires in between them were scrutinized and if there were a chance anything were reusable, we delicately removed them with the steadiness of brain surgeons, forever severing the synapses that once made the house come alive. I felt we were performing lobotomies. It always made me sad.

As for the hardware, we had to unscrew, unbolt, unfasten, unfix, unbind, unratchet, and uncrowbar, every last piece. This was the nuts and bolts of the whole thing. This was the stuff that held everything together and we were there to take it apart. We put aside each hinge, nut, bolt, bracket, brace, and screw in their assigned coffee cans for use in their next incarnations.

Brick by brick, wood by wood, glass by glass, metal by metal, we amassed an impressive stockpile of reusable material. We were truly the most anal-retentive demolition company in The City.

In the meantime, Zietar, with the help of the Good Dog guys at the Free Garage, found a beat-up, but promising 1955 Jeep pickup. Four-wheel drive, motorized winch up front, even the rifle rack still attached across the rear window. It was a most macho vehicle if ever there were one. Richard made love to it like it was some drunken stevedore at his disposal. Unlike the sweetness and gentility he had shown Zwagen in rebuilding *her*, Jeep was a *he*, and required some brutish force, a bit of rough-housing. Manhandling. Deep tissue massage followed by a rather forced entry. But as usual, Richard had his way with him, and rebuilt him into a vehicle that served us extremely well, albeit in an S&M sort of way.

We had a contest to see who could come up with the best name for our jeep, but no one could agree on any of them. Nick just wanted to call him Jeep. But Larry and Richard wanted something more distinctive. Lily, cradled in Nick's swaying arms, had the last word. She was still in the gurgling, gooing stage, but Psylvia and Nick insisted she was talking… Lily-talk. In sporadic outbursts between her spitting up and drooling, she loudly spurted a few baby-epithets that I didn't understand. Like "waaah" and "eee" and "meeah" and "naah." But Larry and Ziets understood immediately.

"Wilhelmina!" Richard translated. "Lily wants to call the jeep, Wilhelmina!" Larry agreed and said he loved the name. Nick couldn't rebuff a "word" that had come out of his own, obviously precocious daughter's mouth. His paternal pride overruled his previously macho stance. "Wilhelmina" became the jeep's name. Who could argue with a baby? We all tickled Lily and thanked her for her creativity. Wilhelmina had a sex change and for *her* transsexual, slavish loyalty, Wilhelmina deserves a place in Hunga Dungan history.

Throughout the rest of the winter, most of the work happened at our neighboring commune, Flo Airwaves. Their basement was already a well-equipped workshop, thanks to the Woodworker's Collective, whereas our basement was full of stuff the landlord was storing. Divine wasn't too happy about this development, but Rolli, Travis, Danny, and the woodworkers were happy to let us use the space. I don't think at the time, however, Flo Airwaves knew how much noise a radial arm saw makes, but they were soon to find out.

Good thing Little Richard was our accountant, bookkeeper, and dispenser of funds. At family meetings, we would trudge through the usual variety of issues. Alvoye and Luc wanted to go to Paris. Lana thought that if anyone should go to Paris it should be her. After all, it was she who had fucked Maxime, a fact Lana insisted on reminding us of, repeatedly.

Tom and Brandon announced they loved us but wanted to find a place of their own and could we excuse them from pooling their money that month.

Psylvia wanted to go to school to be a plumber. She also told us that Lily, now over a month old, insisted upon a fixed schedule so she would know in advance, which crazy person was going to be taking care of her that day. She needed to prepare herself psychologically.

Richard suggested we create a fund for those who wanted to go to Paris. "We'll start off with 60 dollars a month. OK? Can everyone live with that? Is there anyone who can't live with that? Good. The Paris Fund is hereby begun."

Tom and Brandon were another story. People bemoaned the idea of them leaving. It was a personal affront to some of us. To Richard and Lizzie, it was all of that, in addition to being a decrease in the monthly coffers. But who was anyone to stop them from leaving? Besides, I'm sure more than a few minds were scrambling for a persuasive argument why they should get to stay in the cabin after they left. I just plugged this event into my increasing feelings that things were unraveling.

"Hunga Dunga is a state of mind," Baird began. "It has nothing to do with living under the same roof. We are an idea of how the whole planet should work." As usual, Baird had his way of elevating any conversation to a philosophic one. Bobby and Alvoye hated when he did that. I rather enjoyed it. He was so often right on. If only he were a bit more humble in his delivery.

"So many have come and stayed for varying lengths of time in this big Blue House, and then left. When they were here, they were Hunga Dunga. And when they left, we can only hope they shared our vision and remained Hunga Dunga."

I heard Larry and Ellen whisper, "Oy gevald!" to each other and stifle a laugh. Baird ignored them.

"Remember, even those of us who might be in Twisp under the auspices of the Church of Manna will still be Hunga Dunga. The non-principles we don't live by will still be…."

Richard interrupted him. "Yeah, yeah, yeah! Tom and Brandon, we are sorry to see you leave. Leave with our love, but could you wait until next month to stop pooling money? Can you live with that? Can everyone live with that?" And when no one answered, it was a done deal.

Then Nick turned to Psylvia. "What's all this bullshit about becoming a plumber?"

"It's not bullshit, Nicky. We're all getting by pretty well here, but I want to make sure Lily has everything she needs. You don't contribute a cent to Hunga Dunga and I'm not on crazy pay. I just get a split of the meager profits at The Yin-Yin. Plumbers make good bucks. Female plumbers are a shoo-in."

"Let's hear it for affirmative action!" Ellen cheered, and the two of them started chanting, "Sexism sucks! What do we want? Sex! When do we want it? Now!" Lana and Trudy joined in. "What do we want? Sex! When do we want it? Now!"

Nick did not think it was funny. "Psylvia, only dykes want to be plumbers! I knew you shouldn't have been hangin around those lezzies at the Yin-Yin so much!" Everyone was stunned to hear Nick use those words and in that tone.

"Oh Nicky!" Psylvia said with the disgust and disappointment only she could deliver with such devastation. "Just go and fuck your little flower girl across the bridge. I hear her purring for you!" Psylvia stood up with Lily in her arms and left the room. Nick followed, muttering something about being sorry and stupid, but he couldn't help it that he liked smooth legs. Lily started crying. A gloom fell upon those that remained as her cries disappeared into the back yard. No one said anything for what seemed a very long time.

"OK, then," Zietar finally continued. "I suggest we enroll Psylvia in the trade school of her choice. And that if Ellen agrees, she can be Lily's personal secretary and oversee her social calendar. Ellen?"

Ellen answered, "I'd be honored."

"OK, then," Richard said, "can everyone live with that?" This time, instead of silence, there were outbursts of approval. "Absolutely! Right on! Go for it Psylvia! Unclog those drains, girl!"

"Well, that does it guys. We're through." Then just when everyone was in an upright position, more than ready to leave, Richard stopped them before they could take another step.

"Oh, just one more thing." Everyone halted in place and reluctantly turned around. "I'm going to buy a nice used radial arm saw and some other power tools for the Woodworkers Collective. Can everyone live with that?" Richard scanned each set of eyes just waiting for someone to say "no," daring them to say "no." No one dared say anything. No one wanted the meeting to last one minute longer. They couldn't take any more. They were already psyched up to leave. He was such a little sneak! And so intimidating for such a short guy! But I'd have to say that of all the people who were Hunga Dunga, no one was more revered than Psylvia and Little Richard.

And that's how the workshop in the basement of Flo Airwaves became even more well equipped, and how all the unexpected expenses connected with the land got paid: through sleight of hand, or in Richard's case, sleight of mouth.

CHAPTER 77
Winter 1973

When "The Dome Book" arrived, Nick, Ziets, and I gushed over it like a porn magazine. We drooled over pictures of domes of every conceivable kind in every conceivable place. The unique features of a dome, according to Bucky Fuller, were just too good to be true: an even air temperature throughout, the most efficient structure when it came to heating, strong as an egg on its end, and quick and easy to build. It was this last attribute that really horned us up. Quick and easy. We liked quick and easy.

But when we delved into it further, we found it wasn't going to be that quick or that easy. Depending on what kind of dome you wanted, the complexity could vary greatly. The simple domes that could be set up in a day, looked like star-trek housing or some kind of futuristic trailer park. Their frames were very angular and used high tech stuff like PVC pipe and flexible rubber hubs. If the skin weren't canvas or ripstop nylon, or just plain plastic sheeting, it was usually some kind of noxious form of foam or fiberglass. None of these appealed to us.

It became clear that building a dome with traditional materials was going to be a challenge. But that's what we had to work with, that's what we wanted to do, and we were determined to build a tasteful little Victorian dome that would blend in nicely with the neighboring farms.

We decided on a four-frequency, five-eighths truncated dome, 36 feet in diameter. It would be anchored to a circular deck that sat on pilings just tall enough to give us a crawl space. The higher the frequency, the more the structure approached a perfect sphere. However, four frequencies were the highest Zietar and I were willing to go without having a mathematical breakdown.

Although Nick was adequate with numbers, Richard and I could recall our trig and solid geometry. And even with the indispensable tables provided in the book, engineering the thing was going to tax our feeble ATD minds. We decided that Richard and I would do the math independently. When we came up with different answers, we worked on them until they jived. When we agreed the numbers were right, we translated them to Nick in real construction-guy terms.

"OK, Nick. We're gonna have to start thinking in terms of triangles divided into smaller triangles, divided into smaller triangles."

He furrowed his young brow and worked at concentrating.

"This two-by-four has to have three angles on each end. On this end, the face angle is forty-six and a half degrees. The side angle on the left is twenty-two and a half degrees. And the one on the right is thirty-six degrees. Now on the other end the angles are…."

Nick just looked at us dumbfounded. His eyes glazed over when we broke the bad news that there were going to be four different lengths of struts with a total of 32 different angles. Both ends of each strut had to have a quarter-inch notch in the face angle, no more than two and three-quarter inches deep, in order to accommodate the steel hubs. Ellen's uncle was going to forge them for us, as soon as we provided templates for drilling the holes.

This, of course, meant being able to drill through the struts at the precise spots where the holes would align with the holes in the hubs so we could bolt them together. And of course, the holes would have to be countersunk so we could later put the skin on, whatever that was going to be.

As we passed our calculations on to Nick, complete with our own childlike diagrams, we too, started to feel overwhelmed. But at the same time, we were awed by what we had managed to accomplish as we began to understand the mathematics of Buckminster Fuller. We were attempting to build a finite object on an infinite continuum, an imperfect object that approaches, but never reaches, a perfect sphere.

For Hunga Dunga, as in so many examples from our real lives, designing and building the dome was truly a cosmic undertaking. It became a metaphor for our lives in general, but we never spoke of it, because by tradition, "everything was needless to say." It was another one of those deliciously subtle reminders of what Hunga Dunga was supposed to be about. Trying to make the imperfect, perfect. Trying to make a bunch of sticks, look like a sphere.

It was truly inspiring to watch Nick's brain digest, organize, and apply all this information. Nick, the Man! From the gentle, do-nothing fawn Psylvia brought back from Yosemite, to this man becoming more capable and surprising every day. We didn't like the way he treated Psylvia, but until she told us to hate him, we would mind our own business. Unless, of course, we could hint at his unacceptable behavior using the Socratic Method. Questions, to which he either had no answer or ignored them.

Nick applied our math to those two-by-four struts in the most ingenious ways. He color-coded everything. He spray-painted different colored dots along each two-by-four, designating its length and all its different angles. Then he fabricated jigs for the radial arm saw, one jig for each of the four kinds of struts, another jig for the drill press, and still others for the table saw. After a few days of experimentation and fine-tuning, he had it down to where any one of us, when we had spare time, could grab a two-by-four, look at the poster on the door that explained each color, and cut its length, six angles, two notches and two three-quarter inch holes without hardly thinking about it. He amazed us. He knew it. He knew we couldn't get along without him.

The basement of Flo Airwaves became a humming little factory and a source of never-ending curiosity to the other woodworkers in the collective. Even Travis and Rolli got into the swing of things, helping whenever they could, trying to keep Divine at bay. It was her constant whining and yelling at us that lent impetus to working as fast as we could. On one clear mid-winter day, we had enough struts, hubs, and bolts to take one section down to Dolores Park to see if it worked. Three large pentagons attached together. Wobbly. We had to shore it up with our bodies. But we could see where it was going. It worked beyond our wildest expectations. It gave us the kind of rush I expect those people at NASA get when they launch a rocket, and everything is A-OK! We felt the same.

By the end of winter, everything had come together. And we had thought of everything we could think of. Wilhelmina was in perfect running order with a brand-new coat of bright white paint. All the struts for the dome were ready, with extras of each kind in case some broke during the building process. We picked out the best of the recycled materials that might come in handy, and tents and tipis for temporary shelter.

Our goals were to tear down Slim's house and barn for the rest of the materials we'd need to build the dome. We needed to get our dirt road graded and drivable. Then we would build a temporary outdoor kitchen and a rudimentary, gravity-fed water system from the spring. Next, we would have to build the deck, assemble the struts, put a plywood skin over the struts, weatherproof it, and call it good for the season. That's all.

As we actually wrote these goals down, we realized how ambitious it was. There would be Nick, Ziets, Psylvia, Lily, Trudy, Chuck, and me. No one else was interested in coming. They only wanted to visit after there were some creature comforts. We had our work cut out for us.

Shortly before our departure, Rolli and Travis asked if they could come along. And Katie, Lee, Bianca, and Scott from Kaliflower wanted to convoy up with us. This was great! Our pool of labor was increasing, as were the kinds of skills we'd need. Which was everything. As word spread, friends from other communes promised to come up and help. This seemed like a fine idea though we wondered if this would compromise the low profile we wanted to keep in the valley.

By the end of April a caravan of vehicles was double-parked outside Big Blue waiting for the last of the Twispians to wriggle their bodies into some kind of comfortable position. Wilhelmina led the convoy, with Nick and me in the cab, and the bed of the truck brimming with camping gear, tools, clothing, books, and whatnot.

Hitched to Wilhelmina was a six-foot-high by eight-foot-long, wood-frame trailer, loaded with building materials and our beloved struts, which overflowed the top and had to be strapped down tightly.

Behind Wilhelmina, Zwagen idled with the rest of the crew sitting between suitcases and backpacks and mostly Lily gear, diapers and the like. Zwagen's makeshift roof rack was piled high with boxes labeled "kitchen stuff."

Rolli's split-window VW bus lingered behind Zwagen. It was very fantastically painted with images from Grateful Dead songs and wild swirls of psychedelia. Last in line was the step-van waiting to transport the Friends of Perfection contingent.

It probably looked to most "normal" people what the top-heavy, overcrowded buses in India looked like to Jon, Rosie, and me. At that time, it made us think everyone in the subcontinent was crazy. At this time, it made me think of Jon and Rose and how much I really missed them and how I wished they were doing this trip with me, us.

The remaining family members of Hunga Dunga and Flo Airwaves stood on their respective front porches, all waving wildly and wishing us best-of-lucks, drive carefully-s and we love you-s.

All except Divine, who yelled the loudest, "Good riddance! And don't come back soon! Ya damn hicks!"

CHAPTER 78

Spring and Summer 1973

City slickers no more! After tearing down Slim's house and barn, a breeze compared to the Victorians in The City, we had lumber and building materials up the wazoo. And in the process, we'd gotten to know the lay of the land, so to speak. We became regulars at the Mercantile, the True Value, Hank's Market, and the bank.

"Church of Manna?" the pretty, young teller asked as she looked at Richard and me and handed him our new checkbook. She smiled broadly. She couldn't have been cuter! "I see you live up Poorman Creek. Any kin to the Second Mile Ranch? Those folks are just the greatest!"

"We are kin of the Spirit, I am sure!" Richard smiled, his cherubic face aglow.

"Well, you're the kind of people we want movin' here to the valley. Even though some don't understand you're just trying to live exactly like the Lord did… ya know with the long hair and beards and all." She was so Pollyanna-ish. If she were any more gracious and cheerful to us, I would have suspected her of being the front man for an Antlers' hit squad.

Richard kept smiling, his face always so full of light, but he was so stumped by this unexpected welcome, his jaw dropped. Could it be that a mere change in name, from Hunga Dunga to The Church of Manna, had changed the perception of who we were, and therefore how we were treated? Now were we respectable, if still not likeable? Legitimate, if not illegitimate? Christian, if not the Anti-Christ? Treat them nice. Why take any chances?

I politely stepped in front of Richard before he could blow the cover the teller had made for us. I looked at her nameplate. "Jo Ann, we have got one nasty road goin' up to where we want to build our meeting place. Do you know of any good road builders that can smooth her out a bit?"

Jo Ann brightened even more, so eager to help, almost thankful! "Well sure! You want to go see Sam up at the end of Airport Road. Big barn, lots of big equipment. He's the best dirt handler around!"

"Thanks, sister!" She beamed at that moniker and gave a tiny wave. I started to leave, grabbing Richard's elbow, but turned to ask one more question. "Jo Ann, we got any other kin here in the valley?"

"Well sure! There's a couple more small churches like yours, parishes of the Universal Life Church or something like that, and quite a few non-profit organizations have accounts with us, and just a few regular folk, lookin' just like you, livin' in the way of the Lord, up in the woods. I love them all!"

She scared the hell out of Zietar and me. What kind of cruel, demonic device was this? What kind of deranged lunatic could see our long hair as anything other than the trademark of a hippie? I thought she was part of some right-wing plot and was going to pull a gun out at any moment and shoot us all! And with a big smile on her face, at that!

But Bob at the Broken Spoke recognized us for who we were immediately. Not that there wasn't some truth to Jo Ann's image of us, but from that first breakfast when Nick, Trudy and I found the land, Bob knew we were de-Flower-ed Children and wanna-be space angels and true-blue stoners with a bent for egalitarianism. He had only been aloof to us because of Ferlin, the local policeman. Otherwise, he was very friendly, especially when there were no town officials or cops around. He turned us on to red beer, or tomato beer as some called it. I never really liked the taste of beer and only drank it now and then to be part of the gang. Red beer was a boon to me. I loved it! And real men drank it! It wasn't an umbrella drink or anything! But whenever I was back in The City and ordered a red beer, bartenders always looked at me like I was crazy.

We all worked so hard, that after a bath with Dr. Bronner's soap in the freezing Twisp River, and a meal of some vegetable over brown rice, a nice salad, maybe a walk to Zietar's Knoll to watch the sunset; we were all in bed not much later than dusk. The sun ruled our lives. Up at the *break* of dawn, asleep at the *repair* of night.

But one Friday night, Ziets, Chuck, and I went into town to the Spoke. It was empty! It was early, but not that early! Bob said, "Damn! Antlers is having some live music tonight. Some out-of-town country and western band. Valley this small can't compete with that!"

We sat down on the bar stools and ordered our beers. Bob gave me a red one before I could ask for it. I guessed we were starting to be considered part of the "regulars." Bob looked around, brought out some incense of all things, and after lighting it, a pipe, and some weed! We all stared at it and then at Bob. He broke into a big smile. "Aeneas Valley Red!" is all he said as he packed the bowl full and faced the pipe stem toward us.

"Who wants to do the honors?" he asked and gave Chuck the pipe. Chuck looked him in the eye, said "Cheers," and took a toke under the flame of Bob's lighter. Chuck made sure it was fired up good and then passed it to me, while Bob fiddled with some sound equipment under the bar. Suddenly, Pink Floyd's "Dark Side of the Moon" interrupted some *not* unpleasant Bob Wills song, coming through the bar's surprisingly fine sound system.

"Man, you guys have the whole town wondering' what you're up to! Gonna get a crop growin'?" We all looked at each other. "Be careful. Lots of Forest Service planes workin' with the police. Lots of air coverage," he said, almost in a whisper, as if his bar were bugged.

Little Richard answered in what I thought was a convincing voice. I mean it was the truth after all, and we were paranoid enough as it was without people thinking this!

"Hey Bob, that's not what's happening! Really! We're just trying to build this dome and trying to grow some food and trying to enjoy doing it!"

"It's cool, Richard," Bob said assuredly. Then seriously, "I just wish everyone was out there, visible like you guys, doing stuff, workin' hard, being themselves."

We all looked at him with the same expression. "Whaaat?"

"It's like you all came out of nowhere, all at the same time. Except most of ya stay in the woods and only come down into town maybe once a month or so to stock up on stuff. And it pisses me off that ya don't think maybe some of us locals feel the same way about things as you all do, but we don't look the part. Like the Porters and Ben, who're usually the ones playin' down at the Antlers."

Chuck, Ziets, and I looked at each other, then at Bob. We felt guilty that somehow we had hurt his feelings, but by now we were thoroughly stoned and being vacuumed up into the dark side of the moon. Bob was equally stoned and rambled on.

"And only once in a while do I get a few of ya that'll stop in for lunch and then they're always vegetarians, so I make 'em cheeseburgers, hold the burger, extra lettuce. But anyway… your crew! The Church of Manna thing… the 'Dome People' who work on the 'Dome Land,' damn! You guys are notorious!"

"Whaaat?" the three of us replied again.

"Oh, hell yeah! You guys stick out like a sore thumb. Whole valley's waitin' to see if you live up to any of that church stuff!"

Talk about pressure. This was hard to take since we tried to be as inconspicuous as possible. If we were going to stick out, we had to stick out as good examples of how good people behave. At the same time, we wanted to feel we were not alone. We were getting hungry for new faces. We were used to the community of The City. We wanted the same thing but on a smaller, more manageable scale.

Zietar had a bright idea. "Bob! You should hire a hot rock band. There must be one between Tonasket, Wenatchee, and here. Draw those freaks out of the woods."

"There is one," Bob said. "Up in Tonasket. Heard it was great!"

"When the time comes, let us know," I said. "We'll help you put up posters and stuff."

The time came, and the posters went up, and the freaks and locals came down, and it was wild and wonderful, everyone had a really fun time, and the band was happy, and Bob made enough money to want to do it again. Which he did. And he got some really good bands. It became a monthly event. Sometimes more often than that.

As I left one of these events, I could hear the Porter's 3-piece, very tight, very nice bluegrass music coming out of the Antlers and clashing with the wailing guitars blaring from the Broken Spoke. But the people inside both bars were hootin' and hollerin' and dancing up a sweat and having a wonderful time. It made me understand how it was that everyone managed to get along. They all respected and understood hard work and hard play.

We never worked so hard in our lives! There was no division of labor at first, but within a month or so, the women were gravitating to the kitchen and maintaining some semblance of a hygienic operation, while the guys had turned into obsessed pilgrim homesteaders, peeling logs with shaving horses and then splitting them with froes and using other manly, butch, colonial tools.

On occasion, the girls would take up the hammer or shovel and do a fine job. Or

Richard would cook up a stir-fry that was quite tasty. Katie could come up to me and yell, "Hey, Giacco! Let me put up a few struts for a while. You go stir the beans." And that was cool. But unintentionally and inexplicably, the chores wound up split along gender lines. We talked about it. We didn't like it. We didn't understand it. We didn't enforce it. We believed that the role gender plays is determined by how you grow up in a family and in a culture. Skills aren't innate. People develop them through exposure, self-confidence, encouragement, and the assumptions made toward them. We truly believed that.

Nevertheless, Psylvia, Trudy, Katie, and Bianca tended mostly to satisfying the voracious appetites of the guys. Even I could eat four sandwiches for lunch! Until we had our fairly sophisticated watering system in, the girls had to haul water from the spring up near the Saddle Pass, and that in itself was an awesome chore. They came up with some amazing dinners considering the Cenozoic tools at their disposal. And there were always fresh bread and cakes and clean clothes. It was downright weird to find ourselves falling into these traditional roles. But we did and we did them well.

Except for a chain saw, all our tools were hand tools. We had no power and no running water. We were totally off the grid. We liked the image of having gone back in time. We were building a 21st-century building with mostly turn-of-the-century tools. The going was slow, steady, and unending. But the unexpected side effect on all of us was muscles!

We looked great! None of us was ever fitter in our lives and it showed. And the more it showed, the harder we wanted to work. The muscles we were acquiring were so obvious that we worried one side of us would get more muscular than the other. We tried our best to become ambidextrous, especially with the heavy hammers, which were in constant use as we pieced together the deck. This practice increased the incidence of injury at least 400 percent but it was worth it. It was lucky that Katie and Bianca had received first-aid training at Eli's insistence.

Nick looked especially great. His slim body was getting beefier in all the right places, his abs were phenomenal, his muscles incredibly well defined. I wasn't chopped liver either. My Sicilian skin soaked up the eastern Washington sun like a sponge and I was very tan. And my body had become as sinewy and toned as it ever had, and I had put on weight for the first time in years. For the first time I could look at myself naked in a mirror and like what I saw. We liked living in 1903 instead of '73. No need for a gym or fancy foods. A healthy and muscular body was the reward for doing hard work. The best kind of muscles to have.

By the beginning of September, we were assembling the struts. It went quickly. The struts were perfect, and the steel hubs were perfect. Nick's jigs had cut perfect angles. Once we had the first tier assembled and anchored to the deck, the rest went faster with each tier. We got used to these triangular and pentagonal wonders. We were always seeing them one frequency higher in our minds and how they could become a perfect sphere.

It was mind-boggling. But no matter how many triangles and pentagons we put together; the structure never seemed to get any more stable. It was always wobbling slightly as you attached another strut. We worried some of them might crack from the torque as they approached the top and assumed more of a curve. We had to support them from the floor of the deck with long poles. That's just about the time we got our first visitors.

Five men and a woman on horseback ka-clomped their way up our dusty road. We all stopped what we were doing, wherever we were doing it, and watched them approach. They all wore jeans and snap-button shirts, except for one guy all in buckskin, his vest open, showing off his chest. He and the man and woman leading the way seemed older than us, but not by much. The remaining two men were definitely old timers, wrinkled skin, cowboy hats, chaw, the works.

"Howdy," said the woman. Strange how one word could sound so confident and authoritative, yet friendly. "I'm Chettie Porter and this is my husband, Nate," she said, pointing to the man in the saddle next to hers. Chettie behaved, quite naturally, like a Katherine Hepburn aristocrat. Nate looked a bit on the meek side with his thick glasses, face hidden by a full beard and mustache, and the way his shoulders slouched. He said a soft and gentle, "Hi!"

"We own the ranch just upriver, other side, off Twisp River Road," Chettie said as she pointed over the valley. "Can't miss it. Has a big wooden bridge crossing the river to the house. This is our friend, Woody," she said, pointing to the man in buckskin. "He just got back from climbing Mount Everest."

Well, that was quite a statement. Richard and I exchanged glances, wondering if this was bullshit or not. We gave them the benefit of the doubt, mainly because Chettie spoke so nonchalantly about the achievement.

Woody had thin blond hair. He didn't speak but stuttered. Chettie translated for him. His bright, extremely clear blue eyes were a window to an over-active mind that was just out of range of deranged. Chettie seemed to keep him balanced. I felt there was a history between them, and it was one I would never get to learn about.

What I learned about the Porters, I learned from Ben. Many of the townspeople regarded them with awe. Chettie came from an old New England, Mayflower kind of family. The patriarch was involved in politics and the family moved to Washington, D.C., in the mid-1800s, where they became a fixture of Washington society.

Nate, originally from Spokane, was the venerated social studies teacher at the high school. He was famous for his photographic memory and encyclopedic knowledge of everything. He was once a seminarian in a Jesuit monastery, just about to take his vows and enter the priesthood, when he met Chettie galloping her horse through the isolated and hallowed grounds. When Nate stepped from behind a maple tree, the horse reared and threw Chettie into a pile of autumn leaves. Nate, in his brown frock, ran over to see if she were hurt. As soon as their eyes met through his thick lenses, the adrenaline that rushed through their bodies was overwhelming. The rest is history. Or so Ben told me.

Chettie pointed to the two old-timers bringing up the rear. "That's Olie and Dexter. Neighbors of ours. They're brothers. Own the 120 acres upriver from us. Raise some cattle.

Thought you should meet them." And she winked at us as if to say, "May as well know your enemies!"

Olie and Dexter just barely tipped their cowboy hats. They surveyed the scene carefully. There was a lot going on. Some of our gang was out by the kitchen. Others were working in the garden that Little Richard had insisted we plant in the now dry seasonal pond.

The rest of us were loitering around the main attraction, The Dome. Yes, it had become a proper name. Nick sat astride a tall, homemade ladder so he could work the top struts from the inside, Rolli was down on the ground handing material and tools up to Nick. I was culling through the assorted piles of struts we had, picking out the best ones. I'm sure Chettie and her entourage were surprised to see so much activity.

"Ya know when the snows come, that ain't gonna do ya much good!" Olie called out to Nick, who was now standing on top of the ladder, making me nervous just to look at him. He was so fearless.

"Not gonna do you much good a'tall. Gonna come down on your haids and crush ya!" agreed Dexter, with almost a hint of glee in his voice.

Olie dismounted and started for the deck. Some of us gathered around. Olie had immediately recognized Nick as the leader of this particular pack and spoke almost exclusively to him.

"Sometimes we get big snows around here, I'm telling ya. This ain't never gonna take the load," he yelled up.

I got his attention and, opening up the now well-worn Dome Book, showed him numbers about pounds per square inch and all of that and how a dome was stronger than anything else around, even the steep-pitched roofs.

Olie looked up at Dexter. They both shook their heads. Then Olie looked at me. He shook his head and lowered it some. Then he looked up at Nick atop the ladder and he shook his head some more, shielding his eyes from the sun with his cowboy hat.

"You lookee here, son!" Olie said contestingly to Nick. "Look and feel real close!" Then Olie put his big thumb on just one of the struts next to him and pushed a little. Then again. Then some more.

You could see the whole thing start to sway. You could follow it as Olie's thumb firmly pressed one strut and the wave traveled all the way up to the very top. For a moment, we had a sinking feeling that maybe this *wasn't* going to work. It didn't help when Olie jumped up in the saddle again laughing along with his brother. "Oh, my Lordy! This is going to be one interestin' winter!"

And the two of them pulled on their reins and turned their horses around and ka-clomped back down the dirt road. They were still laughing as they turned the first bend.

Chettie looked us over. "Don't pay any attention to them. Nothing would make them happier than to see you fail. But I know you're not going to."

"Me, too," added Nate.

"Thanks for the votes of confidence," said Richard.

"Hey Giacco," Nick yelled down. "C'mon up here and help me get these last struts in place."

I moved one of the tall ladders from one side of The Dome to where Nick was working underneath the very crown. I grabbed one of the tethers we had made, because we learned quickly that the higher we got, the dicier it got. I started up the ladder with the two struts and made my way slowly, one handmade rung at a time. I threw the length of rope over one of the nearby struts and clipped it to my belt. Then delicately, without looking down, I stood on the top rung of the ladder and handed Nick one of the struts.

There was still plenty of play in the structure, and that strut went in with no problem. But the completely wonderful, three-dimensional design we were about to complete seemed more fragile than ever. Seemed that the struts at the top might snap at any moment from the gravity weighing them down. But when Nick and I wrestled in that *last strut*, got those holes lined up and sledged that *last bolt* all the way through, I swear you had to be there to understand it, to grasp the physics of it.

This thing we were building, always swaying to a thumb's push, suddenly locked into place. That last strut turned our recycled two-by-fours into steel. Without the last strut, you had nothing. With it, everything. You could feel its strength. Every strut getting its strength from every other strut. A perfect synthesis.

I fondly thought of Baird. "The most important Hunga Dunga is all of us combined. Individually we are important and equal. Equally weak." The Dome was the perfect metaphor.

Nick and I were so sure of its strength that we knocked down our ladders and just swung from our tethered ropes from one side of The Dome to the other, like chimpanzees hooting and scratching our armpits as we passed each other. Ziets, Chuck, and Lee climbed on the skeleton of triangles and scampered around it like it was a jungle gym. It was strong!

They scurried to the top and the more weight we put on it, pressing or pulling, the more it locked together and the stronger it got. We knew then that we were going to have the last laugh when the snows came. We were so elated, we forgot we still had company.

Nate suddenly became more animated and yelled up to us, "I am so honored that I was here for this event! Buckminster Fuller knew what he was doing! Thank you!"

Then Chettie yelled up, "You guys should come down to the Antlers some weekend."

Nick and I just exchanged glances as we swung by each other. "The Antlers?" I questioned dubiously. "Trudy, Nick, and I almost got our asses kicked last time we went there."

"Oh yes, that's right! Oh! That was nasty." Chettie laughed. "Well, I'm the one playing the banjo, and Nate's on piano, and Ben, whom I hope you will meet very soon, is on every other instrument known to man."

"I thought you guys looked familiar," I said, finally figuring it out. "I am so happy to know you," Richard said. "You sounded great the other night. Giacco and I stood outside the bar and listened. You guys are very good! And you know, in some circles I am known as the 'Ear!'"

"Well, then you must come this weekend. I promise you, no one will hassle you. I promise!"

That weekend we had a great time at the Antlers. We danced, sang, and drank red beer, and most fun of all, met Ben from the Second Mile Ranch. He was a riot and kept us in stitches. The Porters and Ben introduced us to most everyone else in the valley they thought we should know.

People came and went all summer long and into the early fall. We put them to work, and they did it willingly. Friends from The City, hitch hikers passing through, anyone that was willing to work was welcome to *vacation* in The Dome or its vicinity. But it works two ways. They were also bringing part of The City to us.

The big news was this pesky little guru kid Maharaj Ji. His plague, the "Knowledge," had ravaged every commune. Freaks were falling for it everywhere. It was very disturbing, since many of them were really good friends of ours.

"Giacco, you would really like this, I think. This is right up your alley!" Alex from the Good Dog guys said to me one day while we were working on a leak in the water system.

"What makes you think I'd have anything to do with that farce?" I replied.

"I know you, Giacco. I've tripped with you so many times. I know what you've been looking for. I know how you trip. This is it. It's free. You just have to want it enough to ask for it."

"Why don't you just tell me?"

"Because that would mean you don't want it bad enough. A sign you aren't ready."

"You think I'm not ready?"

"Well, if your ego is so big you can't even ask for it, yeah, I don't think you're ready. Why should I reveal a secret if you're so lazy that you won't even go and get it? It's free, man! What more do you want?"

"I want you to tell me the secret, dammit. If you're such a good friend, you'd tell me. But then again, maybe you aren't the close friend I thought you were."

"Now don't go layin' friendship on the line, brother. It's because you're such a good friend that I *can't* tell you the secrets of the Knowledge. Puttin' our friendship on the chopping block… well, Giacco, that's going too far!"

Conversations like this weren't just happening to me. They were happening to Chuck, Richard, Trudy, and Katie. They were happening in Twisp and San Francisco and all over the country, all over the world. We were hearing the same conversations repeatedly from friends whom we would never have described as unsophisticated or naïve. The mere curiosity of it all was contagious. The clincher was when someone said, "Hey, get it, and try it. If you don't like it, fuck it!"

I tried to be the most resistant. I just couldn't allow myself to be part of a mass hysteria. I just couldn't imagine myself being a disciple of someone who had hundreds of thousands of disciples. I just couldn't follow a mere teenager whose secret was called the "Knowledge!" How tacky was that? I just couldn't bear to think how Jon and Rose would look at me if I put so much as one toe in, even if it were just to test the waters. I scrutinized my thoughts and found them to be faulty, based on ego and vanity. Still, I was the most resistant. I would just not let my spiritual immune system be compromised. I just would not let myself be swept up in this epidemic and swoon like some 13-old girl at a Beatles concert.

I was a miserable failure.

CHAPTER 79
October 1973

It started shortly after we had finished putting up the struts and were at the stage of skinning the structure with plywood triangles. Most everyone had moved from their scattered campsites to be closer to The Dome. The Dome already had a magnetic magic about it to which everyone gravitated. Many of us just slept on the deck under the stars. The skeleton of The Dome gave the night sky a frame of reference. We could feel the planet moving beneath us as the stars moved from one triangular frame to another.

We meditated on The Dome, trying to feel it, letting it speak to us. Where it might like to have rooms and how that could happen, if it wanted a second floor or mezzanine. But most importantly, where it wanted windows and doors.

It wanted lots of windows. Pentagonal windows. Every other pentagon, especially on the second tier where the sides of The Dome were relatively vertical, could have windows that would open easily. It demanded a beautiful glass star at its pentagonal crown. But for that, we'd have to use Plexiglas, since tempered glass was so expensive. We really did do our best to use only the recycled materials we had salvaged. But once we tried to sink a few dozen or so recycled nails into old wood, we ended up saying, "Fuck this, let's buy some brand-new nails!" And once you buy a brand-new nail, you may as well buy Plexiglas. Right? That was our logic.

But most fun of all was taking turns reading aloud, Tom Robbins' *Another Roadside Attraction*. It was a beautiful ritual, gathering on the deck when night arrived. Lighting kerosene lanterns and building fires. Getting stoned and letting Robbins' outrageous metaphors take you on a trip. Some of us were better readers than others. Richard was very good, his phrasing perfect, his voice animated. Psylvia was pretty good, too. However, without a doubt, Chuck was the best, and we always looked forward to his turn to read a chapter or two. He was definitely the actor in the family. He brought the characters to life so vividly, and made the plot unfold so easily for us, we never wanted him to stop reading.

That's why we were so surprised one evening when Chuck didn't show up for dinner. In fact, no one had seen him all day. In fact, no one had seen him since the night before. This made us worry. It was not like Chuck to just up and split without telling anyone. Maybe he decided to go for a hike and got lost! There were bears up there! Or maybe a rattler bit him! There were a lot of those around too. We searched for him, yelled for him, but he was gone. We figured it had to be intentional. It was just too hard to disappear on us. A Hunga Dungan was always on the watch for someone whose privacy they could ruin.

We decided to go into town and tell Bob at the Spoke and then up to the Porters to tell them to be on the lookout or give us some advice. There really was nothing more we could do until morning.

The next day, Trudy, Richard, and I were sitting on the edge of the deck, looking out over the valley, waiting for Nick to join our trip to town. We were going to call home to see if anyone there had heard from Chuck. Depending on that call, we might go to the Forest Service office to put in a missing person's report. There was no need to do either.

Chuck was walking up the steep, still ungraded, dirt road, little puffs of dust following his steps. He held his t-shirt in his hand. Sweat was running down his chest from the intense eastern Washington summer sun and the effort required by the grade of the road. But there was a huge grin on his face. I think we all found it very annoying.

He walked steadily and slowly like the turtle, knowing he would get to the finish line eventually, so why worry. It was this attitude that bothered me the most. That, and the fact he was walking toe to heel!

When he got to the deck, he was huffing and puffing, but still smiling. Not the smile of guilt we were expecting and wanting from someone who had been up to no good and Chuck was definitely into being bad. Just a modest, genuine smile. Almost shy, which was rare for Chuck.

Trudy handed him a canteen of water. Chuck took it and gulped it down. "Thanks, Trudy."

"Uh-oh," said Trudy. "What's wrong? You're different."

Chuck just smiled, almost laughing a little.

"OK, Chuck," I said. "Who did you run off with? Tell us about him. Some lumberjack?"

When Chuck caught his breath he said, "I've been with Maharaj Ji!" Trudy and I gasped. "I hitched to Portland where I heard he was going to be. I heard *satsang* at the mission and then listened to Maharaj Ji speak and answer any question you could come up with, and I asked for the Knowledge, and he said yes, and his Mahatma took a bunch of us into another room and gave it to us. And now I'm a *premie*, Jai Satchitanand!"

Trudy and I just stared at him and then at each other. Trudy looked back at Chuck. "Jay-such-a-duh-how much did it cost you?"

"Nothing! I gave him a flower!"

"And the deed to your parents' house? A good Jewish boy like you?" Zietar asked. "Tsk, tsk."

"You don't understand guys! Give me a chance. Try to be a little open about this," Chuck beseeched us, as if for our own good. "For example, one guy said he'd been following Maharaj Ji around from city to city, and still didn't get to receive the Knowledge. So, Maharaj Ji says, 'Maybe you don't want it bad enough.' And the freak says, 'Not true. I want it more than anything!' And Maharaj Ji says, 'OK then, will you cut your hair off for it?' And the guy says, 'Yes, give me some scissors.' And Maharaj Ji laughs and says, 'It's OK! You don't have to cut your hair! You can have the Knowledge!' And the brother is like so hepped up with excitement, the electricity and love sweeps through the crowd.

"And then Maharaj Ji just swings his arm around the room and points his finger at another long-hair trying to look very calm and ready and Maharaj Ji says, 'But you! You must cut your hair now!' And that guy goes bonzo. He just sort of stares and stutters and before he can say anything Maharaj Ji says, 'I can tell you don't want to cut your hair today. It's OK. Come back after you've heard more *satsang* and understand. Come back when you're ready to cut it. I'll bring a baggie for you.' And Maharaj Ji just laughs. That's how he works!"

By this time, Nick wandered over and, after berating Chuck for getting us all worried, fell into the groove of Chuck's storytelling. How the 15-year-old chubby kid went around the room and decided who was and who was not ready to receive the Knowledge. One woman, like so many other people, had been following him from city to city, state to state, across the country. She was refused the Knowledge at every gathering, until Maharaj Ji, picking her out of a crowd, said he had been aware of her presence at each stop all along the way, and now she had proven she really wanted the Knowledge more than anything. She shall have it! And people break into tears when they are chosen, and break into tears when they are refused, but you are always reminded that to give up, means you don't want it bad enough.

"And he is always testing you," Chuck rambled on. "Especially by asking you to give up something you're attached to, like your car, or home, or boat, or money. He'll ask you to give him your car. And if you say yes, he always says he was just kidding. You can keep the car and yes, you can have the Knowledge. But every once in a while, he'll ask someone to do something extraordinary like letting him turn their vacation home into a retreat for his Divine Light Mission, and the person might say 'yes.' And Maharaj Ji, sensing this person was very affluent, might say 'Thank you. Leave the deed and the keys to the house with my brother Raja Ji. Then you may receive the Knowledge.' And more than likely that person would just quietly slip away, though sometimes, someone would actually hand over the deed!"

Chuck continued his storytelling in detail when everyone gathered for dinner and continued it afterwards when we all retreated to the deck. Instead of reading *Another Roadside Attraction*, we asked Chuck every conceivable question we could think of about the Knowledge. Chuck answered to the best of his ability on behalf of "the Goomer" as Psylvia had quickly nicknamed the guru kid.

Psylvia: So, what does the Goomer think about homosexuals?

Chuck: He says once you understand the Knowledge, you'll find it better than sex. But until then, make love, have a good time, and meditate.

Rolli: Does the Goomer say you have to be a vegetarian?

Chuck: No, eat whatever you want. He chooses not to eat meat, but that is just him. It is of no matter. Just meditate and you will know what to do and how to live. And can we please stop the 'Goomer' stuff and call him Guru Maharaj Ji, or at least Maharaji?

Giacco: What does the Goomer say about smoking weed and cigarettes?

Chuck: Oh, this is perfect for you Giacco. You who always say when we're tripping, "It has something to do with the breath, it's like in between the breaths or something..." Maharaj Ji says you should do nothing that would interfere with the breath. Smoking interferes with the breath!

Nick: I think the Goomer is just another con artist!

Chuck: Only meditating on the Knowledge can ever decide that! And you can't meditate on it if you don't have it!

Zietar: Oh, I know there's a flaw in the logic there, pal, throwing in a Catch-22!

Lee: So, is it a religion with do's and don'ts?

Chuck: No. Not a religion at all. Nothing to believe in. Really. It just is. It's a tool. It's a very cool tool. You can use it as you want to or need to. It suddenly makes everything make sense. All the things you've read, all the stuff you've experienced on psychedelics. You can be an atheist and like this a lot. Maharaj Ji would say, "Just meditate." That would be about the only thing close to a commandment.

Giacco: Aha! So, there are rules!

Chuck: Maharaj Ji says the only thing that's a "sin" is to deprive someone from getting the Knowledge or practicing it. So, murder is definitely out.

Giacco: Well at least this kid sounds like he has a sense of humor!

Katie: So give it to us already!

Chuck: I can't. Only Maharaj Ji or his mahatmas can do that.

Giacco: But the Knowledge. Just tell us what it's about.

Chuck: If any of you really want this bad enough, he was in Victoria today, and he'll be in Vancouver tomorrow. But I can't tell you what the Knowledge is. Please don't ask me. It's easy. Just get it!

Ziets: I can't believe you did this, Chuck! How could you get suckered into it! I can't believe that anyone here would fall for it. You know in the end it's gotta be all about the money!

Chuck: Richard, there was no money involved. And this is the best thing I've ever done in my life. Anyway, it's a done deal. Hope you can live with it. Hope you get it!

It was the next statement that snapped everyone out of their temporary enchantment with Chuck's story.

Nick said, "Woooweee. Baird is not going to be happy about this at all!" Richard sidled up next to Nick and seconded the opinion. Psylvia, with Lily in her arms and a tittie out for her to suckle, said to Chuck, "Whatever you do, don't start knocking on doors like Latter Day Saints! Please! That's all I ask."

Chuck looked hurt even though Psylvia was trying to be funny. "Psylvia, how can I not want to share with those I love, something I think is special?"

Psylvia answered a bit less humorously, "Just leave us out of this, OK Chuck? Keep it to yourself. We have too many 'special things' going on here as it is!"

And with that we called it a night.

Except 10 minutes after everyone had dispersed and I was in my sleeping bag, I felt a body lying on top of me. It was Chuck. He was holding me tight. His cheek was against mine. His lips were close to my ear. He was crying, the tears running down his cheek onto mine.

"Chuck," I whispered, "why are you crying?"

"Because I'm so happy, Giacco! Because it's so beautiful, Giacco! You *have* to get this Giacco! This is your Chuck talking to you. I know you. You know me. I'm your brother. You will love this. You have to have this. Trust me. It's not a religion. It's not a mantra. It's not a bunch of mind. It's physical. You'll recognize it immediately. I can't tell you what it is. But you have been very close all along. I know Giacco. Really. This is what you have been looking for."

Then he pushed himself up on his hands and gingerly swung his legs off my bag, like a gymnast dismounting from a pommel horse. He kneeled beside my head, bent down, and kissed me on the forehead. He whispered, "Jai Satchitanand. Truth, Consciousness and Bliss. Isn't that why you followed Jon and Rosie to India? Did you think the truth was meant for just you three?"

CHAPTER 80
October 3, 1973

Trudy, tripping over a can of nuts and bolts lying in the middle of the deck, and the muffled swearing that followed, awakened me at dawn. I raised myself to my elbows. "What are you doing, Trudy?" I asked, my eyes still half closed.

"Shhhh, Giacco, don't cause trouble. Go back to sleep." She was stuffing her daypack with a few items of clothing and a small supply of staples, which for Trudy meant a baggie of granola and some green tea bags.

"I'm not going to cause trouble," I said in a low voice. "I just want to know what you're doing."

"If you must know," she said with that arrogance in her voice she used as a pre-emptive strike whenever she thought someone might question her behavior, "I'm going to Vancouver to find Maharaj Ji. I want to get the Knowledge. I decided after we went to bed last night."

"Well, weren't you even going to tell anyone? Maybe you can use Zwagen."

"Are you kidding? After what was said last night?" She wouldn't look at me directly because she knew I felt her embarrassment. Doing things on the sneak wasn't very Hunga Dungan-like, but given the situation and prevailing attitudes, I could understand. She finally turned her head and looked at me. "I have to do this!" she said with finality.

Trudy and I had that overriding Hunga Dungan love for each other, but neither of us were each other's favorite person in the household. There was always a mutual aversion to the idea of having to pair up for anything, and the very mutuality of it made us love one another in a strange distrustful way.

So, of course, she was shocked when I said, "Hang on. I'm coming with you." Trudy looked at me with those big blue eyes, bigger and bluer than ever. Then looked away. I shoved a change of clothes in my pack, and off we went. We didn't look at each other until we got to the main gate at the bottom of the road.

As I pulled the bolt and Trudy swung the gate open, she looked me straight in the eye and asked, "Are you sure you want to do this?" But really, I knew she was asking for the both of us.

"Look, Trudy. The chances we can even hitch a ride to Vancouver from here and get there in time to find the Goomer are pretty slim. This is my take on it. When in doubt, let the universe decide." And I closed the gate behind us and bolted it shut.

We started walking backwards down Poorman Creek Road, both of us with a thumb out in the air. The first car to come down the road, slowly navigating the hairpin curves, was a late-model Oldsmobile. It stopped beside us, a window slowly rolled down and both Trudy and I bent down to get a look and be looked at.

The man driving the car and the woman with him were both quite elderly. They had bright eyes and snow-white hair and their bodies had been in the process of shrinking for some time now.

Trudy asked, "Are you going as far as Highway 20?"

The woman answered, "Oh, my yes! My husband and I are going all the way to Vancouver!"

"Vancouver, Washington, or Vancouver, B.C.?" I asked, fairly sure that magic was not yet afoot again. I had been doubtful it ever would be. It had been so long.

"Vancouver, B.C.," the old gentleman replied.

This was too much! That at seven AM on a very rural road, a car would drive by and stop. That a very elderly couple, defenseless against anyone who could open a can of chicken soup, would pick up two hitchhikers looking like us. Hey! We were meant to get this ride. This was a very promising opening act. Good juju! Too bad it was Trudy who instigated the whole thing. Damn it!

"If that helps you out any, hop in!" He gave us a big smile when I opened the back door and we slid in. Trudy and I looked at each other. We wanted to pinch each other. A ride right to Vancouver? This was too easy! Maybe magic was afoot! Either that or something very sci-fi was happening. Something out of The Twilight Zone.

The conversations were ostensibly about peaches and other fruits, but I knew they were really extraterrestrials occupying human form. When they started talking about their involvement in the I Am Sanctuary, I was sure of it. Listening to them speak about Saint Germaine and Archangel Michael made the drive go quickly. It felt like we were floating serenely on Interstate 5 with a horde of angels keeping the traffic at bay.

At the border, we breezed through customs. Those Canadians! They are so nice! And though we had no money, we had passports. We were, all of us at Hunga Dunga, seasoned travelers, and always kept our passports within easy reach. Just because we looked like freaks didn't mean we weren't sophisticated. But the Canadian agent at the little booth just looked in the car and saw the angelic light of Grandma's eyes and Grandpa's radiant smile and he completely ignored us in the back seat and waved us through with a stunned smile on his face as if Grandma had zapped him or something. Trudy and I were somewhat disappointed we didn't get to show *our* passports.

At the turn-off to Surrey, where their Sanctuary was located, Grandpa pulled over to the side of the road and said, "OK, you two. Now take care and good luck to you. And let Michael the Archangel watch over you." As we got out of the car and thanked them both very much, I couldn't help but think of *my* Michael, and Nancy Stein calling him the Archangel for taking care of me. Where was that bastard?

Grandpa had just driven off and we had barely resumed our hitchhiking poses when a station wagon pulled over. The window slid down, and a young woman at the wheel with a hippie man beside her, looked us over. "Going into town, eh?" asked the man.

"Hmmm, I think so," I said, "We're really not sure which neighborhood we should be in."

"Well, what're ya looking for then?" asked the woman.

"We heard Guru Maharaj Ji was going to be in town. We need to find him. But we don't know where to look," Trudy explained, getting more desperate with every passing minute. It was already late afternoon of his one day in town.

"You two must have somethin' goin on," the guy said, looking straight ahead and pulling his long hair into a ponytail and tying it off with a rubber band.

"Why do you say that brother?" I asked.

"Cause we're heading to the ashram, to the Divine Light Mission, right now!" He turned to me, and his straight-faced smile slowly turned into a big know-it-all grin. "Maharaj Ji is giving satsang there. I guess you're supposed to hear it. Hop in!"

Trudy and I got in the back seat and off we went in the direction of the Burnaby neighborhood. Trudy and I looked at each other once again. We were thinking the same thing. We were experiencing some kind of synchronicity that only the two of us who shared it would ever understand. One of those experiences you don't even try to make other people believe, because it's too outlandish for your own mind to allow.

We parked right in front of this large brick and log home. Amazingly, there was a space right out in front because there were cars everywhere and some still driving around looking for a spot.

We quietly entered the grand room of the home. Some guy standing at the door told us we were very late and missed most of it. He was just wrapping up. The room was packed with people of all ages, but mainly young guys and girls, sitting on the floor. Almost as tightly as they had sat for Sai Baba in Bangalore.

Maharaj Ji sat on a couple of white cushions on a riser draped in red velvet and all eyes adored him, just as they had when they looked up at Sai Baba and melted at his feet.

Trudy and I wriggled our way to the center of the floor and, just as in Bangalore, the crowd adjusted itself to accommodate us. There must have been 250 to 300 people crammed in there. But all were silent, hanging on Maharaj Ji's every word.

I didn't care for the vibes in the room. They were too worshipful. They were too focused on this chubby kid. OK, so he had a great presence about him. He was still just a kid!

And precisely as I thought that, he spoke about it in very good English, with just enough of an accent to make you have to pay attention to him.

"I see many of you look at me with this reverence I don't want. I don't want it! I personally think it's cuckoo! Give your energy to the Knowledge! I am just a kid! You take the Knowledge my father gave to me. You use it. You practice it until it is second nature to you, and you are doing it while you are buying groceries or filling the car up with gas or making out with your girlfriend or boyfriend. (The crowd giggles.)

"As you understand more and more the infiniteness of this Knowledge, and it brings you joy more and more, then maybe you can thank me sometime, OK? But don't look at me like I'm something special. I am just a kid. I am just a human being. He gestures to people sitting on either side of the riser. This is my mother, Mata Ji. These are my brothers, Raja Ji and Bhole Ji. This is Mahatma Rajeshwaranand, who has been in our family longer than I have. I am just the kid."

The crowd laughed politely, trying to act as if he were normal, but regarding him more than ever as an avatar. I took him at his word. I didn't have any kind of aversion to anything he said or did. There was nothing to disagree with. I tried, but I couldn't fault him on anything. To me he was just a teenager, nothing more. Precocious, yes. He spoke of truths so broad; I couldn't disagree with any of them. But he was no one who made me feel like doing *pranam* at his feet. He was just another teenager who smiled a lot.

"I told you when I first got here," Maharaj Ji continued, "I warned you that this would *not* be a Knowledge session. I just wanted to visit you and thank you for all the wonderful work Divine Light Mission is doing here." He looked over at his older brother Raja Ji. There was a curious smile on his face. Almost a smirk. Raja Ji acknowledged it with a practiced loving smile similar to the one he'd received.

It felt like the rest of the family was promoting him as something more than he was, when what he was, was enough! Would he have the guts to tell his family where to get off when the time came? Like when Krishnamurti came of age and told Annie Besant and C.W. Leadbetter to stop promoting him like he was the second coming of Christ or something! Not that Krishnamurti didn't know a lot! Not that he wasn't a great teacher and philosopher! Not that he wasn't enlightened! It was just that he wasn't the second coming of the Christ. He was just Jiddu Krishnamurti and what he was, was enough.

I was lost in possible scenarios like this when there was a restlessness that swept through the crowd. Desperateness. Maharaj Ji was starting to stand and leave the podium. People sitting on the floor in front of him leaned toward him, hands outstretched as if he would let sacred ash fall from the palm of his hand into theirs. "Please, I want the Knowledge, Guru." "Maharaj Ji, I have traveled so far, please let me receive Knowledge." Others joined in begging for the Knowledge. A respectful pandemonium broke loose.

As if coming back on stage for an encore, Maharaj Ji sat back down on the cushions and held his hands in the air. The crowd quieted down.

Maharaj Ji laughed. "Oh, you are so hungry for the Knowledge. And I recognize faces that have followed me from Los Angeles and Portland and forth and back between Victoria and Vancouver. OK! I give in. I will let Mahatma Rajeshwaranand hold a Knowledge session after I leave. I will pick out 12 people only. You shall be my chosen ones, my apostles. You shall spread the word of the Knowledge."

He held out his hand, extending his index finger, and starting at one side of the room, he slowly swept his arm across the crowd. Every now and then he pointed to someone and simply said, "You!" And then he pointed again to another and said, "You!" He picked a couple of people from the back, a couple from the front. He asked a *premie* who was sitting up front and who lived in the house, how many he had so far. The premie said he needed two more.

Though he had picked no people who sat adjacent to one another, he scanned the room quickly and then pointed to Trudy and me. "You and you!" he said, as he smiled broadly. Trudy and I exchanged wide-eyed glances that confirmed we were thinking the same thing. Magic!

Then looking right at me, Maharaj Ji said, "You shall be my Peter." He hesitated, and then asked, "Or will you end up being my Judas?" He chuckled and the crowd parted as he walked with his entourage out the front door, the enchanted crowd following him outside.

Mahatma Rajeshwaranand took the podium and, in excellent English dusted off with a fine Oxford accent, asked the 12 chosen ones to follow him into a back room of the house.

It was obviously a meditation room, with photographs of Maharaj Ji and his family adorning the walls and icons of all the major religions joining them there. There were pillows scattered on the floor. Mahatma Rajeshwaranand politely ordered one of the members of the household to pile the pillows against the wall and to find 12 folding chairs.

When he and two other guys brought in the chairs, some of us helped unfold them and place them in a straight row across the room, following Mahatma's directions. All three premies sported close-cropped haircuts and wore sports jackets. One even wore a tie. This scared me. They looked so Mormon-ish or Jehovah's Witness-ish. What was with the clean-cut look, when most of the people in the audience were freaks and flower children? Were they going to turn into these robots after they got the Knowledge?

The chairs were all set up. The three premies smiled at us, and then at Mahatma, who turned to them and said, "Jai Satchitanand." That was their cue to leave. In unison they replied, "Bhole Shri Satgurudev Maharaj Ki Jai!" They left the room, closing the door behind them.

The premies sounded just like altar boys responding to a priest's Gregorian command. I felt like an altar boy. An altar boy in training for the Mahatma, as the priest; Maharaj Ji as the Pope. I so easily recognized and denied my strong Sicilian Catholic indoctrination at the early age of 16, that I never went to mass again, much to my parents' constant chagrin, and now here I was, watching rituals, rules and regulations resurrect themselves around me. I made a vow never to let that happen.

It was bad enough Sister Penetrate of the Wood, or whatever the hell her name was back in Catechism class, told us that if we were ever kneeling on the pew during Mass and our ankles were crossed, then our prayers didn't count. We would have to stay and go to the next Mass. And that was true as well if you happened to think a dirty thought or swear word while you were saying the Lord's Prayer or Hail Mary. Then the prayer didn't count, and you'd have to start all over again. And so, it took me forever to say my bed-time prayers. And getting through a rosary? Forget it! Sister Penetrate is the one who gave me an extreme aversion to anything that smacked of religion. The aversion served me very well so far to keep me cult-free and perennially skeptical.

These Sanskrit greetings and praises might have been Heil Hitlers in disguise, spoken by brainwashed Hitler Jugend. I immediately went into my skeptical mode. I didn't go into the "session" with a very good attitude, though Trudy already looked "blissed out!"

Oh, the power of suggestion. The power of mass hysteria, mob behavior, peer pressure. I am above all that. I just want the facts. Just give me the facts, ma'am, just the facts! And that of course means the Knowledge. Just give it to me. That's it, just hand it over. I'll take it from there.

This is what I was thinking as the Mahatma walked around the room lighting candles and incense. He spoke to us in a very serious and intentional way.

"Prem Rawat! That is his family name. He was initiated in the Knowledge by his father, Satgurudev Sri Hans Ji Maharaj, at the age of six. He became Satguru, or Perfect Master, when his father died in 1966. He is now Guru Maharaj Ji. But premies, which is what you will be after you receive this gift, affectionately call him Maharaji."

Mahatma suddenly stopped and turned to a young woman at the end of the row. He asked her in an offhanded way, "What did you bring Guru Maharaj Ji as a gift for this Knowledge you are about to receive?"

She answered, "I brought him a painting I did from photos I took of him last year at the Celebration in Miami."

"And you?" he asked me.

"I brought him these blades of grass from the lawn outside," I answered honestly and without a hint of sarcasm because I meant none.

Mahatma smiled at me. The kind of smile that says, "Hey you, I've got your number."

My smile back said, "I'm still looking for yours. But if I find it, watch out!" We definitely had a gentleman's agreement.

After we were seated, Mahatma told a bit about his own life. Affluent. Studied abroad. A successful lawyer and judge in Bombay for 20 years. Then he received Knowledge from his father. "I gave up everything to devote my life to helping my master's family after he died," Mahatma confided. "I could never show enough gratitude for the Knowledge. Never!"

"And just as Christ sent his apostles forth to spread the word that "Heaven was at hand," once we receive Knowledge, we want to propagate it so eventually the nations of the world will realize peace. And Maharaj Ji has declared you 12 to be his apostles. It is a wondrous honor! And I am honored to be giving you this Knowledge."

Oh shit, I knew there was a catch! By the way, Mr. Mahatma, no way am I going to be an apostle for the Goomer. Not Peter nor Judas. So don't expect me to start propagating for you! Just give me the damn facts and let me out of here!

"Giving the Knowledge will be easy to do," he said as he walked behind our chairs, "because the Knowledge is an immediate and direct experience of the truth, of pure consciousness, of pure love. There are no rites or rituals to perform that separate you from the path. There are no mantras to occupy the mind. Mantras help focus the mind, but it is still a process of thinking, which does not help achieve mindlessness, only concentration."

Hmmm. Nice! I like the way he put that. He's saying all the right things. Like he knows what works on me or something! The way he says them. The references. He's a fucking intellectual! No talking down! Right on!

"The Knowledge is a physical experience. You cannot attain it by reading about it or hearing about it. It must be demonstrated for you and there must be a laying on of hands Maharaji has ordained, such as mine. If you do as I say, you will have a physical response to the Knowledge. Responses vary. Yours may be brief and modest, or it might be overwhelming. The true understanding of the Knowledge comes to different people at different times. It is only with practice that you will truly understand this gift Maharaj Ji gives you."

OK. Are you through with the disclaimers?

"But it is immediate, and you *will* recognize it. It will be an 'aha' experience. Your ancient souls will recognize it and you will call it Divinity."

Alright! We are ready! Lay it on us!

"This is the Divine Yoga. There are four *kriyas*, or techniques. And each technique will produce what seems to be a different sensation. But I tell you they are all part of the one vibration that sustains you, all life on earth, and the universe. It is the energy that permeates everything, but you will feel it in different ways. You can use one technique at a time, all four, or in any combination."

But wait! There's more!

"The more you practice the kriyas, the more internalized they will become, to the point where they will be second nature to you, and that is where you will retreat when there is imbalance or disharmony in your life. The more you practice the techniques, the more you will understand them. You will be able to meditate while you are working, while you are studying, while you are driving, even while carrying on a conversation."

And that's not all. If you call right now…

"And at the moment of death, if you can be in the Knowledge, your passing will be seamless into pure consciousness and bliss. This is the real reason we practice the Knowledge. To be prepared at the time of our deaths."

Now you have my undivided and total attention, Mahatma Rajeshwaranand, Sir!

"But I stress this point. The Knowledge is beautiful, it is everything, it will bring you the answers to all you ask, and it will bring you peace. It is direct, immediate, simple… and a secret!"

Aye, there's the rub! This is where there's going to be trouble. I can tell already!

"Guru Mahara Ji asks that you promise only three things before he gives you this gift." Mahatma walked in front of each of us, making eye contact. "One, to attend *satsang* whenever possible. Two, to give Knowledge a fair chance. And three, not to share these techniques with anyone. Is there anyone who can't promise that?"

Hmmm. I can *promise that… if I* want *to. You didn't ask* will *I promise that! Hey, you're the lawyer. You should know the loopholes!*

"Are there any questions before I begin?" Mahatma asked, having finished circling us and standing once again before us.

I spoke up. I could feel Trudy burning. "Mahatma Rajeshwaranand, if this Knowledge is for everyone, and if it transcends religion, why is it a secret? Why do you make people jump through so many hoops to get it?"

Trudy kicked me, and the other 10 people gave me odd looks, like they were afraid I was going to blow it for all of us. But I figured I was really asking something everyone wanted to know.

Mahatma stepped up to me, squatted down until he was at eye level, and gently said,

"The reason it is a secret, is precisely because it is so simple." Then he looked me in the eyes a long time, as if trying to pass on information. Maybe he was just wondering what Maharaj Ji was thinking when he picked *me* of all people. Trying to figure *me* out. Trying to convince *me* he wasn't a hoax.

He stepped back, stood tall, and in a louder voice stated with absolute certainty, "If anyone, who is not directly appointed by Guru Maharaj Ji to do so, shares these secrets with others who have not been initiated, they will spend their next 10,000 incarnations as a cockroach!"

Well, that was a low blow, and a rapid devolvement from lawyer to practitioner of voodoo and superstition! Shades of Sister Penetrate! You bastard! You know a recovering Catholic like me is going to have a hard time with that one! Just for that, I'm gonna take your damned Knowledge now, *and figure out what to do with it* later! *And think about what you said later! Much later! Maybe later than you think! Now let's get on with it!*

CHAPTER 81
October 3, 1973

"Remember, every time someone takes your breath away, they kill you and your ego does not exist. If it is only for a moment, it may be an infatuation. If it is for too long, it might be murder. But if you are in control of your own breath, you may kill your ego at will, and with great practice, your body as well, when it is time. Now close your eyes and follow my breath. Get your breath in sync with mine. To help you, listen to how my breath sounds. Then listen to yours."

He inhaled deeply, but not strenuously, through his nose. He held his breath. When he exhaled, it was through pursed lips, like a slow, soft and even whistle. He paused then inhaled, a bit slower this time, letting his chest cavity get bigger with every breath.

"If you have trouble finding the sound of your breath, think to yourself '*soooooo*' on the inhale, pause, and then '*huuunng*' on the exhale. Like this." And Mahatma audibly imbedded the sound of '*soooooo*' within his inhale. He paused slightly longer than the previous breath. Then he slowly sounded the '*huuunng*,' hardly noticeable within his exhale.

"*Sooooooo.*" He breathed in. Then an even longer pause. "*Huuunng*," with the exhale. "Once again, I tell you this is not a mantra. Forget it as soon as possible. This is just for now, in the beginning, to get you used to the sound of your breath. Once you are used to it, you must drop this '*soooooo*' and '*huuunng*' and just let the sound of your breath guide you."

If he says soooooo huuunng *one more time, it's going to be impossible to take this seriously! In fact, now I'm so horny, I just want to get it on with one of those buzz-cut premie security guards out front! Hey! Giacco! Stop that! Pay attention! Fuck, I am more in my mind than ever. What am I gonna do with myself? I should be flogged! I gave Josie the benefit of the doubt back in Laguna. Why am I giving this guy such a hard time? I just don't...* Soooooo, *(pause)* Huuunng. Soooooo, *(longer pause)* Huuunng.

I was getting the drift. I was getting into a nice rhythm. My breaths were very even, slowing slightly each time. The space between my exhale and my next inhale was getting longer and longer. And the "*soooooo, huuunng*" really did help my whole body find the sound of my breath and not just my ears.

"Continue breathing so," Mahatma said softly. "This space between the breaths… this is where it resides… the universal vibration. It is very subtle. But as you practice this technique, you will begin to feel the vibration more and more. Between the breaths as those spaces lengthen, you will come to recognize the vibration immediately. You will get to glimpse pure consciousness and love. If you should ever stay there too long, you will die. But with a smile on your face."

Yikes! Tell it like it is, Mahatma! Now this was more like it! Finally, some confirmation I was on the right track all along. I knew it had something to do with the breath! I even knew it had something to do with the space in between the breaths! Damn I'm good. I was so close. I didn't need this. Couple more acid trips under a blanket and I would've had it.

"This is the 'Word' of Judaism and Christianity," the Mahatma explained. "This is what is meant in the Old Testament, when it says, 'in the beginning was the Word, and the Word was with God, and the Word was God.'

This is what Jesus meant when he said, 'The Kingdom of God is within you.' He meant it literally, as he did so many other things that have been interpreted merely as poetic metaphors. He meant the simple reality hiding just beneath the surface of the metaphor. He meant that spot just below the solar plexus. The vacuum there created between the exhalation and the next inhalation. That vibration. You can feel it. Become it. This is where pure energy, consciousness, and bliss reside. This is the Kingdom of God. And you can go there with the Divine Word."

Damn you're good! Man! You just made a whole bunch of books and a whole lot of acid trips make perfect sense. I like that intellectual approach of yours. The way you talk and the way your voice sounds. Like we're all smart! It turns me on. I can relate. Now if you say something about walking in the way of the lord, I'm gonna freak out!

"This is the first and most important of the four kriyas, or techniques. The other three are all facets of the same energy in different forms. Once you understand how to use the Knowledge, it will put you in touch with that which connects us all. That which sustains the universe. That which makes us one. But only if you use the techniques! Only if you practice them!"

Mahatma walked up to the first person in the row. "Keep your eyes closed and keep breathing, slowly, steadily, meditating on the Word. I will place my hands on each of you in turn. You will feel some pressure, but do not back away. When I know it is time to move on, I will replace my hands with yours. Keep them there and be amazed."

As he went down the row, I heard some quiet gasps, a man started crying, and a young girl giggled like a three-year old.

"Look through the center of your forehead. Some of you may see fireworks and stars, others a bright sun, still others a donut with a black hole. Concentrate on the sun. Let it burn as colorfully and as brightly as it wants to."

I felt a strong hand grab my head from behind and a thumb and middle finger each firmly press my eyeballs in and toward the tip of my nose, between my brows. I felt his index finger come gently down upon my forehead and press the center of it just above my nose. My attention was immediately drawn there.

"If you see a black hole, fall into it. Just stare into it. Keep breathing the Word. As your thoughts slow, the black hole will fill with light. It will become the sun. Stay there. Be the light. This is the opening of the Third Eye. This is Divine Light."

Or was it just the stimulation of a plexus of nerves? Phosphenes or something. I'm always seeing things behind my eyelids anyway, for chrissakes! Floaters and stuff. And Mahatma, if anyone is into the Third Eye, it's me! But I'm just seeing some nerve endings being bullied. And what's about if I don't have any hands or arms? Huh? What happens then?

"Some of you may be thinking that this light you see is nothing more than the stimulation of the nervous plexus where the three principal nerves of the body converge. But I assure you, that with practice, you will see this light brighter and brighter, and without using your hands or stimulating the nerves in any way. It isn't needed. This is the opening of the Third Eye, and it has always been there. You just had to be shown."

Damn! Can he hear me thinking? I can see why it's a secret. You really have to want it badly for it to work. This stuff's just too easy! It's begging to be mocked! By anyone with half a brain of how the human body works!

"Once again, this is all part of the vibration that is the Word, but a visual one, the Divine Light. Jesus said, 'If thine eye be single, thy whole body shall be filled with light.' This is what he meant by the single eye, the Third Eye, the Divine Light."

Too much, man! All those acid trips back in New York when we spent hours tripping underneath those blankets. Shit. I've seen that light. So what if I didn't know what it was or what to call it? I know what he's talking about. Does everything have to have a name? This news is no news! Especially since I already read about it in the "Aquarian Gospel of Jesus the Christ," for chrissakes!

I could hear Mahatma coming around the back of the chairs. Once again, he went down the row, letting each person experience his hands on them. When he came to me, he arranged my thumbs just so in each ear and then placed what remained of my hands on top of my head. There they rested quite comfortably. I could almost intertwine my fingers. Then he pushed gently on my thumbs, which pressed on my eardrums. At first, I just heard my pulse beating loudly. Then it quickly became more complex.

Hey fella! This isn't subtle at all! I can hear layers of sounds! No problemo. You can't sing to it, though. That's too bad. And I wish I could adjust the volume. It's a bit loud. It sounds like stuff we might be listening to in the year 3050. Music of the spheres and all that. I bet it's just the aural sensation of blood circulating through the brain, but I say, so what! This is cool!

"This is Divine Music. The more you meditate on Divine Music the more you will hear the richness of the cosmic symphony. But, again, this is just another manifestation of the Divine Word, of that vibration which causes all things to be. None is separate from the other. They are all the same thing, the same energy."

Hell, I knew this back in New York! The place between the breaths, and the trippy light shows behind the eyelids. When I put Kleenex in my ears to drown out the traffic, the sci-fi music waited for me just behind my eardrums. Damn. I should've had more faith I knew what I was doing. At least he hasn't said anything about the blankets yet!

I could feel the Mahatma looking at me. "The last *kriya* is Divine Nectar."

Hmmmm. Nectar, eh? I don't know about this one! It had better be good!

"Simply place the tip of your tongue as far back as it will go along the roof of your mouth. Stretch it until it can go no further. If you keep it there long enough, a sweet, electric-tasting juice will begin to flow. Use this technique with all the others. Especially when meditating on the Word. Soon, your tongue will be reaching back there without even thinking. The Nectar will flow, and you will instinctively meditate on the Word. Whenever you need to be centered in the midst of chaos, that is where your tongue will instinctively go.

To the back of the roof of your mouth. And the Nectar will remind you to become the Word.

Well, I have to admit he had me on that one! Nectar? God! Would've never thought of that one! But three out of four? Not bad. Not bad at all!

"And a personal tip," Mahatma confided, "In the beginning of practicing the Knowledge, it will help to remove as many distractions as possible. Until you have truly internalized all the *kriyas*, you should find a quiet place. Create a meditation room in your home. And if that is not possible, sit underneath a heavy blanket in your room."

Damn him again! Will he leave me nothing to claim as my own? Not even a damn blanket?

He said a few more things about attending satsang often, and only hanging out with other premies, and something about doing service for the mission and propagating the knowledge and stuff, but it sort of went in one ear and out the other.

I got what I came for. Thanks so very much. Really. But I think I must be on my way now. Later, brother Goomer. The Knowledge seems harmless enough, but you gotta get a new ad agency and campaign going! Please! As far as the Knowledge goes, cripes, call it something else! But I will admit, nothing happened to me today that aren't experiences every human on the planet has in common whether they know it or not. So, I guess you could say the Knowledge is the lowest common denominator of humanity. At least we have something in common!

"You are now premies, devotees of Maharaj Ji, keepers of the Knowledge, the highest common denominator of humanity. Some know it; some are waiting to be told. As long as everyone is aware of its existence and how to get it. That is all we ask.

You must keep this Knowledge a secret. Some of you will have friends that will bother you until you give in and give it to them. And maybe you think some of your friends are ready to receive the Knowledge. Only Maharaj Ji can say who is ready and who is not. You may think you do your friend a service when you give him the Knowledge. But no! You do him a disservice! He may not appreciate it because he may think it too simple, too mundane, or too subtle. He may never use it. He will never learn of its infinite depth because it can only be realized by diligent practice. And if he doesn't practice it, you have deprived him of being prepared when he is on his death bed."

On that jovial note, a young man neatly dressed as were they all, walked in and said, "Mahatma Rajeshwaranand. Excuse me. We are late. We must go." We all stood up and gathered around him. I felt him looking obliquely at me.

OK, for the time being I'll compromise. I won't give away the secret, but I also will not spread the word. Deal?

"And so I must go, my dear premies." The Mahatma bowed before us and pressed his hands together in the *namaskar mudra*. "Jai Satchitanand!"

CHAPTER 82
October 3, 1973

Everyone either knew the phrase from attending so much satsang or mumbled something that sounded very much like it in response. I knew that phrase and others that were being bandied about from my travels in India and what was now called Sri Lanka. There the Sanskrit words sounded holy and meaningful. Here, they sounded pretentious.

Most of us were still a bit spaced out from the constant deep breathing, but we did remember our manners and thanked him many times for initiating us. The premie escorted Mahatma Rajeshwaranand to a nice limo waiting out front, the rear door already open.

We "apostles" followed him, stood on the front porch, and watched as the limo disappeared down the street. When we turned to go back inside, we looked at one another for varying degrees of bliss. Or maybe just some kind of validation that something had really happened.

A couple of the "apostles" took pillows on the floor and sat opposite each other re-enacting, confirming techniques for each other, but stopped immediately when someone that lived in the ashram chided them for doing so in public.

I hadn't really studied my fellow recruits before the session began. I realized one of them was a young girl, maybe nine or 10 years old. She seemed the most content, the most fulfilled, the most at ease. As if she "got it" right away.

Another apostle's middle-aged head seemed to float in mid-air. This was partially because he was dressed in a black suit, black vest, black shirt, and a white collar worn backwards around his neck. The minister seemed more than satisfied, as if parts of today's experience could be worked into many Sundays' worth of sermons.

And Trudy. Trudy always had a bit of a stunned look about her anyway, but now she had outdone herself. She walked over to me and said, or rather asked, "Is the Knowledge incredible or what? I mean did he blow our minds or what?"

I didn't mean to question her state of bliss, but I replied, "Well for the time being, I think I'm going to have to say, 'or what.'"

"What?" Trudy asked, not understanding me.

"Never mind, Trudy, it was cool! Really! I liked it. Now let's figure out what we do next."

"Just meditate on the Knowledge," she said. "The answer will come."

For chrissakes! I hope she hasn't gone over the edge!

"Yup, the answer will come," I humored her, as we flopped down on a sofa in the living/stage/satsang/meditation room of the house/ashram/mission. There, small groups of premies or premie-wannabes randomly gathered and spoke softly. I hoped by exertion of the Knowledge now within me, I could make someone take notice of us and ask if they could be of any help. I guessed I'd have to work on it.

Then, suddenly, a young man sitting at the piano, but not playing, turned around as if he knew we were there, his eyes locking on ours, or more precisely, Trudy's. The connection between them was instantaneous and we all knew it. He flashed us a big smile of recognition as if he had some kind of premie radar. It turns out he did, or so he said. He walked briskly toward us, his radiance sticking out like a sore thumb. Trudy and I stood up. It's a good thing he stopped when he did. I was afraid I'd bump into his aura.

"Hello. I'm Jeff. Jai Satchitanand!"

"Hi! I'm Trudy," she said fluidly, with none of the shyness Trudy usually showed when meeting new people. "Jai Satchitanand!" And they gave each other a warm hug. "This is my friend, Giacco."

Jeff stepped in front of me, and we made comfortable eye contact. "Jai Satchitanand Giacco!" he said, with what could only be, despite my desire to be cynical, a genuine smile. I gave him one back. "Jai Satchitanand, Jeff! Good to meet ya, mate!"

He was an attractive looking guy, with a strong face and sweet blue eyes. His smile is what topped it off for me though and made me discount his buzz cut. He hugged me too, and my body suspected that his body was put together nicely. Shame it was hidden by such conservative clothes. Tan sports jacket, white shirt, maroon tie, loose dark-brown dress pants, dark socks, and shiny oxfords. Then again, I always did prefer to undress guys who had lots of clothes on.

"They asked for volunteers to put up any of the out-of-town visitors we were expecting. We knew we'd be swarmed with 'em, eh?" Jeff explained. "Where're you from, then?"

"Twisp, Washington," I answered.

"And San Francisco," Trudy added.

"Oh, Twisp! Down Tonasket way. Other side of Osoyoos. The Okanogan. We're practically neighbors!"

I was warming up to him quickly. I could see the long hair he probably sported not too long ago.

"Well, so if you need a place to stay, you're welcome to stay with me, OK? I live alone in a house in West Vancouver, eh? It's already dark. I take it you drove up?"

"We hitched," Trudy said.

"Oh, well, then it's a definite go, you guys are staying with me! No way could you hitchhike tonight! Cool? We can have a bite to eat, get to know one another and later on meditate together. It's always higher when you meditate with other premies. Jai Satchitanand!"

Damn! I just couldn't stand being referred to as a premie. And this Jai Satchitanand stuff had to go as well. I mean no way could I live with that shit, even though I loved it back in India and Sri Lanka. I wished the Knowledge were called something else if anything at all. Something that would make my life simpler. Not more complex. Something inexplicable. More exotic. Maybe something unpronounceable. Class it up a bit.

And if only I had hitched here with Katie rather than Trudy. If it were Katie, we'd have the makings of a nice three-way tonight. Katie was one of the most delightful and intelligent people I had ever met. She also had one of the hottest bodies and without a doubt, the sweetest vagina I had ever known. And I would have never known how sweet it was if Nick hadn't already tasted the fruit.

One day Nick third-personed me on behalf of Katie, saying she wanted to spend time with me and did I feel the same. And Katie, being a pretty hot lady on all levels, I said, "Sure, why not?" And since then, we have been buddies in and out of bed whenever we found ourselves together. Nothing too serious, but always heartfelt and fun.

Wow! Too bad Katie wasn't here instead of Trudy. Katie on Knowledge! There would definitely be a party here tonight!

Somehow, lost in these thoughts, I found myself in the back seat of Jeff's small car, sitting next to our pile of daypacks. Trudy was in the passenger seat up front. They still smiled blissfully at each other, talking about the different *kriyas*, how beautiful it all was as we crossed the Lion's Gate Bridge into West Vancouver. I realized I had been thinking of nothing but sex for the past 10 minutes, and I had just received the Knowledge! What the hell was wrong with me? Except I knew one thing about myself; that *holy* always made me horny. So maybe this was a good sign. Nevertheless, I just didn't feel blissed out. Just horny!

Trudy wasn't innocent either, even though she looked exactly like Alice on the cover of Through the Looking Glass. There was definitely a noticeable flirt behind each word exiting her mouth. With each breath, she batted her long, black eyelashes like a hummingbird. And Jeff seemed very responsive. But I could never have a three-way with Trudy. And I'm sure it was mutual. If there were to be any heavy breathing tonight besides meditating, it would be coming from Jeff and Trudy. I knew I wouldn't be invited to any after-hours party. And Jeff already knew that, too. I could tell that for sure. But out of a brotherly need to make me feel welcome, he asked, "Well, Giacco. What did you think of Maharaj Ji?"

"He was good, Jeff! I especially liked the part when he talked about how you can even meditate while you're having sex!" Jeff took his eyes off the road just briefly and looked at me in wonder, as if we had been at two entirely different events.

After we settled in at Jeff's very nice home, he lit some candles in the cozy living room and made a fire in the fireplace. We gathered around it, drank some nice hot-spiced wine, and snacked on some cheese and crackers. Jeff started talking up the Knowledge and Trudy was liking it, but I was getting tired of it. When he asked me how my Knowledge session went, I was inclined to be brutally honest.

I told him what I had thought to myself, at every moment during the whole process. I know much of it might have sounded arrogant, but I told him I really felt I had already found three of the four kriyas myself.

Jeff just laughed. "I give up!" He stood up and grabbed some fabric from a shelf. "There is nothing left to say, you just have to do it! Talk means nothing. You just must do it. The three of us together. It will be good! You'll see! We'll do it for about an hour, and then we'll smoke some good bud I picked up at the ashram the other day."

Oh, the old carrot-and-stick routine. What a good incentive. He must've known I needed one.

He tossed some blankets in the middle of the floor and we each took one. They were nice and soft. We sat in an obtuse triangle, me a bit farther away from Jeff and Trudy who sat right next to each other. They sat in full lotus positions. I was doing my best to get into just a half of one. Jeff pulled his blanket over his head until he was a tent. Trudy did the same. And so did I, though I hated giving up the image of Trudy and Jeff as tents. When I was in mine, I knew all too well how ridiculous I must have looked, even though we never gave it a second thought when we were tripping our brains out back in New York.

When we were all in our tents, Jeff said, "I just ask that you try. Really try."

I have no problem with that. Was he talking to me? Wait a minute. Was he saying that just for my benefit?

"We'll start with the Word, and after we're in the zone… you'll recognize it… try going for the Light or the Music. The Nectar should always be on."

He started breathing. *Soooooo.* Pause. *Huuunng.* Pause. *Soooooo.* Pause. *Huuunng.* Pause. I could hear Trudy straightening her back and melding breaths with Jeff's. I joined in as well. Why be a party-pooper.

Soooooo. Pause. *Huuunng.* Pause.

Soooooo. Pause. *Huuunng.* Pause.

After a while, I could hear Trudy crying softly and Jeff chuckling as we delved into the Word and listened to our three breaths stay in surprising rhythm, even as they got slower and slower. The feeling of unison was powerful. The *soooooo-pause-huuunngs* got quieter and quieter until they dropped from earshot entirely.

I tried out the Light. It was better than when the Mahatma showed it to me that afternoon. I could almost plot a graph showing the Light brightening or dimming in a directly inverse proportion to how much I was thinking. What would happen if I ever reached a point where I would not think at all? Not even a smidgen of a thought! Would the Light be too bright to handle?

When I got to the Music it was more incredible than I'd expected, and I thought maybe I had likely licked a sugar cube. If this was acid on the natch, then I had struck gold. But it was the fucking Word that brought me to the ego death, and I surrendered. The ego death may have only lasted a couple of seconds. The moment it did, the Light got more brilliant, the Word stronger, the Music soared, and the Nectar poured, and they all commingled until they were one indescribable experience. I thought I got a glimpse of that elusive god and I burst into tears!

CHAPTER 83
October 1973

As Trudy and I lordwalked up the dirt road, we knew we'd have some major explaining to do. I suggested we keep it very low key. For me, the Knowledge was something to carry around in my back pocket and use whenever I had the inclination or found it necessary. Like a joint. Don't tell people you have one. Wait to be asked about it, especially when your stash is low. That was my take on the whole thing. Be the deep, silent type.

But Trudy was totally smitten, as much with Jeff as with the Goomer. Jeff had driven us to the border. He and Trudy had really connected. I liked him. He was a gentle soul in a very nice body. They promised to stay in touch. I hoped they would. In fact, Jeff promised to come down the next week and help work on The Dome. It so happened that he was an architect and curious about how we engineered it. But I knew the real reason was to get to know Trudy better.

They "Jai Satchitanand-ed" one another many times. I wished they would come up with something less annoying. Why it was so annoying to me, I'm not sure. All these Sanskrit greetings, terms, and chants were bringing me to the brink of aversion. In India, I'd be joining in. Here it bugged the hell out of me. But I knew deep inside it was probably *my* problem, so who was I to tell anyone how to behave?

It was difficult to talk and trudge up the road at the same time, but Trudy managed. She said she couldn't wait to tell Nick and Psylvia about the Knowledge and that I should know how much Little Richard would love the Goomer and it would be selfish of me not to talk about it.

I said that Chuck had probably been giving them satsang all day and night since he got back from Portland, and they had probably already heard more than enough about it!

Trudy said, "But you went around the world searching for this. There's no one with more credibility than you to give satsang!" Oh, the very word was becoming sandpaper on my eardrum. Especially coming from *her* mouth. We stopped in our tracks for a moment.

"Please Giacco, won't you give satsang?" Trudy's voice sanded my eardrum again, this time with a coarser grit. She was patient to wait so long for a reply, because as she stared at me and I stared back, she knew a reply would be long in coming.

Ah, Satsang. Sitting around talking about the Truth, or rather, around it. Telling stories about how lucky we were to have it. The Knowledge? It's completely harmless! It's not a belief. It really isn't! It's not a religion. And it really isn't if you're vigilant enough not to let it become one! It's actually very wonderful. There's nothing to it. It's closer than your own breath. And I can't give it to you so please don't ask!

I looked Trudy straight in the eyes and with finality said, "No!" She looked at me with astonishment but no argument. We turned and continued trudging up the road toe to heel.

It was strange hearing me say "no" because god talk always got me high. I loved being around people who talked about god and altered states and mystical experiences and death. Like Jon and Rosie especially. What were those two up to anyway? Why hadn't I heard from them? What would they think about the Goomer? Would they be mortified? And this Knowledge. Jon would probably want to do the Knowledge on acid. Test it out. Now what we had been searching for had a fucking name and it didn't seem to have the same oomph! The Goomer took the fun out of seeking!

Jon always said you couldn't get there on your own. That you needed a teacher. He was right, I guess. But I really didn't mean for it to be the Goomer! The Goomer of all people! What can I say! That's just the way it turned out. It was supposed to be someone much more exotic and under the radar. Besides, the Knowledge was sort of cool. What was the big deal? There was no thing or belief to disavow. And I didn't have to call it by its name. In fact, I didn't have to have anything to do with Divine Light Mission. Or with Maharaj Ji, for that matter. He said so himself, right? He said all I had to do was meditate. Or would this end up costing me more than the two blades of grass?

I had access to the thing with no name. I could practice it on the sly whenever and wherever I wanted. It was always at my disposal. I wasn't worried about forgetting it from random use or lack of use. I knew what it was capable of and maybe someday, I'd really give it some serious attention. But overall, I really didn't feel any different than I did the day before yesterday.

"Oh, no!" Psylvia screamed when she saw us coming up the road. "Richard was right! He said you two went up to Vancouver!"

"Vancouver and back in two days!" Trudy yelled, as if winning a competition.

"Did you get it?" we heard Richard ask from behind a triangular piece of plywood.

"Of course they got it, Richard! Just look how blissed out they are!"

"I think it's called dehydration, Psylvia!" I yelled, miming for water. Psylvia went into The Dome and came out with a big thermos in one arm and Lily, just up from a nap, in the other. She handed me the thermos. I unscrewed the cap and took a big draught. I passed it to Trudy.

"Yeah, Ziets," I said nonchalantly, "we got it. It's cool. You should check it out sometime."

"Oh, and by the way," announced Richard, "Psylvia and Lily are going back to The City with Lee and Bianca.

"When is all this happening?" I asked.

"You're just in time!" yelled Psylvia.

"In about 10 minutes," Richard replied.

With Lily in her arms, Psylvia walked with Trudy over to Kaliflower's step-van. Lee was rearranging some of the backpacks. Psylvia handed Lily to Bianca and went into the tipi to collect more stuff.

"Who will that leave to finish skinning The Dome and getting it ready for winter?" I asked.

"Well, we've got Travis, Rolli, Katie, and Trudy for another two weeks. And you, me, Chuck, and Nick," Ziets announced, as if it were a roll call.

"Why are Psylvia and Lily leaving?"

"Psylvia and Nick shouldn't be around each other right now."

I didn't probe. I could guess.

"Why are the others leaving?"

"Chuck convinced them getting the Knowledge was more important!"

"Damn!" I said. "We really have our work cut out for us then! But we can do it. We have to do it. We can't leave here until The Dome can make it through a winter. The four of us can do it."

"Well, is it?" Richard asked, not having heard a word I said.

"Is it what?" I asked.

"Is it more important?"

"Is it more important than what?" I answered with another question.

"Is it more important than being here working?" Richard asked, frustrated with me.

"Being here *is* the Knowledge, Ziets!" I said, trying not to sound like I was beating around the bush.

"Stop beating around the bush, Chazan," Richard scolded. "Tell me what the Knowledge is. Not what it's about. What is it?"

"I can't Richard," I heard myself saying. "I'd fuck it up for you."

"No you won't," Zietar insisted. "Just tell me what it is!"

This would be the first real test. My closest friend. A person I deeply loved and trusted. I had no idea what I would do. But my ears heard my mouth saying, "I can't Richard. It's a secret."

CHAPTER 84
November 1973

Chuck, the great giver of satsang, maybe too good, was more shocked than I when Rolli and Travis told us they were leaving earlier than expected, first to The City, and then continue on to Houston.

Rolli uncurled a small poster. It had a picture of Maharaj Ji sitting among some cushions on a couch that curled up into arms on the ends. His feet rested on a large red velvet cushion. The backdrop was as embarrassing as I had imagined it would be. Large shafts of fake red and orange sunlight shooting out from behind him and lots of glitter and shiny stuff. He was speaking into six or seven microphones. He looked high and inspired, though I really wished he would do something about that annoying fuzz of a mustache teenage boys are so determined to wear, even though it looks like shit.

On the top of the picture it read, "Guru Maharaj Ji." Under the photograph was written, "A Thousand Years of Peace for People Who Want Peace. Millennium '73." At the bottom of the poster, it read, "Love is Free, Truth is Free, Admission is Free."

Rolli said with some urgency, "It's happening in the Astrodome. The 8th, 9th, and 10th!"

Travis's voice was excited as well. "We heard Maharaj Ji was gonna knock everyone's socks off! Going to levitate the Astrodome. Katie is going to come with us. And Trudy wants to tag along, too."

But I was more shocked when Nick announced he and Richard were taking Wilhelmina and convoying down with Flo Airwaves. What would we do without Wilhelmina? What would we do without Nick? What would we do without Richard?

Nick was the taskmaster. He had worked us hard and fast, and the weather was working us even harder and faster than Nick. Many freaks had come through for a few weeks at a time since we arrived in the spring, helping any way they could and getting their fix of country in return. Then they'd leave to be replaced by others traveling off the beaten path, or who had heard of a strange clothing-optional church in the hills of the Methow Valley and sought us out on purpose.

Richard was energy personified. From dawn 'til dusk, he worked with an infectious smile on his face, dividing his time between the garden and The Dome. Though we had put in a temporary water system, it yielded only enough gallons per minute for domestic use and then not even enough for showering. Irrigating the land on the part of the bench that got the best sun was out of the question. Besides, it required clearing the land of rocks and boulders and tree stumps, tilling it, bringing in tons of fertilizer and topsoil. No, we resigned ourselves to the fact we would have no viable garden this first year.

Yet Richard was adamant we do the best with what we had. And what we had was a quarter acre seasonal pond. If there were water anywhere, it would be in some kind of aquifer under the pond, or so we thought. That's where Richard lovingly planted his large variety of vegetables. He supervised our more transient brothers and sisters to care for the garden and do whatever was possible to turn that pond into an organic vegetable stand. His ministrations paid off.

When the harvest moon was full, we reaped what Richard had sown. Tears rolled down Zietar's face as we harvested, but the rest of us were in hysterics, or would be if we weren't trying so hard to be sensitive to Zietar's pain. The entire harvest only filled up one large burlap bag. Oh, everything had come up, looked beautiful, and even tasted fine. The only problem was everything was in miniature. The Church of Manna had grown its first crop of cocktail vegetables. They were very cute but would only make us self-sufficient for a few hours, and then only if we took very small bites.

Now, here we were, well into the fall of our first year on the land, and ready to call it the end of our first season. Through it all there was a steady core of about eight of us. We made sure things got accomplished. And we made sure The Dome was completely skinned with plywood and that Chuck and I were up to speed on the tar papering process before the others left. All we had to do was finish it.

Chuck and I liked the idea of getting it done on our own. We were definitely in the work groove and had cutting the tarpaper down to a dance. The only thing that hampered us was the snow in our eyes and the layer of ice on the plywood and ladders during the morning hours, before the sun could hurdle the ridge and warm us up a bit. Other than that, it was a breeze. A *stiff* breeze.

I had always regarded Chuck as a handsome man, yet there was never a sexual attraction between us. Now that we were alone, there wasn't much to do after the sun went down. We read. Sometimes to each other. We meditated together, sometimes facing each other, sitting in lotus positions, knees touching, holding hands, and one big blanket over both our heads. Like little kids playing fort. It just seemed natural that we would end up sleeping together, not only for the warmth it provided on those freezing November nights, but just out of brotherly love.

So, we deliberately became brotherly lovers for a few weeks. It was a lot of fun. At first, the sex was similar to the kind pre-teens might have on a sleepover. Simple, innocent. Just touching got us hard. It was really very exciting and beautiful. When we did begin to explore each other more intimately and more boldly, we confirmed for each other that you *could* meditate while having sex. Or is it you can have sex while meditating? Whatever. You could do both at the same time. The Word came in the handiest. It helped us edge longer. It also helped us really get in tune with the rhythms of our bodies. But the Music, Light, and Nectar also came in handy during certain other sexual acts. We decided we'd keep these to ourselves. Let the others find out on their own. However, if you ever need to come up with a lot of saliva post haste, really want to see stars, or need to get rid of that Karen Carpenter song that's stuck in your head, well…

It was very nice and comfortable, this new love Chuck and I had for each other, even though we were both quick to admit, it was just one of those things and would end the moment we walked into Big Blue. We'd only relive it in our minds when our eyes locked now and then and maybe winked. Our little souvenir from Twisp.

The day finally arrived when we declared The Dome thoroughly winterized. The tipis and tents were folded. Chuck and I both decided that tipis were one of the most uncomfortable shelters ever devised and we were so glad to trade ours in for the five-star hotel of The Dome.

All the tools were gathered and cleaned. And our outdoor kitchen was disassembled and dis-organized. Bedding, mattresses, and foam pads. Books, books, more books, and some board games. Even some clothing. Everything we could find lying around the land that we'd use the next season or would later recycle. All of it now had shelter inside The Dome. Hopefully, by this time next year, we would not only have shelter inside it, but could call it a comfortable home, too.

Now it was time for the luxurious Zwagen to whisk us back to Big Blue, though home was feeling more and more like Twisp to me. So maybe it was the right thing for me to do. A stint in The City. I tried to psych myself up for it.

On the day before Thanksgiving, we crossed the Golden Gate Bridge, drove through the Park, down Geary and into the Haight. That's all it took to be completely infused by the rare psychedelic air of The City. San Francisco had to be one of the most powerful places on the planet. You could almost feel it evolving. I was smitten by it as if I were a virgin, and this was my first time, and Twisp already seemed long ago.

We took Divisidero to the Castro and when we got within a couple of blocks of home, I started looking for a parking space. I made one pass down our block and was surprised to see a spot right in front of our house, behind the Free Food Conspiracy Truck. I turned to Chuck and smiled complacently, "Do we live right, or what?" When we got out and stretched our legs, we saw "Greenleaf Produce" painted on the side of the truck in a very upscale looking font. I wondered what Lizzie was up to.

We ran up the stairs, opened the door and yelled, "Yoooo hoooo, Lucee, we're home!" We were expecting, of course, the usual uproarious welcome. None was forthcoming. Instead, Greg, Ellen, and Baird, walked into the living room from various parts of the house and converged on us. They began to encircle us. They were not smiling.

"Giordano!" snarled Baird. "I know this is all your doing! You want to destroy me and you're willing to destroy the family to do it!"

"Baird! What in god's name are you talking about?" I asked.

"See, already, 'In god's name!' You always wanted to bring religion into this house!"

"Baird, snap out of it," I insisted, "What the fuck are you talking about? I hate religion! Someone, tell me what's going on!"

"They all went!" said Ellen, a bit sourly. "To Millennium. To Houston."

"And they all received the Knowledge!" Greg said angrily.

"And now they are completely unbearable! And this is your entire fault, Giacco!" Baird decided it was I who was the instigator and there seemed to be no way of changing his mind.

Chuck intervened, but I don't think he made the situation any better. "Well, why didn't you all go with them to Houston and get the Knowledge, sillies?"

The floor trembled like that fatal night in 1906. But it was only Baird trying not to explode.

Ellen said sarcastically, "I guess we just aren't the kind of people who want a thousand years of peace."

"The thing is Chuck," Greg said calmly but emphatically, "Ellen and I just don't give a rat's ass one way or another about the Goomer and his toys. It's like a sexual apparatus. Use it in the privacy of your own bedroom. Don't flaunt it!"

"And all of you are flaunting it!" Baird snapped at me.

"Baird, we are not flaunting it. And I don't want to sound like I'm in grade school or anything… but *Chuck* started it!" I laughed, hoping to bring some levity to the scene. "And *Trudy* got it, too!"

"Maybe so, Chazan, maybe so! But I'm holding you responsible!"

"Me? Why me?"

"Because next to me, you understand best how it works," he said.

"How it works? What's that supposed to mean?" I asked.

"How thought manifests itself!"

"Remember what you just said, Baird! It may come back to haunt you soon!"

"This is all your fault, Giacco."

"Not fair, Baird! And it's really no big deal!"

"If you think not, then come with me," Baird said, grabbing my hand and leading me through the kitchen, out the back door and up the path to the cabin. Chuck followed. Greg and Ellen remained inside.

"Peek in through one of the windows."

Chuck and I snuck up to one of the windows and peered through the old, warped glass. There were 12 blanket-tents scattered around the floor. By the light of the many candles, it looked like something out of a bad science fiction movie, pods of alien origin engulfing these innocent bodies. I figured most of them must belong to us, and to the usual hangers-on.

I pulled my face away from the window, turned to Chuck, and whispered, "Oh, my god! What have we done?"

Chuck looked at me in total surprise and with a blissed-out expression answered, "We've done good so far! We've done really good!"

I turned around to face Baird. "Well, I agree Baird. It looks a bit weird. But it'll pass, Baird, I know it."

It didn't help when Chuck went in the cabin, grabbed a blanket, and became a tent.

At Thanksgiving dinner the next night, I thought maybe there would be a return to the zaniness of the old Hunga Dunga, but there were no jokes flying, no scenes of musicals being re-enacted, no indecent exposures. Despite the fact that everyone seemed the same, something was noticeably different.

Richard and Ellen put out two big bowls of colorful salads, one at each end of the long straw mat on the floor that was our table. They left and returned with two large cookie sheets of wonderfully smelling broiled tofu. I guessed it was the garlic that made my mouth water. It might have been the plum sauce.

Nick set up a burner of some sort in the middle of the table. It used a candle for fuel. He struck a match, lit the candle, and put it in the center of the burner's recessed well where it fit just right. Just deep enough to get something hot if it were placed on top of it, but without depriving it of so much oxygen it would extinguish the flame. A delicate balance. Another marvel of civilization.

Lana entered with a big crock-pot of something thick and smelly, but in a good way, and placed it on the burner. Nick returned with two plates of lightly steamed veggies, strange looking forks, and a basket of thin baguettes. The big pot in the middle looked like creamy lava, with chunks of broccoli and cauliflower and small cubes of eggplant, a strip of red pepper surfacing every now and then. Made my stomach growl. Mmmmmm.

The last of the stragglers arrived. As Luc took a seat, he gave us a quick list of the rules of etiquette regarding eating fondue. I was sure everyone would ignore them. It felt great to be at a nice, cheap, innovative, creative, anarchical family dinner again.

We stretched our arms to take each other's hands and observe quiet time as we had always done. I straightened my back and closed my eyes. But no sooner had I taken my first deep breath than I felt a break in the circle. I opened my eyes. Everyone else's were already open. It was Baird. Ellen and Lizzie sat on either side of him, their arms still rocking in mid-air from Baird's quick disengagement.

"Baird! C'mon," said Lizzie. "Hold hands and let's get this over with. I'm hungry!"

"Not until either someone here gives me the meditation techniques, or you stop doing what you're doing!"

"Really, Baird, you are taking this too far," Lana remarked. "You've been doing this all week. It's no big deal."

"I'm sorry, but I can't hold hands anymore when I know there are people doing something besides being quiet, and they won't tell me what it is!"

"Oh, Baird! That is stupid! Can you hear what you're saying?" Ellen asked, shaking her head. "Greg doesn't give a shit what they're doing. As I said before, I couldn't give a rat's ass about it. It's nothing. Shine it on. It'll go away by itself."

"I will not shine it on," Baird declared.

"Baird," Zietar said, sticking his face out from a row of people, "this is ridiculous. We are not doing anything except keeping our eyes closed. We don't know what you're doing when you have your eyes closed! And we don't care! What is the big fucking deal?"

"The big deal," Baird answered, "is that there is a secret in this house. In this house where I thought we had no secrets from one another! You obviously don't trust me or one of you would tell me what the Knowledge is. The collapse of trust undermines all we are as a family."

"Oh, no you don't!" Psylvia spoke up. "Don't get all warm and fuzzy and sentimental on us now, Baird! It's not going to work. If you really want the Knowledge, you just have to walk about three blocks to the ashram and ask for it. You may have to put up with some satsang, but you're the resident intellectual and philosopher around here. You'll probably enjoy it."

"That is beside the point, Psylvia!" Baird's voice was starting to attain its booming quality. "I want one of you to give me the secrets! I don't want it from some flunky of a Madison Avenue guru!"

"Baird," I hesitated to speak, but I had to. "You of all people. So well read. Probably read every bit of esotericism that exists. You know there are references to these kriyas, these techniques, in all religions. All the major ones and many of the primitive ones. And they're always hidden inside metaphors that are so simple and obvious no one ever finds them. And they stay hidden until just the right person comes along and unveils them for you."

"See!" Baird shouted across the mats. "That's exactly what I'm talking about! You don't think I'm sophisticated and intelligent enough to understand and appreciate the power of their simplicity and subtlety! That's what's pissing me off!"

"That's not it," Nick, of all people, said very calmly. "Maybe none of us think we're the right person to do it, that's all!"

Luc timidly interjected, "I yam zo hungreee! Eet eez OK to eat now, yes?"

"Yes, Luc," answered Ellen, "we may as well eat before everything gets cold and the fondue turns into jello."

With that, a dozen hands stabbed veggies with their forks or dipped pieces of bread into the cheesy stew. We passed around the plates of tofu and the bowls of salad. But Baird would not drop the subject. And Lizzie only escalated it.

"What would've happened if Giacco came back from India and he and Jon and Rosie found a guru and the guru gave Giacco a mantra that was secret? You're going to force him to give it to you?"

Baird thought about it for a minute, while everyone else was slopping cheese, broccoli, and cauliflower onto their bread. Normally, Baird would have answered with something like, "I would respect the secrecy of Chazan's mantra because it has the credibility of being given by a respected teacher." But he knew saying something like that would be illogical. This was not a conversation of logic, but one of ego. He avoided answering the question entirely.

He merely said, "I don't give a rat's ass that Greg and Ellen don't give a rat's ass. I do know that they and I don't like seeing all of you under blankets! And I am not going to hold hands any more or observe quiet time until I know whatever it is you are doing! It is a matter of familial preservation that I learn from one of *you* what it is you are doing!

It is a communal imperative that we each have access to the same pools of education and wisdom."

Bobby's hand reached between a tangle of arms and headed for the crock-pot. Just as his baguette contacted the rich sauce, he said, "Baird, isn't it enough that we are all dipping into the same pool of fondue?"

A giggle rippled around the circle. Baird was getting angrier. "This is not a joke! This has serious ramifications! I don't know if I can live in a house where individuals don't share the same beliefs!"

At that statement, I couldn't help but stick in my two cents. "Baird, I thought you and I once agreed that having no beliefs was the only way to avoid conflict. If we believe in anything, it is the creed that you wrote for the Church of Manna." I was trying to massage his ego and at the same time diminish his paranoia. "I promise you this Knowledge, and damn do I hate using that word, these techniques, this *secret*, is not a belief. There is nothing to believe. They are just some little tricks you can play on yourself."

"Tricks you can play only under a blanket?" Baird asked scornfully.

"OK, OK, Baird," Psylvia said with exasperation in her voice. "Even though I believe it is protected in the Bill of Rights somewhere, I promise never to meditate or wear a blanket over my head ever again. Are you satisfied?"

"Oh, Psylvia," Baird sneered across the straw mats, "your humor and sacrifice have no bounds."

"And Baird," Alvoye's voice, so seldom heard, now joined in the conversation over this lovely dinner, "I have been wearing blankets over my head since I was a kid, long before I got the Knowledge. But to keep peace in the family, I *also* will not meditate or wear a blanket over my head."

"How will I be able to tell for sure you're both not meditating behind my back?" Baird asked.

"Oh Christ!" Nick blurted out, "How do you know I'm not saying the Lord's Prayer to myself during quiet time? You'll just have to trust them!"

"Ahhh! Now we come to the crux of the problem," Baird said. "You want *me* to trust *them*, but *they* won't trust *me* to keep a secret by telling me what the Knowledge is."

Even though it wasn't a family meeting, Lizzie said, "OK people, there will be no more meditating or wearing blankets over the head. Can everyone live with that?"

Lizzie expected the usual accommodating responses. Instead, a whole bunch of voices came at him all at once. The loudest came from Chuck and Trudy, who announced in no uncertain terms, they would never stop meditating and they would use the blankets if they found them necessary. Meditating in the cabin out back was about as considerate, discreet, and alone as a person could get in Big Blue, and that Baird was being childish and unfair.

Baird argued that consideration and discretion, blankets, and a cabin, had nothing to do with it. It was the idea of it. How could we be purely communal if some people had something others did not?

The debate could have gone on for days. And it did. But for the time being, a vote was taken and since Baird didn't have enough votes to ban meditating in public, even when you're not sure someone is actually meditating, it didn't pass. And when that happens, the issue is tabled. Life goes on, until someone brews long enough to reach another boiling point.

Nick, for whom Baird had always had a hard on, said, "Baird, if you would just get this Knowledge, there would be no problem. You would understand. You would see how irrationally you're behaving."

Baird answered, "I would only ask for this thing you call Knowledge once I am convinced of its value. And I can't consider its value until someone tells me what it is! If I can't get the information from my own family, I don't want it! As a matter of principle, only one of *you*," he said, sweeping a pointed finger around in a circle, "can tell me the secret!"

No one would and it drove him crazy.

CHAPTER 85
December 1973

The more things seemed to settle down, the more they got out of hand. Chuck and Trudy still spoke about the Knowledge and the Goomer. They gave each other and anyone in earshot satsang. They meditated discreetly, but not secretly, in the cabin. Katie sought asylum at Hunga Dunga from the persecution she was receiving from Eli, as were a couple others of her fellow communards over at Kaliflower. Eli was as irate as Baird over this infestation eating away at his utopian communism and the intercommunal network, he worked so hard to help create. I thought they were getting worked up over nothing. There was nothing to be afraid of.

Nevertheless, most of us, including me, just gradually let it go. We stopped meditating. If we did, no one knew about it. There was no talk about the Goomer except if he were the butt of a joke. Even Trudy soon showed signs of giving in and sublimating what she thought she knew was true for the sake of familial tranquility. Maybe it was just a front.

Baird stopped being so insistent about someone telling him the techniques. I suspect it was because someone *did* tell him what the Knowledge was, or at least a version of it. I also suspected who it was. I hoped they had done a good job. Now he was keeping it a secret from *us*, acting as if he no longer cared; that he was above it all. He may know the kriyas, the techniques, the Knowledge, but would he venerate it, would he practice it? If I were convinced of anything, it was that like any other skill, practice does make perfect.

In a way, I was relieved someone spilled the beans. The 10,000 lives as a cockroach had been as effective as Sister Penetrate instilling me with guilt, and though my intellect knew better, if someone else were willing to do the dirty work that was fine by me. I was amazed at how so many other people could and would keep it a secret. Unless they were Jewish or devoutly Catholic, I wondered where their guilt complexes had come from. Or was it that they understood why it needed to be so. At any rate, I applauded the person or persons who had won the war against guilt and felt free to bring Baird up to date. I figured it would calm things down.

Still, he refused to hold hands at quiet time, which really bugged the hell out of me. We all knew that he knew. But in Baird's perfect world, the way it would have worked was this:

Chuck would have gotten Knowledge, passed it on to Trudy and me and anyone else up in Twisp. Come down to The City. Immediately call a family meeting and turn everyone else on to it. Whether or not they practiced the secrets was beside the point. It was the manner in which the Knowledge was given. Things had not unfolded in that manner, and so this was Baird's method of punishing us.

In many ways, I agreed with Baird. Those that have ears to hear will hear, those that have eyes to see will see, and all that kind of stuff. But deep down I knew it was the person who had made some effort to get it, who asked for it, begged for it, cut their hair for it, or gave their car for it, who got more out of the Knowledge. I don't know why. But I for one couldn't bring myself to do anything more than skirt around it whenever Baird confronted me on the matter.

Right up until Christmas, things seemed somewhat in balance. No outward wars at least. Then at a family meeting, Chuck announced, seemingly out of nowhere, that Trudy, Katie, and he were going to Hawaii to live in a Divine Light Mission in Waikiki.

Chuck asked Hunga Dunga to try to understand that they had to try this, and they hoped if it didn't work out, they could return to Big Blue. If not, so be it. They were going anyway. They weren't going to ask permission because it didn't matter. They just had to go!

Trudy said this was a huge decision for her. She really felt in her heart that being around satsang was more important. She hated leaving Hunga Dunga. Chuck and Katie said that enlightenment meant non-attachment, even to people and family. That living in an ashram where satsang is given openly and continually, reinforces the Knowledge and helps internalize it. Therefore, they had to do this. Trudy had been easily persuaded to join them. Especially when she found out who was living in the Waikiki ashram. They just had to go. They had to give this Knowledge their best shot and they couldn't do it with the current vibes in the house. Then, Chuck had to go and muck it up for me.

"And Giacco," Chuck said, "I really wish you'd reconsider and come with us. I wish you'd re-examine your priorities. I still have a ticket for you."

All eyes turned to me.

"You mean you knew about this all along?" Richard asked in a hurt tone.

"Just what kind of conspiracy is this?" Baird demanded.

Psylvia looked shocked. "Giacco, how could you?" And she "tsk-tsked" me, shaking her head.

That was the stinger. No one could make you know hurt like Psylvia could. No matter who you were, she was your conscience personified. To look into her face was to see all your faults laid out in front of you. Maybe that's what Nick's biggest problem with Psylvia was. Living up to her level of integrity.

Funny. I was able to look right at her and not see any faults of mine mirrored in her eyes. A testament to my good intentions, I hoped. What I did see though, was sorrow. Was it a sorrow for some dark future only she could see?

"I know it doesn't look good, guys," I started off, "but there is no conspiracy at work here. The exact opposite."

"What's that supposed to mean?" Nick asked.

"It means we didn't want to say anything about anything until there was something to say. It was just talk. Just philosophizing. Why open a can of worms if it wasn't necessary? Until Chuck and Katie decided they wanted to do it. And Trudy decided to go along too. And I… well, you know me… I have a hard time making decisions. I haven't made one yet. I guess I've been waiting for the decision to be made for me."

"Oh!" snarled Baird. "But it's OK for you to go around helping other people make their decisions, is that it?"

"Baird, if you keep this up, it might be *you* making the decision for me! If anything, I'm the one who played devil's advocate with them! I'm the one who said what you have is inside you, not in an ashram! I'm the one who said, go next door and hang out with Travis and Rolli if you need satsang. Go to the Park and think about how cool it is that Knowledge doesn't contradict anything. Not even what you wrote for the creed of the Church of Manna!"

"See?" Baird practically lashed me with his beard. "You are so manipulative, Giacco! Stroking my ego, thinking I'll let you get away with this one!"

"You know, Baird," I said, starting to lose my patience, "you are a living contradiction and hypocrisy incarnate!" Baird looked stunned, as did most of the family. People avoided Baird's wrath if they could.

"You sit up in your room admiring the Tibetan prints and study their stories and meanings. You are in the middle of painting beautiful bodies in a classical Greek style, all of them holding a golden rope in their hands, that which 'connects' us all."

"That is art!" Baird declared, "Not a belief system."

"You have no problem with Psylvia going to midnight Mass!"

"That's once a year and I consider it her fucking with the church! I approve of that!"

"You have no problem with Lana practicing voodoo in the upstairs closet and chanting in tongues while spanking the bongos."

"That's performance art, not a religion!" came Baird's stern reply. Lana looked pissed that Baird dismissed her rituals as performance art. Everyone knew who was going to be stuck with needles that night!

I was getting tired of arguing. It was turning dramatic. One of those living soap operas you have no control over. Someone else wrote it and directed it. You are just a player who for some reason feels the need to stay in character.

Chuck said very sincerely, "Baird, I love you. I just don't feel comfortable here anymore. I always feel like I'm walking on pins and needles."

"The only pins and needles are the ones that Lana sticks into her little dolls!" Baird smirked. "The rest is in your imagination! You can't separate the Goomer from the Knowledge. Admit it! It's a religion, just like I told you it would be!"

Chuck took the offensive. "Baird, it's no more a religion than hatha yoga! If I wanted to do yoga exercises, would you forbid that?" Chuck didn't wait for an answer. "I could practice the asanas religiously, but that doesn't mean those yoga positions are a religion. Not to me, at least."

"What's your point?" Baird asked, impatient to continue his tirade.

"The yoga positions are techniques. The Knowledge is just some techniques, not a religion, not a belief system. The Light, the Word, the Divine Music, the Nectar… they are techniques. Just like the plow or the lotus pose! And if you wouldn't let me do yoga in this house, I would have just cause to leave!"

Oh, how I hated that there were now names for everything! Everything seemed ruined by being labeled. I blamed Maharaj Ji for that. Life was much more interesting when we thought there was something unnamable awaiting us. And even if we thought we met it, to name it depleted its strength. Labels were merely a convenience society created for itself to represent the realities hiding involuntarily behind them. It only takes moments for the mind to be tricked into thinking the label is the reality. We slice the continua of nature at whatever point seems convenient enough to manage them, and stuff them into pigeonholes. Society is so fucking lazy. People are so fucking lazy. Labels fucking ruin everything!

"Baird, it's not a religion!" Chuck insisted. "Look at it as if we are going to a Buddhist monastery for a retreat! Would that sound better to you?"

That one stumped Baird. Finally, he said, "Yes, it does sound better. I don't know why."

"I promise you Baird, all we want is to practice the techniques of the Knowledge just like Tom, Brandon, and Ellen do yoga every morning. If we can't do that here, we'll do it somewhere else!"

"Then do it somewhere else!" Baird fired back with the commanding voice he must have used in the Armed Forces. "The mere fact that I feel a disconnect in my logic makes me angry! I suggest we change the subject at once before I lose my temper!"

Bobby, Luc, and Alvoye were getting all teary-eyed. I thought how nice it was they were so sensitive to this historic situation. Then I realized why they were upset.

"We want to go to Waikiki too!" Bobby said.

Luc chimed in, "May weee! I need to go to Hawaii!"

Alvoye hummed so sweetly, "Aloha Ohe," and hula-ed his long brown arms so come-hither-ly, I could swear I heard the ukuleles in the background, and for a moment I was transported to the last time I was in Hawaii. I could almost smell it. And it smelled so fine! Of course, I recalled the best, not the worst, but actually, most of it was pretty cool. Hawaii was a great place to let things happen to you. Suddenly I felt an intense desire to be there. To be passive. To let it all happen to me. To be Hawaii'd.

"Forget it, gang!" Richard said with a nip-it-in-the-bud kind of tone. "We can't afford to be losing Hunga Dunga's money by sending people off on experimental journeys! In Waikiki of all places! If you were really holy, you'd be going to an ashram in Alaska! Then your talk would have more credibility!"

"We're not going to take any of our money," Chuck said. "The money situation stays the same. It all goes in the pot. And Trudy knows someone there. We've been invited there. If I had to, I would go up to Alaska!"

Lizzie and Richard looked relieved. "This is a one-time special situation," Chuck continued. "I borrowed some money from my folks. We know we're leaving but we're thinking we'll probably want to come back in a couple months." Chuck smiled sheepishly and said, "If that's OK. I mean since we're kickin' in our share of the money into the pot and all that. And just think of all the extra room you'll have! Don't get too used to it!" Chuck tried a chuckle.

Trudy added, "Just until we know for sure. But we don't know now. We can't know now." And a look of bewilderment swept across her face.

Chuck stood up. The rest of us followed. Everyone was stretching when Trudy said, "The cab should be here in a few minutes."

Everyone yelled, "Whaaaaaaat?"

"Well, we figured, why delay the pain!" Katie explained.

Everyone started screaming at the same time. Well, it was more like wailing. Mostly about how they didn't want us to go and how could we do this to them. Such short notice. Not enough time for them to process everything. All sorts of pleas to really think over what we were doing. Worst of all, were the few who said nothing, and whose silence was deafening.

Chuck stood next to me and said quietly, "You have your passport and wallet?"

I looked at him and like a robot following orders, climbed to my attic retreat, and retrieved those items, and nothing else. No clothes, no toothpaste, no flip-flops. Nothing. Even less than Rosie allowed us in Colombo. Just the clothes I was wearing, Michael's hishi necklace, and my Ganesh, which always adorned my neck, and my passport and wallet. A sadhu once again. This time in one of the States of the United. By the time I got back to the living room, most everyone was standing on the front porch stairs, still cajoling and begging.

Katie grabbed my arm trying to pull me down the crowded steps. I just stared at her blankly. She said, "Giacco, I know this is hard to do, but think about it? What's more important?"

Richard and Duck grabbed my other arm. "Chazan," Richard pleaded, "Don't go! Stay with us! Think about it! What's more important?"

Psylvia reached in and put her face close to mine. She kissed me on the lips and then winked at me. "Don't worry. Have fun. Give the Goomer a hug for me. Then come home!" She gave me a melancholy smile and turned away.

Larry and Zietar were winning the tug-of-war with Katie. Chuck grabbed Katie and pulled hard. I felt I was being drawn and quartered. I fell into a dream. I heard my voice yelling up to Baird, "Baird, believe me! I'm goin' because that's what's happening!" However, my brain was occupied with thoughts of coconut palms and tropical fruit. "I'm going because it's Hawaii, not because of the Goomer! I'm going for the pali coastlines and exquisite beaches and that rare air so distinct from everywhere else in the world." My voice sounded distant and unconvincing as I watched Baird staring down at me from the front porch. "I'm going because it's a free ticket! I'm going because we've worked so hard on The Dome, I need a vacation!"

Trudy grabbed Chuck's arm and pulled me free from Larry and Richard. We tumbled into the back seat of the taxi. As the driver pulled away from the curb, I looked out the back window. I will never forget the looks of horror on the faces of Zietar, Larry, and Psylvia because I was equally horrified. I can hardly explain how it happened. A spell? Had Lana dipped her pins into plumeria nectar and needled my doll with them? I could smell it already. That rare air. It's fragrance. Or had I been drugged? It seemed so. Already, it was too late. I was being Bali-hai'd.

The last vision I had was of Baird. He was crying. Krishnamurti was standing behind him and shaking his head in disappointment.

CHAPTER 86
January 1974

As soon as we had entered the ashram, we knew we'd made a mistake. A very big mistake. It was mortifyingly boring. It was catechismically frightening. Everyone looked the same. Clean-cut, Christian-ish, quiet. Blissful smiles followed by a spirited "Jai Satchitanand" or sometimes the whole shebang, "Bhole Sri Satgurudev Mararaj Ki Jai!" Chuck and I were losing it fast.

Dinner was served. Mainly yellow and brown. Boring! This was Hawaii for god's sake. Get with it! The Free Food Conspiracy could have done better any day! And then after dinner there was satsang. Oh, yeah, we liked to hear god-talk. It always got us high. But in this setting, it was getting on our nerves. It was god-talk societized, organized. In other words, a religion with rules! Are there any other kinds? Rules, rules, and more rules! I never could discover their source. I never heard Maharaji talk about rules! Just the opposite! So, who deemed that the ashrams should have rules? Maharaji? Not if he were a man-boy of his word! His mom? Brothers? They were all suspect, even the house leader here, himself, some Mahatma-appointed devotee, obviously more devoted to the Mahatma than to the Goomer. He didn't even introduce himself. Chuck and I immediately resented him with every ounce of love we could muster.

There were just too many levels, too many ranks, too many rules. In an effort to make sure no one was distracted from practicing the Knowledge, the house leader reminded us that couples had to sleep separately, no sexual activity was allowed, no smoking of any kind, no this, no that. The ashram existed to make money that could be used to propagate the Knowledge.

Oy veh and oh my god what had we done! I could feel Baird looking down at me again saying, "I told you so!" Worse, I could see Krishnamurti standing behind him once more, shaking his head, his faithful protégé having betrayed him so!

A fair number of people arrived after dinner for the evening's "sermon" followed by "testimonials." I will admit the house leader's satsang was very high and beautiful. But then everyone's satsang was beautiful and true. How could it not be when the topic was nothingness, mindlessness, meaninglessness. When every cloud was now a sign, where every lyric, be it country and western or heavy metal, now held a cosmic truth. When every missed bus was perfect timing because the Knowledge is being in the here and now, and you missed the bus for a reason. The only bright spot of the evening, actually a startling spot, was the satsang of the only other person in the room who had long hair besides Chuck and me. He was a very nice-looking surfer guy, around 19 or so, sun-bleached hair, bright blue eyes, wearing brightly colored board shorts and a torn tank top.

"Hey, I just stopped in to see what was going on Hal. You know, most of us here went to school together or knew each other from the beach or whatever, and now I am convinced this whole thing is totally bogus, dude! If the little guy were here, he'd probably laugh at all of you. He'd probably say, 'What a bunch of idiots! Paradise is right outside their door! Why don't they go get it?' This is fuckin' nuts, man!"

Hal, the house leader, just glared at him and said, "Skip! You do this all the time! If you don't like it, why not just stay away!"

"No mon! I like it!" Skip answered back in mock Rastafarian. "You don't get me bro'! Mariko, Junior, and me just want to say that life is bonzers, and remind everyone mon, when you're in the glide there's nothing like it! Mon, it's irie, I tell ya. Bitchin' nirvana! More fun to live it than to talk it! And walk it, mon. Toe to heel. Get your glide. That's all. Oh, and Jai Satchitanand and all of that! So, get some mirrors in this joint and look at yourselves!"

"Are you finished, Skip?" Hal asked, as if the answer was supposed to be 'yes."

"Just gotta tell ya, the other day I took some mushrooms and meditated for a while and it's bananas man!" Skip said seriously. "Take the Light, man, multiply it by a zillion. And the Word! Talk about *nothing*! In-cred-dibble!"

Skip stood up and walked toward the door. When he reached the back of the room he took a baby boy, no more than a year old, out of the arms of a stunning looking woman. She was exotic, yet demure. The three walked out the front door. Chuck and I watched their silhouettes blend into the shadows.

Chuck and I lasted exactly one night at the ashram in Waikiki. And most of that night was spent whispering in the dark of a small room that at one time must have been used as a pantry or storage room. Now it was used as a guest room, probably so guests wouldn't stay more than a couple days.

The ceiling light fixture was barely filtered by a homemade bamboo shade. The light was so harsh we turned it off as soon as we were finished surveying the space. It was extremely sparse. A couple of futons and light blankets. No windows, but every wall adorned with a picture of the Goomer. We thought we were in solitary confinement in some prison, perhaps during the German occupation of Warsaw.

All we could talk about was escape. Immediate escape. Out into the dark of the Waikiki Jungle. We talked about how we might sneak into the women's dorm and ask Katie if she wanted to come with us. After all, over the past year, Katie and I had a pretty torrid history, both as friends and lovers, but it was a solid relationship that deserved to be saved. And when all was said and done, I guess I really loved her. Nevertheless, we selfishly decided against it. We were too concerned with our own self-preservation. Let her fend for herself for one night. We could always come back in the morning to get her. Some friend and lover I was!

We had already lost Trudy to the awaiting arms of Jeffrey from Vancouver, the guy who put us up that memorable night, the guy who came to Twisp to help us out and obviously got to know Trudy a lot better than we thought. He was the one who sent us the written invitation to come to Hawaii. Ironic that as smitten as they were with each other, this evening they'd have to sleep apart.

Chuck and I were bemoaning the fact we hadn't brought sleeping bags with us so we could just go out and sleep on the beach instead of our claustrophobic closet, when we heard the door open a crack. Just wide enough for a hand to slip in. It held a cigar-sized spliff, the glowing head warm and comforting, the aroma so relaxing.

The smoke turned into Skip's voice. "Get your stuff and follow your nose."

Chuck grabbed his bag. I had nothing to grab. Off we went through the shadows of the quiet house, following the fumes, walking delicately, hunched over, toe to heel, out the front door, onto the beautiful veranda, straightening up, taking deep breaths, and gamboling through the Jungle until we came to a grove of coconut palms.

Skip re-lit the joint, took a big toke, then passed it to Chuck. Chuck passed it to me and that big ol' cigar made three rounds before anyone spoke. Mmmm. Mmmm. It was terrific stuff!

"Pakalolo!" Skip said. "From Maui."

"Very, very fine smoke," I said. "Thanks Skip. I'm Giacco. This is Chuck."

It felt the three of us had known each other for a long time even though we were just now learning each other's names. Chuck and I were completely at ease with Skip. Just an extraordinary kid. One of those rare people for whom everything really *is* needless to say! There's nothing to do but mock everything! Keep things in perspective.

"So, what are we gonna do with you?" Skip asked, as if he were the adult and we were lost kids. With parental authority he said, "You'll stay with us til we figure this out. Follow me."

Skip, Mariko, and their infant son, Junior, lived just a long, wonderful walk from the ashram in Moilili, a neighborhood primarily of university students. They had a very nice little bungalow house with a magical backyard, small, but prolific. There were trees that bore all kinds of tropical fruits, including my favorites: avocadoes, papayas, mangoes, and a big banana tree with cascading bunches of fruit. I learned that bananas were actually an herb and that's why a little herb garden surrounded its base. It was tiny, but all the plants grew so fast, the cuttings used to season every meal grew back in a day. It was like a perpetual motion bio-machine.

A nice variety of vegetables were happy in their raised beds that bordered the house on the two sunniest sides. Many of them I didn't recognize and guessed they had their origin with the coming of the Japanese and Pacific Islanders. I'm happy I got to learn how delicious they are.

Where there was no flora of some kind, there was a piece of yard art. Found objects whimsically put together to be whatever you wanted them to be. Driftwood and shells. Rocks and man-made debris from the sea. I could imagine the three of them, Skip, Mariko, and Junior laughing as they made them. Snapshots of love in motion. I thought they were the Knowledge made manifest, and exactly what Maharaji had in mind for the human race. But who am I to say what Maharaji had in mind?

Though it was only that one night, the ashram felt like a concentration camp, a military school at best. Logically, I understood their intentions and I saw them as well-meaning. Chuck and I just didn't agree with their premises. We didn't even belong on the premises! So, thank the gods for Skip, who snipped the barbed wire and led the escape.

Not only did he rescue us from the physical confinement, but also from the spiritual. Regardless of how much Skip was disappointed by all the hoopla surrounding the Goomer, he thought the techniques were outrageous and "spot on." I guess surfers pick up Aussie slang, or vice versa, but for the briefest moment, I thought I was back in Sri Lanka and Peter or Debra had spoken them.

It was so easy for Skip to sever the kriyas from the ties of the Divine Light Mission, the ashrams and even the Goomer himself, without a shred of guilt. This gave Chuck and me heart. You didn't have to give up anything! You merely had to assimilate it into what you already were.

We spent that first night sleeping in hammocks in the back yard. As the sides of the hammock crept up around me, I felt cocooned and safe, just like when I was a kid back in Lodi, New Jersey, and crept into my sofa cave with no one to see me or hear me. All I saw when I looked up was an amazing sky with billions of stars moving slowly past my stare, or was it me imperceptively falling off the earth?

The next morning, we went back to the ashram with Skip and asked Katie and Trudy if they wanted to stay there or get out. Not only did Katie scream and yell at us for not getting her out the night before, but she insisted on going home as soon as possible. As for Trudy and Jeff, they could not bear sleeping apart. They had already broken the rules and were asked to leave.

Chuck and Katie were back in San Francisco within the week. Jeffrey and Trudy followed soon after, but not until Trudy had lobbied the right people at Hunga Dunga and been assured Jeffrey could stay with her at Big Blue.

Surprisingly, all were welcomed home, albeit to varying degrees. It was a given, that everyone was to ignore the slightest reference to the Goomer, unless it was in a mocking tone. All was getting back to normal, which for Hunga Dunga, of course, meant stretching, to absurd contortions, the relativity of the word.

I decided to stay. Just for a little bit. Another week or two. I was confident that there would be no problem going back to Hunga Dunga. But little events sometimes get out of control and snowball into bigger ones. Even in the tropical heat.

Skip got me a job parking cars with him at the Colony Surf Hotel at the base of Diamond Head. No wages. All tips. We made a hundred bucks a night easy! On a good night, 150. On a fantastic night, 200 smackeroos! Under the table. No taxes. All take home. Fancy cars, famous people. Getting stoned during a lull. Just us two on duty. Man, it was great. Sometimes patrons would leave us a joint in the ashtray as a pre-tip. So cool! They knew we'd be extra nice to their car!

Not only did I *not* need money from home, but I was able to send hundreds of bucks extra to Richard to put in the land fund. How could I leave a job like that! It was doing so many people so much good. That I was having a great time was beside the point. That I was in my element, the tropics, was a minor coincidence. But when you have a job, you start the entrenchment process.

If I were going to have a job, I needed my own space. Mariko and Skip said Junior didn't want me to leave. I framed in Skip's carport and put in a door. Screened in the whole thing. Carefully. Totally bug proof. I found some used rattan furniture in a thrift shop. Mariko got me an extra futon that was at her brother's house. I made a little raised frame for it.

Using skills I learned in Twisp, I made a solar-heated outdoor shower. I used the toilet in the house, but other than that, I was independent. I had the outdoor barbeque grill and a nice propane camping stove that folded open and accommodated two pots. I made some truly gourmet meals for us. Never the same thing twice. I had just about everything I needed. That carport made a fantastic little apartment for me. One of the most comfortable, soothing, and fun I've ever had.

Mornings I'd just walk outside nude. Pick a banana or a papaya off a tree. Have breakfast. Plan dinner for the four of us. Baby-sit Junior while Skip and Mariko went to an afternoon party with their friends, some still in high school! Get more entrenched. Junior and I decorating my *carportment* with stuff we found earlier on the beach. I enjoyed the company of this one-year-old so much. I enjoyed their company so much. Entrench me more!

I was once again amazed at how interchangeable we all are, and how we manage to find the people who will fulfill our needs. That's not to say that every person I've ever met hasn't been a unique experience. They have. And many have been exceptional and wonderful. Yet when we find ourselves displaced, the loneliness can only last so long before we begin to attract the people we need to help us survive. And of course, I'm sure it works both ways.

I fixed up an old bike of Skip's. All he had was the frame. Had to get everything else from the dump and scrap yards. Bought a book on how to do it. Worked great. Was very proud of myself. Made a very solid, sweet, smooth 10-speed. Biked from Moilili to Waikiki roundtrip every day. Enjoyed every bit of it. Enjoyed getting entrenched.

I loved how the Hawaiian breeze passed my body as I bicycled to work. The colors of the setting sun. Lighting the torches around the hotel and on the beach. Driving Jaguars and Bentleys to safe havens and returning them to their inebriated owners a couple of hours later for the gift of 15 or 20 dollars, if they had any class at all… and most did.

Hawaii has a way of suspending animation. One day just seemed to melt into the next. One perfect day after another. One perfect day I actually took the time to look at a calendar and was devastated to discover almost three months had passed! Though I kept in touch with many of my beloved crazies at Hunga Dunga, Richard was my main link with the goings-on at home. My messages to him were always the same. "Ziets! Am coming home any day now!" But any day just became the next and the next.

Job, house, transportation, furniture, food, friends, family. *Entrenchment*! I think that sums it up. It happens so swiftly, quietly. Until it's too late. Almost.

CHAPTER 87
March 1974

Skip didn't realize how much he would break the flow of my idyllic life by suggesting I take a couple of weeks for myself. I had been working every day for months. But it was such easy money. So easy it was hard to give up. But Skip insisted I get out of my delightful rut and check out more of the islands. He assured me my job would still be there when I got back. He suggested the Kalalau Valley on Kauai as a place that might pique my interest.

I went. I easily hitched a ride from the small airport in Lihue to Hanalei and then to the trail head a couple miles beyond Haena. It was 13 miles of questionable path that varied anywhere between one foot and three feet wide, cut into the sharply clawed face of the pali, a couple hundred feet or more above the crashing surf. I passed elephant-leafed plants and orchids and small misty falls that made the path soggy, and me soaked. Sometimes the trail would crumble beneath my feet, making my heart stop and my lungs gasp until the path got firm again, usually just in time.

Finally, the trail wended down into the valley itself. This was home to many a hard-core hippie. Families had built intricate houses, some two, three stories high, into the banyan and other big-trunked trees that grew close to the cliffs.

Fresh water from the pali's falls filled split bamboo aqueducts that provided water to a surprisingly large number of houses in the jungle. The freaks here, though polite, were not inviting. They made their living growing excellent weed. And they gravely protected their privacy.

Farther down as the valley opened and flattened, there were wild apples, tobacco, berries, and volunteer ganja plants. Some folks here had gardens and were growing tomatoes and lettuce and all sorts of vegetables.

The valley became less jungle and more green meadow, until finally it surrendered to the beach. It was surprisingly wide and white. The surf was wild and intimidating and I knew right off that I wouldn't be swimming much.

The cliffs were so breathtaking the way they just dropped into the sand. Some cliffs were riddled with caves. They were recessed deep into the cliffs but were only about four feet high and you had to stoop over to explore them. Wonderful characters made homes here as well. Some homes were so deep in the caves, claustrophobia kept many a stoned head away. But most were shallow caves that gave adequate protection from the weather and still maintained the bay window view. How neat to walk out of your home right onto the beach. Especially if your cave was near the waterfall.

The cave dwellers mingled neighborly with the majority of the people who hung out on the beach. These were just your average freaks, flower-children and space cadets there for a short visit. They brought in the mushrooms and acid, the crystals and tarot cards, their nubile bodies and all the other necessities of life in this land so strange and wonderful, it may have been Atlantis.

The only way in or out of the valley was the wild 13-mile hike that took about nine hours, or by small motorboat out of Haena or Hanalei. That only took a half hour to 45 minutes or so. Or if you had the bucks, by helicopter. In that case, it was mere minutes away. Most everyone hiked in. But during times of the full moon, a lot of hippies took the skiffs in.

There was no place a boat could safely make it all the way to the shore. No ways to actually beach the craft and let the passengers with their supplies disembark. The surf was way too intense. The skipper had to keep that skiff beyond the curling waves or be prepared to go for one hair-raising ride. He'd just keep the boat a safe distance behind the swells, tie the supplies onto large inner tubes and toss them overboard, letting the waves crash the belongings onto the beach where there were always people willing to help grab the stuff before the tide pulled them back out again.

As for any passengers in the boat, they just dove into the water right after their supplies were thrown overboard, caught a wave, and hoped for the best. Body surf if you could, then at the end, just curl up into a ball, and pray. There were always people on shore ready to help pull you in and escort you to the fresh-water falls where you could wash the blood off your knees and face. As long as the drugs weren't damaged. That was the important thing.

The tall waterfall that spilled from the cliffs right onto the beach was a main meeting place, one of two major landmarks. Most everyone gathered here at some time or another during the day, to wash or get water for cooking, or just to play.

It was wonderfully cold and fresh and so nice to watch naked bodies play unabashedly. In fact, that was one of Kalalau's main attractions, the beautiful unabashedly naked bodies and the naked bodies that loved to be stared at unabashedly.

The permissiveness was due to a healthy dose of mind-altering substances of course, the sweetness of the scenery, and most of all, the protection of the Hawaiian gods and spirits who flew along the coastline from their *heiau* at the far northeastern end of the beach.

The *heiau* was the other major landmark. This sacred place was a relatively intact archeological site, and you could still make out the foundations of ancient buildings and the remnants of altars. The ghosts of the *kapu*, the *kahunas* and *ali'i* were present. They were easy to feel and hear. When the tropical breeze decided to swirl suddenly and sensually around my body, I knew it was one of them touching me. But was it love or were they just seeing if I would make a good sacrifice?

Next to the waterfall, the heiau was the most popular meeting place. Many a head spent days at the heiau, meditating, fasting, and de-atomizing. From the beach, look to the left and there was the heiau, a small oval plateau, high atop a spine of green that jutted into the ocean overlooking the crashing surf. Look to the right, the waterfall that fell onto the beach, splashed sapphires during the day and moonstones at night.

The waterfall was narrow at the top and the stream rushing over the stone lip looked like a teapot pouring water into a cup. The water spilled 60 feet or more onto a large, flat stone and splattered like a rainstorm on the surrounding sand, leaving divots that constantly changed their design. Kalalau was a rare combination of natural luxuries: sea, sand, and freshwater. But this waterfall was particularly spectacular.

One day playing in the falls I spied the end of a rope just out of jumping reach, even for those who could dunk a basketball. The rope was in bad shape, but it fascinated me. Stoned on some mushrooms, not too much, just enough, and with my daypack on my back, I persuaded a big, tall freak with wild dreads, to let me stand on his shoulders so I could reach it. I grabbed the frayed rope and wrapped it around one wrist. I pushed my feet against the cliff, keeping my knees slightly bent, trying to mimic climbers I had seen on television. I steadied myself and looked for an obvious climbing route. The guy whose shoulders I had borrowed thought I was crazy but egged me on.

"Hey dude!" he yelled up, "Do you even have any idea how old that rope is or what it's tied to? Dude! Can you hear me?"

The rope skirted the waterfall for the first 20 feet or so, and it was impossible not to get drenched. In fact, it felt great, except it made some of the rocks slippery. I strained to hear my tall friend's voice through the sound of the falls. That's the first time I looked down. That was a mistake. The few people gathered around the falls seemed very far away. And the mushrooms were just starting to come on. It was then I remembered that I had a terrible fear of heights.

"Go for it dude!" yelled the tall one. "Don't fuckin' freeze there man!" he said encouragingly, or was it worriedly? "I'm not gonna come up there and get ya!"

A young water nymph, filling her plastic drinking bottle yelled up. "Man, you are crazy! Come on back down while you still can! You are getting me nervous!"

I had to make a decision. Go for it, or slide back down and hide the rope burns, and hope I didn't break an ankle jumping the last 10 feet to the ground. I climbed. I scrambled. I dug my fingernails and toenails into the cliff. It was a race against time. Make it to the top before the mushrooms kick in too good! Oh, so good!

"Fuck, dude, you sure have a lot of faith!" tall, big guy yelled.

I froze again. Is that what it was? Faith? Did I have faith? Was it faith that made Dennis jump out the window in New York? Countless other images flashed through my mind, mostly of narrow escapes of myself doing stupid things. Death would have been a just outcome for me, but luck kept getting in the way.

Suddenly I had no idea how I'd gotten into this situation. Maybe some kahuna had just picked me up and placed me here dangling from a rope, my body hugging dirt and rock, while the waterfall and wind laughed their heads off around my body.

I wanted to come down. I yelled as loud as I could to tall guy and nymph girl that I was coming down. I figured at worst he'd be able to break my fall the last few feet or so if the rope didn't hold. At best, maybe even catch me, the big lug. I loved him already!

But I guess they never heard me. As I looked down, all I could see was that tall naked guy and water nymph girl were looking into each other's eyes wantonly, and coyly laughing, though I couldn't hear it, just sense it. Their bodies moved closer to one another. He bent his head until his long brown hair mingled with her blond. Then they started groping each other. Then they disappeared into the bushes and by that time I was already a thing of the past.

I looked up. I had about 30 feet more to go. It looked like the trail veered away from the waterfall enough to avoid being constantly splashed. I looked straight ahead. The patch of cliff I stared at was starting to become one of those ever-changing mandalas. I retained enough of my wits and experience with mushrooms to know I had to work fast.

I instinctively shoved my tongue to the back of the roof of my mouth and began taking big breaths through my nose. It seemed so natural and instinctive; I was surprised we ever had to be taught how to do it. And if we already did it, I was surprised we had to be told it was important. It quickly steadied me, focused me. My hands and feet found all the right holds. I climbed to the top with ease.

I noticed the rope was frayed in places where it rubbed against protruding rocks. Maybe even frayed to the degree that were I a heavier person, the rope wouldn't have held. But it did. I pulled myself up over the last few big rocks abutting the top and sat next to the stream spilling over the edge. I looked out over the ocean and beach, captivated by the view, bound to it so tightly, it hurt, and I cried.

And then I closed my eyes and let myself be captivated by the mushrooms and bound to the Word so tightly it hurt. And I cried again until time disappeared.

When time reappeared, the sun was three-quarters through its descending arc. The wind changed slightly and a fine mist from the falls blew my way. At first it startled me. Then I relished in its refreshment and its gentle slap on the face, reminding me there were still things to get together.

I was hungry. And I was a bit scared now that the mushrooms were wearing off and I would soon no longer be in an altered state of mind. I would no longer be a superhero with superpowers. I would just be another vulnerable human being and would have to deal with myself in a real world. What could be scarier than that? The tip of my tongue did another backbend.

Then I realized that I might have to climb down the rope again. I hadn't thought of that. It was a horrible thought. Unacceptable. I'd try to see if I could find another trail back to the beach that didn't involve traveling vertically. I'd have to be quick about it if I wanted to take advantage of the remaining light. I stood up and turned around and for the first time carefully studied the miniature valley through which this narrow stream flowed strongly and steadily until it plummeted over the edge.

This was truly one sweet little valley. I hate to say it, but I have to use the word "cute." It was so cute I could just about burst! It was obvious I was not the first to be here, but I think very few had seen this rare piece of land. Though it was just a beautiful dent in the dirt, I took the liberty of naming it in my honor. I called it "Mai Vallee."

I walked up the valley, the stream as my constantly gurgling companion, and after just a short walk I could see where the valley got higher and flatter and commingled with the forest. Mai Vallee was the exquisite dead end of one of many paths through the dark greens and blacks of the interior. I followed a few of them far enough to tell that none of them was heading downhill back to the beach. My guess was that the climb up the side of the falls was the only way in or out of Mai Vallee.

There was still some light left, and the moon was already rising. It was going to be a full moon. I would have expected nothing less.

As I followed the stream back down the valley, I took more time to look around. The place was already fuckin' homesteaded! What did I expect? Of course, someone had to put the rope there in the first place. Who? How? When? Of course, there had been others who'd climbed the rope and discovered this hidden wonderland. But I figured the worse the rope got, the fewer would try it. Only the most reckless would get to know *this* valley. Only the craziest would want to leave it. So where were they?

One hillside was terraced. Banana trees, all bearing yellow bunches of fruit ready for the picking, grew close to the top of the hill where it was the sunniest. On the terrace below were tomatoes! Big and juicy and lots of them. Lettuce, bok choy, and spinach, took up the third and bottom row interspersed with some marijuana and tobacco! All of them looked more than ready to have a drink of water.

I grabbed a watering can lying on its side in the middle of the bottom terrace, filled it from the stream, and let all the plants drink generously. They seemed to come alive and vibrant before my very psilocybinized eyes. The leaves of the bananas drooped less, the tomatoes swelled with gratitude, the lettuce crisped up nicely. The limp marijuana stems straightened up. I guess I'd arrived just in the nick of time. I felt like Mighty Mouse. Whoever left this place so suddenly must have had faith another would show up. A changing of the guard, so to speak. Freakily cosmic I thought, but in a nice tropical don't-think-too-much kind of way. I felt quite proud that I had been chosen for guard duty.

The hillside on the other side of the stream was dominated by a huge but somewhat deformed koa tree, whose tall and thick trunk was actually rooted somewhere on the other side of the hill in the adjacent minivale, but whose canopy jogged over into Mai Vallee. Low slung and thick limbs just dipped into the notch and sprawled for easy access to anyone who cared to be embraced by this rare wood.

Obviously, someone had. Someone had built shelter here among these strong arms that might long ago have been chosen to be a canoe or a surfboard. Someone had created multi-level living areas defined by platforms made of bamboo and salvaged wood.

The level highest in the tree was the master bedroom. A large, thick piece of foam rubber, wrapped in plastic, lay in the middle of the platform. My mind suddenly reeled with images of the sexual gymnastics of reckless people that had undoubtedly taken place here.

I wondered if I could persuade some reckless, beautiful freak to climb 60 feet above a waterfall to share this lair with me for a while. If I could persuade someone to make the climb, I'd know that, one, they were probably in pretty good shape, and two, they really wanted to be with me to take such a risk. That's always a nice feeling. I was sure that once they were here, the magical setting would do the rest!

I gazed at the panorama of the beach and ocean, the Na Pali coastline, and the canopies of the forests of Kokee. I looked up and the moon was so bright it was bewildering. What a sexy bedroom! And just to make sure it stayed sexy, rain or shine, the room could quickly be covered with a clear plastic tent, not unlike the kind you might see at an outdoor wedding or street fair. They unfurled from the limbs above for those stormy tropical nights when you needed to be waterproof.

But tonight, it was clear. I could see the entire Kalalau valley from the heiau to the waterfall beneath me. I could see the waves crashing on the beach and the trail etched into the side of the cliff. I could see the silhouettes of hikers on the trail, the same trail I had hiked just a few days ago. Or was it more? I was losing track of time.

A bonfire is just starting at the heiau. Little flames peek through a pyramidal pile of wood. A few of the silhouettes take the fork in the trail that takes them directly to the heiau. The others, and there are many, continue on the path into the valley and the expansiveness of the beach. The moon gets higher and brighter and lights up the surf. The heiau on its promontory and I on mine, define the boundaries of the valley. And I can see everything in between.

Freaks ready to party, and the supplies that hopefully will last them a few days, are thrown off the skiffs that brought them here. They hang onto inner tubes and catch waves that throw them all roughly on the beach the first time around. That's unusual! Most times the undertow is so fierce and the surf so strong it takes two or three tries before everything and everyone is accounted for. But even the ocean is mellow this night. Shortly after the skiffs head back to Haena or Hanalei to pick up more passengers, I see a second bonfire starting on the beach, its flames quickly rage, and bodies cast long shadows that dance in between the flickering shards of light.

Then comes the drumming. First from the heiau. Then an answer from the beach. Another message from the heiau. Another reply from the beach. Eventually the entire valley is engaged in a lively conversation using all kinds of percussive instruments, including whatever inventive ways the human body can be used. A few guitars, some flutes, harmonicas, and ukuleles join the seductive beat. The music is intensely sensual. The ear is mesmerized.

A circle of beautiful naked hippie men juggle torches of fire in beat to the drums. They make hypnotic designs in the dark, similar to the designs kids make with sparklers on the Fourth of July, except these are more elaborate, the glow has more oomph and pizzazz, and the designs stay on your retina longer. They throw the torches to one another, and the designs become more complex. Occasionally, a torch is dropped and as the guy goes to pick it up, it highlights the muscles of his naked torso. This image stays on the retina as well.

Loose-hipped freaks dance to the music and its tribal rhythms, their bodies move as if possessed, or in love, or maybe that's the same thing.

The bonfires get hotter and higher. And the people chant and dance into the night, their moves getting wilder as the moon crosses the sky and the flames whip their shadows into frenzy. Sixty feet directly below me, heads are getting stoned. The air is so thick with the smoke of ganja, that even at this elevation I can inhale enough of its delicious fumes to recharge my mushroom high.

From my perch in Mai Vallee, high atop a tree atop a waterfall, I could see that the Full Moon Celebration had begun; the Hawaiian gods, kahunas, and ali'i were most pleased, as was I.

CHAPTER 88
March 1974

When I woke up the next morning I was disoriented. Was I an arboreal animal? And if so, which one? And what did I like to eat? Because I was famished! I also realized I had a blanket around me. That was odd.

As I checked the bananas and tomatoes, and other veggies for ripeness, I also looked for clues as to the history of Mai Vallee, and where the blanket had come from. Who was the most recent settler? Or settlers? Who had domesticated and cultivated this wild little tear in the cliff? Where were they? Who were they? And how soon were they coming back?

It was this last question that intrigued me the most. The place was in such nice condition, it seemed like I missed the last inhabitants by minutes. And if that were so, the changing of the guard could not have gone more smoothly.

I found a hillock of plastic containers in various sizes, from cookie jar to garbage can. They were all various shades of green and unobtrusive against the bushes. Each had its own lid that snapped tightly shut. In one of the larger ones were glass jars of seeds, nuts, rice, polenta, split peas, lentils, and seasonings. A larger container was already opened. In it were blankets, pajamas, and a couple of towels. I didn't recall opening any cans the night before, but it must've been me. I hoped it was me!

All in all, the place was as well stocked as a 1950s bomb shelter, as long as you didn't mind being above ground and totally exposed, and if you didn't expect to live much longer than a few days at most. Ah, but what a few days it would be! However, how they got all this neat stuff up here was a mystery to me, unless it was by chopper. If that were the case, they could be back at any moment.

Kalalau so easily facilitated the achievement of one's glide, I willingly assumed responsibility for Mai Vallee. For the time being, I would consider the entire property mine. If and when the next true owners appeared and laid claim to it, I would graciously give it up.

In the meantime, for that is all there is, I would keep the gardens watered and weeded, sweep clean all the inhabitable spaces of the tree with a broom I made of ragged hala leaves. And in the tradition of Hunga Dunga, try to leave the place in better condition than I found it.

I aired out the foam mattress and some of the linens. Though there was a nice fire pit and wood for burning, and pots and utensils for cooking, I decided not to use any of the food that had been stashed here by whomever. In fact, I decided to go on a fast. This decision was not based entirely on a need to purge toxins from my system, but also on a need to weigh as little as possible when I climbed down that frayed rope.

I eased myself into a water-fast by eating only a banana in the morning and a couple of tomatoes at night for the first couple of days. From then on, it was just water and mind over stomach. I knew the first three days would be the hardest. After that, I knew I'd feel so clean, alert, and energetic, I'd never want to eat food again.

Each morning shortly after waking, I'd drink as much water as I possibly could. I'd climb the limbs of the tree and jump to the top of the southern hill that formed Mai Vallee. I'd piss a beautiful stream, clearer each day, spraying it in wide arcs to minimize the damage my urine might do to the flora. Then I'd climb back onto the tree and make my way down its limbs to the sandy bank of the stream. Though I was about 20 feet from where it disappeared over the edge, I could imagine the wonderful naked bodies below, splashing in the shower of fresh water.

Next to *my* stream, I would do my sun exercises. Maybe some other asanas. Maybe try to make up some of my own. Always with my tongue curled back as far as it would go.

Then I'd stand, legs spread, arms raised to the sky, and let the Angel of Air and the Angel of Light have their way with me. Just like the Gospel of Peace tells you to do. And the Angel of Water would rush over my body as I slowly lay down in the rushing stream, slowly lay down until I could feel the force of the current hit the crown of my head, chill me from there to my toes and make my mind struggle for control over whether my body would shiver or not.

After that morning bath, I tended to the banana orchard and the rest of the garden. Everything was looking happy. I'd lean against a big rock at the edge of the cliff next to where the stream spilled over and spend hours looking at beautiful boys and girls frolicking in the sun and surf, tossing Frisbees naked, body surfing the smaller waves, running up the beach. The water drips from their bodies, the sun glints off their skin. My gaze follows them to where they stand directly below me playing in the water of the falls.

I admire their beauty. I wonder what do I call these incredible human beings? Hippies? Freaks? Flower Children? Heads? Space Angels? Gods? Why would anyone want to do them harm? Anywhere they might be, leave them be. They do the planet good. Encourage them.

And why was I playing the hermit? I was so close, yet so far, from the company of wondrous beings in a magical place. I was so close, yet so far, from weed, drugs, and many other tasty treats. I was so close, yet so far, from wonderful, playful sex. I'm sure of it. So why was I playing the recluse? I became very introspective.

I decided it was a knee-jerk, guilt-ridden response to finding myself surrounded by too much perfection. I could hardly believe I was still carrying around my Catholic baggage! Mea culpa, mea culpa! With everything I had experienced would I never win the war against guilt?

Everything in Kalalau was perfect. The nature and the people. Perfect. I was unworthy of it. So many times, I found myself in wonderful, exquisite places, among so many wonderful exotic people. So lucky, and now this. Too exquisite. Too perfect. Too self-indulgent. That was it! Indulgent! That was the operative word. Mea *maxima* culpa.

I would chastise myself by becoming a penitent. I would make all temptations so close, yet so far, it would be maddening. What better way to atone! I would merely observe from a distance. I would challenge myself to live in my higher chakras. Even if I were forced to do it by this most magical of magic valleys. On the other hand, maybe I was just a borderline masochist.

I sat on the edge of the cliff surveying my domain and noticed that people seldom looked up and when they did, they never noticed me. Maybe I was hidden by the mist that blew over my body with the onshore breeze. Of the many tempting bodies cavorting and pressing flesh to flesh in the falls below, only once did anyone look up and see me. He yelled and I yelled back, but it was impossible to hear complete sentences and he was someone I think I would have liked to have a conversation with.

He understood my invitation and he RSVP'd in the positive. He got his buddies to lift him up to the rope. But just as he grabbed it, I heard him yell something about "crazy" and "ready to snap!" I didn't know if he was referring to his mind or to the rope, but I figured it was the rope when I heard it snap about a quarter of the way from the top. Luckily, he hadn't gotten very far, and he fell back into the outstretched arms of his pals, who all fell into a big pile of tangled limbs. I yelled down, "Need new rope here! Only way down!" But they were already starting to grope each other. And as I yelled louder, they disappeared into the bushes without responding, and by then I was already a thing of the past.

I reflected upon The Four Noble Truths and the Eightfold Path. I wondered if I were a chess piece, where would the Buddha place me on my checkered path to moksha? I had certainly achieved a state of harmlessness. I harmed no one, not intentionally. Not to my knowledge. I had done much good to and for myself. I was never healthier. I was never more content. But had I done any good at all, to or for anyone besides myself? Where and when had I committed deeds of right action?

Was it the extra money I sent back home? The bananas and vegetables would have died without me here to water them. Maybe someone else would have climbed the rope in time, and it was simply my karma that it be me. It was my karma that I should have this monastic time to reevaluate my life, to take the next step.

I was content with my spiritual progress. I didn't have to continue my search for enlightenment. I was already enlightened, wasn't I? But if I were, wouldn't the bodhisattva say to give up my nirvana and go back to help all the others achieve oneness? Wasn't that the way it worked? And if I weren't enlightened? Then what? Oh, yeah! I remembered. I had the tools I needed if I really wanted it.

"If I really wanted it?" Giacco, you asshole. Listen to yourself. Isn't that all you ever wanted? Isn't that what you always told yourself? Your friends? Your folks? Nancy Stein and the Department of Social Services? The United States Government? Jon and Rose? A path to self-realization, god realization? It's all you ever wanted!

Now you have some tools to help you stay on that path. If you used them, you might not be atoning for anything! You would be over all that! You would be in the elusive here and now. Instead, you are talking to yourself like an asshole! You are talking about what you said before you started talking to yourself. Now do you understand?

I had it too good. That was the problem. I knew it. I knew it was payback time. Now was the time to do service. Real tasks. I should be watering our own little orchard up in

Twisp. And weeding a large garden in the buff, out on the bench in front of Zietar's Knoll. And working toward a better America. One that would learn by our example. I wanted to go home. All I had to do was find a way back.

I spent a somewhat restless night in the Koa tree. The bed was comfortable enough and the night air just right for a naked body under a light sheet. But when I awoke at the first light of day, I felt I hadn't slept at all. My mind had been working overtime trying to figure out a way down the falls back to the beach. My desire to be home was so intense, it was interfering with my ability to problem-solve. I was also into the seventh or eighth day of my fast and feeling a bit light-headed, which wasn't helping matters.

I could try to climb down, find an easier descent farther away from the falls, but just the thought of it made me want to jump and get it over with.

I could strike out into the interior and hope one of the paths would take me to a road where cars drove to towns, and not into the Waimean labyrinth of canyons so colorfully viewed from above, and in which, once below, it was all too easy to get lost.

I could try to find a writing implement and some paper and throw SOSs tied to small rocks down to brother and sister hippies playing below, so innocently oblivious to anything other than the beauty of their own bodies and those of others, and the beauty of this waterfall, this rock, this beach, this ocean, this sky, this air.

All I could manage as I considered this last option was to climb down the tree and lay in the stream. My head diverted the current. Water rushed over my naked body. I thrilled at the rapids around my cock, and the froth of white bubbles around my balls as the stream flowed onwards to its sudden plunge.

I stared into the sky, and I felt an ocean breeze blow up between my legs. I looked down the coast to amaze myself at the thousand-foot cliffs that thrust themselves out of the sea. I could definitely feel this place. It had its own vibration. It was sensuous to the body and the mind at the same time. I think that's rare. I'm not even sure it's possible. I just know all of my senses were easily seduced by this very special Hawaiian paradise.

All of me, that is, except for my ears.

I could hear a "whump, whump, whump" getting louder and louder with each "whump" coming up over the Kokee forest behind me. Within seconds, a huge dragonfly with a bubble for a head was hovering above me blocking the sun. On the side it said U.S. Navy. The "whumps" were deafening, and it made such a wind it was a good thing I was already lying down.

A guy with eyes so blue I thought I was looking through him at the sky, stared at me while he threw down some bags and boxes of varying sizes onto the sandy soil. He had a buzz cut and no shirt. But metal tags swung from his neck. "Here, try to catch these!" he said as if I was under his command and the dark side of me wished I were.

I did my best, but I really only managed to break their fall. I figured the bruises wouldn't be noticeable 'til the next day, so my vanity was intact if not my eye-hand coordination. He surveyed the place while he threw a harness over his head and under his arms.

"Hey, bro!" he said smiling big at me while a buddy fed the cable that lowered him down and the pilot expertly kept the dragonfly hovering in place. As he descended, I saw he was wearing camouflage shorts with pockets everywhere and uncomfortable looking boots, which touched the ground with the grace of a ballet dancer.

"Thanks for taking such good care of our place!" He said as he removed the harness and let it dangle there swaying in the breeze. "It's really hard to find a private place like this to get some R&R. Really hard." he said emphatically. "We wanna keep it that way!" He stuck out his hand and looked me hard and square in the eye. "Understand?"

He took my hand and shook it. The strong grip felt good. I stared back at the sexy cleft in his chin, but when he squeezed my hand harder, I met his gaze and let him know I understood completely. "No problem, man!" I said, and for some unknown reason I began jabbering about what a great place they had here and about the rope breaking and being stranded and all, and the fast I still hadn't broken and the wonders of Mai Vallee. But he really didn't pay much attention. He obviously couldn't care less.

He clambered through the tree like a man who knew his way around the place. The annoying "whump, whump, whumps" of the flying creature continued as it hovered incongruously overhead, whipping the water in the stream.

I looked him over carefully. He was definitely an interesting character and just happened to have an equally interesting body. An acrobat or gymnast or maybe even a Navy Seal. I decided if I had to, I would rise to the occasion and share a tree with this guy. But if it didn't work out, what then?

He must've guessed what I was thinking because he was still smiling broadly as he held out the straps of my pack like an aggressive salesman persuading me to try on a sports jacket. His eyes dared me to refuse, so I slipped my arms through the straps, adjusting them over my shoulders.

Then he grabbed the harness that was swinging from the cable. I just looked at him, not quite comprehending. He placed the harness over my head and pulled my arms through it until the harness was firmly under my armpits. Despite the weight of the harness, I felt surprisingly light on my feet. My whole body went slack. My mouth may have been hanging open since I seemed to be eating a lot of the dust the blades were kicking up.

"Need a ride home?" he asked, as his body came so close to mine, I could feel the hairs on his chest brush me. He adjusted the harness to make sure it was secure. Then he looked up at his buddy and gave a thumbs up sign, who gave a thumbs up to the pilot. What was he doing? Didn't he know about my fear of heights? As the copter slowly rose, he steadied my swinging, naked body. I could feel my cock dragging along his chest. Just the briefest of encounters, but enough to make my departure all the more memorable.

I heard the motor of the hoist start and felt the cable pulling me up. I just expected the guy in the open door would grab me under my arms and pull me inside. He didn't. He stopped the hoist, leaving me hanging there several feet below the skids of the copter. I held on tight, my hands glued to the harness, my legs dangling like a limp rag doll. I looked down. I know I shouldn't have, but the navy guy was already naked and waving at me, and well, I just couldn't resist. He was everything one needed to fulfill a particular fantasy. I feebly waved back.

Before I had time to indulge in imagining what might have transpired in the Koa tree, the chopper tilted forward about 20 degrees, and off we went. We were flying over the Pacific Ocean along the northern coast of Kauai. Or should I say *they* were flying! *I* was clinging desperately to the harness on the end of a 6-foot cable hanging out of a steel contraption that was wearing a pinwheel hat.

The "whumping" of the rotor blades was so loud it must have been my imagination when I thought I heard the pilot laughing. I had the last laugh though, because after the initial white-knuckle terror, I fell into that state of grace one experiences after the ego is killed. I flew confidently parallel to the Na Pali coast, enjoying the same view as that of the white-tailed tropicbird.

The vertical folds of the pali are covered in every imaginable shade of green all the way down to the crashing, foamy-white surf. They fall steeply, but some decide to stop their drop at no particular place and curve upwards again into pinnacles of green. Wild goats graze the impossible outcroppings. Sometimes they are so close I swear I can touch them. Maybe I should make the pilot aware of this minor fact. Maybe he is flying in and out and around these little peaks on purpose. Very funny. Ha ha. I trust he remembers the dangling naked guy below him and stays an extra 20 feet higher than usual! I shove my tongue further back down my throat.

There are little dents, tiny valleys like Mai Vallee with rushing streams and cascading waterfalls everywhere. It is a Japanese watercolor over and over again. One of the brush strokes is a small line of people walking smack-dab in the middle of the pali. They see me, the naked trapeze artist swinging oh-so-gracefully in the sky. They wave excitedly. Now, they can't wait to get into the valley. Everything they've heard about it must be true!

They're on the same trail I took in. I follow it with my eyes the best I can. It seems like such a precarious little etching in the cliff. Something scratched there by the fingernail of a god. When you see the big picture, you see how small you are.

I recognize the trailhead and then Haena. I know in a couple more minutes, I'll be passing by Hanalei. My armpits are getting sore, but I figure the pilot is heading toward Lihue and the airport. I could hang on a bit more for that convenience, but I couldn't wait to touch down.

I wanted to see what my pilot looked like. And his pal. If they looked anything like the guy who just evicted me from Paradise, I might have a sudden urge to join the Service! A couple years before, they probably had hair down to their waists and were getting high all the time. Now, after a stint or two in 'Nam, they're *truly* crazy motherfuckers! Certainly crazy enough to let me hitch a ride on this airborne, swinging cable. I may as well have been riding some kind of Acme product in a Roadrunner cartoon.

I imagined that the two guys, riding comfortably in the big bubble above me, were listening to Neil Young, volume cranked, through their headsets. Their buddy was already enjoying the wonders of Mai Vallee in my favorite clothing. Nothing. And who knows? Maybe later in the day these guys would airlift in a nice companion for him. They'd share the foam mattress in the master bedroom. I was jealous.

I decided these guys were buzz-cut airmen only on the outside, but longhaired hippies on the in. Maybe I was wrong. Maybe it was just the collusion of three wild men in the service of their country, but with their own secret getaway to Bali Hai. What a sweet deal. Well, sweet if you're not going to be sent back to 'Nam!

He descended gradually as we approached Hanalei. Or was this Honah Lee, the home of Puff the Magic Dragon? I looked for signs of him. But there were none of the familiar smells of people puffing or draggin' on the *pakalolo*.

We slowed to a crawl and then he gently hovered over the beach and lowered me down in front of the lanai of a popular resort where the guests were all drinking mai tais and acting very South Pacific.

The pilot, with great finesse, descended until all I had to do once my feet touched the sand was extricate myself from the harness. I guess he wanted to get rid of me as soon as possible. He didn't even give me a chance to thank him. All I could see as the rotors kicked up the sand and I backed up to get out of its range, was a friendly smile from the guy reeling in the harness, and the pilot giving me the thumbs up and what I think was another big smile under his big goggles, or maybe it was a smirk. Oh, and a reflection of myself in the bubble.

If the reflection were accurate, I had no clothes on. I had forgotten about *that* little detail. I had been naked for so long it seemed natural. When the bubble got very small and distant, I turned to the crowd on the veranda. Their judgmental eyes seconded my gut reaction that I was, indeed, stark naked. I was not sure what to do, so I took a big bow.

Two big Samoans, genetically predisposed to the occupation of security guards, began to approach me with ominous intent.

I started walking as fast as I could down the beach. Toe to heel, toe to heel. I lengthened my stride. The Samoans lengthened theirs.

I break into a canter, still toe to heel. I aim for that part of the beach where the sand is the most firm. Maybe there the toe will leave a lighter imprint than the heel does. There I can get some lift and push off. It's just a dozen yards away, but as in a nightmare, it never seems to get closer. I am still sluggish in the soft sand. I am as fast as a fucking tricycle. Look at me go! Whee!

I look back. The Samoans have shifted into a full run. So do I. Toe to heel quickly becomes toe to toe. I am as swift as the ocean breeze and thank gods for a tailwind and the fact that I am very afraid. Fear is a very good motivator to make one run fast.

Luckily, Samoans may be big, but they are also all slower than I am. All of them. Especially in sand. Nevertheless, I was relieved when I snuck a look and saw they had given up and turned back. I slowed to a toe-to-heel gambol and finally stopped long enough to rummage through my pack for a pair of pajama pants and a T-shirt.

Then I walked toe to heel up to the road and stuck my thumb out. The very first car that stopped was going my way. To the airport. I was in my glide.

It came as a crushing blow when I told Skip, Mariko, and Junior that I was leaving.

"How can you leave us?" Skip asked in disbelief. "We are family! We love you! Don't you love us?"

I could hardly look into his saddened eyes. "Of course, I love you! I love all of you! You *are* family! You always will be! But I have to do this. I have another family that needs me right now."

Mariko just kneeled in a corner of the room, quiet, her head bowed. She lifted her head and said softly, "What about Junior? He loves you. He's attached to you. He needs you."

I walked over to where Junior was exploring the designs in the linoleum floor and picked him up. I cradled his butt, and he swung his arms around my neck. We looked each other in the eye. "I'll be back, Junior. Sooner than you think. I want to be around when it's time to teach you how to ride a bike," I said excitedly. He squealed happily as if he understood me, and I gently put him down to continue his crawl. I looked up to see Skip looking at me, tears starting to well.

"This is a big blow for us," Skip said, his voice wavering. "As long as you promise to stay in touch and to come back soon."

"How could I not want to come back to you?"

"Promise, Giacco! Say it! Say, 'I promise I'll come back!'"

"I promise, Skip!"

It took over a week to get things in order. Those days weren't the happiest, though we did pretty well putting on a happy face. I played with Junior as if nothing extraordinary were happening, though Junior was so extraordinary, he knew something was in the works.

Kind, gentle Mariko treated me with the grace and humor she always had and surprised me daily with some exotic treat or another like scooped out papayas stuffed with homemade banana yoghurt or mangoes with macadamia nut cookies on the side.

Skip, most times, sat quietly, meditating. When he wasn't doing that, he was funnier and crazier than ever with his stupid jokes and two-year-old antics. He was almost too funny, too crazy. I knew he was over-compensating and both he and I knew he had to. It was the only way he could deal with it.

When they took me to the airport, Skip and Mariko each put a lei over my head. Then Mariko lifted little Junior up so he could put one on me as well. All three of the leis had been hand-made by Mariko.

Skip tried to be light-hearted and said, "Parking cars will never be the same without you, brother."

I laughed and we shared some of our most celebrated parking stories and high-jinks that only a stoned valet could appreciate. Then I got serious.

"Skip, my surfer-guru, thanks for putting it all in perspective for me." He knew what I meant. "You and Mariko and Junior came along at just the right time."

"So did you, Giacco. It was meant to be," Skip said solemnly.

It was one of the most difficult departures of my life. We started crying at the very end, and the hugs were hard and precious. The plane was boarding. I turned around to leave, but Skip grabbed my shoulder and spun me around to give me one last hug. He whispered in my ear, "Jai Satchitanand, Giacco!"

"Jai Satchitanand, brother Skip," I whispered back. And within a few minutes I was boarding the plane. I never heard from nor saw Skip, Mariko, or Junior ever again.

CHAPTER 89
April 1974

I was walking gingerly up Church to 18th Street, my heart beating faster than usual, as usual, every time I found myself returning to Hunga Dunga. I couldn't wait to lay my eyes on the gang and conjured them up in my mind while I walked. Yet images of Skip, Mariko, and Junior kept intruding. It made me reflect for the umpteenth time how everyone is everything.

I turned onto 18th Street and saw Big Blue up the hill. I walked faster and was almost out of breath when I stopped at the bottom of the stairs. I noticed a very big, nice, brand-new truck parked out front. On its side were the words "Greenleaf Produce."

I began my climb, taking the stairs two at a time. I opened the screen door and stood in front of the large, partially opaque oval window that dominated the front door. Normally, I would have just walked in. But for the element of surprise, I rang the bell.

Baird opened the door and when he saw who it was, he stood in the doorway, his big-boned body filling in the space quite completely.

"Oh, it's you," he said disdainfully. He folded his arms and spread his elbows until they were almost touching the frame. "What do you want?"

"Well, 'hi and welcome home' to you too, Baird!" I said, more hurt than sarcastic.

"You are not welcome, and this is not your home," he told me matter-of-factly.

By this time, familiar bodies emerged one by one to find out what was going on. Their faces filled in the few gaps left by Baird's body, and it made for a very wonderful photo. I wished I'd had a camera.

As the faces saw who it was, the screams, hoots, and hollers sprang forth. This was more like what I'd expected. But I did notice the levels of enthusiasm varied. Not that they weren't happy to see me. They were just pondering the storm about to be unleashed.

Psylvia sprang forth and tried to pry Baird away from the door. Baird resisted. Psylvia scurried under his legs, turned around, and rammed her head into his stomach. She scrimmaged with him like a college fullback. "Baird! This is ridiculous. Get out of the way! Let Giacco in!"

Psylvia, with all her might, couldn't budge him, but Baird was not one to stoop down to Psylvia's Three Stooges school of arguing. He knew that through her zaniness, he would end up looking the fool. So, he relented. He stepped back and Psylvia filled in the void. She turned to me, fixing up her hair or so she thought, and yelled, "Giacco, oh Giacco! Welcome home!" Followed by a big hug. "I missed you! Hungry? Come! You look so dark! You look good, Chazan!" And she blazed a path toward the kitchen, managing to bump most everyone along the way with her hips. Questions flew at me from all directions and collided, making it impossible for me to answer any of them.

Even Lily interrogated me, in her own way, with one Lily-question running into the next. She'd become a real chatterbox, two-stepping her way through legs and bodies. When she lifted her arms in front of Nick, he picked her up so she could see what all the fuss was about. I pecked her on the cheek and Nick patted me on the shoulder as I walked by. I followed Psylvia and was gang-humped and hugged by Larry, Ellen, Richard, Lana, Luc, and most everyone else. But not all. Jeff and Trudy gave me a blissful look and mouthed something Goomer-ish that made me feel uncomfortable.

Lana said she was disappointed because she was planning to go to Hawaii in a couple of weeks and was hoping she could hang out with me. I told her I'd go with her anytime. That I'd love to turn her on to my favorite spots, especially Kalalau Valley, which of course I would have never known about had it not been for Skip, but I decided it wasn't the right time to mention him, Mariko, and Junior.

Lizzie just followed me with his signature goofy grin. His eyes seemed brighter than usual. The rest were politely eager to hear about Hawaii. But Baird would only glare and growl.

Duck whispered in my ear, "All is not well in the land of Oz." I shot him a *no comprende* look. Richard tiptoed up to my other ear and sang, "*We got trouble. Right here in River City. We got trouble and that starts with T and that rhymes with P and that stands for trouble, trouble, trouble, trouble,*" his voice faded out dramatically. I looked down at his beaming, angelic face. He had a glint in his eye and a wide mischievous smile. Maybe he had just delivered the punch line to a joke, but I didn't get it.

CHAPTER 90
April 1974

As I sat at the kitchen table savoring a late dinner of lentil soup and home-baked bread, everyone that wasn't out partying or already in bed gathered around and quizzed me about my adventures in the ashram and Hawaii. Why hadn't I stayed in touch more? How could I not fill them in on everything? What a surprise it was to learn only *yesterday* that I was coming home!

I dropped my spoon in the soup. "What do you mean?" I asked. "I stayed in regular contact with you through Richard! I just assumed he passed along all my letters to the rest of you!"

Those gathered around almost simultaneously folded their arms and turned their heads trying to spot Little Richard.

"He knew a week ago I was coming home!" My eyes joined the reconnaissance team. Richard was barely hiding behind the open door under the kitchen sink.

"Richard, we see you!" almost everyone said at the same time.

Richard jumped up from behind the door. His cheeks were so flushed, he looked like the jack out of the box. "I confess! I confess, already! It was me! I just never thought about it! Everything's needless to say and all that!"

"And you only told them *yesterday* that I was coming home?"

"So, it took me a few days. That's better than if I'd just told them this morning. What a ruckus *that* would have caused!"

"And you don't call this a ruckus?" I asked him.

He sheepishly replied, "I've been very busy. I love you. I didn't mean to hurt you."

"Richard, how could you?" Duck chastened, followed by a lot of *tsk, tsk*-ing from the others. "Baird's been on the rampage ever since he found out. We've had nothing but non-stop family meetings!"

"About what?" I asked.

"About you!"

Just then Baird opened the kitchen door and announced, "Remember, as we agreed, he gets to stay here one night and that's it! If he's not gone by tomorrow night, then I am!" He slammed the door behind him.

A long pause. Faces scanned each other's. Mine scanned each of theirs in turn, lingering on them more than they would have liked. "As we agreed?" The words stuck in my throat but came out stronger the second time. "As we agreed?"

Jeff and Trudy had usurped my little attic loft, but Larry invited me to sleep with him. We cuddled and pulled each other's beards. "What else did you all agree to?"

"Oh, Giacco! It's not what you think. Baird is still sore about the Goomer thing and blames you and you alone. You drive him crazy. At one of the meetings he said, 'It's either Giacco or me. Giacco or me! He stays, I go. He goes, I stay. Simple as that!'"

"This is totally ridiculous, Duck. How can this be? Just the money I sent from Hawaii should've been a sign of my intentions! Namely, staying a part of Hunga Dunga."

"Money? What money?"

"I sent Richard hundreds of dollars every month. I had a killer job going on."

"Damn that Richard!" Duck said. "That's what happens when you make one person in charge of all the money! No one ever knows what's really going on!"

"So doesn't that count for something?" I asked.

"Baird would just say no one asked you to contribute money. You did it because you wanted to. And when Trudy came back with Jeff, well, there went your space. We don't rent rooms here, Giacco! You can't reserve one either!"

"Fuck the room, Duck!" I yelled in a volume relative to our whispers and my eyes afire. "I wasn't 'reserving my space.' I am Hunga Dunga! You all know that! I always will be! Once a Hunga Dunga, always a Hunga Dunga!"

"Giacco. You have to consider Baird's ability to confuse people by sounding brilliant, and he only had to confuse a couple of people to get his way."

I didn't doubt Baird's abilities as an orator.

"At a family meeting within days after Chuck and Trudy got back from Hawaii, Baird said that there had been too much disruption to the spirit of Hunga Dunga. The fact that you didn't return with them and chose to stay in Hawaii instead, was a clear message you had better things to do. So was the fact that we never heard from you about what your intentions were. And with the apparent replacement of you with Jeff, it was time we got back on the same wavelength as a family."

"That's bullshit and you know it, Larry! Anarchy's always been our thing. To have so many fucking different wavelengths going on at the same time and somehow managing never to cancel another's out! Until now, or so it seems!"

Larry's explanation was a weak one as far as I was concerned. "Baird reminded us of our tradition that if consensus can't be reached, the status quo prevails. The status quo right then and there didn't include *you* living in the house! He made a point of telling us that a number of times during the meeting."

"Well, thank you all so very much, loving brothers and sisters! None of you protested? None of you supported me? Psylvia? My Zietar? Et tu, Duck?"

"He wore us out, Giacco. We couldn't take it anymore. I'm so ashamed." And Duck did look ashamed in the dark of the room.

"Psylvia put up a fuss for days. But the longer you stayed away, the more she began to believe you really didn't want to be here. And Ziets? He's just been so weird and spaced out lately. Totally useless. Damn that Richard!"

"Damn that Richard!" I agreed heartedly, though I would never love him any less for it. "And you, Duck?"

"Oh Giacco! You know Baird! Blah, blah, blah! None of us took him seriously. We were just humoring him. He never brought it up again and so we thought everything was fine. Until he went ballistic yesterday when he found out you were coming home!"

"This isn't right Duck, and you know it!" I said sharply. "This is not in the spirit of Hunga Dunga!"

"Spirit, shmirit!" was Larry's reply. "Hunga Dunga is not a house. It's an idea. The good news is that you get to stay in Twisp! After all, you're one of the trustees. Baird can't do anything about that!" And he turned around and fell fast asleep, unlike myself. I lay awake half the night. I was home at Hunga Dunga for less than a day when I realized I was being deported to the hinterland. I guess I should use the word "home" loosely, because it seems I no longer had one.

The next morning as I was taking a shower, Psylvia stuck her head in the bathroom and asked me to meet her in the cabin before going anywhere.

I finished up, dressed, and walked out into the backyard. It was small but steep, and that gave ample opportunities for terraces. There were many. Now they were almost ready to burst forth with their spring offerings of flowers, herbs, and vegetables. The backyard always looked and smelled beautiful. I would miss seeing it in full bloom.

I climbed the brick steps to the little front door of the cabin. Chinking was falling out from between some of the logs, but that only added to its charm. I knocked and then opened the door and saw Psylvia sitting in the rattan chair wearing black lace panties and bra. Something was missing besides clothes. It was the hair on her legs. I said nothing.

She stood up and gave me a hug. "You know, Giacco, there's a lot more going on in this house than you know. You just happen to have the honor of being the first."

"The first what?" I asked.

"I have a strong feeling that others will be leaving soon as well. Who knows? I might be next." As she said this, she placed two black silk stockings across the arm of the chair. Then she reached into a big, black patent-leather purse and pulled out a make-up case. In it was a rainbow of colors coming from all kinds of mascara and powders and whatever else women paint themselves with. It looked more like some of Baird's artist supplies.

"You and I go back farther than any two other people in this house, you know," she said, reaching behind the rattan chair for two black stiletto heels that she placed on the table beside the chair. "As far back as you and JonPon."

"What are you talking about Psylvia? I met you the morning after the Cockettes show!"

She was getting frustrated. She glowered at me, a loving glower, but a glower, nonetheless. Without saying anything, she went to the bed and picked up a slinky black cocktail dress hanging from a wooden coat hanger. She held the hanger up to her neck and let the dress fall against her body. She assumed a runway pose. "Now?" is all she said.

"Now what?" I answered, though I felt somewhere in my brain, neurons trying to connect vague memories.

Psylvia was getting upset with me. She reached into her black bag, pulled out a photograph, and shoved it in my face. It was a picture of a tropical isle with coconut palms heavy with fruit. The sky was bright blue with a wisp of cloud, and a seagull flew by. As she pulled the photo away from me, she gave me a long wink.

"Now?" she said.

My mind was in disarray. Too many thoughts about too many things. Psylvia was the last person I would ever want to disappoint but that's just what I was doing. I was scrambling like crazy to put two and two together, but I couldn't for the life of me add it up. I just looked at her with what I'm sure was a pained expression.

"Damn you, Giacco! You are so fucking dense!" she snapped, as she threw everything hastily into the big, black bag, stepped into her bib overalls, and pulled the straps over her shoulders. "Well," she said in resignation, "I've waited this long, I can wait longer. After all, we have forever!"

The fact that she used the word "we" made everything all right. That was all I needed. To be included. As to what she was talking about, I still couldn't say.

"All I can say, Giacco, is consider yourself lucky. You might just be the first to get out with most of your innocence intact!" With that, she walked past me, out of the cabin and back into the house, but not before giving me a peck on the cheek.

As I walked into his room, Lizzie was hunched over his desk. Hovering around him were Little Richard, Luc, Bobby, and Nick. When they noticed me, they abruptly straightened up. Lizzie was the last to notice. When he straightened up, I saw a mirror on his desk with lines of a white powder on it. A few bills of various denominations were curled up scattered around the desk.

"Chazan!" Lizzie cried out. "Oh, my sweet Chazan!" He grabbed me by my hips and pulled me to him. He looked up at me with puppy dog eyes. A smudge of white coated his mustache and one nostril. "This is just temporary. Just to keep the peace. He'll get over it." I hoped he was referring to the cocaine and not my imminent ostracism.

While Lizzie schmoozed me, Zietar bent over the desk tightening a C-note and consuming a long line off the mirror in one powerful snort.

"Giacco," Nick said, "Ziets, Chuck, and me will be up in Twisp by the end of the month. It's no big deal. We'll be together again soon, and it'll be like nothing's changed."

Richard lifted his head. "Jeff and Trudy, too." The *oy veh* roll of his eyes told me everything I needed to know. "Nothing's changed, Giacco. Trust me."

I was fuming inside. It was the illogic of it all. It was unjust. Whenever I don't see logic and justice at work, I get very annoyed and usually speak out. But in this case, the lack of logic and justice was so great, and coming at me from so many people I loved, I was too stupefied to defend myself. I even began to believe I had done something very wrong, and this was my karma, and though I could not see the logic, maybe it *was* just after all.

When Richard backed away from the desk, Nick took his place. I watched this early morning snort-fest and hoped it wasn't a ritual. Lizzie carefully razored a bit of the white stuff into a hefty line on the mirror.

"For you, Giacco," he said as he handed me a rolled-up bill. I leaned over looking at myself in the mirror. I snorted half of it up one nostril and finished it off with the other. It stung, but I soon felt the back of my throat go numb and a nice buzz take over my head. I liked the feel. It was a good thing I had no ready access to it. That's how much I liked it. Heroin and speed were completely *verboten* by Hunga Dungan tradition, but cocaine was considered caviar, having a partially romantic quality to it left over from our love of Cole Porter, and seldom refused when the rare line was placed under our noses. Besides, who could afford it?

"So, how's business, Liz?" I asked in the upbeat mood Lizzie was hoping he'd provided me, more as a way of not having to deal with anything uncomfortable, rather than concern over my well-being. "I see the Free Food Conspiracy has a new truck!"

"It's Greenleaf Produce, Giacco! Legally, it always has been! And we're just getting up a bit of a boost before we begin our deliveries for today."

"No need to get defensive, Liz! Just curious. A refrigerator truck? Pretty snazzy. Hunga Dunga still taking good care of the communes?"

"Of course, we take care of all our clients, Chazan! Including the communes! It's just that we have more paying clients now than ever before!"

"The communes are paying clients, Lizzie," I reminded him. "They pay with their food stamps!"

"Oh, Giacco. You are so silly!" Whenever Lizzie found he had taken an indefensible stand, he dismissed it all by calling you "silly." We had all learned that once Lizzie called you "silly" you might as well be talking to a blank wall.

"Just the other day, I signed up the San Francisco Tennis Club!" He should have stopped while he was barely ahead.

"See you in Twisp, boys!" I said suddenly, as I wheeled around and walked into the hall. Richard followed me.

"Giacco. All is well. Believe me! Just that this thing is taking off!" I didn't know if he was referring to Greenleaf or to his head.

I gave him a big hug. "I love you Zietar! Everything in moderation, OK?" He gave me a strange look.

There was nothing to pack. I had never gotten a chance to unpack. Most of my favorite books and trinkets were already in Twisp, and Nick said he'd bring my guitar when they drove up at the end of the month.

There was little more to say. I had made a point of spending at least a few minutes with everyone, all of whom felt they had betrayed me in one way or another, and yet would do nothing to make it right. At the same time, they felt swindled and blackmailed by Baird's manipulation of our non-rules.

In a last-minute effort to redeem themselves, Psylvia, Richard, Chuck, and a couple of others, offered to call an emergency family meeting. A Hunga Dungan might say at a family meeting that they did not enjoy living with so and so, but they would never feel they had the right to ask that person to leave. The hope was that the person would leave of his or her own accord. If not, we learned to live with it.

But no one was ever pitted against another. There had never been a time when someone said, "Either he leaves, or I will!" No one knew how to handle this one. Everyone withdrew from the possibility of having to choose. In the vacuum of their non-action, Baird would win. And that's what this was all about, antithetical to Hunga Dunga as it sounds. Winning.

"Yeah, let's call another family meeting," cheered Chuck. Everyone else tried not to groan as they said they were for it.

I said, "Thanks, guys, but you know what?"

They just stared at me. Psylvia said, "What?"

"I want to leave of my own accord. This was of my own making. This is my fault."

A hush. Followed by one mea culpa after another.

"No! It was my fault!" screamed Psylvia.

"Your fault? What are you talking about?" I asked.

"Because I became a lesbian while you were gone and shaved my legs, and nobody likes my girlfriend Roxy!"

"We love your butch, Harley-riding girlfriend, Psylvia," ribbed Larry. "It's just that she scares us half to death! And we don't like being around…"

"Psylvia! When did… how did…?"

"Oh, not now, Giacco. I'll explain later… and besides…"

"Besides… it's really Lizzie's fault," insisted Larry. "For getting all capitalistic on us and making us deliver food to those chichi restaurants."

"It was your fault Duck," Richard pointed his finger into Duck's chest. "You never nipped this in the bud and stood up to Baird!"

"Me, why you little… and you call yourself Chazan's best friend?"

I slipped away while they were trying to unravel the mystery of who was most to blame for the discontent in the house. My disappearance lasted but a moment. They caught up to me just as I walked into Baird's room. He was painting. I managed to close the double doors before the gang rushed in.

"Can I speak to you alone Baird?"

"Only if it's to say you're leaving."

"It is. But a few thoughts. OK?"

"Speak," he said, stifling his annoyance.

"You were right," I said. "I was wrong."

He turned from his canvas and looked at me. "About what?"

"The Goomer and stuff. The lingo. The rituals. It must've driven you nuts. For that I am truly sorry and embarrassed." His face softened just enough to look interested. "And you were right about me being the ringleader, even if I wasn't the first to do it, even if I didn't know it myself."

"Go on," Baird said, painting a few strokes in the air with his brush.

"And my actions have caused disruption. Krishnamurti was right as usual. Have no beliefs. And if you do have any, keep them to yourself. I learned my lesson."

"A lesson learned is one that is not repeated," he replied. "And I'm glad you've learned yours, but that's not going to make *us* (he yelled, knowing everyone else had their ears to the door) change *our* minds about your imminent departure!"

"Seems like only yesterday," I reminisced. "You, we, were pronouncing that whoever was in the house at any given moment was a Hunga Dungan. That no one was any more important than another. That everything was everyone's and the only rule was to have no rules."

"Oh, but how you wax poetic my soon-to-be-traveling bard!" Baird said sarcastically.

"I just wonder what really happened. And exactly when? The precise moment."

"You wonder… and wander… too much little Grasshopper."

I tried to smile but it was forced. I began to leave. Baird stopped me and whispered to keep the others from hearing.

"I don't want to live with you in this house, Giacco. But I never said you weren't part of Hunga Dunga."

He opened the doors to a standing-room only crowd. I walked calmly out of the room and down the stairs. I carried my pack in front of me with both hands until I was on the sidewalk. I looked up to see everyone had gathered on the front porch. I could see Baird peeking out his window above us. I studied them as they wished me luck, cried, and told me how much they'd miss me. Nick yelled out some instructions about our gravity-fed water from the spring, the irrigation system, and stuff.

This was the third time they'd stood on the front porch looking down at me, about to go off somewhere. Each leave-taking less lighthearted. What was happening? Why was it happening? Was it a pattern?

I started to walk down the block toward Dolores Park, waving my hand without looking back. I almost got to the corner when I heard Richard yelling.

"Wait! Chazan! I have mail for you!" His little legs made surprisingly good time. He nearly fell into my arms.

"Mail? You have mail for me? And you're just telling me now, you little twerp?" I was practically bending Richard backwards with my anger, though it was always hard to maintain that level of energy with him. He was always so damned disarming. Even now as I was being sent to the outback.

Ziets pushed some letters into my hands. "Oh, I wouldn't be able to live with myself if I did this to you twice in a row!"

"I can tell you right now there'd never be a third time! That's for sure."

I thumbed through them. Some went back almost three months. Damn that Richard! There were two that startled me. In a good way. In a way that made my heart go thump. And my hips go whump. And my thumb stick out far into the air.

CHAPTER 91

May 1974

I opened Jon's letter first. It was postmarked March 7th.

My dear, dear Chazan!

Ayubowan! So long, too long it's been! I hope you still love me. I am lorfing you like mad right now and missing you insanely! I am so sorry I haven't written sooner. I stand on my head buried in the sand in shame and contrition! OK, honey?

I followed Rosie to Jaffna. As I suspected, she beckoned the call of not only Swami Guaribala, but her Australian John as well. Yes! She dumped me! A prize like me! Can you believe it! Florence was right!

I have been a mess. But I made the annual pilgrimage to Kataragama. I trekked all the way from Jaffna. Such a trip! You have to do it to believe it. I am wallowing in madness. Only Muruga keeps me sane.

I am now in Hambantota on the southern coast, on the edge of the Yala Sanctuary. I would tell you all that has happened, but you know Sri Lanka and understand how one day would take a book!

Please, please write me as soon as you can as the mail takes its sweet time getting here as you might guess! I need to know what you are up to!

Write me! C/O General Delivery, Hambantota, Sri Lanka. So much love I have for you!

Jonny!

"Great!" I said out loud from my barstool to the shelves of liquor in front of me. "Another 'General Delivery' return address. Just what I need."

Bob looked at me but continued washing glasses. The Broken Spoke was empty except for us. Unusual, even for this early in the morning.

The second letter was from Michael.

Hi Giacco!

Look brother. I have so much to tell you, but I feel like it's a waste of time. You never write back. I don't know why, and I am at my wit's end. If you get this, I hope you are OK and happy and your life is good. I miss you and think of you all the time.

If you've gotten any of my letters, you know I have been through some drastic changes, bad and good. Right now, things are pretty good for me and the kid. We are both looking forward to heading north. Way north!

Please, Giacco. Write me. Just so I know you are alive! Then I won't bother you anymore.

Love, Michael

Bother me anymore? Yikes! That hurt! How could he think that?

Bob came over and refilled my coffee cup. "Everything alright, Giacco?"

I turned over the envelope. By god, there was a real return address. 922 13th St., Apt. 11B, Lincoln, NE. But the postmark was almost three months ago.

"Yeah, Bob. Things just got a lot better." I said hopefully. "See ya later, pal. Gotta get things done."

"Later," he said as I walked out and went two doors down to the post office.

—mm—

"I need a post office box, Bev," I said.

"Gee, Giacco! This town is so small, all anyone has to do is put General Delivery on it!"

I thought I would have a conniption, but I maintained. "No, Bev, I really think we should have our own box. A big one."

"How about 110?"

"Do you have a 111?" I asked considering the numerological ramifications of our new address for Hunga Dunga North.

"Sure," answered Bev. She wrote on a form, "Church of Manna, P. O. Box 111, Twisp, WA, 98856." I paid for a year, and she handed me a receipt with our new address and a key to the box. I bought a postcard and mailed our Church of Manna address to Hunga Dunga.

I was about to leave when Ben Myers walked in.

"Hey, Giacco! How are you? All settled in?"

"Hi Ben! Hey, thanks for the ride up Poorman Creek last week. Seems like my whole trip up from The City was a breeze. Got rides almost all the way to my front door."

"The Lord must be watching over you!" Ben said.

I hated that he reminded me we lived next door to a Christian enclave. But so far, he seemed pretty cool. Not judgmental in the least… so far. I hadn't met the other Second Milers.

"You heading up to The Dome?"

"Yes," I answered.

"If ya wait a minute, I'll give you a ride."

"Man, that'd be great Ben."

When he had picked up the mail for Second Mile Ranch, and there was a box full of it, we jumped in his beast of a truck and headed up Twisp River Road.

"Thought the rest of the crew would be here by now. You doin' OK up there by yourself?"

"Yeah," I answered. "Chuck, Richard, and Nick were supposed to be here end of April, but it looks like it won't be 'til June now."

"That's too bad. Hard to get anything done by yourself."

"Well, Nick's instructions were great. Got the water system goin' smooth. Dome is pretty tight. Really keeps in the heat from the double-barrel wood stove that your neighbor Ernie made for us last fall. And I stay pretty busy. Getting to know the land and all. Hiking up to the Saddle Pass to spy on you!"

Ben laughed. "If you catch any of us doing anything interesting, let me know!"

"I will. If only I had some listening device."

He laughed again as he took the turnoff for Poorman Creek. "What's so funny is that Wesley, Matt, and I have hiked up to the Saddle Pass to spy on you!"

It was my turn to laugh. "Oh, well you're wasting your time, Ben. You have to wait until the rest of the loony tunes arrive. Then you'll have something worth spying on."

He chuckled and pulled off to the side of the road where our dirt road met the paved. Ben pointed to the cute little house on the other side of the road.

"Have you met Joel and Hallie yet?" he inquired.

"Nope. Haven't seen anyone around."

"Oh! They're in Missouri. Visiting Hallie's folks. They'll be back next week. You'll like Joel."

"Can't wait to meet him," I said as I got out of the truck.

"When the rest of the gang gets here, we'll have you all up for a barbecue or something, OK?"

"Sounds great!" And I slammed the door shut.

"You like parlor games?" Ben asked out the window.

"Sure, what kind?"

"The Porters play Dictionary every Thursday night. You want to go sometime?"

"Sure, anytime," I said. "But I don't know the game. You'll have to teach me."

"It's easy. I'll let you know. Most of the socializin' goes on in the winter around here. Now's the time when everyone has to make hay while the sun shines, if ya know what I mean. But we still make time for fun. See ya later, Giacco. Have a swell day!"

I waved as he drove up the road to the next valley, which is where Poorman Creek Road ended, and the Second Mile Ranch began. I started my climb up the two miles of switchbacks to The Dome. The hike was becoming easier and easier each day. Becoming routine. How easily we adapt.

I opened the door to The Dome. From inside it was all struts, hubs, and triangles. The pentagonal windows were a trip and the starburst window at the top was the best. I could easily imagine The Dome finished. It was going to be even more magical than it already was. And it would be more fun when there were more people, although I was getting used to being alone. In fact, I was enjoying it.

I rediscovered the joys of masturbation. And before answering the letters I got, I took Michael's and held it close to me as I thought of him and stroked.

After a very satisfying release, I meditated for a bit about what I wanted to say, then gathered up some writing materials and began my letters.

I wrote Jon about Twisp. And about the Goomer. I went into some detail about the first, extolling the wonders of our valley. I said very little about the second.

I wrote Michael. I told him I had a shitload of returned mail and someday I would pour into his lap all the postcards and letters I had been sending him since he left Kyle's little garage apartment. I said I was sorry about his wife and all he had been through. I told him how impressed I was that he'd gotten his teaching degree. I asked about his little boy. I wanted details. About his kid and everything that was going on in his life.

I reminded him that the ball had always been in his court since we parted on the interstate after the Celebration of Life fiasco, but I didn't realize how heavy a ball it was. Lots of suffering. Lots of responsibility. I wished I could have helped carry the burden, go through it with him, be there for him. I was always waiting for him to give me the go-ahead.

Then I gently chided him for consistently giving me addresses that didn't work, but I felt good we had re-established contact and that maybe after all this time, we might come full circle after all. I included my new address in Twisp both inside the letter and as the return address on the envelope, just as I had with Jon's.

The next day, I hitched to town, got some coffee at the Spoke and then on to the post office. Bev sold me a roll of 10-cent stamps while she figured out how much it would be to Sri Lanka. That took her a while. She stamped Jon's letter with the proper amount and threw it in a pile behind her. I licked a 10-center and pressed it hard and lovingly on Michael's. I handed it to Bev and crossed my fingers.

CHAPTER 92
May 1974

I surprised myself at how well I handled being alone. I enjoyed the solitude and quiet of the land. It was a pleasant relief from the frenetic energy of Hunga Dunga. I knew it wouldn't last long, so I made the most of it.

Making believe I was an archeologist, botanist, biologist, and geologist, I explored our 120 acres in detail.

First, I walked the boundaries. That was the most difficult because except for the 40-acre bench, everything was steep and dense with old-growth forest. That took a full day, but the views of the Sawtooth Range and their peaks were outstanding!

Then each morning, I'd stand on the deck of The Dome, and scan the slopes for interesting rock outcroppings. There were the rare flatter areas where aspens stood out from the dark green of the firs. I'd choose one of these places as a destination for the day, pack some grub and water, and start hiking.

By the time the gang arrived I knew every flat slab of rock perfect for a nude picnic and every little oasis of soft grasses perfect for making love, and every misshapen tree trunk perfect to lounge in and read a book while the wind blew, and the aspens quaked.

During my wanderings, I couldn't help keeping an eye out for a building site for myself on the off chance we'd ever agree to such a thing someday. I found the original homestead at the bottom of our land. It was near the basin of meadows where the road was flat. It was hidden from view just on the far side of a little hill. The fact that the homesteaders chose this spot led me to believe they had good reasons to build here. Easy access. Greater potential for water. A witcher with his forked stick was unnecessary. You could feel the water not too deep beneath the surface. There was only a territorial view, but I'd take that in exchange for a *casita incognita*.

I have to admit, the perfect building site on the land was the one Little Richard had called dibs on. The little twerp! Zietar's Knoll was cone-shaped, flat at the top, and had a breath-taking view all the way across the border into "The Land Foreign Yet Near."

I imagined that the garden we were going to put in this season would be somewhere between The Dome and Zietar's Knoll. Each day when I walked there, I would clear out as many big rocks and small boulders as I could, knowing we were getting a late start as it was. I carried or rolled them to the base of the knoll.

Eventually they encircled it completely and the piles around the base got higher and higher. The big boulders would have to wait for heavy equipment or oxen or a company of ancient Egyptian slaves. But eventually, we'd have a rock-free couple of acres ready for tilling. We'd also have a nice stockpile of rocks, big and small, to use in making fences, borders, and a big fire pit. Almost as big as the one in Ein Gedi.

Routinely, I'd take a walk to the Saddle Pass and on the way, check the flow of the spring. Whenever I reached the pass, I felt like Julie Andrews in the opening scenes of "The

Sound of Music." From here, I could gaze down at twinkling Poorman Creek and follow it up into the snow-capped peaks of the Cascades. Sometimes, on a moonlit night, I could swear I was in the Alps. I would shiver the moment the peaks came into view. I don't know if it was because they were so majestic or because they made me feel so inconsequential.

I'd hike back to The Dome. I knew anything I could build would never be as incredible as The Dome. I was continually amazed by its geometry, especially from inside where you could see the impressive skeleton of struts. It was hard to believe we'd built this thing.

My mat was on the floor directly under the Plexiglas star. Looking at the stars in the sky through the star in the roof was spellbinding. I looked forward to this time when I could crawl into my sleeping bag and be the astronomer, using The Dome's star as a grid to mark the movement of the heavens. I fell asleep to their crawl from triangle to triangle and I slept soundly every night.

If I did need human companionship, and I did from time to time, I simply hiked over the Saddle Pass down into Second Mile Ranch territory.

In a way, I admired the Second Mile Ranch. Everyone and everything were so productive and orderly. The fields were perfectly rectangular, the gardens were already promising to be bountiful, and the people seemed on a mission. Five recently constructed homes dotted their ranch. Except for Ben and Loretta's, which was the frame house that was already on the land when they bought it, the rest were log cabins. Or rather log houses. Very upscale houses! A couple of them looked suburban!

One belonged to Wesley and Jane Williams. The other to Matt and Cloe Saunders. Bennett and Helen were still finishing up their cabin, and Russell and Leeann were putting the final touches on theirs.

The other members of the Second Mile Ranch chose not to live there, but nearby on their own property. Jim and Andrea Hutch lived across the river almost opposite The Dome. We could see each other clearly through binoculars. The last of the Second Milers were Joel and Hallie Trager. They lived in the little house across the road from where our dirt one started.

The Second Milers bought their spread only a few months before we bought ours. But they worked like a fury year-round, come rain or shine, sleet, or snow. They made us look puny. The men were all rugged jocks and the women were all dutifully subordinate and supportive.

All the men were ex-Air Force fighter pilots. All had done tours in Vietnam. I could only imagine what it felt like to push a button that dropped napalm on innocent villagers. That alone would account for a strong bonding of shared guilt, patriotism, or rationalizations.

All of them were Christians or supposed to be. They were all born-again while stationed together in Greenland. Wes was the self-proclaimed leader and thought of himself as the interpreter of the Word of God and how it should manifest itself. He was the visionary behind the Second Mile Ranch and chief Overlord. He was also the most fundamentalist of the bunch. The rest were on a continuum from fundamental to incidental.

Matt echoed with zeal whatever views Wes had. Bennett pretended to be equally as zealous. Russ was harder to figure out. I definitely got some closet hippie vibes from him, and a restlessness, as if he were always on the lookout for an adventure. He was always hinting about coming up to The Dome and "tripping" out on the "engineering" of it with me. He was a hunky, handsome guy and I encouraged him to do it. After hours, if at all possible. He never did.

Ben was the intellectual, the quick-witted punster, and the incredible musician who made up the third member of the Porters' band. He took the most independent and liberal interpretation of the Bible. He and his wife Loretta were the most fun to hang out with and the ones I felt most comfortable being around. Their house was always filled with music and musicians. They were christian with a small 'c' the way I liked the word "gay" with a small "g."

Jim Hutch was definitely the iconoclast of the group. He really wanted nothing to do with it, because in truth he was an atheist, though he never let on. He kept up pretenses for the sake of his nagging born-again wife. But he liked hanging out with his old Air Force buds and he hated cities. So, he agreed to try it out, but insisted he buy something of his own nearby.

And then there was Joel.

It was a clear and sunny day as I walked down the dirt road to Poorman Creek. I knew once I reached the pavement, I only had to start walking and the first car to come by would stop and ask me if I wanted a ride. Even the cowboys and rednecks would stop. I never missed not having a car. I never waited more than a few minutes for a ride to anywhere. And without a doubt, it was the best way to meet people, so I always looked forward to a trip into town.

I only made it to the paved road.

Across the street at the little house that belonged to Joel and Hallie, a man was working in the yard. His back was to me. He was wrestling with a boulder and oblivious to me staring at him.

He was wearing work boots, heavy socks, and thick gloves. Other than that, he wore only shorts. He was struggling so much; sweat was running down his back. He straightened up and stretched his arms high above him. His shoulder blades almost touched. He put his arms to his side as he turned around and stood at attention, noticing me for the first time.

He was *dashing*. I couldn't remember a time when I'd ever used the word. But for Joel, it seemed appropriate. I imagined him in uniform and could easily see him as the poster boy for the Air Force. I don't know how long he'd been waving when I came to.

"Hi! You must be Giacco!" he said, crossing the street.

"And you must be Joel!" I said. "Ben's talked about you."

"You too," he said.

"Good stuff, I hope."

"Good enough stuff!" he said. "Enough to have me interested in what's going on!" And he laughed.

He asked if I wanted a drink, and we went into his house. He grabbed a pitcher of juice from the refrigerator and poured two glasses.

"So, what's going on?" he asked.

I laughed. "It's a great day to go to town?"

"No, really! What's going on up there at this Dome?"

I tried to be as general as possible, but he would have none of it. He wanted to know everything in detail. At first, I was worried he was interrogating me. But his eyes and demeanor told a different story. He was genuinely interested. He felt he had missed out on something that he didn't quite understand.

I tried my best. But every answer I gave just led to more questions. Then it dawned on me that if we kept going, the answers to his questions would reveal more than I wanted him to know just yet. After all, there was the rest of Hunga Dunga to consider. What I revealed would affect everyone in one way or another.

"I think we're going to have plenty of time to get to the details, Joel. Besides, I have to get to town. Want me to help you budge that boulder first?"

"Sure! That'd be great! Then I'll give ya a ride into town. Gotta pick up some stuff anyway."

The two of us managed to bully the boulder to the side of the yard and we drove into town in his Jeep, one exactly like Father Dan's. I went to the post office while Joel went to the feed store. We agreed to meet at the Spoke when we were through.

I turned the key to PO Box 111 with hope in my heart. Sure enough there was a packet from Richard. A letter from him. And my letter to Michael stamped, "Addressee Unknown. No Forwarding Address." I yelled, "Fuck!" out loud, like a person with Tourette's Syndrome, and then covered my mouth instinctively.

The note from Ziets was more encouraging.

My dear Chazan!

See! Just as I told you. Everything is the same. Nothing has changed. Who am I kidding! But a snort in the morning makes it all worthwhile. Just kidding again! I have replenished the coffers of our account in Twisp, so feel free to take what you need. Looks like we will definitely be up by June. If not, I will shoot myself! We all love you. We are sorry about Baird and all that stuff.

Yours throughout eternity, Zietar.

I went to the bank and took out a hundred dollars, but I had nothing to buy. I was already stocked up on supplies for at least another week. I went to the Spoke. Joel was there drinking a red beer. I sat next to him, and Bob poured me one without asking. Joel looked at me.

"What? You're already an ol' timer?"

Bob laughed.

I laughed. It was good to see Joel drinking a beer. Made me feel like I wouldn't get any puritan drivel from him. He just shined as the three of us made small talk. The only big talk was when he bad-mouthed the war. Then he got red. Bob and I stared at each other.

Could it be he was into Flower Power and didn't know it?

We drove back in his CJ-5 with the ragtop down and J E E P written in big letters on the back. His blond head of hair tried to wave in the wind, but it would require getting a bit longer before it could do that, which it eventually did. There was more soft blond hair on his tanned chest and arms and on his legs, whose muscles tightened with each press of the clutch or brake. His forearm bulged as he shifted. I guess I just have a one-track mind.

Six months ago, this was a man flying over Baffin Bay and the Labrador Sea. A man who spent 14 years in the service. Married. Two little girls. He was a man trying to reinvent himself. *Detoxifying his mind. Wanting to dirty up his brainwash. Just waiting to find something to dirty it up with. This was a man I could be proud of!* And if anyone could provide a little dirt, I felt it was me.

"So, I know you've got no utilities up there," he said.

"That is true," I answered, "but it's OK. I manage."

"Well, if you ever want a hot shower or to do a load of clothes, feel free. *Mi casa es su casa.*"

"Don't you think you'd better check that out with Hallie?" I asked, wondering why I hadn't seen any sign of her or the kids yet.

"I haven't told anyone else, so keep this to yourself for a while. Hallie and the kids have decided to stay in St. Louis."

"Until when?"

"'Until hell freezes over,' I think were her precise words," Joel said crinkling up his eyes and brow, his hands tightening on the wheel. "But Ben and the others think she's just decided to stay with her mom a couple weeks longer."

"Wow! I'm sorry, Joel. Man! What happened? She didn't like the country? Tell me to shut up if it's none of my business."

"Naw! Been coming on for a long time now. Slow, drawn out, tiring. We once thought that when we got home, things would get better. They didn't. We thought moving out to the country with all these Christians would really help. It didn't. It made things worse."

We reached his house and he pulled in the driveway. "Let me unload these things; then I'll give you a ride up the hill."

"Aw, that's OK, Joel, but thanks. I feel like a walk right now," I said, waiting for him to insist.

"Suit yourself, Giacco. Great meeting ya! Come down any time you're bored or need something."

"Thanks, Joel. You, too. Come on up anytime and see what's *really* going on! Whoopee!" And I laughed as I closed the gate behind me and began the two miles home.

I was smoking a joint, lying in my bag looking up at the stars, when I heard the sound of a car coming up the road, and headlights catching trunks of trees every other switchback.

I just had time to slip into some sweats when the jeep pulled up to The Dome. I stuck my head out the door as Joel slammed the car door shut. His eyes were a little red. I guessed he'd been drinking from the way he stumbled up the three steps to the deck. His speech was slightly slurred.

"So what's *really* going on, Giacco?"

"Come on in, Joel," I said.

"I really need to know, Giacco," he said almost pleadingly. "You think I'm just a brain-washed, Christian, Air Force, empty-headed jock! But I'm not! That's not me!"

I grabbed his sleeve and pulled him into The Dome. "Joel, buddy, hang on, slow down! I never, ever thought any of those things."

"Jim Hutch. Me. We aren't under Wes Williams's spell, you know! Now that we're here, we have no idea how we got here!" He plopped on the nearest mattress. The Dome was sparsely furnished, to say the least. A couple of old mattresses on the floor. A big old table and four straight-backed dining-room chairs that Slim and Hannah gave us from their old house. A few other odds and ends. Apple crates for end tables, dresser drawers, and storage. Just like in Michael's garage.

"Is that who you've been drinking with tonight?" I asked. "Jim Hutch?"

"Yup. Good ol' Jim. Only other guy I can relate to. Besides you… I think. He thinks his wife is having an affair with Russ. You know him? Meet him yet?"

"Yeah, Ben introduced me to him up at the ranch. Well, christ!" I said. "Looks like what we have here is one incestuous little Christian community!"

"What's that smell?" Joel sniffed. "Is that marijuana?"

I liked Joel, but just to be on the safe side I said, "You're probably smelling the incense."

"Don't fuck with me! I can't stand any more being fucked with! OK, Giacco?"

"OK, Joel, I get it. Yeah. It's the killer weed. You smoke?"

"Nah, never tried it."

"Want to?" I offered.

"You think I'm scared to try, don't you?"

I picked up the joint I'd been smoking and relit it. Took a big drag then handed it to Joel. "Inhale deep, hold it in as long as possible, and then let it out."

He took a long drag. As he was holding it, I grabbed the straps of the mattress and tugged until he and the mattress were in the center of The Dome, next to my mat. He exhaled.

"What the fuck are you doing?" he asked, as he passed the joint back to me. I took a few small tokes in a row and handed it back. I threw some pillows onto the mattress.

"Lay back. Relax. Check out the Star!"

He inhaled deeply again and held his breath. As he exhaled, he fell back on the pillows and gazed up. "Wow!" was all he said.

We talked long into the night. Getting more stoned while we did. About the search for enlightenment, and the war, and what's important in life, and why does love always suck.

He showed an arrogant side of himself when he divulged how many times he had cheated on Hallie with other officers' wives. How he had a knack for using his good looks to his benefit. His arrogance was accompanied by a confidence I felt was on the shaky side. Vulnerable.

He talked of pussy. I talked in non-gender-specific terms. I had a knack for beating around the bush. That made him even more curious, but luckily, he was too stoned to form a coherent question.

We eventually fell asleep. He on the mattress, me on my mat. Though nothing happened, I felt like I had made someone lose their virginity.

In the morning, we drove down to his house. I took a nice hot shower. When I walked into the kitchen, there was an impressive breakfast in the works.

"Got to keep up our energy," he said smiling.

We worked all morning building a little corral for the two goats Ben gave him. Around noon, Joel said he was going to pick up Hutch and go to the weekly meeting at the Second Mile Ranch. They enjoyed giving Wes Williams a hard time. It was a form of entertainment for both of them. Before he left, I asked if I could use his phone. It was long distance, but I'd pay him back.

"Of course, brother," he replied.

"Brother?" Oh my god, I'm turning him into a hippie!

I yelled, "Thanks!" as he released the clutch, lurched onto the road, and sped off.

I remembered that Michael said "Go Cornhuskers" in his last letter. On a hunch, I tried to track him down. I picked up the phone.

"Operator. The number for the main office of the University of Nebraska, please."

"One moment, sir."

She told me the number and then asked if I wished to be connected. I replied with an eager, "Yes!"

"University of Nebraska. How may I direct your call?"

"I'm trying to find a student. Can you connect me with someone who might help?"

"One moment, please."

A young-sounding voice greeted me. "Student Records. How may I help you?"

"Hi. I'm calling long distance. I'm looking for an old friend I've lost touch with. I think he is a student there. Michael Taylor."

"Let me see." I could hear pages flipping in the background.

"Yes. Michael Taylor. He *was* a student here, but no longer."

"No longer? What do you mean?"

"He finished up his degree last quarter… a master's in education."

"What!" I exclaimed in surprise. "Good for him! I was hoping he'd go for it, but I didn't think he'd go that far! Do you have an address for him?"

"Yes," she replied, "But I am not free to give out that information. Besides, I see there is a line drawn through it as no longer valid."

"In that case," I begged, "if the address were 922 13th Street, could you just say 'good luck' or something?"

She giggled. "Good luck, sir."

"Thanks," I replied. "Just one more thing. Is there any forwarding address? Anything that would give me a hint as to where he might be? He's really a good friend. Really! We just lost each other in our travels."

I touched my Ganesh and my hishi beads, hoping the voice on the other end belonged to a compassionate student. The silence on the other end seemed interminable. Then finally, "I see under his Teacher Placement file that transcripts were sent to Thermopolis, Laramie, Valdez, and the Kenai Peninsula school districts. At least those are the most recently listed. That's about it, sir."

I jotted them down.

"Thank you very much for trying so hard, ma'am. I really appreciate it." I hung up.

CHAPTER 93

June 1974

I politely refused a couple of rides into town because this was the nicest day yet since I'd been here, and I wanted to walk. Not a cloud in the sky. Warm air. Gentle breeze. A bit cooler in the shade or where the road ran directly beside the river. A perfect day for a walk. And definitely the beginning of a delicious summer!

I reached Highway 20. It was busy. Very strange. Maybe they opened up the North Cascades Highway for the season. Normally there was so little traffic, you only looked both ways out of habit. When I looked to the right, I saw a 1955 white Jeep pickup tooling toward me. It was Wilhelmina. The circus had come to town!

They pulled onto the shoulder when they saw me. Nick, Chuck, and Ziets piled out of the cab, stretched and then big hugs all around. How the three of them made it all the way, scrunched up like that, I'll never know. The bed of the truck was covered with a tarp that I suspected hid all kinds of goodies. I couldn't wait to unload it.

I asked if I could drive Wilhelmina up to The Dome. Nick was reluctant, but chivalrously jumped into the bed of the truck and felt for something soft to sit on. Ziets practically sat on the gearshift and Chuck slammed himself in with the door.

"Raise your cheek so I can shift, Richard!" I yelled and laughed at the same time.

"I've gotta stick you can shift!" Richard said and licked my face.

"Stop that, Ziets! This isn't San Francisco, you know!" I said looking nervously around me.

"Oh, Giacco," Chuck said, "just because we're in the country doesn't mean we're going to change who we are."

"I didn't mean change. I meant, well, let's just take it slow. Let's not freak them out all at once, OK?"

"OK," Chuck said, "we'll freak them out one at a time!"

I took the left fork up Poorman Creek. As we came up over the rise, there in the distance was a little house. The sun streamed on the front porch and yard. A blond-haired man in old cut-off jeans and work boots worked vigorously. The sun played with his muscles as he chained up the stump of a tree to his tractor. When his whole body was taught with effort, he looked like the hero on the cover of one of those supermarket romance novels.

"Oh my god!" yelled Chuck. "Do you see what I see?"

Richard just gulped. I chuckled.

"He's hotter than Steve McQueen!" Chuck pronounced.

Richard added, "Now that's a hot tomato if ever I saw one! *Muy caliente!*"

Joel must have heard an engine other than that of the idling tractor. He stopped what he was doing and turned around.

"Quick," yelled Chuck. "Ignore him. Don't look at him. He'll think we're cruising him or something."

As I pulled into Joel's driveway, I said, "Now, Chuck, wasn't it you that just said something about not changing who we are?"

"We *are* cruising him!" Richard said. "Oh, baby!" I could hear his hormones giggling.

"You know him?" Chuck asked excitedly.

"Up here, he's my best friend," I was proud to announce.

I jumped out of the truck, followed by Chuck and Ziets. Nick happily slid off the back. Joel walked over to us all smiles, flushed, and glowing from his labor. His blue eyes sparkled health.

I introduced everyone. Nick was embarrassed at how Chuck and Ziets were eyeing Joel. Especially Ziets, whose eyes were drooling with lust. Richard was just about to rub Joel's tummy when Nick threw him a scowl that made him retreat. Nick scowled even more intensely when I mentioned that Joel had come to the valley with the Second Mile Ranch. Obviously, Nick's first experience at the Antlers had made him a bit cautious of strangers.

I told Joel to come on up later if he liked. Joel took everyone off guard when he said, "Sure. Love to smoke a bowl with you guys later on."

The two stooges and Nick stood there stunned. Maybe they thought this was a sting operation.

Then Joel followed that up with, "And come down here anytime you want to take a hot shower or something. Just like Giacco does. Whenever you want."

"Thanks!" was heard in triplicate.

On the way up the dirt road, Wilhelmina threw us from side to side as I navigated the ruts. Questions were hurled at me, even from the bed of the truck where Ziets was hanging on trying to ride the steed out.

"Hot showers or something? Just like Giacco does? Have you seen him naked? Does he have a big one? Are you making it with him? Can I have him next?"

"Guys, you got it all wrong. We're just good friends. He's married, with kids."

"So what?" Ziets remarked, as if that were a non-issue.

I maneuvered Wilhelmina into a clearing in front of The Dome. As I pulled up the emergency break, Nick looked at me in feigned dismay. "Giacco, you've only been up here for two months and already you're contributing to the delinquency of a Christian. What a troublemaker!"

If it weren't for the fact we all had so much work to do, I'm sure we'd have done a lot more socializing. Nevertheless, Joel fit right in with us and whenever he could, he hung out at The Dome, or we hung out at his place. And through Joel, Hutch, Ben, and the Porters, our circle of friends slowly expanded. This circle had some very interesting people in it, all hiding out in the woods for one reason or another. All waiting, like Hunga Dunga, for the rest of society to catch up to them.

Until then, there was a lot of work to do. Our goal for the summer was to finish The Dome inside and out, plant a garden, and build a shed big enough to hold all our tools and maybe a tractor, if we ever got one. The "shed" ended up being a small barn. It even had a couple of windows for ventilation. Nick was thinking ahead to the day when we might have some big equipment or even a cow or goats.

The first thing we did, though, was to erect the outdoor kitchen again, just shy of Shitter's Hill. Nick made a more permanent solar shower in half a day. It was on a platform he whipped together just to the side of The Dome. It worked beautifully. After the sun had been out a while, the water from the coils of black pipe on the hillside was so hot, we had to mix cold with it to avoid being scalded. It was wonderful to shower naked outdoors. But we often found excuses to go down to Joel's. At The Dome, Richard *selflessly* offered to shower last, in hopes there would be no more hot water and he'd have no other alternative than to visit Joel. The little twerp! We tried our best never to leave Richard alone with Joel. Eventually we felt we had to warn Joel about Richard.

Joel went into fits of laughter. "I'm a big boy, guys. I can take care of myself!"

Slim lent Nick his tractor for a couple of days. Nick had never operated one, but within an hour or so, he was coaxing those boulders, too heavy to move by hand, to the quarry surrounding Zietar's Knoll.

When the field was completely cleared, he attached a tiller to the tractor and churned up the land revealing dark, fertile soil beneath. Then he took Wilhelmina into town and came back with a ton of sheep and chicken manure. The three of us mixed it into the dirt with any tool we could find. By the end of that day, the field was almost black with nutrients, and ready for Richard's magic. And we all smelled like shit!

We paid little attention to the garden because it was Richard's exclusive domain. We knew that in his hands it would respond accordingly, just as it had in Maine. I've never seen Richard work so hard and with so much love. He made long straight rows, and with a sack over his shoulder, planted the organic seeds he brought up from San Francisco. This was the Church of Manna's plan to provide free organic food and it looked like it might become a reality!

We had to set up the tents and tipis again and clear The Dome of the few items inside so we could work on the interior. I chose to build a little platform between four pine trees that conveniently decided to grow within five feet of each other. I draped sheets of clear plastic from some upper branches and attached them to the platform. Then I taped all the seams except for an overlapping one that would be the entryway.

Under Nick's competent supervision, we insulated and then paneled the inside of The Dome. Then we sat down and fiddled with various designs for the interior. We decided we wanted to maintain the openness of The Dome, and still provide enough room for everyone to have a space to sleep. A three-quarter mezzanine seemed to fit the bill. But it was very hard work. And it was slow going. Too slow for our tastes.

Hutch, though an engineer and computer whiz by education and trade, had taken a job as a logger with a local company. Through him, we managed to get a good deal on some logs that were already dried and peeled. Hutch drove the logs up, one afternoon after he got off work. We walked alongside the truck as it lumbered up our rutted dirt road. Every time the bed tilted with a rut, we tensed up thinking a few tons of wood would roll off and crush us all. We decided to keep our distance.

It was slow and precarious going, but Hutch made it up to the bench. Nick told him where to unload. Hutch undid all the straps. The bed lifted slowly sideways, and a mini-forest of giant pick-up-sticks rolled off onto the ground with a thunderous reverberation, and a cloud of dust a couple of stories high.

Hutch looked over our rough sketches and offered his expertise so we would be sure the mezzanine had structural integrity. He came back a couple of days later with an actual blueprint that gave Nick something he could easily work from.

While Ziets tended the garden, Chuck, Nick, and I struggled with the log posts and beams that would support a second floor. It had to be strong enough so that all of us could jump up and down on it without fear. If we got one or two logs in place a day, we were lucky. It was backbreaking work.

Eastern Washington is a very sunny part of the state, with summer temperatures reaching 100 degrees and more. But even on a temperate day, by late afternoon, we were overheated despite the huge quantities of water we drank, sweating like pigs, and so exhausted we could barely climb into Wilhelmina for a ride down to Joel's. Behind Joel's house was a small swimming hole. The Twisp River was icy cold. But damn! It was so refreshing to jump in and shiver later.

Going down to the swimming hole became a wonderful ritual. We'd skinny dip for 30 seconds, then climb onto a hot rock for 15 minutes, and watch the water evaporate off our skin. Then, when the shivering ceased, we'd dive in again. Hutch and Joel often joined us. We'd pass around a joint and get totally blitzed. During the day, we were hard-working men. But at the swimming hole, everyone acted like little kids, cavorting, and splashing each other.

An informal competition began to see who could find the most interesting rocks. Stoned as we were, all of them were interesting. We decided by consensus which ones would stay and which would be thrown back into the river. Many a discussion ensued over which were up to snuff. We were partial to the most colorful ones, but they'd become drab when they dried. So, we'd have to splash water on them to retrieve their colors.

The Rock Museum became famous among those in the know. Whenever we brought someone new down to the swimming hole, the first thing we did was to splash the Museum so the visitors could marvel at our finds. Guests would then start hunting furiously for a rock that would impress us. When they did, it was added to the Museum. Not a rock was ever out of place, and everyone respected the sanctity of the Museum. If a stranger happened upon our secret swimming hole, they would see the chosen ones arranged in concentric circles and probably thought they were akin to crop circles made by aliens.

We'd pass the Dr. Bronner's around while we were still wet and shampoo our hair and soap up our bodies. As soon as anyone was completely lathered, two guys would sneak up. One would grab their feet, the other their hands, and with a swinging one-two-three, toss them into the freezing river, which forced them to stay in long enough to completely rinse off. It was always a stunning and scrotum-shrinking experience. We looked forward to it every day.

CHAPTER 94
July 1974

July brought the much-needed visitors.

One day while Ziets tended the garden, and the rest of us were straining to drag logs into The Dome, we heard the distinctive sound of a VW Bug. We all stopped what we were doing and waited for something to round the bend. It was Zwagen. Richard, being the good communard that he was, knew he shouldn't be upset. But Zwagen and he had a special relationship, and to see Jeff and Trudy in it drove him crazy.

All of us hugged them except Richard, who immediately reached into Zwagen and hugged the keys. Chuck reminded Richard that Zwagen really wasn't his. It was Hunga Dunga's. Or the Church of Manna's. It was for anyone and everyone to use. Nick said we should put up a couple of hooks somewhere, and always leave the keys there in case anyone had to make a trip to town. Richard threw his head back. He had one of the smoothest foreheads I've ever seen. He closed his eyes. He slowly ran his fingers through what little hair he had left. We all took this to be an implicit, if reluctant, agreement on his part.

He did get even, though. When Jeff and Trudy talked about building a little hut on the other side of Zietar's Knoll, Richard put up a fuss. They would be too close to him! With all this land, why someplace where he could see them! Trudy wanted to contest this, but Jeff, being the nice guy, conceded immediately.

I took Jeff aside and told him about some of the secret spots I'd found. I showed him one on the hillside directly above The Dome just 10 minutes away. A berm hid it from sight, yet there were vistas better than any that could be seen from The Dome. And the views from The Dome were awesome!

He liked it and thanked me. "By the way, you still meditating, Giacco?" he asked off-handedly.

"Not like I should, Jeff, but, yeah, I am. This land of ours, I tell ya, you just sit quiet for a bit, and you can't help but be in a state of meditation."

"Trudy and I do, too. We're really into it! But you have to be so damn discreet down there! We're so glad to be up here!"

"And we're so glad you're up here, too. Hope you brought some weed with ya!"

Jeff laughed. "How 'bout some hash?"

"Really?"

"Well, I don't have much. Trudy and I like to smoke a bit before we make love. But we'll get *you* high."

"Gee, thanks Jeff," I said.

But what about the others?

Four days later, Trudy and Richard stood up in the garden, while Jeff, Nick, Ziets, Chuck, and I stood on the deck of The Dome, all of us listening to another Volkswagen coming up the road. A VW bus.

It was Katie, Lee, and Bianca. Katie had hitched from Nevada City where she was living, to visit the Friends of Perfection's farm in Grants Pass, where Lee and Bianca were living. They all decided a trip to Church of Manna land would be fun.

All three had also received Knowledge. Lee and Bianca had the good sense to keep it extremely low key. But Katie, upon returning from Hawaii, was still too blissed out for Eli's taste. He asked her to leave. We related to each other more than ever.

Katie moved in with me in my little, clear-plastic tree house. Not nearly as nice as the one in Kalalau, but a tree house yet again. And yet again, we resumed our off-again, on-again relationship, never quite able to draw the line between platonic friendship and romantic lovers. Still, it was great fun. I hadn't had sex in a very long time, except with myself, and this was a very, very nice development. Especially when Katie decided we should experiment with meditating and fucking at the same time. I did my best to stay in control, but Katie was so damned beautiful and luscious, I could never quite reach that tantric state both of us were aiming for. It was OK though, because Katie couldn't stay in control either. We made love often and always with zeal. Her body drove me crazy. Whether beneath me, on top of me, or in any other position, she squirmed in such a way that my cock was always a stiff, quivering rod aching to shoot. It seemed independent of the rest of my body. Neither of us ever managed not to cum, which was the goal. But after every orgasm, we stared at each other and broke into laughter at how ineffective we were at *tantric* sex. We'd lay back, sweaty, and pleasantly exhausted. Katie, giggling, would say, "I think tantric sex is a cruel joke." She used that line often.

The only tension ever to arise between us was when she said she wanted to have a child, and she wanted me to be the father. "You're obviously not really gay and I can't think of anyone who would make a better father."

"Katie," I said, "you make me feel wonderful. And *you* are wonderful. But I am obviously not really straight either. I would love to have a child and I think I would make a good father."

Katie nodded her head in glowing agreement. I thought of my dear friend Kostas, the elder, and how he would not marry his beautiful Alida under false pretenses. "But Katie," I continued, dousing her fire of affirmation, "I would make a terrible husband. I would never be able to say that *you* were the number one person in my life. Maybe the kid, but not you. I could never promise that someone else wouldn't come into my life who would take your place." Katie looked devastated and embarrassed.

"Katie, I am just being brutally honest. I love you. Really. But don't confuse sexual performance with sexual orientation." She looked glum, so I tried to get a laugh out of her. "You know how bad I am at orienteering." She didn't laugh. I offered a compromise. "If you still want us to have a child together, I'm all for it, but only under the condition that you completely understand the possible consequences, and even I haven't the slightest idea what they might be."

"None of us knows what the future holds, Giacco," Katie replied, and turned away, holding back tears.

With Richard, Katie, and Trudy working in the garden, and the rest of us working on the mezzanine, we hit our stride. The progress we made each day was evident and very satisfying. Sometimes we traded places, but we all knew which teams got the most work done, and we needed to get the work done. Sometimes Joel and Hutch would come up and lend a hand. When they were around, we seemed to accomplish loads. They chipped in as if they were Hunga Dunga. Everyone liked them a lot.

We only had Jeff and Trudy until the end of the month. Lee, Bianca, and Katie were only going to stay a couple of weeks, which meant they would all be leaving around the same time. We wanted to get the most out of them while they were here in Twisp, and they wanted to give us their best.

It wasn't all work and no play, however. Besides the ritual visits to the swimming hole, we'd go to the Broken Spoke, usually on whatever weekend night Bob had hired a band. The red beer flowed, the bands were hot, and everyone danced up a good sweat.

We met even more people. We thought the Twisp River valley was the only valley of any consequence. How egocentric of us. To the south were Libby, Gold, and Cow creeks. To the north were Wolf Creek and the Chewack. Each of these formed their own valley and up each valley were people just as crazy and interesting as the ones that lived up ours.

Most of the time, people stayed within their own little valley and went to town only when needed. In that sense, the topography lent itself to isolation. But whenever there was a big event, a rockin' band, a barter fair, or a political cause, the freaks came out of the woods, and there was a grand gathering. The demographics of the valley were changing and that meant potential political clout.

Of the nearly 900 people that populated the entire Methow Valley, I'd guess 40 percent were rednecks, 40 percent were hippies, or at least extremely alternative, and the remaining 20 percent managed to straddle the two with relative ease.

For some reason, there was a bond between the hippies and the old timers that we never could attain with their adult kids. It may have been all the talk about the ski resort. Their kids didn't want anyone fucking anything up. They knew the hundreds, sometimes thousands of acres their grandparents had homesteaded would be worth millions if Aspen came in. They wanted to cash in on that! The old timers and the hippies wanted to keep things the way they were.

One day, Ziets asked if we could all work in the garden for just one morning. There were so many weeds! But there were also so many carrots. We were already making salads with the lettuce we picked daily. The tomatoes still needed some time but were looking very nice. And of course, the zucchini was already infringing on the rights of its neighbors. The cukes weren't so civilized either.

It was so hot there out in the garden. There was no shade whatsoever. One by one, we shed our clothes until we were naked on our knees, throwing weeds into our pails and every now and then snacking on a green bean or two.

We were all so brown and healthy looking. Katie was very svelte and fit indeed! Lee had one of those skinny bodies with abs so ripped and concave, they made his pecs look big. And Nick was always a sight with his lean torso and shocks of long blond hair.

We were all joking around. Richard started singing something from "Oklahoma" and we all joined in. Then right in the middle of our choral rendition, something buzzed us. It came out of nowhere over the ridge. We saw it coming back. It was a Forest Service plane, flying low over the bench. As he flew over the garden, he tipped a wing so he could get a better view of the naked women, or so I assumed. He came back a third and fourth time, then disappeared.

Word must have gone out over their little radios very quickly and been picked up by every light plane in the county. Every day, crop dusters, smokejumper planes, Forest Service planes, and just plain old planes, decided the airspace above the Church of Manna was the most interesting. Out of principle, we refused to put on clothes. To the contrary. We turned into exhibitionists to spite them. I just hoped the pilots weren't jerking off and would pull up in time to miss the hillside. Eventually, the novelty wore off, and flight paths returned to normal. Thank god. But so much for keeping a low profile. For those that didn't know what we were about, the Church of Manna was now a nudist colony.

We were sad to say goodbye to Jeff and Trudy, Katie, Lee and Bianca. They had decided to all travel together in Lee's bus back to San Francisco and leave Zwagen with us. Richard was ecstatic and relieved by that decision. They were truly amazing friends and with their diligent help, the interior of The Dome was now complete, and we could move back in.

It took forever for everyone to hug everyone else.

Katie cried, but I was grateful she and I parted the best of friends as usual. She never brought up the topic of fatherhood again. I took that as an implicit sign she'd rescinded her invitation. She did admit, however, that what she really wanted was a committed relationship, which I couldn't give her, and she was cool with that. I had a strong feeling, though, we would never be lovers again. That made me sad.

When Lee hugged me, he slipped me a square of tinfoil and said, "Sorry I don't have enough for everyone, but I thought *you* would especially enjoy this." Whatever it was I knew it would be great! "Thanks, Lee!" I said.

But what about the others?

We watched the bus go down the hill, rocking from side to side, some rocks scraping the undercarriage, smaller ones being spit out. Our road was rough on vehicles. Many a pan had already been penetrated, and we were always on the lookout for signs of oil. We watched Lee's bus disappear behind the last switchback but didn't see him come out onto the meadow.

Maybe they broke down. Maybe they were just repositioning things and people. Ziets was about to drive down in Zwagen when Lee's bus popped into view again as it circled the meadow and drove down the draw to the gate.

We were just about to turn around and go back to work when something white caught our eyes walking around the first switchback. Ziets, Chuck, and Nick couldn't make out who it was. He was wearing jeans. He was shirtless and shouldering a backpack. He had a white T-shirt wrapped around his head, Arabian style. He had very long, dark hair, tied back and a bushy beard and moustache. I knew immediately who it was but could hardly believe it.

I ran down the road, trying not to twist an ankle, and took the inside curve around the bank of a switchback. We almost crashed into one another. He dropped his pack to the ground and swung me around and bear-hugged me until I could hardly breathe. He had tears in his eyes. It was just like when we met at Woodstock or in front of the country store in Topanga. When everything was new and for the first time, and we were completely innocent.

"Thank you Lord Muruga!" he cried. "Chazan, how are you? You look great! I am lorfing you so much!"

He picked up his pack and we continued up the hill. "This is great, huh Chazan? So this is the Church of Manna! This valley is beautiful, man!" Then he stopped in his tracks, hugged me again, and planted a big smooch on my lips. "Chazan, I missed you soooo much!"

"And I missed you too, Jonny!"

Joel came up for dinner. Or rather, he cooked dinner. As it turned out, Joel was an excellent chef along with everything else. Combining what he had in his fridge and what we grabbed out of the garden, he put together a delicious veggie stir-fry and an enormous salad. Along with a loaf of Trudy's homemade bread, we feasted not only on food, but on Jon's tales as well.

"I know you guys won't believe this, but I swear to you it is true."

"Go for it," said Nick.

"Rosie was gone. I was depressed. I was so depressed that I was depressed I was depressed. Spiraling down into that dark place, ya know? Why me? How could I let myself get so fucked up? I couldn't focus my mind on anything except Rose and how miserable I was. What to do? What to do? So, I said to myself, 'When in doubt, punch thyself!'"

"So did you?" I asked.

"Of course I did!" Jon boomed, though it wasn't his fault. It was The Dome's acoustics. "I walked almost two hundred miles from Jaffna through the jungles to Kataragama." Jon turned to me. "Oh Chazan! You know how amazing it is!"

He turned back to include everyone. "Anyway, I'm coming out of the jungles into Kataragama. I stay a week, and then totally burned out, head for the coast to rest up. I get myself a room in this little guest house in Pottuvil. It's really nice. Right on the beach overlooking Arugam Bay. It has a cozy café. All the hippies stop there on their way to or from Kataragama. It's a real hangout for freaks and a few die-hard surfers.

"I'm at the Pottuvil post office, and I get a letter from Chazan. I'm so excited I want to savor it. So I go back to the café, sit at a corner table, and order some chai. When it arrives, I open the letter and read it slowly. It's all about you guys and the Church of Manna and Twisp.

"I take a deep breath, lean back, and think about Hunga Dunga. Then I just happen to look up at the wall right next to me. The wall is filled with messages for travelers, advice on where and where not to go, postcards, and the traditional carvings of 'I was here' and all of that. But a large map dominates the wall.

"It's a topographic map of the North Cascades! More accurately, a map of the Twisp Ranger District of the Okanogan National Forest! I stand up, almost knock over the table, and study the map carefully. The town of Twisp jumps right out at me. I can see every valley, river, and creek. I hear Twisp calling me!"

There was total silence. We all sat there blown away, knowing Jon's tales were always true.

"It was a sign, guys! I mean if ever there were a sign, that was it! It was just too cosmic! I couldn't believe it myself, but there it was. I kid you not! Om Shivaya!"

We all knew he was not kidding.

"So here I am!"

CHAPTER 95
August 1974

Jon was in his ascetic body. Traveling through Sri Lanka or India keeps one lean. Sometimes it's from the energy, both nervous and physical, that's involved in getting from one place to another. Other times it's due to something more mundane, like dysentery. Jon's intestines were fine. But the sadness over the loss of his deva, Rose, had stayed in his eyes and every now and then, I caught him crying silently on some hillside near The Dome.

Now he thoroughly poured himself into work around the Church of Manna as a way to rid his mind of her. Now it was physical labor, either on The Dome or in the garden, that kept him fit and muscular. The energy he alone expended daily more than made up for the absence of Lee and Jeff, though the sumptuous meals and sense of domestic order and cleanliness maintained by Katie, Trudy, and Bianca, were sorely missed. It must have been obvious because any time anyone came to visit, they invariably commented on what a bunch of slobs we were.

We lived on Granola and the goat's milk that Nick bought daily from an old woman just outside of town. Lunch was always hit and miss. Sometimes, one of us had the initiative to make some sandwiches. I had forgotten how much I hated peanut butter and jelly. Other times, we just let our stomachs growl until dinner, which came earlier and earlier.

It was Joel who became housemother. He often surprised us with a cooler full of sandwiches made with something other than PB&J. He also brought juice, beer, and soft drinks. Soon, Joel left the soft drinks behind because no one drank them. However, the beer ran freely. We worked so hard and sweated so much in the intense heat of the summer, the beer just poured out our pores as quickly as we could consume it.

Joel was fascinated with Jon, and they became close friends. Jon became friends with almost everyone he met. He just had one of those personalities. No one could match him at being a punster. He could tell joke after joke with the delivery of a professional stand-up comedian.

Jon was so funny; he could keep you laughing until your sides were about to split. I've seen him at the bar making someone laugh so hard they threw up. The vomit on the floor of the Broken Spoke prompted Bob to suggest that Jon open for his band. They were going to play that coming Saturday night. Jon was hesitant, but we cajoled him into doing it. There'd be many friends there who'd provide a laugh track if need be.

That Saturday night, Jon took the stage. He tapped on the microphone, and it sent a chilling squeal throughout the room that made everyone hold their ears. Bob adjusted a fader on the soundboard. I could see beads of sweat on Jon's forehead. I had never known him to be shy in public, but there's a first for everything, I guess.

"Evenin' ladies and gents," Jon welcomed the crowd, and he did a little pole dance around the mic. The crowd hooted and hollered.

"So, a dyslexic walks into a bra…."

Silence. Then a few polite chuckles after a few had figured it out. I could hear a few people leaning over to their friends explaining what a dyslexic was.

"Hmmm. By the way, did you hear about the invisible man who married an invisible woman?" A well-timed pause. "The kids were nothing to look at either!"

A deeper silence filled the room. It was so quiet you could hear the beer pouring out of the tap. Chuck, Ziets, Joel, Nick, and I whistled and clapped wildly trying to have some sort of contagious effect on the crowd, but it was to no avail.

Jon continued, sweat pouring down his face. The spotlight only made it worse.

"I was so disappointed, I went downtown to swill a few beers. That's when the harp seal walked into the club…"

Jon was interrupted by jeers and calls for "Music! We Want Music!" "Hey Bob, where's the hook?" "Get this yahoo off the stage!" Their jeering drowned out our laugh track.

I could see Jon's hands trembling. Could he redeem himself?

"Did ya hear about the guy who walked into the doctor's office?"

Before he could continue, we heard some sarcastic remarks like, "Oh please, please, tell us! Quickly! Very quickly! Please!"

"So, this guy walks into the doctor's office and says, 'Doc, I think I have a problem.'

'And what might that be,' the Doc replies.

'I think I've been watching too many Japanese monster movies.'

'What makes you think that?' asks the Doc.

'Because I think I'm turning into a giant moth!'

'You should see a psychiatrist!' The Doc suggests.

'Well, I was on my way to see one, when I saw your light was on!'"

Total and impenetrable silence except for a two-fingered whistle from Chuck, and a yodel from Ziets. The crowd didn't even have the good taste to razz him.

Jon bombed! I think he was more surprised than anyone that he wasn't a hit. We felt bad that we more or less forced him to do it. However, he rallied and with great fanfare said, "And now, I present to you this evening's main attraction, Bad Bob's Band!"

The crowd went wild. Bob and the four other band members made a big deal about tuning up their instruments. The crowd was so ready to boogie, some people started swinging their hips and arms to the beat-less discord. It took the band about 15 minutes to get all their instruments tuned to middle A.

Then finally, the drummer, Bob's teenage son, started a wicked solo, making sure to bang whatever was in reach, throwing a stick up in the air and holding his hand out to catch it while he kept the bass kicker going. His hand was still in mid-air when the stick came down past his hand and fell on the floor. Embarrassed, he got off his stool and picked it up as Bob scowled at him.

Humbled, the drummer decided against any more acrobatics and kept a simple, steady, but fast four-four beat. With a Pete Townshend-style wide arc of his right hand, Bob came down hard on the first chord and stepping on his toy reverb machine, made that chord bend and wave over the crowd. They went wild.

A few more chord-bending strums and the rest of the band joined in for a rousing rendition of "Rockin' Robin." No one was shy about dancing. The entire crowd started rocking out to the familiar tune. Some danced with a partner. Some danced alone. But everyone was in motion. At the end of the song, the crowd gave them an encouraging applause, accompanied by those ear-piercing whistles I've always wanted to learn how to do.

The next song was a slow country tune. This time only half the crowd danced, while the rest looked for likely partners. The searching got more serious when their next tune was a Patsy Cline why-me, poor-me, love-sucks, oh-the-pain, song. Again, less than half the crowd danced, feeling certain Bad Bob would let loose any time now and they could all sweat away their week's hard work.

Responding to the calls for rock and roll, Bad Bob's Band broke into "Rockin' Robin" once again. The crowd took advantage of it and shook their booties so much, asses were bumping into asses. But when it was over, the band played a Bob Wills tune. Even though the old-timers loved it, few of them were there that night. This young crowd had come from as far away as Tonasket and was expecting a band that would bring the house down.

Soon, a pattern began to develop. A couple of slow country-and-western tunes, followed by "Rockin' Robin." After the fourth reprise of "Rockin' Robin," the crowd turned restless. I don't know where they came from, but without warning, overripe tomatoes were pelted at the band. One hit Bob square in the face. As he wiped it off, the crowd's yells were the loudest yet. The stage was squishy with red. One tomato landed on the high hat just as the drummer came down on it hard with his stick. It splattered all over him. That brought the laughter Jon had wanted. He was envious.

When Bob yelled, "last call," everyone agreed it was one of the best evenings yet at the Broken Spoke. But Bad Bob's Band wouldn't play again until they had added a few more selections to their repertoire, and that never happened while I lived in Twisp.

Jon didn't tell another joke for a week. Even the bizarre and ludicrous behavior of our President couldn't provide enough fodder for his nimble mind. Nevertheless, Nixon had begun the process of bringing the war to an end and many of our soldiers were finally home, some intact, others not. There were no parades to honor them, and they were not received as heroes. Many were cruelly scorned. After what they had been through, regardless of your politics, I thought that was heartless. And they were more confused than ever.

Those few that returned to the valley were strung out on either heroin or speed and probably couldn't march in a straight line even if there were a parade. When there was no heroin or speed to be found, alcohol was the great panacea, as it was for many in the valley.

But we had little time to discuss politics. We were more concerned with putting the final touches on The Dome. Room dividers on the mezzanine. A full kitchen with a stove and sink, and hot water from the copper coils Nick had wrapped around the double-barrel wood stove. We had an outhouse that was more like a fine piece of furniture, though we gathered mullein leaves daily for our toilet paper. Cupboards and cabinets. Shelves and the storage shed. We finally got all systems going and could dismantle the outdoor kitchen. Tearing it down was a milestone. It meant anything else we did, would be purely cosmetic. But we would leave that to Luc, Alvoye, and Bobby, should they ever come up to visit.

We deeply appreciated Jon's efforts. After a week of hard work, his bravado returned. More than the state of hilarity he kept us in, more than the colorful characters he brought up to The Dome for us to meet, were his before-bed tales of traveling and his musings about god.

It was so refreshing to hear about Lord Murugan, Swami Guaribala, and his visit with Baba Ram Dass back in Massachusetts without the specter of Baird looming over us. I do think however, that Baird may have been more amenable to a discussion about the latter, when Jon told us what Ram Dass had confided in him. He told Jon that he hadn't counted on fame as a byproduct of his quest for enlightenment. He hadn't counted on so many young, beautiful, and ardent devotees hitting on him. Male and female. After all, he was only human. After all, he still had temptations of the flesh. Male and female, Jon suspected. Jon also suspected that Ram Dass surrendered to some of those temptations, now and then. Male and female.

It wasn't Ram Dass' sexuality that came as a surprise to Jon and the rest of us, but rather that such a great disciple of the Dharma still battled with desire. The revelation came as a kind of relief, a validation that all of us were equally weak. But somehow, I could just feel it in my bones, that if Jon ever felt compelled to go back to the Subcontinent, it would be in search of Rosie, and nothing else.

Chuck felt obliged to give Jon the satsang of Maharaji, which Jon took seriously, though he made it clear he had no desire to receive the Knowledge. Richard ribbed the Goomer affectionately but would not dismiss him as a charlatan. Nick couldn't care less. I kept my mouth shut.

One day we got a visit from Ben Myers from the Second Mile Ranch. He said the Second Milers had met a spiritually based commune from Seattle, which was in the valley for a few days before heading up to the Aeneas Valley outside Tonasket, where they had friends. The Second Mile Ranch invited them to Sunday dinner and extended the invitation to Hunga Dunga as well. Ben was no lightweight when it came to making puns and he and Jon connected immediately. When Ben asked us how Jon fit into the picture, we just said that Jon was Hunga Dunga, tried and true. That may not have been possible back in San Francisco, but here in Twisp, there was unanimity on this issue. And as far as I was concerned, Joel was being inexorably absorbed into our sphere of influence.

When we arrived at the ranch, there was already a mess of chairs set up in a circle around a fire pit. The Love Family, as they were known, was already gathered around, sitting next to each other, and taking up about one third of the circle. They were all, without exception, handsome people. The men were fastidiously groomed, and physically, well put together. The women were beautiful without the need for make-up. They all wore unisex clothing. Loose blousy shirts and pajama pants. Some of the men wore shorts, revealing legs that were muscled by hard work. They scrutinized us while we happily scrutinized them.

Homemade cheeses and breads and assorted salads graced the plaid tablecloth covering the picnic table. Beside it on the ground was a very large cooler filled with beer, juice, and soft drinks. Jon and Joel helped themselves to a beer, while the rest of us, including all the Love Family, chose juice. None of us was into pop.

Ben and Loretta invited us to take seats and relax. One by one or two by two, the rest of the Second Milers placed food on the table and then joined us in the circle. Ben stood in the middle and asked for silence. He said a very nice prayer thanking his lord for our presence and the hope that peace and love would prevail in the world. To the chagrin of Wes Williams and a couple of other Second Milers, Ben did not refer to Jesus or Christianity. It was a perfectly fine, generic grace, and was all-inclusive, except for the atheists present.

Loretta suggested we all go around the circle and introduce ourselves. She pointed to the presumed leader of the Love Family, who happened to be the son of Steve Allen, the famous comedian, jazz musician and founder of the Tonight Show.

"Hi everyone!" he said jovially. "My name is Love."

The Second Milers and Hunga Dunga exchanged glances. It was probably the first time we were all thinking the same thing. We tried desperately not to show any expressions of mockery on our faces.

Love turned to the woman sitting on his left. "Hi all you beautiful people! I'm Charity."

We heard a few suppressed sighs, but nothing identifiably negative. Then Charity turned to the woman on her left. She was very pretty, but extremely shy. With her head still bowed, she said, "I'm Faith. Hello." The Second Milers nodded with approval at such a nice regular name. She quickly turned her chin to the man on her left.

He was a big brawny guy with a very deep voice. He looked around the circle and said, "Thank you for inviting us. I'm Hope." Once again, many of the Second Milers shifted in their chairs at what they considered pretentiousness. Hope turned to the last member of the family sitting on his left.

He was without a doubt the looker of the group. A handsome stud with beautiful long brown hair. He was sitting directly in the sun and was perspiring. The thin muslin shirt clung to his chest and stomach. He had great pecs and a ripped abdomen. The first three buttons on his shirt were undone, revealing just the right amount of chest hair and the enticing trail heading south.

"I am so glad to be here today, everyone! I'm Integrity."

By now we all got the drift and the rest of us said hello back, without any strange looks. Then Integrity turned to Little Richard, who was sitting on his left.

Richard looked at him and said, "Hi Integrity. I'm Yours!" And the little twerp reached over and rubbed his tummy. Integrity's muscles tightened even more if that were at all possible. He did not know how to react, but he mirrored Wes Williams' expression of utter shock. The rest of we Hunga Dungans were equally embarrassed, but we would never leave Zietar hanging in mid-air.

Jon stood up and said, "Hi! I'm Jon!" Then he proceeded to go up to every person in the circle and rub their tummies. "This is an ancient ritual of the Squeamish Indians that Hunga Dunga has adopted. It is part of their rite of passage into adulthood. Sort of like a walkabout, but the terrain is limited to the human body. An ice-breaker, if you will."

Joel picked up the thread and was incredible in his delivery. "Yes, the Squeamish Indians. A local Northwest tribe, you know. They spoke an obscure form of Eastern Salish. They had a very sophisticated vocabulary of body language. More words than in their spoken tongue." Joel stood up and met Jon in the middle of the circle and they rubbed each other's bellies at the same time and maintained completely deadpan faces.

Then Joel went up to Charity and rubbed her belly. Jon stood next to him and translated. "He's saying, 'Hi, I'm Joel. Glad to rub your tummy!'"

Charity giggled, stuck her hand out, and rubbed Joel's. "Hi Joel, I'm Charity. Nice to rub *your* tummy!"

All I could hear inside my head was the opening theme to Dragnet. "Dum de dum dum. Dum de dum dum, Dum!" What I heard instead was Integrity saying, "Wow, that is so cool!" And he leaned over and rubbed Richard's tummy, much to Zietar's amazement and glee.

Soon everyone was rubbing everyone else's tummies. Even Ben and Loretta. But the rest of the Second Milers found excuses to get a drink.

The Love Family and Hunga Dunga acted as if they were long-lost relatives. Wes Williams grimaced and took Ben aside, I suppose to berate him for putting the rest of them in such an uncomfortable situation. Ben, so kind and affable, just stared at him, and then turned away.

"OK, you guys," Ben announced, "just make yourselves at home while we prepare the entrée!"

Matt and Bennett made a spit over the fire pit and arranged a tipi of wood under it, some briquettes of charcoal at the ready. After the fire was going, flames licking at the spit, Ben disappeared behind a shed. When he returned, he had four cages with two or three rabbits in each one. He placed them along the ground next to the barbed wire fence of the corral.

Matt and Bennett pulled the rabbits out by their ears and tied each one to a fence post. Ten rabbits. Ten fence posts. Ten squirming, screaming little bunnies.

Then Ben walked down the fence with a steel mallet in his hand. As he came to each fence post, he bludgeoned the head of the rabbit. Blood squirted forth as each bunny shivered its last post-mortem shudder.

Charity threw up first.

Our super stud, Integrity, followed her.

I couldn't look after the first blow. Richard was aghast. Jon said, "Oh, this is better. Much better!" Nick, the fearless woodsman, acted nonchalant. Chuck brought up the rear with a vomit of beer and potato salad.

Love stood up. He tried to be gracious, but it was obvious he was horrified. "Ben! The Love Family are vegetarians!"

Jon stood up. "Ben! We are all vegetarians, too! But that is beside the point! Isn't there a more humane way to slaughter them?"

Ben truly did not understand the reactions. "This is more humane than a bullet!"

Love slowly scanned the Second Milers. "No matter how you do it, it's still a slaughter! And you call yourselves Christians?"

Following Love's lead, they all got up and walked to their van. Ben ran after them, telling them Christ was not a vegetarian and this was the country after all and isn't it better to kill what you eat yourself rather than buy it in a market oblivious to the killing that went on behind closed doors?

Love leaned out the driver's window. "Brother! We judge you not. But we are the Love Family, and what we just witnessed was not love!" He put the van in gear, and they drove off.

Lucky them. They could go back to Seattle and never see these people again. But we lived next door! As difficult as it was to watch Loretta and Cloe skin and debone the rabbits, as difficult as it was to watch them skewered and rotated on a spit, we took a deep breath and tried to make the best of it. We agreed in principle that if you're going to eat meat, then you should be able to kill it. It's just that we had never actually seen it being done. Now we had. It made us more vegetarian than ever.

While the Second Milers devoured the rabbits with relish, we relegated ourselves to the salads and side dishes. After dinner, Ben got out his mandolin and Loretta grabbed her fiddle, and their bluegrass music made everything all sunny and bright, even though the sun had already gone down behind the mountains.

Jon tried to be his most delightful and funny. He was most successful with the women. The men regarded him as competition.

Joel kept fielding questions about his wife and kids. He kept giving obtuse answers. They still considered him one of them but reminded him it was the devil's job to tempt, so be careful. They considered him an undercover agent who could tell them what was *really* going on at The Dome.

I engaged some of the men by massaging their egos and picking their brains about Methow Valley stuff. My job was to act clueless. Let them get *me* smart. Things like how to get a permit to cut firewood. Their favorite place to backpack in the high country. What they thought of Aspen trying to come in? Who to see about getting our road plowed come winter? What was the Air Force like?

How many bombs did you drop? How many non-Christian people did you kill? Gee, I wish I could be as much of a real man as you are!

I joined Zietar next to Ben and Loretta. Loretta had a wonderful voice and Ben's, though a bit gravelly, harmonized perfectly with hers. They were playing some of our favorite songs, the ones Richard and I could sing only when we were driving alone in Zwagen. The songs were simple, and the harmonies came easily. These songs always got us high.

We sang the Mamas and the Papas, Dylan, Brothers Four, Patsy Cline. Damn, we were good! Even Ben said so and music was his thing, his training, his life, his soul. He should know. Richard's voice was always so pure and sweet, and I could carry a decent tune. The four of us together, though, made a unique sound. Something more than the sum of our voices. Damn we were good!

More people joined in singing; others just gathered around. As a way of making peace, Jon broke into the song, "Jesus is just all right with me. Jesus is just all right with me…!" Almost everyone sang and harmonized. What song could be simpler? But after the first verse, Ben changed the lyrics. He looked at Jon and as if clinking glasses and returning a toast, he sang, "Buddha is just all right with me, Buddha is just all right with me…!"

All of Hunga Dunga, Ben, and Loretta sang it with equal energy, but one by one, the rest of the Second Milers stopped singing. Ziets began the third verse. "Yahweh is just all right with me; Yahweh is just all right with me…!" We joined in and Richard's voice soared like a flute.

Wesley Williams stood in front of Ben with his arms crossed. With each verse, his face got redder and redder and not from the glow of the coals in the fire pit. Ben just smiled at Wes and kept strumming, though Loretta felt intimidated and stopped fiddling.

We took this as our cue to gather up our things and leave. As we did, Zietar started singing, "Do Lord, oh do Lord, oh do remember me…" and I added the "oh lordy" part. Ben immediately started playing in Richard's key, and all of Hunga Dunga sang the song as we shuffled off to Zwagen parked at the edge of the field.

"Do Lord, oh do Lord, oh do remember me,

Look away, beyond the blue…

Ho-ri-zon!"

CHAPTER 96
September 1974

One of the unusual qualities of The Dome was its acoustics. They were too good. Normal conversation seemed amplified, and the words hit the ear with a slight echo. We got into the habit of counting to two before responding.

There were two sweet spots directly opposite each other about two feet off the floor and four feet from the walls. If a person were low to the floor in each spot, they could carry on a conversation in barely a whisper and yet understand each other perfectly, as if they were whispering right into your ear. The beauty of it was that only those who sat in one of the matching sweet spots could hear what was being said.

If Nick and Jon were chatting quietly in one spot, Richard and I could listen in by going to the other. We listened in as if they were right next to us. It was wireless-tapping. When Richard first discovered it, he tried to explain the why of it to us, but we preferred to think of it as part of the magic of The Dome. We kept the secret of the sweet spots to ourselves. We thought it might come in handy someday.

The acoustics in The Dome were so good that when we lay on our third-hand beds, staring up at the stars through the Star, we could hear each other breathing. Every inhale and every exhale. Every *soooooo* and every *huuunng*. It became a contest each night to see who could fall asleep first, before the snoring started. Many a night, someone with too much on his mind who couldn't get to sleep fast enough, ended up sleeping out on the deck, away from the rhinal racket. Once in a while, the snoring was so bad that the one who snored loudest ended up having The Dome to themselves, while the rest of us camped outside for some peace and quiet.

The acoustics were such that we could hear every yellow-jacket that had gotten in during the day now buzzing around trying to get out. They may as well have been the Blue Angels practicing for a show. We could also hear every creak of the struts against the hubs, settling in place, becoming tighter and more solid than ever. And then one night, we could also hear the scurrying of little feet.

When Richard turned on a flashlight, tiny critters scurried for cover. As they passed through the sweet spots, they sounded like a herd of cattle.

Richard screamed, "Meeces! We have meeces!"

Nick yelled back, "Go to sleep, Ziets! A few mice aren't going to bother you!" However, it was not a night of sound sleep for anyone.

The next morning, we made sure that all our dried goods and other foodstuffs were securely sealed. We scoured every nook and cranny trying to find what treats the mice were after. Richard insisted we go get mousetraps or something lethal. Jon, Chuck, and I said let's just give it a few days. Try to live with them in peace. After all, this was their territory before we got here, right?

"Wrong!" said Nick and Richard. They would have none of it. But we convinced them to wait a few days.

Each night, it sounded like there were more and more little feet scurrying around. After a few days of trying to share our world in peace, we admitted we had a problem. A big problem. It was an infestation. One morning we were jarred awake by someone slapping a shovel hard against the floor. We sat up in our beds and there was Richard running after a mouse with it. The mice were little and so cute, that if there were just one of them, he may have ended up a pet. Instead, Richard's shovel came down hard on one of them frozen in mid-scurry and squished him dead with the back of the shovel. Richard cheered in victory.

Jon objected strongly. "What ever happened to Jainism!"

Nick got up, grabbed the smaller shovel we used for the wood stove, and joined Richard in a frantic charge trying to kill the random mouse trying to get from one side of The Dome to the other. "I don't care who Jane is," he said, tripping over a futon rolled up on the floor.

"What a bunch of hypocrites you are," Chuck yelled. "How is this any different from the rabbits?"

After three sleepless nights, Jon finally said, "OK, that's it!"

Jon, Chuck, and I went into town and bought about 50 non-lethal mousetraps. When we got back to The Dome, the walls were plastered everywhere with notebook paper on which Richard had written in felt pen, "We hate meeces!" "Death to all meeces!" "We hate meeces to pieces!"

We encircled the interior of The Dome with the traps, and slept outside on the deck, which was much, much quieter than inside The Dome. Each morning, we'd take the traps with their catches from the night before and hike them to the Saddle Pass where we would let the bruised or injured, but still-alive mice, free.

It was to no avail. They loved The Dome as much as we did.

The feed store sold us the poison that would end the onslaught of the little ones. We sprinkled it around both the interior and exterior of The Dome. The poison must have been very tasty. The next few mornings were spent sweeping carcasses into a burlap bag and burying them in a pit Nick had dug. After a few days, word must have gotten out and the meeces retreated. The Dome was once again habitable, and a representative of the Rodent Nation signed a peace treaty in blood. Joel reminded us that rabbits were rodents, too.

It's a good thing the Love Family wasn't around.

Nick, Chuck, and Ziets were packing up Zwagen. I had hoped they'd stay longer, but Chuck had to get back to The City to begin rehearsals on a new play.

Ziets loved keeping the books for "Greenleaf." It seemed to give Richard a sense of importance and indispensability. Why he didn't believe we regarded him that way to begin with, I'll never know. But the job gave him a feeling of power. It was a power he used honestly and wisely, but a power nonetheless, and the little guy must've liked that. He worried if he stayed away too long, Lizzie would find someone else to replace him.

Nick was missing his little flower lady, Chelsea, in San Rafael. Being guys, prone to promiscuity if the occasion arose, we could understand Nick. But we still felt badly for Psylvia. We knew how much she still loved him.

So off they went near the end of September, leaving Wilhelmina with Jon and me, and leaving me, finally alone with Jon.

When it was dark and the stars came out, Jon and I each grabbed some cushions and sat under a sweet spot.

He need only whisper and I could hear him at the other side of The Dome. "I miss Rosie, Chazan."

"I know Jon, I miss her too. I think maybe I'll never see her again."

"Remember in Hawaii, Florence said we'd come full circle," he said hopefully.

"She said *you* and Rose would. Not *me* and Rose. But I hope you're right."

"Chazan," Jon asked, "Do you meditate? I mean this Knowledge stuff and all?"

"Don't call it anything, Jon. Makes me feel weird."

"How so?"

"It's just stuff that's been around forever. I guess I could sit in a lotus position and meditate day after day, but I don't. I feel like I'm back where I started. I meditate when I am afraid. I am one of those "black sheep" devotees. The ones that take the good stuff and run. And you?"

"I was jealous of Guaribala at first. Because of Rose. Now I thank her. Guaribala is far out. 'Summu iru, simply be.' I want to be able to sit all day and meditate. I can't!"

"I don't try," I said softly. "Like I said, I feel like I'm where I started. If I'm meant to be enlightened, it'll happen. For me, Jon, it's time to fade down on raja yoga and fade up on karma yoga."

"Uh-oh! I can feel your Catholic guilt surfacing! Duty, service, pay the piper! For me it's tantric yoga. Tantra, you shall rule! Oh, yeah! I can feel my lowest chakra shakin' like a maraca." He laughed. His chuckles reverberated throughout The Dome. "Get it? Chakra, maraca?"

"Yeah, Jon. I got it. Another Wordsworth, you are."

"Hey Chazan."

"What Jonny?"

"This place is amazing! It's so trippy! Magic can happen here! You guys did a beautiful job on this dome!

"So did you, Jon." And we both scanned the intricate geometry of The Dome.

"Hey Chazan!" Jon said leaning back on his elbows and staring up at the Star. "I just realized something."

"What's that Jon?"

"There is no strut in this dome that's any more important than any other! If any one of them snapped, the whole thing would eventually come down!"

Those were such nice days having Jon to myself in The Dome. When we were out and about, a crowd always gathered around Jon. To use the adjective "magnetic" to describe his personality was to use the word literally. Everywhere we would go, the attraction was so strong, people vied to be privy to his jokes, puns, and on the serious side, commentaries about history, politics, and religion.

We often had dinner with Joel, either up at The Dome or down at his place. That was cool. Joel was cool. And the three of us always had a good time together, sometimes talking late into the night. Still, it was a treat when the conversations slowed in tempo, reminding us all how tired we were and either Joel would leave, or Jon and I would go back to The Dome. Alone. The two of us. We'd talk a while, cry about Rosie, berate the gods for not making us holy, and punch ourselves to sleep. It was nice.

It wasn't much later that Jon bowled me over with the news he'd be leaving. I just assumed he was in it for the long haul. And he said he was, just not in Twisp, just not with me. Not this time, at least.

"Chazan, I will always love you. You are my brother! I will miss you like I miss Rosie. Well, almost." He laughed.

"Jon!" I pleaded. "How can you do this to me?"

"Giacco, I have another brother, remember? Rob?"

"Yeah, I remember."

"You think Twisp is rural? Rob and Christy are building a log cabin from scratch, north of Prince George up in central B.C!"

"Wow!" I exclaimed, imagining thick woods and frozen lakes. They stayed in Canada! But why there? Then again, why us here?

"I have to go and help them, Chazan. It's the least I can do." I could hear in Jon's voice the pain of our inevitable separation.

"Christy's pregnant again. You know how hard it is to manhandle a felled tree by yourself. Even if I just help out takin' care my nephew Robbie and the new baby, that would be something. I gotta go! I gotta get up there before winter sets in. I have to make sure they're OK. He's my little brother! Dad would never forgive me!"

"It's OK Jonny," I said, trying to calm him down. "I understand completely. Really. I do!"

It was a somber evening watching Jon stuff his backpack. I can't say for sure if we slept fitfully. I think we were both reminiscing about the same things. About the incredible history we shared. Woodstock. Tucson. San Francisco. Vancouver. India. Twisp. If a picture is worth a thousand words, then an emotion must be worth a million.

I never brought up my feelings about being highjacked out of Nepal, though I did briefly project my brainwork across The Dome wondering if the sweet spots worked as well with thoughts as they did with whispers. I received no mental transmissions back. It was time for me to let those feelings go, anyway. I suspect his obsession with Rose displaced everything else. But I loved him dearly and knew he loved me, too. That was enough.

The only thing he said in the still of that night was, "Just goes to prove that even when you think you're ready doesn't mean you'll get there."

I mentally put that sentence in the "Can of Worms" closet back at Hunga Dunga. It was the only way I could fall asleep.

The next day I gave Jon a ride past Mazama and let him off at a place where he'd be sure to get a ride. It was the nearest road over the mountains to the coast. We hugged a lot. Jon cried. I loved that about him. That he was so big and rugged and yet cried so easily. Even when strangers were around.

I drove away slowly. As I looked in my rear-view mirror, I saw a pickup had stopped and Jon was throwing his pack into the back, but he was still looking at me driving away. That's when I started crying. He stepped into the truck and shut the door and the truck started off. He knew I was watching. But he was too far away to see me bawling. He held out his arm and flashed a peace sign, then joined his index finger to his thumb, the sign for Om.

CHAPTER 97
October 1974

I was alone. Alone in a dome on 120 acres of land. From now on I would watch Hunga Dunga from afar. I would rely on Richard's meager letters to fill me in on the news from The City. As soon as they were gone, I felt the emptiness of their absence, but rather than try to fill the vacuum, I decided to play the hermit for a while. Just as a test.

This was the time to enjoy the mountains. Mosquito and horsefly season had come and gone, as had the tourists. The back-to-nature college kids were back in college, and no longer in the nature. Hunting season was almost upon us, but not yet. It was the perfect time to hit the high country. The challenge I gave myself was to explore the Sawtooth Range on my own. When Lois found out about that, she balked, but if I wouldn't change my mind about going solo, she insisted I take one of her beloved dogs, Pipsqueak.

Pipsqueak got her name because she was the runt of Zoë's last litter. Donald and Lois managed to find homes for all the pups except Pip. So, Pip joined the ever-growing menagerie of cats, dogs, a pig, ducks, and a Shetland pony, that wandered about as they pleased, even inside the house. Lois swore that even the chickens were house trained, but I never got to see that because the cats wouldn't let them in.

None of their animals knew the meaning of the words corral, cage, kennel, barn, or doghouse, though they were available should they need them. Lois just had a way with all of them. They obeyed her every command, sometimes unspoken, with only a look. Their house didn't smell all that good, but no one ever felt they were intruding or overdressed when they stopped by. They were, for all practical purposes, in a constant state of noisy mayhem. They acted as if it was perfectly normal. For all of us who held etiquette and decorum and tranquility low on our list of desirable qualities, Do and Lo's little farm was the place to be.

They also had the most mind-boggling view of the Sawtooth Range. I could see where I would be in a few days from the old back seat of a Chevy they used as a couch on their porch. As I sat there, Pip jumped up on the seat with me. The two of us sat there staring at the mountains. Then she tipped slightly and leaned against me. I thought she was coming on to me she was so affectionate. The air was a bit chilly, but the sun was at just the right angle to warm us both. We bathed in the light as we stared across the valley, and immediately bonded. She listened to me as if I were her best friend. She jumped into Wilhelmina without hesitation and spent the night at The Dome stretched out on the bed with me.

The pack was packed. The sleeping bag was tied to the bottom. Pipsqueak sniffed the outer pockets to make sure I hadn't forgotten the dog food. And off we went. Over the Saddle Pass into the Second Mile Ranch, where Ben and Loretta insisted, I stop and have some tea.

We continued across their field until we picked up the logging road, which was where Poorman Creek Road ended, and had a long but easy climb to Black Pine Lake. We stopped there for lunch, but the lake, as beautiful as it was, was in dense forest, and ringed with cattails, grasses, and very muddy banks. We had no desire to linger longer or make camp there.

We hiked out the backside of the lake and found a trail that, catching a glimpse of it farther up, seemed likely to take us above the tree line, which was my goal for the day. It was rough going. Pip had an easier time of keeping her footing than I did. I could already feel the beginnings of blisters on my feet and hoped that Pip's pads weren't as bad as mine were. She let me check them every few hours. They were fine.

As we climbed higher and higher, the trees thinned, and the chain of mountains came into view. We reached the top and while Pip panted, I gasped in awe. A small wooden Forest Service sign read "Angel's Staircase." There was a conveniently flat area perfect for pitching a tent and it must have been a popular site because there was a very nice fire pit already waiting for someone just like me. I mean us.

I looked down at Angel's Staircase. It was a continuation of the same trail, but it was a steep, rocky descent that would take careful maneuvering. I thought the sign should have read "Devil's Staircase," but then again, I guess it depended on whether you were climbing up it or sliding down.

It flattened out at the bottom when it reached the beginning of the talus, but then it wended its way in a zigzag pattern through the scree. On the other side, the trail was plain as day. It followed the entire curve of the Sawtooth Range just above the tree line. Considering I was in the backcountry, it looked like a superhighway. This was a main trail for the innumerable hiking boots that clomped along it during the summer. I was glad this was the off-season.

When it was about to disappear from my line of sight, I saw where it forked. One trail descended back into the forests, probably to some lake or another. The other fork continued at the base of the peaks still above the tree line. A few alpine lakes glimmered in a receding string of jewels along the trail. The lakes looked close enough to touch from my amazing vantage point, but I knew it might take a couple of days for my, I mean *our*, feet to reach what my eyes could see.

We made camp where we were. Obviously, we were meant to stay here for the night, where we could watch the sun set its oranges and reds on the sides of glaciers, where there was ample kindling and wood for a fire. A delicious dinner of instant oatmeal, some dried fruit, and freshly picked chamomile and mint tea made me feel comfy and content. Pip's dinner made her realize how tired she was, though she had enough energy to lick my bowl and wolf down some of the treats I brought along as a surprise.

Pip slept at my feet on top of the sleeping bag. Her snarls at chipmunks and marmots were just loud enough to let me know she was keeping guard. I slept without worry.

The next morning was a beaut! Gloriously clear skies. The air was clean and thin. When the sun cleared the peaks, it was unusually warm. Maybe it was the altitude that made the sun seem more intense, considering the time of the year.

We carefully navigated our way down Angel's Staircase. One false move by a distracted hiker and they could slip on loose rocks and tumble a hundred feet or more, possibly adding another angel to the sign. Pipsqueak ran up and down the staircase obviously impatient with my overly cautious footwork. My blisters were screaming. Hiking downhill was more painful than hiking up.

The path disappeared for a while through the scree, but we could see where it started again on the other side. Once we were back on the path it was easy going. And it began to get very hot. At least in the sun. When the path ran into the shade, the temperature dropped suddenly, and you could feel the chill of autumn. I played for a minute or two, jumping forth and back between the shade and the sun. There was at least a 20-degree difference between the two. As I followed the trail ahead with my eyes, I saw that most of it was in the sun. That was good. I hated being cold.

But I didn't realize how hot I would get packing 50 pounds across the bowl of mountains whose walls hovered above and around me. Twenty minutes into the hike, I took off my flannel shirt and forced it into a side pocket. Another 10 minutes, and I took off my undershirt but slipped it under the straps of the pack to buffer the chafing on my shoulders.

As far as the eye could see, we had the path to ourselves. My jeans were feeling constrictive. I stopped and let the pack drop off my shoulders. I struggled with my boots but got them off with a modicum of pain. Then I removed my jeans, rolled them up and managed to stuff them in between the sleeping bag and the pack. I never wear underwear, so except for a pack on my back, hiking boots and thick socks, I was completely naked. Pip sat there on her haunches looking up at me. She tilted her head and looked at me curiously as if to say, "What the hell are you doing?"

[1]*Au natural*, surrounded by this scenery was the only way to hike. The feeling of freedom was Adam-and-Eve-like. If only I could lose the backpack. Then I'd really have reason to romp around. I romped as best I could with the weight on my back. On the plus side, it did keep my shoulders back and my chest out. If I had a buzz cut and were in basic training, I would have looked like a model soldier except for the uniform.

We came to a section of the path that curved sharply, hiding from view what might be on the other side. I expected there to be nothing except more path. Instead, as Pip and I rounded the corner, I saw a young, good-looking Forest Service Ranger just about 30 feet away. I sucked my stomach in to go with the shoulders and chest.

Damn, he was hot! And not because of too many layers of clothing! He had his shirt off, slung over one shoulder, along with a small daypack. He wore Forest Service green shorts and when he put his foot up on a big rock and the shorts rode up, I could see the strength of his legs. Probably in his early 30s, he was lean and muscled from his neck to his calves. Long brown hair and a cleanly cropped beard. Eyes as unusually green as the water in the alpine lakes. Some kind of seed hung around his neck on a red string and found a place to rest just above the cleft of his pecs. He stopped and I stopped.

---

[1]

"Hi!" he said, very surprised. I hoped it was a pleasant surprise.

"Hey! How's it going? Perfect weather for a long hike, eh?" I tried to act natural and nonchalant. His eyes left mine and I watched them follow my body down to my boots and then back up. I wondered if he noticed I'd already done the same scan on him. I wondered if he'd even noticed I was naked! He didn't even mention it at first and took it completely in stride. I, on the other hand, had to keep thinking of dead puppies so I wouldn't get a boner.

"What do you do up here?" I asked in as manly and steady a voice as I could muster.

"See that lookout way over there?" He stood right next to me pointing with his right hand, his left shoulder just an inch from mine.

"No," I said. "I can't see it."

"See that little cabin sitting on top of that tower?" he said, bridging the inch between us and actually touching my shoulder.

A chill ran up my body. "Oh, yeah! I see it now! That's where you live?"

"Yup!" he answered. His eyes and mouth smiled proudly at me, especially his eyes. "Three more weeks. Then fire season is officially over, and I can return to civilization!"

"And your buddy?" I asked.

"What buddy? Are you kidding?"

"You mean they put you up there all alone for weeks at a time?"

"You mean a season at a time!" he laughed. "They just helicopter in some supplies every couple of weeks."

"Fuck!" I said. That word always had a nice real-man sound to it. "A good way to go bonkers, don't you think?"

"Nah! I like it. It's good to be alone once in a while. You should be able to relate. You're up here alone. That's a bit unusual, ya know. And not the smartest thing to do!"

"But I'm not alone. I have Pip with me." I looked down at Pipsqueak.

She looked back and said, "C'mon, let's get going already!"

I looked at her sternly. My eyes gave the command to lie down." She did.

"The view from up there must be amazing!" I said.

"It is amazing! Every morning when I get up, the mountains look different. They're always changing. I never get tired of them."

"I can imagine!" I said.

"Why imagine?" He asked, a bit nervously. "If you want, you can see for yourself."

"For real?" I asked, equally nervous. "They allow you to do that? Have guests?"

He laughed. "Hell no, it's totally against the rules! For that matter, so is hiking around naked with a dog! But you do have Ganesh around your neck. So how cool is that?"

That's when I realized the seed hanging around *his* neck was a rudraksha, the eye of Shiva. Jon wore two of them, one for each of his trips to India. "Om Shivaya!" I put my hands together and bowed. He bowed back. When we raised our heads, our eyes met. His unflinching look made me even more nervous, so I looked away and said enthusiastically, "Lead on, brother!"

"Just one thing," he added, "You think maybe you can put on some shorts or something just in case we run into any other late season hikers?"

"Sure!" I said. My nudity had slipped my mind. I dug through my pack and pulled out a pair of shorts so baggy I could slip them on without taking off my boots. "Either that or you could lose the ranger outfit and we could both freak them out!"

He laughed again. "I think not!" he said, as he put on his shirt but left it unbuttoned and slipped his daypack over his shoulders. The shining badge on his shirt pocket made it official. He was indeed a ranger. And the nametag read, "Brian Collier." I tapped it with my finger. "Good to know you, Brian. I'm Giacco."

"Neat name, Giacco! Same here, good to meet you too." He turned and I followed him along the main trail just a short way before he veered unexpectedly onto an overgrown path that would go unnoticed by most anyone else. It dipped below the tree line and kept descending until it opened to large stands of old-growth trees and broad meadows. That's what I liked about the eastern slopes of the Cascades. It wasn't as claustrophobic as the west side.

On the far side of the largest meadow, I saw a trail going back up into the mountains. When we reached the very top there was a large clearing. The tower loomed above us. It was built on solid rock, its legs anchored with steel straps attached to steel footings bored into the stone. A few scrawny pines were scattered around, but none was more than half the height of the tower. Eight guy wires, two from each leg, were strung taut at an angle from the top of the tower to large turnbuckles that disappeared under the brush into the ground. I plucked a wire. It didn't vibrate. But I did.

The lookout cabin sitting on top of the tower seemed to reach for the sky. Luckily, there were real stairs with landings and not just a ladder. Nevertheless, the seven flights of stairs did me in. Pipsqueak had no problem. For a little runt, she certainly had a big-dog stamina and a bigger-dog attitude.

It was only 10 feet square, but the small cabin was well equipped, with a little cook stove that also provided the only heat in the place. The walls came up to the waist on all four sides. The rest was screens and windows up to where the pyramidal roof began. A CB radio sat on a countertop. Across from that was a bed. It was small, yet looked larger than the usual twin bed.

Brian offered me a seat on the bed while he pulled up a stool. He stretched behind him to open a cabinet and retrieved a round, squat, tin can, like one candy might come in. He opened it and pulled out a small pipe resting on top of some green buds with purple hairs. He packed a bowl and held a match over it while he took a few short puffs and then a long one. As he held his breath, he passed it to me.

Two long drags were all it took to get me zonked! Brian's green eyes now had a red tinge to them. Then he stood up and grabbed a pair of binoculars from his daypack. He handed them to me. He held up a second pair lying on the windowsill. The two of us got lost for a while zooming in on all 360 degrees of the breathtaking vistas.

I lowered my binoculars. "Well, with all *this* for company, I can see why being alone isn't all that bad."

"Oh, yeah," Brian said, "But there's nothing like human contact!"

CHAPTER 98
October 1974

We stood there about five feet apart and looked at each other. We smiled at the same time. We raced to see who could get their clothes off first. I won. He had a knot in one of his laces and couldn't get his boot off. I stood in front of him, slipping an ankle behind his, tripping him backwards onto the bed, kneeled down, undid the knot, and pulled off the boot and sock. His shorts were already down to his knees, and I did him the favor of pulling them completely off.

For the next three days, we had human contact. It was some of the most intense human contact I ever had. He made love with every particle of his being.

We experimented with the tantric sex that had always eluded me. I sat in a half lotus position, leaning back slightly and holding myself up with my arms. He lowered himself upon me slowly and carefully, guiding me into him, stopping now and then to breathe deeply, and relax. I slid in effortlessly.

He scissored his legs around my hips and reached forward to grab my shoulders and pull me up to him. Our chests touched and his cock rubbed against my stomach. We held each other tightly as he pushed down harder. I raised my hips and arched my back trying to accommodate him. I thought I would cum any second. When he felt me swelling inside him, he said, "Stop! I'm too close!"

He kissed me hard. Then he said, "Push your chest into mine. Breathe with me."

And we began to breathe together until our inhalations and exhalations were in sync. Our cocks were no less rigid, but we had managed to control ourselves. We stayed in that position a long time. It was wonderful feeling ourselves as one, our bodies clinging to each other, our breaths one breath.

"Feel the energy running up your spine," he said. He slipped a hand between us, grabbed his cock, and pinched it hard just below the head. I couldn't help but clench and unclench the muscles under my balls. I couldn't hold out much longer. When I felt him shudder, I felt a hot river of cum explode from my cock. Or so I thought.

Much to my surprise, there was no cum. I thought that was impossible, but it was true. Neither of us had ejaculated. Yet I felt for sure we had.

"The internal climax!" Brian explained. "The eternal climax!"

We made love often. We made love passionately. But we'd never cum. During the day, we'd walk the nearby trails doing ranger-like things, with Pipsqueak happily following close behind, or running ahead to lead her pack. We checked for glowing embers at every campsite, picked up trash, and of course, always looked for any signs of smoke that might indicate a conflagration in the making. There were none, though we did walk through a scorched area of a small recent fire. It still smelled of smoke and ash and the aroma permeated our clothes.

While we hiked, we talked. I would mention Madras. He would mention Pondicherry. I would talk about Dehra Dun; he'd talk of Hardwar. It seems he had pretty much taken the same routes through India as I had. But his travels were more extensive than mine. He had trekked into the Himalayas, had been to Bali, Borneo, and all sorts of exotic places that I had never been.

We talked of gurus, different spiritual paths, and the Dharma. When I asked him if he had found a teacher, he was very reticent, so I didn't pursue it. Conversation came so easily. Every utterance launched a response, which launched another response, each one getting us higher and higher. Time seemed to stand still. Before we knew it, we had done his rounds and headed back to the lookout.

A large, black rubber bladder hung from the lowest crossbeam in the sunniest part of the tower. The water it held would be at its warmest. There was enough for two short showers or one longer one… if we showered together. That, of course, was the option we chose. It was nice lathering each other up all over, then rinsing off just as the water turned cold and we laughed and jumped up and down trying to shake off the chill. Then we bounded up the stairs in time to watch the sunset. True to his words, the mountains were ever-changing, ever-amazing!

The last night Pip and I stayed with Brian is difficult to talk about because few words can describe it. The CB radio crackled, and Brian fine-tuned it to the right frequency. The supply helicopter would be coming the next day along with his supervisor. It was time to continue the trek I was supposed to be doing solo.

That night, Brian got me totally worked up with a slow and methodical erotic massage. He used a fragrant and slippery oil, and his hands worked every part of my body until my muscles felt like melting butter under his touch. He sat on the bed in a half-lotus and held his hands out to me. His green eyes looked at me with longing. His aura beckoned me; almost hypnotizing me. I straddled him but he sensed my hesitancy. "Brian, brother," I confessed, "I've never been fucked before. This is a first for me!"

"Trust me," was all he said. His eyes locked onto mine, and I did.

The entrance of him, even though slow, was painful. He saw it on my face. He stopped and let me get used to him. He told me how to breathe, how to send the exhalations to the right muscles so they'd relax. Then he pushed in a bit more, stopped, made a motion of pulling out, but pushed back in and went deeper.

I worked hard at total surrender. I finally succeeded, but it was like one of those bad acid trips where it's so scary, you'd rather give up and die than fight it. I knew the secret was to relax. To struggle was hell. To relax, divine. It worked.

He felt good inside me. So right inside me. He grabbed my hips and pushed me down on him as he slowly lifted his hips in the air. I felt bolts of lightning all the way up my spine.

Suddenly I wanted to be an active participant, not just a passive receiver. I felt my ass tightening around his cock and riding it in a nice rhythmic wave. I couldn't tell who was fucking who, which might have been the objective all along. Brian smiled. He knew what was going on. It excited him. His face was ablaze. I grabbed the back of his neck and brought his face up to mine. I pushed my tongue through his already parted lips, and deep down his throat.

"No!" he said breathlessly, pulling away. "I'm so close, Giacco, stop!"

I pressed him to me. I wanted to feel his skin under mine. "Feel my breath. Feel my heart. Breathe with me. Relax."

We stayed there squeezing each other into each other as hard as we could. Almost desperately. And we did get into a rhythm. But it was much faster than previous times. It kept increasing in pace and intensity. Our chests sweaty against each other, our cocks so rigid between us.

We both started breathing harder and making sounds. Nuanced moans and sighs, a rich language in which there were hundreds of words for pain and joy and passion. They were really shouts to each other to become one. To be one person, not two. To feel unity and oneness and connectedness. To become the same person, even if just for a moment.

I couldn't help it, but I had to kiss him again. The tongue can tell so many more things to someone while inside their mouth than it can outside. And I had a lot to tell Brian. I kissed him with a fury, incapable of getting enough. He kissed me back with wide-eyed urgency. The translation to other parts of our bodies was immediate.

With sharp thrusts of his hips, he exploded inside me, and I exploded between us, and both our brains exploded together in a cloud of euphoria that floated to the pyramid hovering above us. And for the first time I got to hear what Pipsqueak sounded like when she howled.

We were up before dawn. The mountains were incredibly beautiful. They put everything in perspective and there was a common understanding that what had transpired between us had been magic. This had been memorable. There were no anticipations. There were no expectations.

Brian walked with Pip and me as far as the meadows. He looked so dapper in his full uniform. He said he was taking a job for the winter on a ski patrol in Vail.

"What? You're not smart enough to get a job as a lifeguard in Hawaii! Masochist!"

He laughed. We exchanged addresses. He hoped he'd be working the Sawtooth again next year. If he did, I'd better be sure to hike up and cause some trouble.

We hugged and exchanged the hippie handshake. He didn't let go my hand but pulled me to him and kissed me with a tenderness that revealed what had gone unspoken.

He said, "Giacco, I'm not trying to sound high falutin' or anything, but you know what we have is permanent, don't you? It's permanent because it's infinite."

In the mountains, all alone, you can do, feel, or say anything you want, and the only reaction might be a shifting shadow.

He started to say more, but I hushed him with my fingers. "Brian, everything is needless to say. Trust me. Everything is needless to say. And for that I thank you!"

I walked backwards a few yards, imprinting Brian on my brain. I yelled, "Peace to you, brother! Be well!"

He called back something barely loud enough to hear. It made me stop in my tracks. I thought for sure it was, "Jai Satchitanand!"

With too many questions roiling around in my brain, Pip and I hiked back to the main trail. So much for the "being alone" challenge. But what a great time! I left feeling I had a much greater understanding of the yin, though I never considered myself a particularly yang person. What Brian taught me would come in handy many a time. With both women and men.

We spent a night at Oval Lake. It was all glacier melt and ice cold. Pipsqueak dove in once after a stick I threw and turned immediately back to shore. As she violently shook herself, she said, "Fuck the stick! It's freezing, you asshole!"

We decided it was time to go home. If I hadn't spent three days with Brian, I would've gone all the way to McAlester Peak and over South Pass. But I would have never had it differently. I'd have years to explore the North Cascades. I may have had only that one opportunity to explore Brian. It's a good thing I took that opportunity, because I never heard from nor saw Brian ever again.

I knew somewhere behind Oval Peak was the Oval Creek drainage, which would eventually lead us to the Twisp River. We could follow that home if we could find the pass. I looked at Pipsqueak and said, "Home, Pip!"

She looked up at me and tilted her head. Then she darted off.

"Wait for me!" I yelled. I followed her over rocks and little creeks and up impossible slopes of loose rock that made you slide two feet down for every three feet up. Eventually she led me to a ridge that flattened out. Actually, it was the hollow between Hoodoo and Oval Peaks. Another half hour and it would be pitch black. We would spend yet another night in the mountains, and I hoped no one was worrying back home.

I plopped down, letting my pack drop off my shoulders. Oh, how they ached. And my poor, poor, little doggies. How they were yelping! I was too tired to pitch the tent. I had just enough energy to feed Pip and feed myself a couple of the okanomiyaki pancakes Lois had made for me. A lifesaver. No one should ever go backpacking without some.

I sat there on the ridge encircled by majestic peaks. In the very far distance, I saw what must have been a lantern. It was Brian's lookout. Was he surveying the trails in search of me? I thought about using my flashlight to send a message. He might be able to see the light through his powerful binoculars. But the only morse code I could remember was SOS. and I didn't want to send him on a wild goose chase in the middle of the night.

The only other option was to start a small forest fire, an option I immediately discarded. So, I sat still and tried to meditate. But my mind was all ragged and jumbled. I thought I could get control over my thoughts through my breathing. I couldn't. Brian kept interrupting me. So, I meditated on Brian.

Pipsqueak was jumping at the bit as soon as the sun rose. She ran forth and back, hurrying me to roll up my sleeping bag and to get going. She trotted over the ridge into some brush. I saw no path whatsoever, but I followed her anyway. If I hadn't had long pants on, my legs would've been bleeding from the deep scratches. At first, I thought Pip was taking a trail meant only for dogs, and I thought that was very inconsiderate of her. But as usual, she surprised me by leading me to a very decent trail that led all the way down to the Twisp River.

We walked down the dirt road that in five miles or so, would become the paved Twisp River Road. At that junction, a truck came by and told us to hop in the back. The driver was an old geezer, maybe one of those cowboys who had come up with Chettie and Nate to mock our Dome. He seemed to recognize me, but I couldn't be sure it was him without his sunglasses and cowboy hat. He let us off at the bottom of the dirt road that led to Do and Lo's farmette. Pip jumped out, immediately knowing where she was. I thanked the old man.

He said, "No problem. Gonna come up there agin' when the snows come, ya know! I gotta see what it looks like all caved in!" He laughed as he drove off.

Pipsqueak ran full speed up the long driveway to announce our arrival. When I caught up, Lois and Donald were standing there along with Joel, Nate, Chettie, and Ben. Their expressions changed forth and back between smiles and scowls.

"We were just about to send out a search party for you!" Lois reprimanded, letting Pip jump into her arms for licks and hugs. "You said you'd be back yesterday at the latest!"

I was very moved to see them all standing there, concerned for me. Missing me. It made me feel that there were people in this valley who would look out for each other. It made me feel loved. I hugged each of them and said I was sorry I made them worry. Do led us into the house. I brought up the rear. As I walked by them into the living room, I patted Susie the pig, lying in the middle of the floor.

Donald said, "Christ, you stink! You'd better take a shower immediately!"

I said sarcastically, "You mean in this zoo you call home, you can tell?"

Lois grabbed me by the collar and pulled me close to her. She sniffed me all over.

"I smell yarrow. I smell fir and moss. I smell campfire. No, wait. I smell forest fire! I'll be damned! I smell forest ranger!"

She brought her face close to mine and just stared, waiting for some kind of response. Lois was one of those rare beauties in face and figure, but with an intuition and intelligence that was almost scary. I simply smiled broadly at her.

She respected my silence.

I gave Pipsqueak a big thank-you hug and let her lick my face. She looked up wistfully at Lois.

"Pip says she'd go back with you into the high-country any time you like," Lois translated.

Joel gave me a ride back to The Dome. He offered to let me take a hot shower at his place and spend the night, but I said I needed to spend the night at home. Joel drove down the hill and I walked into The Dome. I unfurled my sleeping bag on top of the bed. I got undressed and slipped into the bag. I would take a shower in the morning. Tonight, I wanted to smell the forest ranger on my skin.

CHAPTER 99
November 1974

Gradually, almost imperceptibly, new people were entering my life. A new family was forming.

It seemed to be true that everyone was interchangeable. Somehow, I always managed to find the people I needed to fill my needs. Oh, Hunga Dunga would always be the family of my heart chakra. Who could ever replace any of them?

It's just that it *is* all a play, a *lila* in the *maya*, a cosmic dance of illusion, and no matter what or where the theater, characters come forth one by one or sometimes two, just as I need them to fill a particular role. And they, likewise, are more than welcome to cast me in the roles *they* might need. It's nothing manipulative or premeditated. It's organic and natural. It's what humans do. We seek to satisfy our primitive and functional need for connection. Sometimes we do it in the least expected ways. There is a strange magic about it I like.

I still love all the people who have come into my life no matter if I left them, or they left me. I will always love them. But new people were now filling the void and I already wondered if these were the people I would leave, or would leave me in the future. People I will always love. Even if I should never hear from nor see them ever again.

Was Joel going to be one of them? He was my best friend in the valley. We did most everything together. And that was a lot.

This was the beginning of the social season. Except for a few crops, most everything that could be grown and harvested in the Methow's short season, had been. The hay had been baled. The dry wheat scythed. The fruit picked. The root crops cellared; the berries jammed. The handcrafted houses crafted enough to get them through another winter. Now was the time to kick back, have potluck dinners, play parlor games, make music and, in general, party!

Jim Hutch became a good friend. At first, his gruff and bearish manner intimidated me, but after his wife left him for the man she'd been having an affair with, whose wife was having an affair with a man married to the lady at the post office, he was more vocal about distancing himself from the Second Milers, and joining the ranks of the "alternative" ones.

He's the one who turned me on to Ed and Vicki, Jet and Judy, Do and Lo, Mark and Marianne and a lot of wonderful freaks who had been much more successful at keeping a low profile in the woods than the Church of Manna. In fact, as the weather began to turn wintry, all kinds of colorful characters came out of the woodwork. Everyone was surprised to learn that they were not destined to live in isolation, but as part of a growing community of like-minded hippies. In Twisp, long hair or handmade clothes did not define "hippie." It was defined by attitude, politics, tolerance, and, of course, drugs.

The demographics of the valley were changing quickly. However, there were very few middle-of-the-roaders. There were the old, established families: the orchardists, ranchers, farmers, and their kids. Lumped in with them could be the more recent arrivals of Bible-thumping families and gun-toting survivalists.

Then there were the left-leaning, organic, environmentally conscious, socially conscious, outrageously pinko, commie-acting hippies. That was it. Those two groups. I had never lived in a more polarized population.

The only people I can think of who straddled the two groups easily were the Porters. Through their music and community involvement and their well-deserved stature in the valley, as well as their conservative dress, they could speak both languages fluently, and both sides would listen. But they were really hippies at heart.

It was ironic that the fundamentalist Christian community, which comprised the majority of the valley's population, should be so judgmental about the hippies. Many of us, even those with kids, did not believe that a relationship had to be sanctified by a church or a state to be valid. Just love. Hippies had already had their fill of promiscuity and orgies. But the god-fearing "Christians" could not allow themselves to commit such heinous sins. However, they did have a convenient loophole, marriage.

As soon as one began an affair, they felt compelled to get a divorce and remarry. Affairs were always short-lived. Too long an affair was anathema. A short affair, followed by a divorce and a wedding, was considered acceptable. A short affair was a forgivable indiscretion. A long affair was a major sin. The "Christian" community accomplished the same thing the hippies did, albeit through series of serial marriages. But what a series!

In a town so small, it was impossible not to run into your ex and his or her new partner. Therefore, it was in everyone's best interest not to hold a grudge. Many a time I'd go to the Antlers to listen to Nate, Ben and Chettie play, and someone would start pointing out people of interest.

"See that woman over there dancing with the guy in the orange cowboy shirt? Well, the guy in blue dancing right next to them is her ex-husband. He's dancing with his wife who used to be married to the guy sitting next to the piano, who also used to be married to the woman dancing with the man in the orange cowboy shirt." Of the longtime residents of Twisp, there were very few who hadn't been married at least twice. Many had been married four or five times.

Have a brief affair. Get divorced. Remarry. Have another affair. Get divorced. Remarry again. As long as you were married and weren't a "swinger," it was sanctified. In a town so small, people went around the circle so many times it was not unusual for a foursome to be seen around a table in which the two men had been married to each of the women and vice-versa. Unlike those unclean, immoral, living-in-sin hippies.

We preferred to hang out with kindred spirits, which included some of the Second Milers who were christians with a small "c." And even they were surrendering to bouts of what became known as "Methow Madness."

It was in a town so small, suffering from Methow Madness, that Joel and I had our first disagreement. He had heard all my stories and about all my adventures, most in pursuit of self-realization. He felt he had missed out on so much and wanted to make up for lost time. He accused me of not really thinking of him as a hippie but as a dilettante. I strongly objected. But he insisted I give him more credit for being capable of outlandishness and rebelliousness. I thought this was wonderfully strange coming from a military career guy.

I invited him up to The Dome to spend the night. After all, in The Dome, as in the Sawtooth, all alone, you can do, feel, or say anything you want, and the only reaction might be a shifting shadow.

When he arrived, I had two small hills of cushions directly beneath the Star. In between was an upside-down apple crate covered with a batik Lana had made that served as a tablecloth. Naturally, it was a design of flowering phalluses, though you could only tell that if it were hanging on a wall. On top of the cloth was some incense and the little square of foil that Lee had slipped me just before he left. I lit a candle. The aluminum reflected the flame just right.

"Got any beer on tap?" Joel joked as he walked in.

"Nope!" I said. "This is an alcohol-free zone! But I do have some of the finest herb in town."

"Well, light one up," he said, plopping himself down on a hill of cushions and adjusting them until they suited him.

I did. I took a long drag and passed it across the table. The flame of the candle singed the hair on my arm.

Joel said, "Ouch!" for me, as he moved the whole apple crate a foot back.

"What's this square of foil?"

"I don't know!" I said in wonder. "Lee gave it to me before he left, and I haven't opened it."

"Enough, Giacco! Open it. Now!" Joel ordered as if I were a private, or whatever the lowest rank in the Air Force is.

"Yes Sir! Right away, Sir!" I answered mockingly. I carefully unwrapped the foil and laid it out flat. There were two very small squares of plain paper. No design, no cartoon characters, no color. This was unusual, but knowing The Friends of Perfection and their master, Eli, they had probably conscripted Owsley to brew them their own reserve batch. I knew it would be good. But would it be too much for Joel?

"So, what is it?" Joel asked.

"Acid," I replied. "LSD."

"You think I won't take it, don't you? You think I'm not up to it, don't you?"

"This is not a dare, Joel. It's only an opportunity to go on a mission. Should you choose to accept this mission…"

"I do!" Joel shouted.

"This tape will self-destruct in three… two… one…! Cool," I answered, "But knowing Lee, this is going to be too strong for a first trip. Let me get an exacto knife and cut one in half." And those were exactly the wrong words to use.

I got up to rifle through the toolbox. When I came back with knife in hand, there was only one square of paper on the foil.

"Hah!" said Joel triumphantly.

"You asked for it!" I teased. I moistened my index finger with my tongue, picked up the other square, and popped it in my mouth.

It was pure, thank god. Because it was a doozy. It came on so gently that when we lifted our heads an hour later to see how the other was doing, neither of us could talk. I was the first to regain the power of speech.

"You OK, Joel?"

"When my eyes are open," he struggled to form the words, "I keep falling into the Star. I'm afraid I'm going to break through the glass and die. When I close my eyes, I get sucked into this whirlpool and I can't get enough air. But I'm on top of it, Giacco. Don't worry."

"Don't be on top of it, Joel! That's the secret!" I said, hoping he trusted I was a good guide. "Fall into the Star, go down the whirlpool. I promise the other side will astound you. Just let go. I am here to catch you."

"Thanks Giacco. I do trust you. But do me a favor, please?"

"What's that, Joel?"

"Could you either turn down the stereo or put on a different album."

I started laughing so hard I thought I would asphyxiate myself. We had no stereo! We didn't even have electricity! Joel was definitely on a trip. But I got up and went to the far end of The Dome, made some noise, and flipped a dinner plate over. I returned and said, "How's that? Is that better?"

"Much better!" He said. "That's much, much better!"

I lay back down on my cushions stifling a giggle. We listened to the Quaking Aspen's new album. I let him trip and allowed myself to go to the other side. It was clarity beyond clear. Everything was needless to say. I felt we were both peaking at the same time. I raised myself up just a bit to check on Joel. His eyes were closed. I watched as a voyeur. He opened his eyes and looked right through the Star just as a big three-quarter moon came into view.

I watched as his eyes flooded with tears that flowed like rivers down his cheeks onto the cushions. He whispered, "Oh, my god!"

He looked over at me. His eyes said it all.

After the peak, coming down is sort of nice. Still high enough to really trip out on things without freaking out, it's often a feeling of well-being and total ablution. We took a walk around the deck, marveling at the wind through the trees, and the moon, bright enough to see across the valley. We saw what a truly beautiful place this was. We saw the beauty in each other. We went back inside and tripped out on the knots in the logs, the magic of the "sweet spots," the taste of freshly brewed mint tea.

And through it all, Joel kept saying, "Don't you feel it, Giacco?" Thinking he meant what a trip all these things were, I kept saying, "of course." We lay back down on our cushions. "I mean don't you feel it? Aren't we in sync? Don't you feel what I'm feeling?"

"Joel, really, I think so!"

"Well, why don't you do something about it then?"

Now I was lost and didn't want to be. "Uh, uh… what am I supposed to do?"

"Damn you, Giacco! You know! Do I have to make the first move?"

"Ah, ah… hmmm, hmmm." Light bulbs were going on in my head. Then off again. Then on again. Could this be happening? Joel was the kind of man you kept for fantasies. Fighter pilot, military uniforms, tractors, and Jeeps, bib overalls with nothing underneath, a logger with an inner-thigh wound that was in desperate need of attention and I'm the only one around. Flash Gordon! Tarzan! That's who Joel was. I wasn't sure I was ready to have a fantasy become a reality. But I had no choice.

Before I knew what was happening, Joel was unbuttoning my shirt, removing my shoes, and unbuckling my belt.

"If I haven't read you right, then just please remember you could destroy my life here in the valley if this ever got out!"

"If you have the slightest doubt, then stop!" I said.

"I can't, Giacco! Can't you feel it? As strong as I'm feeling it?"

He was naked by the time he said the sentence. He hovered over me, ready to do a push-up, but gently lowered himself down until his body was covering mine. Almost as soon as his cock touched my stomach, he came all over me.

"Oh, my god, Giacco! It was too exciting! I couldn't help it! I'm sorry!"

"Whadya talkin' about? I came too!" I lied, and surreptitiously smeared his cum all over my chest to make it look true. "See?"

In relief, he let his full weight rest upon me. We lay there cheek to cheek.

He whispered in my ear, "Now am I a Hunga Dungan?"

The next morning, we drove down to Joel's house, where we took a hot shower together. We scrubbed each other all over, but when I went to give him a kiss, he turned his head. I would be patient. The kiss is the most difficult for a curious straight man. He was new at this. He had made a huge leap. I wouldn't push it.

The phone rang and it was Wes Williams. He said they were having a very important meeting at the Ranch, and it was essential he be there. I thought the timing was extraordinary and hoped Joel had completely come down from the acid. The meeting was at 10. We had a breakfast of fried eggs and russet potatoes. I washed the dishes while Joel went up to the Ranch.

When he returned, I'd never seen him more angry or worked up. He was ranting and raving until I calmed him down enough to get the skinny on what had happened.

According to Joel, when he arrived, the chairs were already in a circle. All the Second Milers were there except Hutch, who had officially disassociated himself from the group. One chair was vacant. It was for Joel. He took a seat and looked around the circle.

"So what's up, guys?" Joel asked. "What's the meeting about?"

Wes Williams spoke. "Joel, all of us are very concerned about your welfare. We spoke to Hallie and know she is filing for a divorce. First Jim and Andrea, now you and Hallie.

This can't go on. This is not the Lord's work."

"And this is not any of your goddam business!" Joel lashed out. "What's between Hallie and me is between Hallie and me. Stay out of it!"

Wesley tried to stay composed and ministerial. "Joel, we want to pray for you. And we want you to pray with us. Together, we can bring you back into the Lord's fold." Wes bowed his head and the others followed. "Dear Lord," Wes began…

Joel stood up. "You guys are a bunch of loonies."

Ben looked hurt. He said, "Even me, Joel?"

"OK," Joel said, looking at Ben. "Maybe you're the least loony of the bunch, but you're all brainwashed. Either that or Wes put something in your drinking water!"

Wes was starting to get hot under his invisible chaplain's collar. "And that's the other reason we've asked you here. We know you've been doing drugs. What kind, we don't know, but we know you are falling into a hell, that we can help you out of… if you let us."

"Drugs! Is that what this is all about? You think I'm taking drugs? That I'm getting high?"

"Yes!" said Wes confidently. "You are spending too much time with Hunga Dunga. You are spending too much time with Giacco. You have fallen into their devil's trap! We can help you fight the addiction! With the Lord's grace, we can stop the drugs!"

Joel went ballistic. "So you think I'm into drugs and that I spend too much time with Hunga Dunga and Giacco? Do I have that right?"

Once again, Wes nodded in the strong affirmative. Joel paused just long enough to achieve the greatest effect. Then he blurted out, "You're absolutely right."

A slight gasp went around the circle.

"Not only am I smoking weed and taking LSD, but Giacco and I are lovers! We have as much sex as we can, every day! So put that in the middle of your prayer circle and pray for it!"

Joel tossed the folding chair aside as he walked stiffly out the door. No wonder he had come speeding down the road, skidding into the driveway. No wonder the hairs were still upright on his forearms.

"Joel," I said, "we had sex once! What you said took a great deal of courage, but it may have also been stupid. And dangerous!"

"I thought you were into the truth, Giacco. Be true to yourself and all of that! You mean we aren't lovers?"

Maybe I wanted it to be true. Maybe I didn't. I was confused, but I didn't want to say it wasn't true if in time it might turn out to be true. I felt there was a glimmer of hope, Joel could prove to be the one. The only man there had ever really been for me was Michael. But I'd heard nothing from him or from the school districts I'd written. Could I take the chance of losing something in the here and now when I knew I might never hear from nor see Michael ever again? I selfishly hedged my bets.

"Yes, Joel, we are lovers." After what he'd done, I couldn't very well leave him looking foolish.

As if to clarify our relationship he said, "So we only had sex once. We'll have it again tonight. And tomorrow night. And the next night. And we'll be lovers, right?"

"Sounds like the adventure of a lifetime to me, Joel."

He ran out the front door to his Jeep. I ran after him. "Where're you going?"

"May as well get it over with right now!" he said putting the Jeep into gear and driving off. I didn't know exactly what that meant until late that evening when he finally showed up.

"Where have you been? What've you been doing?" I asked looking at the clock. He told me.

He had gone to every friend we had in common to tell them the news. If he saw them in town, he'd go right up to them and announce that he and I were now lovers. He never really waited for a reply or reaction. He just told them the fact, and left.

He drove up and down the valley, bursting in through each door and with the maximum shock value his voice could deliver, he said, "Giacco and I are lovers. I hope you can deal with it!" Then he'd leave as excitedly and quickly as he had arrived.

He ran into the Porters' barn where they were feeding the geese. Joel took Chettie and Nate by the elbow and said in the most dire earnestness, "Giacco and I are lovers. We just want you to know that!" He turned around and left before Nate had a chance to give his historical account of Alexander the Great. But Joel never stayed long enough to do more than shout the headline like a newsboy.

Joel loved the whole idea of shocking everyone with the news. He relished in his own rebelliousness and outrageousness. The more shocked he might make people, the more satisfied he felt.

There was just one problem. Except for the Second Milers, no one was shocked. Then again, all the friends we had in common were freaks. Even macho Hutch didn't flinch. He just said in his southern drawl, "Oh, that's nice." But Joel was already out the door on his way to "shock" the next household, or so he believed.

I did move in with Joel, though we spent an equal amount of time at The Dome. And we did sleep together every night. I loved feeling his body next to mine, draping an arm across his chest, having the lover's privilege to explore the speed bumps of his stomach on my way to his groin or most any other part of his body. The ass and the lips were off limits. Fucking was no big deal to me. But kissing was not part of our repertoire and I loved to kiss.

Our repertoire consisted of me getting him hard, then he rolling over on top of me, furiously dry-humping a while, and cumming all over my stomach within a few minutes. It was OK though. It was the idea of him. And I thought in time he'd learn. I thought more acid trips would help, but he insisted that one trip was enough to last a lifetime.

After he informed everyone he could think of, he waited for the bomb to explode. For the sky to fall. For the shit to hit the fan. He steeled himself and hunkered down for the inevitable doom. And he dared any one to give him flak!

I had images of being beaten up and tortured in as many ways as my active imagination could come up with. Maybe tied to the train tracks, except Twisp had no trains. Maybe shoved into a woodchipper. Maybe roped and hog-tied like a calf in a rodeo and then dragged through Barnaby thistle. Whatever the method, I was sure the men at the Antlers would be sadistically inventive.

How fortunate it was that after telling all these many people about our torrid love affair, Joel decided he needed to drive to St. Louis as soon as possible so he could be there for Thanksgiving. He sorely missed his kids and couldn't wait to see them. He also had divorce stuff to sort out with Hallie. He couldn't wait a day longer. How fortunate he was taking a trip at just this time. How very fortunate. For Joel!

He left me to face alone, whatever repercussions or recriminations he had expected or projected. And he had expected and projected the worst. I was paranoid for the first few days. I was angry with Joel for making me so vulnerable. Just my luck I'd have an encounter with some homophobic redneck. I had to be extra careful when I went into town. I was nervous about staying up at The Dome… where no one could hear you scream! At Joel's, at least there was a phone!

Much to my delight, but not surprise, our friends not only accepted us, but actually embraced us. And they knew that in this particular valley, they had been given a great responsibility. They were so protective of Joel and me, they abided, without exception, by the old saying, "Loose lips sink ships," or in our case, "If word gets around, they'll be run out of town."

Up at the Second Mile Ranch the same thing happened. Ben and Loretta pleaded with Wes and the rest that what Joel had told them was said in the confidence of the Lord. To violate that confidence was to put Joel and me at physical risk, a sin that would be as difficult to forgive as throwing lions to the Christians. Their emotional and eloquent challenge to be true Christians trumped anything Wes could come up with. If Wes were to maintain authority, he needed to be the best of the best. Which meant the quietest.

I spent Thanksgiving with Do and Lo, Jet and Judy, Mark and Marianne, and Jim Hutch. Large acorn squash stuffed with a medley of vegetables and swimming in butter and melted brown sugar, corn bread, salad, and green-butter brownies for dessert. Yum!

As we all relaxed, and I mean totally relaxed, into the cushions on the couch and chairs, we talked, joked, and felt very, very good. The lack of a turkey's triptophanic sleep-inducing qualities was adequately replaced by the trippiness of the brownies. When we were all totally blitzed, Lois said, "It's really too bad Joel couldn't be here."

Hutch leaned to the left and fell against my shoulder. I looked over at him. He said, "Men! What are ya gonna do with 'em!" And then we drifted into the rainbow prism of "The Dark Side of the Moon."

CHAPTER 100
Winter 1974-1975

It was going to be a white Christmas. A very white Christmas. The valley glistened. For those of us who lived in the hills, the snow was so deep, people had to climb out their second-story windows to shovel the snow away from the front door.

Up at The Dome, the snow was higher than the deck, which meant it was at least four feet high without drifts, and it would stay that high all winter. During the day, it would melt a little in the bright winter sun. Then it would freeze again at night so the next morning, the area you had already shoveled, was so slick that walking just a few yards was a frustrating and tiring affair. Then thankfully, a few inches of fresh snow would fall and bring back a little traction.

I thought getting around the valley would be a huge chore. But instead of being stranded on our own little forested islands, the snow provided a wonderful mode of transportation. So much so, that the town did not plow the two-block long main road but packed it down flat with a grader.

In front of the Antlers, snowmobiles angle-parked. They were such obnoxious things, but I admit, useful at times. In front of the Broken Spoke, pair after pair of cross-country skis leaned against the building. The skiers and the snowmobilers glared at each other. Each accused the other of ruining their trails.

The snowmobilers were of course the upstanding citizens who considered themselves natives of the valley with unlimited access to everything not fenced in. The cross-country skiers were the unclean intruders with second-class status. Any self-respecting citizen had a snowmobile. Snowmobilers were the salt of the earth. We just hoped they didn't salt the trails on their way.

Donald gave me an old pair of wooden cross-country skis he had lying around. He taught me how to ski the Nordic way. He taught me about waxes and how to wax them properly. I learned how to ski well. I loved it.

He tried to teach me how to telemark. I did not learn that at all. No matter how much I practiced, I never learned to telemark. It was *my* ineptness. Donald was an excellent teacher. In fact, back in New England, he used to *be* a teacher. A graduate of Brown with a degree in literature, his first job was teaching high school English in a rural New Hampshire town. I asked him why he stopped teaching as we skied down the hill. Donald filled in the blanks.

Lois was a junior in that high school. As soon as they saw each other, there were fireworks. Lois was one of those unusual beauties. At seventeen she was luscious! Not perfect, but remarkably sexy. Incredibly, they managed to carry on an affair in secret almost until Lois' graduation. They were caught just before the big event. Lois' parents threatened to press charges.

It was so ugly, that his teaching contract wasn't renewed. Donald had to skedaddle as far away as he could. Self-banishment to the nether regions… namely, Twisp. He was probably driving up the Methow Valley at the same time Lois' class was moving their tassels from one side to the other. Their caps flung into the air, all of them except one.

Lois took *her* cap off and held it at her side. The tassel swung glumly. As her classmates stepped down the bleachers, Lois was left standing alone. Her gown stuck out from her belly in a beautiful dome. Her parents were stunned. The crowd all stared at her. Murmurings, whisperings. Lois ran across the football field, wailing loudly and crying all the way home.

She ran in the front door and up the stairs to her room. She removed her gown, untied the pillow, and let it fall to the ground. She laughed, and then grabbed a small suitcase that was already packed. She hastily threw a letter on the dining room table and ran out the back door. Her best friend K.C. waited for her behind the gas station. K.C. drove her to the Greyhound bus station in the next town, which took her to Boston. There, she boarded a flight to Seattle with the ticket Donald had sent her.

"The rest is history, my sweet Giacco," Donald said, as we began to ski into town. I had never been called "sweet" before. It sounded nice, though I would have preferred something more like "rugged" or "intrepid."

Our feet in their bindings pushing forward toe to heel, we trudged up hills and then crouched low with our poles under our arms to glide down them as fast as we could, building up momentum for the next hill. Nate Porter came by on a snowmobile. He slowed down to say hi. Do and I thought Nate was more of the cross-country skier type than a snowmobiler. Then we saw he was pulling a trail groomer behind him.

"Need a tow?" he yelled while tossing out a rope. Donald grabbed on first, and then I grabbed on behind at a safe distance. Nate went a bit faster, always looking behind to see if we were still upright. So far, we had only made our own trails through deep snow. Skiing on a groomed trail seemed effortless in comparison! I would almost use the word "groovy," but I won't.

We let go of the rope on the long hill into town and waved bye to Nate as he sped off. The trail he was making made it so easy. And Nate made it so easy for a few other snowmobilers to emulate him. And that was a typical, beautiful, Porter way of bridging the two seemingly distinct groups. Soon there were groomed trails everywhere. Snow became the rapid transit system in the valley.

We skied from farm to farm up and down the valley. We skied up Elbow Coulee to Patterson Lake and up the Chewack and Wolf Creek trails. Sometimes during the day, skiing high on a hillside, the sun was so bright and the reflection off the snow so strong, we could take off our shirts and come home with a tan. The exercise made everyone healthy and glowing, and the valley seemed like Eden even in winter.

Jet and Judy were having everyone up for a winter solstice celebration. They lived farther up the valley than anyone else we knew. However, Hutch had a snowmobile too, joining the very few who could talk sense to the most recalcitrant rancher. Between Nate and Jim, six of us managed to get towed all the way to within skiing distance of Jet and Judy's octagonal log cabin set way back in the woods, without having to spend a night camping on the way.

They invited Sadie, someone we'd heard about all summer, but hadn't met. She was a perfect addition to the tribe. She was cute, funny, athletic, and a woman of many practical skills that I wished I had. Like plumbing, welding, and bricklaying. She was also a burned-out activist lawyer. It was something she tried her best to keep secret.

But everyone had a secret. For all practical purposes, I was gay, and maybe Joel was, too. Donald was technically a statutory rapist on the lam. Sadie was an ACLU trouble-maker with credentials. We all grew pot in some secret place or another. We all had secrets. We all got along perfectly fine.

We wondered what Jet and Judy's secrets were. We found out one of them when Jet pulled out a guitar and started strumming. When he was warmed up, he performed some fancy finger work. We were all very impressed. On cue, Judy started singing the Patsy Cline song, "I Fall to Pieces."

Everyone perked up and paid attention. Judy, who looked like a perennial 14-year-old with rosy cheeks and pigtails, had a voice that made the rafters ring. She had perfect pitch and great range. Jet was a masterful guitarist and sensitive accompanist. In addition, during the bridge, he yodeled. He began softly and got louder as the yodel got more intricate. Then the yodels circled down the scale, fading to the precise note with which Judy began to sing the next verse.

We hooted and hollered. I took a toke on the pipe that was being held out to me. I exhaled. Judy melted into the female counterpart of Zietar! I thought of how we used to drive around The City putting on a harmony. Zwagen's windows rolled up, we'd sing at the top of our lungs. What fun!

I got up my courage to do a harmony with her. It sounded like we sounded great! To me. But even if we didn't, it didn't matter. It got us so high! She naturally soared above me, but I have one of those barbershop quartet voices that sound best in a supporting role. We really did sound good.

The food was delicious. The company delightful. The conversation titillating. And the entertainment a truly unexpected surprise. What other surprises lay in store?

Before we left, we told Sadie about our full-moon ski trips.

"A week from tomorrow," Judy said.

"Usually we start out at Joel's," Nate said.

"You mean Joel and Giacco's," Lois corrected.

"Oh. Sorry," Nate said. Sadie gave me a knowing and understanding look. I suddenly felt very conspicuous.

"Then we snow-shoe or side-step up to The Dome," Hutch took over. "I think snow-shoein' is easier. Carry the skis on your shoulders."

"Nah, I like the herringbone. Bet I'll beat ya!" Sadie said, already excited by the idea, and letting us know she wasn't a novice.

Hutch laughed. "You got a bet, woman! Anyway, when we get up to The Dome, we throw down a few shots of cognac or tequila or whatever comes along, smoke some weed, and head out over the Saddle Pass."

"It's sweet from there," I told Sadie. "All downhill around the Second Mile Ranch, down the Black Pine Lake road to the bridge where Poorman Creek Road ends and crosses the river. That puts us on Twisp River Road, and from there it's a gentle hill down to Lo and Do's."

"Takes about five hours if we don't get hung up in The Dome," Donald added. "But it's worth it. The peaks are absolutely amazing in the moonlight!"

"And if we do get hung up in The Dome, which is easy to do," Lois warned, "the dawn is incredible."

We gathered at Joel's on the evening of the 29th. The trip was more wonderful than any of us had described. Who could adequately describe a moonlit, snow-covered night, surrounded by glowing peaks, unless they had the time to describe every individual snowflake and every crater on the moon? A Currier and Ives print might be a good beginning. The iconic beauty of that trip made us euphoric. It may also have contributed to the beginning of a romance for Jim and Sadie.

Though it would be only our second full-moon skiing party, it was already a tradition that would be resurrected every winter for years. The only thing that bothered me was that when the witching hour came and it was time to go home, everyone went home with a partner or spouse. I was the only one who went home alone to an empty house or an empty Dome. I didn't even know in which one I really belonged. The Dome represented communal. Joel's house represented community. We were part of a very loving and supportive community. When we needed help to stand up a wall or put on a roof, help was readily available, much like an Amish barn raising. I couldn't help think that maybe this was devolution and not evolution. That we were turning back to the nuclear family unit, held in such high esteem by the Flag.

If we could stop the regress just where it was, that would have been bearable. But should it disintegrate any further, we'd fall right into the hands of Uncle Sam's dream: where individual initiative, and of course, lots of consuming is required by the corporate overlords. It's our patriotic duty to climb the social and economic ladder and buy, buy, buy, despite who might get hurt along the way. If that happened, then all of this had been for naught.

Being alone at this time was not healthy for me. It gave me too much time to think, and though I had the means to stop thinking, I seldom did. That's why that fifth day of the New Year, I was so glad to see Joel's Jeep coming up the road. I ran outside.

He jumped out and ran to the front porch. He hugged me and swung me around. It felt great! Maybe this trip had been just the right absence he needed to sort himself out.

He filled me in on the details of his trip. He had told Hallie that she could have everything. He would contest nothing. There was no need for lawyers. The only thing he wanted in return was permission to visit his kids and maybe, when they got older, they could come out and spend part of the summer with him.

Hallie agreed. That was enough for Joel to return a seemingly happy guy.

I filled him in on our full-moon ski parties, and winter solstice at Jet and Judy's. I told him we'd been invited to the Porters to play Dictionary Thursday night, and the following night, dinner at Do and Lo's. In fact, the calendar on the kitchen wall was circled with all kinds of get-togethers and the refrigerator magnets held in place hand-made invites to parties celebrating made-up holidays. Like the après solstice party at Mark and Marianne's or the milking party at Ed and Vicki's, where you could milk a goat and drink a glass fresh from the udder.

In the middle of the fridge door was a poster announcing the debut of the "Right Up Your Valley" trio, the 1st of February at the Spoke. On it was a black and white photo of Jet, Judy, and me, but the quality was so poor it looked like a large head with two small appendages peeking out from behind.

At first, Joel was pleased with our very full social calendar. But every event we attended; we were treated as a couple. Instead of the ostracism Joel had been waiting for, we had been treated with respect and hospitality. Being a couple was a non-issue. Even Ben and Loretta had surreptitiously invited us to have dinner with them.

The effect it had on Joel was completely opposite of what I had expected. Instead of being relieved there were no explosions, he freaked out. He hated us being a "couple." The word "partner" was even worse. "Sidekick" was the most he could handle, even though no cowboy worth his bowed legs would ever think to question that moniker. How quickly he had forgotten that he was the one who called us "lovers!"

Joel had the good sense not to go around reneging on the "confession" he had made to our small world. He knew it would make him look bad. But with the right logistics and precision bombing, he could at least balance everything out! He brought a whole new definition to the word "ambiguity." To keep people guessing which way he was bent, Joel went to extremes.

He'd leave me at the house, drive into town, and get looped. He became a regular at the Antlers and the Spoke. He'd pick up any available lady and fuck her. He was extremely successful due in part to his undeniable sex appeal, and the fact that his intoxication made the most homely of women seem desirable. He also felt compelled by Christian mores to sleep with each one at least a few times in a row before finding a way out and going on to the next conquest.

His reputation as a ladies' man spread quickly. He had such charm to augment his good looks, just a seductive smile flashed across the bar at some similarly inebriated lonely woman would seal the deal.

I got used to him not coming home until mid-morning the next day. I never questioned him. On the nights he was too tired to go out, he would slip into bed with me. I could tell our sexual relationship was nearing an end, because I sensed he was fighting hard not to develop an aversion to my touch.

Lois and Marianne felt sorry for me. They were privy to the gossip meant only for the ladies, but they shared it with me. Among the women, Joel was a catch. Women vied for his attention as soon as he entered the bar. He always entered exuding a rough, self-reliant, country-like confidence. It must have taken a lot of energy.

It wasn't really necessary. Just a small circle of friends knew about us. Most of the townspeople didn't, and Joel was considered a man's man. Among those who *did* know about us, including the Second Milers, there was incredulity. Maybe it was just a passing phase. Maybe he was overcompensating. Maybe he was just sorting things out. Whatever it was, he mystified all of us. And that was his mission. His goal. To re-invent himself into a man of such mystery, he would defy classification. He was eminently successful.

This went on all winter. Our friends looked to me to give them a clue as to how to act toward Joel. My clue was to ignore his wanderings and play ignorant and let things unfold as they might. I only spoke highly of Joel. He was a good man. He was my best friend. And I felt one day, he would find the true balance he sought.

But I wanted out.

One night Joel came home alone. A rarity. I wasn't there. He waited a bit, then snowshoed up to The Dome. When he burst in, he was winded, his cheeks all red, his muscles all pumped. I was reading, or rather rereading some passages by Krishnamurti and when I saw him, I fought not to melt and let my attraction to him veer me in a direction different from the one I was intent on following.

"What's going on, Giacco? Why aren't you down at the house?"

"We need to talk, Joel."

"You hate me, don't you? I disgust you! I disgust myself!"

"No way, Joel! Don't say that!"

"Well, what then?" he asked.

"I just want to be best friends again," I said. Joel actually looked hurt, which surprised me.

"Does that mean you're not coming back to the house?"

"I'm staying up here, Joel. The snows will be melting soon. I need some alone time again before the gang comes up."

"Do you think we can really rewind the tape and go back to being best buds?" he asked.

"I'm sure of it, pal. Rewind it to the night we took acid and pause it there. One night of being gods. Now a lifetime of being friends."

"Giacco. How do you know for sure we can do this? That *you* can do this. What we've been through and all. How do you know for certain we can be best friends?"

"Because, Joel," I answered, "all my lovers end up being my best friends."

CHAPTER 101
Spring 1975

Richard had been unusually incommunicado all winter. I noticed he made regular deposits into the Church of Manna account at the bank, but other than that, nothing.

It didn't matter. Writing or forwarding mail had never been his strong suit, and I was sure I'd see Zwagen any day now, bouncing up the dirt road and packed with Hunga Dungans. Instead, one day I saw a red Honda hatchback with two people in it. I didn't recognize them through the clouds of dust until they were almost at The Dome.

It was Trudy and Jeff! They jumped out of the car and hugged me. Jeff looked better than I remembered him. His hair had gotten longer, and he seemed more buff. Trudy looked just the same, wide-eyed Alice in Wonderland. But she was not one to let a looking glass decide her adventures. Beneath that exterior of surprised innocence, I could hear the gears of her mind working, and they always worked so the results would benefit *her*. But I was glad they were here. I had spent enough time alone.

"Damn, are we glad to be here!" Jeff said in relief. "The City was getting way too much for me. Especially Big Blue."

"Totally nutso." Trudy said. "We're up here for good! We told Hunga Dunga we weren't coming back and if they wanted to see us ever again, they'd have to come on up to The Church of Manna."

All of a sudden, my desire to be alone came back. I could go screaming into the hills like a lunatic, or I could be a reasonable guy and just shoot myself. I did neither and helped them unload the car, smiling as much as I could. This was better. Much better.

As soon as they settled in, Jeff started designing a little cabin where he and Trudy could be alone. After all, we had 120 acres of land. Why crowd into one dome.

I was all for it, for selfish reasons. But I wondered if this didn't require an act of consensus from Hunga Dunga. When I asked about that, Trudy just stared at me and said, "Giacco, you know that would just be opening a can of worms!" I took that to mean they had made a unilateral decision, and I was not to question it.

Looking over Jeff's shoulder as he drafted plans for their shelter, I could envision the time when the land would be dotted with many little cabins. I thought that's what I wanted, too. My own little cabin down at the old original homestead. However, seeing Jeff actually planning to make it happen shook me up. We'd just all be neighbors. Maybe good neighbors, but where would it go from there? To the individual? I, me, mine? Shouldn't the focus be on the communal? The common good? Community was OK, but communal was better. To focus on the individual was definitely going backwards. We should be expanding from the communal to the global! What was happening? I was sure it was a government conspiracy of some kind.

Over the next few weeks, I introduced Trudy and Jeff to the rest of the valley. By the rest of the valley, I mean the part that liked us.

Most of my friends liked Trudy and Jeff simply because they were Hunga Dungans. But Lois withheld judgment until she got to know them better. Lois had an intuition bordering on the psychic. Trudy seemed to gravitate more readily toward those she thought might be of use to her, even if she didn't particularly like them. Lois was the first to recognize this trait in her. It would take others longer to see it, but eventually they did.

Shortly after their arrival, I asked Trudy to take a walk with me to the Saddle Pass. I was so hungry for detailed news of what was going on at Big Blue. In her incredibly organized brain, she gave me the lowdown in outline form, as if she were preparing for a thesis. I took mental notes.

Psylvia was no longer a lesbian. Roxy had been abusive to her and Hunga Dunga refused to let Roxy in the house. Little Lily was more their concern than Psylvia. Lily had been exposed to about the most eccentric people there were, but without exception, all their eccentricities were expressed with love.

Roxy didn't care at all if Lily were present or not when she would lash into Psylvia, which was recently fairly often. I think it was the first time Hunga Dunga ever kicked someone out and banned them from the house. It was a shame. I really thought Hunga Dunga needed a few lesbians. We might learn a lot. It would balance us out. A few more straight men would be nice, too. But once again, it reminded me not to generalize. Big mistake. There was good and bad in every group.

The only ironically beneficial result of Psylvia's affair, was that she got electrolysis and had all her body hair removed. That explained the smooth legs the last time I saw her. Now she was a Madison Avenue billboard beauty, as Roxy *insisted* she be. Her beautiful trophy bitch. We couldn't figure it out. Psylvia knew she was always beautiful to the rest of us, hairy legs, mustache, and all. Fuck billboards.

It was also ironic because Nick would have loved Psylvia to shave her legs once in a while, as well as her upper lip, but he was too sensitive to Hunga Dunga's political correctness and rampant feminism to ask her to do anything without fearing a backlash. In a way, while others were still holding a grudge toward Nick for cheating on Psylvia, I knew where he was coming from, though I'd be hard pressed to say he wouldn't have cheated on her anyway.

After a couple of weeks of skulking around the house, Psylvia became her old wonderful self. Her new body attracted many men. Hot men. Nice men. Hot nice men. She had her male suitors by the basketful. She kept her ladies in waiting. And bisexuality never had it so good.

Affirmative action greased the wheels for Psylvia to become an apprentice plumber. It was a union job and paid well. In fact, she became the first female *master* plumber in the state of California. Unfortunately, shortly after achieving the rank of *master*, she hurt her back. But the L&I claim was eventually approved and she lived comfortably on that, and like a good communard, gave all her earnings to Richard.

She also announced that though she would continue to support the Church of Manna in Twisp, she herself had no interest in going back up to the land ever again.

Oh, how not surprised I was as I listened to Trudy tell me the next piece of juicy news.

Lizzie had come home one afternoon all excited, and acting the clown as only he could do, called a family meeting, and announced he had bought Big Blue from our landlord.

The family let that sink in. It took a while. Then all hell broke loose.

"What the fuck!" Bobby screamed.

Baird was at his heels and to show his shock, called Lizzie by his given name. "Matthew Ridgeston, do you fully understand what you've done?"

"Don't freak on me!" yelled Lizzie. "Look at it this way. Instead of Hunga Dunga paying rent to some stranger who only tolerates us because we keep the place up, and pay the rent on time, now the rent comes to *me*! I'll charge only what it costs to cover the mortgage. And I have great ideas for remodeling. With Nick's skills, this place could be a palace! It's going to be a win-win situation! And the house is ours!"

Nick perked up when he heard his name. How easy it was to stroke his ego.

"You mean it's *yours*!" Baird corrected. "It's in *your* name, not Hunga Dunga's. More importantly, where did you get the money?"

"Baird, you didn't think my *pater* would lend me money if I were going to buy property in somebody else's name, now did you?" He said it with the air of an aristocrat. "Be real! And besides that, Greenleaf is doing fantastically!"

"You mean *The Free Food Conspiracy*, don't you?" Larry interjected angrily.

"Larry. The legal name on the license is Greenleaf. Remember? So we could cash food stamps? The Free Food Conspiracy is only what *we* called it!"

Ellen leaned in to add, "And some of us still do!"

Larry and Ellen got up and left the room.

David screwed up his face at Lizzie and said, "Ya know, Lizzie. Sometimes I just don't get you. What happened to 'eat the rich'? You can just go eat your chichi clients and choke on them for all I care!" And David left the room.

Greg, as usual the unruffled one, said, "Listen folks. It's no big deal. We just traded one landlord for another. We just have to separate Lizzie into playing two roles. As a part of Hunga Dunga and as our landlord. Is that so difficult?"

With that, everyone went to wherever they chose to dwell on an answer. Or not.

"What did Ziets say?" I asked Trudy. "Wasn't he outraged?"

"Oh, Giacco!" Trudy looked genuinely concerned. "There is so much cocaine in that house it's scary. Lizzie's really gotten into it, but he handles it OK. He says a line in the morning gets his workers energized. But Richard is doing way too much. He doesn't know when to stop. And Richard, of all people, is keeper of the books as well as the coke, except for Lizzie's private stash.

"When Lizzie gave his spiel about buying the house, all Richard meekly asked was, 'Can I still keep the books?' Lizzie assured him nothing would change."

"Damn! That is not like Richard!" I said. "I need to get him up here for a while!"

"I wish you could!" Trudy seconded. "Anyway, all he does is stay at the warehouse and play with numbers while everyone else is out working. God knows what he's doing when he's alone!"

I let out a big sigh. "Is that it? Any other surprises for me?"

"Lana's gone," she said.

"Lana! What happened?"

"After that family meeting, things were never the same. One morning, Lana walked into the kitchen and simply announced she was leaving. She said, 'People, I love you all. But I can tell the curtain is slowly closing on this little show. Besides, there are just too many goddam queers in this city! I need some real men!'

Some people looked hurt, especially Bobby and Alvoye. 'Nothing personal, jeez!' she added before she walked out the door with a carpetbag and a backpack."

"Wasn't Luc offended as well? And Larry? Baird?"

"Luc had visa problems. He went back to Paris. Baird knew of Lana's sexual frustrations and nymphomaniacal tendencies, so he definitely wasn't offended."

"And Larry?"

"Oh, this'll really kill you!"

I couldn't take much more anyway, so likely it would.

"Duck moved to Santa Rosa."

"Santa Rosa? Why Santa Rosa?"

"Just because it's not in The City but he wants to be close to it. It's a new place."

"Did he move in with anyone I know?" I asked.

"No. He just rented a little cottage all to himself."

"But why?"

"He said he couldn't take the infighting any longer. He wasn't going to put up with it and he wasn't going to fight any more. He was just going to remove himself from it all. He asked Richard to come with him, but Richard said he needed to keep the books."

Trudy and I walked back down past the spring to The Dome. Jeff was all excited. He wanted to show Trudy the spot he thought would make a great building site. I was a bit put out that he didn't bother to consult with me, but I figured I'd wait to see where it was before putting up a stink, just on principle.

It was at the far end of the bench in a small grove of aspens. It was totally out of sight unless you stood on Zietar's Knoll. It was a very pretty place, though the exposure was less than optimal.

Our land *was* truly beautiful, with thick forests and vistas all the way to Canada. The other side of the Twisp river tended to be more barren until you got way up the river near Jet and Judy's. But city slickers that we were, we didn't realize the prime land was really on the other side of the Twisp, the side with the southern exposure. Plus, it had better views.

Maybe we should have looked around a bit more. But what was done was done. We knew we had no right to complain. We did get smart in enough time to build The Dome and grow the garden in the very best spots for maximum sunlight. So, we did good after all, I guess.

Besides, no matter where the land was, what side of the valley, or what the exposure, the cost of it was skyrocketing. Speculation had wildly inflated the market. What originally cost us 350 dollars an acre was now easily worth three or four times that much. It made me secure to know that we had ironclad articles of incorporation that prevented us from selling the land, except as a whole, and only to another nonprofit corporation approved by all the trustees. I was one of them.

Trudy interrupted my thoughts. "You don't have a problem with us building something here, do you?"

"I think it's a thoughtful site, Trudy. And a pretty one."

Jeff approached. "Like it, Giacco?"

"Sure, Jeff. It's great!"

"Great place to meditate, eh?"

"I'll take The Dome any day," I said.

"Yep, she's a trippy one, she is. Hey, listen. Looks like there's not going to be a garden this year, so I'm going to sink a holding tank and run some PVC pipe to here. Makes sense, eh?"

Somehow I felt this conversation wasn't thoroughly soliciting my input, yet sad as it was going to be, I didn't see a garden happening without Richard, Chuck, and the usual gang, and who was I to deny them water.

"Yeah, sure. If for some reason we decide to put in a garden later, we can always figure something out."

I tried to avoid all possessive pronouns. All of us at Hunga Dunga did, or at least used to. I always did around Trudy, in particular. She had a quick sense of ownership, which I refused to encourage. It was as if she were always trying to call dibs on something before anyone else could. Then again, Richard had called dibs on Zietar's Knoll, and that hadn't bothered me. I did my best not to be a hypocrite. I'd have to give some thought as to why Trudy always seemed to press my less-than-enlightened buttons.

I told Jeff, "Put a T-fitting where the pipe ends at the garden, and cap it off for the time being. Then we always have the option if we need it. Are you going to buy the pipe you need to extend it from the garden way out here?"

Jeff and Trudy just stared blankly at me. Then Trudy spoke up. "The Church of Manna has money, doesn't it? When we left, we told them no more pooling of our money except the percent that goes into the land fund. You have a checkbook. You can write checks."

The Church of Manna account, down at the bank, was very solvent. I hadn't drawn much on it at all. But this didn't feel right to me. I wish a few of the others were up here.

"Gee, Trudy, I think for that to happen, we need to call home." Trudy knifed me with her eyes.

Jeff said, "Giacco, that is our money in that account. We've been contributing all this time!"

Trudy turned to Jeff. "What do you mean *we*, oh blissed-out one? You haven't put in a Canadian nickel!"

"Trudy," Jeff said quietly, "I think you should remember the Word."

I could see Trudy breathe hard and fast. And not in the *soooooo-huuunng*, calming sort of way. I felt a fight about to erupt.

"We'll come up with something," I said, hating to see the peacefulness of our surroundings disrupted. "Let's draw up a list of materials for everything you need and figure out how much it's going to cost."

Jeff, being an engineer and analytical, thought that was reasonable and was placated. Trudy quietly seethed.

"Hey," I said, trying to lift the mood. "It's Friday night. I gotta bring you guys into town. You won't believe it. It's a whole new Twisp!"

That night the Spoke was rockin'! Bob had booked a really tight band from Wenatchee. Just a cover band, but they did maintain a very hot, body jangling, bumping, grinding beat with little pause between songs. They worked themselves up into a dripping sweat and the crowd even more so. The vibes in the place were exceptionally friendly and everyone was dancing with everyone else.

Trudy and Jeff had such a great time, they started going there every Friday and Saturday night. I went with them sometimes. Other times I chose the Antlers because I liked the bluegrass of Ben and the Porters. When I tried to get Trudy to go into the Antlers, her first experience of it came hurtling back into her brain, and the frightening memories she had suppressed, resurfaced. No matter how much I tried to persuade her that it was safe now, she refused to enter the bar with me. She peeked inside and saw lots of cowboy hats and women in crinoline, and it freaked her out.

She said, "No way, Jose! I'm sticking with the longhairs!" That was a shame. The Antlers had really become fun. The rednecks still had red necks, but the influx of hippies and other newcomers had turned their fists into merely good-natured ribbing. As long as the discussions didn't turn to politics, everything was "apples," as Peter and Debra used to say. However, because of that first scary night we had at the Antlers, Trudy developed such an aversion to the bar she seemed scarred for life. She would only walk on the other side of the street, rather than in front of the place.

One reason Bob's Broken Spoke was doing so well was due to the new group of settlers from the coast. Most of them sincerely wanted to live in a peaceful, crime-free, healthy, beautiful place. For the most part, they were decent folk, humble, and hard working. But they were all very tight-lipped about how they were being funded. The truth was most of them were recipients of trust funds or just plain wealthy.

Then there was the specter of the ski resort, which had overly inflated the real estate market, and it was still inflating. This attracted speculators who were buying up as much property as they could afford, thinking they would make a killing when ground broke for the resort. Even those who just wanted to carve out a little niche in the country couldn't help being persuaded to buy more land than they needed if they had the moola.

The old families of the valley didn't know what to make of all these sudden newcomers and all this disposable income floating around town. They weren't hippies. They were all well-educated. The men didn't sport long hair and the homes they were building were not simple log cabins. Some were works of art. Five thousand square feet of art! The business owners didn't care if they were social liberals. Businessmen are true-blue capitalists. As long as the newcomers spent lots of money. As long as the newcomers employed their kids. That's all that mattered.

Most of this new wave of hip-but-not-hippie people chose the Spoke as their watering hole of choice. And this gave Bob the cash he needed to hire better and better bands, the result being larger and larger crowds. It was sad sometimes to go to town on a weekend and see the Spoke packed and hopping, while down at the Antlers, the same old crowd two-stepped to the three-piece band. It was a major indicator of the shift in valley demographics.

This shift allowed my crowd to walk forth and back between the Spoke and the Antlers with aplomb. If the Porters and Ben took a break, we'd go back to the Spoke. When the band there took a break, we'd go back to the Antlers. If both bands were taking a break at the same time, we went into the back alley where the smell of marijuana filled the air.

Jeff had given me a list of materials and estimated costs, which I sent off to Hunga Dunga. I expected an answer from Richard, but instead I got a letter from Baird. This was a good sign. For all of our disagreements and all the pain Baird had caused me, I knew he would be true to the traditions of Hunga Dunga. In short, Jeff and Trudy's requests were denied.

I tried to explain to Jeff. I admitted I didn't understand all the dynamics taking place in The City, but he and Trudy had to think of the Church of Manna as an extension of Hunga Dunga. Spending money on any development of the land, which didn't benefit everyone, went against the grain. Though Lizzie had been all for it, he was overruled. Besides, everyone had unanimously agreed to the Church's articles of incorporation, so what was there to argue about?

Jeff looked resigned, but Trudy was beyond irate. She insisted I return all the money she had given to Hunga Dunga that had been earmarked for the land. I ignored her. Instead, I walked Jeff about 45 yards past Shitters Hill, to where there was a big tarp covering a pile of leftover building materials. I pulled the tarp back. There were plenty of extra logs, and pieces of plywood and two-by-fours, and all kinds of hardware and bolts and stuff.

"Hey, Jeff," I asked, "with your creativity and ingenuity, don't you think you can piece together something suitable for you and Trudy?"

Jeff scavenged through the pile carefully. Actually, he was surprised we had so much left over. He said, "Ya know what, Giacco. This might do just fine!" But when he told Trudy, she was a stuck record.

"This is my money! I'll use it as I see fit!" But I had the checkbook. She didn't. And though I didn't lord it over her, she resented me for it.

"Trudy, really," Jeff implored, "we can make this work just fine. You'll see. I'll make this work!"

"You are such a wuss!" Trudy yelled at Jeff. "I thought you had a backbone! Obviously, Canadians are just too wimpish to fight for what's theirs. Or should I say mine!"

That was absolutely the worst thing she could have said. But Jeff quietly started hauling logs with Wilhelmina over to their building site. I helped Jeff as much as possible. I kept trying to appease Trudy by saying that if she would just rephrase her request to Hunga Dunga that they were building a "guest" cabin, that anyone could use and not a private home, she'd score points with everyone and probably could have her way.

Trudy would have none of it, even though I told her it would be simply a matter of semantics. No "guests" were going to come up. No one seemed likely to evict them while they were visiting. It would be virtually theirs, if not literally. No. She wanted her own piece of the pie called the Church of Manna.

While toking on a doobie behind the Spoke, Trudy met a man named Blake. They fell in love in a fog of smoke. It was a wonder he could see those big blue eyes, but he must have, because he was smitten with her exaggerated demureness and spiritual humility.

Not more than a week later, Jeff met Lueta. Lueta was a new arrival who had just divorced, after the briefest of marriages, the man whom Andrea had married after she divorced the man for whom she left Hutch.

Each of them moved in with their new partners. Lueta owned the old hotel in town. It was the largest building in Twisp and the only hotel, though defunct. It needed major repairs, but it could be restored to its original turn-of-the-century beauty with the right skills and lots of money. With the coming of the ski resort, it might turn into a lucrative business.

Blake owned the 40 acres adjoining Do and Lo's. At the bottom of his land, right on Twisp River Road, was a cute little house in good condition. That's where Blake lived. Trudy moved in, but her dream was to have a big home at the top of the hill where the views would come close to those of Do and Lo's. She cajoled Blake with her long eyelashes, and made it clear she expected him to make her dreams come true.

After short affairs, Trudy eventually married Blake, and Jeff married Lueta. I found it perfect that each of them had married a person who was independently wealthy. It was just too predictable. No one ever found out where Lueta or Blake got their money, but it never seemed to run out.

The pile of logs remained at their building site. Jeff had only gotten as far as peeling them. The clearing he made for the cabin soon grew over again. Except for the logs, and a small temporary lean-to, there was no trace anything had gone on or was even in the works.

By the time summer was in full swing, I was once more alone in The Dome on 120 acres of land.

CHAPTER 102
Summer 1975

One day in July, Sadie saw me downtown and called me over. She said that a group of people was organizing to stop the ski resort. They needed a meeting place and since Hunga Dunga had been the first truly "alternative" group to spearhead the invasion of other like-minded people into the valley, she thought The Dome was both for practical reasons and symbolic ones, the best place to meet.

Ellen and David would have approved immediately. That's all I needed to know. Sadie even paid for our road to be graded so no more oil pans would be slashed, and thereby removed the only deterrent to accessing The Dome.

I could not believe the number of hippies who showed up at that first meeting. Where had they all come from? From Libby Creek, Lower Beaver Creek, the three forks of Gold Creek, Cow Creek, and French Creek way down in the south valley of the Methow. They came from the small valleys whose rivulets drained into the Chewack. Some people came from as far away as Mazama itself, at the far north end of the valley, where the planned ski resort was to be built.

I was stunned. The Dome had never been filled before with such a crowd of longhairs. It felt like old times, though old was only a couple of years ago. Not surprisingly, neither Trudy and Blake, nor Lueta and Jeff, attended.

People who'd never been up to The Dome before were impressed. It really was a perfect place to meet. Far enough away from prying eyes or eavesdropping, large enough to hold a hundred, and acoustics that didn't require yelling to be heard. The Dome became headquarters for the Council and meetings became more frequent as the fight became more intense.

Sadie was remarkable. Without her, nothing would have happened. She filled us in on what was really going on. She had access to, or knew how to find, the information about everything. Permits that had been filed, environmental impact statements, the names of the people on the board of the Aspen Corporation, statistics on how Aspen's other developments had impacted those communities. We were quietly gathering evidence.

The Aspen Corporation, in cahoots with small town realtors suddenly catapulted into the role of developers, started an organization called Citizens for Planned Growth, which was really just a euphemism for "rape the land." They had tons of money and spent it on PR campaigns meant to persuade the old families, who had thousands of acres to sell, to join their side. Some did, others were skeptical. But the sons and daughters of those old-timers realized this was their chance to become millionaires.

First thing we had to do was raise some money. We all donated as much as we could and realized it was not enough to do much with, except print and post a few flyers around town. We did realize we had enough money to buy a roundtrip ticket to Hawaii. So, we bought one and held a raffle. We sold tickets under the auspices of the Methow Valley Citizens

Council, a name Sadie came up with and that sounded very respectable. Even people *for* the ski resort bought tickets, not fully understanding where the money was going. Bob at the Spoke sold a slew of tickets for us. He was perfectly happy with the crowds he had and feared that if a destination ski resort were built, complete with bars and restaurants and hotels, he could easily lose out.

After subtracting the cost of the ticket to Hawaii, we'd made almost $13,000. With that money, and Sadie's contacts, we were able to hire independent hydrologists and geologists, unlike those that were on Aspen's payroll. We would make our arguments based solely on science and not on any personal preferences of how the valley should look in the future.

Aspen told the Citizens for Planned Growth that unless they could build a resort that handled 50,000 skiers a day, it wouldn't be cost-effective for them, and they would move on. Citizens for Planned Growth squirmed at the thinly veiled threat.

Fortunately, both Nate and Chettie Porter were regular contributors to the Methow Valley News, and their reporting or commentary was always considered fair, balanced, and bipartisan. When they published the findings of the independent hydrologists and geologists, the valley may as well have experienced a magnitude 8.0 earthquake. It split the valley down the middle.

The findings indicated that the water table was already very low. As it was, the valley had experienced frequent droughts over the last 50 years. There was no way the water resources could handle 50,000 skiers a day. Ten thousand was the max. More would destroy the shallow aquifers. Just the human waste alone generated by so many people, would end up polluting the streams and ground water upon which so many people depended, since most everyone except those that lived in town relied on wells. In conclusion, the independent study strongly advised that Aspen downsize its plans.

You couldn't go into town without overhearing discussions and arguments about the revelations. The tensions ran so high, the mayor called a town meeting at which Aspen could defend its position of building a resort that had to accommodate 50,000 skiers a day.

The gymnasium at the high school was packed to standing room only. The mayor asked Sadie, as representative of the Methow Valley Citizens Council, to speak. She lobbied for a more reasonable solution to the valley's desire for growth. She was calm, succinct, and eloquent. With her confident and firm demeanor, she let Aspen know they'd met their match. When she finished, whistles, hoots and hollers rolled through the crowd. Or half the crowd.

Then the representative of the Aspen Corporation took the podium. He was already flustered as he walked up the stairs to the stage. He told his side. He presented his statistics. He gave an impassioned speech about how many people would benefit from a destination ski resort. But people weren't stupid. They knew only a handful would truly benefit. For every seductive statistic he gave, Sadie was able to quash it with statistics derived from a more reliable source.

His face got beet red. His job was on the line, to say nothing of the millions Aspen had already spent buying up land where the "village" was to be built. At one point, he was actually making some headway among the old-timers. They imagined a comfortable retirement. Their children imagined buckets of money, which took priority over buckets of safe drinking water. Then he made a fatal mistake.

He said, "Look, people. This is not a vote. We have the permits to break ground!"

Sadie stood up. "Correction! You only have the permits pending EISs done by an *independent* agency, not your own employees! Maybe we should have a vote to see where everyone stands!"

The Aspen rep blew up. "Listen, little lady! I don't know who you think you are, but we are so big, that if need be, we can relocate 3,000 employees into this valley. In a month, they'll be eligible to vote, and we will totally outnumber all of you tree-huggers and regressive hippies. And did you ever hear of deodorant? Well, use it!"

The children of the large landowners yelled, "Yeah! Tell it like it is!" However, their parents looked across the gym at one another and suddenly felt a huge dislike for the man standing at the podium and all he stood for. How dare he threaten them! And the old timers sniffed their armpits to see if they were the ones he was talking about. Their saying was, "If ya don't smell, ya aren't workin' hard enough!"

At the next meeting of the Citizens Council up at The Dome, we were stunned to see among the crowd a number of older people, ranging from their 60s into their 90s. A strong coalition formed between the old timers and the freaks. The divisiveness in the valley, which had slowly been disappearing, reappeared with a vengeance. The vengeance this time, though, was between fathers and sons, mothers and daughters, corporate capitalists, and the environmentalists. The length of your hair, or if you had electricity and a TV, was not a factor.

Aspen brought in its attorneys. Sadie brought in her pro bono lawyer friends. Each step Aspen moved forward, we pushed them back two, with injunctions and endangered species and letter-writing campaigns to the paper, legislators and anyone who could forestall Aspen if only for a while. It became a matter of who could outlast whom.

We won. By the end of the summer, Aspen left for a valley north of Vancouver, Canada. They didn't leave without telling us how sorry we'd be when we saw what they would do at Whistler. Real estate prices stopped artificially inflating, but there was still so much interest in the valley, that land values continued to increase, though at a much slower rate.

Sadie was spent from her efforts, but we were all grateful to her. She said she couldn't have done it without us, and took us off guard when she said she'd be leaving. She was renting out her farm and going to Harvard to get another law degree. This time in environmental law. But she promised she'd be back. We did not dissolve the Methow Valley Citizens Council but kept it alive just in case. We had given shape to an amorphous and scattered group of people, and we felt we just might need it in the future as an entity around which to coalesce.

The Dome was once again quiet. I very intently lordwalked to the Saddle Pass and sat for hours contemplating my life and what I was doing with it. What would Miss Nancy Stein or the Department of Social Services say if they knew they were now paying me to be a political, environmental, and anti-corporate capitalist activist? I liked to think they would have approved.

Summer was almost over. Joel and I began hanging out together again, comfortably, as "sidekicks," without any questioning stares. Anywhere. We were once again each other's best friend. I confided in him that I felt I was being a slacker now that I wasn't in The City, and that there would be no Hunga Dungans coming up to work the land.

Joel just said, "Well, Giacco, maybe it's time you got a job!"

A job! Now that was a novel idea. But what kind of job? Even though there seemed to be some disharmony at Big Blue, I clung desperately to the values of Hunga Dunga. I felt deep down that those were the true American values, and the ones I wanted our country to have. They were the ones I wanted the planet to have. I was sure that values such as tolerance, selflessness, generosity, and kindness, would end all disharmony in the world.

Damn! Why not just post the Boy Scout Oath, Laws, Motto, and Slogan on every telephone pole and get it over with. If only they'd remove the word "straight" in the Oath, I'd feel a little better. And the "obedient" part under the Laws could do with a little revamping. But the Motto and Slogan were right on!

I was sure Hunga Dunga would work out their problems one way or another. But if Hunga Dunga couldn't maintain and live the values I thought we shared, I would sure as hell try my best to keep the traditions alive on my own.

CHAPTER 103
October 1975

One Monday in early October, Joel and I went into town. Much to my surprise, I had mail.

First, there was a postcard from Jon. On the front were two hippies standing in the foreground, a colorful bazaar behind them. They both had very long, matted hair. The guy was bare-chested wearing a lungi and had pierced ears and nipples. The woman was in a gold and red sari, with a tilak on her forehead. She wore a gold hoop in one nostril and a slinky of rings that extended from her ear lobes up to the top of her ear. She reminded me somewhat of Debra. Blond, radiant. The man looked anemic and in need of medical help, but he was smiling. Underneath them it read, "Greatings from India!" I thought two things. Much better! Now we're a tourist attraction! And damn, if they're going to print thousands of postcards, can't they afford a proofreader?

I turned over the card. It was postmarked a month earlier.

Dear, dear, Chazan,

I am back in India. I guess you can tell that from the card. Cute, aren't they? What the fuck! That should be me and Rose on the front. But I'm having a wonderful time and wishing you were here. Really! I really do wish it. On my way to Trivandrum and then catch the ferry to…

The rest was smeared and unreadable, but I knew he meant he was going to Sri Lanka. I was pissed. Well, not pissed, but jealous. Well, not jealous, but envious. Well, not envious, but damn that Jon!

There was also an official looking letter from the Thermopolis School District in Wyoming. I almost threw it out, but remembered it was one of the four school districts I'd written inquiring about Michael. It was stamped in red all over. It had gone to Hunga Dunga where who knows how long it withered before someone had the Boy Scout *trustworthiness* and *helpfulness* to forward it up to Twisp. To say nothing of the slogan, "Do a good turn daily!" It was postmarked about two weeks after I had originally sent out the letters. But I may as well have thrown it out because it read:

Dear Mr. Giordano,

We are sorry we can be of no help to you regarding your request. We have no Michael Taylor teaching in this district. We do have an application from him in our file and we did offer him a position, but it was never accepted. By law, we may not give out any of his personal information.

I hope this has been of some help to you. If you are employed by a school district in an administrative or teaching position, please let us know. This may allow us to forward his application to your superintendent.

Sincerely,
Mrs. Mary Quint,
Secretary to the Superintendent
Thermopolis School District #1
Thermopolis, WY 82443

Oh, yeah. Big help. I screamed at the letter, "You have been no fuckin' help at all!" Bev looked up at me over the counter. "Sorry, Bev." I tore the letter into tiny shreds, threw them in the trashcan, and stormed out.

By the time I got back to Joel's Jeep, he was already in the driver's seat. I had calmed down some, but Joel could tell something was wrong.

"What's up?" he asked.

"Aw, nothing! Just a letter from some school district."

"What? You thinking about becoming a teacher?"

"No," I answered, as I climbed in. I was getting unduly perturbed with all this "job" talk.

"You know, you'd make a great teacher, Giacco!"

"Thanks, Joel, but I don't think anyone would hire me looking like this, and I have no intention of cutting my hair."

"OK! OK! Don't get riled up at me! Just my take on things. Want to drive up to the Porters with me? I gotta pick up some eggs Chettie's saving for me."

"Sure," I said, "let's go."

I may have sulked for a few miles, but between the letter from Thermopolis and Joel's remarks, a seed had been planted and I decided to nurture it just a bit to see where it led. I had so much compost swirling around in my brain, there was enough to fertilize all sorts of seeds.

When we drove over the bridge that connected Twisp River Road with the Porters' farm, a feeling of peace came over me. Theirs was the perfect picture-postcard place. Geese, ducks, goats, chickens, two dogs, a cat, and a horse. Unlike Do and Lo's, where their menagerie wandered wherever it pleased, the animals here had their specific places to hang out. The chickens had their coops, the ducks their fenced-in pond, the dogs their houses, the horse a half a barn full of hay, the goats the other half. Only the geese ran around freely.

The house they lived in still had the original, red-flocked wallpaper in the living room, giving their home the distinct look of a brothel. They often joked about it but liked it that way and had no plans to redecorate.

Chettie and Nate greeted us enthusiastically, offered us a drink, and then Joel went with Chettie out to the chicken coop.

After they'd gone out the back door, Nate said, "Giacco, I'm taking a leave of absence this winter. Chettie and I are going to Central America."

"Nice!" I said, just a miniscule of envy hiding behind my voice.

"Chettie and I were wondering if you'd be interested in taking care of our place."

This was a wonderful opportunity, though I hated the thought of The Dome being vacant all winter.

"Nate, I know so little about animals and you have so many, but if you teach me what to do, I'd love to stay here while you're gone."

"Don't worry too much about the animals. Woody is staying in our little log cabin down by the river. He'll take care of the animals. But Woody prefers to stay in the cabin. He's almost unbearably eccentric at times. We just need someone here to keep the home fires burning." He thought about what he'd said and laughed. "That's just a metaphor, by the way. We do not want to come home to charred beams with only the chimney standing!"

I laughed, too. "Well, it does sound like a sweet deal!"

"You can help yourself to any of the canned fruit and veggies, and the root cellar is stocked with potatoes and carrots and turnips. You'll have a fresh supply of eggs every day and if you can master milking a goat, you'll have fresh milk, too."

Ed and Vicki taught me how to milk a goat and I loved fresh, cold goat's milk. Closest thing to mother's milk, not that I had an Oedipus complex or anything.

"You can use the snowmobile if you want to go up to The Dome. If not, we have skis and snowshoes."

"It sounds great, Nate!" I said. "And when is this all happening?"

"Oh, not for a while. We'll be here until Christmas vacation, and then we're off until spring. Don't worry," he laughed," we'll get in at least one rousing game of Dictionary before we leave."

I laughed, too. Nate knew how much I liked that game. And it was an honor to be invited to play because Chettie would only play with people who could really make it interesting and fun.

Chettie and Joel walked into the house.

"Giacco's going to do it!" Nate said, as if it took a great deal of persuasion.

Chettie said, "Oh, Giacco! That's great! We'll be able to enjoy ourselves so much more knowing the homestead is in good hands."

Chettie brought Joel up to date.

"Oh, man!" Joel said excitedly. "Just think of the parties we can have!" Then before Chettie could cast him a nasty look he held up his hands and added, "Only kidding! Only kidding! By the way, Nate, who's going to take your place at the school?"

Nate looked at me but answered Joel. "I wish it were Giacco! He'd be great in my Contemporary Problems class. But he doesn't have his teaching certificate. Shucks!"

Nate was a very cool guy and I have met none more intelligent. Jon came close, but

Nate was even more remarkable for immediate cerebral access to historical facts. But he just could not bring himself to swear. Maybe it was a leftover from his days in the seminary, but for the life of him, he could not utter a foul word. He'd try, but any words other than "shucks" or "phooey" or "darn" were not part of his swearing vocabulary. He slipped now and then, but always immediately covered his mouth with his hand as if that could stop the word from flying out of his mouth. Fortunately, Chettie was much more comfortable swearing and she made up for both of them. I thought they were a great couple.

Joel needled me, "See, Giacco! I told you you'd make a great teacher."

"Were you thinking about it?" asked Nate.

"I don't want to go back to school. Besides, where would I go? I'd have to move to Seattle and deal with all that crap, I mean phooey, and, well, I just don't know if I'm ready to take on such a chore."

Nate surmised, "Giacco, I bet most, if not all of your courses from Georgetown will transfer to any college around. Shucks, teachers are in such demand, colleges will do just about anything to get more of them out there. Some states are even starting programs where if you have a degree of any kind and teach for a full year, that at the end of the year they'll give you a teaching certificate."

"No joke?" I asked in surprise.

"It's true," Chettie said, "Washington has something like that. So do California, Idaho, Alaska, and I bet a few others. Nate gets monthly newsletters from Gonzaga with all the job openings in the Northwest. You should look them over."

Were these signs? Had I forgotten to pay attention? Had I been lordwalking more, would I have heard more distinctly, first Joel, then Nate, then Chettie talking to me about teaching? The hoe and rake in my brain started tilling the compost around what was now a seedling.

Joel and I hopped in the Jeep and waved bye to the Porters. Nate yelled, "We'll talk more about it when you come over to play Dictionary!"

"When is that?" I yelled back.

"The first Thursday in November! Put it on your social calendar! Can you make it?"

"You know I will, Nate. See ya later! Thanks!"

We took the back road over the Christianson's bridge to Poorman Creek Road, past the Second Mile Ranch, and back to Joel's.

"Want to hang out for a while?" Joel asked.

"Thanks," I said, "But I think I'll go up to The Dome. I need to do some thinking."

Even though I hadn't written Brian and hadn't heard from him either, I decided I needed some alone time to sort things out. I stuffed my backpack, grabbed some granola, instant coffee, dried fruit and condensed milk, my Swiss army knife, a flashlight, and my sleeping bag.

Once again, I hiked over the Saddle Pass, up to Black Pine Lake and headed toward Angel's Staircase. I wished Pipsqueak were with me, but this trip was unplanned, and I was anxious to get back into the Sawtooth.

I followed the main trail and had to hike forth and back a while before I found that short cut that led into the big meadows. I kept my clothes on this time.

I finally found it, and it was a quick downhill stumble to the meadows. On the other side I saw the trail that led to the lookout tower.

As I approached, I saw a ranger with binoculars to his face, searching the forests for signs of smoke. Looking up from this acute angle, I couldn't make out much. He was so intent on scanning the panorama, he was surprised when I yelled up to him.

"Brian! Is that you?"

He let the binoculars fall, walked out to the railing, and looked down.

It wasn't him. This guy was probably in his late 40s and though his hair was disheveled, it wasn't long and blond, and his eyes didn't have that glacier-green sparkle I was longing to see. I was disappointed.

He motioned for me to come up, though he was already starting down. I left my pack at the bottom. We met halfway at a landing.

"Hi!" he said. "You need help? Anything wrong?"

"No," I answered. "Everything is fine. I'm just looking for a friend of mine. He was the lookout here last season. You know him? Brian Collier?"

The ranger sat on a step and gestured for me to do the same.

"Yeah, I knew Brian."

"Knew? Did he quit?"

He looked down at his shoes and cleared his throat, then up at me again.

"Were you good friends?" he asked me.

I wasn't sure how to answer that. Does friendship require a defined length of time? Does the degree of a friendship depend on how well you know the details of someone's life? Or do a few days of intimacy warrant the title of "good" friend? I went with my heart.

"Yes, he's a good friend of mine, but we haven't been in touch since last fall."

"Well, no way to put it nicely," he said. "Brian was killed in a skiing accident last winter."

"What?" I cried.

"He was patrolling the areas off limits to skiers when some yahoo came out of nowhere and cut him off. He made a sharp turn to avoid him and ran smack into a tree. Died instantly."

It was my skin that first remembered Brian. His touch. His body on mine. His lips. Then my heart remembered Brian, and I dwelled in that memory a while. What a wonderful spirit he had. What a kind and loving person he was. I couldn't believe I would never see him again.

I tried to thank the ranger but had trouble getting the words out. He understood anyway and patted me on the shoulder in a well-intentioned but awkward attempt to comfort me. I climbed down the stairs, retrieved my pack, and started back up the trail.

I heard the ranger yell, "I'm sorry, guy. Really, I'm so sorry. It was a loss to all of us."

By the time I reached the main trail, I was crying so much, I could barely see where I was going. I thought that maybe I could metamorph myself into Pipsqueak and sniff my way to Oval Creek Pass. I only made it to Oval Lake, at the base of the mountain.

I sat down on a small rock at the edge of the lake and leaned back, letting my pack fall off my shoulders to the ground. I stared into the water. It only reminded me of Brian's eyes. I relived every detail of our three days together. And I cried some more.

I hadn't formally meditated in a long time. I thought this was the time and I wondered why it always took fear or sorrow to make me meditate, rather than joy or happiness. Why the incentive to meditate was always my path of last recourse. When all else failed, I always had *soooooo*, *huuunng* to still my truly rattled and baffled mind.

I held my fingers to my eyes and pushed hard. Then I started breathing slower with each inhale and exhale. I almost managed to free myself of thought. To free myself from emotion.

I failed miserably. I only got as far as concentrating on a mantra I'd been given when I was a kid. The mantra was the Boy Scout motto, "Be Prepared."

Be prepared for sorrow and pain.

Be prepared for the unexpected.

Be prepared to die.

Isn't that what the Goomer said in Vancouver?

Lois was leaning against her truck as I hiked the last few yards to the trailhead that ended in a tiny campground off Twisp River Road.

"Well, it's about time!" she said in mock chastisement, her arms akimbo.

"Lois! How did you know I was up in the Sawtooth? How long have you been waiting here?"

"Because whenever you can't be found, I know you're up there somewhere. I've been here about 20 minutes."

She walked over to me and gave me a big hug. I couldn't help it. I started crying again.

She sniffed me up and down. When she got back to my face, she hugged me again and said, "It's OK, Giacco. It happens sometimes. It happens to all of us. I'm sorry, really I am."

I had never told anyone about Brian. Though she may not have known the specifics, she knew enough. She never ceased to amaze me.

She gave me ample time to pull myself together. Then she said, "OK, now, hop in the truck. We're going to pick up Donald and then we're off to the Barter Fair.

"I'm wasted! I'm a mess! I just want to go home!" I protested.

"Giacco, the Barter Fair is just what you need. Get in!"

And off we went. We picked up Donald who looked at me in surprise, then at Lois.

"Lois," he said, with deep love in his eyes, "I just don't know how you do it!"

Lois wriggled over and shared the passenger seat with me. Donald hopped in behind the wheel. The back of the truck had sacks of garlic, onions, some crates of pears and apples, and I was sure somewhere, hidden appropriately, a nice variety of herbs, including our favorite one.

We drove over Loup Loup summit down to Highway 97, then north to Tonasket, where we took the turn-off west, back into the mountains. Near Blue Lake, we took another fork in the crushed gravel road until the gravel became dirt and the dirt became ruts and the ruts got deeper as if a wagon train had recently come through.

Finally, the road blended into a large grassy meadow beneath the towering peaks of the Pasyaten. In the distance was an enormous circle of tipis. Smoke drifted in small columns into the air, which was heavy with the smell of burning wood and incense.

Around that inner circle were tents, lean-tos, and other makeshift shelters. Hundreds of people were walking around from one camp to another.

The outermost circle, though it was more like a giant squiggly, if there is such a geometric form, was made up of a stunning variety of vehicles including decal-festooned VW buses, psychedelic school buses, horse trailers, trucks, cars, and motorcycles.

We found a place to park. That was easy. Anywhere you wanted was fine. We simply set up a camp in front of the truck. Lois put out some signs advertising what we had to barter.

That was what the Barter Fair was all about. There was absolutely no money allowed. Only bartering. It was like an Indian bazaar without the rupees. Complete with haggling, as required.

That's why there was so much continual movement. Freaks went from one camp to another to see what they could trade. Garlic was traded for potatoes. Apples were traded for plums. Echinacea was traded for mushrooms. Pot was traded for someone else's pot, or beadwork, artwork, or most any kind of craft imaginable.

Services of all kinds were offered from masseurs and masseuses to fortunetellers, herbologists, acupuncturists, reflexologists. Whatever service was needed, someone was there to provide it. And there were freaks who rambled about in the full regalia of whatever storybook character most changed their lives.

Or maybe it was the mescaline I traded for my canteen. I never saw so much buckskin in one place. Most of it sitting on horseback. Rugged, handsome cowboy hippies, their long hair blending in with the fringes on their vests. Princes and princesses in blousy pants made of batik or tie-dyed. Superheroes without their super costumes, all naked and powerfully beautiful. Wandering minstrels and poets looking like they had just walked out of Sherwood Forest. It was part renaissance fair, part wild-west show, and part rock festival without the rock, just mellow ballads, and bluegrass.

We had to barter for everything. A song might cost a hit off a joint. A massage might cost giving one back in return. A hand-carved pipe might cost a bag of mushrooms. A magic trick might cost whatever someone threw at the magician's feet.

We didn't even have to think of cooking. There were booths everywhere bartering veggie burgers, burritos, and frittatas. Pies, jams, and jellies. Chocolates, cheeses, and magic cookies.

We were hungry and went up to the burger stand. Lois said, "Hi! I'm Lois. What do you want for three veggie burgers?"

The woman answered, "Hi! I'm Suzan, with a 'z,'" She had a slow Southern drawl and emphasized the 'z.' "Where you people coming from?"

"We're from Twisp," Donald replied and introduced himself and me.

"Twisp! I've been thinking of moving down there soon! Good to know ya! Now what you got for my luscious burgers?"

Lois brought out a sack of garlic from behind her. She opened it up and the woman peeked inside.

"Garlic! I have garlic coming out of my ears! What else ya got?"

"That's all I have with me. I have some other stuff back in the truck. Onions, fruit. Maybe some weed?"

"I got weed coming out my ears too!" the woman laughed, "But I sure am into beads! You got any beads?"

"No," Lois answered in disappointment.

"Well, lemme see." Suzan pondered the situation, and then said, "Lois, I sure do like that blouse you're wearing!"

Lois stared at her. Then at Donald. Then at me. She shrugged and took it off, leaving her topless. Oh, that Lois. She was always the kind to take her shirt off her back for someone, though usually it was metaphorical, not literal. This time she literally took off her blouse and handed it over the counter. The woman put three paddies on her grill along with three opened buns to the side. We each walked away with a delicious burger and a drink in our hands. As we looked for a nice place to sit and eat, a few men looked at Lois, but admiringly, not lasciviously. Most of the women there were topless and it was no big deal. The same was true for the naked superheroes soaring around the crowd. We sat in a circle and enjoyed our meal.

We were there two full days and part of a third, and we were high on one thing or another most of the time. Lois promised that next year she'd bring exotic beads, lots of vintage clothing because that seemed in high demand, along with homemade ciders and wines, and anything else that might alter your consciousness.

But the bartering wasn't restricted to food, trinkets, and drugs. Some bartered on a much larger scale.

A VW bus in good condition traded for a plane ticket to Kathmandu. An acre of land was bartered for a pair of llamas. A large yurt was exchanged for a classic Airstream trailer. And one evening, as we walked around the inner circle, Donald and Lois persuaded me to trade my nice down sleeping bag for an hour with a Native American shaman. I didn't mind. We had lots of extra sleeping bags back at The Dome.

I entered a small wickiup. The dark-skinned man inside was dressed in beaded buckskin. He wore a feathered headdress and sported a small silver ring pierced through his nose.

He sat cross-legged in front of a large fire pit of glowing coals. The coals surrounded big rocks piled in the center. He looked up at me and offered a seat on the narrow hand-woven carpet opposite him. At his knees lay little piles of sacred herbs. Willow bark, sage, sweetgrass, tobacco, and shavings of cedar were the few I could identify.

He studied me for a long time. A slight look of arrogance settled into a trance-like stare. Without looking, he picked up some tobacco and shavings of cedar. He threw them on the coals. They smoked and filled the hut with an aromatic veil. Then he sprinkled some sage and a fungus-looking thing on top. The aroma was pungent but transporting.

"You have a dilemma," he said. "Why do you carry this burden? It is not necessary."

"Help me, please," I said. "Sometimes I don't trust my own mind."

"Dis-ease, illness of the mind or body, is only a dis-ease, or illness of the spirit," he said. "When the spirit is out of balance, the mind is thrown into the sky of confusion, where clouds crest and break, churn, and boil. No light is to be found."

"What can I do?" I asked.

"The black void of nothing and the brilliant void of everything is the same void. They are neither, they are both, they are one. One cannot exist without the other. But our custom is to teach our children from an early age to choose only the light, though they know the dark exists."

He stood up, walked behind me, and closed the flap to the wickiup. He put some charred wood into the fire pit. Soon they were flaming and joining the coals beneath in an orgy of heat. The rocks in the middle almost glowed.

"Take off your clothes," he said casually.

As I started to remove my jacket, shirt, and undershirt, he fanned the flames and began a chant. The air around me was getting warmer. He removed his headdress and set it aside. His cheekbones looked more prominent. He was a good-looking man. Deep eyes. Hypnotic eyes.

He removed his buckskin shirt. His skin looked smooth and soft except for a few battle scars. When he removed his moccasins and took off his pants, I did the same, revealing the long-johns I'd been hiking in and hadn't taken off since I was in the mountains.

Now he wore only a loincloth, which disappeared with a wave of his hand. I pulled the waistband of my long-johns down past my knees and then reached down and pulled them off my feet. I put everything in a pile near the edge. I resumed my cross-legged position opposite him. He kneeled, his legs under him, his cock relaxed between them. Then he leaned over the rocks and closed his eyes so his cheeks could gauge their temperature. When he stretched, he filled his chest with air, pushing out his pecs, pulling back his shoulders, to inhale as much as he could. He remained so for a minute or more.

He forced his stomach to cave as he exhaled, bringing his shoulders in, and slowly releasing the very last molecules of his breath into the redolent air. He was a beautiful man. He opened his eyes to find mine admiring him. He smiled and resumed a slow but steady breath that was unmistakably *soooooo, huuunng*.

He brought out a mortar and put in some herbs. As he ground them with the pestle, he added a slippery, translucent gelatin from a wide-mouth jar. He spooned it in, letting it drip slowly into the bowl. I thought I smelled a hint of grape-seed oil, but it had the thickness of saliva. He ground all of the ingredients together while saying a prayer in Salish. When the mixture was a uniformly thick sludge, he placed it on an outer rock of the fire pit.

Then he grabbed a gourd painted with strange symbols and poured a small stream of water slowly over the inner rocks. The water exploded into clouds of steam. He chanted something with increasing gusto, trying to coax spirits from the mist. He stoked the coals and pushed them against the rocks.

He poured another stream of water and once again, clouds of steam filled the little shelter. I was starting to sweat a lot. I hoped I didn't smell too bad. I could barely make out the shadow of him as he moved around the fire pit. He grabbed my hips from behind and pulled me sideways on the little carpet until his knees pressed against my ass. He sat on his haunches and began to smear the ooze all over my back, continually calling upon the spirits to guide him, to become a medium for me.

He lay me down and stretched out my arms and legs. He spread the stuff all over me, even my cock and balls, my armpits, the bottoms of my feet. He gave me a full body massage in the process, even rolling me over on my stomach so he could do my back. It felt wonderful. It was better than the massage I'd had in our hotel room in New Delhi, except this time… I wasn't aroused, I was completely relaxed.

He rolled me over once more on my back. The last part of my body he worked on was my head. He closed my eyelids and smeared his creamy potion on my face, neck, and ears. Then he kneeled beside me and ran his hands slowly down my body, not touching it, but an inch or two above it. He ran his hands forth and back, chanting, calling the toxic spirits out. In the middle of his chant, he whispered in English, "You are merely energy thought into form. To energy you shall one day return." Then he began his chant again.

Whatever it was, the oozy stuff covering my entire body felt warm and getting warmer with each pass of his hands. The gritty particles of herbs seemed to absorb the negative spirits. I lost track of where I was. I just fell into the warmth of his ointment; the hypnosis of his chant.

I don't know how long he chanted over me, but I came to when he reached under my shoulders and sat me upright again, facing the fire. He returned to his spot, rolled the inner rocks over, and scattered them among the remaining hot coals. He poured a third stream of water over the whole fire. The steam was intense. The sludge of herbs was washed off my body by the sweat pouring from my skin, the sweat from my skin washed off by the condensing steam.

When the steam had cleared enough for his face to come into view, he said, "Remember. The dark and the light are the same. The positive and the negative are the same. You may choose whichever one you want, but never forget the other exists. Let go the reins! Ride my horse Ayauaska. Hold your hands high and let him fly you into the light."

He closed his eyes. I dressed quietly and undid the flap to what I now realized was a sweat lodge. He stopped me before I left.

"One last thing, my friend... to help you stay in the light."

"What's that?" I asked.

"Walk like we do through the woods. Toe to heel."

I smiled at him as I left. Toe to heel.

CHAPTER 104
November 1975

The snow once again blanketed the valley and once again, it was stunning. It wasn't a heavy enough snow for cross-country skiing or snowmobiling, but it was beautiful nonetheless. For the time being it was good enough to have a four-wheel drive. I hoped that soon more snow would fall and reignite our full moon skiing trips.

I walked down from The Dome and had dinner with Joel. Then we picked up Do and Lo and drove to the Porters. Ed and Vicki showed up right behind us. Woody and Ben were already there. Just the right amount of people for a good game of Dictionary. More would have made it too slow, less would have made it uninteresting.

Chettie already had the chairs, pillows, and cushions, arranged in a circle, and the most enormous dictionary I had ever seen. I'm sure they had a team of oxen haul it in. It should have come with wheels attached it was so heavy!

Dictionary is a wonderfully humorous game. Everyone is given a stack of scrap paper. The person whose turn it is thumbs through the book, finds the most obscure word they can, and asks if anyone is familiar with it. If no one is, the word finder writes down the real definition while the rest write down their fabricated ones, as true to dictionary form as possible, complete with phonetic pronunciation and origin.

Everyone folds up their small pieces of paper and puts them in a bowl. The person who provided the word picks from the bowl one scrap of paper at a time and recites that definition as authoritatively and deadpan as possible. When all are read, including the real one, each person votes out loud on what they think the true definition is. The word finder then reveals the true answer.

More often than not, especially with this crowd, made-up definitions were often chosen over the real ones, regardless of how absurd or outrageous they might sound. When that was the case, a toast of wine, which everyone had to drink empty, duly honored them. The glasses were refilled before each round, but it was the praise, more than the points awarded for such a feat, that counted.

As the wine did its work, the definitions became more creative, more elaborate and fantastic, yet always plausible. One turn, Chettie thumbed through the book and asked, "Has anyone ever heard of the word, 'hoise?'" No one had, and as Chettie wrote down the real definition, the rest of us scribbled our own. When all the slips of paper were in the bowl, Chettie read them. They were all so ingenious and all of them likely definitions. The only one no one thought a possibility was: "Hoise. From the Middle Dutch, *hischen*. To be blown up by one's own bomb."

It sounded ludicrous and when Chettie read it, we all laughed that the wine must have destroyed her brain cells. We all dismissed it as absurd. Any of the others offered a more likely sounding definition than that! No one voted for it.

Chettie stood up and did a little jig. "Hah!" she cried. "I stumped all of you! The real definition is 'To be blown up by one's own bomb!'"

To be blown up by one's own bomb? We only believed her after we read it for ourselves. It was one of those words that scars the brain and is forever there. We were all so anxious to use it now that we had added it to our vocabulary. We tried to use it whenever we were having a conversation with someone. We searched for opportunities, even if sometimes they were contrived.

The first time I got to use it was when Bob down at the Spoke said something to the effect that if Aspen hadn't left town, he was prepared to resort to guerilla warfare. I said, "Just watch out you don't get hoised!"

He looked at me curiously. "You mean watch out I don't get hosed?"

I laughed. "No, Bob, I mean hoised!"

"Damn, Giacco," he replied. "You're never going to lose that Jersey accent of yours, are ya!"

I gave up. I never forgot the word, but I never used it again, except in my mind when I wished someone or other would hoise themselves and get out of my life.

I left the Spoke and walked down to the bank to withdraw some money. When I pocketed the cash and looked at the balance slip, I realized no money had been deposited in our account for a couple of months. It wasn't like Richard to be so remiss. I went back to the Spoke and used the pay phone outside. Ellen answered.

"Oh, Giacco! I'm so glad to hear your voice. We miss you!"

"I miss you, too, Ellen," I said, "The whole gang… well most of them."

I told Ellen about the sudden cessation of funds, and she said she'd get on Richard's case right away.

"Giacco, I hate it here! There are so many bad vibes in this house! Richard is a case and a half! If he didn't truly deserve ATD at first, he sure deserves it now! A real space cadet!"

"Tell Lizzie to stop with all the coke, already!" I ordered. "This has gotten way out of hand. I'm telling you, send Richard up here for the winter! I'll straighten him out!"

"Ziets is hell bent on keeping his job at Greenleaf. He thinks he doesn't exist without it. It's become his whole identity. He'd never leave. He's afraid Lizzie will find someone else to take his place."

"You have to make him, Ellen. Even if it means abducting him and shipping him in a crate via UPS!"

I could see Ellen smiling on the other end. "Oh, Giacco, if only we could! By the way, Nick moved out."

"What?" I yelled into the mouthpiece.

"Yeah! He started a custom cabinet business using the Woodworker's shop and already has some good clients, thanks to Lizzie."

"So why did he move out?"

"A couple of things," she said. "One, both he and Lizzie told us they were no longer going to pool all their money. They would only contribute what they thought fair, meaning a twelfth of the expenses each! They included you, Trudy and even Lily in their calculations!"

"And their reasoning for that?" I asked, getting angrier.

"They said it wasn't fair because Lizzie was bringing in thousands of dollars a month and Nicky's business was starting to be very profitable."

"Oh, better. Much better." I said. "And Baird? He didn't rant and rave?"

"I don't know what's going on, but Lizzie seems to have Baird under his thumb. He just walked away from the meeting without saying a word."

"And the second reason Nick moved out?" I asked.

"Remember Chelsea, that florist lady of his up in San Rafael?"

"Yeah, what about her?"

"She told Nick that if they got engaged, she probably could persuade her dad to give him one of his smaller warehouses to use as a shop and start a real business."

"And he did?"

"Yep! He left the house so fast, I thought there was an earthquake!"

"Fuckin' A!" I yelped. "What the fuck is going on down there?"

"Oh, Giacco. It's like a tornado all the time. Get this. Lizzie has 20… you heard me… 20 refrigerator trucks and about 50 employees. And Greenleaf has stopped delivering food to the other communes!"

"Oh, no! What did Kaliflower say about that?"

"They've given up on us. They won't speak to any of us anymore!"

"I don't blame them, but they shouldn't take it out on the rest of you."

"And the house is filled with all these gorgeous half-naked carpenters tearing down walls and rewiring everything, fixing up the attic. God, it's mayhem! David and I can hardly stand it anymore!"

"And when Nick left, what did Lizzie say?" I probed further.

"Oh, Lizzie was *so* magnanimous! Lizzie said that because Nick left and would only contribute his share of the mortgage on the land, Lizzie would agree to contribute an *eleventh* of the expenses. Psylvia said that Lily shouldn't count because she was just a toddler. And Lizzie said in his joking way that maybe it was time Lily got a job! Psylvia grabbed Lily and stormed out of the room!"

Before we hung up, I told Ellen that she could count on me to make sure nothing like that happened up on Church of Manna land. I hoped with all my heart I would never have to eat those words.

We didn't need a weatherman to persuade us this was going to be an unusually hard winter. One fierce storm followed another at regular intervals. In between them, the valley was white and quiet. It was during one of these lulls, when the snow settled and turned the roads into powdery ribbons, that we had the first full-moon ski of the season.

More people than ever joined us. Word had gotten out about our ritual treks and friends of friends from Mazama and Winthrop joined us to see what the excitement was all about. We all marveled at the views and stopped often for a nip of brandy out of a few flasks that were passed around. I could feel the alcohol coursing through my body. It was warm. When I looked at the others, they were huffing and puffing, but smiling broadly. I didn't know if their cheeks were red from the exercise or from the booze. Whichever, they all had a healthy glow.

Those that joined us for the first time were thrilled. They understood now why Nate and Hutch and sometimes Ben were seen every day, specks in the distance on their snowmobiles, forging their way through the deep snow. They dragged wide and heavy graders behind them packing it down and grooming the trails for us. It was hard work, especially the first time around, but once the trails were established, they were easier to maintain.

It was going to be a great winter and the Farmer's Almanac promised us that we might get in four or possibly five wonderful full-moon trips that season. Smaller groups of twosomes and foursomes used the trails during the day, but nothing could be as splendid as a clear night when the moon was full. We took a brandy break at the highest point of the trail above the Second Mile Ranch before schussing down that long logging road to the Christianson's bridge over the Twisp River.

The view was too beautiful for words. A hushed silence, except for some labored breathing, fell over the group. Then one of the guys from Mazama spoke.

"This is too much!" he said. "We should do this up in Mazama!"

"Mazama?" a woman from up the Chewack said. "We should do this throughout the valley!"

Nate just smiled. It was as if he had foreseen this natural development all along. As if he knew by *doing* instead of *talking*, this simple yet inspirational recreation would catch on without fanfare or meetings.

The guy from Mazama and the woman from the Chewack, though both had moved here before Aspen arrived, had turned their farms into bed and breakfasts in anticipation of the ski resort. The woman had even built a few cabins surrounding her farmhouse. When Aspen showed up and displayed a rendering of the "village" they planned, complete with hotels and restaurants, their hopes had been dashed. They would be too far away from the action to reap any of the benefits. The benefits would go solely to the businesses backed by Aspen and the only residual effect upon the locals would be service-related jobs. Waiters and cooks, maids and security guards, etc. Minimum wage kind of jobs.

The Chewack woman said, "Can you imagine groomed trails all the way from Mazama to Twisp?"

The guy from Winthrop added, "Yeah! And the trails could go from one bed and breakfast to another. This valley was never meant for a downhill ski resort, anyway. But it's perfect for cross-country skiing!"

Nate's smile grew broader. This is just what he and Chettie had in mind. This is what Sadie had dreamed of, and the Methow Valley Citizens Council unanimously embraced that dream. A decentralized and gradual development of the valley into a cross-country skiing paradise. Instead of a corporation getting all the profits, the influx of tourist money would be spread out among people all up and down the valley. Groomed trails would connect one B&B with another. Guides would lead tourists on treks lasting several days, and the skiers would stop at a different B&B each evening. Most importantly, it would be environmentally sound.

As their vision got more grandiose, with talk about how many jobs could be generated, I saw Chettie turn to Nate with a knowing look of love and pride. It was auspicious that the two up-valley people were very influential in their own communities. They both promised to start grooming trails up and down their own hills and valleys. And they did. In weeks to come, snowmobilers could be seen in the distance, but instead of the usual hot-rodders, they were slowly and methodically carving out trails by pulling heavy steel plates behind them. Who knows? But I thought maybe one winter in the future, there would be hundreds of miles of groomed trails all up and down the valley with small rustic lodges near the trails, welcoming guests at the end of a tiring but exhilarating day of cross-country skiing.

We stuck our poles under our arms and scrunched down, leaning forward a bit, trying to eke out as much speed as possible from our skis. We raced down the hill taking turns passing each other until the gentle rise to the bridge almost slowed us to a stop and forced us to herringbone our way up to the center of the span. We stopped to catch our breath.

When we got to Do and Lo's, Chettie hopped on the snowmobile and along with Hutch and Ben, towed everyone who needed a ride to their cars parked at Joel's. Chettie dropped Nate and me off at their house. Nate invited me in for a nightcap and said when Chettie got back he'd give me a ride up to The Dome. Late as it was, this was a good time to talk about some small chores connected with my imminent house-sitting.

With a snifter of warm cognac in our hands, Nate showed me parts of the house I'd never seen before, including the guest bedroom where I'd be sleeping. It was so cozy, paneled in knotty pine with a window that looked out over the river.

Nate said they get lots of mail, and please be sure to pick it up every day so the mailman doesn't get upset. Then he took me into his office off the living room. It also was paneled in knotty pine, but you could hardly see it through the bookcases that covered two entire walls. I thought I had entered an eccentric professor's office at a university. Papers and files lay strewn across his desk, and above it maps of the world were thumb tacked to the knotty pine. Photos and folk art of previous travels hung wherever there was a space. One in particular caught my attention. It was long and narrow and framed in black lacquered wood. Ten small prints were individually matted within the frame. It grabbed my attention immediately and I walked over to study them. Each of the prints seemed primitive and minimalist, but easy to interpret once Nate started explaining them to me.

"You like?" he asked.

"Yes, very much!" I said. "But what are they? They look Japanese."

"You're right, Giacco," Nate said. "These are the famous ox-herding depictions of the 10 steps to enlightenment in Zen Buddhism. They go back to the 15th century."

I studied them more carefully. I could tell the steps went from left to right. As I moved from one print to another, I could almost recite the story. But the ninth print stuck out from all the rest. There was no longer an ox-herder in the picture. It was just an obviously hand drawn empty circle, the kind a calligrapher would paint in one steady stroke with black ink on a thick brush.

"This must be where the ox-herder achieves enlightenment," I guessed.

"Right again, Giacco! The achievement of mindlessness."

"The only thing I don't get is this last print. I would have thought the series would end with the empty circle."

"To the contrary," said Nate. "It's not enough to achieve enlightenment. The master can't hide away in a cave and bathe in the light of his own awareness, meditating away the rest of his life."

"But I thought that was the goal. Reach the light and stay there."

"Absolutely not!" Nate contradicted. "The master may not stay in the light. It's his duty to return to the village and teach what he's learned to the others. Only when everyone's achieved the same consciousness as he, can he rest."

I joked. "Well, that's going to be one tired ox-herder!"

"Yep. I think so. But that's what it takes. You cannot achieve a true state of bliss unless you bring everyone else along with you, no matter how long it takes. The truly enlightened one knows he must forsake the peace he's attained and go back to work. By example, he'll lead the others along the same path he took. And each person who gets to this ninth print must move on to the tenth and do the same, until all the people of the earth have walked the same path and experienced the same state of pure consciousness."

I knew then that when I started house-sitting, I would spend a considerable amount of time ruminating on these prints.

Nate interrupted my fascination.

"If it's not too much trouble, just pile the mail as it arrives, here on the desk. Oh, and by the way, every month I get a notice from the Gonzaga placement office. It lists all the teaching positions currently available from all over the Northwest and Alaska. It's just stapled shut, so feel free to open it up and look them over. Never can tell what you might find."

"Thanks, Nate. Will do!"

We heard Chettie as the snowmobile sputtered into the driveway and almost stalled. She put it in neutral and revved it up a bit. Nate and I walked out. I hugged Chettie goodnight.

I lashed my skis upright to the back of the snowmobile and sat on the back waiting for Nate to straddle the saddle. Instead, he motioned me to scoot forward, and he hopped on behind.

"May as well learn to drive this thing. No one around. Perfect time to master the beast!"

It was not unlike the Honda 250 dirt bike Ben had lent me for a couple of days last spring. In fact, it was easier. Especially on the roads. Nonetheless, I took my time getting the feel of the thing. When we got to Joel's I told Nate I could snowshoe the rest of the way, but he insisted we go up to The Dome.

That road was the real test. It gave me a much better appreciation for the work involved in grooming trails. Some sections were rough, and the snowmobile bucked like a bronco. I almost missed a switchback but compensated just in time. I thought I'd done an admirable job. But when we reached The Dome and I looked at Nate, he was white with fear. I burst out laughing.

"Well, Giacco," he said, trying to be encouraging, "we didn't crash into anything, and we didn't fly off a cliff. But when you move into our house, take the snowmobile out into the fields and practice with it until you're perfectly comfortable, OK?"

"I was perfectly comfortable," I said.

"Yeah, but I wasn't!" and he laughed nervously. "I'm sure you'll get it down." He slid forward, said goodbye, and rode down the hill, the single headlight looking like a miner navigating his way through the labyrinth of a coalmine.

CHAPTER 105
Winter 1975-1976

Nate and Chettie left for Seattle on the 15th of December. I settled in over the next couple of days amazed at their library, their art, and the photographs of Chettie's family, some of whom were pictured with Presidents and other famous politicians. I knew I would not be bored and looked forward to the rest of the winter. Do and Lo were within walking distance, and it made me realize how isolated The Dome really was.

The next moonlight ski was coming up and I figured I should help groom the trails. I hooked up the small grader and drove the snowmobile up to The Dome. I had no sooner walked in the front door, when the storm hit.

The big white flakes fell so quickly that our double-barrel wood stove couldn't generate enough heat to make them melt and stop piling up on the roof. It quickly covered up the view of the sky through the Star. All the other windows were clear, but the Star was completely white.

I decided to play it safe and wait until the snow stopped before heading back to the Porters. I'd have to wait longer than I thought. By Thursday afternoon, I knew the moonlight ski would be canceled. The snows fell harder all through the rest of the week and into the weekend. It snowed so much that everyone was captive wherever they happened to be. Especially those that lived upriver, or like me, high over the valley. But what better place to be a captive than The Dome. It was exquisitely peaceful. It was the most transcendent I'd ever seen it.

I watched as the snow endlessly fell, drifting up to and over the deck. When I purposely walked off the deck into the snow, I fell up to my armpits. It was a blast. I shook the spray of flakes off my face, invigorated. I fought my way through the drifts until I was far enough to turn around and get the overall view. The Dome looked more like a cone on a gnome. It was hilarious. I wished I had a camera, but I didn't, so I went back inside to settle down for the night.

I was sound asleep in my bright red one-piece long-johns. The old-fashioned union suit kind with the flap in the back. I woke up when I thought I heard strange crunching sounds coming up the road. It sounded like a horse clomping. I was sure it was a horse when I heard a loud neigh.

I reached for the flashlight and looked at the clock. It was 3:30 in the morning. I got out of my sleeping bag and walked to the window to take a cautious peek. The full moon and the reflection off the snow made the dark of the night a soft blue daylight. Even with the snow falling, I could see pretty well.

It *was* a horse! And riding him was a guy wearing jeans and a sheepskin jacket. Scraggly dark hair snuck out from under his cowboy hat. His beard was frosted over. He looked familiar but he was swaying forth and back so much I couldn't place him. He was drunk as a skunk. He was hanging on to the saddle horn by instinct, trusting his steed to figure out that there was a road under all that snow.

When the horse faltered slightly, he threw the cowboy's head back into the light. I struggled to place him. Finally, I remembered. He was a regular down at the Spoke. Never met him though. He always sat down at the bar wherever there were the least people. And if the bar got crowded, he'd move to the corner of the room where there was the most space. He caught my eye a couple of times just because he looked like such a character. But he never looked approachable. In fact, he looked downright scary. He always left well ahead of the crowd. And he always left drunk.

Bob told us his name was Wagner. He didn't know if that was his first or last name. He was just called Wagner. He was a dry-wheat farmer along with his sidekick Duane. They were both from old families that originally settled this area. The families raised their kids, generation after generation, to farm their two sections of land way up Beaver Creek.

They'd been friends since childhood. Neither of them ever got married. Duane was seldom seen in town. Wagner was the socialite, Bob sarcastically guessed. If they had friends, Bob didn't know who they were. People speculated about them, but they were such loners most people never gave them a thought. For the most part, they were invisible.

Except this time.

I quickly lit a lantern, put on some clothes and my boots and, toe to heel, went outside holding a fireplace poker behind my back, just in case.

The horse came to a stop right in front of me, funnels of steam snorting from his nose, his eyes big and wondering. I grabbed his reins and held them firmly. Wagner halfway opened his eyes and asked, "Giacco?" His dismount consisted of falling off the horse flat on his back, a foot deep into the snow.

I found a post of the deck and secured the horse. Then I retrieved the cowboy hat that had fallen off and I dragged Wagner into The Dome. It was a job. He was a beefy guy and dead weight. The snow actually helped. I dragged him near the stove and stoked it, adding a few logs. I threw a sleeping bag around him.

I didn't know what to do with the horse. I was afraid the poor thing would freeze out there. I really didn't know too much about horses, except I'd always wished they'd sleep lying down instead of standing up. It took some doing to get a door open, but I did and I led him into the shed. I was glad we hadn't bought a tractor or a cow. There was ample room. I tied him up and wiped him hastily down with some old towels I found on a shelf. I had no idea how to remove a saddle. I gave him some carrots and granola in a washbasin. I filled another with water. I hoped that would do.

I went back into The Dome. Wagner was shivering crazily. He got me scared. What made him do such a thing in weather like this? I pulled back the sleeping bag and felt his pants. They were soaked. I opened his jacket. His shirt was drier but not by much. I pulled off his boots and socks. Phew! Undid his big belt buckle, undid the buttons of his fly, and tugged the pants off him. I unbuttoned his shirt. Then I got behind him and pushed as hard as I could until he was in a sitting position so I could get the jacket and shirt off him.

I pulled a mattress closer to the stove and managed to roll, push, and pull him on top of it. As I covered him with a sleeping bag, I realized his thermal underwear was wet, too. One might say he was chilled to the bone, he was shaking so violently. I grabbed a wool cap off the hat rack near the door and pulled it down over his head.

I quickly put a large pot of water on the stove. Got out some teas. Thought about a bit of whiskey I had around. Then thought better of it.

I wasn't a medic, but I figured this was hypothermia and I'd better do something, anything. I yelled at him, "Wagner, wake up! Wagner, it's Giacco! Say something! Do you know where you are?"

A few twitches and more shivering. I began gently rubbing his legs and feet, his hands, his arms, his fingers, while I waited for the water to boil. His underwear was ridiculously damp. I knew if I were wearing them, I'd want someone to rip them off me. So I said what the fuck and pulled his thermal shirt off and then the pants.

Now that the snow had fully melted into my clothes, I realized I was soaked, too. So I took everything off except my long-johns, and along with his clothes, hung them on the stairs of the mezzanine to dry.

I rubbed his skin harder. It was like rolling and kneading sinewy clay. His forearms, his chest, calves, thighs. I kept talking to him, trying to get a response. All he did was shiver and quake. I heard the water boiling. I tucked a couple of down sleeping bags tightly around him.

I put more wood in the fire, then poured some water into a teapot filled with mint and chamomile. I poured the remaining water in a basin and soaked some washcloths. When they were lukewarm, I pressed them gently all over his body and then dried him off with a towel. I threw the sleeping bags back over him. I could still see him shaking under the sleeping bags. Damn, how I wished I had that CB radio that Hutch wanted to set up for me exactly for emergencies like this!

I lay on top of the sleeping bags and tried to hold him tight, hoping my body heat would help but wondering if he could feel it through two layers of goose feathers. When the tea was ready, I got up and poured a cup. I knelt next to his head and lifted it, bringing the cup to his lips. I don't know whether he got a sip down or not, but I hoped so.

For no reason at all I suddenly thought of Peter and Debra and how we'd cuddle in the "nip" to keep warm. There was nothing like a naked body next to you to raise the temperature. Medically, not sexually.

I unbuttoned the front of my long-johns and pulled them off. I untucked one side of the two sleeping bags and slid in on top of him, pulling the bags back over us. Then I put my legs on the outside of his and scissored them tight. I forced my arms under his back and hugged him with all my might. I could still feel him shaking under me. I hugged him harder. The shivering lessened. I let my body sink into his. The shivering stopped.

I felt his arms wrap around me so tightly I thought he'd break a rib. He spoke for the second time. "Giacco?" This time it was as if he were asking permission for something. I felt the big muscles in his legs tighten. I felt him briefly harden beneath me. Then he started crying.

He was sobbing as if he had been relieved of an enormous burden. He spoke my name over and over, each time more quietly. Then he kissed me gently just before passing out.

I was shoveling snow at the bottom of our road where it opened onto Poorman Creek Road. Another full moon and we were expecting more people than ever to join us. We needed to make more parking spaces. Joel was in town picking up some goodies to snack on when we took our first break at The Dome, and some brandy to wash them down.

An old beater of a pickup rattled up the road. I didn't recognize it. It pulled off to the right side of the shoulder. A guy wearing a plaid cowboy shirt and cowboy hat stuck his head out the window. He had straw-blond hair and ruddy cheeks beneath gray-blue eyes. He could have been anywhere between 30 and 40 years old, I guessed. He looked gruff at first, but as he approached, I detected a kind of sweetness in his face. And it was a face I'd never seen before. In a valley this small, that was rare.

He stepped out of the truck and walked toward me, a sturdy looking man, slightly bow-legged. He asked, "You the guy called Giacco?"

"Yep, that's me," I answered.

"That The Dome up there?" he asked pointing up our road.

I just nodded.

"I'm Duane," he said.

A gulp was my response. I wished Joel would get back. I thought this guy was going to beat me up. I did my best not to show any fear. He approached to within six inches of my face and looked intently into my eyes. I did my best to hold my ground.

It took some hemming and hawing, but eventually he said, as if confiding in me, "I just wanted to thank you."

"Thank me? For what?"

"For saving my buddy's life," he replied.

"Aw, I don't know that that's true," I said.

"Sure 'nuf is!" he insisted. "You kidding me? Wagner was so drunk that night! If it weren't for you, he would have frozen to death in that storm. He was just damned lucky he made it up to your place."

"I just did what I could," I said, wondering if he knew the details of that evening.

"Well, that's not all," he said. "Somethin' else. Don't know quite how to say it."

"Duane," I said, trying to make a preemptive move, "nothing happened up there. He just crashed for the night."

"No," he said, "somethin' happened up there. I don't know what it was exactly, but somethin' went on!"

"What makes you say that?" I asked nervously.

He was even more nervous than I was when he answered. Though there was no one else around he leaned over to whisper in my ear.

"Giacco! I been sharin' a bed with that guy for goin' on 20 years. He never stays out all night. I was worried somethin' fierce with that storm and all. When he got home the next day, he was just quiet, wouldn't say nothin'"

"I swear, Duane, nothing happened up there."

"Oh, yeah… somethin' happened up there. I know it!"

"Duane," I tried to explain, "Wagner had some kind of breakdown. I don't know. He was drunk."

"Damn, Giacco! Don't you get it? It wasn't a breakdown. It was a break*through*! I don't know what went on and I don't care what went on! All I know is whatever happened, when we went to bed that night, for the first time ever in all the years we been together he turned to me and said, 'I love you, Duane!' I been waitin' for that so long!" His eyes watered up. "Not only that. He's stopped gettin' drunk!"

A drunk Wagner is the only one I ever knew. All I said was, "Damn! That's nice!"

"We been so scared all our lives," he continued. He started to choke up. "I gotta go. Just wanted to say, 'thank you.' My grandma used to say, 'What goes around comes around.' I wish that for you, buddy. Everything good." And he started for his truck and hopped in.

I thought only hippies had the trademark on Grandma's phrase! She must've been one cool lady!

"Hell, thanks Duane," I yelled, and then changed it to, "thanks *buddy*." He looked back and flashed me a grin. When he smiled, he turned handsome.

I ran across the road. "Hey. Duane! Wait up!" He rolled down the window and looked at me, his gray-blue eyes all red now. "You know how to cross-country ski?"

"Damn! You kidding? Course not!"

"You and Wagner got any interest in learnin'?"

"We don't do nothin' 'cept farm, Giacco!"

"Not in the winter ya don't!"

He didn't have a comeback for that. "I'm staying up at the Porters. You know where that is?"

"Sure do."

"You and Wagner get bored, you come up to the Porters, OK? We got lots of extra skis. I'll teach ya what I know. We'll practice out in the back fields."

"Gee, bud, just don't know about that."

"Think about it. Surprise me. C'mon down some time. The two of you can even spend the night in the house. It's a cool place. You'll like it and it'll be fun."

"OK, bud, we'll think about it. Thanks buddy."

He started the truck and was making a U-turn when some of the skiers drove up the road with Joel right behind them. They stopped while Duane made a slippery three-point turn, giving all of them plenty of time to get a good look at the cowboy behind the wheel. Duane held his hand out the window with a wave as he drove away.

While we skied that night, one by one, each person sidled up to me and asked who that cowboy was. I told them it was Duane.

"The mystery cowboy?" they asked in disbelief.

"One and the same," I answered.

"Did he give you any trouble? You OK?"

"I'm better than OK. I'm great!" I waited for the inevitable question.

"So are the rumors true?"

"What rumors?"

"C'mon Giacco! You know what we mean! Are they more than 'sidekicks?'"

"I have no idea," I said. "I just know they're good guys."

They prodded but couldn't get more out of me. We left it at that. What went on between Wagner, Duane, and me would remain a beautiful secret that warmed me every time I thought about it.

The moonlight ski was as beautiful as expected. The snow was dry and powdery. It just blew off our clothes and gloves like sparkling dust.

When we got to the bridge, instead of going to Do and Lo's we skied up Elbow Coulee to Patterson Lake and back. The Winthrop contingent had persuaded Sun Mountain Lodge to let them incorporate their existing trails into the new ones. Sun Mountain agreed in hopes they would be considered one of the lodges cross country skiers might stay in.

Sun Mountain profited from the ever-increasing miles of groomed paths and wound up being one of the most vocal supporters of a valley sewn together with a network of cross-country trails. The Winthrop skiers had groomed trails all the way from Sun Mountain Lodge to Twisp River Road. It felt like the first transcontinental railroad finally joining tracks. It felt historic.

When we got back to Twisp River Road, I took a left and skied to the Porters. The others went down to Do and Lo's where Hutch and Ben towed them back to Joel's.

I was just about to go to sleep when the phone rang. It was Joel.

"OK, Giacco! Spill the beans. I want to know what's really up!"

I said, "Joel, the only thing I know is that soybeans are up, but pork bellies are flat!"

He hung up on me.

I spent most of February reading, writing, and doing my best to keep the house in order. I had no idea that geese could be so violent and mean. Whenever I stepped out of the house, they would run for me and nip at my legs. It hurt! After the first attack they sensed my fear and became even more aggressive. It got to the point that I wouldn't leave the house without a rake and shovel, which I swung forth and back, crossing them over each other to keep the damned geese at bay. Still, some of them managed to attack me from the rear.

I was performing this odd maneuver when two guys came driving up. They were wearing cowboy hats. They came up a few times and even spent a night after we'd stayed up late talking.

One time as they were leaving, Duane handed me a folded piece of paper. Duane said, "This is something I wrote the night Wagner didn't come home. This is just between you and me, Giacco!" When they were out of sight, I opened it. It was a poem.

I crawl in and lie
On my side.

I can smell you.
Maybe it's time to wash the sheets,
But I like the aroma.

Under the covers
My nose slides
From the head of the bed
To the foot
And starts back again,
Savoring the scent
In every thread of the fabric.

The flannel is infused with you.
I linger awhile and then return
To the beginning.

I wake up to find myself
On your side.

I was totally blown away. Again, I had to learn that every human is a novel unto themselves, with stories some share, and others don't. It doesn't make the ones who don't any less fascinating. It just requires more patience. I had met my first Cowboy poet.

That next and final full moon ski found two new people in our group. They were shy at first. When the brandy was passed around, Wagner waved it off, but Duane took a slug. As we climbed the Saddle Pass, Wagner kept hanging on to Duane's shirttails flapping under his jacket. That made them both fall a number of times, always laughing heartily like little kids and making us laugh as well. By the time we schussed down the Black Pine Lake road to the bridge, they were completely at ease and talked readily with anyone, though they were usually men of few words.

After all, everything *is* needless to say.

CHAPTER 106
Spring 1976

Nate and Chettie returned the middle of March. They found their house in almost exactly the same condition they left it except for a few open bulletins of job openings from Gonzaga's placement office.

After regaling me with stories of their adventures and some incredible photos Chettie had taken, Nate asked me if I had found anything interesting in the way of teaching positions.

"Well, you were right," I said. "I didn't realize just how many there were. But I didn't come across any that offered a job without a teaching certificate."

"I'll keep a look out for some," Nate offered. "In fact, if I were you, I'd put together a resume and get some copies of your transcripts ready just in case something comes along."

"Excellent!" I said. "I'll get right on it."

"If you need to use a typewriter, feel free to come down here, Giacco," Chettie added.

"Thanks, Chettie," I said. "Except for your gladiatorial geese, it was a real treat!" They laughed.

"Anytime you need a house sitter, just yell."

"You got it, Giacco," Nate said. "It's *you* we thank."

"You can thank me by having another Dictionary session as soon as possible," I laughed.

"We'll do our best," Chettie said. "First we need to recuperate from our trip."

"Listen, Giacco," Nate said just before I left, "I went to school with a lot of people who are now superintendents. Mind if I make a few calls?"

"That would be great!" I said. "Wait until I get you my transcripts and resume, though. You might need ammunition."

"Good idea. Get on it."

And I went back to The Dome to write a rough draft of my resume and a letter to Georgetown requesting my transcripts. Then I settled in for the "working" season paid for by the State of California. I promised myself that if I should get a job, I would immediately call Nancy Stein and tell her, "Thanks for the help but I'm better now."

I was so glad to be back up at The Dome even though electricity and a phone had spoiled me. I hoped that this season, some Hunga Dungans would come up. Certainly, they'd come up. Why wouldn't they?

With Joel's tractor, I managed to till the garden that had been fallow for a year. I planted some lettuce, carrots, bok choy, string beans, and eggplant. The tomato starts were inside The Dome. I'd wait until it got a bit warmer before putting them in the ground.

The Dome had held up superbly for three winters now, though some of the planks in the deck were starting to warp. I walked around the building trying to hammer them back into place. I was at the backside of The Dome when I heard some vehicles coming up. I walked to the front and saw Blake and Trudy driving up the road, followed by a pickup with a couple of men in the cab and a bunch of chainsaws in the back.

Blake and Trudy stopped at The Dome. They seemed surprised to see me and quickly directed the pickup behind them to drive to the far end of the bench.

"What's going on?" I asked, perturbed at this intrusion that obviously did not bode well.

Trudy spoke first, Blake always being the submissive one. "Jeff designed a wonderful log house for us!" She rolled out a large poster-size piece of paper. It was a big house. Two-storied atop a full basement.

Two wings with double-hipped roofs angled out at 45 degrees from each side of the "great room." It was unique for a log home. I was impressed with Jeff's skills. I hoped he knew as much about structural design as he did about renderings.

"We came to get some logs," Trudy said, as if she stupidly thought I'd allow that. "Don't worry, we're not going to clear-cut or anything. We'll pick them out carefully."

"Let me see. How many things are wrong with those sentences?" I asked irritably. "First of all, you're not going to pick anything thicker than a yarrow stalk. Second, by picking them out carefully, I assume you mean the oldest and the best. Thirdly, what gives you the goddam right to think you're entitled to any of them?"

"I told you so, Trudy," Blake said softly, but with an edge. "You know the Church of Manna rules. You said, 'Even Giacco won't be a problem.' You didn't even expect him to be here, did you? You thought he was still at the Porters, didn't you?"

Trudy bristled. "Shut up, Blake." She whipped her head back to me, killing some gnats with her long, tough hair. "Lizzie said I could cut down some logs. What we need doesn't come close to what my share is. That's what Lizzie said."

"Who the fuck does Lizzie think he is?" I exploded. "He has no right to give permission for anything up here! It's got to be a unanimous decision. You're not going to do a thing until I call home and…"

I heard the pull on a chainsaw and saw one of the loggers revving it up and adjusting the carburetor until he was satisfied with the annoying, grating roar.

I ran as fast as I could screaming, "Stop! Stop it!" I tried to scream louder but I was running too fast and getting winded. I ran past Zietar's Knoll as I hit the wall, the endorphins kicked in and I was flying toe to toe, zigzagging through the trees. I got there just in time to stand between the intended victim and the saw.

"What the fuck!" he yelled and let the chainsaw sputter to a stall and drop to his side while I tried to catch my breath.

"You will get in big, big trouble if you touch any of these trees," I managed to get out. "They do not belong to either of them. I suggest very strongly they *prove* to you that they own this land before you do a thing."

The two loggers looked at each other. They didn't know whether to take me seriously or not. By this time, Trudy and Blake had caught up.

The guy who seemed to be in charge looked at Trudy and asked, "Do you own this land? Just a 'yes' or 'no' will do."

"Of course, I own this land!" Trudy said.

"Ask her to prove it. If she can, then you can cut down the whole fuckin' forest!"

The logger said, "Damn, if yur willin' to go that far, you must know somethin.'" He turned to Trudy. "Can you prove you own this land, ma'am?"

Trudy was going for it. "Of course, I can prove it!"

Blake said, "No you can't, Trudy. And you even lied to me. You said everyone had agreed. You didn't even have a family meeting, did you?"

"Guys, listen up!" I yelled. "Follow me back to The Dome. I can show you a document that proves she has no claim to this land."

The head logger said, "Bud, that ain't necessary. I believe you. This is one lying...." He mumbled a word that I suspected started with a "b." He glared at Trudy and then yelled over his shoulder to his buddy. "Let's get goin' Cody. We're outta here."

Trudy was livid. She stormed off without looking at me. Blake followed and just shrugged his shoulders as he passed me by. I was about to follow when I looked at the tree they were going to cut down. It had a red X on it. I scanned the immediate area. There were red X's everywhere. It looked like maybe a hundred or more. They were all mature, good-sized trees. Some were probably destined to be milled into boards and timbers. Others were just the right thickness and straightness to be dried, peeled, and used for the logs themselves.

As I picked up my pace walking back to The Dome, I realized they must have come up here when they knew I wasn't around so they could mark those trees for the loggers. If that was the sneaky way to do it, it was because she knew I'd stop her dead in her tracks. I was fuming when I stood in front of their car and stopped them from leaving. I walked over to the driver's side. Trudy rolled down the window just halfway but didn't look at me.

"I don't even know where to begin," I said. "I guess a good place to start is to say you are really one helluva disappointment."

Inside my head, I was less kind. I wished that she would get hoised!

I looked past Trudy to Blake, and said, "Blake, you have my sympathies."

With that, Trudy put the car into gear and spun off, kicking stones and dust in my face. It was a small price to pay.

I was afraid to leave The Dome. For a week, if I had to go into town, I made the trip as quickly as possible. In Twisp, going to town for a quart of milk usually took a couple of hours. It was impossible not to run into friends and talk and talk and talk. Fortunately, it was that time of year when everyone was busy taking advantage of the growing season, and the building season. We were forced to bite our tongues every now and then and keep the conversations to a minimum if we were ever to get anything accomplished.

On one of those quick trips into town that week, I called home. Fortunately, David answered the phone. I told him what happened. David shouted so loud I had to hold the phone away from my ear. "This is the last straw! What nerve! This has gotten way out of hand!"

"OK, Dave, that's all I wanted to know. Just wanted to make sure all of you were in the dark as much as I was."

David said somewhat mysteriously, "Well, Giacco, I think most everyone here was in the dark about this, but things have gotten so secretive, I wouldn't be surprised if a couple of other people knew about this."

"Like whom?" I asked.

"Well, Nicky for one," he answered.

"Nick isn't even living there anymore," I said.

"Yeah, but Lizzie and Nicky are always gabbing on the phone, so who knows? At any rate, I'll spread the word. Thanks for filling us in. Christ, all hell is gonna break loose."

"OK, Dave. Thanks. Sorry if it causes more trouble. I feel like I'm being left out of the loop. Just because I'm up here doesn't mean I don't have a say in what's going on. Right?"

"I agree, Giacco. Don't worry. We'll handle this. In fact, you might be getting some big news soon."

"What? Tell me."

"Can't," he said. "Not until it's a done deal. Patience my friend."

"OK, Dave. I'll try. And thanks. Give my love to everyone."

"Everyone?" David laughed.

I laughed back. "OK, everyone you know that I love!" And we hung up.

On the way back up Poorman Creek, I stopped at Slim and Hannah's. They greeted me warmly. Hannah offered me a cold drink.

"Thanks, Hannah." I said, taking the glass.

"So what's up?" asked Slim.

"Not much really. Was just wonderin' if anyone from San Francisco was in touch with ya. Or if maybe Trudy had talked with ya."

"No," he answered. "The only thing I get from San Francisco is the mortgage payment. Always on time. And Hannah and I really appreciate it."

"Well, that's great to hear. Just thought I'd stop to say hi and make sure everything was in order."

"Everything is fine, Giacco. Becoming land barons now, are ya?" He laughed.

"Land barons?" I quizzed.

"Yup! Well, I mean first Lizzie buys 60 acres adjoining the Church's land. Ya know where the bench wraps around the hills to the north?"

"The Church bought it?"

"No, Lizzie bought it. On his own."

"Oh," was all I could get out.

"And ya must know that Nick bought 20 acres in the meadow at the bottom. It butts up to the old homestead."

"No, I didn't know that," I tried to say without too much astonishment. "I didn't even know it was for sale!"

"Well, it wasn't, but he offered me such a good price, Hannah and I decided to let it go."

"Oh, that's interesting."

"So now you guys have two hundred acres. In this small valley, that's a lot of land!"

"Yep, sure is." I said, forcing a smile. "Well thanks, Slim. Thanks, Hannah." I handed the empty glass back to her and they waved as I hopped in Wilhelmina and drove up the road. I wished I'd had this information when I called David. It would have to wait.

I was paranoid every time I left The Dome. I thought about putting a padlock on the gate. I thought about having some big boulders set in a row at the beginning of the bench, with only enough space to let a small tractor through. I thought of posting signs warning people to stay out. Everything I thought of was contrary to Hunga Dungan tradition. I was frustrated.

As I drove up our road, I stopped at the meadow. It was just 100 feet or so from the old homestead that I liked so much. I always coveted that meadow because it was a builder's dream. Boulder free. Flat. Easy access. It was the only part of this bowl, surrounded by forests and mountains that stayed green all the time, except in winter. It obviously wouldn't require drilling too deep before you'd hit water for a well. And not too expensive to have power and phone lines brought in. Damn that Nick!

I went up to The Dome, rifled through a box of documents, and retrieved a copy of the articles of incorporation and the deed. I studied them carefully. Ellen's lawyer friend had done an excellent job and covered every conceivable loophole. It was indeed an ironclad contract. I felt a sigh of relief.

I worked in the garden the few remaining hours of daylight and then made a delicious dinner of polenta and parmesan cheese, covered with a vegetable stir-fry. After dark, I grabbed a thin foam mat and a sleeping bag and went up to the Saddle Pass. I tried my best to meditate and calm the agitation I felt building inside me. I finally succumbed to the beauty of the peaks and the valleys and slept under the stars. Not soundly, but I slept.

I woke up with the dawn. I traipsed back to The Dome and had some granola with apple juice. Then I hopped in Wilhelmina and drove to Joel's. He was an early riser, too, though I guess my arrival interrupted a morning tryst with a lonely housewife. She hurriedly dressed and kissed Joel goodbye, saying she'd see him later in the day.

Joel smiled at her. When she wasn't looking, Joel looked at me, screwed up his face and whispered, "Giacco, what the hell am I going to do now? *Fuck me!*"

Then he waved lovingly at her as she drove off. When she was out of sight, Joel shook his whole body, as if cringing at the thought of having to spend any more time with her. But he laughed and shrugged his shoulders.

"So, Giacco, just in time for breakfast."

"No thanks Joel, I just came by to use the phone if that's OK."

"Of course," Joel said. "By the way, did ya bring a joint with ya?"

"Sorry Joel, no. But later on I'll go and get some or you can come up."

"Good enough. C'mon in."

I told Joel about the incident with Trudy, and Lizzie and Nick buying land next to the Church's. He was surprised. He regarded Hunga Dunga as the model communal experiment. Joel, of course, would casually pass the information on to all our friends, and soon, whenever Trudy walked down the main street, some people would only look at her with a sideways glance.

I called the Porters. Chettie answered. I asked if I could come over and type up my resume. She said, "Naturally! C'mon over!"

I was there in 15 minutes. I was almost finished with it, and Chettie looked over my shoulder and made some editorial suggestions. When we were through, the resume made me look better than I could have ever thought, thanks to her. I pulled the paper out of the typewriter.

"Leave it here," Chettie said. "When you get your transcripts, Nate can make copies of them both at school."

"Chettie, you and Nate have been so good to me!" She blushed, unusual for her. "I don't know what I'd do without you!" I gave her a big hug and left.

At the post office, I mailed my letter to Georgetown asking for my transcripts. There was also a letter for me. A long one. From Larry, who had never written me before!

Dear lovely Giacco,

I am missing you terribly. Santa Rosa is nice, but I'm getting lonely. Now sit down for the rest of this letter. Are you sitting down? OK.

A few weeks ago, I went into The City to see the gang. It was mayhem. They were in the middle of a family meeting, and it was terrible. Even our wonderful Psylvia was disgusted. David and Ellen didn't even attend the meeting. They have removed themselves completely from the fracas. They get too upset. You know me. I seldom get angry, but I just yelled at them, "I can't stand this anymore! How can you live like this? Why not just split up?"

Well, guess what? They're going to do just that. David and Ellen have been looking for over a month for a place. They found a nice Victorian on Waller Street in the lower Haight. Not too far from Hunga Dunga. A nice walk. Anyway, it's three-and-a-half-stories! The third floor is a beauty. Small, but with a little bedroom and even a small bathroom. And above that floor, tucked into the attic, is a charming munchkin room, with a killer view.

David, Ellen, Psylvia and Lily are moving in. They asked me if I wanted to move back to The City. I said I would if I could persuade Richard to move in too. And guess what! He agreed! On the condition that he got the munchkin room, of course. We said OK.

And I guess you know by now that Chuck moved out. He got his own apartment. He said he'd had it with everyone, and it was time to go solo.

Anyway, my sweet, I think I owe you a huge apology for not sticking up for you when you came back from Hawaii. I am so so so so sorry. Can you ever forgive me?

Giacco! We are saving a room for you. If you want to live with us, we would love it. Think about it. Please. Baird hinted he'd like to move in too, but he was not invited. We love Baird, but we don't want to live with him. We love Chuck and we hope he visits us a lot.

And get this. Richard came up with a phone number that spells the word "UNIFIED!" (Maybe he was inspired after his fifth line of coke in a row! What are we going to do with him?) Anyway, the phone company said we could have that number. Is that cool or what?

We are going to move at the end of May. Ellen, David and Psylvia have already given their "landlord" notice. Our phone should be installed by then. Give a call. Remember. Area code + U-N-I-F-I-E-D!

(Unified? Are we ever going to get a second chance?)

Always with you, Duck

I was touched. The letter made me sentimental. I thought back to that Halloween night when Lizzie and Trudy brought me back to the house in the Haight. What beautifully crazy people. What magic! In terms of years, it wasn't all that long ago and yet so much had happened it seemed like a lifetime.

Duck's letter sounded very upbeat and optimistic. A new beginning. Maybe this would help wean Richard off the coke. I hoped it would with all my heart.

CHAPTER 107
Summer 1976

It was so hot we were getting temps in the low 100s before it was even officially summer. The Dome was uninhabitable during the day. It retained the heat too well. It was so efficient during the winter and so inefficient in the summer. I wished we'd made the Star so its triangular windows could open. It wasn't until the early hours before dawn that it was comfortable enough to sleep inside. Often, if not always, I slept outside on the deck.

Everyone carried plastic half-gallon milk containers filled with water wherever they went. They carried them to drink from and to splash over their faces and heads. Large cowboy handkerchiefs came in handy. Easy to wear as a scarf pulled tight across the forehead and tied behind the neck so it looked like a skullcap. The word *babushka* comes to mind, but I've no idea from where. Stick the head under a faucet and get that colorful kerchief soaking wet with cold water. Ah, it felt so refreshing even though it evaporated three minutes later.

I hate hats with a passion. But I wore a ridiculous looking straw one when I was out in the garden. I was afraid if I didn't, someone would find me dehydrated and unconscious in a row of beets.

Regardless of the heat, everyone went about their required tasks, many of which required help from neighbors and friends. But no one really had to ask for help. They just had to let it be known.

"Yep, me and Judy are gonna rebuild the front porch this Thursday."

Ten friends would show up early Thursday morning, ready, willing, and wanting to work. And when we thought Hutch could use a hand or two, Jet and Judy were there along with the usual gang of freaks and old-timers.

Around the circle it went. It felt good. Maybe "community" wasn't so bad. As long as we never forgot the "commune" in the word.

I was inspired when some of the women got together and started a collective kitchen. They were canning jams and preserves at home, just as carefully as their great-grandmothers had done before them. But as soon as they tried to sell them to the tourists at the Saturday street fair, the Health Department stepped in.

"You can't sell any preserved foods that haven't been prepared in a commercial kitchen," the man from Okanogan said.

None of the women had the money to install a three-sink, up-to-code, commercial kitchen. He knew that. But the women were resourceful. They pooled their money and rented a small building down by the bowling alley. It didn't take long for word to get out. A crew of men and women of all ages, lifestyles, and skills showed up. They installed the plumbing and brought the electricity up to spec. A trip to a restaurant-supply store in Wenatchee yielded three used stainless-steel sinks and an industrial oven. A cheery paint job, some shelves, and folk art on the walls, made it a happy place to be.

Soon the kitchen was buzzing with activity, chitchat, and flies knocking themselves out on the windows, trying to get at the up-to-code goodies. Now the women could sell their jams, jellies, and pies not only at the street fair, but to restaurants, markets, and roadside stands, as well.

While the guys who had been doing the heavy work were taking a break, they walked two doors down to a vacant building and looked inside. When the Collective Kitchen was finished, the men and women who loved working with wood began on the Woodworkers' shop.

They pooled all their tools except those needed around the house. Some guys had been storing power tools at their places for years, even though they had no power. Now, collectively, they all had power. And, collectively, they had radial-arm saws, routers, drill presses, lathes, some very specialized tools for doing fine finish-work, and lots of other dangerous looking equipment I didn't want to be around.

Both the Collective Kitchen and the Woodworkers' Collective were very cost-effective and gave both the men and women involved the opportunity to do together what they could not accomplish alone. And they accomplished a lot. The best tasting treats and the finest furniture and cabinets. Once the needs of the community were met, the collectives were free to sell their wares… most often to the ever increasing numbers of tourists. It actually provided the members with a decent living.

Maybe a stretch of my imagination, but in its organization, the valley reminded me of the intercommunal network back in The City. In the valley a family, even with only two people in it, was a commune unto itself. The collectives were the equivalent of the Free Food Conspiracy and the Free Bakery and the Free Garage. Well, maybe with the "Free" removed.

If this "collective" thing caught on, well maybe, just maybe…

The days were long, and some took advantage of them by working through dinnertime. But most said, "OK, that's enough!" And off we'd go from wherever we were, to converge on whatever was our favorite swimming hole.

Get naked! Dive in! Oh, brrrr! So cold but so nice! We'd climb onto a sunny rock and shiver, but only for a minute or two before the sun hung us out to dry and warmed us up. When we got too warm, we dove back in. And of course at Joel's swimming hole we always added only the most stunning rocks to the Rock Museum. Among the locals, it was practically becoming a tourist attraction. Admission was the price of seeing the shriveled penises of grown men with beards and long hair, all acting like five-year olds. Only the bravest dared look.

I got to the post office just before it closed. My transcripts from Georgetown had arrived. I immediately took them up to the Porters. Nate was feeding the geese. As soon as they saw me, they attacked. I ran into the house but one of them left a nice mark on my ass before I got inside. Nate, of course, was in hysterics.

My emergency entrance surprised Chettie.

"OK, Giacco, just what in hell did you do to those poor geese while we were gone?"

"Animals love me, Chettie! I can't explain why the geese don't like me, but I am very insulted!"

She giggled. "Maybe they know you sleep in a down bag!"

I made a face. She laughed. Nate walked in wiping his hands on a rag. He saw me holding the manila envelope.

"Those the transcripts?" he asked more excited than I had been.

"Yessir! Here they are!" and I handed the envelope to Nate. He opened it and took out the two stapled pages. He studied them carefully.

"Yikes!" he shouted. "Your GPA is incredible. But look at these courses. I don't get it. You have enough credits here for a Master's degree."

"Yeah, well, it was a pretty intensive program."

"Damn! I mean darn!"

I smiled. I was such a good student with such a promising career with the State Department or the CIA, what with being the deep, silent type and all. A shame Vietnam and LSD came along. Or was that my mother's voice I was hearing in my head?

Nate looked up at me. "I'm going to make copies of your resume and transcripts. I'll write a letter of introduction. If I see any positions come our way, we'll be quick to respond."

"Thanks Nate," I said. "That would be great. Really nice of you. I appreciate it." And I appreciated the way he used the word "our."

"Giacco, you trust me?"

"Of course I do, Nate!"

"You mind if I do some searching on my own?"

"Not at all, but hey, you got your own life to worry about, not mine."

'It's no problem. A few phone calls. We got to get on this! Some districts are starting the school year earlier than usual."

"You're the expert," I said, and he was.

"You have any geographical preferences?"

"Yes. Yes, I do, Nate," I answered. "I'd like a tranquil community on a tropical island where clothing is optional."

He and Chettie laughed.

"Au contraire, mes amis! I am dead serious!"

"We'll keep that in mind," they said at the same time.

It was my turn to laugh, but as I ran down the driveway to Wilhelmina, a gaggle of geese nipped at my hamstrings and made me yelp.

I rounded the last switchback to The Dome and saw Blake and Trudy's red pickup parked in front. When I saw who was sitting on the deck, I nearly ran off the road. It was Lizzie!

I tried to be very happy to see him. "Lizzie! Finally! Someone from home! When did you get here?"

He tried his best to be equally happy to see me. "I've been here a few days. Been staying with Trudy."

I looked around for signs of them.

"They're not up here. I came alone. They lent me their truck. I sure wasn't going to bring my new toy up here!"

"What kinda toy might that be?" I asked him.

He sputtered out a German name with a long model number. I was obviously ignorant. "It's a sports car, Giacco. Jeez, don't they teach you anything up in these hills?" He laughed. I knew my trucks, but sports cars eluded me. I wondered why he waited so long to come up and visit but decided not to ask.

"Giacco, you look great. The Dome looks great. Zietar would be so proud of you with the garden and all."

"I wish he were up here, Liz. He's the master at it."

"Well, old Richard's having some problems, Giacco. I even had to fire him."

"Fire him? After all he's done? He made it so none of us ever had to think about bills or utilities or taxes and stuff. Same with the Free Food Conspiracy. And with *your* Greenleaf! He always got you the best produce at the best price. You learned everything you know from Richard."

Greenleaf is a big business now, Giacco. I don't think anyone at Hunga Dunga really understands how big. We're talking close to a million in revenues last year!"

"That's nice," I said, truly and completely unimpressed.

Lizzie looked miffed. "Richard was doing OK at basic bookkeeping. But now I have a certified accountant who really knows the ins-and-outs of taxes. And I have one of the best lawyers around, as well. I had to let Richard go. It's the big time, Giacco! You gotta move on!"

"Does 'moving on' mean you leave people behind after you've used them up, or step over them if they're in your way? You couldn't find some way to keep him on? You had to fire him? Humiliate him? He made Greenleaf happen, not you! You're good at getting the clients, but they sure wouldn't stick around if Richard didn't do all the follow up. I can't believe it. You fired him! You know how much that meant to him?"

Lizzie was getting angry. "Are you through telling me how to run my business, Giacco? Richard was shootin' up in the back room. Getting other guys to do it with him. When I caught him, stoned out of his mind trying to get into the pants of one of my employees, that was it."

"Gee," I said innocently, "I thought *you* were the one who had to get them coked up, hoping to get into their pants. In fact, wasn't that one of your criteria before hiring them? You were always the great casting director. I bet every single one of them is a looker. And I bet every single one of them is a man."

"OK, Giacco. Enough. Let's not argue. Let's take a walk. Show me around."

I walked quickly toward Zietar's Knoll. I slowed my pace when I realized Lizzie was way behind. When he caught up to me, we walked side by side.

"I guess I should get all the stuff I know is going to upset you out of the way, and then get on to the cool stuff, OK?"

"Shoot!"

"OK, then. Don't freak on me."

"Spill it already!" I sharply replied.

"Richard no longer has power of attorney for you. I have it now. I cash all the checks. I pay all the bills."

"What? How did you swing that?" How can you do that without my authority?"

"But I always had your authority. Remember when Ziets, Psylvia, Nicky, and you went to the Celebration of Life? We added my name as a power of attorney so I could deposit checks and pay bills when Richard wasn't around. Remember? Besides, I have a good lawyer. And we found Richard in a most accommodating mood to delegate his. *Authority*, that is."

He fully believed me when I said, "Lizzie, I'm telling *you* that I'll call Social Services this afternoon. I'll tell them to send my checks directly to me. In fact, I might just tell them to stop the checks completely."

"And how will you pay your portion of the mortgage and the money it costs us to keep this place going, and you fed and dressed?"

"Forget the food and clothes. You just figure out what my share of the mortgage and expenses is, and I'll send you the money every month. I'll get a job." I was getting really bummed by all this talk. "The mortgage is only a hundred twenty-five fuckin' bucks a month. Divided by 10 trustees, that's $12.50 each. I think I can handle that!"

"Yeah, I suppose so," he said. "But that's what everyone who's moved out said. And of them, the only one who has any real interest in the land is Ziets. You watch. They'll stop sending money one by one, and I'll end up making up the difference."

"Lizzie, stop projecting. Wait until that happens, then worry about it. Hell, you're bringing in thousands of dollars a week and you're worrying about a measly one hundred twenty-five? Man, it's true. The richer they get the more tight-fisted they become."

That stung Lizzie. He had a very high opinion of himself. He usually paid no attention to the opinion of others, but this hit home.

When we got to the end of the bench, I pointed out some trees that still had a red "X" painted on them. They looked like concentration camp Jews wearing Star of David armbands. I said, "Can you believe they wanted to cut down trees *here* to build a house over *there*!" I pointed to the other side of the valley where Blake and Trudy lived. I cupped my hands into a cheerleader's megaphone and yelled at them, "What nerve you had, Trudy!" I turned to Lizzie, feigning complete ignorance of his involvement.

Lizzie looked at me trying to read between the lines. He let the matter drop without admitting to anything. I led the way down the hill in the direction of the old homestead.

"Wow! A hundred twenty acres of land is a lot of walking!"

"Yeah, it's really more than we needed, but it's nice to have the privacy." We reached the obvious remains of a foundation and fireplace and a few charred beams.

"This the original homestead?" Lizzie asked.

"Yep. This is just about my favorite part of the land. No incredible views, but then again, the peaks spoil us. We forget that even the hills have their own personality and beauty."

Lizzie was taken off guard by that and he seemed to remove a couple of masks. He was looking almost genuine. But then again, he was an actor by profession, and I was way beyond the point where I trusted him. He didn't seem to realize that fact yet.

Lizzie said, "You really love this place, don't you?"

"Yeah! You just figure that out? Isn't it obvious? I would go crazy happy if everyone agreed I could build a little house down here."

"Or if we could *all* agree to sell the place and split the money." Lizzie said, finally getting to the point.

I looked at him in amazement. "This is the Church of Manna, Lizzie. That would never happen."

We walked along the road that skirted that beautiful meadow just below the old homestead. When we reached the fork that led back to The Dome, Lizzie grabbed my elbow and stopped me in my tracks.

He looked at me as if lightning had struck his brain and he had just come up with the idea. "I have it, Giacco! I know how I can get you that land or money to get some other land or whatever. It's only fair. You deserve it for all the time and work you've put into this place. If only you won't nix it for the rest of us."

I watched as he put his masks back on. They fit so well. The concerned one, the business one, the greedy one.

"Here's a surprise for ya, Liz!" We began to hike again as he waited for it. "I'm not your problem," I told him. "I'm not the obstacle. You don't have to convince me of anything. I'm not going to stand in anybody's way. Whatever everyone else wants to do, I'll do. If everyone wants to sell the land to another nonprofit organization that we can all agree on, I will not stand in the way."

"Oh, very sarcastic, Giacco. Get real! You know it'll never happen that way. We'll never get everyone to agree, and if we do it'll take years."

"So?" I said. "What's the hurry?"

"Besides," he said, ignoring the question, "We'd have to sell the land as a whole. We can't break it up. None of us would get to have our favorite piece."

Now it all became clear.

"Well, except for you and Nick," I said.

Lizzie turned red. "I specifically told Trudy not to…"

"It wasn't Trudy, Liz. I got it directly from the source. Like I always do."

When he finally spoke, it was penitently and pleadingly at the same time. "Giacco, please don't be so stubborn. Try to understand. We're sitting on a half million dollars!"

"I'm not being stubborn, Liz. I already said I'd go along with whatever everyone else wants. As long as it's unanimous."

"Unanimous!" Lizzie said, putting on his smarmy face. "This is all Baird's fault."

Thank god for Baird!

When we were almost back at The Dome, Lizzie said, "Giacco, listen, I know how to make it happen. I know how to get out of that stupid contract. God, we were so naïve!"

I just looked blankly at him.

"Now that Richard's no longer writing the checks, maybe we can talk Slim into a deal."

"What're you talking about, Liz? What kind of deal?"

"We go to Slim and tell him we're going to default on a mortgage payment or two. We make it worth his while to foreclose on us immediately by giving him a cash gift for his efforts. Then he turns right around and sells it back to us as individuals for what's remaining on the mortgage, as if nothing were different except the names of the owners on the deed. The people that don't care about land and want the money instead, we'll give 'em the money. Everyone'll be happy."

I stared at Lizzie in disbelief. "Very inventive. Like I told you before, Liz, I don't care what we do. I would even agree to that doozy of a scheme. As long as it's done in the spirit of Hunga Dunga, OK? As long as we *all* agree to it. If Hunga Dunga is going to fall apart, let's make it as graceful as possible, OK? Let's make it end as beautifully as it started."

Lizzie stared back like I was a child living in a fantasy world. "Giacco, there is no Hunga Dunga. There's Big Blue, Waller Street, Chuck's apartment, and Nick Cantrell's Cabinets. And the Church of Manna. Which right now, is just you!"

He hopped in the truck and drove down the bumpy road. I could see him grimacing at me in the big side-view mirror. The next morning, I imagined him taking the sharp curves in his new toy, speeding over the North Cascades Highway and down I-5. Knowing Lizzie, the first chance he got he would cut over to the coast. He was always one for thrills and drama.

It is not beyond the realm of possibility, irony and the cosmic confluence of events being what they are, that as Lizzie was crossing the Golden Gate Bridge into The City, another vehicle was speeding out of The City over the bridge. The difference was that Zwagen only made it to mid-span when it slammed on the brakes, almost causing an accident. A small, balding man, with a cherubic face ran from the white VW, and without hesitation, climbed the railing. Witnesses say he was yodeling as he did a swan dive into the Bay.

CHAPTER 108
September 1976

Joel lent me the money to fly down for the funeral. When Zietar's body was retrieved they found a couple of syringes that amazingly hadn't been dislodged by the impact. It was David and Ellen who had to go identify the body. I'm sure it was the most gruesome task they had ever been asked to do. The coroner said there was so much cocaine in him, that had he not died from the jump, he would have died from an overdose.

I stayed at Waller Street, in Zietar's room no less. Although they had already done their best to clean his room of all incriminating items, Psylvia asked me to give it a once over. I did a thrice-over. If he had hidden any X-rated materials or toys, they had already been discovered and discarded. The only things of interest I found were in a nightstand. A bunch of packets of vegetable seeds and a photograph of a rock. I put the seeds in my backpack and went into the kitchen to ask about the strange photo. Larry said all he knew was that Richard said it was his favorite rock on the land. It didn't seem worthy of the Rock Museum, but it was shaped like a seat just right for his small frame. I put the photo in my shirt pocket.

Everyone walked around like zombies. We all knew Richard was doing way too much cocaine, but it was beyond us how he could maintain such a level of secrecy as to the true extent of his addiction. It was too soon to talk about it. To analyze it. To understand it. We were numb.

I wore my denim jacket with Richard's embroidered duck on the back. It was a closed-casket funeral. We shared our grief and condolences with Richard's folks who had flown out from New York. We found it almost impossible to meet their gaze. Their piercing looks seemed to accuse all of us as being guilty. Of being his murderer. It was easy for the rest of us to blame Lizzie, and many did, but deep inside we all knew we were equally guilty, and the self-flagellation would go on for a long time, either because we thought we hadn't done enough to prevent it, or because we had been accomplices by indulging in it ourselves.

Ellen took it upon herself to ask a favor of Richard's parents. Well, not really a favor, but a wish, that although never written down, was something Richard had mentioned often.

If ever he should die, he wanted his remains to be cremated and spread out over Zietar's Knoll. They balked at the idea. Even if it were his dying request, they would have none of it. It would be as if they had condoned this social experiment all along. No! They would have the body flown back to New York and buried in the family plot. Moreover, how dare any of us call him "family!" That *really* hurt!

It was a real testament to what a lovely man, and what a loved man Richard was, that so many people showed up at the funeral. Trudy flew down as well, but she stayed at Big Blue with Lizzie. That made sense. Looking at the two of them, standing there across from me, seemed strange and ironic. Standing there, arm in arm, just as they had when they first met me at the Cockettes show. Standing there, arm in arm, just as they had when they brought me home to the beginnings of Hunga Dunga. And now, here we were, at the endings. I guess the lesson to be learned was that karma intervenes in our lives in unknown ways. If they hadn't brought me home that Halloween night, god only knows how different my life might have been. In retrospect, I don't think I'd have had it any other way.

All the communes, or what was left of them, came to the service. Lee and Bianca drove down from Grant's Pass. They stopped by Nevada City to pick up Katie, still looking as sweet as ever. Lee and Bianca had started a recycling center and Katie was going to nursing school. It was good to see them.

Alvoye and Bobby arrived, wrapped in black silks. Baird gave an eloquent eulogy that made everyone weep. Bobby and Alvoye wailed with the ululations of a *zaghareet*. Richard's folks turned around, stared in amazed disgust, especially since they were Jewish, and considered it an insult.

The schism between Big Blue and Waller Street had grown so wide, many of our friends who wanted to pay their respects, get stoned, or tell stories, had to make two separate visits. One to Waller Street, another to Big Blue. I think Eli, from The Friends of Perfection, was the only one who refused to visit Big Blue.

I spent most of my time walking around The City, revisiting old haunts. It no longer had the magical appeal of just a few years before. As I shuffled aimlessly up and down the Haight, hippies hung out half-conscious in doorways, or jazzed up on meth talking a mile a minute. Where had the flower children gone? If this is what we had come to represent, no wonder we were reviled. Even the buildings looked dilapidated, with many windows and doors boarded up.

I went to visit Flo Airwaves one day. Most of them were in the middle of moving to a house they bought in the Mission. Travis and Rolli had come down for the funeral from their land in Willits where they were building a cabin. Glenn, I mean Divine, was already a star, and John Waters the toast of both coasts.

One morning all of us at Waller Street, plus Chuck, Tom, and Brandon, walked the entire way through Golden Gate Park to Land's End. It was an unofficial memorial service, though little was said. We stared at the beautiful Golden Gate Bridge in silence. Some small talk, banter. Catching up. Larry had started school to become a court reporter. David was trying to get a job as a truck driver. Ellen was going to grad school to become a nurse practitioner. Psylvia was using her disability pay to study computer repair. We never could get a hold of Jon or Rose, but we knew how devastated they would be when they found out. In between the news items, we were silent and stared at the seductively shining bridge. It was comforting being in each other's company. Richard, Little Richard, Zietar, Ziets, was pretty much the embodiment of the spirit of Hunga Dunga. At least up until he became infected with Lizzie's malignant, capitalistic tumor. With his plummet off the bridge, so plummeted much of what we thought we all had stood for.

We agreed, or at least hoped, that some of the ideals and dreams and activism would return, but it looked like we were in for a long period of mourning. In the meantime, maybe trying to work within the system was the way to go. If we chose to do that, we'd refuse to consider it a capitulation, and promised to honor the flower child hippie in each of us because we knew that was our true nature.

The real test of something being true, is if it's true under every conceivable circumstance. Then it is absolute truth, not conventional truth, convenient truth, or any other twist, turn or spin of the word. We could not come up with a scenario in which the ideals of love, peace, and equality would not result in a planet revolving in harmony. Sitting on that hillside, overlooking the bridge, we realized it was time to reenter the establishment. We would. But we'd bring with us, unsullied, the hippie inside, though it might have to stay in remission for a while.

Until the rest of the world caught up, we promised always to cherish the values of that golden time. We laughed, hearing each other speak of the "golden times" as if they were decades ago! Chuck reminded us of the time we all went to see "Yellow Submarine." The part where the Beatles blow your mind by showing just how much a person can experience in a minute. Sixty seconds! That's what the past millions of minutes had been like for me, each one crammed with experiences. I was a collector of experiences. I wondered how *that* would look on a resume!

Psylvia stood up and stretched. The others did the same. We huddled together as the fog rolled in. We huddled closer, trying to stifle our tears. Before turning our backs on the view and heading home, Psylvia spoke to no one in particular, quoting Little Richard. "Everything is needless to say."

Before I went back to Twisp, I made a visit to the Department of Social Services. The wheels of a bureaucracy work slowly, and I thought a few more checks would arrive before I could get them stopped. I requested they be sent in care of Joel's address. That's how distrustful Lizzie and Trudy had made me. They had access to the post office box and until I got my own, I didn't want anyone to have access to what was mine. I heard myself use the word "mine." Bummer, it had come to that. I punched myself in honor of Jon and Rosie.

Then I asked for Nancy Stein. She was no longer employed there. The reasons for her dismissal weren't clear but a colleague intimated she was "too generous." I was disappointed, but very proud of her and hoped she was doing well. Now I would have to tell my story from the beginning to a stranger. When I did get to sit down with a social worker, I got right to the point. I said I no longer needed their services or money and to please stop all the checks. I asked him to thank The City and the State of California for me for their help in my time of need, but I was just fine now.

The young man looked through my file and said, "I'm sorry, Mr. Giordano, but according to your file you have *organic* brain damage and are incurable. I don't see how we can stop sending the checks."

"That is utter nonsense!" I replied, getting a bit worried that this would haunt me the rest of my life. "Just for the record, put in my file that I requested I be taken off the rolls."

He just looked up at me, shaking his longish hair forth and back in disbelief. "I have to tell you Giacco, this is a new one on me. Most people come to me to complain they've been denied ATD, not to be removed from it! I'll put a note in your file, but I think this'll take the expertise of someone higher up than me."

I stood up, thanked him, the insincerity in my voice obvious, and walked away. I would just sign the checks over to a charity or something. I would get a job. I would re-enter the establishment, but it had to be in a way that I could personally contribute to society without compromising the hippie I forever wanted to be, even if I had to keep it in hiding.

CHAPTER 109
October 1976

Joel picked me up at Sea-Tac. We took I-90 east, then over Blewett Pass to 97 north. It was beautiful but not as spectacular as the North Cascades Highway. I asked Joel why we weren't taking the scenic route. Joel just said I-90 was faster and we had to get back to the valley as soon as possible.

Nate Porter had a job for me! Joel didn't know the details, but Nate told him to get me home as quickly as possible. We didn't get in until after dark but there was a message waiting at Joel's. It said to come up first thing in the morning. The earlier the better.

I spent the night at Joel's and must've been in a deep sleep because I was startled awake by Joel roughly shaking me and shouting, "Get up Giacco, we have to get going!"

Without even so much as a cup of coffee, he shoveled me into his Jeep, but I insisted we take a quick trip up to The Dome, where I put Richard's seeds in a cupboard. I would plant them for him next spring. Then we walked through the barren garden still bordered by rocks, a beautiful frame with no picture. I held up the photo and scanned the field. It was so obvious. The large rock sat in a corner of the frame. A section of the rock was broken off, forming a little seat with a back. I could imagine Ziets sitting there admiring the results of his green thumb.

I persuaded Joel to help me roll it, push it, lug it up to the top of Zietar's Knoll. We positioned it to face the Pasayten Wilderness. I sat in it and admired the view. Joel took his turn. When he stood up, I saw he was crying, which made me cry, too.

Through his tears, Joel said, "C'mon Giacco. We have to go." So we hopped back into the Jeep, took the dirt road down the hill, sped up Poorman Creek, over the Christianson's bridge, up Twisp River Road, and across the little bridge to the Porters.

Nate and Chettie had been up since dawn, as usual, and were bubbling with excitement when they saw us drive in. Chettie poured Joel and me a cup of coffee that I almost spilled as Nate tugged at my arm leading me into his office.

"Giacco! I have the *best* news!"

"Well, I like that adjective," I said, trying to come out of my stupor. The black coffee was helping. "So tell me. What is it, Nate?"

Nate could barely contain himself. "I am somewhat jealous," he said. "This is going to be the adventure of a lifetime!"

"OK, OK," I laughed, "you know I am always up for an adventure. Now tell me what it is."

"I called an old friend of mine who's now the Superintendent of Schools for the Yukon-Koyukuk School District. His name is Cal Kreidler. I told him about you. He said to send up your resume and transcripts and he'd be happy to look them over, pass 'em around to all the principals in the district, see if anything pops up."

"Well, thanks Nate," I said. "Thanks for going through all that trouble."

"No trouble at all. I was actually very surprised when he called back so quickly. But I guess they have a high turnover rate and no-shows. He's expecting you to call him as soon as possible. I think he's going to offer you a job. You can use the phone in my office."

Joel, Nate, and I all tried to get through the door at the same time. Chettie waited patiently. "OK, you Three Stooges. Enough slapstick. It's too early in the morning!"

"So, where the hell is this Yukon-Cluckacluck school district anyway, Nate?"

"Yukon-*Koyukuk* school district," he corrected, and then wrote it down on a notepad. "It's here." he said, reaching high on a map of North America tacked to a wall. "It's the largest school district in the United States!"

I saw him trace an area in Alaska just south of the Brooks Range that encompassed almost the entire interior of Alaska north of Fairbanks, from the state's eastern border with the Canadian Yukon to the Bering Strait. I took a closer look. I froze.

"Nate, this is the Arctic Circle you're talking about! I hardly call that tropical!"

"Well, no, that's true. But you said if you were going to get a job, you wanted it to be something different, something exciting. The Inuit! The Athabaskans! What could be more exciting? This is the stuff National Geographic is made of! Besides, this may be part of the establishment, but just barely."

"It looks totally on the fringes of it, that's for sure," Joel interjected.

"Giacco," Chettie said, "give them a call. You haven't even been offered a job yet and if you are, you can always refuse."

"Well, OK," I agreed. "Where's the number?"

"Right here," Nate pointed to a phone number circled in red on his desk calendar.

"Cal here," the voice announced.

"Cal Kreidler?" I asked. "Superintendent of the Yuk…"

"Yeah, yeah, that's me. "Who's calling and how can I help ya?"

Gee, they must be a really loose organization up there.

"This is Giacco Giordano, friend of Nate Porter."

"Giacco!" I could almost feel him straighten up in his chair. "Giacco Giordano, finally!"

I could hear voices starting to murmur in the background at the mention of my name.

I could see his hand covering the mouthpiece, but to no real effect as he yelled, "Shut up guys! Don't you have anything better to do?"

Then back to me, "Giacco, I have a teaching position open and it's yours if you want it."

Damn, he was almost too quick to get to the point. "Well sure I'm interested, but I imagine school has already started up there, right?"

"Wrong!" Cal answered. "But any day now! We need a teacher up in Allakaket."

"Allakaket?" I repeated. As I said it, Nate found it on the map and pointed to it.

"Well, actually, Allakaket and Alatna."

"Alatna?" I repeated. Nate looked closely at the map but just shrugged his shoulders.

"Yeah, they're two villages on opposite sides of the river, right where the Alatna comes down from the Brooks Range and meets the Koyukuk. See it?"

"OK, Cal, I'm looking at the map. Or rather, I'm looking at Nate who is pointing to things on the map. He says 'hi' by the way."

"Tell him 'hi' back. Has he found the Alatna?"

I asked Nate to find the Alatna River. He did and traced it south from the Brooks Range.

"Tell him to follow it down to where it meets the Koyukuk."

I passed the instructions on to Nate and followed his finger as it traced the rivers.

Nate stuck a thumbtack at the confluence.

"OK, Cal, we have them pinpointed."

"Damn! That Porter must have one great map. Most maps don't even have stuff that small on 'em."

I hoped he didn't hear me gulp when I said, "Well, that's right on the Arctic Circle!"

"Well anyway," he continued, dismissing my remark, "school doesn't start until the rivers freeze thick enough so the kids who live in Alatna can safely cross to Allakaket where the schools are. And only the village elders decide when it's safe."

Wow! That was different! In fact, maybe it was too different!

I think he felt the hesitation on my end.

"The elders said it was safe this past Monday. So we're ready to boogie. Are you?"

Boogie? Was this guy for real? Could a school-district superintendent really be so laid back?

I wished I could be a fly on his wall to really see what the hell was going on in that room.

"Well, what grade would I be teaching? What subjects? How many kids? How do I get there? When do you want me up there?"

I couldn't explain it, but I sensed other faces sidling up to Cal's, trying to listen in. There was a hint of stifled laughter. I thought maybe someone was playing a joke on me.

"Hold on, hold on. One question at a time. You'll be *the* high school teacher, grades nine through 12. You'll be responsible for all subjects. You will have… hold on Giacco."

He put his hand over the mouthpiece again and asked the same question of some guy standing behind him. Then he got back to me.

"Fourteen. Fourteen high school kids. Three from Alatna, the rest from Allakaket. And to answer your last question we'd like you up here by tomorrow."

"Tomorrow?" I yelled.

"Tomorrow?" Nate yelled.

"Tomorrow? Chettie yelled.

"Tomorrow?" Joel yelled.

"Cripes, Giacco, you in an echo chamber or something?" And his hearty laugh made me feel very comfortable. I could also hear two or three other voices on his end stifling outbursts of laughter.

"I told you to keep it down, fellas!" The laughter abated. "OK, I guess tomorrow is a bit too much to ask. Be real nice though if you could get up here by the end of the week. You'd have the weekend for someone up there to get you settled in and up to speed, meet some of the important elders and stuff. The head guy is also the middle school teacher. You, him, and a young Inuit woman who teaches the elementary school kids. That's it. You three."

"Sounds like a cozy little community," I said.

"Yeah, that would be one way of putting it," he laughed. "So listen, Giacco. Don't worry about anything. Just get your ass up here ASAP! There'll be a plane ticket waiting for you at the Alaska Airlines desk at Sea-Tac. It's the early bird flight, so get there the night before, OK. We'll pick up the tab for the hotel. You should be getting into Fairbanks no later than 1 PM. Someone will meet you and drive you to Nenana."

"Nenana?" I asked as Nate found it on the map.

"Yep, that's HQ for the YK. It's really just a few miles outside Fairbanks. Fill out some paperwork, then one of our pilots will fly you out to Allakaket."

"Fly me?"

"Hey Giacco. There are no roads to any of these villages. The school district has two Cessnas and two full-time pilots. Hope you don't have a fear of flying in the bush!" More laughter in the background.

"Not that I know of," I tried to say with equanimity, though my heart was beginning to race.

"Hmmm. Let me think. Anything else you should know?"

I let him think for a minute.

"Nope, I can't think of anything else. Well, just a couple of things but I don't want to scare you off cause everyone who looked at your resume and stuff really liked what they saw. We had a number of openings we could have offered you, but our guy in Allakaket called dibs on ya. He insisted upon it. Said you were just the right guy for the job, the only guy."

"What made him think that?"

Cal stuttered, "Well, uh… because, uh…"

His hand was back over the mouthpiece. I heard a lot of urgent whispering in the background. Then in a tone of certainty, "Oh, yeah… Nate's letter of introduction. That's what it was. I think it was the cross-country skiing part… or something like that."

It sounded too vague, but then this whole conversation was surreal to begin with.

"So Giacco, just get your ass up here! You'll like it! Takes a special kind of guy to make it up here, but I think you'll do just fine. Be on that Alaska flight Friday morning. That's *this* Friday. We'll have you in Allakaket before sunset. I'll make sure someone's there to meet you. Gonna radio the principal right after I finish up with you. That is, if we have a deal."

"Ya know what, Cal? I think we do. But the couple of other things you were going to mention?"

"Well, I guess it's only fair you know that besides no roads, there are no phones, no running water, and only a honey bucket for a toilet. But the teachers each get a nice log cabin with an oil stove that puts out mucho heat. The school has its own generator which also provides electricity for the teachers' cabins, even though it's only a few hours a day. But on the plus side, if you finish the school year out, you'll have a teaching certificate. And the pay for a first-year teacher is the best in the country!"

I heard someone in the background say, "It's called hazard pay!" And everyone who was in that room burst out laughing in unison.

As he was hanging up, I heard Cal yell, "I thought I told you guys to shut up!"

ARCTIC CIRCLE
October 1976

I feel debris and branches rushing under my feet as the current whisks them by. A log snags my flight suit and rips me from the feeble grasp my leather mitts have on the edge of the black hole in the frozen river. It tries to take me for an underwater ride. I instinctively cling to it with the tenacity of a cowboy riding a bronco. It drags my face on the underside of the ice, but it hardly seems a bother. I notice the bottom of the ice is rougher than the top as it scrapes and cuts my forehead, nose, and chin. I notice the water is so cold, yet so warm at the same time.

My eyelids are tightly shut but my eyes are open. I hear almost inaudible rock music coming out of invisible speakers. I see through my eyelids a light on my face. I see that it is Psylvia's and she is gazing at me with smiling eyes that are outlined with black kohl. She winks a wink that is forever. On her eyelid is the most beautiful tropical setting I've ever seen. Pillow clouds. A wide, sandy beach. Coconut palms heavy with fruit. A seagull flies by. The surf is warm and gentle.

Suddenly the log surfaces like a submarine in distress, breaching nose-first at an acute angle through another hole in the ice. I take a gasp of air. And then another as we come down with a soft thud and my water-logged steed bucks me off onto the ice. I spread myself out to cover as much area as I can. I am so glad I am a Boy Scout and remember my training. I am really only a few yards farther downstream. I can still see the bonfire and silhouettes of some bodies walking forth and back between a cabin and the bonfire. I want to be in the light of that bonfire. I want to be a silhouette.

I can see the flickering lights in the few cabins up ahead. And I realize I want those flickering lights, no matter how dim.

I'll settle for this wasteland backdrop of ice and sky. It is *some* thing and not *no* thing. I can try for the tropical island later. I shimmy and squirm toward the bank. It's only a few yards away, but I am traveling about one inch a minute. As the bank gets closer, I think I might actually make it. I want to make it so much. That's when I feel the panic start and the adrenaline surge.

I want to make it so much that I jump to my feet and take a slow, deep, painfully cold breath, and walk toe to heel, carefully testing the ice before I commit myself. *Toe to heel, in the way of a native stalking his prey. Toe to heel in the way of a baby taking its first steps. Toe to heel in the way of the lord.* I don't care which one.

I feel synchronized with everything in the universe and notice all I am supposed to. I notice a conveniently arranged assortment of ice chunks and logs that could get me up to the top of the bank. The flight suit is soaked. It's worth its weight in lead. Climbing the few feet to the top seems like climbing a mountain peak. But I do it. And I look back at the log and the trail I had chosen and realize I have a past. And if I have a past, I have a present. And if I have a present, then maybe I have a future. And if I do, then I am alive.

And if that's for better or worse, I don't know. I could have gotten the ultimate answer we were all searching for. Whether death is a void, or whether there *is* something. Pure light, pure energy, pure love; and if I would be conscious of them. *No mind, never matter. No matter, never mind.* If it's all just a part of the cosmic *lila*, then let me dance to it until I don't want to, because dying is too easy.

I start dancing toe to heel toward the bonfire, which seems to be dimming now. I notice the locus of points in each move I make with my arms and legs. I wish Joel's flight suit were made of dayglow material and the bonfire were a black light. Then perhaps they would notice a strange design in the distance reaching out for them.

I try to yell, but the air, now a stiffening wind from the north, stings my lungs with a million icy barbs. I manage to get out a few desperate sounds as loud as I can. I can see the locus of points of my movements slowing down. The flight suit is starting to freeze. I am starting to freeze. I move a knee forward and I can hear and feel the material cracking. I am so close yet so far. This is not fair! I am freezing in place. I wonder if they will eventually find me here, frozen, standing in midair on one toe.

The image of that inspires me to yell one last time with all I have left, which is very little. I tip over and lay in the snow. A freezing sleep is trying to blanket me. I let it tuck me in. I take a nap and wait to see if I will wake up.

Smell was the first sense aroused. Fur. Dead skin. Steamy tea. Burning wood. Jack Daniels.

The second sense was that of touch. I was naked and felt animal skins wrapped tightly around me, as if I were rolled up in a rug. Hands were rocking me forth and back and rubbing me up and down. They were reaching inside the bearskins and moose skins and touching my naked skin. Six hands. One pair, knobby and hard; one pair, small and smooth; another pair, big and strong. Their hands were rubbing my body all over in the way a mother rubs her child's cold hands between her own warm ones.

Sound was the third sense to come alive. A crackling fire, a basin of water being filled, voices.

One voice was old and had an odd accent. "What a stupid man. What a stupid white man. This is what we get for a teacher?"

"It's not his fault." A different voice responded, "Why didn't they let us know he was coming in today?" The voice sounded young, Midwestern, out of place. *Maybe I was hallucinating?*

"You are the principal!" The old voice said, speaking slowly and emphasizing each word. "You should know these things. He almost died!"

"Grandpa Oscar," the young man said, "I just talked with them by radio two days ago. There must've been a fuckup. They're always fucking up back in Nenana. What do they care? They may as well be in the lower 48!"

"Yah, Blah, Nah! Hey Giacco, go make some tea." Grandpa Oscar ordered.

I was barely conscious.

"How can they expect me to get up and make tea in my condition?"

"OK," I heard a little voice say.

"No," said the young Midwesterner, "I'll get it. Giacco, you go rub his feet and hands, OK?"

"I was supposed to rub somebody's feet? The old man's?"

"OK," said the little voice in the same heartland accent as the young man's. Little hands crept up the bottom of the roll of bearskins and moose hides and started rubbing my feet. His hands felt so warm.

Am I dead? Is this the reality of the void that is not real because there's nothing there? But this is something. This is not nothing. Is it an alternative afterlife?

"Grandpa Oscar, how many times do I have to tell you he's only five! Don't tell him to make tea!"

"You white people. So soft." Grandpa Oscar replied.

His voice trailed off as the young man's voice got closer. He resumed rolling me forth and back while the little boy's hands were now massaging mine.

"Is your brew ready yet, Grandpa?"

"Lemme look."

Two minutes of silence. Just rocking and rolling and tiny massages.

"Yes."

"Well then bring me a cup please. Giacco, go get a towel for daddy, OK?"

Oh, great. Now they want me to go get a towel? And what's this "daddy" stuff?

"OK." And little feet walked across the wood floor.

Hands loosened the skins around my head, and one reached under my neck and lifted me up. The other placed a warm cup against my lips and tried to part them with the edge of the cup. "Here. Drink this, Giacco. It'll make you feel better." I heard the toddler scooting on his knees behind me. His little hands tried to help hold my head up.

The fourth sense that woke up was taste. I felt the warm tea entering *my* mouth, and *my* tongue giving way to it, and *my* taste buds thawing and the warm liquid sliding down *my* throat.

I opened my eyes, awakening the fifth sense, sight.

A face was close to mine. I studied it for a long time. A lamp backlit him so much I couldn't see his face in detail. But I felt he was looking at me with such love and concern, that he knew me. The little boy came up and put his arm on his dad's shoulder. Above him hunkered a little old man wearing a hefty coat with a hood edged with fur. His face was so deeply wrinkled I couldn't make out the color of his skin. He leaned in to get a better look, as if he were ice fishing. His line of sight was the fishing line, the opening at the top of the carpet of skins was the hole in the ice. And I was the fish. He studied me with kind eyes. Nate was right. He looked just like a picture of an Eskimo out of a National Geographic magazine.

"Who is he?" the little boy asked, his russet hair sticking out of a knit cap.

Placing the cup to the side, the dad turned to his son and said, "Giacco, meet Giacco." Then the dad turned to me. He broke into a big grin as he backed up and sat on his haunches. He held my hands between his. The lantern glimmered on a tear falling from his eye. I watched it roll down his cheek until it was caught by his smile. There was the shadow of a scar on his upper lip. His hands reached to fondle the hishis around my neck, and then let Ganesh rest in the palm of his hand. He leaned in until his face was close to mine, and he kissed me on the forehead.

"I'm the guy who called dibs on ya," Michael whispered in my ear.

I felt the corners of my mouth crack slightly as I smiled at him.

It just doesn't get any better than this!

ACKNOWLEDGMENTS

I cannot thank enough my remarkable editors, Larry Brinkin, Jonathan Hawley and Tim DiMarco. I welcomed their ideas and contributions so much, that I looked forward each time we met to discuss my work. Their labor of love was accompanied by great humor and sensitivity. I was honored and flattered they offered their help.

In addition, I would like to thank the many friends, too many to name here, who offered suggestions, jogged my memory regarding chronology and anecdotes, researched topics, verified the substantive accuracy of historical accounts and, most importantly, had the utmost faith in this project, demonstrating it with continual support and encouragement.

I wish to thank Tim DiMarco, who, for the decade it took me to write this book, put up with a manic, obsessive, compulsive, and certifiably crazed man. He did so with a kindness and generosity that continues to amaze me, and the constant reminder that this was a book demanding to be written.

Finally, I would like to thank Mary Jane Charas for putting wings on my prayers.

About the Author

Phil Polizatto is a graduate of the School of Foreign Service, Georgetown University. He has been a feature writer for UPI, a copywriter for CBS, and an award winning corporate film producer. He wrote the score, lyrics and book for the off-off-off Broadway musical, *Organic Matter* and immortalized the songs of Cowboy Bob in the unforgettable CD, *Cowboy Bob: The Morbid Years*. Mr. Polizatto is a regular contributor to a number of alternative arts and literary journals. He resides in the Pacific Northwest where he is working on a collection of short stories and poems. Mr. Polizatto regards this book as more history than fiction. He hopes you will enjoy the trip and find a few truths along the way.

Books by Phil Polizatto

Hunga Dunga, A True Novel
Confessions of an Unapologetic Hippie
C'est Une Maison Bleu, Les Arenes, Paris (French Edition)
The Unapologetic Hippie

Saltydog (penned under Budd Connor)

www.ingramcontent.com/pod-product-compliance
Lightning Source LLC
Chambersburg PA
CBHW080528300426
44111CB00017B/2646